THE
Which? Wine
Guide 1996

ABOUT THE EDITOR

Harry Eyres is drinks editor for *Harpers &
Queen* and author of *Wine Dynasties of
Europe* and the *Viking Guide to Cabernet
Sauvignon Wines*. He is also series editor of
the Viking guides to grape varieties. His
enthusiasm for German wines began at the
age of eight, and his wine education
continued at Cambridge University, where
he twice won the individual prize in the
Oxford *v* Cambridge blind tasting match.
He then worked for a time as Michael
Broadbent's assistant at Christie's wine
department. Harry is also a theatre critic,
teacher and poet.

T H E
Which? Wine Guide 1996

Edited by HARRY EYRES

CONSUMERS' ASSOCIATION

Which? Books are commissioned by
Consumers' Association and published by
Which? Ltd, 2 Marylebone Road, London NW1 4DF
E-mail address: guidereports@which.co.uk

Distributed by The Penguin Group:
Penguin Books Ltd, 27 Wrights Lane, London W8 5TZ

Contributing editor: Simon Woods
Acknowledgements to: Stephen Brook, Jim Budd, Philip Eyres,
Carol Johnson, Giles MacDonogh, George Sarahs, John Wheelwright

Designer: Paul Saunders
Cover photograph: Johanna Fernihough
Illustrations: Christine Roche
Index: Marie Lorimer

British Library Cataloguing in Publication Data
A catalogue record for this book is available from The British Library

ISBN 0 85202 590 4

Typeset by Saxon Graphics Ltd, Derby
Printed and bound in Great Britain by Biddles Ltd,
Guildford and King's Lynn

CONTENTS

CONTENTS

Part III   Where to buy wine

Part IV   Find out more about wine

INTRODUCTION

In the volatile world of wine things can change quickly as the events of the past year have shown. Who would have guessed not so many months ago that in the middle of 1995 we would be experiencing a worldwide shortage of quality wine? Who would have guessed that Australia, the guiding star of wine-exporting countries, would suffer a decline in sales for two months at the end of 1994?

The shortages and the sudden, dramatic deceleration of the growth of Australian wine imports have been caused by a single factor: the weather and in particular serious drought in many wine regions of the world. Reduced harvests have been experienced not only in Australia (down 25 per cent on expectations in 1995) but also in Spain (the sherry harvest is expected to be at least 40 per cent down for the second successive year, and drought has wrought havoc in La Mancha), Eastern Europe (especially Hungary), Italy and California. Suddenly, in parts of the world such as Andalucia, people are wondering whether ecological crisis is not already upon us, in the form not of global warming but water shortage.

These shortages are having a knock-on effect, driving up demand and prices, especially for wines from South Africa and South America. The resurgence of South Africa has been a fine thing to behold, but the kind of pressure now being exerted on Cape wine-producers could have damaging effects on quality. South Africa, a wineland of immense promise, still needs to develop a strong image of its own, and any compromise on quality to meet short-term demand could be disastrous. Chile ('the France of the New World', according to Allan Cheesman, recently reinstalled as director of off-licence buying at Sainsbury) seems to be coping well with increased demand and the spotlight has now fallen on

Argentina. Argentina is one of the world's largest wine-producers but so far only a small proportion of production is of international export quality. All these developments, and those we discuss below, are charted in the revised and updated Wines of the World section of this year's Guide.

Another unexpected news item in 1995 was the increase in French wine imports to the UK in 1994. This did not signal a revival of France's old classic wine regions, but rather the continuing success of France's backyard New World, Languedoc-Roussillon. Fortunately, 1994 was a much better vintage in the Midi, with most grapes picked before the rains which for the fourth successive year fell heavily in September. An interesting development in Languedoc has been the partnership of Penfolds and Val d'Orbieu. This has produced not the somewhat one-dimensional single varietals favoured by some other Australo-Gallic operations, but more complex multi-varietal blends – perhaps the most exciting way forward for the Midi.

Bordeaux has blown the trumpet for the 1994 vintage, certainly the best since 1990, but equally certainly not a great vintage, and many UK merchants have been offering the wines *en primeur*. Few expect anything like the bonanzas of the late 1980s.

All in all, this has not been the easiest of years for the UK wine trade. More or less unrestricted cross-Channel wine-buying, at vastly lower rates of duty, is the bugbear which the trade has to grin and bear (see the revised and expanded feature). The possibility of mail-order purchase from the continent is another matter altogether. Several merchants are watching with extreme interest developments in the ongoing Death cigarette case (the producers of these cigarettes have applied for judicial review against a ruling prohibiting them from selling by mail-order in the UK at continental duty rates). If the Death merchants win their appeal, Simon Loftus of Adnams reckons many independent wine merchants would either go bust or cross the Channel.

For most merchants at time of writing, however, far more worrying even than cross-Channel wine-buying is the seemingly unstoppable fall of the pound against the French franc and Deutschmark. Though recession is over, the British economy is not exactly buoyant, and certainly not in the mood to absorb hefty price rises. In fact the pressure on prices seems if anything to be downwards: ASDA are offering wines at £1.99 as we go to press, prompting mutterings about loss-leaders from their competitors. The extreme obsession of all the supermarkets with particular price-points, especially £2.99 and £3.99, combined with the falling pound and shortages of quality wine, can mean only one thing for the customer: sacrifice of quality to price. Why must wine, unlike most other foodstuffs, be tied to rigid price-points? The question deserves to be asked. Restaurateurs and caterers buying meat, fish or cheese expect to pay the market price: there is no reason why the same rule should not apply to wine.

In the first of the Guide's two features, we examine another aspect of the supermarket wine scene, analysing the prevalent cult of extremely young wines, and lamenting the virtual disappearance of mature wines from supermarket shelves. The second feature gives more light-hearted, but still practical and helpful, advice on how to organise a wine-tasting at home.

The wine scene in the middle of the 1990s may be more uncertain and unpredictable than it was in the 1980s, but it is equally fascinating. The compensations for less than wonderful vintages in some classic areas have been some scintillating newcomers and some unsung old-stagers. South Africa, New Zealand and Chile are striding ahead, most importantly in quality as well as quantity, and Burgundy and Germany are two classic areas blessed with better-than-average vintages in the 1990s. There may not be too many Burgundian and German bargains around, after price rises and currency woes, but there are still some superb wines from the 1993 vintage in particular at fair prices. Please peruse the extensive directory of UK wine merchants and take your pick of wines, from what is still an unparalleled wealth of choice.

THE WHICH? WINE GUIDE AWARDS FOR 1996

The competition for these awards seems to become fiercer each year. Don't be at all surprised if you find several of the merchants listed below have excellent ranges from areas other than those where an award has been won.

Bordeaux Specialist Award
Justerini & Brooks
This is not the easiest of times to be selling Bordeaux, but Justerini & Brooks remain just ahead of the opposition owing to the depth of older vintages.

Burgundy Specialist Award
Howard Ripley
For single-minded devotion to his chosen area, a good overall range and some affordable older vintages, Howard Ripley just pips a host of close contenders.

Rhône Specialist Award
Croque-en-Bouche
There are other good Rhône lists around, but none matches the encyclopaedic selection of this restaurant-cum-wine merchant.

Italian Specialist Award
Enotria Winecellars
This company not only supplies the bulk of all Italian wine ranges at merchants around Britain, but also offers an unbeatable range including older vintages.

German Specialist Award
Berry Bros & Rudd
Whenever the market for fine German wines revives, Berry Bros & Rudd is most ably placed with a great range of wines from top estates.

Spanish Specialist Award
Moreno
Moreno continues to scour Spain for newer wines,
but still offers the classics in some depth.

Australia/New World Specialist Award
The Winery
A great selection from Australia, California and
many other places besides in some of London's
most welcoming surroundings.

Fine Wine Specialist Award
Raeburn Fine Wines
A fascinating source of good and interesting wines
not only from traditional areas but also from some
of the New World's most individualistic producers.

Best Supermarket Award
Waitrose
While others worry about buying to fixed price
points, Waitrose concentrates on maintaining quality.

Best High Street Chain Award
Oddbins
Despite keen competition from Bottoms Up,
Oddbins retains its premier position because of its
consistently exciting wines and the best staff around.

Best Mail-Order Merchant Award
The Wine Society
The £20 life membership for The Wine Society is one
of the best investments in the wine world.
Intelligent and stimulating mailings backed up by a
fine range.

Best Independent Merchant Award
Noel Young
One of the newest kids on the block, but already
showing flair, enthusiasm and a highly personal
approach to the world of wine.

Best Out-of-Town Merchant Award
Lay & Wheeler
One of the blue chips of the wine trade, Lay &
Wheeler offers impeccable wines supported by
impeccable service.

We are living in an age when it is possible to put together a very reasonable range of wines just by buying from a few different wholesalers. The following merchants stand out for going the extra mile and offering more interesting and unusual wines backed up by high standards of service.

CENTRAL ENGLAND
Gauntley's of Nottingham
The Rhône is a particular strength, but Gauntley's offers a well thought out selection from many other regions besides.

EAST OF ENGLAND
Adnams
Never predictable, never less than entertaining, Adnams is always in the vanguard of good taste.

NORTH OF ENGLAND
D. Byrne
Keen prices, a range which has few gaps and a warren of a shop which has few rivals north or south.

SOUTH-WEST OF ENGLAND
Nobody Inn
For the unusual premises, the impressive range and the wit and passion of a real enthusiast, The Nobody Inn is one of the country's hidden gems.

NORTHERN IRELAND
Direct Wine Shipments
Continuing improvements to the range, together with great enthusiasm make this Belfast merchant an exciting place to buy wine.

SCOTLAND
Ubiquitous Chip
A hard-fought category as ever, but Glasgow's best pokes its nose ahead of the competition.

WALES
Tanners
The main stronghold may be over the border in Shrewsbury, but Tanners provides an excellent service to all wine-lovers in the Principality.

Part I

Features

YOUTH CULTURE AND SUPERMARKET WINES

In Aldous Huxley's *Brave New World* age is the ultimate obscenity.
Increasingly our culture seems to share that view. As tennis players
burn out before 20 and bond dealers hope to retire at 30, youth is
seen by many as the ultimate, or sole, value. How is this cult of
youth rubbing off on wine, and in particular on the choice of wines
available in the supermarkets?

DRINK IT YOUNG

For a couple of years now Liz Robertson, head of wine-buying at
Safeway, has been enthusiastically promoting the message that we
should all be drinking young wine – relatively inexpensive wine
that is – the younger the better. 'It all starts with the new
technology,' she explains. 'In the old age of wine-making extraction
was not carefully regulated and reds were unnecessarily tannic.
Whites tended to be palate wines – not especially aromatic. Now
we make whites which have wonderful aromatic properties, and
with reds tannins are controlled – there is no need to wait for the
tannic walls to crumble.' Indeed, with these modern wines, it can
be a mistake to wait. 'Having less tannin, reds are less well
protected and need to be drunk younger. As for whites, youth is
really their most attractive feature; they have a lovely flowering
when they are young, but a gentle decline can begin quite early.'

In accordance with these ideas, Ms Robertson and Safeway have
been working to 'turn customers on to the latest vintage'.
Robertson believes in clear-cut distinctions between vintages, and
is opposed to the 'received wisdom of the old wine trade that it was
kinder to customers to mix vintages over the year divide' – in other
words, blend back younger wine into the older wine. This is a
practice vigorously defended by other supermarket wine-buyers,
such as Claire Gordon-Brown at Sainsbury who feels that around
Christmas a 14-month old Liebfraumilch from the previous vintage
will be tasting tired, and will be greatly improved by the addition
of some 2-month-old wine. It is an important part of Robertson's

new vintage philosophy 'to insist that producers substitute the new vintage for Safeway at the earliest possible moment'.

It may be worth pausing here to consider the implications of this revolutionary thinking. Gone are all those headaches about whether a wine is ready to drink, gone are the intricate comparisons of vintage to vintage. 'Keep it young, On the tongue', as one of those rhyming jingles in Huxley's *Brave New World* might have run, 'Old wines are a pest, Young wines are the best.' This new way of thinking is also an old way of thinking – a return to the norms of the Bible and Middle Ages, when the best wine was the young wine which had not had a chance to go off. It goes against the grain of the great ages of wine connoisseurship – the Roman period, when vintages like that of the famous Consul Opimius (121 BC) were thought to improve for upwards of 150 years, and the modern age, when traditional buffs lovingly laid down claret and port for 20 or 30 years.

Of course, the wines to which Liz Robertson is referring are not old vintage wines. Her message mainly concerns wines costing around £4 or under, and is aimed rather more at whites than reds. In the case of such products as Chilean or South African Sauvignon Blanc, whites whose aromatic, varietal characteristics notoriously wear off in a matter of months, there can be no doubt that this policy is doing the customer a favour. Could there be a danger of the new thinking extending too far, into areas where youth, and its corollary, simple fruit, are not necessarily the prime virtues?

Julian Brind of Waitrose, generally considered the most traditional of supermarket wine-buyers, is not especially worried. 'The success of Australia has had an impact on winemakers in Europe. Australians regard fruit as the number one priority and even in traditional French areas such as Bordeaux wines are being made to come round sooner. You could say fruit-driven wines were

the current fashion – in my view, on the whole a very attractive one. Cheaper wines are now much easier and more enjoyable than they were 20 years ago, when there were a lot of tough wines, and wines with volatile acidity. Of course there should be a place, at the top end of the market, for wines which will age – but fine old wines are something of an esoteric subject: you've got to have considerable knowledge to understand them. My only real regret is the virtual disappearance of old-style, oak-aged, slightly oxidised and volatile, but wonderful white Rioja, like Murrieta.' Brind, in fact, has outdone even Liz Robertson in the youth stakes by offering a clutch of 1994 clarets as early as spring 1995 – a dubious achievement, given these wines' high levels of tannin.

At ASDA, the new head of wine-buying, Nick Dymoke-Marr, takes a broadly similar view. 'We really don't sell wine for people to keep: 90 per cent of our wine is sold for pretty imminent consumption. We do look for youthful fruit indicators – we find people now want to taste the grapes, the fresh fruit in their wine. And wine is only worth keeping if it gets better: we find that Australian wines, on the whole, don't tend to age especially well. They don't seem to convert their ripe fruit into elegance – they remain chunky.' Dymoke-Marr is prepared to admit , however, that the fashion for youthful fruit might have some highly convenient economic motivations. 'There are economic pressures favouring early consumption: flying winemakers, for example, want to come in, make the wine as quickly as possible, and have it out of the winery certainly before the next vintage. There's no space in most wineries these days to store wine.' He also worries that as older vintages of, for example, Bordeaux, become more and more difficult to obtain at a reasonable price, the supermarket customer will be left without a smooth progression of wines moving up from the basic, new vintage varietal to the wine of more quality, complexity and – it may be embarrassing to mention, but here goes – age.

This is a problem which Sainsbury addressed with considerable forethought in 1992 and 1993, when, having seen that neither 1991 nor 1992 would offer much high-quality Bordeaux, the company invested heavily in *crus bourgeois* of the 1989 and 1990 vintages. 'It took a good deal of persuasion by the wine department,' recalls Claire Gordon-Brown, marketing manager. 'The company had not really addressed the question of whether supermarkets should buy wines to lay down. It certainly is difficult to find affordable wines of older vintages. At the moment our oldest wines are six or seven years old, and that is probably as good as it will ever be. On the other hand, many of our customers are suspicious of older wines – they think that there may be something wrong with a wine that is, say, eight or ten years old. The populace is involved with fruit.'

FRUIT AND YOUTH

Supermarkets always claim to follow public taste, but there is no question that they also help to form it. With their dominant share of the market, and their equal dominance of the media (encouraged by food and drink editors who, while happy to provide coverage of the most exclusive and elite restaurants, seem to enforce a bargain-basement approach to wine), supermarkets have immense power. At the moment that power is being put fairly and squarely behind fruit and youth. However, fruit is only one dimension of wine – and some brave iconoclasts would say, not the most important one. After all, if pure fruit flavours are what you are after, why not buy Ribena instead of Cabernet Sauvignon, or a fruit salad rather than some New World Chardonnay?

THE CASE FOR AGE

Cheese-makers divide the aromas and flavours of cheeses into three categories: first, the primary flavours which come from the grass, herbs and flowers eaten by the cows, ewes or goats; second the aromas and flavours of fermentation; third the aromas and flavours which evolve during maturation. Wine is in many ways similar to cheese: no accident that France has the most developed culture of both. Indeed, wine is capable of infinitely longer maturation. Six to nine months is about the limit for most French cheeses, whereas some wines are still developing and improving, gaining complexity and subtlety of aroma and flavour, at fifteen years of age. But from the way the supermarkets, and the pundits who depend upon them, speak of wine these days, you might think it was only the primary flavours – plus additions of obvious oak – which counted. Is such a one-dimensional approach doing justice to wine's multidimensional richness?

In the case of some wines, certainly, primary fruit flavours are their best feature. Many New World wines fall into this category, especially those made from such grape varieties as Sauvignon Blanc and Merlot. The old-fashioned classics, however, red Bordeaux, red burgundy, fine Rhône, white burgundy, fine German Riesling, vintage champagne, Barolo and Barbaresco from Piedmont, are wines whose greatest delights lie beyond the primary realm. The finest wines made from Cabernet Sauvignon, Syrah, Pinot Noir, Riesling, Nebbiolo, as they age, become less and less tied to simple primary fruit flavours, more and more complex, subtle and elusive. It is no accident that supermarkets do not offer the most rewarding selections of these wines.

Take Bordeaux, of all these areas the one where supermarkets try hardest. Sainsbury's initiative in buying substantial stocks of 1989 and 1990 *crus bourgeois* was a commendable one, but looks unlikely to be repeated. The oldest clarets available at the time of writing from any supermarket, with the exception of a couple of wines offered by the admirably unageist Tesco, are from the 1988 vintage, whose better wines have yet to emerge from a dumb, tannic adolescence. Around Christmas 1994 Safeway released a couple of 1990 *crus bourgeois*, which quickly sold out: the only problem was that the wines, stranded between youthful charm and more developed complexity, were not particularly rewarding to drink. The virtues of fine Bordeaux are the virtues of maturity; under-age claret may be all the supermarkets can ever offer.

Much the same applies to the great northern Rhône reds, which, Claire Gordon-Brown admits, are even more difficult to obtain at a reasonable state of maturity than Bordeaux. Indeed, Sainsbury's list at time of writing offers nothing at all in this category.

The case of fine white wines which positively require ageing may be still more desperate. There is even less public understanding of the need to age some white wines than certain reds. However, the greatest white burgundies such as the Meursault of Jobard or *grand cru* Chablis may be almost undrinkable until they reach six or seven years of age. Of course, new oak is often added to these wines nowadays as little more than a sweetener. Top German Spätleses and Ausleses from quality-conscious estates likewise need time to develop their wonderfully many-layered, honeyed, floral aromas and flavours. The little-known, great white wines of the Rhône likewise only offer their true glories after about six years. The best vintage champagne (and even non-vintage champagne is not a primary fruit wine) can take a decade to reach harmonious maturity. Once again, a trawl through supermarket lists reveals depressingly little good mature white wine, or champagne.

So what is the solution for the lover, or would-be lover, of multidimensional mature wine, who shops for wine at a supermarket? In terms of red wine, the answer would always have been, and to some extent still is, Iberia.

Rioja has traditionally been a region where producers have taken on the burden of maturing their wine, both in barrel and bottle, before releasing it for sale to the customer. But Rioja seems to be undergoing something of a crisis of identity, in which youth (*juventud*) has become all the rage, to the detriment of the region's special strength in mature wine. In the fashionable region of Ribera del Duero, also, there appears to be a Gadarene rush to produce *joven* wines of primary appeal, when the obvious potential, shown by Vega Sicilia and Pesquera, is for wines of grand dimensions, needing time to soften. Under these circumstances, most supermarkets' offerings are restricted to one or two Rioja *reservas*, with the odd maverick mature wine such as Tesco's Cabernet Sauvignon from La Mancha.

In a wine scene where the supermarkets are healthily complemented by high-street specialists and independents, it might seem that the dominance of youth culture in supermarket wines was perfectly acceptable. The supermarkets, however, are where most people today begin their journey into the world of wine. If there are no longer even any pointers beyond the somewhat infantile realm of primary fruit, with the odd dollop of oak, how will these voyagers become acquainted with wine's other dimensions? Have we arrived at a brave new world of wine, where, in the words of Mustapha Mond, one of the Controllers from Huxley's novel, 'people are happy: they get what they want, and they never want what they can't get . . . We have sacrificed the high art. We have the feelies and the scent organ instead. They mean a lot of agreeable sensations to the audience.' End of story?

HOW TO ORGANISE A WINE-TASTING

The ancient Greeks knew a thing or two about wine-tastings. Mind you, symposia, as the Athenian tastings were called, had certain features guaranteed to raise eyebrows among polite wine-bibbers in Surrey or Perthshire. Respectable women, for example, were banned from these occasions, which were only for men and not entirely respectable, or solely musical, flute-girls. Then there was the custom of mixing the wine with water, to a proportion dictated by the symposiarch, or master of the wine-tasting. As a further diversion there was *kottabos*, a game which consisted of flicking the dregs in your wine glass at a bronze disk balanced on a tripod.

THE THEME

The Greeks, however, at least knew the most important factor about wine-tastings: they must have a theme. In the most famous symposium of them all, Plato's, the theme was love; but in these more specialised days we would expect the theme to have something to do with wine. Before determining the guest list, the date, the time, the venue, the type of glasses, the arrangements for lighting and temperature control, the first step when organising a tasting is to decide on a theme. What aspect or aspects of wine is this tasting meant to illustrate? Just opening a few bottles at random is the equivalent of a conversation which leaps about from topic to topic without ever settling down – unsatisfactory.

What might be possible themes for an informal tasting with at least a semi-serious purpose? Perhaps the most obvious these days would be based on grape varieties: a selection – six to ten wines is a fair number for an informal tasting at home – of Cabernet Sauvignons, Chardonnays, Sauvignons or Merlots from around the world. You can always go more recherché, with Viognier or Zinfandel, or more specialised with a clutch of South Australian Chardonnays or Cabernet-based wines from Bordeaux. You might wish to establish a theme within the theme, such as South African *versus* Chilean Cabernet Sauvignon, or Burgundy *versus* Oregon and California Pinot Noir.

This is the moment to ask yourself whether you are going for a blind tasting (that is with the bottles obscured, not the guests blindfolded) or one with bottles visible. Blind tastings are undoubtedly better for learning and testing your tasting ability, and provide an element of suspense, but some may find them intimidating or simply too much hassle. A good theme for a blind tasting is the identification of different grape varieties.

Apart from grape varieties, there are our old friends the vertical and horizontal tastings. These terms do not refer, as some wags have thought, to the postures taken by participants, but to tastings of, first, different vintages of one particular wine, and, secondly, a single vintage as refracted through a choice of different wines. The vertical tasting obviously works best with wines of some quality designed to age, and a range of say Château Latour going back to 1961 might stretch your budget. Horizontal tastings, especially of fairly recent vintages, probably offer more scope in the middle range of price. Sometimes Cinderella vintages such as 1987 or 1991 – that is, vintages considered disappointing in Bordeaux, even though they are often quite adequate in other regions – make excellent bets, not least because the wines are cheaper, and probably mature quicker than those of 'great' vintages.

There are myriad other possibilities. You might want to focus on a country – a selection of German estate-bottled wines from the Mosel-Saar-Ruwer, Rheingau and Rheinpfalz, for instance – or a region – Bordeaux from *petits châteaux* up to *grand cru classé* – or on a topic such as oaked *versus* unoaked Chardonnay, or indeed Chablis. The fundamental point is that you have to come up with a theme which will enable you to choose between six and ten interesting wines which illustrate your theme in varied ways, and provide stimulating points of comparison and difference.

BUYING THE WINE

Now comes probably the most enjoyable part of the whole business – choosing and buying the wines themselves. You may have a wine merchant to whom you are monogamously faithful – in which case we hope he or she is one with a list recommended in this Guide; or you may be utterly, gloriously promiscuous. We would, without counselling immorality, advise you to shop around a little; if you normally do all your wine-buying at Sainsbury or Tesco, spare a thought for your high-street specialist, Oddbins or Wine Rack, and even the maverick independent who operates from a converted dairy down the road. In particular, if your theme leads you to a particular country or region, think about merchants who specialise in that country or region (Winecellars or Valvona & Crolla for Italy, La Reserva, Moreno or Laymont & Shaw for Spain). At this point you will also have to decide on quantities, which will be determined by the number of tasters, which may in turn be decided by the amount of space at your disposal. While as many as 20 tasting samples may with care be poured from one bottle, it would be prudent to assume that your guests will wish to retaste. As a general rule, one bottle will be enough for five or six guests.

LOGISTICS

You have decided on your theme and bought or ordered your wines; the rest is logistics, which for wine-tasting require some careful planning. The first thing to consider is space. There is nothing worse than a cramped tasting with no room to move your elbow, either in order to bring the glass to your lips or to write notes. So there needs to be room for everyone to sit comfortably at a well-lit table – trestle tables are an idea if existing tables are not big enough or are too precious. The table needs to be the right height and firm enough to write notes on. Ideally, it should be covered with a white cloth to enable tasters to judge the colour of each wine. Fluorescent lighting is highly undesirable as it gives wine an unnatural colour.

Temperature control, especially for white wines, is vital and cannot easily be improvised at the last minute. Remember that wines will warm up quickly in the glass in a fairly crowded room, so it is better to start with wines which are slightly too cold than too warm. Contrary to some opinions, it is advisable to keep a dry

white wine in the fridge for at least three hours, and sweet whites for longer. Fine reds should not be served too cool: keep the bottles in a warm room or airing cupboard for a few hours before tasting.

Glasses come next. For a serious wine-tasting you would provide a separate glass for each wine. If you cannot match this ideal, there should be at least three different glasses, so even if not all the wines can be compared at once, flights of three may be tasted. The type of glass is important, though if it has a reasonable-sized bowl and a stem, and is clean and polished, tasting should at least be possible. George Riedel of the well-known Austrian firm of glass manufacturers, Riedel, has been busy over the last decade designing glasses suited to particular types of wine. He is very persuasive on the subject of why Riesling and Pinot Noir need to be tasted from glasses with curling rims (to counteract acidity) and other refinements: you may not believe all he says, but his Vinum range of machine-made glasses is excellently designed and not prohibitively expensive. Another recommended tasting glass is the widely available ISO (International Standards Organisation) glass. Any decent wine merchant will hire out glasses, usually at no cost, though there may be a deposit and you will be expected to return them clean.

At this point come two very important interrelated matters: the order of wines to be tasted, and the tasting sheet on which the wines are printed and on which guests will record their tasting notes. The classic rules regarding order of wines are dry before sweet, light before heavy, simple before complex, young before old. These rules are not absolute, but the first three are broken at peril. Sometimes, however, a very powerful young wine – young vintage port, for example – will obliterate a delicate older one. Here you may wish to consider whether to pour each wine separately, with an appropriate interval for tasting and note-taking, or whether to pour wines in pairs or flights. It is a good idea to provide plain water biscuits and drinking water; this helps to clean the palate in between wines.

If your tasting is conducted blind, you will need to prepare two tasting sheets, one with the numbers of the wines, and space to write notes, and then a key putting the names of the wines to the numbers. Otherwise, give the fullest possible information about each wine – vineyard, grower, vintage – on a single sheet and do not cramp your guests who want space to write notes. Some people believe in prescribing categories for tasting notes, such as appearance, nose, palate and assessment, which can serve as useful prompts for the fledgling wine-taster; others prefer to leave a few blank lines. Clipboards and pens may smack of a junior sales conference, but your guests will thank you for providing them.

Now you are almost ready to begin – and, we hope, after the headaches of organisation, to enjoy the wines. There are just a few final considerations. The first concerns that delicate matter – spitting. To spit or not to spit? Serious tasters do it, at least in England and America, and if you want to keep your wits about you, or if you are planning to drive home after the tasting, it is obviously the sensible but much less enjoyable policy. In which case spittoons, which may be sawdust-filled wooden boxes (one between two tasters), or simply quite deep bowls (one for each taster), should be provided. If people find spitting offensive, they are probably not ready for the raw, dangerous pursuit which is wine-tasting. Smoking, strong perfume and aftershave are other potentially delicate matters, but the answer here is simple: ban them.

Now it really is time for your friends to arrive, and for the wine-tasting to begin. The purpose of the tasting is partly to learn something about wine, but above all to have good conversation, initially about wine but then spreading to many other subjects under the sun, or the moon. The ancient Greeks, for all their peculiar ideas, did know a thing or two about good conversation, and having a good time. So bring on the flute-girls.

CHECKLIST

▶ Decide on theme

▶ Determine number of guests

▶ Select and order wines

▶ Decide on order of wines; print tasting sheets

▶ Organise space – tables, chairs, lighting

▶ Temperature control – cool whites, reds at room temperature

▶ Glasses (clean and polished, right number)

▶ Biscuits and water

▶ Clipboards and pens

▶ Spittoons

CROSS-CHANNEL WINE SHOPPING

Harry Eyres

Customs allowances within the EU were abolished from 1 January 1993, thus allowing Britons to bring back almost any amount of wine from abroad at virtually duty-free prices, while maintaining duty on wine purchased within the UK at punitive levels. This was a decision implemented by Norman Lamont, but his successor Kenneth Clarke, has not endeared himself to the wine trade either, though his decision to raise duty in the wake of the government's defeat on VAT on fuel might have been taken with some reluctance. (The current UK duty on table wines between 5.5° and 15° alcohol is around £1.05 a bottle; on sparkling wine it is around £1.72. VAT is also payable on this duty.) French duty is around two pence a bottle.

Cross-channel wine-buying seems to be here to stay: as we go to press a huge new Tesco is scheduled to open at the French entrance to the Channel Tunnel, putting to shame Sainsbury's slightly undersized effort within the Mammouth hypermarket in Calais, and Victoria Wine has just announced that it is to open a shop in the same centre.

No one knows exactly how much booze is being bought in Calais, Boulogne and other Channel ports for consumption back in the UK: the Wine and Spirit Association's figure of 10 per cent of all wine drunk in the UK has been challenged by the independent consultants London Economics, but the latter organisation also predicts that the UK will have to bring down its rates of duty. For the time being, the Treasury seems to have no intention of doing that. The incentive to buy in France remains, and the range of outlets is now considerable, especially in Calais and Boulogne.

It is with some ambivalence, therefore, that we offer advice to those wishing to buy abroad: we may be considered as traitors by some sectors of the wine trade, but our primary responsibility is to our readers.

Fortunately, the British wine trade has shown its customary spirit of enterprise and adventure by taking on the French merchants at their own game. Following the success of the pioneers, The Grape Shop, The Wine Society, La Maison du Vin and others, the supermarkets, led without much flourish by Sainsbury, and Allied's Victoria Wine have crossed the Channel. British travellers to the Continent can now buy wine at several British-run outlets, and at a considerable saving on prices in the UK. The French, somewhat belatedly, have responded to this invasion with increasing inventiveness, and the best of the French shops are worth serious consideration. Below, we offer more detailed listings of the main outlets.

Customs & Excise guidelines for alcohol purchases in an EU country

- You are only allowed to buy drink for your personal consumption. Buying for resale is illegal and Customs & Excise claims to have been bringing one prosecution a day on this score. Buying-rings and groups are also illegal, so it is not advisable to tell Customs officers that you have bought drink on behalf of a group of friends.
- There is a minimum indicative level (MIL) of 90 litres (of which no more than 60 may be sparkling wine) of wine per person. This, however, is not a legal limit. You are entitled to import more than this if you clear it with Customs in advance and can prove that the wine is for your personal use. If you are buying wine or champagne for a party or wedding, you should be able to name the date and venue (though presumably Customs does not have the power to enforce this in the event of an absconding bride or bridegroom). You may also purchase 10 litres of spirits, 20 litres of fortified wine and 110 litres of beer.

Brits abroad

We recommend the following British-run outlets:

- Calais Wine and Beer Company, rue de Judée, Zone Marcel Doret, 62100 Calais (tel: 21 97 63 00). A Majestic-inspired, warehouse-type operation offering reasonable, if not inspired selection of around 500 wines.
- The Grape Shop, Gate Maritime 85-87 rue Victor Hugo, 62200 Boulogne-sur-Mer (tel: 21 33 92 30 and 30 16 17). A splendidly characterful selection by Martin Brown, based on his successful shop in Northcote Road, London SW11. Particular strengths are growers' champagnes, French country wines and the New World, but very few lines will disappoint. There are now two

shops, much the larger being situated next to the Seacat terminal. The original shop, in the centre of Boulogne, offers parking in an underground garage.

- La Maison du Vin, 71 avenue Carnot, 50100 Cherbourg (tel: 33 43 39 79; fax: 33 43 22 69). The directors of this venture are Anthony Wills and Richard Harvey MW, of Richard Harvey Wines, Wareham, Dorset. Mr Harvey's buying skills are in evidence in a smallish but well-chosen selection of French growers' wines, with some good Australians. Now also at 12 rue Georges Clemenceau, Saint-Servan, St-Malo (tel: 99 82 69 54; fax: 99 82 69 56).
- The Wine Society, c/o Distilleries Ryssen, 1 rue de la Paroisse, Hesdin, 50km south of Boulogne (for membership enquiries telephone The Wine Society in Stevenage on (01438) 741177). Last year The Wine Society (life membership £20) did a deal with a local distillery to allow members to buy and collect wine in France. Now it has opened a small shop. The range on offer is limited (100 wines) compared to the grandiose full list, and prices are on the high side.
- J. Sainsbury Bières, Vins et Spiritueux, Mammouth Hypermarket, Route de Boulogne, 62100 Calais (tel: 21 34 04 44, ask for Sainsbury's). A relatively small store (3,000 square foot) modestly tucked away inside the Mammouth Hypermarket, offering a selection of some 300 wines and beers from the JS range. Wines work out at least £1 a bottle cheaper than in the UK.
- Tesco, Cité de l'Europe, Channel Tunnel. Opening as we go to press, this is a vast (22,000 square foot) store promising a 'huge' range of wines.
- Les Caves de Roscoff, Zone de Bloscon, Ateliers 7,8,9, 29680 Roscoff (tel: 98 61 24 10). A reasonable selection of mainly French wines from Andrew Bruce and Tim Hanbury.

The French hypermarkets and merchants

French hypermarkets such as Auchan (Route Nationale 42, direction St-Omer, 62200 St-Martin les Boulogne), Continent (Quai de l'Entrepôt, 50100 Cherbourg) and Mammouth (Route de Boulogne, 62100 Calais) are notorious for buying wine almost entirely on price, and certainly offer nothing like the range and variety of a good Tesco, Sainsbury or Safeway. However, Bordeaux is one area worth studying, especially at Auchan and Mammouth, where some excellent wines can be found. Three worthwhile French wine merchants are:

- Bar à Vins, 52 Place d'Armes, 62100 Calais (tel: 21 96 96 31). Very good French country selection. Also a café and wine bar.
- Le Chais, Quartier Brequerecque, rue des Deux Ponts, 62200 Boulogne-sur-Mer (tel: 21 31 65 42). The best French warehouse-style operation, selling by the case of six or twelve. Selection rather dominated by *négociants*.
- Perardel, Zone Marcel Doret, rue Marcel Doret, 62100 Calais (tel: 21 97 21 22). Remarkable fine wine selection and good champagne offers, though a move downmarket is reported.

Car-loading tips

With such a fragile, and heavy, cargo, making sure that you load sensibly could avoid a costly disaster. *Which?* motoring experts advise that you secure bottles firmly but they don't recommend using a roof rack. Hypermarkets don't always provide spare cartons so it may be wise to take some empty ones with you. The following tips should help you ensure that both you and your purchases reach home in one piece:

- your car manual or dealer will provide maximum weights. For example, a 1992 Ford Escort 1.4L takes approximately 450kg and a Ford Sierra 2.0LX 555kg
- allow an average 70kg for each adult and an appropriate amount for luggage
- a case of still wine weighs about 15kg and a case of champagne about 20kg
- check appropriate tyre pressures for increased loads
- once the vehicle is loaded, check both steering and braking, which may feel different.

Wine-buying tips

Things worth bearing in mind:

- check the rate of exchange so you have a clear idea of prices
- if possible, have an idea of what you want to buy before you go and take a note of comparable prices in the UK
- check duty-free prices on the way as some purchases (especially spirits) may be cheaper en route than on land
- remember to check vintages: in cheaper wines, younger is usually better, for whites and most reds
- if you are unsure about what you're buying, it may be wise to buy a mixed case or two to decide what you like and then plan another trip to stock up. Remember that 90 litres is 120 bottles – that's a lot to get through if you make an imprudent purchase

- note that more expensive wines are often competitively priced in the UK and that the range may be wider at home
- some outlets may offer the chance to taste before you buy
- keep all receipts in case you are asked to show them at Customs
- don't attempt to resell any wine.

Part II

Wines of the world

THE LOOK, SMELL AND TASTE OF WINE

THE LOOK

Wine appeals to more than just our sense of taste. In our sight-centred culture, it is the appearance of wine which will strike us first. A great deal of information, as well as pleasure, can be gleaned from our first glance at the wine poured into a glass (not cut or coloured glass, please).

White wines, you might think, all look pretty much alike. Not true: there are all kinds of subtle variations, from the palest off-yellow of a modern, cool-fermented white from Italy or South Africa, through the pale green of a fine Mosel to the mid-yellow of a Pinot Blanc, Vernaccia or lightly oaked Chardonnay, to the richer golden yellow of mature white burgundy, and deep burnished copper of old Sauternes. Dullness of colour is always suspect, as much in white as red wine, often indicating oxidation. Cloudiness is simply unacceptable.

With red wine, the colour is more obviously part of the experience. The range is enormous, from the deep purple of youthful Dolcetto through the dark, blood-red of claret to the faded (but not dull) orangey-brown hues of mature Gran Reserva Rioja or old burgundy. Red wines generally start off with a purple or even blue hue in their youth, becoming first redder and then browner, at the rim, with age.

Rosé wines, so often scorned, depend more on their colour than any others. Here too the range is great, from the palest onion-skin of a Cabernet rosé from Bordeaux, through the brighter, but still pale, pink of a young Cabernet Franc rosé from the Loire, to the frankly lurid colour often achieved with Grenache in Australia or the Languedoc.

Wine is best stored in a cool, dark place where the temperature is steady at around 11°C. If you intend to keep the wine for more than three months store the bottle on its side so that the cork and the wine remain in contact.

THE SMELL

Some experts claim that as much as 80 per cent of the sensory content of a wine is picked up by the nose. Perhaps these experts (including the legendary José Ignacio 'the Nose' Domecq) are proboscically better endowed than most of us, but they certainly have a point. The scent of a wine can often be the most exquisite part of its personality. To knock back a glass of fine burgundy, say, without even a sniff is a crime. A preliminary nosing is also an important safeguard against ingesting liquid which may prove unpleasant or even noxious.

White wines can be divided into the aromatic and the non-aromatic, but this does not mean that the non-aromatic lack smell. It is simply that certain grape varieties, especially Gewurztraminer, Muscat and Viognier, are more obviously scented than others. Chardonnay would be classified as non-aromatic, but the finest Chardonnay wines develop the most fascinating and complex aromas with age. Here, the influence of oak is clearly important. New oak barrels impart both scent and flavour to wines which are fermented or matured in them.

The aroma of fine, mature red wines is best appreciated when they are drunk from glasses with ample-sized bowls. Red-wine aromas develop even more markedly than those of fine whites such as Rieslings and Chardonnays. In their youth, red wines tend to smell of fruits, cherry in Valpolicella, blackcurrant in Cabernet Sauvignon from Bordeaux or Chile, raspberry in the case of some young burgundies. As the wine matures, the fruits deepen into roots, spices and a great complexity of other aromas, sometimes suggesting a whole room-full of smells.

THE TASTE

For most of us, wine must be taken into the mouth, and indeed tipped down the throat, to be fully appreciated. Taste is the most intimate of all the senses. Once we have got past the infant, exploratory stage of oral contact, taking something into our mouth is not something we do lightly. It is a sign of trust. Wine should deserve that trust – sadly, this is not always the case. Good and great wines, however, richly reward it.

As for what we are looking for in flavour, the first element is probably what we loosely call fruit. Fruit is a much more slippery concept than it might seem. All wine is made from grapes, but not many wines actually taste, or should taste, of grapes in their raw form. Wines made from Muscat, Gewurztraminer, sometimes, Riesling, do taste of grapes. Wines made from Chardonnay,

Cabernet Sauvignon and Pinot Noir emphatically do not. After all, if you want the taste of grapes, buy them fresh. Wine is something else: fermented grape juice, in the course of its magical transformation into an alcoholic drink, takes on or reveals many other flavours.

Common fruit flavours often detected in wines include apple, pear and peach (with white wines), cherry, strawberry, raspberry, blackberry, blackcurrant, plum and damson (with red wines). A useful distinction between red and black berries can sometimes be made between red wines of different provenance or different years. We find that the red Bordeaux of 1985 usually suggest red-berry fruits while those of 1982 or 1986 suggest black-berry fruits.

After fruit, or in some cases even before, the most common flavour element looked for in a wine is sweetness or dryness. Red wines are usually expected to be dry, but the two best-selling types of white wine in the UK, Liebfraumilch and (white) Lambrusco are on the sweet side. In wine parlance, of course, medium means sweet. There are many grades of dryness and sweetness, especially with white wines. Brut champagne, the driest style, for instance, can contain up to 15 grams per litre of residual sugar (sugar not converted into alcohol), which puts it into the semi-dry category of still wines. Many white wines which purport to be dry, such as many vins de pays des Côtes de Gascogne, actually contain fair amounts of residual sugar. Even some Chardonnays, such as Glen Ellen, are by no means as dry as their purchasers probably like to think.

THE TEXTURE

Texture is an extremely important element of the taste of wine. It is also perhaps the hardest to talk about. Thinness is less desirable in wines than in people and fatness, or at least plumpness, can be most attractive. White varieties such as Sauvignon Blanc and Riesling tend to give leaner wines than Chardonnay or, at the extreme of plumpness, Viognier. Great red wines are usually rich and many-layered in texture, while great sweet wines can be viscous.

Acidity

Acidity, although it may not sound very attractive, is essential to all wines, but especially to white wines. Acidity keeps wines fresh. Of course, excessive acidity is unpleasant, but some white burgundies, for instance, require to be aged for some time to lose the harsh edge of acidity. If they did not possess that acidity, they would quickly fall apart and become flabby, like many California and Australian Chardonnays. German Riesling, grown in a cool climate, famously possesses high levels of acidity, often softened by discreet balancing with residual sugar.

Tannin

Tannin, to some extent, is to red wines what acidity is to white wines. This extract from the grape-skins and pips is a preservative, essential for allowing long life but often less than pleasant in the first few years. Traditionally made Bordeaux and Barolos are two types of red wine which are likely to contain high levels of tannin. The trend in wine-making these days, however, is to extract less tannin, or to extract what some claim is a chimera, soft tannin, to make red wines more drinkable in their youth.

Oak

Oak, already mentioned as a component of smell, is the only influence on the flavour of most wines which does not derive from grapes. New oak barrels, especially French oak, are expensive, but are highly prized by winemakers for their ability to enhance the taste of wines with a sweet spiciness, or chocolatey richness. American oak has a more obvious taste than French, sweet and vanillin: this taste is probably the main reason for Rioja's popularity, but it is scorned by many sophisticated winemakers. Oak connoisseurship is a complicated subject, involving oak from different forests, made by a variety of coopers who employ different levels of toast, or char.

Age

The average age at which even fine wines are consumed has almost certainly dropped considerably over the past decade. Most wines, of course, are bought for immediate consumption, which is perfectly natural. However, the ability of many wines, not just red, to gain new dimensions of flavour with age is sadly seldom recognised. White wines are by no means always best drunk very young. Fine white burgundy, for instance, can require at least seven years to reach optimal maturity, and if that sounds snobbish, it is meant to be helpful: some young Meursault, which will one day taste majestic, is positively unpleasant at two or three years of age. Riesling, another grape which can gain immensely from bottle-age, is rarely given the chance.

Red Bordeaux is the type of wine most associated with laying down. Perhaps in the past there has been excessive emphasis on the need to keep fine claret for twenty years or so before drinking. Recent vintages, however, under the influence of Professor Emile Peynaud, have been vinified in a less austere style, and many fine Bordeaux seem approachable after seven years or even fewer. Vintage port needs more time than any other commonly available wine – fifteen to twenty years is a good guide.

GRAPE VARIETIES

If you walked into a supermarket wine department and asked about grape varieties 15 years ago you would probably have been directed to the fresh fruit section. Alsace, to be sure, had been identifying its wonderfully pure clean wines by grape variety for decades, but few had noticed. Bulgarian Cabernet Sauvignon, Australian Shiraz, California Chardonnay, New Zealand Sauvignon Blanc and the rest changed all that. Grape varieties were suddenly in vogue. They continue to be in vogue as new or regenerating wine countries such as Chile, South Africa, Romania and Moldova bombard us with an unstoppable barrage of well-targeted varietals. Some may be becoming almost indistinguishable from each other, but at least they present a basic wine style in a logical, unambiguous and unpretentious manner. If the concept is still unfamiliar to you, think of apples. Everyone knows the difference between a Cox's Orange Pippin and a Granny Smith. The difference between Chardonnay and Riesling is just as obvious and significant.

What follows is a guide to 15 of the world's most fashionable varieties, with brief notes on the best of the myriad others. We should note here that while varietals have won many new friends for wine, they also have their detractors. The more aristocratic of the French wine-growers, in particular, tend to curl their lips at the notion of *cépage* (grape variety) predominating over *terroir* (vineyard site). The château-owners of Bordeaux will say 'I make Pauillac (or Mouton, or whatever), not Cabernet Sauvignon' – and they have a point. No Bordeaux red wine is a 100 per cent varietal. More strangely, a leading Burgundian such as Lalou Bize-Leroy, formerly director of Domaine de la Romanée-Conti, will assure you that her wines do not taste of Pinot Noir, despite being made entirely from that variety. These people are not just being snobbish. Narrow-minded concentration on single varietals can lead to boring sameness, and, indeed, to wines which lack intrinsic balance. Still, the success of a country like Bulgaria, whose state-run wine industry had the foresight to plant Cabernet Sauvignon and Chardonnay, can hardly be overlooked. At a fairly basic level, the pick of the French varieties simply provide a more pleasant and popular drinking experience than certain native grapes whose survival has nothing more noble to sanction it than ignorance and inertia. Some worry that the fashionable duo of Chardonnay and Cabernet Sauvignon are extending their empire too widely. They should be consoled by the fact that Chardonnay still accounts for less than half a per cent of the world's vineyards. Recent trends in Italy offer further reassurance. A few years ago the intrusion of Cabernet Sauvignon into the heartlands of Chianti Classico and even Barbaresco was seen as a betrayal of native Italian tradition. But the scare was exaggerated: Cabernet did not prove to be a grey squirrel of a grape, ousting the handsome native red. In fact, it seems to have achieved a pretty harmonious minor position, and has even brought about, paradoxically, a better appreciation of the qualities of the great Tuscan grape, Sangiovese.

1. CABERNET SAUVIGNON

Cabernet Sauvignon is like one of those maddeningly successful people at school who always comes top of the form, and is also good at games and music. It seems to exude a smug superiority, which provokes envy. What is so special about Cabernet? You might well argue that other grapes are more exciting, overwhelming or subtle. But Cabernet wins the prizes. It is more complete and consistent than any other red grape. Its wines have deep colour, body, cedary, faintly herbaceous or tobacco scent, blackcurrant fruit, sometimes gum-puckering tannin and sufficient acidity. No other grape makes wines which age so satisfyingly.

Cabernet Sauvignon owes its worldwide popularity to its success as the leading grape of Bordeaux, the area where fine red wines made to age in bottle were first produced in large quantities. Bordeaux red wines, refined, often reserved, sometimes dustily dry, yet harmonious and able to age, are the ones which have been imitated all over the world. Cabernet is relatively easy to cultivate and pretty hardy, and it preserves its blackcurranty, cedary, cigar-box character remarkably well wherever it travels.

Wine styles; vinification; blending; oak

Cabernet Sauvignon may be a high-class grape, but its wines cover the entire price spectrum. You can pick up perfectly acceptable examples from Bulgaria or Chile for less than £3. Australia, California and the south of France begin to pitch in with their ripely fruity versions from £3.50 upwards. Bordeaux also begins around this price range, then proceeds upwards through the sometimes rustic, artisanal *petits châteaux*, the solid professional world of the *crus bourgeois* to the ultimate aristocrats of wine, the suave, silky, elegant *crus classés*.

No Bordeaux red wine, traditionally, is made from 100 per cent Cabernet Sauvignon. Blending is the rule in the region, and the main blending partners for Cabernet Sauvignon are Merlot (which gives softer, jammy fruit), Cabernet Franc (providing perfume and finesse) and Petit Verdot (adding four-square solidity). Cabernet Sauvignon is also blended successfully with Syrah/Shiraz (Provence, Australia), Sangiovese (Tuscany) and Tempranillo (Penedés, Navarra).

Wines made to age longer will have gone through longer fermentation and maceration (see glossary), and will, in their early years, hide much of their richness behind protective tannin. Most of the world's best Cabernet Sauvignons have been aged in the small oak barrels called *barriques*, preferably made of French oak, though certain great California Cabernet Sauvignons stick with American oak to wonderful effect.

Cabernet Sauvignon is rather more versatile than many claret-lovers realise. It can be vinified using the whole-berry carbonic-maceration technique to produce vividly fruity *primeur*-style wine (Mitchelton's Cab Mac, for instance). It also makes excellent rosé (in the south of France, especially). And Yalumba has proved that sparkling Cabernet is not just a Monty Python spoof.

See under: France – Bordeaux, Languedoc, Provence; USA – California, Washington State; Australia; Eastern Europe – Bulgaria, Hungary, Moldova, Romania; South America – Chile, Argentina; Italy; Spain; Portugal; South Africa; New Zealand.

2. CHARDONNAY

Perhaps the world's passion for Chardonnay has lost its first madly romantic flush, but there is every sign of a long and satisfying relationship. The world-weary wine writers who complain of Chardonnay fatigue syndrome are way out of step with most of their readers. The elite wine-drinkers of post-war Britain fell in love with white burgundy, so it is hardly surprising that today's vastly expanded society of wine-drinkers should relish the white burgundy grape, even if their appetite means supplementing the tiny production of Burgundy with New World imitations (often excellent).

Wine styles; vinification; oak

For many people, Chardonnay is synonymous with dry white wine. If you were to ask them to describe the particular Chardonnay taste, they might find it difficult. There is, to be sure, a roundness, a peachiness, sometimes a butteriness, a nuttiness... But this is the ultimate winemaker's grape, the one which cries out to be shaped and moulded into whatever form the winemaker's desire may take. Chardonnay, by a combination of the timing of harvest and techniques of vinification, with or without malolactic fermentation, with or without oak, can be made in a huge range of styles, from light and lemony-fresh to nutty and extremely rich. It's hard to avoid those sexist old wine writers' analogies, comparing different styles of Chardonnay with the voluptuous blonde or the anorexic Twiggy-clone. Chardonnay seems able to satisfy all (yes, male) fantasies, from the *Sun*-reader's D-cup to the intellectual's buttoned-up blue-stocking. Chardonnay has even been compared to Madonna, but will remain desirable for longer.

Chardonnay's origins lie in Burgundy, where it is by far the most important white grape. Chablis and the Côte d'Or still produce the world's supreme Chardonnays, together with many which are substandard and overpriced. The Mâconnais is a source of fair-to-good medium-priced Chardonnay. In Champagne, Chardonnay is the most sought-after of the three grapes, and 100 per cent Chardonnay Blanc de Blancs, though difficult to make, is highly fashionable. But Chardonnay's name, paradoxically, has been made by the New World: first California, then, with even greater success, Australia have hijacked the white burgundy grape. Ripe New World fruit combined with obvious oak have created a hugely popular style, now imitated, by a reverse process, in southern France as well as countries like South Africa, Chile and New Zealand.

Chardonnay has a particular affinity with the nutty, spicy flavours of new oak. Top Chardonnay-makers around the globe now agree that fermentation, not just ageing, in barrel is essential for the flavours of fruit and oak to marry harmoniously. Less ambitious producers still like to get some element of oak flavour in their wine, even if that means suspending a bag of oak chips in the vat during fermentation. Unoaked Chardonnay (of which Chablis has a proud tradition) has been out of fashion, but may be set for a comeback. Italy is proving a good source of clean-limbed lighter styles. Decent sparkling examples are cropping up all over the wine world.

See under: France – Burgundy, Champagne, Languedoc, Loire; Australia; USA – California, Oregon, Washington State, New York State; New Zealand; South Africa; South America – Chile; Italy; Spain; Eastern Europe – Bulgaria, Hungary, Moldova.

3. PINOT NOIR

Pinot Noir has probably given rise to more myths, dubious claims and purple prose than any other grape. The first myth is that the temperamental red grape of Burgundy does not travel. The sensitive, thin-skinned Pinot Noir is undoubtedly more difficult to handle both in the vineyard and in the winery than the thicker-skinned Cabernet Sauvignon. So far, its international successes, in still red wine rather than sparkling form, have been limited. But if Pinot Noir is the Holy Grail of modern wine culture, the Burgundians who guard it had better watch out. There are knights in shining armour approaching from several directions. Oregon, with its amiably eccentric, small-scale wine industry, was for a time considered the New World region most likely to get there first. Even Oregonians now admit, on the whole, that most of the best Pinot Noirs from America are coming out of California. Australia's Yarra Valley is another source of exciting, raspberry-scented Pinot Noir, and New Zealand seems poised for success with the grape. South Africa already has one first-rate producer.

Wine styles; vinification; oak

Pinot Noir is a component of two of the world's greatest wine styles, red burgundy and champagne. Though more sensual, earthy, animal even, than Cabernet Sauvignon, it is not a plebeian variety. You will search in vain for good Pinot Noir in the bargain basement (though Romania produces acceptable inexpensive wine from the grape). Red burgundy is scarce, and top-quality red burgundy even scarcer. Uncertain weather, subdivision of properties into tiny parcels and rustic wine-making still make the purchase of burgundy a high-risk business. It is only the overwhelming reward of great burgundy – its aromas of hung game and roots as well as red fruits, its voluptuousness of texture – which can justify that risk.

Pinot Noir from elsewhere carries less risk, though the rewards are relatively smaller. California's sun-blessed climate, especially when tempered by cool Pacific breezes, can deliver Pinot Noir of seductive, fleshy appeal, and, increasingly, a measure of rooty subtlety. Oregon is almost as chancy as Burgundy, but can be magnificent at its best (currently represented by a Burgundian, Robert Drouhin). Certain cool corners of Australia (including Tasmania) and much of New Zealand are producing, or will soon be producing, world-class Pinot Noir.

Sensitive in all things, Pinot Noir demands the lightest touch in the use of oak. Heavily charred American oak simply swamps the subtlety. Tight-grained French oak is essential, but should not be over-used.

Then there is sparkling wine: Pinot Noir is the backbone of nearly all the world's best sparkling wines, though 100 per cent Pinot Noir sparklers can be too big and meaty for modern tastes.

See under: France – Burgundy, Champagne; USA – California, Oregon; Australia; New Zealand; South Africa; Germany; Italy; Spain; Eastern Europe – Romania; South America – Chile, Argentina.

4. RIESLING

Riesling is the world's most abused and misunderstood grape. This is actually one of the noblest of all grapes, but its name has been taken in vain by unrelated pseudo-Rieslings such as Laski Rizling from Slovenia, Welschriesling (not the Ebbw Vale tipple) from ex-Czechoslovakia and Riesling Italico. It has also been associated with Liebfraumilch, the bargain export sugar-water from Germany, which is made mainly from Müller-Thurgau and other new crossings, not from Riesling. The result is that the great Rieslings, above all from the Mosel-Saar-Ruwer, Nahe, Rheingau and Rheinpfalz in Germany, also from Alsace, Austria, New Zealand and in a very different style from South Australia, are scandalously underrated. The time for a revival of this superb grape is overdue – as wine writers have been repeating for years.

Wine styles – dry and sweet; vinification

Put simply, the problem with wines produced from the white Riesling grape is that people think they are sweet. Of course there are the great sweet botrytis-affected Rieslings, the Beeren- and Trockenbeerenausleses, and the Eisweins made from frozen grapes, but those are probably not what such people have in mind. Apart from those luscious rarities, all the world's best Rieslings are either dry or balanced between sweetness and acidity. This sweet-sour piquancy is Riesling's great secret. The grape is naturally high in acidity – much higher than Chardonnay, for instance – and in the coolest climates may be unbearably austere without some tempering sweetness (achieved either by stopping the fermentation early or by adding unfermented grape juice). The steep slatey valleys of the Mosel and its tributaries are the place where this delicate balance is most perfectly poised, and combined with appley fragrance.

Rhine Rieslings tend to be bigger and earthier: minerally and intense in the Rheingau, softer in the Rheinhessen and more exotic, even tropical, in the Rheinpfalz, where Germany's best dry Rieslings are made. These are some of the most satisfying and versatile food wines in the world. French Alsace is a southern continuation of the German Rheinpfalz (or *vice versa*), but Gallic wine-making traditions lead to a fuller-bodied, less grapey style. Dry Alsace Rieslings can be great, but sometimes need years to reveal their aromas and flavours. Austria is a relative newcomer to the making of fine dry Riesling, and her versions can err on the side of harsh austerity.

South-eastern Australia has a very different climate from the Mosel Valley, so it should come as no surprise that the Rieslings of the Barossa, Clare, Eden and Goulbourn valleys are powerful, ripe wines. The lemony or limey acidity is still present, to balance the richness, and no less a luminary than Brian Croser is just as proud of his Riesling as of his Chardonnay. The best New Zealand Rieslings, though even further away geographically, are much closer in character to the great German and Alsace Rieslings. This is a style to watch. California has had markedly less success, or probably interest, in Riesling production, with the exception of the superb, exotically spiced botrytised Rieslings from producers such as Château St-Jean and Phelps. Other areas of the USA, such as Washington State and New York State, may prove more suited to fine Riesling production.

See under: Germany; France – Alsace; Austria; Australia; New Zealand; USA – California, Washington State.

5. SYRAH/SHIRAZ

Syrah is indisputably one of the finest of all red wine grapes. If it is less well-known than Cabernet Sauvignon, say, that reflects the tiny yield and relative obscurity of the northern Rhône wine villages which produce the greatest Syrah wines, rather than the quality of the grape. Syrah still has, perhaps, a faintly rustic aura, but there is nothing rustic whatsoever about Guigal's Côte Rôtie, Jaboulet's Hermitage La Chapelle or Penfold's Grange Hermitage. There is something wild, yes, indeed: Syrah is almost overpowering in its pungency, which combines more scents than any other grape – violets, wild herbs, all sorts of berries, pepper, tar, leather, the list could go on. Syrah's happy combination with Cabernet Sauvignon is a partnership of opposites: the suave, reserved gentleman in harness with the wild, charismatic bandit.

Wine styles; blending; vinification; oak

The greatest Syrah wines are wines for keeping, massively concentrated, dark in colour (Côte Rôtie somewhat less so), time-bombs of flavour with long fuses. But Syrah can also make more modest, yet still highly flavoured and aromatic, wines, ready to be drunk within a year or two of the vintage (the lesser Crozes-Hermitages and St-Josephs from the Rhône, and most Australian Shiraz). At the bargain end, single-varietal Syrah from the south of France or Shiraz from Australia will often provide character, but sometimes calls out for a blending partner. Syrah wines vinified by carbonic maceration tend to have a coarse, boiled-sweet flavour, and suggest that the grape is not suited to making light Beaujolais-style wines. Syrah's strong, occasionally overbearing, character has always made it an extremely useful blending grape. In the southern Rhône Syrah makes an invaluable contribution to the blend of the top Châteauneuf-du-Pape and Gigondas wines, made mainly from Grenache (q.v.) as well as to wines from lesser appellations such as Lirac, the Côtes-du-Rhône-Villages and also to basic Côtes-du-Rhône. The grape is widely planted as a *cépage améliorateur* (a variety used in small quantities to add quality and character to a blend) in Languedoc and Roussillon.

In Provence, Syrah combines with Cabernet Sauvignon to wonderful effect in wines such as Domaine de Trévallon and Château Vignelaure. But the Cabernet-Shiraz partnership has really blossomed in Australia; the warm, sometimes minty, often caramelly qualities of Australian Shiraz complement the tighter, bonier structure of Cabernet and fill out its 'hollow middle'. The greatest Australian Shiraz wines, though, such as Grange Hermitage, Henschke's Mount Edelstone and Hill of Grace and Lindemans' old classics from the Hunter Valley, are simply some of the world's most majestic red wines. Also from Australia come magnificently idiosyncratic sparkling and fortified Syrah wines.

Syrah has made little impact in the Americas, though California's Rhône Ranger school has produced one or two fine examples (especially Qupé). Nor has the northern Rhône grape travelled widely in Europe: experiments in Tuscany look promising but remain isolated. Spain's lack of interest in the grape seems strange.

See under: France – Côte Rôtie, Hermitage, Cornas, St-Joseph, southern Rhône, Languedoc, Roussillon, Provence; Australia; USA – California; Italy.

6. SAUVIGNON BLANC

Sauvignon Blanc is a more versatile grape than is sometimes realised, but for most contemporary drinkers there is one style which epitomises it: fresh and aromatic, scented with the almost tangible smell of crushed blackberry leaves or nettles, and clean as a whistle, with a gooseberry-tartness. This style originated in the upper Loire Valley, around the towns of Sancerre and Pouilly, but for many (most?) drinkers it now conjures up a different landscape: pointed, receding mountain ranges by a southern sea. New Zealand's Cloudy Bay, followed by a host of imitators, made this style of aromatic Sauvignon perhaps *the* cult wine of the mid- and late 1980s.

Wine styles – dry, sweet, oaky; blending

Sauvignon actually originated in Bordeaux, where it is used to make sweet, botrytised and dry wines, sometimes of superlative quality. Until recently, most dry white Bordeaux, made from a blend of Sauvignon, Sémillon and Muscadelle, was dull, cardboardy stuff. Temperature-controlled fermentation, a technique pioneered in the New World which came to the aid of the Old, changed the picture. Sauvignon in Bordeaux may never achieve quite the gooseberry intensity it manages in Sancerre and New Zealand, but some very decent, fresh, dry Sauvignon is issuing in increasing quantities from the stainless steel fermentation vats of Entre-Deux-Mers. Sauvignon also makes tiny quantities of great dry wine in the Graves region, usually as an equal partner with Sémillon, but, occasionally – as at Domaine de Chevalier – as majority shareholder.

Sauvignon is one of the grapes used in the production of Sauternes and Barsac, the world's most celebrated dessert wines made from botrytised grapes. Here, Sauvignon is very definitely the junior partner, accounting for only 20 per cent of the blend at estates such as Yquem and La Tour Blanche, and a mere 5 per cent at Lafaurie-Peyraguey. Sémillon is preferred because it is more susceptible to botrytis and gives richer wine.

A third style of Sauvignon, this time dry, involves fermentation or ageing in new, or newish, oak barrels. This style has a curious history. The Californian Robert Mondavi coined the term Fumé Blanc to describe this kind of oaky Sauvignon, believing that it was typical of Pouilly Fumé. In fact, oak flavours were probably never sought deliberately by growers in Pouilly until Mondavi's wine, and others like it, gave them (especially Didier Dagueneau) the idea.

Mostly, Sauvignon in California seems uncertain of its identity, torn between oaky richness and attempts at buoyant freshness. The latter are seldom entirely convincing, because the hot Californian climate makes it difficult to pick the grapes at a mid-point between asparagussy unripeness and tropical blowsiness. Australia has the same difficulty, and has not succeeded in mounting a serious challenge to New Zealand Sauvignon. Chile makes large quantities of mostly mediocre Sauvignon, though new plantings in the Casablanca Valley are delivering exciting results. Odd corners of Europe provide the occasional interesting Sauvignon (Collio in Friuli, Rueda in Spain), while Eastern Europe supplies the bargain basement.

See under: France – Sancerre, Pouilly Fumé, Touraine, Sauternes, Barsac, Entre-Deux-Mers; New Zealand; USA – California; Australia; Italy – Friuli; Spain – Rueda; Eastern Europe – Bulgaria, Hungary.

7. SEMILLON

Sémillon is a strange, chameleon-like grape. It seems to change character, depending on where and how it is grown, to such an extent that a single description of its taste is almost impossible.

Wine styles – dry, sweet, oaked

In Western Australia and New Zealand, Semillon can produce herbaceous, almost asparagussy wines which are practically indistinguishable from Sauvignon Blanc. In the hotter Hunter Valley, Semillons at first powerful, dry and unaromatic develop an extraordinary honeyed, lanolin richness with age (up to 20 years). In Bordeaux, Sémillon combines with Sauvignon to produce two potentially great styles: dry, barrel-fermented Graves and luscious Sauternes. Perhaps this highlights Sémillon's two great advantages for the winemaker: its natural affinity with new oak and its susceptibility to botrytis. Beyond that, it is hard to characterise this somewhat inscrutable, but undeniably useful, variety.

See under: France – Bordeaux, Graves, Sauternes; Australia; New Zealand; South America – Chile.

8. MERLOT

Merlot tends to get a raw deal. It is always mentioned as the less noble partner of Cabernet Sauvignon – generous, fruity, a good sort, but somehow lacking the aristocratic reserve and class of

Cabernet. In fact, Merlot is much more widely planted in Bordeaux than Cabernet; it is also the grape used to make one of the world's most expensive wines, Château Pétrus; and, more significantly for a good many drinkers, Merlot is a far more attractive, easy-going proposition than its often crusty, unapproachable senior partner.

Wine styles; vinification; oak

Merlot is an earlier-ripening and budding variety than its relative, Cabernet Sauvignon, and gives wines of good colour, alcohol, supple, softish fruit (often strawberry rather than blackcurrant) and considerably less tannin than Cabernet.

Not all Merlots, however, are a complete push-over. Château Pétrus hardly falls into that category, nor do many other top-class St-Emilion and Pomerol wines which are made mainly from Merlot. North Italian Merlots are stronger on charm than backbone, but California Merlot can be as big and butch as any Cabernet. Australia, for some reason, has never favoured Merlot (though some is planted in Coonawarra), and New Zealand's efforts, so far, err on the grassy side. South Africa, on the other hand, is beginning to produce Merlots of greater fruit and charm than most dusty Cape Cabernets.

See under: France – Bordeaux, Languedoc; Italy; South Africa; USA – California; Eastern Europe – Bulgaria.

9. CABERNET FRANC

Cabernet Franc probably suffers even more than Merlot from the opprobrium of being a lesser partner to Cabernet Sauvignon. People dismiss Cabernet Franc like some fickle, lightweight, under-achieving family member – charming, potentially fine, but lacking bottom. There is some truth in this patronising assessment, but some equally weighty counter-evidence.

Wine styles

French Cabernet Franc wines tend to be aromatic – with that delicious note of woodland leafiness which the French call *sous-bois* – with raspberry-fruit flavours, but are lighter in body than those made from either Cabernet Sauvignon or Merlot. However, it can be difficult to say how much of this character derives from the *terroir* – the cool marginal vineyards of the Loire Valley – and how much from the grape itself. Northern Italian Cabernet Francs (when the term Cabernet is used in Italy, unqualified by

'Sauvignon' or 'Franc', it normally means Franc) are also light and grassy. In Bordeaux, however, one supreme Cabernet Franc-based wine, Château Cheval-Blanc, demonstrates what magnificent, ample, voluptuous, balanced and long-lived wine can issue from Cabernet Franc. Surely it is time for some producers in the New World to start to follow the example of Cheval-Blanc: so far, the call has been heard in one or two corners of California.

See under: France – Loire, Touraine, Bordeaux; Italy – Trentino, Alto Adige, Friuli; USA – California.

10. GRENACHE/GARNACHA

Grenache (or Garnacha, as it is called in its land of origin) is the grape which epitomises the warm south. When Keats called for a 'draught of vintage... tasting of dance and Provençal song, and sunburnt mirth' it was surely a Grenache wine, a Gigondas, a Châteauneuf-du-Pape, even a Catalan Priorato, he was imagining. Loose as the girdles of his Grecian nymphs, these are sensual, hedonistic wines, far from the intellectual rigour of Bordeaux. But though structure is not their strong point, certain Grenache wines can achieve greatness through sheer density and weight of texture.

Wine styles

Grenache is a versatile grape. It can be vinified in many different ways to produce wines as contrasting as the light, fresh rosados of Navarra and the heavyweight monster reds of Châteauneuf-du-Pape and Priorato, capable of ageing for a decade and more. Grenache also makes superb fortified wines in Banyuls and Australia.

The fashion nowadays favours lightness, and, even in Châteauneuf-du-Pape, many wines are being vinified partly or wholly by carbonic maceration to emphasise up-front, sweet fruit. Some delicious wines in this style are now coming out of Australia's Barossa Valley (from Charlie Melton and Rocky O'Callaghan) and California's Santa Cruz mountains (home of Randall Grahm's idiosyncratic Bonny Doon).

See under: France – southern Rhône, Châteauneuf-du-Pape, Gigondas, Languedoc, Roussillon; Spain – Penedés, Priorato; Australia; USA – California.

11. MUSCAT

One of the best things about late summer and early autumn is the arrival in our markets of Muscat grapes, mostly from Italy. Muscat (or Muscatel, Moscato or Moscatel) grapes are the ones which smell grapey – with wonderful, overpowering, and, yes, musky perfume. Wines made from any of the extensive family of Muscat grapes preserve the same scent and taste – unlike most wines, which actually taste of other fruits, rather than the grape.

Wine styles – sweet, dry, sparkling, fortified

Most wines made from Muscat aim to preserve its essential, uncomplicated, sweet grapeyness. Many are fortified, such as the Muscat de Beaumes de Venise and Muscat de Rivesaltes of southern France, the Muscat of Samos, the treacly liqueur Muscats of Rutherglen in Australia, or the Moscatel de Setúbal of southern Portugal. Some of the most delicious are sparkling, made around Asti in Piedmont by the Charmat or *cuve-close* method, preserving a considerable amount of residual sugar and keeping alcohol low at around 5–9°. Just a few are bone-dry, and of these the most refreshing are the Muscats of Alsace, which make perfect aperitifs for a warm summer evening. Some of the best-value sweet Muscats come from Valencia in Spain.

See under: Italy – Asti Spumante, Moscato d'Asti; France – Alsace, Muscat de Beaumes de Venise, Muscat de Frontignan, Muscat de Rivesaltes; Australia; Spain – Valencia; Greece – Samos; Portugal – Moscatel de Setúbal.

12. GEWURZTRAMINER

Gewurztraminer is probably the most intensely aromatic of all grapes and, therefore, the easiest to recognise. Its scent is not so different from that of Muscat, but closer to lychees. Its heavy muskiness, like some perfumed houri, can either seduce or repel.

Wine styles

Gewurztraminer is almost synonymous with Alsace, where it is usually vinified as a powerful dry wine, sometimes with a hint of residual sugar. The rich *vendange tardive* wines can be sweeter, and are certainly more alcoholic; the rare *sélection de grains nobles* are intensely, sometimes cloyingly, sweet. Alsace's northern neighbour, the German Rheinpfalz, also makes good Gewurztraminer, often lighter in style and with higher acidity.

Europe's other centre of Gewurztraminer is Italy's German-speaking enclave of Alto Adige (Südtirol), where the grape may, in fact, have originated. These versions are closer to the German than the Alsace style, fresh, scented and not over-heavy. Of the New World countries, New Zealand, with its cool climate and Germanic tradition of white wine-making, looks to have the best potential.

See under: France – Alsace; Italy – Alto Adige; Germany – Rheinpfalz; New Zealand; USA – California; South Africa.

13. CHENIN BLANC

Chenin Blanc is few people's favourite grape, yet it thrives in many parts of the world, and is remarkably versatile, excelling at dry, sweet and sparkling styles. In Vouvray in Touraine and Savennières in Anjou the grape achieves indisputable greatness. Poor, unripe Chenin, on the other hand, is one of the least agreeable of all wine experiences.

Wine styles – dry, sweet, sparkling

Chenin is the main white grape of the central Loire Valley, around Angers, Saumur and Tours. The *vignerons* of this northerly region have learnt to ring the changes with their often ungracious grape, adjusting levels of sweetness and using the most acid grapes to make fair-to-excellent sparkling wine (Saumur, Vouvray). In certain favoured vineyards, Chenin ripens to produce superbly flinty, long-lived dry wine (Savennières), or becomes affected by botrytis and achieves marvellous intensity combined with refreshing acidity (Coteaux du Layon, Bonnezeaux, Quarts de Chaume). These wines can age for up to 50 years.

Chenin is also the main, workhorse white grape of the Cape in South Africa, where it often goes under the name Steen, and turns out hectolitres of acceptable, fresh, clean, but not very characterful, white. There is a lot of Chenin in California, but very few attempts are made to do anything more ambitious than turn it into everyday blending material. In Western Australia, a potentially exciting new, oaked style of Chenin has emerged in the form of Hardy's Moondah Brook.

See under: France – Loire, Anjou, Touraine, Vouvray, Coteaux du Layon, Savennières; South Africa; Australia; USA – California; New Zealand.

14. PINOT BLANC/PINOT BIANCO

Pinot Blanc has often been confused with Chardonnay – in parts of northern Italy the confusion remains – but it is actually a mutation of the red Pinot Noir. Its flavour could be described as a muted version of Chardonnay – soft, rounded, lowish in acidity but distinctly lacking in positive flavour characteristics. One place where this is not seen as a disadvantage is northern Italy, where neutrality in white wines is highly prized. It is no surprise then that the world's most expensive Pinot Biancos come from Friuli.

Wine styles – still and sparkling

There is one basic Pinot Blanc style – dry, unassuming, but moderately fruity, and highly versatile. Not for nothing has this been called the ideal wine bar white. In Alsace, where a good deal of very decent Pinot Blanc is produced, no one makes great claims for the variety, and as a result Alsace Pinot Blancs can be excellent value. Most northern Italian Pinot Biancos are also good everyday drinking whites, but a few producers in Friuli stake a high claim for their concentrated but still neutral and, frankly, often overpriced versions. Pinot Bianco is also employed in north Italy for sparkling wine purposes. Germany's most southerly region of Baden claims to specialise in the variety, which certainly achieves remarkable ripeness in those parts – often too much, since Pinot Blanc (or Weissburgunder) at 15° alcohol is top-heavy. Few New World producers have shown any interest in the variety, but one of the world's most remarkable and long-lived Pinot Blancs is made at Chalone in California.

See under: France – Alsace; Italy – Friuli, Veneto; Germany – Baden, Rheinpfalz; USA – California.

15. PINOT GRIS/PINOT GRIGIO

Pinot Gris is another mutation of Pinot Noir, and its name derives from the fact that the grapes are not so much white as pink-brown, or even grey. This is certainly a strange grape, poised between white and black in colour; it is widely cultivated throughout Europe but vinified in a bewildering variety of styles, light, powerful, dry and sweet. The grape's flavour is also difficult to pinpoint – it can vary from extremely neutral to quite musky in perfume, but perhaps Pinot Gris's strongest characteristic is a satisfying fatness of texture.

Wine styles – dry, sweet

Most Pinot Gris is vinified as a dry white; light and neutral in much of north Italy, much richer and more concentrated in Alsace. Some Alsaciens consider this their noblest variety and a fine match for their cuisine: the subtly flavoured, faintly smokey wine (traditionally called Tokay d'Alsace) can be magnificent. In top years some Pinot Gris will be left on the vines for the attention of botrytis and used to make luscious sweet wine. Sweet Pinot Gris is also made in Germany's Rheinpfalz, Nahe and Baden (where the grape is called Ruländer or Grauburgunder) and Hungary (Szürkebarát). Very little interest in Pinot Gris has been shown by New World producers apart from a few in Oregon.

See under: France – Alsace, Loire; Italy – Friuli, Alto Adige, Veneto; Germany; Eastern Europe – Hungary, Romania, Czech Republic; Switzerland; Austria; USA – Oregon.

THE BEST OF THE REST

Barbera has the distinction of being the third most planted grape in Italy. A native of Piedmont, it has languished in the shadow of Nebbiolo. Barbera is usually planted in the less good vineyards where Nebbiolo does not ripen. In the right conditions Barbera can produce delicious, dark, lively, redcurrant or cranberry-flavoured reds, some of which can benefit from a touch of new oak. California has considerable plantings and potential in Barbera, as yet little realised.

Carignan/Cariñena is widely planted in France's deep southern regions of Languedoc-Roussillon, and also in eastern Spain. The grape is distinctly unfashionable, but in the right hillside vineyards, with low yields, it can deliver marvellously warm, fruit-cakey reds.

Cinsault is another unfashionable southern French red, mainly used for bulk production. It also thrives in South Africa (as Cinsaut), and is one of the parents of Pinotage, South Africa's most distinctive red wine grape.

Colombard is a workaday white variety which does not aspire to the heights, but in South Africa and Gascony it can yield pleasantly fresh and fruity dry or off-dry plonk.

Dolcetto is Piedmont's answer to Gamay, producing inky-dark, yet soft, reds for quaffing, not pondering.

Gamay is famous as the grape of Beaujolais, where it is usually fermented by the whole-berry, carbonic-maceration technique to make seductively gluggable reds which smell of cherries and bananas. The best Beaujolais *crus* can actually aspire well beyond this level, and benefit from some oak-ageing, but fashion currently decrees that all Beaujolais should be light and unserious, even if not *nouveau*. Gamay is also grown in Touraine and other pockets of central-eastern France, but has not shone in other countries.

Mourvèdre/Mataro is a black grape of Spanish, or Catalan, origin, which has crossed the border and flourishes in southern France, especially Provence. It is a useful part of the Châteauneuf-du-Pape blend, providing warm body and spice, but it really comes into its own in Bandol, whose reds are perhaps the only satisfactory wines made entirely from this variety – though Bonny Doon and other California Rhône Rangers are turning out some delicious Mourvèdre blends. In Australia it is called Mataro and is used mainly in blends.

Nebbiolo produces some of Italy's – many would say the world's – greatest reds, in the form of the majestic Barolos and Barbarescos of Piedmont. It is a tricky, late-ripening variety, awesomely high in tannin, and the wines generally need several years to reveal their subtle, smokey, truffle-like complexity. Perhaps for those reasons few New World producers have tried to tackle it.

Palomino is the white grape used to make the great, authentic sherries of southern Spain. Vinified as dry unfortified white, however, Palomino shows little class or interest. It is only the combination of fortification, oxidation and the action of the porridgy yeast – flor – which converts Palomino base wine into pungent, tangy finos and manzanillas, and rich, rare amontillados, palo cortados and olorosos.

Sangiovese is the classic black grape of central Italy, especially Tuscany, and, within Tuscany, of Chianti. Sangiovese always gives a certain rasping asperity, but in the greatest Chiantis, Brunellos and 'Super-Tuscan' vini da tavola, combines that with rich, concentrated dark cherry fruit. Such wines can age magnificently. Lighter versions bearing the variety's name come from Emilia-Romagna. Sangiovese is now being cultivated in parts of California.

Tempranillo, the red grape of Rioja, also appears under different names in other northern and central Spanish regions, such as Ribera del Duero (Tinto Fino), Navarra, Toro (Tinto del Toro), La

Mancha and Valdepeñas (Cencibel). The fruit is strawberry-soft but surprisingly capable of ageing, and combines wonderfully with the sweet vanilla spice of American oak. Safeway's Young Vatted Tempranillo is a delicious, uncomplicatedly fruity version.

Touriga Nacional, by common consent the best grape for making port, is also partly responsible for red Dão. The tough, unappealing character of most Dão should not be blamed on the grape, which, though deep and powerful, can certainly make superb, age-worthy table wine as well as port in northern Portugal.

Trebbiano/Ugni Blanc is by far the most widely planted white grape in Italy – not a statistic to induce pride among Italian wine-growers. Under its French name, Ugni Blanc, this neutral variety is used to make the thin acid base wine for Cognac and Armagnac. Much Italian Trebbiano suggests distillation would be a kinder fate than table-wine production.

Viognier is one of the world's most interesting, though little-known, white grapes. Its obscurity, as the grape of the tiny appellations of Condrieu and Château Grillet, may soon be a thing of the past, as growers in Languedoc rush to plant this scented, peachy variety. There are also plantings in California.

Zinfandel is California's one significant original contribution to viticulture. This dark, bramble-sweet black grape may be the Primitivo of southern Italy – who knows, who cares? The point is that when taken seriously by growers in the Napa Valley or the Santa Cruz moutains (Ridge, above all) it can deliver wines which burst with exuberant fruit yet satisfy with layers of smokey density.

FRANCE

You can understand why the French are so chauvinistic and protective about their wines. French wine is, after all, one of the greatest achievements of Western civilisation. Other countries have excelled in other arts and sciences (the Germans with philosophy, the English with literature, the Italians with art and design); but modern wine was developed in France, using French soil, French grapes, French hands and French palates.

The French are unique in being analytical hedonists. The northern European races tend to be analytical but not hedonistic, the Latin ones hedonistic but seldom analytical. The French, however, as they never tire of telling us, have developed the perfect balance. The reason why French wines, in almost all cases, have become the models copied throughout the world, is that at all levels of French society the pleasures of the palate are taken extremely seriously. Traditions can be wonderful or deadly, depending on the intelligence and care with which they are constantly re-examined. France's vinous traditions have survived and flourished because generation after generation of wine-farmers, winemakers, wine-brokers and wine-lovers have worked to refine them.

Now French wine is facing a challenge, perhaps the greatest since phylloxera in the late nineteenth century. The New World is eating into a contracting wine market. French wine sales may have increased slightly, relative to the market, in 1994, but the recent trend of French wine exports is steadily downwards. Far-sighted French analysts are worried. France's complicated hierarchies, and even more complicated place names, contrast starkly with the simplicity, reliability and perceived value for money offered by the New World, especially Australia. The top names may be basking in international adulation, fuelled by the enthusiasm of Francophile foreign wine journalists such as Robert Parker. In the middle and lower levels, however, the competition is fierce. What is the future for indifferent Mâcon or Bordeaux, mass-produced by less than brilliant co-operatives?

Much of the competition to France's established areas is coming from France's own deep south, the rejuvenated wineland of Languedoc. This is where the greatest challenge to the system of *appellation d'origine contrôlée*, so proudly developed and guarded, and subsequently copied, is being mounted, in the form of the varietal wines pioneered by Robert Skalli. At the cheaper end, Eastern Europe, South America and South Africa are poised to take market share away from France's workaday producers.

Our sympathies are somewhat mixed. International competition has already had an enormously beneficial effect on the way many French wines are made. Bordeaux has woken up to the fact that Cabernet Sauvignon and Merlot can be vinified in a more overtly fruity, less austerely tannic style, without sacrificing quality. Perhaps these wines will not last quite as long as some of their predecessors, but then, when you consider that the 1870 clarets reputedly came round only when their original purchasers were dead, this may not be a bad thing. The use of new barrels to ferment Sauvignon Blanc and Sémillon in Graves has led to an exciting renaissance. Even the Burgundians have realised that their artisanal methods could be rendered somewhat less hit-or-miss.

The new international free market sanctified by GATT, and then freely interpreted by the EU, is a tough environment. One can have much sympathy for French farmers attempting to defend a traditional way of life which has added so much to the world's culture and pleasure. But there can be little future in producing excessive quantities of indifferent wine, in a world which increasingly regards wine as something to be savoured, not glugged.

At the same time, it would be madness, destructive madness, not to recognise the enormous strengths of the French tradition. At the heart of that tradition is the notion of *terroir*. *Terroir* means nothing more than the recognition of the special viticultural qualities of certain patches of the planet. As such, it is equally central to the wine culture of Piedmont or Germany's Mosel Valley as it is to Burgundy. All the best New World producers, no longer grouped behind Bill Jekel's war-cry of 'Soil is dirt', now recognise the importance of *terroir*. So the competition, between winemakers defending their special patches with equal care, should be fair and beneficial. France's wonderfully diverse yet stylish and (an over-used word, but unavoidable here) elegant wines will always be hard to beat.

FRENCH WINE LAW

France's strict wine laws are currently being challenged more forcefully than at any time since their introduction in the 1930s. The top category of French wine, *appellation d'origine contrôlée*

(AOC), which accounts for around a third of all French wine, is based first on delimitation of territory, and then on control of grape varieties, pruning methods, yields and methods of vinification – in the words of the founders, '*usages loyaux, locaux et constants*', or time-honoured, traditional, local practices.

This is a system of which the French are justifiably proud, but it is not perfect. The biggest drawback for the foreign consumer is simply that AOC, while guaranteeing that a wine comes from a certain place and is made in a certain, more or less traditional, way, does not guarantee that a wine is good. Perhaps no wine law can do that; for the time being, the only guarantee of quality in a wine is a skilled, conscientious producer.

The other complaint against AOC is its excessive rigidity. In particular, the outlawing of certain grape varieties in certain places – for example, Cabernet Sauvignon in most Languedoc-Roussillon AOCs – forces experimental, innovative producers outside the system. The INAO, the body which controls the AOC system, recently reinforced its view, in relation to the appellation Touraine, that the name of the grape variety must be in smaller letters than that of the appellation. M. Berger, director of INAO, declared that 'the varietal is not our identity', but many export-oriented producers of AOC wine must have groaned.

Beneath AOC, in the French wine hierarchy, comes VDQS, the category of *vins délimités de qualité supérieure* (demarcated wines of superior quality). This is seen very much as a transitional category, a staging-post for aspiring AOCs, and accounts for a small percentage, less than 3 per cent, of production.

The third tier of the system is made up of *vins de pays* or country wines. This is by far the most dynamic segment of French wine at present. *Vins de pays* is a loose concept; three regional denominations, Jardin de la France, d'Oc and Comté Tolosan, cover the whole of France. There are also departmental *vins de pays* and much more precise denominations covering quite small areas such as Collines Rhodaniennes. Crucially, *vins de pays* offer much greater freedom of choice of grape varieties than AOC (as well as higher yields), and permit the naming of those varieties, though, absurdly, only one at a time, on labels. This is why so many producers in Languedoc have been happy to label their varietal wines as Vins de Pays d'Oc. According to the bureaucrats of INAO, this is fine as long as these plebeian wines take their place beneath AOC in the hierarchy. However, in Languedoc, at least, the hierarchy has been overturned, with varietals often, if not usually, commanding higher prices than AOCs such as Corbières.

Finally, comes lowly *vin de table*, a category which deserves to have a rather poor future, though still accounting for nearly a quarter of all French wine. There seems no reason why most *vin de table* should not upgrade itself to *vin de pays* in the next few years.

BORDEAUX

In 1993 it looked as though Bordeaux might be on the brink of another major collapse. Not only did some of the most prestigious names in wine (Châteaux Latour and Gruaud-Larose) change hands, at, it is said, comparatively knock-down prices, but the major *négociant*, SDVF, got into serious financial difficulties. Then the 1993 vintage, yet again, was diluted by heavy rain during the harvest. Earlier in the year Bordeaux's ruling wine body, the CIVB, had revealed the extent of its unhappiness in a document entitled *Breaking the Silence*. Amazingly, the world's grandest fine wine region was complaining of neglect and unfair competition from the mass-produced, standardised wines of the New World.

In 1994–5 Bordeaux recovered to some extent from this nadir. Despite another flawed, rain-affected vintage in 1994, the market began to bounce back. Demand, not just for reds but also for the unloved dry whites, began to exceed supply and prices for basic red Bordeaux jumped by around 30 per cent. The main worry now for Bordeaux merchants selling to English supermarkets was that these wines might price themselves out of the market, with the pound at its weakest point against the franc for many years.

Bordeaux may be breathing again, but it has still a long way to go (and we may be thankful for this) to regain the triumphalist euphoria of the late 1980s. World recession is one factor, but another has been the obstinate refusal of the weather gods to deliver the kind of vintages which became almost commonplace in the 1980s. Despite the much-publicised collapse of the Hungerford Wine Company, *en primeur* made a modest comeback with the 1993 vintage in spring 1994. However, leading merchants admitted that quantities sold were modest indeed compared with the bonanzas of 1989 and 1990. The 1994 campaign may fare better, but punters should beware of excessive claims made for this vintage. It certainly looks better than the lightish, if often charming 1993, but the respected Bordeaux analyst Bill Bolter calls it a vintage of good, not great wines.

On the positive side, vintages like 1992, 1993 and 1994 have undoubtedly benefited from improved wine-making techniques, especially at top properties. Winemakers have learnt to cope with wet harvests: the best wines are usually those which aim for fruit and elegance rather than big structure. Some 1992 *crus classés* have already appeared on the market and the best are very attractive forward wines. The challenge now is to extend these improved wine-making techniques from the glamorous *crus classés* down to the lower levels of Bordeaux's hierarchical structure. Much basic red Bordeaux wine-making remains lamentably rustic.

Improved wine-making techniques have probably had a still greater effect on Bordeaux's dry whites (outnumbered by the reds by over four to one). Here there has been quite a transformation: gone, for the most part, are the oxidised, cardboardy whites which gave Graves a bad name. The new Bordeaux whites are usually impeccably clean and fresh, but often characterless. To counter this shortcoming, much work has been done in the areas of skin contact, barrel fermentation and ageing. Bordeaux's dry whites certainly deserve more attention than they are getting.

Bordeaux cannot afford to rest on its laurels. The rapid export growth of Australia's youthful wine industry has rung alarm bells even in the Médoc. The top Bordeaux wines are probably not threatened, for the time being: their extraordinary subtlety and complexity, and their ability to acquire nuance through ageing in bottle, can still be matched only by a few determined New World producers. In the middle and lower parts of the Bordeaux pyramid, however, there can be no complacency. Bordeaux wines are competing in a free, international market, and they must offer value for money, just like any others. With good *terroir*, good-sized properties (unlike Burgundy), reasonable land prices and, above all, the skill, expertise and will to succeed, Bordeaux, on the whole, has favourable prospects.

Some change, however, to the overstratified and hierarchical structure of the Bordeaux trade is probably needed. One development we view with great interest is the appearance of high-quality Bordeaux branded wines, such as Jean-Michel Cazes' Michel Lynch and Bruno Prats' Maître d'Estournel, following in the footsteps of Baron Philippe de Rothschild's pioneering, much-derided, but recently improved, Mouton Cadet. Brands have a bad name in general in the UK, but brands which are based on quality, and which provide information on grape varieties and vineyard provenance, could surely have an important role in cutting through the excessive complexity of Bordeaux's myriad châteaux.

Red wines – styles and grape varieties

Bordeaux is most famous, of course, for the classic red wine traditionally known in the UK as claret. Red Bordeaux is fascinatingly varied and complex: it has a wide range of incarnations, from simple and uncomplicated to hyper-sophisticated and complex, yet it retains a certain distinctiveness of character. Bordeaux reds are seldom as obviously ripely fruity as, say, most Australian Cabernets. Herbaceous and tobacco notes vie with blackcurrants and other fruits on the nose, even in youth. With age come even more complex, elusive aromas and flavours. There is usually a certain reserve, a sense in the young wine of something withheld. Tannin levels are traditionally quite high but many wines nowadays are being vinified for early consumption.

Red Bordeaux owes its basic character to two grapes in particular, Cabernet Sauvignon and Merlot, with additional input from Cabernet Franc, Petit Verdot, Malbec and the rare Carmenère. No Bordeaux red is a 100 per cent varietal (though some, such as Pétrus, at 95 per cent Merlot, come close), and the idea of *cépage* (grape variety) predominating over *terroir* is scorned by most of Bordeaux's leading producers. The habit of blending is rooted in practicality: as Bruno Prats of Château Cos d'Estournel explains, the reason why certain parts of the Cos d'Estournel vineyard are planted with Cabernet Sauvignon and others with Merlot is that experience has proved that each variety does better in a particular place. It is not because the winemaker decided beforehand that he wanted that particular blend.

Cabernet Sauvignon is the Bordeaux grape which gives the classic blackcurrant and cigar-box aromas and flavours; its thick-skinned grapes also provide depth of colour and the tannic backbone which allows great Bordeaux to age for decades. Merlot, perhaps surprisingly, is considerably more widely planted in the Bordeaux area than Cabernet Sauvignon, accounting for 32 per cent of the vineyard area as against Cabernet's 18 per cent. Merlot, in general, gives softer, less tannic wines, suggesting strawberries rather than Cabernet's blackcurrants. A blend of the two is often ideally harmonious. Merlot, the dominant variety on the right bank of the Gironde and Dordogne rivers, can rise to greatness in St-Emilion and, especially, Pomerol.

Not many of the vineyards in the Bordeaux area seem ideally suited to Cabernet Franc. This grape is used, however, in the Médoc to add finesse and aroma to the blend, but it really comes into its own in parts of St-Emilion and is the main component of one of Bordeaux's greatest wines, Cheval-Blanc.

Petit Verdot has a reputation as a difficult grape which hardly ever ripens, but it has its (perhaps growing) band of supporters, who admire its strong, full-bodied character. Malbec or Cot is out of fashion nowadays and Carmenère, once an important quality variety, is now seldom seen.

Appellations

The basic Bordeaux Rouge appellation covers the entire vast region of around 100,000 hectares. Wines which carry this appellation must have a minimum of 9.5 degrees of alcohol. Quality can range from very basic indeed to really quite good – it all depends on the commitment of the grower and winemaker. Bordeaux Supérieur is similar in all respects to straight Bordeaux, except that an extra degree of alcohol is required. As a result, the wines are likely to be somewhat more concentrated. Many wines under these basic appellations will be marketed as own-labels or brands, but others will be single-property wines – the so-called *petits châteaux*. Choosing the best of the *petits châteaux* is one of the most useful functions of the specialist wine merchant.

The left bank: Médoc

The most famous portion of the Bordeaux vineyard area consists of part of the long Médoc peninsula, which stretches north from Bordeaux along the left bank of the Gironde, bordered on the west by pine forests and the Atlantic. Here are found many of the well-drained gravel *croupes* or outcrops which force Cabernet Sauvignon vines to send their roots deep into the subsoils. The great vineyards, such as Lafite, Latour, Mouton-Rothschild, Cos d'Estournel and others, are situated on these *croupes*.

Médoc appellations are Haut-Médoc, Listrac, Margaux, Médoc, Moulis, Pauillac, St-Estèphe, St-Julien. The Médoc appellation, in practice, covers the northern end of the Médoc vineyards, where wines tend to lack finesse, though, when serious commitment is in evidence, as at Potensac, quality can be excellent. The most famous appellations, Margaux, St-Julien, Pauillac and St-Estèphe, cover the best vineyards running north from the outskirts of Bordeaux quite close to the river. The differences between them have been the subject of learned discourse for centuries: Margaux has been considered feminine, but can be tough and tannic – certainly the soils are poor and the harvest earlier. St-Julien is perhaps the *beau idéal* of claret, cedary and elegant. Pauillac makes some of the most powerful, Cabernet-dominated and indeed greatest wine of all Bordeaux. St-Estèphe has richer, more clay-dominated soil and the wines can have an earthy edge. Haut-Médoc, in theory, means the higher-lying heart of the Médoc, but, in practice, it covers certain vineyards around the northern and southern fringes of the four famous village appellations. Moulis and Listrac are villages further inland, and are considered to have a slightly rustic character.

Pessac-Léognan and Graves

These appellations cover the original cradle of Bordeaux viticulture on the southern and western fringes of the city. Many vineyards have indeed been swallowed up by Bordeaux's urban sprawl, and some very famous ones, such as Haut-Brion and La Mission-Haut-Brion, eke out an existence among ringroads and airport runways. In 1987, following the determined lobbying of M. André Lurton and others, the northern and most highly regarded part of the large Graves region broke off and formed its own appellation, Pessac-Léognan. This move does not seem to have harmed growers and winemakers in the southern part: some of their wines can offer excellent value for money. Pessac-Léognan and Graves wines tend not to be quite so Cabernet-dominated as those of the Médoc, and sometimes have a slightly rougher, earthier texture. Maurice Healy described the difference between Médoc and Graves wines in terms of the difference between 'glossy and matt prints of the same negative'.

The right bank

The vineyard areas on the right bank of the Dordogne and the Gironde have a different feel from those of the Médoc. The scale is more human, the atmosphere, lacking the often cold seigneurial grandeur of the Médoc, more typically French. Still more important, the soil and balance of grape varieties are different – more clay and more Merlot.

The two highest-quality right bank appellations are St-Emilion and Pomerol, one large (5,000 hectares) and confusing, the other very small and concentrated. AOC St-Emilion, centred on the charming medieval town of the same name, has hundreds of properties, of which no fewer than 200 can call themselves *grands crus*. There are a further 63 *grands crus classés* and 11 *premiers grands crus classés*, perhaps stretching the point somewhat. The major geological distinction in St-Emilion is between the *côtes* vineyards, situated on a limestone plateau and adjoining slopes, and the *graves et sables* vineyards, consisting of a mixture of gravel and sand. There is quite a variation of styles both within and between these: the *côtes* wines tend to be firmer and more structured, the *graves* wines flatter in youth and sometimes lack staying-power. Encépagement (the choice of grape varieties) is also important, and, while Merlot is predominant almost everywhere, wines with a relatively high proportion of Cabernet Sauvignon (Figeac with 35 per cent has one of the highest) take longer to develop.

The small appellation of Pomerol has come to prominence only in the past 20 years. What is now the most fashionable of all Bordeaux appellations was an obscure rustic region until the 1960s.

Even Château Pétrus was at that time known only to a small band of cognoscenti. The great Pomerols combine velvety lushness of texture and ripeness of fruit with amazing staying-power, perhaps what has made them the cult Bordeaux wines of the 1980s and 1990s.

Both St-Emilion and Pomerol are surrounded by less prestigious satellite appellations. AOC Lalande-de-Pomerol includes some excellent châteaux, while mostly useful, sometimes quite exciting wines come out of AOCs Lussac-, Montagne- and Puisseguin-St-Emilion.

Other right-bank appellations AOCs Côtes et Premières Côtes de Blaye and Côtes de Bourg cover quite a large, hilly area on the right bank of the Gironde facing the Haut-Médoc. For some reason, these attractive south-facing slopes have never enjoyed the renown of their neighbours across the stream, and, as a result, the investment and effort needed to make really fine, as opposed to pleasant, red wine have been absent. One or two properties seem to be trying harder: these could be AOCs to watch.

Fronsac and Canon-Fronsac to the north-west of Pomerol have a different history: these were once highly regarded vineyard areas, but they fell into neglect in the last century. Recently there have been efforts to revive them, most notably by the famous *négociant* firm of J-P Moueix. Quality still seems patchy, however.

Côtes de Castillon and Bordeaux-Côtes de Francs are two unpretentious areas on the fringes of St-Emilion, offering straightforward, softish wines. The Premières Côtes de Bordeaux area, situated on the right bank of the Garonne, is best known as a source of inexpensive sweet whites, but also produces much lively, fruity red Bordeaux.

The château concept

Before going any further it is necessary to explain the concept of the château, which is central to the production and marketing of all the better wines of Bordeaux. What is a château? It is not, on the whole, a castle, though one or two moated and drawbridged properties, such as Olivier and d'Issan, do exist. It is more often a fairly modest Second-Empire villa, but may not even be a house. Cos d'Estournel has a very splendid, exotic set of outbuildings but no dwelling. The château, in fact, may refer to no construction at all except a mental one – try finding Château Clairefont (second wine of Château Prieuré-Lichine), for example, on a map.

Even more strangely, 'château' does not necessarily refer to a particular piece of land. It may mean, rather, as Hugh Johnson has put it, 'the property on the land' – in other words, the estate. The point about this is that estates can grow and diminish. Comparison of current production figures of leading Bordeaux *crus* with those given in an early edition of *Cocks et Féret*, the Bordeaux bible, will show that most have grown very considerably in the past 50 or 100 years.

Even if the château is a rather slippery entity, there can be no doubt about the success of this method of marketing fine wines. Bordeaux châteaux are, in a way, high-quality brands: they guarantee a certain style and consistency. They are also, of course, brands which are linked to particular vineyards, even though the boundaries of those vineyards may shift.

The 1855 classification

There are so many châteaux in Bordeaux, several thousand in fact, that some form of classification is clearly useful, if not essential. The classification of the major Médoc *crus*, together with the solitary Graves Haut-Brion, undertaken by the Bordeaux Chamber of Commerce for the Paris Universal Exhibition of 1855, was by no means the first attempt to rank Bordeaux châteaux. Previous classifications had been made by Jullien (1816), Franck (1824) and Paguierre (1827). However, the 1855 classification of some 60 châteaux – the *crus classés* – in five classes has acquired a quality of immutability which its own compilers never intended. In fact, their conclusions were based pragmatically on market value, taken over a considerable period. Most Bordeaux experts would agree on a dozen or so châteaux which deserve relegation and a further dozen or slightly more which ought to be promoted. So far, the only change has been the promotion of Mouton-Rothschild from second to first, achieved in 1973 after decades of lobbying by Baron Philippe. The truth is that the venerability and aura of the 1855 list serve the image of Bordeaux rather well, and any attempt to change it leads to the most unseemly in-fighting.

The *crus bourgeois*

Relishers of contradiction may be amused by the continuance of a rigid, almost feudal, class structure among the Bordeaux châteaux, in the land which gave the world *'liberté, égalité, fraternité'*. Even to this day, the Médoc's *crus bourgeois*, worthy professionals barred forever from the glittering world of the *crus classés*, seem to nurture an entirely understandable chip on their collective shoulder. The situation is, in fact, quite as absurd as the hereditary privileges and abuses rampant in the France of Louis XVI. Why should a wine like Henri Martin's Château Gloria, created from fragments of existing *crus classés* and quite as good as many fifth and even fourth growths, be forever condemned to *bourgeois* status? It is enough to turn a Girondin into a *sans-culottes*.

Fortunately for us drinkers, the strict and unchanging classifications of Bordeaux mean that there are many good-value wines in the Médoc *cru bourgeois* and *petit château* categories. The best of these employ exactly the same techniques of viticulture, vinification and *élevage* (maturing the wine in 225-litre oak barrels called *barriques bordelaises*) as their aristocratic neighbours.

Second wines

The idea of the *grand vin*, or principal wine, of a château goes back 200 years to the beginning of Bordeaux's history as producer of modern, bottled wine. This idea seems to imply the existence of a second, not-so-grand wine. However, the widespread marketing of 'second wines' by well-known châteaux is a recent phenomenon. The pioneer here was Château Latour with Les Forts de Latour, first marketed in the late 1960s with the 1966 vintage. A stream of other châteaux followed suit in the 1980s.

The idea was, and is, that you are getting a wine with many of the same characteristics as the *grand vin*, but somewhat lighter and quicker to mature, for around half the price. The reality is slightly more complex and needs careful consideration. Most second wines of leading châteaux are blended from vats of wine rejected during the selection for the principal wine – a selection which has tended to become much more rigorous in recent years. The quality of these reject vats will vary from the very good (in excellent vintages) to the frankly sub-standard (in rain-affected vintages). The choice of vintage is therefore especially important with second wines. Years such as 1985, when there was simply too much good wine, produced many seductive second wines (Les Fiefs de Lagrange, for example, was utterly delicious). Second wines from the rain-affected 1987, or from 1991 or 1992, on the other hand, should be approached with extreme caution.

There is a further type of second wine, which consists not of reject vats but the produce of a subsidiary vineyard. Château de Marbuzet from the Cos d'Estournel stable and Haut-Bages-Avérous from Lynch-Bages fall into this category. These wines are likely to be more consistent in mediocre vintages.

A final point to be made about second wines is that they are largely the product of the 1980s, a decade of excess and abundance. The future of second wines, in the light of recession and the difficult vintages of the 1990s so far, where strict selection was necessary to make wines of any concentration, must be uncertain. Meanwhile, second wines from vintages such as 1988, 1989 and

1990 may offer the only affordable entrée into the world of the *crus classés* – even if it is via the tradesmen's entrance.

Château profiles

L'Angélus, *grand cru classé*, St-Emilion. Much-improved, aromatic St-Emilion, with high proportion of Cabernet Franc. String of successes in the 1980s (1985, 1986, 1988).

D'Angludet, *cru bourgeois*, Margaux. The home of Peter Sichel, co-owner of Château Palmer and leading Bordeaux merchant. Deep, serious wines of *cru classé* standard. Promising 1993.

D'Armailhac, *5me cru classé*, Pauillac. This is Mouton-Rothschild's little brother or sister, formerly called Mouton-Baron(ne)-Philippe, and now reverting to its original name. Very stylish in top vintages (1961, 1982, 1986) but can be weak in poor years.

L'Arrosée, *grand cru classé*, St-Emilion. High-class, rich, powerful wine with 35 per cent Cabernet Sauvignon. Worth seeking out.

Ausone, *1er grand cru classé*, St-Emilion. Supposedly one of Bordeaux's greatest wines, especially since revitalisation by Pascal Delbeck (from 1976), but made in such tiny quantities and sold at such ludicrous prices that most of us will never know if quality matches hype.

Batailley, *5me cru classé*, Pauillac. Solid, dependable wines made by the likeable Emile Castéja, who regrets the way most *crus classés* have priced themselves out of professionals' pockets. Good in 1985, 1986, 1988, 1990.

Beaumont, *cru bourgeois*, Haut-Médoc. Good chunky wine, recently improved (1988, 1989, 1990) and marked by new oak.

Beychevelle, *4me cru classé*, St-Julien. Grand and beautiful property with wines which look and taste like second growths; rich and chocolate-flavoured with lots of oak.

Branaire-Ducru, *4me cru classé*, St-Julien. Strangely variable wine which used to display chocolate flavours, then became lean, even light, in mid-1980s.

Brane-Cantenac, *2me cru classé*, Margaux. Large, recently improved second growth owned by Lucien Lurton. 1993 shows the Margaux perfume and breed.

Calon-Ségur, 3me cru classé, St-Estèphe. Solid, earthy wine which takes time to show its best qualities, though never great. Improved in late 1980s.

Camensac, 5me cru classé, Haut-Médoc. Full-flavoured but rather coarse wine lacking true class.

Canon, 1er grand cru classé, St-Emilion. Top-quality St-Emilion of great concentration and lovely texture. Needs time to open up.

Cantemerle, 5me cru classé, Haut-Médoc. Very stylish, elegant wine greatly improved under Cordier management since 1981; sometimes, as in 1993, on the light side. Second wine: Baron Villeneuve de Cantemerle.

Cantenac-Brown, 3me cru classé, Margaux. Despite investment from AXA-Millésimes, this chunky, fruity but somewhat coarse wine still fails to convince.

Certan-de-May, Pomerol. Tiny but magnificent Pomerol producing wonderfully lush wines. Superb 1985.

Chasse-Spleen, cru bourgeois, Moulis. Prime candidate for promotion to *cru classé.* Superb, full-flavoured wines made by the late-lamented Bernadette Villars who died in a climbing accident in 1991. Second wine: Ermitage de Chasse-Spleen.

Cheval-Blanc, 1er grand cru classé, St-Emilion. Splendid, flamboyant wine with very high proportion of Cabernet Franc, which can be very flattering when young but ages for at least twenty years. 1988, 1989 and, especially, 1990 all brilliant.

Chevalier, Domaine de, Graves-Pessac-Léognan. A wonderful, hidden property producing both red and white wines of highest class. Reds are subtle, civilised, harmonious. On a par with best second-growth Médoc. Oddly light in 1993.

Cissac, cru bourgeois, Haut-Médoc. Very consistent, reliable *bourgeois.*

Citran, cru bourgeois, Haut-Médoc. Once modest *cru bourgeois* bought by the Japanese in 1987 and now showing star quality. 1991 outstanding.

Clarke, *cru bourgeois*, Listrac. Huge Rothschild-owned vineyard in Médoc backwoods, making increasingly good, sinewy wines.

Clerc-Milon, *5me cru classé*, Pauillac. Belonging to same stable as Mouton-Rothschild and making good, powerful wines.

Clinet, Pomerol. After a problematic period in the 1970s, this is now one of the best wines of Pomerol.

La Conseillante, Pomerol. Very consistent and fine wine.

Cos d'Estournel, *2me cru classé*, St-Estèphe. The best *cru* of St-Estèphe, and surpassed by few in Bordeaux. Wines combine power and refinement, and fully deserve 'super-second' status. Second wine: Château de Marbuzet.

La Dominique, *grand cru classé*, St-Emilion. Very good, rich wine.

Ducru-Beaucaillou, *2me cru classé*, St-Julien. Classic, cedary claret from one of the Médoc's finest estates. Approaches first-growth quality in some vintages (1961, 1970). There have been some recent murmurings about a possible barrel problem, but the 1991 seems back on course.

Durfort Vivens *2me cru classé* Margaux. Previously under-performing second growth but showing lovely style in 1993.

L'Evangile, Pomerol. One of the top wines of the *appellation*, powerful yet silky.

De Fieuzal, Graves-Pessac-Léognan. Excitingly revived in 1980s, and making some of the best and richest Graves. Wonderful 1988.

Figeac, *1er grand cru classé*, St-Emilion. Large and famous neighbour of Cheval-Blanc, with highish proportion of Cabernet Sauvignon. Seems to have taken another step forward in late 1980s.

La Fleur-Pétrus, Pomerol. Very good, silky Pomerol just below top rank.

Giscours, *3me cru classé*, Margaux. Large Margaux property making soft, lush, quite oaky wines. Some slippage in 1980s after very consistent 1970s, but return to form in 1989 and 1990.

Gloria, cru bourgeois, St-Julien. This is the creation of the late Henri Martin, put together from sold-off chunks of neighbouring *crus classés*. Soft, gracious wines, accessible when young.

Grand-Puy-Ducasse, 5me cru classé, Pauillac. Dependable and quite good-value Pauillac. Consistent in recent vintages.

Grand-Puy-Lacoste, 5me cru classé, Pauillac. Another style of Pauillac, brambly, powerful, earthy, needing time to show its best. Under Xavier Borie's management now worthy of at least third-growth status.

Gruaud-Larose, 2me cru classé, St-Julien. One of the Médoc's finest vineyards, making classic, deep, cedary wine. Top years (1961, 1982) match first growths in quality. Second wine: Sarget de Gruaud-Larose.

Haut-Bailly, Graves-Pessac-Léognan. Wonderfully silky, underrated Graves, possibly because tannins are never obtrusive. 1970 still splendid. Fine 1993.

Haut-Batailley, 5me cru classé, Pauillac. Very elegant Pauillac in cedary St-Julien mould, on the light side, but savoury.

Haut-Brion, 1er cru classé, Graves-Pessac-Léognan. The only Graves château to be classified in 1855, and most historic of all Bordeaux growths, now almost engulfed in Bordeaux's urban sprawl. Sometimes deceptively light-seeming, suave and civilised, with wonderful caramelly nose, but ages superbly. More consistent than some other first growths.

D'Issan, 3me cru classé, Margaux. Greatly improved in 1980s, with more new oak and lovely perfume. Still requires patience for flavour to soften.

Lafite-Rothschild, 1er cru classé, Pauillac. Generally regarded as the greatest of all Bordeaux wines, but can be elusive. Great qualities are perfume and balance, not overwhelming power. Seemed unsure of itself at times in 1980s. Second wine: Carruades de Château Lafite.

Lafleur, Pomerol. Legendary small Pomerol growth said to be almost on a par with Pétrus. Most of us can only guess.

Lagrange, *3me cru classé*, St-Julien. Under-performing until 1983, then dramatically turned around following purchase and massive investment by Suntory. Vintages from 1985 are splendid, cedary and seductive. Second wine (also very good): Les Fiefs de Lagrange.

La Lagune, *3me cru classé*, Haut-Médoc. Distinctive, rich, chocolatey wine always strongly marked by oak. Extremely consistent second-growth quality.

Langoa-Barton, *3me cru classé*, St-Julien. Smaller of the two classed growths belonging to Anthony Barton, making lovely, cedary, classic claret, especially since 1982. The 1985 is special.

Lascombes, *2me cru classé*, Margaux. Large and fragmented property owned by Bass Charrington, who have invested heavily in cellar equipment. Wine can be very good, quite soft, but seldom really special.

Latour, *1er cru classé*, Pauillac. The most uncompromising, Cabernet-dominated, forthright claret of all. Used to take two decades to become approachable; attempts to make style more modern in 1980s resulted in one or two less-than-classic vintages. Back on form from 1989. Second wine: Les Forts de Latour, almost a second growth in its own right, and third wine Pauillac de Latour to ensure quality of Les Forts.

Léoville-Barton, *2me cru classé*, St-Julien. Very traditional, classic, dry wine from smallest part of great Léoville estate. Made by Anthony Barton, and improving greatly since 1981. Recent vintages are superb and reasonably priced.

Léoville-Las Cases, *2me cru classé*, St-Julien. Largest and most famous portion of the Léoville estate, under perfectionist direction of Michel Delon. Wines can be very tannic and austere in youth, with an almost bitter twist, but repay long keeping. Second wine: Clos du Marquis.

Léoville-Poyferré, *2me cru classé*, St-Julien. Once most highly regarded of the Léovilles, which went into long decline, to some extent reversed since 1981 though still lagging behind other Léovilles.

Lynch-Bages, *5me cru classé*, Pauillac. Has been described as the poor man's Mouton. A splendid, powerful, rich, minty, Cabernet-dominated wine, no longer for paupers, but deserving second-growth status. Second wine: Haut-Bages-Avérous.

Magdelaine, 1er grand cru classé, St-Emilion. One of top wines of St-Emilion, possessing great style and finesse. Made by J-P Moueix.

Malescot-St-Exupéry, 3me cru classé, Margaux. Rather austere and light-coloured Margaux which used to be hard to like. Change of consultant in 1990 may improve matters.

Margaux, 1er cru classé, Margaux. Under the inspired management of Paul Pontallier, probably the best wine in Bordeaux on current form. Wonderful combination of scent, finesse and power. The 1983, 1986 and 1987 may all be best wines of the vintage; 1990 reputedly superb. Second wine: Pavillon Rouge du Château Margaux.

Meyney, cru bourgeois, St-Estèphe. Extremely reliable, solid, earthy wine from excellent property meticulously run by Domaines Cordier; better than many fifth growths.

La Mission-Haut-Brion, Graves-Pessac-Léognan. Neighbour of Haut-Brion in much more chunky, tannic style but of almost equal class, now under same management. Greatly increased proportion of new oak is apparent from 1988.

Montrose, 2me cru classé, St-Estèphe. Very well-placed property which used to be known for brambly, slightly over-extracted wines, good but often clumsy. The 1990 is a surprise star.

Mouton-Rothschild, 1er cru classé, Pauillac. Not just a triumph of public relations, but also one of the very best wines in Bordeaux. Extraordinary, intense aroma, likened to lead pencils, and blackcurrant richness from high proportion of Cabernet Sauvignon in best years. 1982 one of the greatest Bordeaux ever. 1986 almost as good.

Palmer, 3me cru classé, Margaux. Certainly the second best wine of Margaux, and in some years (1961, 1966) as good as any in Bordeaux. The 1980s and 1990s have not been quite so brilliant as at some other properties.

Pape-Clément, Graves-Pessac-Léognan. Famous and historic property, greatly improved since 1985, and running into top form with 1988.

Pavie, 1er grand cru classé, St-Emilion. Large *côtes* property, until recently below top level, but revitalised since 1985.

Pétrus, Pomerol. Now by far the most expensive of all Bordeaux wines, though little known before 1962 when J-P Moueix took a half-share. Only for plutocrats.

De Pez, cru bourgeois, St-Estèphe. Very traditional and fine, long-lasting *bourgeois*, made with care and repaying patient keeping.

Pibran, cru bourgeois, Pauillac. Exciting *bourgeois* growth from same stable as Pichon-Longueville. True, blackcurranty Pauillac density since 1988.

Pichon-Longueville, 2me cru classé, Pauillac. Great property, neglected until purchase by AXA-Millésimes in 1987. Jean-Michel Cazes and Daniel Llose have effected a stunning transformation, and wines since 1988 are magnificent, complete clarets. Second wine: Les Tourelles de Longueville.

Pichon-Longueville-Lalande, 2me cru classé, Pauillac. Perhaps the best-run property in Bordeaux during the 1970s and 1980s, thanks to inspired direction of Mme de Lencquesaing. Wonderfully silky, perfumed wines of highest class. Second wine: Réserve de la Comtesse.

Le Pin, Pomerol. Tiny new superstar from Thienpoint family. Very rich, very oaky, very delicious, but horrifically expensive.

Pontet-Canet, 5me cru classé, Pauillac. The largest *cru classé*, still struggling to find consistent style, despite considerable investment. Promising 1988.

Poujeaux, cru bourgeois, Moulis. Excellent wine of great elegance, perfume and staying-power. Classed-growth quality.

Prieuré-Lichine, 4me cru classé, Margaux. Very much the creation of the late Alexis Lichine. Some years, such as 1983, show true Margaux perfume and style, but others can be hard and charmless.

Rausan-Ségla, 2me cru classé, Margaux. This famous property had been under-performing for decades until it was transformed following major investment in 1985. Vintages since and including 1985 show classic style, concentration and breed but 1993 is not great. Second wine: Château Lamouroux.

St-Pierre, *4me cru classé*, St-Julien. Once very obscure property, regrouped in 1982 by Henri Martin. Very good vintages in 1980s, with high proportion of new oak – tannic and needing time to open up.

Siran, *cru bourgeois*, Margaux. Charming, elegant wine often of classed-growth standard. The 1966 drank beautifully at 20 years old.

Soutard, *grand cru classé*, St-Emilion. Very old-fashioned but quietly impressive St-Emilion, making sturdy wines built to last.

Talbot, *4me cru classé*, St-Julien. Another of the meticulously made Cordier wines, classic, cedary St-Julien in style and often very good value. Second wine: Connétable Talbot.

Du Tertre, *5me cru classé*, Margaux. Strangely little-known *cru* from same stable as Calon-Ségur. Beautiful violet scent and piercing blackcurrant fruit make this one of the best, and best-value, Margaux wines. Exceptional in 1983 and 1986.

Tertre-Rôteboeuf, *grand cru*, St-Emilion. Serious, small property using high proportion of new oak and making wines of perfume and structure.

Trotanoy, Pomerol. One of the most highly regarded Pomerols, making opulent, caramelly wines with sufficient structure to age.

Vieux Château Certan, Pomerol. Supposedly second-best Pomerol after Pétrus, but leaner and less opulent in style. Needs time to show its best.

Red vintages

1994 For the fourth year running rain soaked the harvest in the Gironde, and for the second successive year a potentially great vintage became merely useful-to-good. Ripeness levels were perhaps a degree higher than 1993, and Cabernets in particular were riper, so properties which managed to harvest in between showers may have made some really good wine.

1993 It rained and rained during the harvest, after a promising mid-summer, spoiling the chance of a wonderful vintage. All the same, some very attractive, medium-weight wines have been made, especially by châteaux not trying too hard to make blockbusters. The Merlot-dominated right-bank wines have the most flesh and weight, but Margaux (especially) and St-Julien also performed well, with some real charmers. Overall, better than 1992 but probably less good than 1994, and certainly not a great vintage. Careful selection will be required as some wines are disappointingly dilute.

1992 The wettest summer in Bordeaux for half a century, and the least sunny one since 1980, was hardly propitious for quality. Despite attempts to reduce the crop, a huge, diluted harvest resulted. Complicated-sounding new techniques such as 'inversed osmosis' and 'cold concentration under vacuum' were tried out at some smart properties, but few will have managed more than mediocre quality. Some charming lightish wines, however.

1991 This was the year of the devastating April frost which killed off infant buds on vines all down the western side of France. There was talk (surprise, surprise) of another super-concentrated 1961, especially when August turned out to be the hottest on record, but the vintage was seriously affected by rain. Really conscientious producers who picked before mid-October made decent-to-good wines, especially in the Médoc, but all too many are dilute. The right bank was devastated by frost and very little wine was made.

1990 The last blessed vintage of the great decade (1981–90), and in some ways the most blessed of all. This was an extremely hot year (you may remember it was hot even in the UK) – so hot, in fact, that many vines became stressed and ceased to photosynthesise. This actually meant that, despite higher temperatures, the vintage was later than in 1989. Because of the heat, vines planted on more clay-dominated soils, in the north of the Médoc and on the right bank, were in general happier than those planted on well-drained gravel. That would suggest a Merlot year, but there are many magnificent Médocs, and one of the best wines of the vintage is the mainly Cabernet Franc Cheval Blanc. Prices of these wines have been moving upward quite sharply as the market sniffs another exceptional vintage. Just a few critics warn that truly classic Bordeaux wines are made in summers that are not abnormally hot. However, the 1990s appear to be endowed with good acidity, promising long life.

1989 This pre-hyped vintage, the earliest since 1893 and one of the hottest on record, came to symbolise the incredible good luck of Bordeaux in the 1980s. It was also the last vintage to be sold under boom conditions. The circumstances were hardly normal in other respects; the early ripeness of the Merlots, in particular, took many producers by surprise, and some were picked overripe, very full of sugar and low in acidity. The Cabernets, by contrast, ripened beautifully. It is really too early to say quite how the top wines from an unusual vintage will turn out: some have already defied predictions by closing down into a tannin-protected bunker from which they may take a long time to emerge. It is certainly a super year for *petits châteaux*.

1988 This looks far more like a classic Bordeaux vintage than either of the two remarkable ones which followed. Cooler conditions are reflected in wines of great poise, which balance ripe fruit with greener, herbaceous notes. Tannins are quite hard, in general, sometimes uncomfortably so. Perhaps the most successful appellations are Graves and Pessac-Léognan, which produced a sheaf of successes, showing the world how much progress was being made in those parts.

1987 September and October rain diluted a healthy crop ripened by a warm summer. The resulting wines, especially the Merlot elements, are often full of charm and ideal for early, lunchtime drinking: they are not serious wines for laying down, but the 1980s produced no shortage of those. Most 1987s should be drunk now.

1986 The very best wines of this vintage are great Bordeaux classics for the very long haul. They do not have the obvious charm of the 1985s, but their plum and blackcurrant fruit has a wonderful dark solidity. The top wines will require considerable patience, and so are recommended only to serious collectors.

1985 This was a vintage of delightful, precocious charm and balance all over Europe. The red Bordeaux smell and taste seductively of red fruits – raspberry, redcurrant, strawberry – rather than the more usual blackcurrant. This is thought of as an especially good year for the right bank, but there are many beautiful Médocs. Most can be drunk now.

1984 The ominous year of Orwell brought lowering skies and cool conditions to Bordeaux. Merlot suffered badly from *coulure* (the berries dropped off early), but Cabernet Sauvignon fared much better. These wines have aged more gracefully than many predicted and the best are drinking well now.

1983 A strange vintage which we feel has never fully lived up to its reputation as a classic Bordeaux year. There are some stunning wines, especially in Margaux, but others browned early and have an odd, burnt aroma. St-Estèphe was markedly less successful than more southerly Médoc appellations.

1982 This might be dubbed 'le millésime Parker', since it launched the career of the American wine commentator and perfectly matched his particular taste for big, burly, ripe, muscular wines. To our taste, many of these wines seem more Californian than typically Bordeaux in style and a number are, frankly, clumsy. Ripeness is not all, in our view. However, *petits châteaux* are certainly full and delicious. Top wines are currently going through a dumb, tannic adolescence and should be kept a while.

1981 A year immediately overshadowed by its much-hyped successor, but very typical of Bordeaux in medium-weight, balanced style. Some wines are undernourished but the best are very satisfying. To be drunk from now on.

Previous fine vintages: 1979, 1978, 1976, 1975 (very tannic, but some excellent), 1971 (drink up), 1970 (perfect now), 1966, 1961 (some beginning to dry up), 1959, 1955, 1953, 1949, 1947, 1945.

Dry white wines – wine styles

Dry white Bordeaux has always suffered by comparison with the much more famous and important red. On top of that, white burgundy, Sancerre and Pouilly Fumé, even Muscadet, have all acquired greater cachet as whites of style and substance, or as simply having a spring in their step. Dry white Bordeaux still sounds dowdy. The fact that the greatest dry white Bordeaux come from the Graves region, known mostly for pretty dire sweet wines, has not helped. But dry white Bordeaux has certainly been making a comeback. Temperature-controlled fermentation, careful timing of the harvest, and restraint in the use of sulphur have helped the simple wines express lively, bouncy fruit, while barrel-fermentation and experimental work with yeasts and lees have created an exciting renaissance of high quality in the Graves and Graves-Pessac-Léognan.

Grape varieties

All white Bordeaux, dry and sweet, is made predominantly from Sémillon and Sauvignon, usually in that order of importance, with small additions of the aromatic Muscadelle and, occasionally, Ugni Blanc. A lively debate rages over the relative merits of the two major grapes. The fashionable, aromatic Sauvignon is certainly on the increase, and has forceful proponents, such as André Lurton and the team at Domaine de Chevalier, but others are convinced that the softer and more neutral Sémillon can offer greater complexity and interest in the long run.

Appellations

The basic Bordeaux Blanc appellation covers a wide range of mostly unexciting dry-to-medium wines, made from some 10,000 hectares of vineyards dotted around the vast Bordeaux area. Within this sea of mediocrity there are some islands of quality. The rare dry whites made in Sauternes, such as Ygrec from Yquem and R from Rieussec, and the Médoc, including Pavillon Blanc du

Château Margaux, Caillou Blanc de Talbot and Loudenne Blanc, only qualify for the basic AOC Bordeaux Blanc. Better value may be had from some of the increasingly good branded blends offered by *négociants* such as Peter Sichel (the barrel-fermented Sirius Blanc), Bruno Prats (Maître d'Estournel) and Dourthe Frères. A little-known source for some of the grapes used in these blends is Blaye, which has its own small white AOC, Blaye Blanc.

AOC Entre-Deux-Mers, covering a large and charming rural area between the Garonne and the Dordogne, is the source of most of Bordeaux's best lively, fresh, unoaked whites.

The most serious of Bordeaux's dry whites, as we have said, come from the Graves region and especially from the northern AOC Pessac-Léognan. Great, complex, age-worthy wines have been produced in tiny quantities at Haut-Brion, Laville-Haut-Brion and Domaine de Chevalier for decades. The 1980s saw a more widespread revival in the region. The introduction of barrel-fermentation at properties such as Fieuzal and La Tour-Martillac has led to exciting results. Unfortunately, quantities are very limited.

Château profiles
Bonnet, Entre-Deux-Mers. Excellent, fresh, lively, mainly Sémillon white made in quite large quantities by André Lurton.

Carbonnieux, *cru classé*, Graves-Pessac-Léognan. Important property whose 60 per cent Sauvignon white is much more exciting than the red.

Chevalier, Domaine de, *cru classé*, Graves-Pessac-Léognan. Very remarkable 70 per cent Sauvignon, 30 per cent Sémillon barrel-fermented white which seems to disprove theories that Sauvignon does not age. Amazing, tight concentration and length of flavour, needing at least a decade to open out.

Couhins-Lurton, *cru classé*, Graves-Pessac-Léognan. Very good, barrel-fermented 100 per cent Sauvignon wine from the André Lurton stable made in tiny quantities.

De Fieuzal, *cru classé*, Graves-Pessac-Léognan. Half-and-half Sauvignon and Sémillon white, fermented in new oak since 1985 and offering almost tropical richness of flavour. Exciting wines.

Floridène, Clos, Graves. Excellent barrel-fermented wine made in small quantities by white-wine-making guru Denis Dubourdieu.

Haut-Brion, *1er cru classé*, Graves-Pessac-Léognan. Small quantities of white, 55 per cent Sémillon and 45 per cent Sauvignon, fermented in new oak and exceedingly rich. Also exceedingly expensive.

Laville-Haut-Brion, *cru classé*, Graves-Pessac-Léognan. Very complex, long-lived wine, 60 per cent Sémillon, made at La Mission-Haut-Brion and sold at stratospheric price.

La Louvière, Graves-Pessac-Léognan. Very fine, barrel-fermented, mainly Sauvignon wine made by André Lurton.

Malartic-Lagravière, *cru classé*, Graves-Pessac-Léognan. A well-known Graves *cru* making both red and white wine. The white is 100 per cent Sauvignon, vinified in stainless steel and matured for one year in oak. Very attractive Graves in a fresh style.

Rahoul, Graves. Château associated with yeast guru Peter Vinding-Diers, making rich, barrel-fermented 100 per cent Sémillon.

Smith-Haut-Lafitte, *cru classé*, Graves-Pessac-Léognan. 100 per cent Sauvignon wine, cool-fermented in stainless steel then aged in oak. Fresh and pleasant but lacking complexity.

Thieuley, Bordeaux. Very good, fresh, 100 per cent Sauvignon white, to add to red and clairet from same property, made by oenology professor Francis Courselle.

La Tour-Martillac, *cru classé*, Graves-Pessac-Léognan. Very traditional estate belonging to historian Jean Kressmann. Barrel-fermentation for the 60 per cent Sémillon white was introduced in 1987, and subsequent vintages are of exciting quality, spicy, rounded and complex.

White vintages

1994 Because of earlier picking, the whites from this vintage are better than reds, and show excellent balance of ripeness and acidity.
1993 Early-picked whites look promising, with clean fresh flavours.
1992 The whites, especially from Graves, were the most successful wines in this cool, sodden year. The break in the rain in September allowed growers to pick healthy, if somewhat dilute, grapes, to make pleasant fresh everyday whites.
1991 April frost led to a greatly reduced vintage. Many wines are quite concentrated and of good quality.

1990 Very hot conditions were a mixed blessing. Many wines, especially from Graves, lack acidity. Choose with care.
1989 Too hot for comfort in many areas, and some wines are flabby. Early picking essential to retain acidity.
1988 Very dry summer retarded ripening and some wines are almost too green. However, the best Graves are absolutely superb.

Sweet whites – Sauternes, Barsac and the rest

Sauternes enjoyed a renaissance in the 1980s. Before that time, few of the châteaux specialising in top-quality sweet white Bordeaux, made from nobly rotten Sémillon and Sauvignon grapes, could be relied upon to justify their position as *premiers* or *deuxièmes crus classés*. Some made light, pale, sweetish wines which were, frankly, a disgrace to their appellation. True Sauternes, or Barsac, as the very similar but supposedly lighter wines of that commune can be styled, is difficult and expensive to make. It relies first upon the presence of the noble rot, botrytis, which does not affect the grapes every year, and then upon very meticulous and costly harvesting by repeated *tries*, or selections.

Fortunately, the affluence of the 1980s meant that prices could rise, and with higher prices quality-oriented investment was possible. By the end of the decade, nearly all the classified growths of Sauternes and Barsac, and some unclassified ones as well, were making truly classy wines. Nature helped, delivering a wonderful trio of vintages in 1988, 1989 and 1990 (see later), in which botrytis and ripeness were both present.

The trouble is that there has not been a really good vintage in Sauternes since 1990. Despite growers' prayers, 1994 turned out to be no better than average – some decent botrytis came in October, but quantities are once again small. 1991 was the year of the great frost. The eventual harvest was good in quality: the few grapes remaining on the vines were healthy and mature, but production was so low that many producers did not bother to bottle the wine. Both 1992 and 1993 were, with very few exceptions, dire. Rain was constant, and although some estates, by exercising the most severe selection in vineyard and winery, did finally emerge with some decent wine, the problem again was one of quantity. Suduiraut is the only one of the *crus classés* to have bottled no wine at all in 1991, 1992 or 1993, but many properties have not bottled two of the three vintages.

Mouldy flavours were all too common in 1993, as rot of the non-noble kind ravaged the vines. Some producers tried their hand at the new technique of cryo-extraction in 1993. This involves chilling the wet grapes to rid them of unwelcome moisture, and was first used widely in the wet but healthy 1987 vintage. Admirers of the technique claim that it enabled them to salvage part of the crop and to avoid excessive dilution. In 1993 its use was more controversial. A few growers reported satisfactory results, but most said the unhealthy condition of the fruit made it dangerous to use cryo-extraction, which can concentrate unwelcome flavours as well as healthy ones by the drying process.

The current run of mediocre vintages is proving yet again what a risky business Sauternes-making is. Suduiraut has been bought by the powerful insurance group AXA, and so can probably afford to sit out another year or two. Some other properties, such as Rayne-Vigneau, Coutet, Rieussec and Yquem itself, can make small quantities of dry white wine in poor vintages, but the prices they fetch are far lower than those for Sauternes.

The lesser sweet white appellations

Sweet white wines from Sémillon, Sauvignon Blanc and a little Muscadelle are also made in AOCs Cadillac, Cérons, Loupiac, Ste-Croix du Mont, Graves Supérieures and Premières Côtes de Bordeaux. Athough much cheaper than Sauternes and Barsac, they are not often great bargains, partly because conditions are simply not as conducive to botrytis as in Sauternes and Barsac, and partly because the production of fine sweet wines takes care and money, neither commodity being super-abundant in these zones. However, there are one or two sterling producers, such as Clos St-Georges in Graves Supérieures, which consistently makes good sweet wine, and in a year such as 1990 the general success rate was much higher than usual. Here, too, we can mention the sweet white wine of Monbazillac, near Bergerac, which once again seldom achieves any real quality.

Château profiles

Bastor-Lamontagne, Sauternes. An impeccably run estate, offering very well made wines at fair, sometimes bargain, prices.

Climens, *1er cru classé*, Barsac. Many Sauternes lovers justifiably regard this as the finest estate after Yquem. It has consistency, elegance, breed – and high prices.

Coutet, *1er cru classé*, Barsac. After some disappointing vintages, Coutet is back on form, with delicious 1989s and 1990s at reasonable prices.

Doisy-Daëne, *2me cru classé*, Barsac. A light Barsac, but always stylish and pure in flavour. Reasonably priced.

Doisy-Védrines, *2me cru classé*, Barsac. An atypically rich Barsac, scrupulously made by former *négociant* Pierre Castéja. An outstanding 1989.

de Fargues, Sauternes. Made by the Yquem team in the Yquem style, this *cru bourgeois* is expensive but well worth looking out for.

Gilette, Sauternes. The most eccentric wine of Sauternes, made only in top vintages and aged for twenty years in large tanks before release. Rich, old-fashioned, expensive, but ready to drink on release.

Guiraud *1er cru classé*, Sauternes. A revitalised *premier cru* of growing quality and consistency, but perhaps too pricey compared to other top estates.

Haut-Bergeron, Sauternes. The 1990 here was one of the bargains of the vintage, rich and oaky but inexpensive, reflecting the obscurity of an estate that is rapidly reaching classed-growth quality.

Lafaurie-Peyraguey, *1er cru classé*, Sauternes. Classic Sauternes, rich but balanced, oaky but elegant.

Lamothe-Guignard, *2me cru classé*, Sauternes. This *deuxième cru* gets better with every vintage, and the 1990 is superb. Reasonably priced.

De Malle, *2me cru classé*, Sauternes. Of average quality until 1988, de Malle has greatly improved. Medium-weight wine of great panache, sensibly priced.

Nairac, *2me cru classé*, Sauternes. Changes of winemaker make judgements precarious, but Nairac, at best, is an oaky wine of tremendous flair and staying-power.

Rabaud-Promis, *1er cru classé*, Sauternes. Very stylish, medium-bodied Sauternes, including a gorgeous 1990 and exquisite 1988. Fair prices.

Raymond-Lafon, Sauternes. Made to exacting standards by the former winemaker at Yquem, this wine is very oaky, very rich and very expensive.

Rayne-Vigneau, *1er cru classé*, Sauternes. Superb vineyards and ultra-modern cellars should take this once mediocre estate to great heights.

Rieussec, *1er cru classé*, Sauternes. Rothschild investment and expertise is restoring Rieussec's reputation as one of the region's top wines.

Suduiraut, *1er cru classé*, Sauternes. Always good, sometimes great, Suduiraut can look forward to a glorious future under the eye of the ambitious Jean-Michel Cazes.

d'Yquem, *1er grand cru classé*, Sauternes. Absurdly expensive, but in great vintages no Sauternes can match Yquem for opulence, power and complexity.

The great trio of vintages – 1988, 1989 and 1990

The consolation for consumers is that it is still possible to locate bottles of the great trilogy of vintages from 1988 to 1990. No one can recall three such successive vintages in the region. The Sauternais raised their prices excessively in 1989, by up to 40 per cent, with predictable consequences: buyers baulked. The 1990 vintage came down in price, and there has been some discreet discounting of the preceding two vintages.

1989 is the most voluptuous of the three – fat and unctuous, oozing with sumptuous botrytis flavours. But the 1990 is even finer, with levels of richness and sweetness rarely paralleled this century. This is unquestionably a great Sauternes vintage.

Not as flashy as the 1989 or 1990, the 1988 should not be overlooked. It too had excellent botrytis character and an impeccable balance. For those looking for elegance as well as power and richness, this is the vintage to go for.

Earlier fine Sauternes vintages: 1983, 1976, 1975, 1971.

Rosé

Poor rosé almost always gets tacked on as an afterthought. This may not be surprising in Bordeaux, a region which produces so much magnificent red and white wine, but Bordeaux rosé and clairet (a strange style somewhere between rosé and red) should not be overlooked. Bordeaux is an excellent source of these styles of wine, made from Merlot and Cabernet Sauvignon, which are often more vibrant and exciting than their white equivalents.

Château profiles

De Sours, Bordeaux. Ex-Majestic man Esmé Johnstone has shown what smart marketing can do with a modest Bordeaux property. He makes red and white as well, but the shocking pink, delectably fresh and fleshy rosé is the star.

Thieuley, Bordeaux. Francis Courselle makes a speciality of clairet, which has its own AOC, Bordeaux Clairet. Quite full-bodied but very refreshing.

BURGUNDY

Burgundy is so often infuriating. Nowhere else are excessive price tags attached to mediocre bottles with such nonchalance. Value for money, you feel, is something many inhabitants of the Côte d'Or either do not understand or regard with contempt. For them, the sacred *terroir* of Puligny or Vosne sanctions anything, including daylight robbery. For the consumer, the risks and complexities of this small and excessively sub-divided region are daunting. Venture into this territory without the advice of a specialist burgundy merchant, and your chances of escaping a fleecing are slight. Even the best advice will seriously damage your pocket. Hardly surprising, then, that so many consumers give up on Burgundy and espouse the reliable quality and vivid fruit of Burgundy's New World imitators.

Why does anyone bother? The answer lies in those rare but marvellous bottles which cause a divine dissatisfaction with almost any other liquid. If you have ever tasted a great mature Meursault from Jobard, say, or a Chambertin from Armand Rousseau, you will always be hankering for more. Burgundy may be infuriating, but it is also a place of miracles. The growers who allow these miracles to happen could hardly be more different from the very secular technocrats who dominate much of modern wine-making. People such as François Jobard or Jean Grivot are the true descendants of the monks who once tended the vines of Burgundy; quiet, ascetic men who speak of wines possessing grace and spirituality. Their wines compel assent to such terms.

The top growers' wines continue to be in huge demand, but the recession years of the 1990s have certainly caused a major shake-up among the burgundian merchants. Prices finally rose, by 51 per cent for reds and 40 per cent for whites, at the 1994 Hospices de Beaune auction but too late to save the famous house of Bouchard Père et Fils. After 260 years the Bouchard family handed over control of the company to Henriot of Champagne in April 1995.

Another Bouchard house, Bouchard Aîné, hit the headlines in 1994, when it was purchased from receivers by Frank Boisset, whose managing director Bernard Repolt promptly poured 90,000 bottles down the drain. Boisset, who also bought Jaffelin from Robert Drouhin (even Burgundy's most quality-conscious *négociants* have been feeling the pinch), now has huge influence. It is good to report that quality in the basic burgundy styles seems much more of a Boisset priority these days. All the same, Burgundy needs conscientious *négociant*-houses such as Jadot, Drouhin, Faiveley, Rodet and Latour (for its whites), who can combine quality and reasonable quantity in basic Bourgogne and village appellations, in a way simply impossible for small growers, however excellent.

Meanwhile, apart from the aforementioned *négociants*, the best bet for the consumer seeking reasonable value for money is probably lesser appellation wines from conscientious growers – those who have turned away from the excessive fertilisation and yields of the 1970s. One piece of unqualified good news is Burgundy's recent run of good vintages, less trumpeted, but possibly still more remarkable than those of Bordeaux. Burgundy has been much luckier than Bordeaux, weather-wise, in the 1990s. In particular, 1992 has produced some ravishing whites and seductive, fleshy reds but the 1993 reds are considerably better – almost up to 1990 standards. As ever, though, expert guidance through the maze of vineyards and properties is essential. Good, not to mention great, burgundies from the Côte d'Or are made in lamentably small quantities. As the worldwide market expands, it is probably unrealistic to expect bargains. Miracles do not come cheap.

The scattered vineyards of the Côte Chalonnaise to the south repeat the conditions of the Côte d'Or, albeit to a slightly watered-down degree – prices of the best wines are lower, but quality never reaches the same sublime heights. North, in Chablis, and south, in the hilly expanses of the Mâconnais and Beaujolais, the picture is somewhat different. Chablis prices have tumbled in the past couple of years, as the vineyard area has expanded. This region still seems unusually divided, between adherents and opponents of oak, and those who support the vineyard expansion and those who do not. There is also the important presence of the forward-thinking La Chablisienne co-operative which vinifies nearly one-third of all Chablis.

The Mâconnais and Beaujolais are regions which, on the whole, do not aspire to boutique status and prices. Their role has been to supply wine in the middle and lower-middle price ranges. They, above all, need to rethink their priorities in the light of falling market-share and New World competition. Mâcon, of course, has a huge potential advantage, in the form of large plantings of its native, now ultra-fashionable, Chardonnay. Some corners in the south of the Mâconnais, in Pouilly-Fuissé and elsewhere, can produce Chardonnay of the highest quality – Vincent's Château Fuissé Vieilles Vignes shames many Côte de Beaune *grands crus* in blind tastings. Just a few growers are defying the appellation hierarchy and showing that there is nothing intrinsically lower-class about these *terroirs*.

As for Beaujolais, it is still the victim of the success of a particular marketing stunt – Beaujolais Nouveau. The best *cru* wines (which, by the way, can be declassified into Bourgogne Rouge), when made by growers of skill and heart using oak *foudres* for maturation, are some of France's most undervalued. The *cru* of Morgon has taken an admirable step by introducing the category of Morgon Agé for wine kept 18 months before release. Another piece of good news is the excellent 1993 vintage, followed by the equally promising 1994.

Classifications and quality levels

Burgundy, excluding the Mâconnais and Beaujolais, has probably the most complex hierarchy of classifications and appellations in all France. At the top come the *grands crus* (15 for white, 25 for red), which each has its own appellation. These are the greatest, historically renowned vineyards in the region, accounting for only a tiny percentage of all production.

The next level down consists of the *premiers crus* – still privileged sites, whose nomenclature is horrifically complicated. The best *premiers crus* can be on a par with the *grands crus* and are almost always substantially cheaper.

After the *premiers crus* come the village wines (e.g. AOC Chassagne-Montrachet) from less-favoured vineyards, which are still considered worthy of these famous names. Bourgogne Hautes Côtes de Beaune and Hautes Côtes de Nuits cover high, backwoods vineyards in the Côte d'Or, not traditionally known for quality. These wines can be good value.

Finally, come the cover-all appellations, Bourgogne Rouge, Bourgogne Blanc, Bourgogne Passetoutgrains (for reds with a higher proportion of Gamay), and Bourgogne Grand Ordinaire (the lowest quality level for reds). Wines labelled Bourgogne Rouge or Bourgogne Blanc from a good Côte d'Or grower will come from vineyards which do not qualify for a village appellation. They may be right next door to the *premiers crus*, but have slightly different soil, and the wines are often the best-value burgundies of all. A small amount of Pinot Noir rosé is also made in the village of Marsannay.

Fortunately, things are somewhat simpler in the larger southerly regions of the Mâconnais and Beaujolais. Here there are village appellations (including Pouilly-Fuissé and the ten Beaujolais *crus*) but no *premiers* or *grands crus*.

White wine styles and grape varieties

All the best white burgundy is made from Chardonnay: reduced plantings of Aligoté produce a rather thin, sharp wine which can be flintily refreshing (perhaps best known as the classic base wine for Kir), while small plots of Pinot Blanc and Pinot Gris (called Beurot in Burgundy) are of curiosity value only. A solitary Burgundian outpost of Sauvignon exists around St-Bris, making wines not far from Sancerre in quality and style.

Chardonnay is a notoriously malleable grape, and even within the confines of Burgundy it can display a Protean ability to change shape, both through response to *terroir* and via different methods of vinification. In both Chablis and the Mâconnais, much white wine is made in neutral vessels and never sees oak, but the results are very different – green-glinting and minerally in Chablis (or at least in traditional Chablis), soft and buttery in the Mâconnais. The barrel-fermented style of complex, powerful Chardonnay which has conquered the world was born in the Côte de Beaune. The best growers of Meursault, Puligny and Chassagne still turn out the world's most fascinating and satisfying Chardonnays, the best of which take a decade or more to reveal their glory. All too many are killed off before they reach their prime. And far too many *négociant* wines bearing these names are mediocre and overpriced.

Regional and village appellations

Chablis is situated well to the north of the main Burgundy wine regions. The climate can be cruel, and May frosts are a particular danger. Traditionally, this harsh climate produced quite severe, minerally wines with a pronounced greenness which you found either enticing or off-putting. In recent times, however, Chablis seems to have changed, and at the same time to have become rather contradictory in character. Many wines are now much softer and more buttery than before – hardly distinguishable from Mâcon, in fact. At the same time, a debate rages over the use of oak, especially for the top *grands* and *premiers crus*, which are the pride of Chablis. Very fine wines are made by both camps, oakers and non-oakers, so it is perhaps best for an outsider to remain neutral. Two further points to note are the reduction in size of the Petit Chablis appellation, which used to cover vineyards not sited on the famous Kimmeridgian limestone slopes, and the creation of new *premiers crus* out of woodland. The La Chablisienne co-operative markets declassified wine as Jeunes Vignes.

The greatest white burgundies come from the Côte d'Or, which, in terms of white wines, means the Côte de Beaune – the tiny quantities of Chardonnay produced on the Côte de Nuits are not of serious interest. Here are the world's most famous white wine villages – Meursault, Puligny-Montrachet, Chassagne-Montrachet – and the world's most admired white wine vineyards – the *grands crus* Le Montrachet, Bâtard-Montrachet, Chevalier-Montrachet, Corton-Charlemagne – and the hardly less good *premiers crus* – Puligny-Montrachet Les Folatières, Meursault-Genevrières, Chassagne-Montrachet Les Embrazées, and several others. Unfortunately, the total production of white wine on the Côte d'Or is considerably less in an average year than that of the single Beaujolais *cru* of Morgon. There is just not enough to go round.

Wine writers like to generalise about the differences between these villages – Meursault, rich and nutty, Puligny, peachy and refined, Chassagne, full and robust – but the truth is that such generalisations are very crude. A Meursault-Blagny, from a cool, high vineyard, for instance, can be much leaner than a particularly ripe Puligny. In the end, the grower (the only guarantor of quality) is more important than the *cru* – though any conscientious grower will be proud of the difference between his or her various parcels.

For the majority who, sadly, cannot afford Le Montrachet or even good Meursault, there may be consolation in the less-renowned Côte de Beaune appellations, especially Auxey-Duresses, St-Aubin and (to a lesser extent) St-Romain. Failing those, there is Bourgogne Blanc from an excellent producer – still classy Chardonnay.

Leaving the Côte de Beaune, we come first to the scattered vineyards of the Côte Chalonnaise. Some excellent white wine is made here, but, just as in the Côte d'Or, unfortunately, not very much. Chardonnay makes up only around 10 per cent of the vineyard area of the Côte Chalonnaise. The most important village appellation here is Montagny (all of which, oddly, qualifies for *premier cru* status), though perhaps the best, most complex wines come from Rully and Mercurey.

The Mâconnais is lucky in having commercially significant resources of Chardonnay, but the co-operatives which make the majority of the wine seem, for the most part, to be unaware of this good fortune, and oblivious to the New World competition which is eating into its market. Basic AOC Mâcon Blanc has no pretentions to greatness, and much of it is pretty ordinary stuff, vinified by co-ops and marketed by the big Beaune and Nuits *négociants* who are more interested in money than quality. With

Mâcon-Villages, and the individual village wines, there is sometimes, but not often enough, more effort and individuality. The biggest name is Pouilly-Fuissé, whose wines have gone on a roller-coaster ride of prices in recent years, mainly because of the important but fickle American market. M. Vincent of Château Fuissé is a standard-bearer, showing that Pouilly-Fuissé can match the best of the Côte de Beaune. Unfortunately, he stands almost alone. One or two other producers, such as Thévenet (Mâcon-Clessé Bon Gran), Merlin (Mâcon La Roche Vineuse) and Guffens (Mâcon-Pierreclos), in the south of the Mâconnais, make whites of high class.

Finally, AOC St-Véran covers most of the Chardonnay vineyards in the far south of the Mâconnais bordering on the Beaujolais, and has for the most part replaced the now rare AOC Beaujolais Blanc. Quality in St-Véran is more consistent than elsewhere in the Mâconnais.

White burgundy vintages

Chardonnay ripens with much greater regularity than Pinot Noir in Burgundy, and, most years, decent wines are made and chaptalisation should not be necessary.

1994 Wet weather in early September, after an excellent summer, caused some problems but a generally successful white harvest is reported, though quantity is down in Chablis.

1993 Mixed summer weather leading to fair, if somewhat under-ripe, harvest. Heavy September rain may have caused dilution.

1992 Classic year for white burgundy, enticingly floral yet with structure to last. Lovely wines which will be approachable early.

1991 Not a great year, though the best growers made decent, early-drinking wines.

1990 Very good year marked by high and sometimes unripe acidity, but the best will be long-lived classics.

1989 The situation was reversed between whites and red in 1990 and 1989: the 1989 whites, like the 1990 reds, are great classics. The best are monumental and do not lack acidity.

Previous fine years: 1988 (somewhat underripe in places), 1986, 1985, 1983 (rot-affected, but the best wonderfully rich), 1982, 1979, 1978, 1973, 1971.

Red wine styles and grape varieties

Red burgundy made from Pinot Noir is the world's most tantalising wine. Long after they have succeeded with Cabernet

Sauvignon and Chardonnay, the best wine-making talents of the New World are still struggling with what they call the Holy Grail of wine-making. Pinot Noir is a notoriously temperamental and sensitive grape – it is literally thin-skinned (like so many sensitive people), prone to mutation, prone to rot, requiring the most careful handling in the winery. The rewards are aromas and flavours of indecent voluptuousness.

Burgundy has an advantage with its centuries of experience of growing and vinifying Pinot Noir, but the complacency sometimes displayed in the Côte d'Or is quite uncalled-for.

Gamay is Burgundy's other black grape, hardly to be mentioned in the same breath as Pinot Noir, but well-suited to the granite hills of Beaujolais. With age, the better Beaujolais *crus* can come to taste almost indistinguishable from mature Pinot Noir.

Regional and village appellations
In the Yonne region, not far from Chablis, small amounts of Pinot Noir are grown around Irancy, which has its own AOC, and Coulanges-la-Vineuse, whose reds qualify only for AOC Bourgogne Rouge, giving light-coloured, fragrant wine for early drinking.

Great red burgundy comes from the Côte d'Or. The northern section, the Côte de Nuits, is almost entirely planted with Pinot Noir, and it is on the east-facing, marl slopes running from Gevrey-Chambertin down to Nuits-St-Georges that most of the best red burgundy vineyards are sited. The greatest concentration of *grands crus* is in the villages of Gevrey-Chambertin and Vosne-Romanée, but the top *premiers crus* of those villages, and others, such as Morey-St-Denis, Chambolle-Musigny and Vougeot, are scarcely inferior. These wines combine power and finesse, overwhelming scents of red fruits, roots, spice and other less mentionable things, and a silkiness of texture. They can age for almost as long as great claret, but are usually approachable much earlier (from around their fifth year).

The Côte de Beaune, more evenly split between Pinot Noir and Chardonnay, has only one red *grand cru*, the great hill-vineyard of Corton, but marvellous red burgundies, slightly franker and softer (more feminine?) than their Côte de Nuits counterparts, come from the top sites of Beaune, Pommard and Volnay. Pommard wines tend to be powerful (though some very disappointing *négociant* wine is sold under this appellation); Volnay is perfumed and elegant; and Beaune combines scent and fleshy body. Chassagne-Montrachet makes reasonable quantities of robust red, much less highly valued than its white; and Santenay (full and fruity), Savigny (tannic when young), Auxey-Duresses, Monthélie, St-

Aubin and St-Romain are other second-division villages whose wines can offer good value. The backwoods vineyards of the Hautes Côtes de Beaune and Hautes Côtes de Nuits are planted mainly with Pinot Noir, which is worth looking out for in good vintages.

Pinot Noir is the main grape planted on the Côte Chalonnaise, and Mercurey and Givry, in particular, are red burgundy villages, producing wines as good as many in the Côte de Beaune.

The main black grape in the Mâconnais is Gamay, but some 7.5 per cent of the vineyard area is covered by Pinot Noir. Mâcon Rouge is much less well-known than either Mâcon Blanc or Beaujolais, but it seems to be making a low-key comeback.

The beautiful Beaujolais hills are the home of Gamay, intensively planted and producing twice as much wine (nearly all red) as the rest of Burgundy put together. Most is very ordinary, and huge quantities have been vinified for early consumption as Beaujolais Nouveau or Primeur. Now, it seems, that hugely successful marketing strategy is on its last legs. This may be no bad thing, for Beaujolais's best wines have always needed at least a few months and sometimes a year or three to reveal their plummy fruit. The best wines come from the northern parts of Beaujolais, known collectively as Beaujolais-Villages, and within that area from the ten privileged villages known as *crus*. These *crus* – Brouilly, Chénas (small and underrated), Chiroubles, Côte de Brouilly, Fleurie (overpriced), Juliénas, Morgon (needing a year or two to reveal its special cherry bouquet), Moulin-à-Vent (the most powerful, burgundian wines), Regnié (the newest recruit) and St-Amour – carry their own name but not that of Beaujolais. From a skilful grower, who may well mature his wines in large oak *foudres*, they can be quite delicious and excellent value. It it worth perusing the list of the Beaujolais specialist Roger Harris, as well as the widely available selections from Duboeuf and the Eventail de Vignerons-Producteurs.

Red burgundy vintages

1994 Mixed results are reported from a rain-affected harvest.
1993 The best of the reds, picked before the rain which started on 22 September, are magnificent – deep-coloured, full of aroma, fruit and power. Not all growers managed to avoid the rain – beware.
1992 Large vintage of easy, attractive wines, but only the most conscientious growers have achieved real concentration.
1991 Small vintage reduced by hail damage and affected by vintage-time rain. Some very concentrated reds were made – choose carefully.

1990 Magnificent vintage, for once justifying the hype. Less austere than 1988, more structured than 1989 or 1985, the balance is perfect.
1989 Very attractive, soft reds for earlyish consumption. Nothing like as good as the whites, however. Côte de Beaune wines best.
1988 A great, tannic, long-lasting vintage. The best wines require patience but will reward it.
1987 Much under-rated, attractive, fruity vintage for the medium-term, better in the Côte de Beaune than Côte de Nuits.
1986 Somewhat hard and charmless wines, but the best are well-structured and not lacking in fruit.
1985 Over-hyped vintage of precocious charm and lovely raspberry fruit. Many have turned out to lack staying-power.

Earlier fine vintages: 1983 (many wines ruined by rot), 1978, 1976, 1971.

Pick of the Burgundy and Beaujolais producers (red and white)
Angerville, Domaine Marquis d' Famous aristocratic estate in Volnay, one of the pioneers of estate-bottling. Light-coloured, elegant wines.

L'Arlot, Domaine de Nuits-St-Georges domaine much improved since purchase by AXA-Millésimes in 1987. Winemaker Jean-Pierre de Smet aims for fruit and elegance.

Boillot, Domaine Jean-Marc Conscientious producer of white Puligny-Montrachet, Meursault, Chassagne-Montrachet and Bourgogne Blanc, red Beaune, Pommard, Volnay and Bourgogne Rouge.

Bonneau du Martray, Domaine Great aristocratic producer of some of the finest Corton-Charlemagne.

Bouchard Père et Fils Recently taken over by Henriot. Best of the Bouchard *négociants*, with some fine wines from the Domaine du Château de Beaune, including Le Montrachet, Chevalier-Montrachet, Beaune Clos de la Mousse and Grèves Vigne de l'Enfant Jésus. Sometimes disappointing in bottle.

Buxy, Cave Co-opérative Good Montagny from this well-distributed co-op.

Carillon, Domaine Louis Magnificent, subtle Puligny-Montrachet (especially Les Referts). Perhaps the best estate in Puligny.

La Chablisienne Deceptively girlish name for the huge Chablis co-op which vinifies one-third of all Chablis. Quality very good considering scale.

Clair, Domaine Bruno Excellent domaine at Marsannay on the Côte de Nuits, run by one of Burgundy's leading young Turks. Especially good Gevrey-Chambertin Clos St-Jacques and Savigny-lès-Beaune La Dominode.

Coche-Dury, Domaine Jean-François One of the very greatest white burgundy producers, especially of Chevalier-Montrachet and Meursault-Perrières.

Dauvissat, Domaine René & Vincent Better of the two Dauvissat estates in Chablis, with exemplary oaked wines from *grands crus* Les Clos and Les Preuses, and *premiers crus* Les Vaillons and La Forest.

Delorme, André Both a *négociant* and large vineyard-owner in the Côte Chalonnaise, especially Rully. Good, if not exciting, quality.

Drouhin, Joseph Certainly one of Burgundy's best and most quality-conscious *négociants*, run by the fastidious Robert Drouhin, who also owns large holdings in Chablis, and is responsible for the vinification and *élevage* of the famous Le Montrachet, Marquis de Laguiche. Fine white Beaune Clos des Mouches. Reds also good.

Duboeuf, Georges Hugely successful Beaujolais and Mâconnais *négociant*, with good-quality selections.

Dujac, Domaine Excellent Côte de Nuits estate run by Jacques Seysses, with important holdings of *grands crus* Clos de la Roche, Clos St-Denis and Bonnes-Mares, all at Morey St-Denis.

Faiveley, Maison Improving whites and solid, sometimes heavy-handed reds at this quality-conscious *négociant*.

Fèvre, Domaine William/Domaine de la Maladière Large and important Chablis domaine, leading spokesman for barrel-fermentation, at least for classic Chablis *premiers* and *grands crus*.

Fuissé, Château de Jean-Jacques Vincent produces towering Pouilly-Fuissé Vieilles Vignes and excellent St-Véran.

Gagnard, Domaine Jean-Noël Probably the best of the many Gagnard domaines, producing superb Bâtard-Montrachet and Chassagne-Montrachet *premiers crus*.

Gouges, Domaine Henri Famous estate at Nuits-St-Georges, one of the first to bottle its own wines, which suffered decline in 1980s, but now showing signs of revival.

Grivot, Domaine Fine estate at Vosne-Romanée, making some of the best Clos Vougeot and Richebourg, also *premiers crus* of Vosne-Romanée and Nuits-St-Georges. Etienne Grivot also makes the wines of Domaine Jacqueline Jayer (his aunt), including superb Echézeaux.

Guffens-Heynen Remarkably concentrated Pouilly-Fuissé and Mâcon-Pierreclos (tiny quantities) from this Belgian duo. Also *négociant* wines under Verget label.

Guillemot, Domaine Michel Lovely pure Mâcon-Clesse Quintaine and remarkable sweet, botrytised Sélection de Grains Cendres.

Hospices de Beaune Great medieval charitable foundation in Beaune with large holdings of mainly *premiers* and *grands crus* in the Côte de Beaune. These are sold as *cuvées* named after benefactors at a special auction in November, once thought to be a benchmark for burgundy prices in general. Unfortunately, quality is very variable, not just between *cuvées*, but from sample to bottle.

Jadot, Maison Louis Most people's pick of the Burgundy *négociants*, benefiting from the inspired wine-making of Jacques Lardière. Wonderful domaine Chevalier-Montrachet Les Demoiselles and Puligny-Montrachet Les Folatières. Very fine red Beaune Bressandes and Theurons.

Jaffelin Good-quality *négociant* previously owned by Drouhin, recently sold to Boisset.

Jayer, Domaine Henri The most famous small red wine domaine in Burgundy, thanks to superb stewardship of the recently retired M. Jayer. Wonderful Echézeaux and Vosne-Romanée *premiers crus*.

Jobard, Domaine François Relentlessly traditionalist Meursault producer, whose subtle, demanding wines take an average of a decade to open up. The sublime Genevrières, Poruzot and Charmes are well worth the wait.

Juillot, Domaine Michel Excellent producer based in Mercurey, who makes impressive Corton-Charlemagne as well as fine red and white Mercurey.

Labouré-Roi Better-than-average *négociant* whose whites are at least inoffensive, and reds rather better.

Lafarge, Domaine Michel Exemplary producer of Volnay of elegance and class.

Lafon, Domaine des Comtes Very high-quality, if over-fashionable Meursault and Volnay domaine, with superb, oaky *premiers crus*.

Laroche, Domaine Huge Chablis domaine owned by *négociant*-house of Laroche, which also runs Chablis house of Bacheroy-Josselin. Fair-to-good quality.

Latour, Domaine et Maison Louis The famous Beaune *négociant* also owns vineyards in Corton, and makes superb Corton-Charlemagne and Chevalier-Montrachet Les Demoiselles. Some *négociant* selections of Meursault, Puligny-Montrachet and Chassagne-Montrachet can be excellent. Famously pasteurised reds are much less impressive.

Leflaive, Domaine Very famous but, in our view, disappointing producer of Puligny-Montrachet, often lacking fruit.

Leflaive, Olivier Youthful *négociant*-house founded by nephew of the late Vincent Leflaive of Domaine Leflaive. Attractive, but often over-oaked, wines.

Leroy, Domaine Some of the priciest wines in Burgundy, produced from this recently created domaine by Lalou Bize-Leroy, former director of Domaine de la Romanée-Conti, cultivated using bio-dynamic methods.

Lugny, Cave de Reliable co-operative producer of Mâcon.

Méo-Camuzet, Domaine Vosne-Romanée domaine with excellent vineyards, especially *grand cru* Richebourg, run by same team as at Domaine Henri Jayer.

Merlin, Domaine Olivier Exciting young producer of Mâcon La Roche Vineuse. Cuvée Vieilles Vignes is outstanding.

Michel, Domaine Louis Leading proponent of unoaked Chablis *grands* and *premiers crus*. Splendidly pure, minerally, long-lived wines prove their point.

Morey, Domaines Bernard, Jean-Marc A classic example of the fragmentation caused by French inheritance laws. Two brothers have inherited the excellent Chassagne-Montrachet domaine of their admirable vigneron father Albert. So far, quality seems not to have suffered.

Ramonet, Domaine Legendary producer of *grands crus* Le Montrachet, Bâtard-Montrachet, Bienvenues-Bâtard-Montrachet and a superb range of *premiers crus* from Chassagne-Montrachet. Some of Burgundy's best and most complex whites.

Raveneau, Domaine Jean-Marie Highly regarded producer of Chablis, poised between oaked and unoaked styles, including *grands crus* Les Clos, Blanchot and Valmur.

Rodet, Antonin Large *négociant* and vineyard-owner in the Côte Chalonnaise. Mercurey, red and white, from Château de Chamirey, can be excellent.

Romanée-Conti, Domaine de la Late-picked, powerful reds can be sublime, but prices are a deterrent. Le Montrachet from Burgundy's most celebrated domaine is probably the world's most expensive dry white wine. Not for mere mortals.

Rouget, Domaine Emmanuel Rouget is the nephew of the great Henri Jayer, who helps with vinification.

Roulot, Domaine Guy Very good, rich, typical Meursault.

Rousseau, Domaine Armand Great Gevrey-Chambertin domaine with substantial holdings in *grands crus* Chambertin, Chambertin-Clos de Bèze, Charmes-Chambertin, Mazy-Chambertin and Monopole Chambertin Clos des Ruchottes.

Sauzet, Domaine Etienne Famous Puligny-Montrachet estate, with holdings in *grands crus* Bâtard-Montrachet and Bienvenues-Bâtard-Montrachet. Finely made, concentrated wines.

Thévenet, Jean/Domaine de la Bon Gran Most eccentric producer of Mâcon, and also one of the best. Bon Gran is harvested very ripe, often with considerable botrytis (sometimes a separate Cuvée Botrytis is made), and can last for decades.

Thivin, Château Fine Côte de Brouilly, expressing all the vividness of Gamay.

Tollot-Beaut, Domaine Rich, chocolatey, approachable reds with lots of new oak. Especially good-value Chorey-lès-Beaune.

Villaine, Domaine Aubert de The scholarly co-owner of the Domaine de la Romanée-Conti makes what is probably Burgundy's best Aligoté here at Bouzeron.

Vogüé, Domaine Comte Georges de The most famous producer of *grands crus* Le Musigny and Bonnes-Mares. Wines have not always lived up to reputation.

CHAMPAGNE

Stung by the dramatic slump (following the great boom) of the early 1990s, Champagne set about a remarkable public washing of dirty linen. It started with Bollinger's Charter of Ethics and Quality, an admirable document which, unlike certain other recent charters, seemed genuinely committed to a new policy of openness and to the maintenance of certain standards (for instance, elimination of the *deuxième taille* or third pressing, and refusal to allow *sur lattes* or buying of ready-made champagne). Bollinger is a small house. The largest house of all, Moët et Chandon, surprised almost everybody in 1994 by following suit and sticking a back-label on its best-selling Brut Impérial stating the exact mix of grape varieties (including no less than 39 per cent Pinot Meunier), the vintage of most of the blend, the period spent on the lees (three years) and the percentage of reserve wine. Wasn't this like revealing the formula for Coca-Cola? Haven't we always been told that the *assemblage*, the final blend of a house's champagne, was the ultimate trade secret?

One thing you can be sure of is that the Champenois, those master-manipulators of image, have well-considered reasons for removing one, or several, of the veils of mystery surrounding their product. Richard Geoffroy, the young master-blender who initiated the Moët back-label, speaks of 'a new era of information: people want to be more aware, richer in knowledge'. He is undoubtedly influenced by his experience working for Domaine Chandon in Australia. The champagne houses initiated the development of premium sparkling wines in the New World, and now, not before time, the New World is rubbing off on them, with its philosophy of directness and simplicity. Australian wines score on flavour and value for money, not mystique. Champagne has taken note.

However, one of the most important aspects of this prolonged clean-up of image is proving resistant to the most energetic of detergents. Two years ago we were told of the imminent reorganisation of the Syndicat des Grandes Marques – the association of what were, in theory, the top houses. The man in charge of the operation, the engaging Jean-Claude Rouzaud of Roederer, admits that it is proving far more difficult than expected. He has what sounds like a stringent list of 20 criteria, including banning the sub-contracting of vinification and insisting on a minimum stock level of three years. At the moment, around 15 houses comply, and the arguments surround five or so more. Watch this space.

Meanwhile, champagne sales have improved markedly after a disastrous 1992 and flat 1993. After the excesses of the 1980s, has a new era of moderation and good sense dawned in Champagne? Grape prices seem to have stabilised, for the time being. Stocks are at a healthy level, allowing no excuse for the premature release of harsh, green wine which marred the reputation of at least one top-quality house in the late 1980s. The recession certainly sobered up a region which had become drunk with euphoria. A new generation of winemakers, many with experience of working in New World sparkling-wine operations, is aware of the New World attitudes which have revolutionised the wine scene.

At bottom, though, despite a run of rain-sodden vintages, the Champenois still feel pretty confident. New World premium sparkling wine is still a small sector, compared to champagne – less than 5 per cent, according to Richard Geoffroy. The quality gap may have narrowed – in some cases, it may have been reversed, for who could claim that Mumm Cordon Rouge is better than Mumm Cuvée Napa? – but the image gap remains.

Grape varieties

Champagne is made from three varieties, two black – Pinot Noir and Pinot Meunier – plus the white Chardonnay. Pinot Noir, the great grape of the Montagne de Reims and the Marne Valley, is the backbone of most blends, providing power, body and length; the often-scorned Meunier, when correctly pressed and vinified, gives fragrance and lift, while Chardonnay, the best of which comes from the Côte des Blancs south of Epernay, provides perfume and finesse, but not usually much power or length. Most non-vintage blends, as the new-look Moët proves, contain a highish proportion of Meunier, which continues to be the most planted grape in Champagne (42 per cent of the vineyard area). Many vintage wines dispense with Meunier.

Styles

Blanc de Blancs Champagne made entirely from Chardonnay. Fashionable, but difficult to make.

Blanc de Noirs Champagne made from black grapes.

Brut The term for dry champagne with less than 15 grams per litre of residual sugar.

De luxe cuvée/prestige cuvée A top-of-the-range product, offering (in theory) the highest quality and (invariably) glitzy packaging. Moët's Dom Pérignon was the pioneer.

Demi-sec Confusingly, this means sweet.

Dosage Addition of sweetness just before the wine is recorked for release, calculated according to style. Non-dosage wines are therefore totally dry.

Extra-dry Dry, but not as dry as Brut.

Non-vintage The producer's standard blend, which accounts for the vast majority of champagne sales. This can be as young as one year old, though quality-conscious houses are aiming for a minimum age of three years. It is often claimed that non-vintage champagne will improve with keeping: the problem here is that the wine must be good in the first place. Cheap, basic-quality champagne will get worse, not better, with keeping.

Récoltant-Manipulant (RM) The term for a grower who harvests and makes his or her own champagne.

Rosé Pink champagne, most commonly made by adding small amounts of red Pinot Noir wine from Bouzy or Aÿ to the blend.

Vintage A champagne from a single, better-than-average year.

Pick of the producers

Billecart-Salmon Small, quality-conscious, family-owned house which specialises in long, cool fermentations to make fine-grained but not weak wines. Excellent rosé and vintage.

Billiot, Henri Grower in Ambonnay making superb, powerful, fruity, 100 per cent Pinot Noir Brut and Rosé.

Bollinger One of the most traditional of all houses, still fermenting most wines in small barrels. Wines need time to show at their best, but have superb power and ageing ability. A speciality is RD or recently disgorged vintage wine which has spent nearly a decade on its lees.

Deutz Admirable, smallish firm taken over in 1993 by Roederer. Very good, consistent non-vintage.

Gosset Often overlooked but excellent small house.

Gratien, Alfred Small house which ferments in barrel and makes wines of rich, yeasty character.

Heidsieck, Charles Much-improved house, now using up to 40 per cent reserve wines for non-vintage of great character.

Krug The Rolls-Royce of champagne. Grande Cuvée is meticulously blended to achieve power with finesse, Rosé is magnificent (though not pink), Clos du Mesnil is a single-vineyard Blanc de Blancs of astonishing price.

Lanson Great dowry of vineyards has been sold off following 1991 purchase by Marne et Champagne, so the future of this house, once notable for firm vintage, is in doubt.

Laurent-Perrier The most consistent in quality of the bigger houses. Non-vintage is always fresh and satisfying; Ultra-Brut is successful non-dosage wine; *de luxe cuvée* Grande Siècle is a blend of three years.

Moët et Chandon By far the largest house, now galvanised by promising new spirit of openness. Non-vintage Brut Impérial, once bland, looks set for somewhat more characterful style. *Prestige cuvée* Dom Pérignon, from Moët's own vineyards, combines power and fragrance.

Mumm Champagne's greatest under-performer, with short and disagreeable Cordon Rouge. *Blanc de blancs* Crémant de Cramant is light but attractive.

Perrier, Joseph Under-rated, small house maintaining good standard with fresh non-vintage.

Perrier-Jouët Once highly regarded house now owned by Seagram and living on reputation.

Piper-Heidsieck Much improved quality recently from this large house. Attractive, fresh non-vintage.

Pol Roger Traditional family-controlled house, maintaining good quality, especially with vintage and *de-luxe cuvées* PR and Sir Winston Churchill. Very good Chardonnay.

Pommery One of champagne's great names, much affected by recent changes of ownership. Winemaker Alain de Polignac is a man of integrity, so quality may improve.

Roederer, Louis Quality-conscious house, sourcing 75 per cent of grape requirements from own vineyards. Beautifully judged, quite rich non-vintage, superb vintage and *de luxe cuvée* Cristal.

Taittinger House noted for chic, but also perhaps the best *blanc de blancs*, Comtes de Champagne.

Veuve Clicquot Famous, large house still achieving distinctive, rich character with non-vintage, vintage and *de luxe cuvée* La Grande Dame.

Vintage guide

1994 Rain started falling in early September, spoiling a potentially great harvest. Severe problems of rot.
1993 Large but rain-affected crop. Quality seems fair, though much diluted, where not affected by rot.
1992 Very large crop, with rain causing some rot.
1991 Large quantities despite spring frosts. Vintage will be released by some houses.
1990 High-quality, ripe harvest, forming the basis of many current non-vintage wines.
1989 Very ripe, very good quality. Some vintage wines are already being released, too young.
1988 Good quality vintage, released as vintage by most houses. Attractive, firm, fruity style.
   Previous fine vintage years: 1986, 1985, 1983, 1982.

ALSACE

Alsace used to be so simple. This was the one French (yes, it is French, even though the names, the bottles, even the styles, are Germanic) region which, long before Australian Chardonnay was even a gleam in the eye of Murray Tyrrell, decided on the revolutionary idea of naming wines exclusively by grape varieties. There was a single appellation for the whole compact region, on the eastern slopes of the Vosges, four major and two or three other grape varieties, reliable co-ops, *négociants* and just a few determined, individualistic growers.

   No wonder that Alsace's pure, fruity, yet dry, whites became so successful, at least on the French market, accounting at one time for

40 per cent of all AOC white wine consumed in Paris. On the export markets, Alsace was praised for its reliability, and in Britain gained a reputation as the ideal wine-bar white: safe and sound, but not very exciting. You can understand the frustration of Alsace's growers, who knew that Riesling, Tokay-Pinot Gris and Gewurztraminer from their best, steep vineyards were as good in their way as any white wines in the world. So they decided to complicate matters.

The introduction of the Alsace *grands crus* has been a controversial business. No one has ever denied that some sites in Alsace were better than others – indeed, these notable vineyards are surrounded with as much history and tradition as any in Europe. Even the *négociants*, who now oppose the *grand cru* concept, often stated vineyard origin for top *cuvées* – Trimbach with Clos Ste-Hune, Hugel with Sporen. It is more the manner in which so many vineyards – 50 at the present count – have been classified at the highest possible level which has caused the argument. Johnny Hugel's often-quoted line that the introduction of dozens of complicated Germanic names may further confuse customers already unsure whether Alsace is really French or German should not be taken too seriously. Tom Stevenson, however, surely has an excellent point when he suggests that the vineyards might first have been established as *premiers crus*, allowing the best to emerge in due course and be promoted to the top rank.

In any case, the *grands crus* are a *fait accompli*. In their favour, it must be said that they have encouraged a new generation of growers to express the full possibilities of their marvellous vineyards in wines of great individuality. Perhaps they have also caused a polarisation, in a region which seems increasingly split between major co-operatives (some admirable) and ambitious growers aiming for boutique prices. The quality *négociants*, once the backbone of Alsace, have lost ground. All the same, Alsace, which has enjoyed better-than-average vintages in the 1990s after the spectacular 1980s, offers world-class white wines, as well as many which are more straightforwardly enjoyable. Reliability remains a great plus point.

Appellations and quality levels

The single Alsace AOC used to cover all the still wine made in the region – 95 per cent of it white – until the delimitation of the first 25 *grands crus* in 1983, leading to the introduction of AOC Alsace Grand Cru, which now covers 50 sites, but only about 4 per cent of Alsace production. AOC Crémant d'Alsace covers the region's champagne-method sparkling wines, often of high quality.

Quality levels are something of a bugbear in Alsace, especially among the *négociants* who bandy about terms like *réserve spéciale* and *cuvée tradition* in the usual vague French manner.

Two more precise higher quality designations exist:

Vendange tardive The term means late-harvest, and wines in this category must be made from grapes with high natural sugar levels and may not be chaptalised. Unfortunately, it does not give a clear idea of the style of the wine, which can be anywhere from completely dry and alcoholic to medium-sweet. Unsatisfactory.

Sélection de grains nobles This refers to wines made from nobly rotten grapes. Botrytis does not occur with any regularity in Alsace and these wines are therefore very rare and expensive. The best, from Hugel and Marcel Deiss, can be magnificent.

White wines – the major grape varieties

Gewurztraminer
This is Alsace's most famous and distinctive grape. Its extraordinary perfume, combining lychee fruit with an animal muskiness, is its strongest point, but not everyone will like it. As a wine, Alsace Gewurztraminer can often be clumsy, high in alcohol and low in acidity. However, it can come into its own as a partner for smoked fish.

Muscat
Much the rarest of Alsace's four 'noble' grapes, Muscat produces wines which smell of the grapes but taste dry. They tend to be light and delicate.

Riesling
Considered by Alsace producers to be their greatest grape, Alsace Rieslings often seem excessively dry and austere. Not as perfumed and fruity as German Rieslings, the best develop magnificent, oily, honeyed, yet still fresh, richness.

Tokay-Pinot Gris
This is the most mysterious and elusive of Alsace grapes. Even its name is confusing: the Tokay has nothing to do with the sweet Hungarian wine. Tokay-Pinot Gris wines are not as perfumed as Gewurztraminer or as fruity as Riesling or Muscat, but have a subtle smokiness and a fascinating richness of texture.

Other white grape varieties
Pinot Blanc is used to produce much attractive, soft, fruity dry
white wine, mostly for quaffing, though some versions can taste
surprisingly intense. There is some confusion in Alsace between
Pinot Blanc and Auxerrois, which, although a different grape, with
a sweeter, buttery taste, can be mixed in with Pinot Blanc. Sylvaner
has lost ground, and its earthy flavour seems unfashionable.

Red wines

Pinot Noir is the only black grape cultivated in Alsace; it satisfies a
local demand for light, cherry-flavoured reds, which account for
some 5 per cent of Alsace production. Some producers try harder to
make serious, burgundian red, but their efforts seem misguided.

Blends
Alsace has traditionally been known for easy-drinking blends,
known as Edelzwicker or Vin d'Alsace. Such blends can mix, say,
the softness of Pinot Blanc with the backbone of Riesling to
satisfying effect, but they are on the decrease.

Pick of the producers
Deiss, Domaine Marcel Superb wines, especially Rieslings from
Grands Crus Altenberg and Schoenenbourg, from this fanatically
quality-minded producer.

Dopff au Moulin *Négociant* maintaining high standards with simple
varietals and also excellent Domaines Dopff wines, including
Riesling Grand Cru Schoenenbourg.

Faller Frères/Domaine Weinbach Some of Alsace's most seductive
Riesling, Tokay-Pinot Gris and Gewurztraminer, always beautifully
poised, is made by Collette Faller from excellent vineyards in the
Grand Cru Schlossberg.

Hugel The greatest name among Alsace *négociants*. Known for quite
fat, rounded wines; the higher qualities, especially Réserve
Personnelle, are often outstanding,

Kientzler, André Excellent, sure-handed grower in Ribeauville,
making superb Grand Cru Riesling Geisberg and Osterberg and
Grand Cru Kirchberg Gewurztraminer.

Kreydenweiss, Marc Talented grower in the unfashionable northern part of Alsace, whose firm, steely Riesling Grand Cru Kastelberg and Wiebelsberg are outstanding.

Kuentz-Bas One of Alsace's best *négociant*-houses, with 12 hectares of fine vineyards.

Ostertag, André Eccentric, voluble young grower who has been experimenting with *barrique*-ageing, to sometimes bizarre effect. Fine Riesling and Tokay-Pinot Gris from Grand Cru Muenchberg.

Rolly Gassmann Dedicated husband and wife team of grower-winemakers who specialise in a rich, oily style with considerable residual sugar. Especially good Auxerrois.

Schlumberger, Domaines The largest vineyard-owners in Alsace, with massive holdings in Grands Crus Kitterlé, Saering, Kessler and Spiegel, all in the village of Guebwiller. The wines tend to be big and rich with a distinctive earthiness. Late-harvest wines a speciality.

Trimbach Traditionally the great rivals of Hugel, making much more austere and elegant wines. The top Rieslings, Clos Ste-Hune and Cuvée Frederic Emile, though they can taste harsh and forbidding when young, develop beautifully and are, with those of Deiss, the greatest of the region.

Turckheim, Cave Vinicole de Perhaps the most dynamic co-operative in Alsace, which has taken the British middle-market by storm. Especially good Gewurztraminer from Grand Cru Brand.

Zind-Humbrecht, Domaine The greatest *grand cru* specialists in Alsace, making outstandingly concentrated, if sometimes excessively rich and fat, wines. Tokay-Pinot Gris from Grand Cru Rangen is a spicy marvel, and Riesling from Grand Cru Brand and Gerwurztraminer from Grand Cru Hengst and Goldert are almost as wonderful.

Vintage guide

1994 A very hot summer led to high hopes; some were dashed by September rain but October sun redeemed the situation for late pickers. Some very ripe Gewurztraminer and Tokay-Pinot Gris.
1993 Above-average-quality but not great vintage. Tokay-Pinot Gris seems especially good. Riesling less so.

1992 Huge vintage of soft, early-drinking wine.
1991 Better quality than in many French regions, though diluted by rain at harvest.
1990 Magnificent, ripe, healthy crop. Superb quality.
1989 Amazingly ripe vintage, declared by many (not hyperbolic) growers to be their best ever. Extraordinarily high proportion of *vendange tardive* and *sélection de grains nobles*.
1988 Very good, ripe vintage of muscular wines.
Earlier fine vintages: 1985, 1983, 1981, 1976, 1971.

LOIRE

The Loire Valley is the most quintessentially French of all France's wine valleys. The long, slow-moving river more or less divides the country in half, as it flows in a great arc from the northern slopes of the Massif Central through the rich flatlands of Bourges, the woods and fields of Touraine and Anjou, and finally the green vineyards around Nantes where it meets the Atlantic. Wine is made patchily along much of its 600-mile length, but after the thinly spread country areas of Côtes du Forez, Côte d'Auvergne, Côte Roannaise, St-Pourçain and Châteaumeillant, the first vineyards of serious note occur around Sancerre and Pouilly. Touraine and Anjou are important, historic wine regions, producing fine reds from Cabernet Franc and whites from Chenin, which go all the way from bone-dry to intensely sweet. Near the river's mouth is Muscadet country, producing sharp dry whites designed to partner the region's fine shellfish.

It is difficult to generalise about such a long and varied wine-river. For most drinkers, Loire wines probably mean Muscadet, Sancerre, Pouilly Fumé and Rosé d'Anjou, possibly not in that order. The whites are certainly more familiar than the reds, and the most fashionable of the whites are made from Sauvignon Blanc. Some who buy at Oddbins may even think that Sancerre and Pouilly Fumé are French imitations of New Zealand Sauvignon Blanc (rather than vice versa).

Loire wines, in common with almost all the wines of France's classic regions, are currently facing a challenge from the New World and new European producers. South Africa, with its crisp but ripe whites from the Loire's own Chenin Blanc, may pose a particular threat. Sancerre and Pouilly Fumé face obvious, though not cheap, competition, and have acknowledged the fact by forming a Central Vineyards promotional organisation (though, for the moment, Pouilly is declining to join!). Muscadet has fought back from a low-point, and reports healthily rising sales – a surprise

to many wine journalists who felt that the region's thin whites might have outlived their usefulness. The Loire's reds, though much less well known, have a considerable advantage in being made mainly from Cabernet Franc, a variety very seldom planted in the New World. Touraine, Saumur and Anjou producers should be shouting louder about this.

The Loire's *vignerons* have also been severely tested by the weather gods in the 1990s. The frost of April 1991 devastated vineyards especially in Muscadet, Anjou and Touraine, reducing the crop by as much 80 per cent in places. In contrast 1992 was a huge harvest: the vines rampaged back after their year off and many vignerons failed to apply the pruning-knife with sufficient rigour. Fortunately, 1993 was a very good year, with the best reds since 1990, and fine, flinty Sancerre and Pouilly Fumé. 1994 could have been a cracker, after a sweltering summer, but September rains mean careful selection will be necessary. In the great sweet wine areas of Anjou and Touraine, still relatively little-known to the world at large, some fine concentrated dessert wines were made in both 1993 and 1994 by patient growers who waited until November.

White wines – grape varieties, appellations

The white grape most associated with the Loire nowadays, Sauvignon Blanc, is actually a relative parvenu, only introduced to the central vineyards of Sancerre and Pouilly around 1910. Having established classic styles of mainly unoaked Sauvignon, which have gone on to conquer the New World, in those two towns, Sauvignon has crept westwards into Touraine, where it now accounts for some 60 per cent of all Touraine white. Sauvignon Blanc is also the white grape of the small AOCs of Menetou-Salon, Quincy and Reuilly, and flourishes in the large Haut-Poitou area south of Anjou.

Chenin Blanc has a greater claim than Sauvignon to be the classic white Loire grape. Chenin's heartland is Anjou, Saumur and Touraine, where the ungracious grape shows its versatility in producing dry, medium, sweet and sparkling wines of quality. The dry whites of Savennières are stern in youth but develop fascinating minerally complexity; the dry, medium (*demi-sec*), sweet (*moelleux*), lightly sparkling (*pétillant*) and *méthode traditionelle* wines of Vouvray show the full gamut of Chenin's possibilities. Good sweet wines are made in Montlouis and great ones in certain favoured corners of Coteaux du Layon, especially Bonnezeaux and Quarts de Chaume. Chenin is also responsible for the dry and sparkling whites of Saumur, often good value when not excessively harsh.

The third of the major Loire trio of white grapes is the seldom-praised Melon de Bourgogne, the grape of the greenish, tart, at best, deliciously crisp, Muscadet. The best Muscadet comes under the Muscadet-de-Sèvre-et-Maine AOC, and carries the suffix *sur lie*. This is supposed to mean that the wine comes straight off the lees, and should (but does not always) guarantee freshness and a touch of CO_2. A new AOC Muscadet Côtes de Grandlieu, covering a small area south-east of Nantes, was announced in November 1994. The even tarter, thinner Gros Plant, Muscadet's junior partner, is made from the grape of the same name, also called Folle Blanche.

Apart from these, Chardonnay has a considerable presence, especially in Haut-Poitou, and can be sold as vin de pays du Jardin de la France. Mention can also be made of the Chasselas wines of Pouilly and the Pinot Gris, known locally as Malvoisie, of Ancenis in the west.

Red wines – grape varieties, appellations

All the best Loire reds are made mainly from one grape, Cabernet Franc, which produces wines of highly distinctive character – sometimes tart and tannic in youth, but possessing all the aromas of a summer wood after rain – with the ability to age for a decade and gain considerable complexity. Cabernet Sauvignon is also planted and often forms 5-10 per cent of a blend with Cabernet Franc. The Touraine AOCs, Chinon, Bourgueil and St-Nicolas de Bourgueil, produce most of the best Loire reds, though the increasingly fashionable Saumur-Champigny can be equally delicious. Straight Saumur, Anjou and Anjou Villages reds can be rather tough and rustic, though there are notable exceptions.

Apart from Cabernet Franc, the burgundian Pinot Noir and Gamay are cultivated in places – the former in Sancerre and Menetou-Salon, the latter in the upper Loire and Touraine. The Pinots tend to be light and thin, the Gamays rough and earthy.

Rosé wines

The most commonly seen bottles of Loire wine in British shops are probably still pink-orange in colour and contain medium-sweet Anjou Rosé. The best that can be said about this AOC is that it is inexpensive. Much better, largely because the wine is dry, is AOC Cabernet d'Anjou (Rosé), which can be leafily refreshing.

Pick of the producers
Baumard, Domaine Wonderful sweet Quarts de Chaume in top vintages such as 1989 and 1990, and dry Savennières.

Bouvet-Ladubay Good sparkling Saumur from this Taittinger subsidiary.

Brédif Good Vouvray, especially at the sweeter end.

Couly-Dutheil Large but reliable estate producer of Chinon, which ages gracefully. *Négociant* wines from other Loire regions.

Dagueneau, Didier Fanatically quality-minded producer of Pouilly Fumé, including *barrique*-fermented Cuvée Silex.

Druet The top name in Bourgueil, producing much deeper and more serious wines than the lightish norm.

Fesles, Château de Magnificent sweet Bonnezeaux from this top-class estate, under new ownership but same stewardship.

Filliatreau, Domaine Perhaps the finest producer of Saumur-Champigny.

Huet Fine producer of Vouvray, mainly *demi-sec* and *moelleux*, also *pétillant* and *mousseux*.

Joguet Charles Joguet is, if not the king, then the cardinal of Chinon, a goatee-bearded perfectionist who specialises in single-vineyard bottlings.

Joly Eccentric, if not downright crazy producer of Savennières-Coulée de Serrant, dry white Chenin which gains complexity with age. Biodynamic methods involve much moon-gazing.

Ladoucette (Château de Nozet) Celebrated producer of Pouilly Fumé, including over-priced Baron de L. Also owns reliable Comte Lafond estate in Sancerre.

Langlois-Château Reliable Saumur house owned by Bollinger of Champagne, and best-known for drinkable sparklers. Less well-known still red and white Saumur is worth looking out for.

Oisly-et-Thésée, Confrérie des Vignerons d' One of the Loire's most respected co-ops, responsible for nearly two million bottles of Touraine varietals, especially Sauvignon and Gamay.

Pellé, Henri Excellent producer of 100 per cent Sauvignon Menetou-Salon, better than much Sancerre and Pouilly Fumé.

Poniatowski Princely estate in Vouvray, specialising in wines on the dry side.

Sauvion Quality leader in Muscadet-de-Sèvre-et-Maine, 80 per cent of production being *négociant* wines, 20 per cent estate-bottled.

Vacheron Top estate in Sancerre, making wines of flinty character in most years.

Vatan Quality-conscious young grower in Sancerre.

RHONE, PROVENCE, CORSICA

The Rhône Valley

The Rhône is a long river. Ignoring the Swiss bit, and the stretch which brings the water off the mountains and into Lyon, it divides viticulturally at the River Drôme. North of this line, wines are the products of small plots of vines perched up high on breathtaking slopes. The size of these estates gives the northern Rhône an almost Burgundian structure, and the story of the northern Rhône can be told for the most part with reference to a small band of individual growers. To the south of the Drôme, domaines have the space to spread themselves out to the east and west. The land is much flatter and the style of wine-making warm and Mediterranean. Turn the corner into Provence and you'll even find a touch of Latin sloppiness.

Until recently, the only bond which linked the two halves of the Valley were the *négociants*. A few of these were based in the south, but most were to be found in the twin town of Tain-Tournon, tucked under the great rock of Hermitage. A generation ago these *négociants* exercised enormous power up and down the valley, where growers had to choose between selling to them or to the co-operative. Few people made wine themselves. In the past decade, however, more and more of the younger generation have decided to break loose from this system; and these growers are currently the centre of attention in the northern Rhône.

It would be wrong to write the *négociants* off. They still make some of the best wine in the Rhône Valley. Guigal's *crus*, La Mouline, La Turque and La Landonne, are the most sought-after wines of the region. In Hermitage, the houses of Jaboulet and Chapoutier have tended to juggle for the place at the top of the league, while Gérard Chave sits in splendid isolation as the one private individual with sufficient land to ensure supplies of a world-class wine. In the past few years, Chapoutier has tended to win the laurels, especially since the launch of the Le Pavillon 'brand' as the top of the Chapoutier range. Michel Chapoutier is rare in being a Grenache fanatic. His La Bernadine Châteauneuf-du-Pape was always a good bet, but he has now launched a new 100 per cent Grenache wine called Barbe Rac: his attempt to imitate or even surpass the (allegedly) 100 per cent Grenache wines of Château Rayas.

The northern Rhône – appellations

The most famous of the northern Rhône's red, Syrah-based appellations is **Hermitage**, which also produces a small amount of white from Roussanne and Marsanne. Hermitage is carved up among the big *négociants* with a small amount of unreliable wine being made by the second division of fruitcroppers-cum-growers. This is less true of the small red appellation of **Côte Rôtie**. Marcel Guigal, for example, has been frustrated in his attempts to expand his holdings in La Landonne, despite offering dizzy sums to his next-door neighbour. There is more talent about here than in Hermitage. Names which are consistently worth a punt in this most elegant of Syrah wines are the Barges (father Pierre and son Gilles, who make individual wines), Bernard Burgaud, Clusel-Roch, Gerin, Rostaing and Vidal Fleury's Côte Blonde La Chatillonne (also owned by Guigal).

If Guigal is having problems securing a larger slice of the Côte Rôtie cake, he has been more successful in the leading northern Rhône white AOC of **Condrieu** (100 per cent Viognier), where his purchases in recent years have made him the major landowner. Condrieu has expanded from a mere 30 ha in recent years to something nearer 100 ha. There must, therefore, be a lot of new vines around which have yet to realise their potential. Growers have also taken to flavouring their wines with new oak (*caveat emptor*).

Old men retire. Some even die. The valetudinarians have been disappearing in **Cornas**, the other top-quality Syrah AOC of the northern Rhône, and changing the nature of the place. Guy de Barjac makes very little wine these days; Noël Verset has hung up his *sécateurs*. New men have come in to look after the vines. One of the best is Sylvain Bernard, whose main interests are in **St-Joseph** and the small white sparkling and still wine AOC **St-Péray**. Thierry Allemand has been hailed as the great white hope, but he makes atypically light wines for Cornas. With the vines he acquired from de Barjac, Jean-Luc Colombo has been making wines with greater concentration since 1990.

Jean-Luc Colombo doesn't just make Cornas. Together with Alberic Mazoyer he runs Rhône Vignobles, an organisation which offers oenological and marketing services to growers. Through Rhône Vignobles a number of talented young growers have emerged and, in particular, redeemed the reputation of the AOC **Crozes-Hermitage**. Crozes is now one of the most dynamic appellations in France, with superb wines being made by Alain Graillot, Etienne Pochon, Albert Belle and Laurent Combier. Over on the other side of the Rhône there has been an improvement in the overall quality of AOC **St-Joseph**, once one of the most hopeless wines in France. This is largely due to the replanting of the slopes high above the river. Names to look out for here are Courbis, Coursodon, Chave (who makes minuscule quantities of one of the best St-Josephs of all), Gripa, Grippat and Florentin.

The southern Rhône – appellations, vins de pays

Colombo is also active in the southern Rhône, consulting with a number of estates in **Châteauneuf-du-Pape** including Château Fortia. Châteauneuf's growers are, however, a notably independent, sometimes eccentric band, and are resisting trends towards excessive use of new oak. Most are agreed that Grenache (which despite increasing planting of Syrah and Mourvèdre still makes up 80 per cent of the average Châteauneuf blend) and new oak do not make a harmonious partnership. Carbonic maceration, introduced at Nalys in the 1950s, is also very much on the retreat:

the current fashions are for extremely long fermentation (*cuvaison*) and *pigeage* (a burgundian method of plunging down the cap of skins into the fermenting juice), leading to big, meaty, edible wines. Despite unkind vintages in 1991 and 1992 (1993 is better and 1994 will be excellent from the best producers) standards in Châteauneuf seem to be improving, and there are one or two rising stars such as Aimé and Christophe Sabon's Domaine de la Janasse. Domaine du Vieux Télégraphe has begun producing some excellent new Châteauneufs at its recently acquired Domaine de la Roquette. White Châteauneuf only accounts for around 8 per cent of the total wine made, but the best, such as Beaucastel's sublime Roussanne Vieilles Vignes (barrel-fermented) and the Avrils' quite different, unoaked but ageworthy Clos des Papes blanc are wonderful.

AOC **Gigondas** can certainly match Châteauneuf-du-Pape for warm, rich spicy reds, but much wine-making here is rough around the edges. There is also considerable potential in the best of the villages which make up AOC **Côtes-du-Rhône-Villages** – the islands of quality in the great sea which is AOC **Côtes-du-Rhône**. **Vacqueyras**, which has had its own AOC since 1990, and **Cairanne** are two names which usually deliver quality. Here, too, can be found the most fashionable of southern France's white *vins doux naturels*, the delicious Muscat de Beaumes de Venise.

AOCs **Lirac** and **Tavel** are perhaps best-known for fleshy rosé, but the former's violet-scented reds can match most Gigondas and there are even some attractive whites. AOCs **Coteaux du Tricastin** and **Côtes du Ventoux** offer lighter-style Grenache-based reds, often made using *macération carbonique*. **Côtes du Lubéron**, from Peter Mayle country, is definitely Provençal in character, loose and holiday-ish. **Clairette de Die**, a small appellation on the east side of the Rhône, produces sweetish sparklers based on Muscat and Clairette, rather in the Asti mode.

On the other, western, side, known as **Coteaux de l'Ardèche**, but not yet considered worthy of AOC, there have been successful plantings of such fashionable varieties as Cabernet Sauvignon and Chardonnay (controversially pioneered by Louis Latour of Beaune).

Rhône vintage guide

Since 1990, the weather has not been as kind to the Rhône as in the previous decade. Rain in September has been the pattern, as in Bordeaux, for the last four vintages. 1991 was actually a very good year in much of the northern Rhône, but is to be avoided in Châteauneuf-du-Pape. In 1992 there were floods in Vaison-la-

Romaine (over 30 people drowned), and the wines are best avoided, though the very best estates in Châteauneuf made attractive lighter wines. 1993 was substantially better in the south and 1994, though variable, has produced some excellent bottles.

Provence

Outside Bandol, there are few estates of exciting quality in Provence, which lives from tourism, and whose best-known wine is the usually dreadful rosé. In and around the tourist trap of Les Baux de Provence there are one or two serious red-wine producers, such as Les Terres Blanches and the Domaine de Trévallon, which can now use the new AOC **Les Baux de Provence**, one of the few in the south of France to sanction Cabernet Sauvignon. Sadly, one of the great pioneers here, the Château de Vignelaure, is not what it was. In the late 1980s, a succession of superb vintages in Bandol pushed growers to use even greater amounts of Mourvèdre in their wines. The results were a revelation: Bandol could be one of the best red wines of southern France. Probably the best estate today is the Château de Pibarnon.

Three other tiny AOCs, Bellet, Cassis and Palette, close to the Côte d'Azur, command high prices which are justified more by their locations than their quality, though the whites of Cassis can be good, firm and powerful.

Corsica

The legendarily beautiful but somewhat morose Mediterranean island has belied its backward reputation recently with some exciting and forward-looking vineyard and wine-making developments. Reds, from the native varieties Nielluccio and Sciacarello, as well as recently planted Cabernet Sauvignon and Syrah, are the best bet by far, with Grenache-based rosés usually much more appealing than the whites. Vin de Corse is the overall AOC, to which various names such as Calvi or Coteaux du Cap Corse can be added, and there are separate AOCs for Ajaccio and Patrimonio. Wines outside the AOC system go by the romantic name of vin de pays de l'Ile de Beauté. The well-known Chablis house of Laroche has been making varietals on the island.

Pick of the producers – Rhône, Provence and Corsica
Beaucastel, Château de Meticulously made Châteauneuf-du-Pape of power and depth, made from all 13 permitted grape varieties. The Perrin family also produces one of the best Côtes-du-Rhônes, Coudoulet de Beaucastel, from nearby vines.

Chave Gérard Chave is the uncrowned king of Hermitage. Wonderfully silky wines combining power and finesse.

Chapoutier Big Tain-Tournon *négociant*-house long considered to lag well behind Jaboulet, but recently revitalised under Michel Chapoutier. Hermitage La Sizéranne used to be non-vintage but is now fine, as is Châteauneuf-du-Pape La Bernadine.

Clape Auguste Clape almost singlehandedly put Cornas on the map as a high-quality Syrah appellation. The wines seem to have lost a little in intensity and excitement of late.

Clos de l'Arbalastrier Emile Florentin's tiny estate in AOC St-Joseph produces wonderfully traditional reds and a few uncompromising whites.

Clos des Papes Paul Avril and his son Vincent are responsible for the best-heeled, most elegant, traditional wines in Châteauneuf du-Pape.

Clusel-Roch, Domaine Estate to watch in Côte Rôtie; the owners, Gilbert Clusel and Brigitte Roch, are advised by Jean-Luc Colombo.

Font-de-Michelle, Domaine The Gonnet brothers are serious rugby players but make red Châteauneuf of considerable finesse, and fresh, pear-scented white.

Galantin, Domaine de A middle-sized estate in a touristy location in Bandol, which succeeds in making top-quality Mourvèdre wines. A name to watch.

Gerin, Jean-Michel Another very fine Côte Rôtie estate which has come to the fore. The best wines are labelled Les Grandes Places.

Graillot, Alain A former marketing man who has become the salvation of the moribund AOC of Crozes Hermitage. Excellent simple Crozes and a new wonder-weapon called La Guiraude.

Grand Tinel, Domaine du One of the unsung heroes of Châteauneuf. Elie Jeune's wine-making is meticulous and his wines live long.

Guigal Hugely respected *négociant*-house in Ampuis, specialising in Côte Rôtie, both from own vineyards and bought-in fruit. Crus La Landonne, La Mouline and La Turque command dizzy prices; at the other end of the scale, generic Côtes-du-Rhône is usually a good buy. Guigal has recently bought the small, but good, *négociant*-house of Vidal-Fleury.

Jaboulet, Paul (Aîné) The Rhône's best-known and respected *négociant*. There is a wide range, but the stars are Hermitage La Chapelle, consistently one of the Rhône's greatest reds, and Crozes Hermitage Domaine de Thalabert, an excellent wine which is remarkable value. Côte Rôtie Les Jumelles and Châteauneuf-du-Pape Les Cèdres, both *négociant* wines, maintain a good standard.

Michel, Robert Owner of 10 per cent of Cornas. His top wines are bottled under the La Geynale label. The vines are anything up to 70 years old.

Pallières, Domaine les The best estate in Gigondas; the mostly Grenache vines are planted on the limestone slopes of the Dentelles de Montmirail.

Perret, André Coteaux de Chéry, Condrieu. Probably the best of the bunch in Condrieu, at present. Perret makes less interesting wines from the Clos Chanson as well as some St-Joseph.

Pibarnon, Château de Since Henri de Saint Victor started making a virtually pure Mourvèdre wine here in the late 1970s, Pibarnon has succeeded in surpassing even the wines of Lucien Peyraud's Domaine Tempier.

Rayas, Château Eccentric hermit Jacques Reynaud could write a book on Zen and the art of Grenache-making, if he had any desire to communicate. Rayas, second wine Pignan and the wonderful Côtes-du-Rhône Château de Fonsalette can be marvellously pure and vibrant, but consistency is not Reynaud's middle name.

Rostaing, René The Côte Rôtie's leading light after Guigal. Rostaing bottles a fine Côte Rôtie, a Côte Rôtie Côte Blonde, and a La Landonne single *cru*. He has recently acquired some of Marius Gentaz' vines.

Tempier, Domaine Very fine Bandol from the family estate which led the revival of the Mourvèdre-based Provençal red.

Trévallon, Domaine de Remarkable, elegant wine made from 60 per cent Cabernet Sauvignon and 40 per cent Syrah grown on the north side of the Alpilles; recreates the 'Hermitaged' clarets of the nineteenth century.

Vieux Télégraphe, Domaine du Sure-footed Châteauneuf-du-Pape of medium weight and considerable style, belonging to the Brunier family, who have recently acquired a new estate, Domaine de la Roquette.

LANGUEDOC-ROUSSILLON (FRANCE'S NEW WORLD)

These two southern regions, extending in a great sickle from Nîmes south-west to the Spanish border, used to be more or less complete no-hopers. They account for no less than a third of the French vineyard area and produce an almost unimaginable 2,200 million litres of wine – five times as much as Australia. Some of this great flood still goes for EU distillation, but a combination of severe market pressure caused by the decline of wine-drinking in France and a new spirit of pride and optimism have produced a remarkable renaissance of quality.

Languedoc, in particular, has become the most dynamic of all French wine regions. If a revolution is occurring in French wine, its epicentre is Montpellier. The proud Girondins of Bordeaux are being upstaged by the *sans-culottes* of the south. What is being challenged by the iconoclasts of the south is no less than the whole structure of *appellation d'origine contrôlée*, the quality system of which the French are so proud.

AOC hardly existed in Languedoc and Roussillon until the late 1970s. Even when appellations were created, they did not command much of a premium. More particularly, the southern appellations have insisted on the traditional southern mixture of grapes, including the unfashionable Carignan and Cinsault. The way was clear for an enterprising individual to decide that AOC was an irrelevance, and to set about planting fashionable grape varieties – not giving a fig if they ended up labelled as *vin de table* or *vin de pays*. That individual was Robert Skalli, president of Skalli-Fortant de France. A shrewd businessman, who had made a fortune from pasta, Skalli realised that Languedoc-Roussillon offered a potentially winning combination of reliable warm climate and relatively low land and labour costs.

Between 1980 and 1992, mainly because of Skalli's initiative, which was followed by other forward-looking groups such as Les Vignerons du Val d'Orbieu, nearly 35,000 hectares of vineyards were converted to noble grape varieties such as Syrah, Merlot,

Cabernet Sauvignon, Chardonnay, Muscat and Sauvignon Blanc. The result has been to create a mini-, or not so mini-, New World in France's own, previously uncherished, backyard. The shock-waves are being felt all over the wine world. If France has applied Australian strategies in its southern wineland, the Australians, in a kind of reverse colonisation, have set up shop themselves in Languedoc, led by Hardy with Domaine de la Baume, closely followed by Yalumba with La Porcii, and now Penfolds in partnership with Val d'Orbieu.

At the moment, it seems as if two quite different and perhaps contradictory wine systems are operating in Languedoc-Roussillon – the traditional French system of *appellation d'origine contrôlée* based on *terroir* and tradition, and the New World philosophy based on varietals. Can the two meet? The answer may be yes, if you consider such landmarks as Aimé Guibert's pioneering Mas de Daumas Gassac (though this has not yet been granted appellation status), the efforts being made in the best estates of Corbières and the development of *terroir*-based Chardonnay in the Limoux area. In other words, it may be possible to loosen the crippling restrictions on grape varieties imposed by the appellation system without losing sight of the importance of *terroir*. At the moment, everything is up for grabs, which is probably as it should be. More important, there is a new generation of wine-growers which believes, for the first time in decades, in the potential for quality in these ancient, beautiful wine regions. Fortunately, the last two years (1993 and 1994), despite September rains, have been kinder weather-wise than the uncharacteristically sodden 1991 and 1992. 1994 was one of the earliest vintages ever, and quality looks excellent, though quantity is down.

Red wines – grape varieties, vins de pays, appellations

Languedoc-Roussillon, as you would expect, is overwhelmingly red-wine country. Furthermore, despite the efforts of Robert Skalli et al, it is still dominated by Carignan (with nearly half the total area under vine), Grenache, Cinsault and Aramon – not the world's most exciting group of grape varieties. Cinsault and Aramon, in particular, have very few convincing defenders, but Carignan, when grown in the right areas (hillsides, poor soils) and when the vines are mature, can give wine of fruit-cakey richness. Grenache, as the world knows from Châteauneuf-du-Pape, can also in the right conditions be a quality grape. However, the black varieties used for the new *vins de cépages* (varietal wines) are Syrah, Merlot and Cabernet Sauvignon. These are famous and fashionable names, and can give good results in Languedoc, though many of the 100 per cent varietals can seem one-dimensional. The south of France has always been an area where blends of grape varieties have been used; perhaps an Australian-style Cabernet-Syrah blend would be more satisfactory at a basic level than either variety on its own.

Absurdly, French regulations currently prohibit the naming of two varieties on the label, even of *vins de pays*. Interestingly, Penfolds in its new partnership with Val d'Orbieu has opted for multi-varietal blends, not single varietals.

Vins de pays

Most of the new varietals from Languedoc are sold as vins de pays d'Oc. *Vin de pays*, though theoretically a lowly level only one step up from *vin de table*, has the great advantage of allowing freedom over grape varieties. This seems to have brought about the great success of this category, by far the most dynamic in French wine at present. Vin de pays d'Oc is the catch-all designation for all the *vins de pays* of Languedoc-Roussillon, and Provence. More localised categories also exist – though whether these are helpful or simply cause confusion is open to question.

Appellations

Placing AOCs, the summit of the French quality pyramid, after varietals and *vins de pays* might seem provocative. However, it merely reflects their relative unimportance in the Languedoc-Roussillon scheme of things. They account for around 10 per cent of total production, and, in many cases, command lower prices than varietals and *vins de pays*. However, the picture is more complicated than that and requires a closer look at the AOCs to separate the worthwhile from the redundant.

Collioure A small Roussillon AOC for concentrated reds.

Corbières An AOC with a split personality: the mountain wines, with substantial input from Syrah and Mourvèdre, grown on hillsides surrounded by *garrigue* scrub, can have marvellous warm aromas of wild herbs, but there is also a lot of very ordinary red from Carignan grown on flatter land.

Costières de Nîmes The newest of Languedoc's AOCs, this is in fact the old Costières du Gard. It represents some powerful but somewhat coarse reds, with Carignan dominant, but with increasing amounts of Grenache, and some Syrah.

Coteaux du Languedoc This is an AOC to watch. There is a lot of interesting experimentation going on in the 12 *crus* which make up this AOC. Reds, from a mixture of Carignan, Syrah and Grenache, range from light, carbonic-maceration styles to deep and powerful, with some amazing minty aromas. AOC Faugères tends to be quite big, though soft, while St-Chinian is lighter and spicily aromatic.

Côtes de Roussillon and Côtes de Roussillon Villages These are the two major red wine AOCs of Roussillon, the French part of the old Catalan kingdom which continues on the Spanish side of the Pyrenees. Here, Carignan reigns supreme, but produces better wines than the norm in Languedoc. They are usually good value, too. Of the villages, Caramany specialises in the technique of *macération carbonique*.

Fitou One of the best-known names in Languedoc, thanks to the efforts of the local co-op with their well-distributed Cuvée Mme Claude Parmentier. Mme Parmentier went through some indifferent periods, but most Fitou, made from 70 per cent Carignan, is of reasonable, warm, sturdy quality. Look out for oak-aged *cuvées* from Mont Tauch co-op.

Minervois An AOC in the hills north of Corbières, Minervois tends to produce lighter reds than its neighbours, with attractive peppery forward fruit.

White wines – grape varieties, vins de pays, appellations

Traditionally, the dry white wines of Languedoc-Roussillon have been scarcely more than an atoll in the ocean of red – not a very distinguished atoll at that. The varietal revolution in Languedoc has had, relatively, an even greater impact on the whites than on the reds. *Vin de pays* varietal Chardonnay, Sauvignon, Muscat and even the rare Viognier, from Skalli-Fortant de France, Hardy's Chais Baumière, Hugh Ryman, Domaines Virginie and others have proved infinitely more appealing than the traditional southern French white varieties such as Macabeo, Grenache Blanc sanctioned by the AOCs Corbières Blanc, Coteaux du Languedoc and others, though some recent efforts with Bourbolenc and Picpoul (de Pinet) have been successful. A combination of fashionable varieties and high-quality *terroir* is in evidence in Limoux, whose Chardonnays are now allowed AOC status.

Sparkling wines

Languedoc-Roussillon has one well-known sparkling wine in the form of Blanquette de Limoux. This *méthode-traditionelle* wine from a high cool area in the upper Aude valley can be one of the best of France's non-champagne sparklers. Increasing amounts of Chardonnay are being used for both sparkling and still wines.

Vins doux naturels

Sweet fortified wines, both red and white, are a speciality of Languedoc-Roussillon, with a long history. The whites are made from Muscat (both the high-quality Muscat à Petits Grains, and, more common, Muscat d'Alexandrie). Muscat de Frontignan, Muscat de Lunel, Muscat de Mireval, Muscat de Rivesaltes and the more interesting, less sickly, Muscat de St-Jean-de-Minervois are all quite similar to the fashionable Muscat de Beaumes de Venise from the southern Rhône. More intriguing and complex are the fortified red Grenache wines from Banyuls, Maury and Rivesaltes in Roussillon. Some are aged in the open air in demi-johns called *bonbonnes* and acquire fascinating, oxidised, nutty aromas and flavours.

Pick of the producers
Abbaye de Valmagne Very good Coteaux du Languedoc reds from this property based on a former Cistercian abbey.

Cazes Frères Leading family *négociant* in Roussillon, producing reliable red Côtes du Roussillon and fine *vins doux naturels*.

Chais Baumière/Philippe de Baudin The South Australian company Hardy's acquired the 68-hectare Domaine La Baume in 1989. It produces a range of New World-style varietals, among the best in the region, including Chardonnay, Sauvignon, Merlot and Cabernet Sauvignon, from its own and bought-in grapes.

Fortant de France/Skalli The pioneering *négociant* business specialising in varietals. Chardonnay comes in unoaked and more complex oaked styles, also Cabernet Sauvignon and Syrah.

Herrick, James Sleek well-balanced Chardonnay produced by English winemaker Herrick from vineyards near Narbonne.

Château de Jau Producer of Côtes du Roussillon Villages with higher pretensions than most.

Mas de Daumas Gassac Remarkable estate and wine created in special *terroir* near Aniane by ex-leather manufacturer Aimé Guibert. Red, mainly Cabernet Sauvignon, is massively concentrated and can develop marvellous *garrigue* aromas with time. White is influenced by Viognier.

Mas Julien Olivier Julien is probably the Languedoc's most talented young vigneron, producing wonderful concentrated reds from old, old Carignan, Grenache and other vines.

Ryman, Hugh The peripatetic English winemaker and his growing team are much in evidence producing ripe, peachy-oaky Chardonnays from various domaines, including some in Limoux.

Tuilerie, Château de la Impressively well-run estate making good sturdy Costières de Nîmes.

Val d'Orbieu, les Vignerons du Huge conglomerate of Languedoc growers and co-operatives, now making interesting if rather expensive multi-varietal Laperouse blends in conjunction with Penfolds.

JURA, SAVOIE, BUGEY

The wines of France's eastern mountain ranges, like some rare Alpine chamois, have retreated into obscurity. The Jura was once widely famed for its vineyards, which covered nearly 20,000 hectares before phylloxera struck in the 1880s. Now there are fewer than 2,000 hectares of vines, and the wines are, in truth, no more than curiosities. Savoie's light but sometimes exhilarating wines, less eccentric, may be more familiar, at least to those who frequent the ski-slopes of the French Alps.

Jura appellations, grape varieties and wine styles

The vineyards of the Jura, which cover an 80km stretch of foothills between St-Amour and Salins, are divided into four different appellations: Arbois, Côtes du Jura, L'Etoile and Château-Chalon. The first covers light reds made from the local Poulsard and Trousseau as well as Pinot Noir. Côtes du Jura covers the entire region, and can be red or white. L'Etoile is a small appellation for whites made from Chardonnay and the local Savagnin. Château-Chalon is the appellation which specialises in *vin jaune*, a unique wine created by a combination of a curious local variety, Savagnin, and a layer of yeast similar to the flor of Jerez. The result is much more oxidised, nutty and strange than fino sherry, and, we have to say, less appealing. Appropriately, *vin jaune* comes in bottles holding an entirely idiosyncratic quantity, 62 cl.

Savoie and Bugey – appellations, grape varieties

The cover-all appellation for France's beautiful Alpine region is Vin de Savoie, which is mostly white, made from the local grapes Jacquère and Altesse (known locally as Roussette), and Chardonnay, with some light red Pinot Noir and Gamay and the more serious deep-purple Mondeuse. Within this appellation, it is worth looking out for the *crus* of Apremont and Abymes, which grow delicate, crisp white wine from Jacquère. Roussette is rounded and fuller, and there is good sparkling wine made under the appellation Seyssel. Bugey is a tiny VDQS known for crisp Chardonnay and lively sparkling wine, hardly ever seen in the UK.

SOUTH-WESTERN FRANCE

The vineyards of France's soft, hidden south-west suffered until very recently from their relative inaccessibility. The great port of Bordeaux ruled the roost and called the shots, and actually prevented the up-country wine of Cahors from being exported until all the Bordeaux had left the docks. Phylloxera compounded the problems of the put-upon small *viticulteurs* and *vignerons* of these rural areas, and many vineyards disappeared. The survival of so many is one of the greatest tributes to the extraordinary resilience of what, without wishing to cause offence, we can only call the French peasant tradition.

In the past couple of decades, there has been a remarkable revival, especially in Gascony, where the innovative Plaimont co-operative and certain growers hit on the inspired idea of turning grapes no longer needed for Armagnac distillation into crisp dry white wine. This has now become the point of reference for accessible yet characterful dry whites in the bargain category – everyone's favourite house white and arguably better value than anything from Australia. Bergerac, Côtes de Duras and Gaillac are three other appellations revitalised, especially in their white form, by new technology and an outward-looking approach.

Once in the bottle a cork can last for decades but eventually it becomes brittle and crumbly with age.

White and rosé wines – appellations, vins de pays, grape varieties

Bergerac and Côtes de Duras

These country areas form part of the Bordeaux hinterland, both geographically and stylistically. Whites are made from Sauvignon, Sémillon and Muscadelle, with the first very much on the increase; the best have a refreshing grassiness and lightness of touch often missing from their Bordeaux counterparts.

Gaillac

Gaillac is much further from the sea (not far from Toulouse), a remote area which has mainly persevered with local grape varieties. With whites, this means, among others, Mauzac, a grape which shows appley fruit and quite powerful vinosity. Gaillac comes in dry, sweet (*moelleux*) and slightly sparkling (*perlé*) versions.

Gascogne

The best-known of all the names for south-western whites, Gascogne is not an AOC but a modest *vin de pays* (des Côtes de Gascogne). The supposedly boring Ugni Blanc and Colombard grapes have been brilliantly used by the Plaimont co-op and growers such as Grassa to make crisp, almost sharp white with just a touch of residual sugar to soften the acidity. The VDQS Côtes de St Mont, making similar wines, has been almost completely upstaged.

Jurançon

Jurançon, in the Pyrenean foothills, is the aristocrat among south-western whites. The intense, apricot-scented sweet white (*moelleux*), made from Petit Manseng grapes left to turn into raisins on the vines, is certainly one of the greatest in France, which is to say the world. Leading producers are also experimenting with barrel-fermentation and ageing for the dry white Jurançon, made mainly from Gros Manseng.

Pacherenc du Vic-Bilh

The obscure white AOC of the Lot valley is not a great wine, but it is a wonderful name.

Pick of the producers

Cauhapé, Domaine de The leading name in Jurançon, with fabulously rich, oaky, concentrated and expensive sweet Quintessence.

Grassa, Domaine Very important family estate in Côtes de Gascogne, including Domaine de Planterieu and Château du Tariquet, with successful oak-aged version.

Jaubertie, Domaine de la Bergerac estate recently bought from father Henry by son Hugh Ryman and Esmé Johnstone with high-class 100 per cent Sauvignon.

Labastide de Lévis, Co-operative By far the largest producer of Gaillac, with much-improved white.

Larroze, Château Leading estate producer of crisp Gaillac.

Plaimont Co-operative The co-op which more or less created vin de pays des Côtes de Gascogne. Also producing AOC Côtes de St-Mont.

Red wines – appellations, grape varieties

Bergerac

Under the heading of Bergerac we include its top-quality enclave of Pécharmant, Côtes de Buzet, Côtes de Duras and Côtes du Marmandais, all AOCs of the Bordeaux hinterland producing reds of generally similar, Bordeaux-like style from Merlot, Cabernet Franc, Cabernet Sauvignon and Malbec. The best Pécharmant is more serious and structured, not unlike good St-Emilion, while Côtes de Buzet is lighter but often very attractive. Côtes de Duras and Côtes de Marmandais, where non-Bordeaux varieties Fer and Abouriou are used in the blend, are pleasant but light reds.

Cahors

The famous 'black wine' of the Lot valley, made from the Malbec grape, known locally as Auxerrois, is historically important, but now mostly coarse and lacking in breed. Some fine examples from Château de Cayrou, Clos Triguedena and others.

Côtes du Frontonnais

This AOC, not far from Toulouse, features the deep-purple, soft-flavoured Négrette grape. The result is something like a French Dolcetto.

Gaillac

Gaillac produces considerably less red, mainly from the local Duras grape, than white, though some can be quite elegant.

Irouléguy
This appropriately wild-sounding AOC of the French Basque country makes pretty heavy, rough red from the Tannat grape.

Madiran
The best red of Gascony is made from roughly 50 per cent Tannat, with the rest mainly Cabernets – a full, ripe wine good for a winter evening but tending to lack class and breed.

Pick of the producers
Bellevue-la-Forêt, Château The best-known producer of soft, juicy red Côtes du Frontonnais.

Court-les-Mûts, Château Well-made red Bergerac and excellent rosé.

Cros, Domaine/Château Larroze Elegant red Gaillac from this quality-conscious domaine.

Jaubertie, Domaine de la Reds perhaps a little less exciting than whites from the Ryman domaine.

Montus, Château Leading estate in Madiran, using some new oak.

Peyros, Château Much-improved producer of Madiran, with vivid fruit and new oak.

Tiregand, Château du Elegant Pécharmant of real, cedary class.

GERMANY

As the world commemorates the end of the Second World War and
the defeat of Hitler, perhaps we should remember one of the less
obvious casualties of those events. Post-war Germans have turned
their backs on their nation's finest wines: modern Berliners,
Hamburgers, Düsseldorfers seem happy to drink any wine
(Chianti, Bordeaux, Rioja) so long as it is not Rhine or Mosel
Riesling. Meanwhile, the reputation of Germany's noblest wines on
the export markets has been destroyed by Liebfraumilch.

The main explanation for this neglect lies in the legally induced
contradictions of the world's most divided wine industry. Most
major wine countries see their wine production as a kind of
pyramid, with a broad base of ordinary wine supporting higher
levels of quality. The French pyramid is the most admired one. The
image of French wine is projected, like the beam from a lighthouse,
from near the sharp point at the top of the shapely structure, a
beam which can be translated as *cru classé* claret, *premier cru*
burgundy, champagne. Château Lafite is not tarnished, but
supported by the lowly *vin de table* from the Midi.

In Germany, this structure has been turned on its head. Instead
of supporting the higher echelons of quality, everyday German
wine bears down on them, crushes them, reduces them to near-
invisibility. Perhaps a better image is that of a flood. Liebfraumilch
has flooded the market for German wine in Britain, submerging the
high peaks of the Mosel, the Rheingau, the Rheinpfalz, until they
are little more than memories, mythical landmarks for which the
map has been lost. And the law has actively assisted this process,
especially the 1971 German Wine Law, one of the most disastrous
pieces of wine legislation ever framed. According to this law, over
95 per cent of German wine production qualifies as quality wine.
Now this, in a part of the world near or beyond the margin of
possible wine-making (the same latitude as Mongolia or northern
Newfoundland), stretches credulity. But there is worse to come.
The single most damaging provision of the 1971 law was the
invention of the *Grosslage*, an utterly discreditable entity which
takes the name of a single, reasonably high-quality vineyard and

stretches it to include a much wider area which has no historic or qualitative link with it.

The most notorious example is Niersteiner Gutes Domtal. This was originally the name of a small, 34-hectare vineyard in Nierstein; now the name can be used for the produce of 1300 hectares of vineyards in 15 villages. It is almost as bad as allowing any producer of simple Médoc to use the name Lafite or Latour. No more effective way of destroying the good name of famous wine villages could have been devised.

The good news, or the distant gleam of good news, is that consultations have been going on since 1992 about possible changes to the 1971 wine law. However, the one proposal which seems sure to go ahead, for a new category of *Ursprungswein* or QbU, may well only add to the current confusion. QbU is designed as a way of safeguarding the traditional character of a regional style. It will not replace existing categories of QbA (wasn't that meant to safeguard regional character?) and QmP, and according to the innovative producer Rainer Lingenfelder is 'simply another unnecessary storey built on a shaky edifice'. Proposals to abolish *Grosslage* seem to have been shelved. Not for nothing did Hugh Johnson once suggest that there should be a faculty of German wine philosophy at one of Germany's universities.

Democratically minded readers may feel this introduction to German wine is elitist. Liebfraumilch has, after all, introduced thousands of drinkers to the joys of wine, and is in itself the most innocuous of substances. Liebfraumilch is, in some ways, a remarkable phenomenon, one of the most noteworthy achievements of post-war German technology and industry. It has been something of a technological miracle – an example of *Vorsprung durch Technik* – to produce millions of hectolitres of acceptable, if sweetish, wine, from flat vineyards in the Rheinhessen and Rheinpfalz, where grapes struggle to ripen. Two techniques, in particular, have made this possible: first, the breeding of new strains of *Vitis vinifera* designed to ripen early and produce large yields, and, secondly, the ability to stop the fermentation while retaining considerable amounts of residual sugar, without using excessive sulphur.

Liebfraumilch has had its place in the post-war wine market. Whether it will retain that place is more open to question. Savage price-cutting battles have driven many producers to the wall. More fundamentally, with cheap dry wine made from French varieties, and ripe grapes, now pouring in from all over the globe, the future of a product which depends on residual sugar to make it palatable must look rather bleak. Rapidly falling market share seems to confirm this diagnosis.

The tragedy would be if Liebfraumilch not only sank without trace, but also dragged fine German wine down with it. Fortunately, there is a whole, bright new generation of German wine-growers and winemakers (in Germany, as in Burgundy, these two activities are usually combined) which is absolutely determined that shall not happen.

Gloom, in fact, is by no means the only expression on the face of German wine. Two of Germany's eleven – or now, with the former east German regions of Sachsen and Saale-Unstrut, thirteen – wine regions, in particular, have been fired with an exciting, quality-minded spirit. These are the Mosel-Saar-Ruwer, where the flame of quality, guarded by estates such as J.J. Prüm and Maximin Grünhaus, never died, and the Rheinpfalz, once thought of as a distinctly poor relation of the lordly Rheingau, but now, with estates such as Lingenfelder and Müller-Catoir, leading the production of drier wines.

Just when such dynamic producers needed a little extra encouragement, nature came to their aid and delivered an almost unprecedented string of fine vintages. Much has been said about Bordeaux's great run in the 1980s, but Germany's run since 1988 has been possibly even more remarkable – and, what is more, the royal flush has continued into the 1990s.

Altogether, there is every reason to shake off largely ignorant prejudice and give fine German wines a chance. They are wonderfully appetising, remarkably versatile with food, usually, but not always, lighter in alcohol than their French or Australian rivals, and above all they deliver a completely different range of sensory pleasures.

The German quality system

Before embarking on a discussion of styles and varieties, it is necessary to explain the complicated, confusing German quality system. The first two categories, *Deutscher Tafelwein* and *Deutscher Landwein*, are more or less irrelevant since they account for only 5 per cent of German wine production, though some new heavily oaked, fashionable *barrique* wines fall into the *Tafelwein* category. Ninety-five per cent of German wine falls into the category of *Qualitätswein*, or quality wine. This in turn is divided into *Qualitätswein bestimmter Anbaugebiete* (QbA), meaning quality wine from specific regions, and *Qualitätswein mit Prädikat* (QmP), or quality wine with a specific attribute. An important difference between QbA and QmP wines is that QbA wines can be chaptalised (see glossary) while QmP wines cannot.

As if all this were far too simple, QmP is further divided into sub-categories, based on the ripeness of the grapes at harvest, as follows:

Kabinett is the lowest grade of QmP, usually referring to light, delicate, fresh wines, very low in alcohol.

Spätlese, the second grade, means literally late-gathered. These wines can be either dry, balanced or quite sweet, but they will have been made from ripe grapes.

Auslese, meaning selected, brings us into the realm of sweeter, usually botrytised, wines, though these can range from delicate to rich.

Beerenauslese wines will have been made entirely from botrytis-affected bunches, and will usually be intensely rich, but not cloying.

Trockenbeerenauslese wines are great rarities, made in theory from individually picked botrytised berries. They are even richer than Beerenauslesen and need to be kept for many years. A recent trend is to make both TBA and BA wines more alcoholic and less sweet than formerly.

Eiswein is the category for wines made from frozen berries, left on the vine until the first heavy frost of the year, sometimes as late as the January after the normal harvest. Concentration by freezing leads to a different structure from concentration by botrytis, with sharper acidity, and a longer lifespan.

Wine styles and varieties

Riesling: dry, balanced, sweet

Germany's great grape, indisputably, is the white Riesling. Riesling is a late-ripening grape, which, partly by accident, partly by design, can be vinified in a wide variety of styles. Up until the 1970s, the 'traditional' style of German Riesling, below Auslese level (see above), was balanced between sugar and acidity. The feeling was that, without some sweetness, the tartness of Riesling's acidity made the wine unpalatable, but the intention was not usually to make a sweet wine, or even a 'medium' example (and what is 'medium' but a euphemism for sweet?).

This view of tradition was challenged in the 1970s by a new wave of producers who saw that the success of French white wine was based on dryness, and felt, perhaps naively, that what France could do, Germany might emulate. They also argued that German Riesling wines had, until the Second World War, been mainly dry. The early Trocken (German for dry) Rieslings were generally more suitable as industrial cleaning fluids than beverages. They were thin, bone-dry and sharp as sour lemons.

In the 1980s, a less extreme doctrine of dryness was promulgated by the Charta group in the Rheingau, whose Rieslings fell into the category called rather awkwardly Halb-trocken (half-dry). In the same decade, however, it was not the aristocratic estates of the Rheingau but the more modest ones of the Rheinpfalz which proved that balanced, drinkable dry Rieslings could be made in Germany.

Riesling is also a grape on which the noble rot, botrytis, can work to marvellous, transforming effect. German Rieslings of the Auslese level upwards (sometimes the Spätleses, too) are usually to some extent botrytis-affected. Once again, there are wide variations in style between a delicate Mosel Auslese, suitable as an aperitif, and a super-rich Rheingau Beerenauslese or Trockenbeerenauslese, a concentrated nectar to be sipped at the end of a meal in heaven.

Other white varieties

Müller-Thurgau, a crossing between the Riesling and Silvaner grapes, is actually the most planted grape in the German vineyards. Great swathes of the flatter vineyards of Rheinhessen, Rheinpfalz and Baden are planted with this early-ripening grape, which gives flowery, scented, easy, unmemorable wine.

Silvaner is an ancient, traditional and rather underrated variety, seen at its best in Franconia (Franken), where it gives dry, earthy and quite intense wines which go very well with food.

Ruländer/Grauburgunder, the French Pinot Gris, is capable of making spicy, rich dessert wines and powerful dry whites, especially in Baden.

Weissburgunder is French Pinot Blanc, quite widely planted in Baden, where it can produce big, alcoholic dry wines.

Scheurebe is by far the best of the *Neuzüchtunge* or man-made grape varieties; it is a crossing of Riesling and Silvaner, bred as long ago as 1916 and accounting for around 4,000 of Germany's 99,000 hectares. Scheurebe first came to fame for its magnficent dessert wines, but it can also make shapely dry wines, especially in the Rheinpfalz, when the grapes are ripe.

Gewürztraminer, when grown in the Rheinpfalz or Baden, is intriguingly lighter and more flowery than in Alsace.

Chardonnay, would you believe it, is beginning to be planted on an illegal or experimental basis. Who needs it?

Red wines
Germany is hardly known as a red-wine producer, and, indeed, less than 10 per cent of German production is red. Most of this finds a ready market within Germany, and little stands up to the searching light of international competition. However, one or two really interesting Spätburgunder or Pinot Noir wines are emerging from the Rheinpfalz and Baden; Dornfelder can be Germany's answer to Gamay or Dolcetto; and Württemberg's spicy Lemberger is worth a try.

Sparkling wine – Sekt
Germany produces a good deal of fresh, grapey sparkling wine which we in Britain have obstinately failed to take to our bosoms. The best wines, made from Riesling or Weissburgunder, can be of high quality.

The regions

Mosel-Saar-Ruwer
This north-westerly region of spectacularly vine-clad valleys deservedly takes pride of place for quality, and because it produces the most distinctive, super-fine, apple-scented Rieslings of all. Fortunately, the tide of Müller-Thurgau seems to be on the ebb, and Riesling is once again recognised as the peerless grape. Most of the best producers realise that totally dry Mosel Riesling is almost impossible to bring off, and discreetly balance their wines by stopping fermentation before all the sugar is converted.

Rheingau
Germany's most aristocratic and Riesling-dominated region has somehow failed to make a concerted push for even higher quality in the 1980s and 1990s. However, the Charta group of estates, including Graf Matuschka's Schloss Vollrads, has made some headway – especially in Japan – promoting its medium-dry wines designed to partner food.

Nahe
An often forgotten, idyllically rural valley region between the Mosel-Saar-Ruwer and the Rheingau, the Nahe can produce some of the most wonderfully racy, pure, minerally Rieslings of all.

Rheinhessen

This large region on the left bank of the Rhine epitomises the split personality of the German wine industry. On the one hand, there are thousands of hectares of flat vineyards formerly planted with potatoes and now used for Liebfraumilch; on the other, facing the Rhine, there is a strip of top-quality, sloping vineyards where spicy, soft, intensely honeyed Rieslings are made.

Rheinpfalz

This large and generally unpretentious region has perhaps become Germany's most dynamic. Quality has come from a group of small, hard-working estates with no laurels to rest on. Names such as Lingenfelder and Müller-Catoir, unknown 15 years ago, are now ones to conjure with. The big so-called 'Three B' estates of Buhl, Bassermann-Jordan and Bürklin-Wolf were always known for quality, but must now struggle to keep up with the youngsters.

Baden-Württemberg

Most of the wine from these southerly regions is consumed within Germany, but the large co-operatives of Baden have begun to export increasing amounts of their soft, fruity, but dry, whites, and occasional good Spätburgunder (Pinot Noir). Most of Württemberg's red and white wines are drunk around Stuttgart.

The rest

The Ahr, Mittelrhein and Hessische Bergstrasse are very small regions which export little, though the Ahr's thin reds are sometimes seen. Saale-Unstrut and Sachsen are two small wine-producing regions within the former East Germany. So far, a talking-point, little more.

Pick of the producers

Bassermann-Jordan On current form, the best of the 'Three B' estates of the Pfalz, making beautifully balanced, stylish Rieslings, never too sweet, never too dry.

Becker, J. B. Excellent Rheingau estate making full-flavoured, concentrated Riesling and fine Spätburgunder (Pinot Noir).

Buhl, von The least consistent of the 'Three Bs', because of troubled ownership, but owning superb vineyards in Forst and Deidesheim.

Bürklin-Wolf Largest of the Pfalz 'Bs', Bürklin-Wolf maintains a very consistent standard with its elegant, Rheingau-like Rieslings. Balance is sometimes on the sweet side.

Charta Estate Association Group of leading Rheingau estates, including G. Breuer, Knyphausen, Schloss Vollrads, Wegeler-Deinhard, which has promoted a semi-dry (Halb-trocken) style of Riesling designed to partner food.

Deinhard The famous shipping firm based in Koblenz has three estates, one in the Mosel, the second in the Rheingau and the third in the Rheinpfalz. Quality is usually reliable.

Friedrich-Wilhelm-Gymnasium Historic Trier-based Mosel-Saar-Ruwer estate consisting of vineyards bequeathed to Karl Marx's old school. Beautifully made, traditional-style wines, always good value.

Haag Wilhelm Haag is one of the Mosel's greatest winemakers. Superb, concentrated, long-lived wines from Brauneberger Juffer-Sonnenuhr.

Heyl zu Herrnstein Excellent Rheinhessen estate based in Nierstein, pioneering organic methods of viticulture and producing superbly elegant wines, dry and traditional.

Juliusspital Famous Würzburg estate belonging to a hospital. Full, earthy, dry Silvaner wines.

Karthäuserhof Famous estate in tiny Ruwer valley, almost sunk after fraud involving illegal addition of sugar, now restored to pride and excellence by Christof Tyrrell.

Kesseler Leading Rheingau producer of fine, rather oaky Spätburgunder (Pinot Noir).

Kesselstatt, Reichsgraf von Large Mosel-Saar-Ruwer estate now owned by Reh family and run by expert taster Anne-Gret Reh. Look out for monopole Josefshöfer wines.

Künstler New Rheingau star, making finely structured Riesling.

Lingenfelder Dynamic Rheinpfalz estate run by master-winemaker and innovator Rainer Lingenfelder. Especially good dry Scheurebe and Riesling, fine *barrique*-aged Spätburgunder and controversial new Silvaner.

Loosen, Weingut, Dr Family estate at Bernkastel on the Mosel, revitalised by Ernst Loosen. Substantial wines from low yields, and superb Ausleses from Erdener Prälat monopole.

Müller-Catoir Fine estate in southern Rheinpfalz, making tremendously powerful and characterful dry Riesling, Scheurebe and Weissburgunder wines.

Müller-Scharzhof, Egon Famous estate on the Saar, producing traditional-style wines of great purity and longevity, especially Auslese and above.

Pfeffingen, Weingut High-quality Rheinpfalz estate at Ungstein, making remarkably pure Riesling and Scheurebe wines.

Prüm, J. J. Greatest of the estates belonging to the Prüm family in the Mosel-Saar-Ruwer, run by perfectionist Dr Manfred Prüm. Wonderfully pure, flavourful, racy, long-lived wines from Wehlener Sonnenuhr vineyard.

Richter, Max Ferd. Some of the best dry Mosel Riesling made by quality-enthusiast Dr Dirk Richter.

Saarstein, Schloss Fine Saar estate, making impressive, concentrated wines.

Schönborn, Schloss Large, aristocratic Rheingau estate. Wines variable, but often magnificent.

Schubert, von Splendid former monastic estate of Maximin Grünhaus on hill above the Ruwer. Peerlessly fragrant and delicate Rieslings sold at high prices.

Staatliche Weinbaudomäne, Niederhausen-Schlossböckelheim Very long name for one of Germany's greatest, state-owned, estates, at Niederhausen on the idyllic Nahe. Wonderful racy, minerally Rieslings, not too dry in style.

Thanisch, Dr (VDP) Confusingly, there are two Dr Thanisch estates in Bernkastel, but this is the better, with substantial holdings of famous Bernkasteler Doktor. Look out for the VDP sign.

Wirsching, Hans Excellent estate in Steigerwald region of Franconia (Franken), making fresh but powerful Silvaner and Riesling.

Vintage guide

1994 A very wet September after a hot summer spoiled the quality of early-ripening grapes such as Müller-Thurgau, but a golden autumn encouraged botrytis and some of the greatest Beerenauslesen and Trockenbeerenauslesen seen since 1976.

1993 Much better than in most of Europe, a fine vintage with high proportion of Spätlese and Auslese.

1992 Variable, but very good in Middle Mosel, producing elegant, racy Spätleses.

1991 Small vintage with some concentrated Kabinett wines in Mosel-Saar-Ruwer.

1990 Superb vintage all over Germany, combining ripeness with racy acidity. The top Ausleses need keeping for several years.

1989 Very warm and fine vintage. Great Saar wines. Some others lack acidity.

1988 Good, typical vintage, not as hot as the two following ones, but producing wines of great breed in the Mosel-Saar-Ruwer.

Previous fine vintages: 1985, 1983, 1979, 1976, 1975, 1971.

ITALY

Nineteen-ninety-four and 1995 were supposed to be great years of change in Italy. In 1994 a whole generation of politicians was discredited; the party which had ruled the country for nearly 50 years fell apart, rotten with corruption. The improbable alliance between northern separatists and southern neo-Fascists, led by the media tycoon, Silvio Berlusconi swept to power in the March 1994 elections from a standing start in less than three months only to unravel almost as quickly. The changes promised by Signor Berlusconi did not materialise. As the Mafia retook control of Palermo it was the same old story but with a different label.

A major change in Italian wine was expected in 1994 and 1995. The new Goria wine law, passed in January 1992, establishing a framework for an improved system of wine regulation, was supposed to begin to make itself felt by 1994. Has anyone noticed the difference?

For years, perhaps the greatest problem with Italian wine has been that so little of the huge harvest comes under any form of regulation. The DOC (*denominazione di origine controllata*) system came into being in 1963, with the higher-quality level of DOCG added in 1983, but 30 years on it still accounts for only about 10 or 12 per cent of Italian wine. The Goria law establishes the new category of IGT (*indicazione geografiche tipici*), supposedly the equivalent of the very successful French *vins de pays*. It is hoped that around 10 per cent of the Italian harvest will come into this category.

IGT could still provide a valuable middle ground between the DOCs and the oceans of *vino da tavola*. Also, the Goria law's stated objective of reducing yields and tightening up quality in DOCG, DOC and IGT could pay dividends. All will depend on the spirit in which the law is interpreted by the various regions and appellations. So far the signs are mixed. The big co-operatives and merchants in the Veneto appear to have sabotaged any chance of decisively improving the names of Soave and Valpolicella. On the positive side, however, the new DOC for Sassicaia, a long overdue recognition of outstanding quality achieved by individualistic means, could herald the end of the absurd stand-off by which so many of Italy's best wines flew the ironical banner of *vino da tavola*.

Promised new regulations in Chianti allowing 100 per cent
Sangiovese and zero Trebbiano also sound hopeful.

Moving away from the law and politics, Italian wine continues to
present a kaleidoscopic, confusing picture of massive fecundity
shot through with shafts of brilliance, but leaving an impression of
frustration and disappointment. The country called the land of
wine – Oenotria – cannot fail to produce many wonderful things in
its 800-mile, vineyard-rich length. Any year of tastings reveals
several noteworthy discoveries. But there is also the feeling that too
many allowances are made for Italian wines. Would any other
country get away with the tough, stringy reds and characterless
whites which are still too frequent, and always excused by besotted
Italophiles with the line: 'Oh, but it tastes so marvellous with the
regional cuisine.' How many Chiantis, Brunellos or Barolos are
actually attractive enough to non-Italians to command world-class
status? Italians may love neutral white wines, but can they
persuade the rest of the world to love them equally?

It would be wrong to let exasperation dominate this impression
of Italian wine. Many talented winemakers are at work, as you
would expect in this most creative of countries. The South and the
islands of Sardinia and Sicily, however backward they may appear
to Umberto Bossi leader of the Northern League, have been
surprising us with excellent, characterful wines at fighting prices.
The real challenges now lie in the vineyard, not the winery.
Wineries can be built in months, but the conversion of vineyards
can take a generation. The next few years will see how this
challenge is being met, in Chianti, in Soave and Valpolicella, all
over the land of wine.

REGION BY REGION

One of the keys to Italy is, of course, that this is an intensely
regional country (not a country at all until the mid-nineteenth
century) and, if Signor Bossi has his way, perhaps not a single
country in the future. The wine cultures remain regionally diverse,
which adds charm, as well as causing confusion.

The north-west – Piedmont, Lombardy, Liguria, Aosta

The north-west is home to perhaps Italy's proudest wine culture,
that of Piedmont, but it is not a culture which has been very
amenable to outsiders. The fizzy sweet white Asti Spumante (now
known simply as Asti) and Moscato d'Asti are almost too easy to
appreciate, but Piedmont's noblest reds – Barolo and Barbaresco,

made from the reserved Nebbiolo grape grown in the bumpy Langhe hills near Alba – have deterred many attempts to understand them. Both can be among the world's greatest, most complex red wines, developing extraordinary scents of tar and truffle, but the thin line between excessive tannic austerity and oxidised blowsiness is difficult to find. Angelo Gaja's innovative methods and use of new oak have certainly gained both publicity and dizzy prices, first with his Barbaresco *crus* and now with his more recently acquired Barolos, but the greatest Barolos are made by less overtly flamboyant winemakers such as Aldo Conterno.

Carema, Gattinara, Ghemme and Spanna are four other Piedmontese Nebbiolo-based reds which may serve as an easier introduction to this difficult grape, but quality in these DOCs is sadly unreliable. Another option is Roero, from the north side of the Tanaro river close to Barolo and Barbaresco.

Barbera is the often-maltreated workhorse black grape of the north-west, but a few growers have shown that with the right treatment, including a touch of new oak, it can look like a thoroughbred, with vivid cranberry fruit and aromas of roasted beans. Barbera's name is linked to a number of Piedmontese DOC localities, of which Barbera d'Alba is the most distinguished. The same applies to Dolcetto, which is hardly a thoroughbred, but this deep-purple, sweet-scented grape can give much uncomplicated pleasure.

Piedmont's whites are very much an afterthought to the reds. Gavi is the most famous name, but it is not nearly as interesting a wine as that made from the revived Arneis grape – soft and musky – or from the pear-scented Favorita.

The populous region of Lombardy is much less proud of its wines than Piedmont, and, as a result, can deliver some pleasant, reasonably priced surprises. Franciacorta, which uses a Bordeaux mix of grape varieties (Cabernets Sauvignon and Franc, and Merlot), is the pick of the reds, while the whites of Lugana, on the southern shores of Lake Garda, can be much more interesting than the better-known Soave of Veneto. Lombardy is also a source of much sparkling wine from Pinot Bianco and Pinot Noir (Nero), and is sometimes elegant.

Liguria, along the Italian Riviera, and Valle d'Aosta, the remote Alpine province, are the two other regions of Italy's north-west, but neither produces much wine of interest to the export markets.

Piedmont vintage guide

1994 and 1993 look better than the rain-affected 1992 and variable 1991. 1990, 1988 and 1982 are classic vintages for Barolo and Barbaresco.

The north-east – Veneto, Friuli-Venezia-Giulia, Alto Adige-Trentino

The extensive vineyards of Italy's north-east provide the great majority of the country's best white wines, together with attractive light reds and one or two more serious examples. Friuli, on the Slovenian border, and Alto Adige, the German speaking Südtirol, are the leaders in quality for white wines. Friuli uses mainly French or central European grapes, with Pinot Grigio and Pinot Bianco much in evidence, as well as the less exciting Tocai Friulano. Friuli's whites are the most highly prized on the home Italian market, which makes them often seem over-priced. However, the best Pinot Grigio and Pinot Bianco from Collio can be fine indeed, and DOCs such as Isonzo and Grave del Friuli can offer good value. Friulian reds are mainly based on the Bordeaux trio of grapes (see earlier), and are made in a lightish style.

Alto Adige rings the changes between the Germanic Riesling, Müller-Thurgau and Gewürztraminer (which may in fact have originated in the Alto Adige village of Tramin), the French Chardonnay and Cabernets, and the local red Schiava and Lagrein (the latter two actually make up the bulk of the production). Trentino, the southern continuation of Alto Adige, is more Italian in character, with somewhat warmer and often very productive conditions, not always geared towards quality. Trentino's distinctive red DOC, Teroldego Rotaliano, somewhat on the lines of *cru* Beaujolais, is widely distributed in the UK. Another speciality is good-quality sparkling wine featuring Pinot Bianco and Chardonnay.

The Veneto produces far more DOC wine than any other Italian province. Sadly, the names of white Soave and red Valpolicella in particular became perhaps the most debased in the whole DOC structure in the 1970s, when planting extended to fertile flatlands, and industrialised wineries were content to churn out bulk. This strategy ran into difficulties in the late 1980s as Italian wine consumption declined and the market demanded better quality. It took a few small houses in Soave (Pieropan, Anselmi), Valpolicella (Allegrini, Masi, Quintarelli) and Bardolino (Guerrieri-Rizzardi, Fraterna Portalupi) to show the way forward with wines of character – almondy in the case of Soave, bitter-cherry in those of Bardolino and Valpolicella – and concentration. Some of the bigger Veronese companies, such as Bolla and Pasqua, have begun to go down the same road, and standards of Soave and Valpolicella have risen, though not enough. Meanwhile, a challenger to the white domination of Soave has arisen in the shape of DOC Bianco di Custoza – often a better bet.

The top-quality, serious reds of this area, Valpolicella Amarone (dry) and Recioto (sweet), pose different problems. Made from concentrated grapes dried in lofts, they reach awesome degrees of alcohol and are almost too rich in flavour for modern tastes.

The central and eastern parts of the Veneto have a rather different wine culture, with more emphasis on imported varieties, and on sparkling wines, especially the Prosecco of the hills around Treviso. Chardonnay, among the whites, and Merlot, among the reds, are making advances, often in unregulated, *vino da tavola*, form. One admirable outpost of quality exists in the form of the Maculan winery in Breganze, which makes admirable, concentrated reds and luscious sweet Torcolato.

North-east Italian vintage guide

The 1994, 1993, 1992 and 1991 all produced some good whites, with 1991 especially good in Friuli. Many 1993 reds, including Amarone and Recioto, are superb, possibly as good as the fabulous 1990.

North-central Italy – Emilia-Romagna

These twin regions, straddling a belt of north-central Italy from Piacenza to the Adriatic coast, have always been known for their gastronomy. For some reason, the wines have never matched the food in quality. Co-operatives dominate the scene, making 70 per cent of the wine, and the most famous name of Emilia is the frothy

Lambrusco. Most Lambrusco drunk in Emilia is dry, quite unlike the sugary stuff sent by Riunite for export to the UK and the US, but it cannot be claimed as anything very special. Romagna stunned the wine world by gaining the first white DOCG, the highest rung of the Italian wine ladder, for its rather ordinary Albana. Elsewhere, the fashionable French varieties – Chardonnay, Cabernet and Merlot – are very much on the increase, and one excellent producer of French varietals has emerged in the form of Terre Rosse at Zola Pedrosa near Bologna.

Central Italy – Tuscany

Tuscan red wines – Chianti, Brunello di Montalcino, Vino Nobile di Montepulciano, Bolgheri, Carmignano

To international eyes, Tuscany appears to be the centre of the Italian wine scene. It produces the reds which, at their best, epitomise Italian wine for most drinkers – Chianti Classico and Brunello di Montalcino. Essential to these wines is the classic central-Italian black grape, Sangiovese, which is grown all over these regions but reaches its apogee in the heart of Tuscany. Sangiovese, with its slightly rough texture and often harsh tannins, is not everyone's favourite grape, but it now seems to be better understood and more in favour than at any time in recent memory.

Both Chianti and Sangiovese were in a bad way in the 1970s. After the dismantling of the old system of share-cropping, vineyards were planted in industrial style on the productive flat land, not the favoured but awkward slopes. Vines were selected for productivity, not quality. The result was a catastrophic decline in quality, price and reputation. Piero Antinori and his winemaker Tachis deserve much credit for their quality initiatives in the late 1970s, including the introduction of some Cabernet Sauvignon (not entirely new to the region and already flourishing at Piero's cousin Mario Incisa's Sassicaia vineyard) and the creation of the first 'Super-Tuscans' Tignanello and Solaia, which began a dramatic turn-around in the fortunes of Chianti.

Chianti now has many fine, quality-minded estates, but the region is facing a significant challenge as the vineyards are substantially replanted for the first time since the 1970s. A project called Chianti 2000, involving research into the best clones of Sangiovese, rootstocks and training methods, was launched in the late 1980s. The real key, however, lies in the use of the best vineyard sites. Another problem is that four of the seven Chianti sub-zones still allow up to 15 per cent of grapes to be brought in from other Italian regions – hardly a recipe either for quality or regional identity. Some observers feel that the name Chianti should be restricted to the Classico heartland and the other top-quality zone of Rufina.

Much progress has certainly been made in Chianti in the past two decades. The role of white grapes, which used to dilute the wine, has been reduced to a minimum. Cabernet Sauvignon has made its contribution, but has not proved the dangerous interloper many feared. The best of the Chianti producers have shown that Sangiovese can produce world-class wines of piercing, rasping fruit, even if they have often chosen to stand outside the DOC and DOCG system with their 'Super-Tuscan' *vini da tavola*. All that may change if the promised changes allowing 100 per cent Sangiovese come into force.

Perhaps unfairly, Chianti tends to dominate discussion of Tuscan wine. Brunello di Montalcino has always had a reputation for producing some of Italy's greatest, biggest, most tannic reds – not always a deserved reputation, though the small DOCG, with its warm microclimate, has recently been enjoying something of a renaissance. The grand old, but much-declined, name of Biondi-Santi has been knocked off its perch by younger pretenders, especially Altesino. For those who find the tannic style of Brunello too much to take, the junior appellation of Rosso di Montalcino for lighter red from the same grapes has proved attractive.

Vino Nobile di Montepulciano probably suffers from its long name and potential confusion with the lower-grade Montepulciano grape of Abruzzi and elsewhere. This is high-quality Sangiovese wine. Other interesting Tuscan reds from Sangiovese include the intriguingly minty Parrina and the rather Bordeaux-like Morellino di Scansano.

Even more Bordeaux-like, of course, are the Cabernet Sauvignon-, Cabernet Franc- and Merlot-based wines made at Bogheri by the cousins Niccolò Incisa (son of Mario) and Lodovico Antinori (brother of Piero). Incisa's Sassicaia was the mould-breaker; even before Piero Antinori's Chianti-based Tignanello, the maverick Incisa showed what could be achieved in an obscure part of coastal Tuscany with the classic Bordeaux grapes. Lodovico Antinori tried his hand too, on his section of the ancestral Bolgheri estate, creating Ornellaia, a lusher wine with a higher proportion of Merlot. Now these have been brought under the DOC wing. It remains unclear how this surprise move will affect another attempt, initiated by Ruffino and others, to set up a separate classification system, Predicato, for Super-Tuscans and wines based on French varieties.

The last Tuscan red of note is Carmignano, where, according to Ugo Contini Bonacossi of Capezzana, who more or less created this

DOCG, Cabernet Sauvignon has flourished since the eighteenth century. Here the mixture of Sangiovese and Cabernet produces wines of great structure and ageing potential.

Fine Chianti and Brunello vintages: 1990, 1988, 1986, 1985.

Tuscan white wines – Trebbiano, Sauvignon Blanc, Chardonnay, Vernaccia, vin santo
Tuscany's white wines present a rather feeble, pallid impression after the rich gamut of reds. The main culprit is the omnipresent Trebbiano grape. Faced with its hopeless dullness, some producers in Chianti and Bolgheri have turned to French varieties such as Sauvignon Blanc and Chardonnay, while there are minor attempts to revive other Italian varieties such as Malvasia. A fashionable DOC for whites upgraded to DOCG in 1993 and allowing 10 per cent Chardonnay, is Vernaccia di San Gimignano, whose proponents are probably affected by the beauty of the tower-spiked hill-town, since the wines are pretty uninteresting. Tuscany's most famous white is the sweet *vin santo*, made from dried grapes and fermented for years in tiny barrels, which can be wonderfully spicy but is too often simply oxidised.

Umbria The quiet beauty of the Umbrian countryside and the artistic riches of the hill-towns are matched by few wines of great quality. The best known are the rather dull white Orvieto, which comes in both dry and sweet (*abbocato*) forms, and the Sangiovese reds of Torgiano, a DOC created by one of Italian wine's great individualists, Giorgio Lungarotti. Antinori has shown faith in the Umbrian Grecchetto grape, producing a rich, barrel-fermented Grecchetto and Chardonnay blend, Cervaro della Sala. A powerful red with exciting potential is produced from the Sagrantino grape in the DOC Montefalco.

Lazio/Latium The region which revolves around Rome is one of Italy's least distinguished in wine terms. The great bulk of wine production is made up of Frascati, the golden wine of the Alban Hills, and Est!Est!!Est!!! di Montefiascone, perhaps the world's prime example of hyperbolic nomenclature. The vast majority of Frascati and other Colli Albani whites is pretty dull stuff, made from Malvasia and Trebbiano and lacking either freshness or character, though a few producers, such as Fontana Candida, who add a bit of Chardonnay, and Villa Simone, try harder. Increasing plantings of Chardonnay and Merlot can only improve matters.
Marche, Abruzzi, Molise These three regions on the Adriatic side of the Apennines do not play star parts in the Italian wine scene. The three wines quite widely seen in the UK are Marche's Verdicchio

dei Castelli di Jesi – a white of oddly variable character, which can range from entirely pale and neutral to rich and golden, and is always said to go well with seafood – and two sturdy, stalwart reds from the untrendy but satisfying Montepulciano grape – Rosso Conero and Montepulciano d'Abruzzo. Rosso Piceno is another slightly gamey Marche red made from Sangiovese and Montepulciano and can offer good value. Molise's one DOC of note, though only for red, is the Montepulciano-based Biferno.

The south and the islands Not very long ago, even the most determined Italophile merchants came back from Italy's southern third shaking their heads, quite unable to unearth anything of note there. The outposts of quality in Campania, Taurasi's reds and the whites of Greco di Tufo and Fiano di Avellino (all mainly produced by one family firm, Mastroberardino), were already mapped. Sicily and Sardinia were slightly more promising, the former with its admirable branded Corvo and one or two go-ahead co-operatives and aristocratic estates, the latter with its interesting native grape varieties and its seminal modern wine estate, Sella & Mosca.

In the past five years, a small revolution seems to have occurred in parts of the south, especially in Puglia. This region alone produces more wine than Germany, yet only a fraction qualifies for DOC status. Much still goes for distillation by the EU. However, from DOC Salice Salentino, especially, and to a lesser extent from DOCs Copertino and Squinzano, there have emerged greatly improved reds of gamey elegance from the local Negroamaro grape. Chardonnay has also been planted, and the New Zealand winemaker Kym Milne is active in the area.

Sardinia continues to put most of the southern peninsula to shame. The latest wines of interest to emerge from Sardinia's unusual wine culture, influenced by centuries of Catalan domination, are splendidly rich Carignanos from Santadi. The red Cannonaus and white Nuragus are usually good value.

Sicily seems less dynamic, but can offer remarkably good everyday whites (surprisingly, white grapes outnumber reds by four to one in Italy's largest wine region). In Marsala, on the western tip of the island, Marco de Bartoli continues to wage his one-man crusade against the bastardisation of the once-great fortified wine. His dry, unfortified Vecchio Samperi tastes something like a very fine amontillado sherry. De Bartoli also makes extraordinary sweet Moscato from Zibbibo wines grown on the windswept island of Pantelleria, halfway to Libya.

Pick of the producers

Allegrini Leading producer of Valpolicella Classico of style and substance.

Altesino Possibly the best producer of Brunello di Montalcino, not as tannic as some, but beautifully balanced. Also fine Rosso di Montalcino.

Ama, Castello di Highly innovative Chianti Classico estate, experimenting with Merlot and Pinot Noir as well as Sangiovese.

Anselmi Dedicated producer of much-better-than-average Soave, including *crus* Capitel Foscarino and Capitel Croce, and oak-influenced Recioto dei Capitelli.

Antinori Hugely influential Chianti company, which helped change the style of the wines by adding Cabernet Sauvignon and launching the Super-Tuscans Tignanello and Solaia. Innovation continues, with excellent single-estate Chianti Classico Pèppoli and exciting Greccheto and Chardonnay white made at Castello della Sala in Umbria.

Avignonesi The best producer of Vino Nobile di Montepulciano, also Super-Tuscan I Grifi, and Chardonnay.

Badia a Coltibuono Historic abbey estate in Chianti Classico making firm, long-lasting reds.

Banfi Vast new estate and winery outside Montalcino built with money made from exporting Lambrusco. Wide range, including Brunello and Rosso di Montalcino, Sangiovese/Cabernet blend, 100 per cent Cabernet Sauvignon Tavernelle and Chardonnay Fontanelle.

Bartoli, de The great maverick of Marsala, who makes wonderful dry Vecchio Samperi outside the DOC system, and Moscato di Pantelleria.

Ca' del Bosco High-profile, but also top-quality, estate in Lombardy run by Maurizio Zanella. Excellent Cabernet-based *vino da tavola* and traditional-method sparklers as well as DOC Franciacorta.

Capezzana, Tenuta di The beautiful family estate which created DOCG Carmignano, making wines of class and structure. Also Cabernet and Merlot-influenced Ghiaie della Furba.

Collavini Leading producer in Collio and Colli Orientali del Friuli, specialising in clean, shapely whites.

Conterno, Aldo One of the greatest producers of Barolo at Bussia Soprana which does not sacrifice all fruit to tannin but has awesome staying-power. Lighter Nebbiolo-based Favot.

Corvo-Duca di Salaparuta Remarkably reliable branded white and red wines from this long-established Sicilian firm, now complemented by excellent *barrique*-aged red Duca Enrico.

Enofriulia Excellent Friuli merchant operation run by Vittorio Puiatti, making DOC Collio and *vino da tavola*, especially Chardonnay.

Felsina-Berardenga Fine producer of structured Chianti Classico and Super-Tuscan Fontalloro.

Frescobaldi Historic, aristocratic Chianti estate in Rufina. Castello di Nipozzano is the main name. Also DOC Pomino and Cabernet-based Predicato Mormoreto.

Gaja The man who introduced glitz, new oak and dazzling prices to Barbaresco. Now owns vineyards in Barolo also, as well as producing some of Italy's best Chardonnays and slightly less convincing Cabernet, Darmagi. Wines are hardly seen in the UK.

Giacosa, Bruno Fine traditionalist Piedmontese producer, making excellent Barbaresco, Barolo, Barbera and white Arneis.

Guerrieri-Rizzardi Aristocratic Veneto estate making better-than-average Bardolino, Valpolicella and Soave.

Isole e Olena Unshowy Chianti Classico estate brought into top rank by the very talented Paolo de Marchi. Both Chianti Classico and 100 per cent Sangiovese *vino da tavola* Cepparello are among the best of their kind. Recent experiments with Syrah show promise.

Jermann, Silvio Highly talented and individualistic Friuli winemaker who specialises in *vini da tavola* blends such as Vintage Tunina, a rich blend of Sauvignon, Chardonnay and other varieties. Fine Chardonnay with kitsch name, 'Where Dreams Have No End...'.

Lageder High-quality house in Alto Adige, making fine Chardonnay and Cabernet.

Lungarotti Pioneering estate which created DOCG Torgiano, with especially good Sangiovese-based Rubesco riserva. Cabernet Sauvignon also features, as a varietal (di Miralduolo) and in blend with Sangiovese (San Giorgio).

Maculan Outstanding producer in Breganze, Veneto, with both DOC and *vini da tavola*, including Cabernet, Chardonnay and Sauvignon Blanc. Superb sweet Torcolato.

Mascarello Taciturn maker of magnificent Barolo (Monprivato), Barbaresco and Dolcetto, more serious than most.

Masi Dynamic Verona firm specialising in ripasso style of Valpolicella, made with a proportion of dried grapes, sold under *vino da tavola* Campo Fiorin. Also excellent Valpolicella Classico, Amarone and Recioto.

Mastroberardino Highly respected family estate in Campania, almost single-handedly responsible for the fame of white DOCs Greco di Tufo and Fiano di Avellino, and red Taurasi, all capable of ageing.

Ornellaia Lodovico Antinori decided to compete with his cousin and neighbour Niccolò Incisa of Sassicaia, and, with help from André Tchelistcheff, has produced a delicious, lusher wine from Cabernet Sauvignon and Merlot, as well as good Sauvignon Blanc Poggio Alle Gazze, and rare 100 per cent Merlot Masseto.

Pieropan Unusually dedicated producer of Soave, characterful and concentrated from low yields, and luscious sweet Recioto di Soave.

Prunotto Respected *négociant*-house in Piedmont, now owned by Antinori. Reliable Barolo, Barbaresco and fine oak-aged Barbera Pian Romualdo.

Quintarelli Maverick producer of great Recioto and Amarone di Valpolicella, including some from Cabernet Franc, and Valpolicella Classico quite out of the common run.

Regaleali Aristocratic estate near Enna in central Sicily, producing fine, deep red Rosso del Conte.

Riecine Small, perfectionist Chianti Classico estate run by Englishman John Dunkley, making wines of great polish.

Santadi Excellent Sardinian co-operative specialising in classy Carignano, including *barrique*-aged version.

Sassicaia Remarkable estate at Bolgheri on the Tuscan coast where Mario Incisa created an Italian 'first growth' using Cabernet Sauvignon and Cabernet Franc, now run by his son Niccolò.

Sella & Mosca Vast private estate near Alghero in Sardinia, run on modern lines and producing good DOC Vermentino and more exciting *vini da tavola*, including remarkable sweet red Anghelu Ruju.

Talenti Excellent small estate at Brunello making top-class DOCG Brunello di Montalcino and fine DOC Rosso di Montalcino.

Vajra Admired estate producer of Barolo, Barbera and one of Piedmont's best Dolcettos.

Voerzio New-wave Alba producer of Barolo, Barbera, Dolcetto and Arneis, with new oak much in evidence.

Volpaia, Castello di Fine Chianti Classico estate at Radda, making excellent DOCG Chianti Classico and *vino da tavola* Coltassala, from Sangiovese and Mammolo.

Cork was used by the Romans to stopper jars and amphorae but after the Romans its use was forgotten until the middle of the sixteenth century.

SPAIN

TABLE WINES

We were all so excited by Spain in the 1970s and early 1980s. There was the death of General Franco in 1975 and the peaceful transition to democracy, and then there was Rioja, offering mellow delights at modest cost, and Torres Cabernet Sauvignon beating the world in blind tastings. Twenty years on some of the excitement has subsided. Spain seems a touch stagnant both on the political and vinous fronts. Rioja and Torres, leading the way in Penedés, continue to thrive, but how many of Spain's 38 other *Denominaciones de Origen* (DO) are widely known, apart from Jerez, Navarra, Montilla and possibly Ribera del Duero?

Is this the fault of unadventurous merchants and drinkers, or a true reflection of the state of Spanish wine? As it happens, neither explanation fits the bill. Enthusiastic wine merchants have scoured Spain and returned with interesting and unusual finds, such as the fruit-cake rich Prioratos of southern Catalonia and the flowery-scented Albariños of Galicia. The innovative supermarket chain, Safeway, has persuaded wineries in the great bulk-producing region of La Mancha, using modern equipment, to create a deliciously fruity style of Tempranillo. Imports of Spanish wine into the UK are rising at a healthy rate – though they may be halted in their tracks by the disastrously short 1994 vintage, decimated by late frosts and torrid summer heat. Perhaps the main problem is ignorance – ignorance by the British of a country they visit in their millions, and ignorance by the Spanish producers of the export possibilities open to them, if they paid a little more attention to the international competition.

One of the first characteristics which strikes anyone travelling in Spain is the country's regional diversity. The Romans referred to *Hispaniae*, Spains, and their plural view was correct. Many Catalans and Basques, who speak their own ancient languages, are not satisfied with the limited autonomy they enjoy at the moment: they do not consider they belong to Spain at all. Galicia and Valencia are other regions with their own language and culture – and their own distinctive wines. Given this reality of regional diversity, covered by a deceptive mask of national identity, it may not be surprising that outsiders fail to get a grip on the wide variety of Spanish wines.

Spanish producers, however, must take a large part of the responsibility for failing to make their wines better known for quality. Why does the enterprising, typically Catalan firm of Torres still remain virtually unchallenged as an internationally reputed exporter of a top-quality range of wines? More Spaniards, or Catalans, should be asking themselves that question. One intractable problem is certainly that many of Spain's most interesting, lesser-known wines, such as Priorato or Albariño, are produced in such small quantities that there is hardly enough to satisfy the home market. Another, perhaps even more serious, is the dullness of Spain's dowry of native grape varieties. Spain is one country which does not need to be alarmed about the spread of Cabernet and Chardonnay. Having said that, why is greater use not being made of national treasures such as low-yielding Monastrell (Mourvèdre) in Jumilla?

However, there are many signs of progress in the Spanish wine scene. Denominations such as Toro in the north-west and Somontano in the Pyrenean foothills of Aragon have fully justified their DO status in the past decade. Gallons of very decently made wine are pouring in from Valencia. The shortage is of really dedicated, quality-minded small- to medium-sized producers. Spain needs more wines like Pesquera – the brilliant, chocolatey rich Ribera del Duero from Alejandro Fernández – or the meticulously crafted estate Navarra wines from Bodegas Guelbenzu. Nor does this apply only to less well-known regions. Rioja itself, one of the great wine export success stories of the past twenty years, cannot afford to rest on its laurels. Rioja needs more firms like Martínez Bujanda, experimenting with new styles of white wine, and more quality-oriented single estates like Remélluri and Contino.

Wine classification

Spain's equivalent of French *appellation contrôlée* is *denominación de origen*, or DO for short. DO delimits the boundaries of wine-producing areas and controls matters such as grape varieties, pruning, maximum yields, and minimum levels of alcohol. For all that, many of Spain's 40 DOs produce little or no wine of true quality. In 1991, a further category called DOCa, or *denominación de origen calificada* was introduced. So far, only Rioja is eligible, and it is difficult to detect any qualitative change since its promotion to DOCa. Below DOCa and DO come the increasingly important categories of *vinos de la tierra* (equivalent of French *vins de pays*) and, bottom of the pile, *vino de mesa* or table wine.

The regions – North-West Spain

Rioja

Rioja remains by far Spain's most important quality-wine region, or perhaps we should say quality red-wine region. Considerable quantities of white Rioja are made, mainly from the Viura grape, and much is now clean, modern, acceptable and boring. The most interesting white Riojas are old-fashioned and aged in oak, giving an extraordinary caramelly richness to offset their citric bite.

However, for most consumers Rioja is red – and marked by the sweet vanilla spice of American oak. In fact, there is a strong move away from oak-ageing in many *bodegas*. Only around 40 per cent of Rioja falls into the *crianza*, *reserva* and *gran reserva* categories which stipulate oak-ageing. This is creating something of an identity crisis, for without oaky spice, the soft fruit of the Tempranillo and Garnacha grapes in *sin crianza* (unoaked) Rioja can taste pretty plain and unremarkable.

The best Rioja, in our view, does see oak, even if it has not been kept in ancient barrels for over 20 years, like some of the *gran reservas* from the ultra-traditional Bodegas Marqués de Murrieta. Perhaps around two years – as with the best Bordeaux, which inspired the makers of Rioja in the last century – is the right amount of time in barrel for top-quality Rioja. For all that, traditional *bodegas* such as La Rioja Alta continue to age their *reservas* and *gran reservas* for between five and seven years, and the results have such lovely harmony and wild strawberry fruit that criticism is disarmed. A relatively new fashion is for French oak, used by Palacio, Baron de Ley and others, which certainly gives more refinement.

Rioja is dominated by large *bodegas*, but there has been an encouraging growth of small, single-estate producers in the past few years. The main problem for the moment is a shortage of grapes: the Riojanos lobbied the EU for permission to plant but no new vineyards have been authorised for the past three years.

Another question which Rioja does not seem to have answered concerns the status of Cabernet Sauvignon. It is well known that Marqués de Riscal has had Cabernet planted since the nineteenth century, and many others use the grape unofficially, but the authorities, for the moment, regard Cabernet as an undesirable interloper.

Vintage guide

1994 Very good quality, but 10 per cent below average quantity.
1993 A wet harvest, only average quality.
1992 September rain spoiled a potentially excellent harvest. Early-picked grapes were healthy, but rot became a problem later. Wines will be early-maturing.
1991 A cool spring and early summer was followed by a hot end to the season. Small crop of good-quality wines.
  Previous fine vintages: 1990, 1989, 1988, 1987, 1986, 1985, 1982.

Navarra

Rioja's northern neighbour has traditionally been considered a poor relation, in wine terms – best known for light rosados – but concerted research and innovative thinking have made Navarra very much a region to watch. Unlike Rioja, the Navarra DO has sanctioned the planting of Cabernet Sauvignon, and the benefits seem obvious in Tempranillo/Cabernet blends, combining sweet strawberry fruit and refined, cigar-box Cabernet scent and firm Cabernet structure.

  Navarra's reds are coming on in leaps and bounds, but that is no reason to neglect the delicious rosés (rosados, claretes) made from the Garnacha grape. These are some the world's best and certainly best-value dry rosé wines. Unfortunately, ill-founded prejudice continues to militate against them in the UK market.

Ribera del Duero

Spain's most fashionable wine area received its DO only in 1982, at which time its sole quality producer was the legendary Vega Sicilia. Alejandro Fernández's Pesquera, improbably described by Robert Parker as Spain's answer to Pétrus, shot to stardom in the mid-1980s, and was followed by a number of other producers. At their best Ribera del Duero reds, made from the Tinto Fino (Tempranillo) grape, combine power and intensity of flavour as only great wines can, but standards of wine-making still leave much to be desired, and there is an irritating lack of consistency and reliability. Some producers are misguidedly pursuing a light, *joven* style, when the region's strength is in powerful, stalwart yet balanced reds.

Other North-Western regions

Toro is a DO in the province of Zamora, near the Portuguese border, which produces inky-dark, powerful reds from Tinto de Toro (alias Tempranillo). The oak-aged wines from Bodegas Fariña are excellent.

Rueda, in nearby Valladolid province, is one of Spain's few interesting DOs for white wines. The main grape is Verdejo, but Sauvignon Blanc is also permitted, and Marqués de Riscal makes an enjoyable, fresh version. Flying winemaker Jacques Lurton also operates in the area.

The Basque country has a solitary, unusual white, the prickly, pale, apple-sour Chacolí (from Guetaría or Vizcaya).

Further west, Galicia has its own traditions, which have much more in common with those of northern Portugal than any part of Spain. Galicia's answer to basic Vinho Verde is Ribeiro, a DO making both red and white wines, the latter usually slightly pétillant (sparkling). Good-quality native grapes such as Loureira and Treixadura are gradually gaining ground on the dull Palomino.

Galicia's, and perhaps Spain's, best white grape is Albariño, thought to be a grape of German origin brought over by Cistercian monks in the twelfth century. Good dry Albariño from the Rías Baixas DO can bear a remarkable resemblance to German or Alsace Riesling.

Eastern Spain – Catalonia, Aragón, Valencia

Catalonia

Catalonia is and has always been Spain's most forward-looking, industrious region – which begs the vexed question of whether Catalonia is part of Spain at all. When you look at dynamic firms such as Torres and the big Cava producers, Codorníu and

Freixenet, you can understand the irritation many Catalans feel at being shackled to the slow-moving, backward centre and south. These firms, admittedly, have had the fairly large Spanish internal market at their mercy, but the best of them have relished the challenge of competing on the international stage.

Penedés, stretching east from the outskirts of Barcelona, is Catalonia's premier wine region, and so innovative that it sometimes seems to belong more to the New World than to old Spain. The terrain here is very varied, ranging from hot flatlands near the Mediterranean, suitable only for liqueur Muscat production, to high, pine-covered uplands, where snow falls every winter. In the middle is excellent vine-land, planted mostly with the three white grapes, Parellada, Macabeo and Xarello, used for the production of Cava (DO Cava covers all bottle-fermented Spanish fizz). The headquarters of the Cava industry is the small and functional town of San Sadurní de Noya, housing the cellars of Codorníu, Freixenet and nearly all the major firms.

Penedés has also been highly successful in producing still wines, mainly white, but also red, both from indigenous varieties, such as Parellada, Garnacha, Ull de Llebre (Tempranillo) and Monastrell, and from French varieties such as Cabernet Sauvignon, Chardonnay and even Gewurztraminer, introduced by Miguel Torres and Jean León. The Penedés DO permits these French varieties, and the best Cabernet Sauvignon and Chardonnay wines from Torres and León are world class. Several other producers, some of them offshoots of the big Cava companies, are following in Torres' footsteps with fair success. Miguel Torres himself moves ever onward; not content with exciting results from Pinot Noir and Merlot, he is now conducting research into traditional Catalan varieties.

Outside Penedés, Catalonia has a number of DOs, which range from interesting to ordinary. Ampurdán, the wind-scoured plain in the north, struggles to produce wine of any quality. Over in the east, a single exciting producer, Raimat (offshoot of Codorníu), has made excellent use of Cabernet, Chardonnay and Pinot Noir on its vast, irrigated estate. The DO Costers del Segre is simply an acknowledgement of Raimat's excellence, for no other producer in the region deserves recognition. In the south, the Tarragona DO has been known mainly for fortified wine (it still supplies communion wine to the Vatican), but offers good-value reds, especially Falset. Two smaller DOs within Tarragona province are the rustic Terra Alta and the extraordinary Priorato, the latter making some the world's most potent reds. Finally, there are the high-altitude inland vineyards of Conca de Barberá, elevated to DO status as recently as 1989, including the spectacular Torres single-vineyard Chardonnay Milmanda (strangely, this used to appear as Penedés on the label). Hugh Ryman is now consulting with a winery in this area, producing inexpensive red and white wines.

Aragón

Aragón is one of the least-visited parts of Spain, and its scattered wine regions are hardly household names. Cariñena and Catalayud do not deserve to be, but Somontano (DO since 1985) in the Pyrenean foothills is one of Spain's most interesting up-and-coming regions. Good reds are made from traditional varieties, but exciting results are coming from experimental plantings of Chardonnay, Chenin Blanc and Gewurztraminer.

Valencia

This region accounts for nearly half of all imports of Spanish wine into the UK, yet, if anything, it is probably best known for sweet Muscat. Most Valencia wine is white and, as so often in Spain, suffers from being made from a less-than-thrilling grape variety, in this case, Meseguera. Where Valencia does score is in value for money and reliability, for the large export *bodegas* are well equipped. The inland DO of Utiel-Requena makes good, if luridly coloured, rosés and improving reds from the Bobal grape.

The centre and the south

The great south-central plateau of La Mancha gave birth not only to Don Quixote but also to most of the gallons of plonk poured down the throats of Spanish Sancho Panzas since time immemorial. This is the country of the white Airén, the world's most widely planted and possibly most boring grape. Red wines (sadly, only 10 per cent of total production) made from Cencibel, the local name for Tempranillo, are much more promising, and can indeed be delicious, strawberry soft. When made in a modern style, as pioneered by Safeway with its Young Vatted Tempranillo, the strawberry can deepen to plum, with youthful vivacity. Valdepeñas is a DO enclave within La Mancha, traditionally known for better quality and producing some of the best-value, soft reds in Europe. Sadly, these account for only 15 per cent of production; there are currently not enough black grapes to meet demand. One day, perhaps, growers will have the sense to grub up a proportion of the vast acreage of Airén and replant it with Cencibel. Almansa, on the border with Valencia, makes decent reds from Monastrell, Garnacha and Tempranillo.

Murcia, the small autonomous region in the south-east, has one reasonably successful and well-known DO, Jumilla, which spreads across the border into Castilla-La-Mancha. Around 80 per cent of the powerful Jumilla red wine still goes for blending (and who knows where exactly it ends up); the remaining 20 per cent can be good value, if you like really dark, slightly rough reds. The other Murcian DO, Yecla, is a non-starter in the export stakes.

Andalusia, the great southern region where the Moorish presence lasted longest and left its still-magnificent legacy of architecture and social custom, is known above all for the great fortified wines of Jerez (see below), and the less-great fortified wines of Montilla-Moriles and Málaga. Not very much table wine is made in Andalusia, apart from the average-quality whites of Condado de Huelva near the Portuguese border, and the odd unfortified Palomino white made by sherry producers such as Barbadillo; the latter is of no more than local interest.

Pick of the producers
Abadía de San Campío Small producer of excellent Rías Baixas Albarino.

AGE Very large Rioja *bodega*, making well-known Siglo Saco Rioja, with hessian-coated bottle, possibly to distract attention from average-quality wine inside. Romeral is another, undistinguished, label.

Alella, Marqués de Leading producer of tiny DO in northern outskirts of Barcelona. Decent fresh white Alella Classico and good Chardonnay.

Amezola de la Mora Exciting new single-estate Rioja. Reds have lovely plush, strawberry fruit.

Bach, Masía Nothing to do with the German composer, this is a large Penedés producer of table wines now owned by Codorníu. Used to be best known for sweet white Extrísimo Bach; reds now much improved.

Barbier, René Penedés table-wine producer owned by Freixenet. Reds best.

Barceló, Hijos de Antonio Good, if patchy, new export-oriented Ribera del Duero *bodega*.

Berberana Large Rioja *bodega* purchased in the 1970s by the notorious RUMASA company, later expropriated by the government. Wines have stayed surprisingly consistent, with some good *reservas* and *gran reservas*.

Beronia Smallish, good-quality Rioja *bodega* owned by González Byass of Jerez. Especially fine, long-lasting *reservas*.

Bilbainas, Bodegas Ultra-traditional Rioja *bodega*, currently searching for a more modern style.

Bodegas y Bebidas Huge wine group, now Spain's largest, owning such names as Campo Viejo, Vinícola Navarra and Señorío del Condestable in Jumilla.

Cáceres, Marqués de Enterprising *bodega* founded in the early 1970s by Enrique (Henri) Forner. Grapes are supplied by an association of growers and vinified in ultra-modern facilities at Cenicero. Whites are unusually fresh and reds rather French, fruity, not oaky, in style.

Callejo, Felix One of the leading *bodegas* in Ribero del Duero.

Campo Viejo By far the largest Rioja *bodega*, keeping commendably high standards with *crianza* and *reserva* reds.

Chivite Leading Navarra producer, family-run for three centuries. Generally good, clean wines, though reds can be over-oaky.

Codorníu Giant cava producer based in Gaudiesque cellars in San Sadurní de Noya. Basic wines are unexciting, but Chardonnay-influenced Ana de Codorníu is above average.

Contino Splendid single-vineyard wine from Rioja Alavesa, vinified by winemakers of CVNE (see below) in style emphasising full, plummy fruit. All wine is sold as *reserva* or *gran reserva*.

Coto, El Good Rioja *bodega* making elegant, strawberry-scented red.

CVNE (Compania Vinícola del Norte de España) One of the very best and most consistent of Rioja *bodegas*, making good oak-aged white Monopole, excellent Viña Real Reserva and outstanding Imperial Gran Reserva.

Domecq The famous sherry firm also owns a *bodega* and vineyards in Rioja. Red Domecq Domain is fair, but seldom exciting.

Fariña, Bodegas Excellent producer of hearty reds in Toro.

Faustino Martínez Large but consistent *bodega* in Rioja Alavesa, making excellent Faustino I Gran Reserva.

Freixenet Huge cava producer based in San Sadurní, making reliable but not brilliant Cordon Negro and other wines.

Griñon, Marqués de Maverick aristocratic estate near Toledo making excellent, rich, chocolatey Cabernet Sauvignon (with advice from Emile Peynaud) and interesting white Rueda.

Guelbenzu, Bodegas Exciting family-run estate in Navarra, making serious, hand-crafted reds, based on Cabernet Sauvignon and Tempranillo and aged in French oak.

Juvé y Camps High-class, family-run cava producer in Penedés, charging top prices for well-made Reserva de la Familia Extra Brut.

León, Jean Ex-Hollywood restaurateur and pioneering producer of Cabernet Sauvignon and Chardonnay in Penedés. New World-style wines.

López de Heredia Vying with Marqués de Murrieta for title of most traditional *bodega* in Rioja. Very distinctive, long-oaked Viña Tondonia red and white. A style either to treasure or deplore.

Los Llanos, Señorío de Very good, exceptional-value reds from probably the best producer in Valdepeñas.

Martínez Bujanda Admirably innovative and quality-minded Rioja *bodega*, making fresh fruity Tempranillo red and Valdemar red and white, and excellent Conde de Valdemar *crianza*, *reserva* and *gran reservas*. New, modern-fashioned barrel-fermented Conde de Valdemar white is one of Rioja's best.

Monistrol, Marqués de Penedés *bodega* owned by Martini, though vineyards are still owned by the eponymous Marquis, making both decent, fresh cava and still wines, of which whites are better than reds.

Montecillo Admirable Rioja *bodega* owned by the sherry and brandy firm Osborne. Long-lived, elegant, not too oaky reds.

Mont Marçal High-quality Penedés producer of mainly still and some sparkling (cava) wine. Cabernet Sauvignon and Chardonnay among the best of the region.

Muga Very traditional, artisanal Rioja *bodega* making attractive, soft, but harmonious, reds.

Murrieta, Marqués de Prestigious, traditional Rioja estate and *bodega*. Extraordinary, oaky whites and reds, sometimes over-oaked to modern tastes.

Navajas, Bodegas Good, unpretentious Rioja *bodega* making exceptional oak-aged white Crianza.

Ochoa Highly innovative Navarra *bodega*. Good-quality range, with reds influenced by Cabernet Sauvignon.

Parxet Excellent small cava producer. Wines have more finesse and fruit than most.

Paternina, Federico Large Rioja *bodega* owned by Marcos Eguizábal, making decent red Banda Azul.

Pérez Pascuas Excellent family *bodega* in Ribera del Duero. Fresh, fruity Vino Joven, sophisticated *crianza* and *reserva* Viña Pedrosa.

Pesquera Cult Ribera del Duero red, made by Alejandro Fernández. Excitingly rich and oaky, but not quite the Pétrus it has been claimed to be.

Raimat Remarkable, huge estate in dry, barren land near Lérida, Catalonia, owned by Raventós family of Codorníu and irrigated with water from the Pyrenees. Excellent New World-style varietals, especially Cabernet Sauvignon, Pinot Noir and sparkling Chardonnay Cava.

Remélluri One of the best of the new wave of single-estate Rioja producers, owned and run by a young brother and sister partnership, Telmo and Amaya Rodríguez. Powerful, complex reds, now less heavily oaked.

Ribera Duero Large co-operative in Ribera del Duero, making wines of variable quality, some marked by musty, off-odours.

Rioja Alta, la Admirable, traditional Rioja *bodega*. Viña Alberdi and Viña Arana are quite light, Viña Ardanza is rich and powerful, Reserva 904 and Reserva 890 are among the greatest examples of the long-oaked style.

Riojanas, Bodegas Traditional Rioja *bodega*, making especially good, powerful, fruity Monte Real Reserva.

Riscal, Marqués de Historic, controversial Rioja *bodega*, the first to plant Cabernet Sauvignon in Spain, back in 1864. Despite this, the reds have been curiously light and oddly scented. White Rueda, made from Sauvignon Blanc, is attractive.

Scala Dei Innovative *bodega* in Priorato, breaking the mould by aiming for lighter, fruitier style, containing a proportion of Cabernet Sauvignon.

Segura Viudas Well-known cava producer, now part of Freixenet group, making pleasantly fresh, dry style of cava.

Solis, Felix Leading producer in Valdepeñas, maintaining good standard, especially with Viña Albalí Reserva.

Torres Catalan family firm which leads the pack in terms of innovation and quality. Constantly refined and expanding range includes red Coronas (Tempranillo and Cabernet Sauvignon), Gran Coronas (mostly Cabernet Sauvignon), Châteauneuf-lookalike Gran Sangredetoro, white Viña Sol (100 per cent Parellada), Chardonnay-influenced Gran Viña Sol and Gewurztraminer-plus-Muscat Viña Esmeralda, plus exciting single-vineyard range including world-beating Cabernet Sauvignon Mas la Plana and Chardonnay Milmanda.

Vega Sicilia Legendary producer of long-oaked, long-lived and extremely expensive reds in what is now DO Ribera del Duero (Vega Sicilia was there long before the DO). The least-expensive wines are called Valbuena, the top of the range, formerly matured for ten years in barrel, Unico. Cabernet Sauvignon is set to increase from 25 per cent to 40 per cent of the blend, dominated by Tinto Fino (Tempranillo).

Yllera Usually good-quality Ribera del Duero red which does not qualify for DO.

FORTIFIED WINES

Sherry

For most of the past two decades, the outlook for Spain's greatest wine has been depressing. The rush to plant new vineyards on the chalky, light-flooded Jerez hills in the 1960s and early 1970s seemed more and more misguided as the sherry market entered an apparently terminal decline. Exports slumped from over 16 million cases in 1979 to 9.6 million in 1991. Thousands of hectares of the new vineyards were grubbed up and turned over to sunflowers, or whatever was on the current EU menu. Excess stock became a grave problem, although nature has helped here by drastically reducing the harvest in 1994 (40 per cent down on normal).

The reason for this decline was perfectly obvious. Most of the sherry exported to England was dark, heavy, treacly-sweet – more of an alternative to central heating than an appetising aperitif. This was the sherry kept in the decanter on the sideboard by Great-Aunt Rose, and drunk as a sort of sacrificial burnt offering. Great-Aunt Rose's great-nephews and nieces, understandably, did not care much for this outmoded beverage. Sherry's great problem is a declining, elderly market for an old-fashioned drink.

There is another way of looking at this problem. The kind of sweetened, dark or medium sherry we have been talking about scarcely exists on the Spanish market. Ninety per cent of the sherry drunk in Spain is pale, light and dry – fino and manzanilla – and goes wonderfully well with seafood and tapas of all kinds. When the sherry producers commissioned a market research survey in the early 1980s, the conclusion was that the only viable future for sherry lay in these lighter, drier styles.

Unfortunately, and despite the explosion of tapas bars in London and elsewhere, which you would think were ideal outlets for fino and manzanilla, the move towards the lighter styles in the UK is proceeding slowly. Fino and manzanilla account for only 16 per cent of the market, still dominated by cream and pale-cream sherries. All the same, in 1994 there was an encouraging growth in fino shipments of over one per cent, and the tiny manzanilla market also moved upwards.

Fino and manzanilla, now mostly at 15.5° and appreciably lighter and more wine-like as a result, are more widely available and more reliably fresh than ever before. The increasing interest in Spanish cuisine is bound to rub off on these marvellously versatile wines: perhaps the most important single message for the consumer is that sherries are wines, to be drunk with food as well as on their own, and with gusto.

Jerez, and the other sherry towns of Sanlúcar and El Puerto de Santa María, have much to offer besides fino and manzanilla. The greatest sherries are the deeper, nuttier, but still dry, amontillados, palo cortados and olorosos. A difficulty here is the absence of a graduated system of classification in Jerez. Take the horribly abused name of amontillado. The sherry producers have only themselves to blame for bastardising the term – which should only be used for a rare old wine which has metamorphosed from fino into something rich, nutty, yet dry – and sticking it on the labels of sweetened-up, youthful, low-quality blends. There is no obvious way for the consumer to distinguish a low-quality supermarket amontillado from a splendid, authentic, aged wine, such as Hidalgo's Napoleón or González's Amontillado del Duque, except by price. One suggestion is the introduction of age bands such as exist for tawny port. This might be hard to reconcile with the famous *solera* system, by which older wines are constantly refreshed with younger vintages, but it might be possible to establish approximate ages. For the moment, the great aged wines of Jerez are among the world's most under-valued. In May 1994 González Byass surprised the sherry world by offering vintage-dated old dry olorosos for sale at Christie's.

Styles

Pale and dry – fino and manzanilla   These types of sherry, usually made from first pressings of good-quality Palomino grapes, are affected by the famous yeast-like fungus, flor. Flor forms on the surface on the wine in barrel and protects it from oxidation, while feeding on some elements in the wine and making it finer and more pungent.

There are considerable differences between finos matured in Jerez and those matured in El Puerto de Santa María, nearer the sea. Puerto finos are influenced more by flor and tend to taste lighter and fresher. Sanlúcar's fino-style wines are called manzanilla, and have the strongest flor influence of all. Manzanilla at its best is pungent yet fresh, delicate but full of flavour. In the past, the best manzanilla was considered to be manzanilla pasada, aged for upwards of a decade in the *solera* system, but these days lighter, fresher manzanilla fina is all the rage. Jerez finos are, typically, more powerful, sometimes with a slightly oaky character. There has been a trend for Jerez *bodegas*, led by Domecq with La Ina, to give their finos an almost manzanilla-like lightness, probably not unconnected with the current fashion for manzanilla within Andalusia.

Longer-aged and richer dry styles – amontillado, palo cortado, dry oloroso   Amontillado should be a fine, aged dry wine which started out as a fino, then developed a deeper, nuttier character, and was fortified from 15.5° to 17 or 18°, thus killing off the flor. Unfortunately, as we have indicated, most amontillado on the market is nothing of the sort, but is sweetened young wine of the lowest quality.

Palo Cortado, oddly called Jerez Cortado in Sanlúcar, is the rarest and most mysterious of sherries. It is perhaps best described as a cross between a very fine old amontillado and a dry oloroso.

Dry oloroso is a splendid, powerful winter drink, aromatic, sustaining and inspiring.

Sweeter styles – medium, pale cream, cream, Pedro Ximénez
Medium, pale cream and cream are sweet styles of sherry developed for the export market and never seen in Spain. The sweetness tends to mask any distinctive character, though some cream can contain good-quality, rich aged oloroso. Pedro Ximénez, a grape which reaches incredible sugar levels, especially in the Montilla region, is also the term for treacly sweet sherries which can age into distinction.

Pick of the producers
Barbadillo Much the largest Sanlúcar *bodega*, making most own-label manzanilla and good-quality Solear manzanilla, somewhere between fina and pasada in style.

Caballero Successful growing company based in El Puerto and selling good Puerto fino under Burdon label.

Domecq Most famous of Jerez *bodegas*, recently merged with Allied-Lyons. Excellent, delicate La Ina fino, fine Rio Viejo and, very old and rare, 51-1A dry amontillados.

González Byass Large and distinguished Jerez *bodega*, now linked with IDV-Grand Met, maintaining the highest standards with Tío Pepe fino (more typically Jerez in style than La Ina), Alfonso dry oloroso and wonderful rare dry Amontillado del Duque and sweet Matúsalem.

Hidalgo Family-owned *bodega* in Sanlúcar, making excellent manzanilla La Gitana (more fina than pasada) and superb old dry amontillado Napoleón and Jerez Cortado.

Lustau Important Jerez *bodega* supplying own-label market, but also offering exceptional range of almacenista (see glossary) sherries, from private stores of well-to-do Jerez, Sanlúcar and Puerto families. Now controlled by Caballero.

Osborne Giant family-owned company in El Puerto, with huge brandy interests, but also offering fair-quality fino Quinta.

Valdespino Great traditionalist family-owned *bodega* in Jerez. Fino Inocente is the best and most typical Jerez fino, amontillado Tío Diego is extremely dry and pungent.

Montilla-Moriles

Montilla-Moriles, the wine from the hills south of Córdoba, still carries around the accusatory, albatross-like tag of being the poor person's sherry – a tag which only becomes more burdensome as sherry's own reputation declines. There is also a self-fulfilling quality in this description, for while Montilla continues to command such bargain-basement prices it can never hope to shake off its depressing image. Cheap Montilla is rather a depressing drink, but better-quality aged Montilla in the amontillado (the term actually comes from Montilla in the first place) and oloroso styles can be very good – if you can find it.

Málaga

Málaga, as a high-quality, exported fortified wine, has become nearly extinct, one of wine's dodos. One or two producers, especially Scholtz Hermanos, continue to keep some sort of flame burning: Scholtz Solera 1885 balances burnt richness with tangy acidity, rather in the manner of Bual madeira, and makes a fine partner for chocolate.

When opening a bottle cut through the capsule just below the lip of the bottle, then wipe the lip with a damp cloth. This is particularly important for bottles with lead capsules since wine can pick up lead contamination from the bottle rim as it is poured.

PORTUGAL

TABLE WINES

The steam engine which used to drag the slow train up the Douro Valley in northern Portugal was called 'Paciencia'. Many visitors have been charmed by the patience and quiet courtesy of the Portuguese (shown everywhere except on the roads). Rapid development has appeared alien to the nature of this dreamy country. Portugal's conservatism has both positive and negative results for wine: the country has a great reservoir of valuable native grape varieties, but until recently skill in the winery has been conspicuous by its absence.

All that is changing: generous EU funds are being usefully employed, especially by some commendably forward-thinking co-operatives in the Ribatejo, Oeste and, above all, Alentejo. Two or three Australian winemakers resident in Portugal, notably Peter Bright, have also made a difference out of proportion to their number.

All this means that exports of Portuguese wine to the UK have been surging ahead at a near-Australian lick in the past couple of years until supply problems in 1994 forced on the brakes. In volume terms, that is; unfortunately, the increase in terms of value has been almost embarrassingly small. Not that there is anything to be embarrassed about in the quality of wines such as Leziria (the red, especially) from the Almeirim co-op, or the Do Campo range made by Peter Bright for Sainsbury's. It is simply that at such low prices it will be difficult for these wineries to take the step forward in quality which is within their reach.

It may seem strange that the Alentejo, Ribatejo and Oeste should be leading the new wave of Portuguese table wines, because these are not regions traditionally known for quality. Portugal's premier northerly table wine regions of Dão and Bairrada are currently lagging behind the arrivistes of the south and centre. There are some encouraging developments, most notably the efforts made by Portugal's largest and most innovative producer, Sogrape (Mateus, but much, much more besides), in its £6 million new winery in the Dão, and with its exciting barrel-fermented white Bairrada Reserva. Too many producers in Dão and Bairrada, however, are locked into low-priced production, which does not create enough profit for investment.

Portugal is still, by European standards, a poor nation. The home market does not generate a demand for top-quality, glamorous wines. The number of small, high-quality estates remains small, and none so far has appeared (Miguel Champalimaud might object) which can challenge the Super-Tuscans or Bordeaux *crus classés*. This will perhaps only be a matter of time, for money is pouring into Portugal, and enriching the growing middle-class. A final piece of good news is that after the near-disastrous 1993 vintage, which produced only half the usual crop in many areas, 1994, though still very much on the small side, has provided some excellent quality.

Appellation and quality wine system

Portugal now has 18 DOC (equivalent to the French AOC) regions, including four newly promoted ones from the Alentejo, and 29 IPR (equivalent to French VDQS) regions. The IPRs, like the French VDQS, are a staging-post on the way to DOC. Below IPR comes a category called *vinho regional*, equivalent to French *vin de pays*.

Wine styles, varieties and regions

White wines

Portugal's most famous white wine is Vinho Verde, from the northern region of Minho. In fact, over half of Vinho Verde is red, or inky purple in colour: the *verde*, or green, refers to the character rather than the colour. The Vinho Verde we see in the UK is all white, and most of it, unlike the authentic article you would drink in Braga, is sweetened. Authentic dry vinho verde made from the Loureiro and Alvarinho grapes is beginning to be seen more widely, and its flowery scent and freshness are most appealing. The other northern regions of Douro, Dão and Bairrada all make some white wine, but most is, frankly, dull, apart from the excellent oak-fermented Bairrada made by Sogrape. Increasingly good whites, including one or two Chardonnays, are appearing from the southern and central regions of Oeste, Ribatejo and Alentejo. A speciality is the fortified Moscatel from Setúbal, near Lisbon: the firm of Pires also sells a well-known, refreshing medium-dry Muscat.

Red wines

Traditionally, the premier red wine-producing regions have been Dão, a hilly region of vineyards cleared among pine forests, and Bairrada, nearer the sea. Most of the Dão seen here until recently was hard and charmless, its fruit (partly from the Touriga Nacional grape also used for port) leached out by prolonged ageing in ancient barrels. Bairrada, made from the tannic Baga grape, was not much more attractive. Sogrape has pioneered a much more modern approach to Dão, emphasising forward fruit, and Luis Pato has shown that Bairrada can give excellent-quality, if tannic, reds. More and more table wine from the Douro is being seen, as the authorities take steps to counter overproduction of port.

Many of Portugal's best reds, however, are now coming out of the less well-known regions around Lisbon, the Oeste, Ribatejo, Arrabida and Palmela, and from the Alentejo on the Spanish border. It is in the former regions that French varieties such as Cabernet Sauvignon and Pinot Noir (as a blending component) are being cultivated, to complement native grapes such as Periquita, also known as Castelão Frances. The Alentejo is a home of traditional Portuguese varieties, ripened to hearty strength in the baking summers, and now mostly vinified in modern, EU-funded wineries, rather than the traditional *talhas*, or clay jars.

Rosé

This category includes, of course, Portugal's most famous wine, Mateus, the inspired invention of Salvador Guedes. Perhaps this celebrated brand has squeezed out other, more authentic styles, which are very seldom seen, though Sogrape has once again shown the way with its dry Bairrada rosé, Nobilis.

Sparkling wines
Bairrada produces a good deal of quite competent fizz, hardly ever encountered in the UK.

Pick of the producers
Abrigada, Quinta de Good-quality single-estate red from Alenquer area north of Lisbon.

Almeirim Co-operative Situated in the rich alluvial soils of the Ribatejo, the Almeirim co-op might be content to churn out bog-standard bulk. However, cool fermentation and interesting use of grape varieties, including some Pinot Noir, have made the Leziria wines deservedly popular.

Arruda Good hearty reds from this co-op north of Lisbon.

Bacalhoa, Quinta da Historic estate near Azeitão, making rather tough Cabernet Sauvignon vinified by João Pires, until recently under direction of Peter Bright.

Borba Co-operative One of the admirable co-ops of the rolling, empty Alentejo, which has achieved a dramatic turn-around in quality. Good hearty reds and surprisingly refreshing whites.

Carmo, Quinta do Single estate in the Alentejo, recently purchased by the Rothschilds of Lafite. Promising mellow red.

Carvalho, Ribeiro & Ferreira High-quality merchants specialising in the maturing of fine Garrafeira (see glossary) wines from the Ribatejo.

Champalimaud Maverick Douro producer in the less highly regarded Baixo Corgo who, as well as irritating the British port producers, makes excellent Douro red table wines, Quinta do Côtto and Grande Escolha.

Esporão, Herdade do Huge estate at Reguengos in the Alentejo, recently revitalised under wine-making direction of Australian David Baverstock.

Fonseca, J. M. da Not to be confused with Fonseca International, makers of Lancers, or with the well-known port shipper, this is one of Portugal's best table-wine producers. Especially good Tinto Velho from Rosado Fernandes estate in the Alentejo and successful Cabernet and Periquita blend, Camarate.

Pancas, Quinta de Beautiful estate at Alenquer, north of Lisbon, making promising, oaky Cabernet Vinha Maior, fair Chardonnay and good second-label Quinta de Parrotes.

Pato, Luis Leading producer of red Bairrada, built to last.

Pires, João One of Portugal's most-innovative table-wine producers, based at Palmela near Setúbal. Wine range, including excellent, powerful red Tinto da Anfora and semi-dry white Muscat.

Redondo Co-operative Another admirable Alentejo co-op, making excellent-value reds and whites.

Reguengos de Monsaraz Co-operative Powerful reds from this
Alentejo co-op are among Portugal's best.

Sogrape The Guedes family has not rested on its laurels since
inventing Mateus. This huge but cunningly diversified firm is at the
forefront of developments in Dão (Grão Vasco), the Douro (Villa
Regia and Sogrape Reserva) and Bairrada. Excellent inexpensive
new Vinha do Monte range from Alentejo.

PORT

The great fortified wine of the Douro valley both is and is not a
Portuguese wine. Port, as we know it today, was invented by
British merchants in the seventeenth century. The survival of this
extraordinary, powerful, sweet, dark wine into the late twentieth
century, supposedly an era of lightness (but not sweetness) in all
things, is something of a miracle. Port has, in fact, risen phoenix-
like from the ashes of more than one slump already this century.

After the great boom decade of the 1980s, the 1990s started as a
difficult decade of readjustment in the Douro, with prices slipping
dramatically, to provide great buying bargains for consumers, but
hardly a decent living for farmers. Still, after the longest gap since
the Second World War, 1991 was declared as a vintage by most
major shippers in the summer of 1993. The wines, deep, scented
and brooding, appear to have sold better than many gloomsters
had predicted. Prices of the 1980s vintages, especially 1983, still look
pretty cheap but there has been a dramatic hardening in the price
of the great 1970 vintage. Port has also benefited from the lobbying
of the sherry producers, which has led to a single duty band from
15 to 22 degrees, and also to a progressive reduction of duty on
fortified wines from the beginning of 1993. Port sales actually
boomed in 1993 and 1994, and the biggest increase of all has been
in the, admittedly tiny, vintage port sector. After a terrible 1993
vintage, shippers are expressing barely concealed optimism about
1994 as a very likely general vintage declaration. Once again, port
seems to be bucking the trends and defying the gloomsters.

Styles

White port
This is almost a contradiction in terms, and certainly most white
port is far less interesting to drink than good fino sherry. Attempts
to produce light, dry white port have been misguided. The best

white port is made exactly like red port, but from white grapes, by Niepoort.

Ruby
Ruby is the name for inexpensive red port aged for a couple of years in barrel. It should have youthful attack, fruit and fire, but do not look for complexity or refinement.

Tawny
This confusing term is used for two very different kinds of port. One is cheap and usually blended from white and red port. The other is aged for a considerable time in oak barrels, until it reaches a lovely, fragrant, nutty mellowness. Aged tawny comes in 10-, 20-, 30- and 40-year-old styles: paradoxically, the ideal age for tawny is thought to be 15 years. Some excellent tawnies, such as Delaforce's His Eminence's Choice, Niepoort's Senior and Warre's Nimrod, do not carry a precise age tag. Colheita is a Portuguese style of tawny from a single vintage, bearing both a vintage and a bottling date: do not confuse the two.

Vintage character
This is a dubiously named category since it claims to have the character of a vintage port but, in reality, it is a good-quality ruby.

Late-bottled vintage (LBV)
Late-bottled vintage is an even more controversial style – or rather two styles. This must, of course, be the wine of a single vintage, and all LBV is aged for between four and six years (as opposed to two for true vintage port) in barrel. However, there is a world of difference between most commercial, heavily filtered LBV and the superb, unfiltered traditional LBVs of Warre and Smith Woodhouse.

Crusted
Crusted port really is vintage-style wine (but of course, given the logic of port nomenclature, doesn't say so), unfiltered, but blended from more than one year. This can be excellent value.

Vintage port
Here is the *crème de la crème* of port, the top 2 per cent or so from the best vineyards, bottled after two years in barrel. Only two or three high-quality vintages are 'declared' by each major shipper in a decade. Vintage port repays its purchasers, if they wait for up to twenty years, by delivering one of wine's most overwhelming

experiences – scents of herbs, flowers, fruits and other rich and many-layered flavours. Many shippers make a so-called Single Quinta vintage from a particular farm in non-declared years.

The major port houses

Cálem Up-and-coming Portuguese house making much-improved Vintage, excellent Single Quinta, Quinta do Foz and – a speciality – wonderful old Colheita Tawnies.

Churchill The most recently founded house, a brave venture by John Graham of the family which founded the famous shippers Graham's, now owned by the Symington family. Good-quality, reasonably priced wines, especially Vintage Character.

Cockburn Part of the British Allied group, and best known for the market-leading Special Reserve. Vintages have returned to top form since 1983.

Croft Something of a sleeper among major houses, owned by IDV-Grand Met, and making fragrant, light Vintages and Tawnies.

Delaforce Another house owned by IDV-Grand Met and best known for His Eminence's Choice Tawny.

Dow A top house owned by the ubiquitous Symingtons, with deep, long-lasting Vintage based on grapes from Quinta do Bomfim, now marketed as Single Quinta in non-declared years.

Ferreira A leading Portuguese house owned by Sogrape, making excellent Vintage.

Fonseca Under the inspiring direction of Bruce Guimaraens, this house, part of the Taylor's group, is making arguably the greatest Vintage ports of all. Second label, Guimaraens, for scarcely less good Vintages from non-declared years.

Graham Pride of the Symington stable, and making marvellous, sweet, strawberry-scented Vintage. Single Quinta: Quinta dos Malvedos.

Niepoort Small Portuguese house making hand-crafted wines of great distinction, including powerful Vintage, excellent Vintage Character, superb Colheita, and, a speciality, Garrafeira wines aged in glass demi-johns.

Offley-Forrester Unfairly overlooked house, perhaps because it is owned by Martini. Single Quinta Boa Vista wines are often excellent.

Noval Highly reputed Portuguese shipper recently bought by French AXA-Millésimes company. Owns beautiful Quinta do Noval, which produces feminine, scented Vintage and exceptional Nacional from ungrafted vines.

Ramos-Pinto Innovative Portuguese house especially strong on aged Tawny (10-year-old Quinta da Ervamoira, 20-year-old Quinta do Bom Retiro). Controlled by Louis Roederer.

Real Vinicola/Royal Oporto Controversial, troubled giant Portuguese house, making disappointing light Vintage and fair Tawny.

Rosa, Quinta de la Farm owned by the Bergqvist family and now selling Single Quinta port and good table wine.

Sandeman Seagram-owned house struggling to achieve top quality with Vintage.

Smith Woodhouse Second-division house owned by Symington group which can surprise with excellent Vintage and traditional LBV.

Taylor Most prestigious of all port houses, making fine Vintage and Single Quinta, Quinta de Vargellas.

Warre Top-quality Symington house, making beautiful, blackberry-scented vintage and Single Quinta, Quinta da Cavadinha.

Vintage guide

1992 Declared by Taylor, Fonseca, Niepoort and Delaforce. The best wines, ample and fruity, were made by the houses which delayed picking until the grapes had absorbed much-needed rain in September.
1991 Climatically very dry year declared by most major shippers. Excellent, concentrated wines of perfume and class. Drink from 2010 onwards.
1985 Much-hyped year declared by all major shippers. Priced too high when released, but the best wines, such as Fonseca, Graham, Cockburn, will be magnificent. Drink from 1998 onwards.

1983 Powerful, concentrated wines which will repay keeping.
Initially expensive, but now remarkable value. Warre, Dow,
Graham, Cockburn all excellent. Drink from 1997 onwards.
1980 An underrated vintage, now extraordinarily good value.
Warre, Graham best. Drink from now onwards.
1977 Magnificent vintage declared by almost all major shippers,
excluding Cockburn. Wines still need keeping. Drink from 1997
onwards.
1975 Most disappointing vintage of past 40 years, but best wines,
such as Fonseca, are very agreeable. Drink up.
1970 Magnificent vintage, strangely underrated in early days.
Wines have everything, power, balance, class. Drink from now
onwards.
1966 Very good vintage, firm wines. Taylor very good. Drink up.
1963 Great vintage of huge, massively constituted wines, some of
which still need keeping. Fonseca classic. Drink from now
onwards.

Earlier fine vintages: 1960, 1955, 1948, 1945.

MADEIRA

A few years ago, the wine of Portugal's Atlantic island looked set
on the path to near-oblivion already taken by other fortified wines
such as Marsala and Málaga. By the early 1980s, the vineyards of
the steep, verdant isle had become seriously neglected. According
to Hugh Johnson's estimate, less than 10 per cent of the island's
vineyards were planted with the four noble varieties of Madeira:
Sercial, Verdelho, Bual and Malmsey. The most widely planted
Vitis vinifera variety was Tinta Negra Mole, but more alarming was
the spread of the hybrid Jacquet, outlawed by the EU. Nor was
anyone taking any trouble to give the marvellously tangy, long-
lived, unique wines of Madeira a push in the market-place.

The energetic Symingtons of Oporto took up the challenge: in
1988 they purchased a substantial, later to become controlling,
share in the Madeira Wine Company, previously wholly owned by
the Blandy family. With the Madeira Wine Company, the
Symingtons took control of such famous brands as Blandy's,
Cossart Gordon and Rutherford & Miles.

Better marketing of brands was one step, but the Madeira
problem went deeper. Fortunately, the regional government, with
the help of a team of German viticulturalists, has also been paying
attention to the crucial question of planting the right vines in the
right places. Now the Madeira Wine Company has a new winery
under construction but it has been pipped at the post by the rival

firm of Henriques & Henriques, which opened its new winery in June 1994. Madeira has probably been saved for future generations.

This is wonderful news, because the destruction of madeira would have been one of the worst wine crimes of the twentieth century. These really are irreplaceable wines, with an astonishing combination of richness and tangy freshness. They also cover a surprisingly wide range, from the dry, fine-pointed Sercial through the soft, delicate Verdelho to the rich, yet superbly balanced, Bual and Malmsey.

STYLES AND VARIETIES

The naming of madeira styles is being given close attention by bureaucrats in Brussels. What had happened was that the names of varieties were used to denote styles of wine which very often did not contain a single grape of the stated variety – hardly surprising, since the proportion of Madeira's vineyards planted with the four noble grapes had declined so catastrophically. The EU rule is that any varietal wine should contain at least 85 per cent of that variety. Madeira has got to do some catching up, at speed.

Basic styles of madeira are usually around three years old. The next step up in quality is the 5-year-old, followed by the 10-year-old. There is often a very dramatic step up in quality between the 5- and 10-year-old wines, more than justifying the price jump. After this come the very rare Solera and Vintage wines, which sometimes take over 50 years to reach maturity. Traditionally, these are not subjected to the *estufagem*, or heating, which gives most madeira wines their slightly burnt character.

Sercial
This is the driest style of madeira, which, when made from the Sercial grape, should have racy elegance and refinement, as well as the ability to age decades.

Verdelho
Verdelho wines are softer and slightly richer than Sercials, but can be deceptively powerful. Some of the greatest vintage madeiras are made from this variety. Cheap Verdelho is simply a medium-sweet wine made from Tinta Negra Mole.

Bual
These wines are rich, but the best have a marvellous cheesy tang which balances the sweetness.

Malmsey
This, the most famous of madeira styles and grapes, is also the sweetest. Again, the best examples have tremendous cleansing acidity.

CENTRAL AND EASTERN EUROPE

AUSTRIA

Austrian wine deserves both our sympathy and our serious interest. The so-called anti-freeze scandal of 1985 damaged exports of Austrian wine much more profoundly than the infinitely more serious Italian scandal – the murderous methanol affair – affected the wines of Italy. Fortunately, that whole story is a thing of the past. Austria has some of Europe's most stringent wine regulations (reducing yields in 1986 and again in 1991), but, even more important, Austria can offer some unique and attractive wines in several different styles: dry white, sweet white and red. At the moment, retailers are having some success selling Austrian wines at very low prices – around £3.50 – but finding it much harder to persuade punters to pay more, even though they would be amply rewarded, and, as always, would get much more wine value for their money. Here is a wine country which calls out to be explored, especially by those whose tastes extend beyond Chardonnay and Cabernet.

Although Austrians speak German, their country is historically and culturally much closer to Hungary and other parts of the former Austro-Hungarian Empire. This is also true of the wine and even the climate. Austria may be relatively northerly, but the climate is continental, and summers are hot enough to ripen black grapes consistently. Austrian wines are not so much Germanic as central European in style – fiery, hearty and full-bodied. One of Austria's great attractions is the spicy white Grüner Veltliner, an ideal partner to the paprika-spiked dishes which form the Magyar strain of the national cuisine. Austria's red wines are surprisingly good and certainly not pallid weaklings. Perhaps the country's greatest wine endowment is the microclimate of the broad, shallow Neusiedlersee, which encourages noble rot as reliably as any place in the world.

Altogether, Austria's medium-sized wine industry has a great deal to offer the curious consumer. Not the least important aspect of that industry is a small group of perfectionist, and sometimes eccentric, wine producers, prepared to be innovative and determined to push quality to its limits.

Wine styles, varieties and regions

Dry white wines
Austria's main strength lies in its white wines, made from an
intriguing spread of grape varieties. Grüner Veltliner, not the
easiest grape to vinify, but most attractive at its best, has already
been mentioned. The Pinots, Blanc and Gris (alias Weissburgunder
and Rülander), both flourish, and sometimes attain quite
frightening degrees of alcohol. Riesling is a relative newcomer, but
is showing exciting steely form in the steep vineyards facing the
Danube in the Wachau and also in Kamptal-Donauland. Among
other varieties, Gewürztraminer (or plain Traminer) and
Muskateller have more chance of distinctiveness than the
ubiquitous Chardonnay and Sauvignon.

Sweet white wines

Luscious botrytis-affected wines made from a cocktail of varieties, including Bouvier and Muskat-Ottonel, are produced on the shores of the Neusiedlersee. Austrian categories of sweetness are slightly different from the German, and demand higher levels of ripeness: there is an extra category, Ausbruch, between Beerenauslese and Trockenbeerenauslese. Some of these wines are just too sweet and sickly; the best have a backbone of acidity.

Red wines

Austria's reds may never mount a major challenge on the international stage, but the best are seriously good. Blauer Zweigelt is a man-made cross, usually vinified in a light, quaffing, 'Beaujolais-esque' style, emphasising cherry fruit, but capable of considerable depth when matured in oak. St-Laurent, one of the parents of Zweigelt, is perhaps Austria's most interesting black grape, tricky to grow but capable of real complexity and distinction. Blauburgunder, the Austrian name for Pinot Noir, shows some promise, as does Cabernet Sauvignon. Some of Austria's best reds are *cuvées* of different varieties. Other black grapes cultivated include the lighter Blaufränkisch, which can show lovely cherry flavours, and Blauer Portugieser.

Pick of the producers

Heinrich Powerful, quite serious oak-aged Blauer Zweigelt is a speciality of this Neusiedlersee producer.

Klosterneuburg Famous abbey and also wine college and estate north of Vienna, which markets exciting St-Laurent Domäne.

Kracher, Alois Wacky pharmacist and immodest part-time producer of equally eccentric and sometimes brilliant botrytised wines.

Lenz Moser Large dynastic family firm which sells a wide range, from reasonably priced if unexciting Grüner Veltliner to high-priced Bordeaux blend from the Knights of Malta estate in Mailberg.

Loiben Very fine Riesling from this Wachau co-operative.

Mullner Excellent producer of both white and red wines, especially soft, Muscat-scented Grüner Veltliner and subtle Blauer Zweigelt.

Muster Remarkably good, intense yet ripe Sauvignon.

Opitz, Willi Austria's leading eccentric and part-time producer of marvellously intense Neusiedlersee sweet wines.

Pöckl Serious producer of red wines, including Pinot Noir and Cuvée Admiral Barrique, good but over-oaked.

Salomon, Fritz Conscientious producer of fine steely Riesling and Traminer from the great Steiner Hund vineyard in Kamptal-Donauland.

Seewinkler Impressionen Artistic labels should not distract attention from this enterprising co-op's splendidly rich Neusiedlersee dessert wines, made in distinctive, quite oxidative, style.

SWITZERLAND

Some fine Swiss wines are made from the country's 1400 or so hectares of vineyards. Of these, the most commonly seen (hardly at all in the UK, it must be said) are the reds from Pinot Noir and Gamay – often blended together and called Dôle – which come from the Valais, the mountain-guarded upper part of the Rhône valley. Chasselas is the most common white variety. Swiss wines are almost always fresh, lightish and expensive.

LUXEMBOURG

Before reaching its stretch of glory between Trier and Koblenz in western Germany, the river Mosel (or Moselle) passes through Luxembourg. Luxembourg wines have much in common with those of the German Mosel, but generally lack the piercing distinction of flavour of the best German Mosels. Grape varieties are partly to blame: the Luxembourgeois have planted a good deal of Müller-Thurgau (Rivaner) and Elbling, and not much Riesling. Decent tank-method sparkling wine from Luxembourg is imported by one or two UK merchants, including Eldridge Pope.

EASTERN EUROPE

A whirlwind of change is sweeping through the wine industries of the former Soviet bloc countries, including Russia itself and Moldova. This change needs to be seen in the context of more general political and economic upheaval. At the moment, there are winners and losers. Among the former, Hungary stands out, no surprise to those aware of Hungary's long-standing wine culture and also the country's relative enthusiasm in embracing free-market capitalism (despite the recent election victory of the socialists). Bulgaria, the great wine-exporting success story of the Communist bloc, is going through an uncertain period, which includes the virtual disappearance of its largest export market, and the subsequent grubbing up (pulling up) of many vineyards. Moldova has made a surprising entrance on to the international scene, as a result of investment from the Australian giant, Penfolds. The losers include the countries of the tragically war-torn former Yugoslavia, except for Slovenia, and Russia itself. Eastern Europe can still offer some remarkable wine bargains; we are just beginning to see the signs of emerging quality.

BULGARIA

The Bulgarian wine industry has had some serious rethinking to do following the collapse of the Russian export market, to which so much of its production was geared. Bulgarian wine, especially the ubiquitous plummy Cabernet Sauvignon, remains an important player in the UK market, but a move up-market, promised by some importers, is scarcely evident at the moment. The much-trumpeted privatisation of some wineries and the establishment of an independent importing company, Domaine Boyar, may in due course yield improved results. The newly privatised Lovico Suhindol winery looks promising, especially for Merlot. Perhaps the most exciting development of the past couple of years has been pioneered by the supermarket chain Safeway, which has persuaded a winery in the Russe region to vinify Merlot and Cabernet Sauvignon in sealed vats. These vibrantly fruity wines are quite a revelation, and other Bulgarian wineries would be crazy not to follow suit. Bulgarian whites continue to disappoint – though Kym Milne's international-style versions available from Thresher are much better than most – and higher quality levels such as Controliran and Reserve offer, in the main, tired, clumsily oaked veterans when the market calls out for vigorous young warriors.

HUNGARY

At the moment, Hungary is some way ahead of the other Eastern European countries in wine development. A Hungarian would probably tell you there was nothing new in that: Hungary has an appetising spread of native and imported varieties and produces one of the world's most famous wines, Tokay. For all this, the Hungarian wine industry is in a period of flux. Like Bulgaria, Hungary relied heavily on exports to the former USSR. Now that these have dried up it is estimated that the vineyard area may contract from 130,000 hectares to around 80,000. Formerly state-owned wineries are being rapidly privatised. If the future lies in increased home consumption and exports to the West, the omens, so far, are encouraging. Exports to the UK are currently forging ahead. As substantial investment from abroad, including France, Germany, Spain and Italy, enters the Hungarian wine industry, the question will be whether Hungary follows the international, Chardonnay and Cabernet route or, like Portugal, remains faithful to local traditions. A mixture of the two looks likely and no doubt desirable.

Classification system

Hungary's equivalent to *appellation contrôlée* is Minőségi Bor (quality wine).

Wine styles and varieties

White wines
Hungary, like Austria, is predominantly a white wine country, though its leading export wine, until recently, was the red Bulls Blood. It has a number of interesting and unusual white varieties, including Furmint, Hárslevelü and Kéknyelü, but we are more likely to encounter international-style Sauvignon Blanc and Chardonnay vinified by travelling British or Antipodean winemakers such as Hugh Ryman (Gyöngyös estate) or Kym Milne (the Chapel Hill range for Balatonboglar). The 1994 vintage

produced some excellent fresh whites. Hungary's greatest wine is Tokay, made from botrytis-affected Furmint, Hárslevelü and Yellow Muscat grapes in the north-east corner of the country. Tokay can be both dry and sweet: the intense, long-lived dry version is called Szamarodni (though Szamarodni can also be sweet). Sweet Tokay, which should always be balanced by intense acidity, comes in different grades or Puttonyos, named after the container for adding Aszú or nobly rotten grapes to the rest. Five Puttonyos (Putts for short) means a very sweet, concentrated wine. The highest grade of all is called Eszencia. Tokay has recently been revitalised by foreign investment: Jean-Michel Cazes of AXA, Jean-Michel Arcaute of Château Clinet, Vega Sicilia of Spain and the British-Danish Royal Tokay Wine Company are all making Tokay in a more or less modern, non-oxidative style. The best sweet wines from the 1993 vintage, especially from Disznoko (the AXA label) and Châteaux Megyer and Pajzos (the two labels of Arcaute's GAN company) are splendidly pure, lush yet fresh. The dry white Furmint, Chardonnay and Oremus from Château Megyer and Disznoko are also mouth-filling and distinctive.

Red wines
Hungary makes good red wine from a mixture of grapes, including the local Kékfrankos and Nagyburgundi, as well as French stars such as Cabernet Sauvignon, Cabernet Franc and Merlot. The Cabernets from Balatonboglar are particularly impressive, more refined and structured than all but the very best from Bulgaria.

MOLDOVA

This newly independent state bordering Romania has come into the international wine spotlight mainly as a result of a joint venture linking Hugh Ryman and the largest Australian firm, Penfolds, with the large state farm at Hincesti. Moldova has vast plantings of Cabernet Sauvignon, as well as some Chardonnay and Pinot Noir, most of which used to go to Moscow. Some of the older Cabernets, rather like good, old-fashioned *cru bourgeois* claret, caused a stir when they appeared over here a couple of years ago. They represented the last of the *ancien régime*; the new wave comes in familiar, Ryman-style, fresh and fruity, and sometimes oaky, whites – some made from the most interesting local variety, Rkatsiteli – and lightish reds. It is still early days and various problems have needed to be tackled, including the disappearance of large quantities of grapes just before the vintage. However, the potential, for decent whites and very good reds, certainly exists. The

Chardonnays are showing progress, with 1994 the best yet, surprisingly big and rich.

ROMANIA

Romania undoubtedly has the potential to make excellent wines. Even under the despised and corrupt regime of Nicola Ceauşescu, decent Cabernet Sauvignons, Pinot Noirs and waxy-sweet white Tamaioasas were coming out of the relatively modern vineyards and wineries of the Dealul Mare region. Unfortunately, little progress appears to have been made politically since Ceauşescu's demise, and the prognosis for the wines must be more of the same – unambitious, reasonably good value plonk – for the time being.

SLOVAKIA AND CZECH LANDS

Slovakia is the warmest and, in wine terms, most interesting part of the former Czechoslovakia. Angela Muir (the British MW, merchant and consultant) has been involved in developments and good red St-Laurent and white Pinot Blanc show promise.

SLOVENIA AND FORMER YUGOSLAVIA

Slovenia, unaffected by the bloody conflicts in the rest of former Yugoslavia, continues to churn out the popular, semi-sweet Lutomer Laski Rizling and dull, cardboardy Pinot Blanc and Chardonnay. Reds from the Istrian peninsula in Croatia and from Macedonia are also seen, but do not compare favourably with the international competition.

ENGLAND AND WALES

English and Welsh wine has progressed in the past twenty years from being the expensive hobby of a few retired majors to the status of a respectable, small pioneering industry. The pioneers have needed a Job-like patience in the face of adversity – mainly the obvious adverse weather, but also a testing combination of public indifference and bureaucratic obstruction.

There are now over 1000 hectares of vines, producing, in 1993, over 1.7 million litres of wine – not much in French or Italian terms, less, in fact, than the production of a single Beaujolais *cru*, but still enough to trigger a Brussels ban on further planting. Most of the vines are German crossings designed for cool conditions, so the wines tend towards flowery aromas and thin body. Recently, the larger producers have been attempting to bring greater body and richness to the wines, using a combination of different grape varieties (including Chardonnay) and oak. At the moment, the future of the quality-wine scheme introduced in 1991, mainly in a vain attempt to avoid the ban on further planting, is uncertain. Currently, the English wine producers are up in arms over a proposed EU scheme to raise the minimum levels of natural alcohol from 5 to 6 per cent for table wine and 6 to 7.5 per cent for quality wine, and, at the same time, to reduce the permitted level of natural sugars used in wine-making (chaptalisation), possibly to 2 per cent. They say that up to half the English grape crop might fail to reach these levels. The unkindest cut of all, surely, is the crazy situation brought about by the British government, which means that English wine is cheaper to buy in Calais than in Sussex.

Grape varieties and styles

Müller-Thurgau is by far the most widely planted variety in England and Wales, covering some 250 hectares. In cool English conditions this Riesling-Silvaner cross can produce dry white wines which combine flowery aroma with good acidity – less flabby than much German Müller. Seyval Blanc is technically a hybrid grape, and therefore banned under EU quality-wine regulations, but it proves the stupidity of bureaucrats by delivering some of the best, dry, Loire-like English wine. Other varieties planted in England include the remarkably rich Schönburger, Reichensteiner, Madeleine Angevine, Pinot Noir (used to make one of the only English reds), Chasselas and Chardonnay. Given England's cool conditions, Pinot Noir and Chardonnay are probably best employed in making sparkling wine – after all, the southern English downs have very similar soil structure, and not dissimilar weather, to Champagne.

Pick of the producers

Breaky Bottom Wonderful perfectionist producer of dry, age-worthy Seyval and Müller-Thurgau in a hollow of the Sussex Downs.

Bruisyard Delicately scented medium-dry whites from Suffolk.

Carr-Taylor Commercially successful range of dry and medium-dry whites and *méthode-traditionelle* sparkler.

Denbies Estate Largest vineyard in England (250 acres), near Dorking, producing good, consistent dry white from mixture of grapes.

Lamberhurst For years the leading English vineyard, making good dry white from Müller-Thurgau, Seyval, Schönburger, and *méthode-traditionelle* sparkler.

Sharpham Remarkably full-bodied dry white from Devon.

Tenterden Serious producer of good range, especially Seyval.

Thames Valley Former Penfolds winemaker John Worontschak makes cleverly crafted dry white and red wine, using some oak, from vineyards near Twyford, and also from bought-in grapes under other labels such as Stanlake.

Three Choirs Leading producer of sweeter-style wines, from Gloucester, Hereford and Worcester vineyards.

THE EASTERN MEDITERRANEAN

GREECE

Where are the heavenly nectars celebrated by the Greek lyric poets and enjoyed by the gods on Olympus? Most Greek wine today seems a sorry disappointment, not just to those brought up on the classics but also compared to wine from other EU countries in the southern Mediterranean. There are exceptions: Château Carras, which created the Côtes du Meliton (note the French style) appellation in Halkidiki, makes excellent Bordeaux-lookalikes from Cabernet Sauvignon, and the firm of Boutari puts most other Greek producers to shame, with pleasantly fresh whites and solid reds. The sweet Muscat of Samos is reasonable, if oily. Finally, there is Retsina, Greece's most distinctive contribution to modern wine, made with the addition of pine resin. Some of the best comes from the Peloponnese.

CYPRUS

Cyprus is a significant exporter of wine – indeed, exports account for 75 per cent of Cyprus wine. Much of this is Cyprus 'sherry', heavy and medium-sweet. There is also Cyprus' most famous historic wine, the sweet, raisiny, brown Commandaria. The quality of the ordinary table wines, white and red, is hardly exciting, though the modern firm of Keo at Limassol makes acceptable, hearty red (Othello) and less impressive white (Aphrodite).

TURKEY

Turkey has a vast acreage of vineyards, but almost all the grapes go for table consumption. Turkish wine, surprisingly you might think in an overwhelmingly Islamic country, does exist and can be quite good, especially the Villa Doluca label. The red includes some Cabernet Sauvignon.

LEBANON

Peace seems to have returned to this beautiful small country. Serge Hochar's Château Musar must now compete for media attention simply on the basis of its quality and value for money. Hochar makes several blends, of which the mainly Cabernet Sauvignon Musar, designed to be aged for a decade and more, is the flagship. This wine develops wonderful gamey aromas. There is also a *tradition* blend, with a higher percentage of Cinsault, softer and lighter and meant to be drunk sooner.

ISRAEL

Israeli wine used to be peculiarly unpleasant, partly as a result of being boiled to comply with kosher regulations. One excellent winery, Yarden, has emerged in the cool Golan Heights, which Israel won from Syria after the 1967 war. California wine-making and intelligent marketing have created a fine range of international varietals, with especially good Yarden Cabernet Sauvignon and Chardonnay. The Gamla label is used for lighter but still well-made wines.

AUSTRALIA

The Australian wagon has turned into a juggernaut. In the past
nine years imports of Australian wine into the UK have increased
from under one million litres (barely a blip in the statistics) to over
50 million litres. Granted, the extraordinary rates of growth
registered in the late 1980s and early 1990s slowed down markedly
in 1994, but this was bound to come some time. Australia, from
being the target of Monty Python ridicule in the 1970s, has become
the wine country most admired and feared by competitors. The
rate of growth of imports may have slowed down in 1994, but the
average price of a bottle of Australian wine rose to over £4 – a
figure most countries could only dream about. The only real
problems experienced recently by Australia have been caused by
shortage – a sequence of drought-affected vintages leading to
inability to meet demand. The new vineyard plantings due to come
on stream in the next two or three years should help to ease this
difficulty.

What does Australia have that other wine countries do not?
There are three things: reliable sun, pragmatism, and – until very
recently – the absence of regulatory control. The Australian wine
industry, in its current form, is extremely young. Table wine
production only overtook fortified wine production in 1970; at that
time there was not a single Chardonnay vine in South Australia.
Lack of appellation control (except in Mudgee) meant that the big
companies which control most of Australian wine were able to
assess what the market wanted and plant, or graft over,
accordingly.

The Australian wine industry, despite a few ups and downs,
continues to spot what the market is looking for. It delivers simply
styled wines full of ripe, primary fruit flavours, and, where
appropriate, the vanillin spice of new oak. Although the
Californians were there before them, it is the Australians who have
succeeded in cutting the Gordian knot of wine snobbery, showing
millions of Britons that you do not need to have been to Oxbridge
to enjoy wine. In reducing complexity, however, have they also
removed much of the magical mystique of wine? Fortunately, that
is a question which the most far-sighted of the Australian wine-

growers and winemakers are asking themselves. The important commercial question is whether pressure on supply may price Australian wines out of some markets. Some British supermarkets are already expressing doubts about Australia's continuing ability to deliver the value for money which has made Australia's name.

GRAPE VARIETIES *VERSUS* VINEYARD SITES

Australian wine is firmly based on grape varieties. Chardonnay, Cabernet Sauvignon, Shiraz, Semillon, Sauvignon Blanc and certain others have proved remarkably easy and successful points of recognition for a limited number of basic wine styles. Varietals are clear and simple; combined with Australia's reliable climate and high-tech, industrialised wine industry they also inspire confidence. If you buy a bottle of Australian Chardonnay you pretty much know what you are getting. You are unlikely to be disappointed, as, sadly, you so often will be when you buy an unknown name from France or Italy. The only worry is that, after a while, you might become bored.

This is not too much of a worry, after all. For Australia has impressive, individualistic, widely scattered riches to offer, if you become sated with the standard, mass-produced styles. A remarkable fact about the Australian wine industry has always been that the very biggest companies produce some of the greatest wines – Penfolds' Grange Hermitage, Lindemans' Pyrus and old Hunter Semillons, Orlando's St Hugo. That continues to be the case, but in the past few years the smaller Australian wineries, based in particular localities, have come increasingly to the fore. Such producers are aware of the intimate connections between grape-growing and wine-making. They no longer subscribe to the old Promethean myth of the winemaker as hero, able to transform neutral base material, trucked in from god-knows-where, into great wine by computer-controlled wizardry. Instead, they are mindful of the special qualities of microclimates (cool ones especially), the importance of low yields and the undesirability of chemical fertilisers and pesticides. They are the essential pioneers and pathfinders for the whole industry.

Meanwhile, Australia has signed the long-awaited bilateral wine agreement with the EU. This means that Australia will phase out certain European wine names for Australian products, such as Chablis, Burgundy, Beaujolais, Chianti etc., and, in return, will secure important concessions, such as the right to export botrytis-affected wines and the recognition of Australian sparkling wine as quality wine. This is also a significant step towards appellation control, since the agreement stipulates that 85 per cent of each wine labelled as a single varietal or single regional wine must come from that variety or be sourced from that region. There are likewise precise stipulations for multi-varietal and multi-regional blends. At the time of writing, a system of Geographical Indications is under construction, but it seems likely that this will resemble the Californian AVA (approved viticultural areas) scheme more than the prescriptive European systems of appellation control.

Wine styles and grape varieties

White wines

Most Australian vineyards are situated in warm areas. For white wines, in particular, this poses problems. Innate fruit balance and complexity, necessary for the greatest white wines, are difficult, if not impossible, to achieve when temperatures are torrid. The leading intellectuals in the Australian wine industry, such as Brian Croser, James Halliday, Adam Wynn and Andrew Pirie, are united in their search for cool-climate vineyards. All the same, it is remarkable how good the Chardonnays, Semillons and even Rieslings from hot regions such as the Hunter, Barossa and Clare Valleys have been and continue to be.

Chardonnay is, of course, the most fashionable white grape, and Australian Chardonnay is the most fashionable kind of Chardonnay. Much Australian Chardonnay continues to be big, bold, rich, ripe and oaky. However, the country's most sophisticated winemakers increasingly seek subtlety of fruit and moderation in the use of oak, a tendency which has culminated in Shaw and Smith's Unoaked Chardonnay.

Semillon is in many ways a more interesting grape, in Australian terms, than Chardonnay. Semillon either from the Hunter Valley or from Margaret River is quite unlike anything else in the wine world – the former gaining incredible lanolin and lemon richness with age, the latter being fascinatingly subtle and leafy. Semillon is also widely blended, with Chardonnay, Riesling and Sauvignon, to make very palatable commercial wines.

Riesling was until very recently the most widely planted white grape in Australia, and continues to be responsible for many of the country's greatest wines. Top-quality Australian Riesling, after years out of fashion, is enjoying a comeback, at least in Australia. Rieslings such as Petaluma, Delatite, Mitchelton and Mitchells, though more full-bodied than their European counterparts, age brilliantly and are just coming to their limey, oily best at an age when most Chardonnays have fallen apart.

Only a few Australian producers have succeeded in making Sauvignon Blanc of aromatic flair. More interesting is the Rhône variety Marsanne, which makes powerful, original whites in central Victoria. Australia has large plantings of Muscat and Trebbiano, used mainly for bulk wine, and some Chenin, which looks promising in Western Australia.

Red wines

Australia's heat, you would think, would be more of a boon for red wine-making than white. The grape which most enjoys it is Shiraz, strangely undervalued and often employed for undemanding bulk production, though also responsible for the country's greatest, most complex and long-lived wines, Grange and Henschke's Hill of Grace and Mount Edelstone.

The received wisdom is that the best Cabernet Sauvignon comes from the relatively cool vineyards of Coonawarra, though many examples taste excessively vegetal and austere. Big, burly Cabernet comes from McLaren Vale, intense minty versions from Central Victoria, and subtle, silky examples from Margaret River and the Yarra Valley. Cabernet and Shiraz combine magnificently in blends which fill out Cabernet's hollow middle with the caramelly richness of Shiraz. Merlot is strangely uncommon, though the occasional example such as Grant Burge's highly attractive plummy version from the Barossa is sometimes to be found.

The quest for the perfect Pinot Noir has led winemakers to two special spots – the Yarra Valley near Melbourne and northern Tasmania. The results are highly promising.

Australia's considerable plantings of Grenache were until recently considered something of an embarrassment, until Charlie Melton and Rocky O'Callaghan produced their marvellously seductive versions. Mataro (aka Mourvèdre) is another unfashionable southern grape which may yet be revived.

Sparkling and fortified wines

Australia is becoming increasingly well known as a producer of good, medium-priced, as well as some excellent high-priced, sparkling wine, much of it made from Chardonnay and Pinot Noir. Once again, cool-climate complexity is at a premium, and the very best sparklers, such as Domaine Chandon's Green Point Vineyards and Croser, come from the cool Yarra Valley and Adelaide Hills. A different approach is shown by Seppelt's Salinger, which features typically Australian ripeness. Fortified wine is Australia's traditional strength, now ironically undervalued, though the liqueur Muscats of Rutherglen have a connoisseur following.

Regions

South Australia – warm *versus* cool-climate viticulture

South Australia is far and away the most important wine state, producing half of Australia's wine. The state's vineyards go from one extreme to the other, from the very hot, flat, irrigated vineyards of Riverland, which churn out the bulk, to the very cool, marginal, top-quality area of Coonawarra, a cigar-shaped strip of special red soil in the far south-east which produces many of Australia's greatest Cabernets. In between come areas such as McLaren Vale, the cool Adelaide Hills and the warm and historic Barossa and Clare valleys. South Australia, in effect, has everything that a wine country could want, and excels in all leading varieties. For good measure, it is also home to such seminal winemakers as Brian Croser and Adam Wynn, and to Australia's leading wine school, Roseworthy College.

The area is one of the centres of the controversy over the best climates for grape-growing. For nearly two decades, Brian Croser has been insisting on cool growing sites for certain varieties. His Piccadilly winery is situated in the cool, damp Adelaide Hills, and he now sources all the fruit for his famous Chardonnay and his increasingly successful *méthode traditionelle* Croser from his own Piccadilly vineyards. Not far away, Adam Wynn, with his Mountadam winery high on the wind-scoured Eden Ridge, needs to employ more land in preserving water than in farming grapes.

The Barossa Valley is one of Australia's most historic wine regions, home to the Barossadeutsch, Australia's answer to the horny-handed French *vignerons*. The Barossa is hardly cool, but it has always made great wines, especially from Shiraz, and now has a group of splendidly individualistic small-scale producers (Charlie Melton, Rockford, St-Hallett) determined to prove they can match any Australian region for quality.

New South Wales comes second after South Australia in terms of wine production, but it contains probably Australia's most famous wine area, the Hunter Valley, north of Sydney (fortunately, spared significant damage by the terrible bush fires of 1993). Despite the fact that most of New South Wales is pretty warm, white grapes outnumber black by roughly three to one. Hunter Valley Semillon is, with Shiraz, Australia's most distinctive wine style. We fervently hope that following Penfolds' takeover of Lindemans in 1990, Lindemans' tradition of ageing top Hunter Semillon for up to 20 years will be continued. The Hunter was also the area where Australian Chardonnay first saw the light of day, in the form of Murray Tyrrell's 1971 Pinot Chardonnay (sic) Vat 47. Tyrrell's wine and others which followed established the deep-yellow, rich, bananas-and-cream style of Australian Chardonnay which is still the most familiar.

Mudgee; Murrumbidgee Irrigation Area; Cowra Mudgee is a little-known, interesting and anomalous wine region in the hills west of Sydney. The interest is, especially, in the deep powerful reds, from Cabernet Sauvignon and Shiraz (though Chardonnay can be excellent too); the anomaly is the extremely tight system of appellation control devised and run by the Mudgee producers. The irrigated plains of the Murrumbidgee Irrigation Area, Australia's second-largest, warm, bulk-producing region after Riverland, could hardly present a more different picture, though De Bortoli's botrytis-affected Semillon, now free to enter the EU, is of exciting quality. Finally, Cowra, south of Mudgee, produces luscious, ripe Chardonnay of such high quality that Brian Croser formerly employed it for Petaluma Chardonnay.

Victoria
Victoria is in many ways Australia's most diverse and exciting wine state. Its wine industry, once Australia's largest, has fluctuated in fortune, and took a very long time to recover from the combined blows of the end of the gold rush and the coming of phylloxera. Now, Victorian wine is very much back in business, with a wealth of offerings from the good-value bulk production of Sunraysia/Mildura (the Victorian segment of the Murray River irrigation scheme) to the boutique wineries of the Yarra Valley.

Warm regions – North-west and North-east Victoria The hot, flat, irrigated Murray River region, as in the South Australian and New South Wales sections, produces thousands of tons of sound, ripe fruit, largely for sultanas. There are, surprisingly, only 342 hectares of Chardonnay in this region. North-eastern Victoria, though also hot, is different wine country, best-known for the production of marvellous fortified Muscat.

Central Victoria – Goulbourn Valley, Bendigo, Pyrenees, Great Western These diverse regions produce fine table wines – Mitchelton and Chateau Tahbilk in the Goulbourn representing new and old schools – and, in the cool Great Western ranges, excellent Chardonnay base wine for some of Australia's finest sparklers.

Around Melbourne – Yarra Valley, Mornington Peninsula, Geelong
The cool wine-growing regions around the state capital of

Melbourne are experiencing a major revival. In the lead, both for quality and publicity, are the boutique wineries of the Yarra Valley, such as Yarra Yering, Coldstream Hills and Yeringberg. The Mornington Peninsula, not far from the bungaloid sprawl of Melbourne's southern suburbs, presents a less certain picture. Pressure on land from developers and resulting high prices have created economic difficulties for leading wine-growers such as Garry Crittenden.

Western Australia

This is a country – almost a continent – in itself. Europeans find it hard to imagine the sheer scale of this slice of land – roughly ten times the size of Britain – not to mention its isolation from the rest of the country. The Western Australian wine industry is of modest proportions, but in the Margaret River region it scales the heights of quality. Perhaps because of its isolation, Western Australia breeds some of Australia's most proudly individualistic wine-growers, epitomised by the Cullen family, David Hohnen of Cape Mentelle and Keith Mugford of Moss Wood. Apart from Margaret River, the huge Lower Great Southern Region features fine producers such as Goundrey and Plantagenet, the Swan Valley near Perth houses important wineries such as Houghton and Sandalford, and a few bold pioneers are producing warm, silky wines from the gum-cloaked Perth Hills.

The rest of Australia – Tasmania, Queensland

The island state of Tasmania provides Australia's ultimate opportunities for cool-climate wine-growing. Some see a perversity in deliberately seeking such hardship, but the best, super-fine Chardonnays and Pinot Noirs from Pipers Brook and Heemskerk, appear to justify the risk.

Queensland's Granite Belt is at the other extreme, though high altitude tempers the heat. Wines are promising but have yet to establish a consistent style.

Pick of the Australian wineries

Berri-Renmano-Hardy's Mega-conglomerate resulting from 1992 merger between Berri-Renmano, the huge Riverland co-operative, and Hardy's, one of Australia's largest and proudest wine companies. A bewildering range of wines, from inexpensive Riverland plonk to that ultimate in Australian refinement, Eileen Hardy Chardonnay. Houghtons in Western Australia is also part of the group, making excellent white Supreme and the new, oak-touched Moondah Brook Chenin Blanc.

Brown Brothers Long-established family winery in northern Victoria making sound varietals, including new Beaujolais-lookalike Tarrango.

Cape Mentelle Idiosyncratic Margaret River winery run by David Hohnen of New Zealand's Cloudy Bay fame, now owned by Veuve Clicquot. Austere but age-worthy Cabernets, delicious Semillon and Zinfandel.

Chandon, Domaine Moët offshoot in Yarra Valley, run by talented Tony Jordan, and now producing perhaps the New World's best fizz, Green Point Vineyards.

Coldstream Hills Top-quality Yarra Valley winery specialising in Chardonnay and Pinot Noir (perhaps Australia's best), run by wine writer James Halliday.

Cullens Top-quality yet splendidly eccentric Margaret River winery run by self-taught Di Cullen and winemaker daughter Vanya. Powerful, flavoursome Cabernet, Chardonnay and Sauvignon Blanc.

Goundrey Enterprising winery in the sheep country of Mount Barker, Western Australia. Very good Cabernet and Chardonnay.

Heemskerk Small Tasmanian winery specialising in lean, lemony Chardonnay.

Henschke Most experts' choice as finest small winery in Australia. Magnificently consistent range, especially Mount Edelstone and Hill of Grace Shiraz, and Semillon, from Eden Valley in South Australia.

Knappstein, Tim Intelligent, talented winemaker based in Clare Valley, making superb long-lived Riesling and fine Chardonnay. Company once part of Blass, now owned by Petaluma.

Leeuwin Showpiece Margaret River estate, specialising in splendidly long-lived Chardonnay. Cabernet less consistent.

Lehmann, Peter Improving range made by Barossa winemaker from bought-in fruit.

Lindemans Now part of Penfolds' group, and the subject of much reorganisation. Very good value Bin 65 Chardonnay, more expensive Padthaway Chardonnay and remarkably lean, Frenchified Coonawarra Cabernet and Shiraz (Limestone Ridge, St George, Pyrus) unlikely to be affected by changes. Subsidiary brand Rouge Homme.

McWilliams Famous Hunter Valley company with greatly improved, competitively priced range.

Melton, Charles A laconic individualist of the Barossa, specialising in Grenache-based Nine Popes and marvellous Shiraz, both still and sparkling, all from old, dry-farmed vineyards.

Mildara-Blass Merger between Mildara and Wolf Blass, the former with holdings split between Riverland and Coonawarra, the latter a flamboyant master-blender of supple, oaky reds.

Mitchelton Underrated, modern winery in Goulbourn Valley, central Victoria, with consistent range, especially superb limey Riesling and minty Cabernet.

Moss Wood Brilliant, small Margaret River winery making marvellously opulent Chardonnay, subtle oaked Semillon and suave, silky Cabernet and Pinot Noir.

Mountadam Exciting Eden Ridge, South Australia, estate winery of multi-talented Adam Wynn. Very burgundian, barrel-fermented Chardonnay, and fine Pinot Noir. David Wynn range of reliable, though not always exciting, mid-priced varietals from bought-in fruit. Some wines are organic.

Mount Langi Ghiran Remote winery in Great Western, Victoria, making magnificent peppery Shiraz and fine Riesling.

Orlando Huge Barossa-based company of awesome reliability. Jacobs Creek range irreproachably sound, St-Hilary Chardonnay and St-Hugo Cabernet both excellent. Also owns large Wyndham Estate group based in Hunter Valley.

Penfolds Now the largest presence in Australian wine, owned by South Australian Brewing Company since 1990. Runs from cheap and cheerful own-label to the summits of Bin 707 Cabernet and Grange, with too many labels to list in between. Whites used to be much less good than reds, now improving fast (good Coonawarra Chardonnay). Pioneering Organic Chardonnay/Sauvignon introduced in 1993.

Petaluma Highly respected winery of Brian Croser, Australia's most intellectually gifted winemaker. Superb Riesling from Clare Valley, meticulously crafted Chardonnay from Adelaide Hills, red Coonawarra and sparkling Croser, made from Adelaide Hills Chardonnay and Pinot Noir. Second label: Bridgewater Mill.

Pipers Brook Fine-tuned Tasmanian winery of academic Dr Andrew Pirie, specialising in lean Chardonnay and Pinot Noir.

Plantagenet Pioneering winery in Mount Barker, Western Australia, run by Englishman Tony Smith. Minty, lean Cabernet and Shiraz.

Rockford Another Barossa individualist, Rocky O'Callaghan, extracting the most from dry-farmed Barossa fruit. Splendid Basket Press Shiraz and irresistible sparkling Shiraz.

Rosemount Hugely successful Hunter Valley operation specialising in rich Chardonnay, Show Reserve and single vineyard Roxburgh. Quite good, but less exciting Cabernet.

Rothbury Estate The creation of Len Evans, large Hunter Valley estate and winery noted for extremely rich Chardonnay and good Semillon.

St-Hallett Third of the trio of Barossa individualists. Fine Old Block Shiraz from dry-farmed Barossa vineyard.

Saltram Often-overlooked Seagram-owned company based in South Australia. Pinnacle Selection and Mamre Brook reds are fine.

Seppelts Great historic South Australian company known for sparkling and fortified wines, now part of Penfolds group.

Shaw and Smith New alliance of winemaker Martin Shaw (ex-Petaluma) and Master of Wine Michael Hill-Smith, making one of Australia's best, refined Sauvignons and excellent, lean, Chardonnay Reserve.

Tahbilk, Chateau Perhaps Australia's most old-fashioned winery, in central Victoria. Tannic Cabernets built to last decades, fascinating Marsanne. Temperature-controlled fermentation not a speciality.

Taltarni Excellent Victorian winery run by Dominique Portet, son of the *régisseur* of Château Lafite. Like his brother Bernard at Clos du Val in California, Dominique makes French-inspired wines which age into grace and beauty, especially Sauvignon and Cabernet.

Tyrrells Outspoken winemaker Murray Tyrrell is one of the great characters of Australian wine, and his Hunter Valley wines can be great too, especially Vat 47 Chardonnay. Long Flat Red and White usually sound and good value.

Wynns Pioneering Coonawarra company, now part of Penfolds group, making superb Cabernet, especially top-of-the-range John Riddoch.

Yalumba (S. Smith & Co) Large and dynamic family-owned company based in South Australia. Big range of mainly good table wines, especially Pewsey Vale Riesling, Adelaide Hills Cabernet, Heggies Vineyard. Oxford Landing range commercial but sound. Hugely successful Angas Brut and Rosé sparkling wines.

Yarra Yering Perhaps Australia's most eccentric winery, in Yarra Valley, run by retired viticulturalist Dr Bailey Carrodus. Dry Red no. 1 (Cabernet), Dry Red no. 2 (Shiraz) are extraordinarily complex, while Underhill Shiraz is more straightforwardly magnificent.

Yeringberg Top-class Yarra Valley winery making extremely long-lived Chardonnay, Cabernet and Pinot Noir.

Vintage guide

Most Australian wines are best drunk in their vibrant, fruity youth. But there are exceptions, and not just among the top Cabernets and Shiraz wines such as Grange (undrinkable until eight or ten years old). One of the saddest aspects of the contemporary wine scene is the public lack of awareness about the need to age certain fine white wines. Top Australian Rieslings, in particular, benefit enormously from two or three years' bottle age. Certain Chardonnays, such as Leeuwin and Petaluma, will also acquire fascinating layers of complexity if allowed to evolve.

1995 Early reports suggest that though quantities are short in certain regions, quality should be high.

1994 A smallish crop of generally high-quality grapes in most areas, following another slow, cool-ripening season.

1993 This looked like being the year which finally dented Australia's reliable image. A very wet, cool summer delayed the harvest by as much as five weeks in some places. Unaccustomed summer rain brought outbreaks of mildew, which many growers were ill-prepared to combat. However, in almost all areas, a fine late-ripening season saved what might have been a disaster.

1992 Rather mixed conditions in the ripening season, including some unseasonal summer rain in South Australia, but generally good quality. The Hunter Valley, however, had a very difficult time, with torrential summer rain.

1991 Warm, early-ripening conditions in most areas.

1990 Late, slow-ripening season leading to some exceptional quality Cabernet and Shiraz.

NEW ZEALAND

Everyone knows a few things about New Zealand: the All Blacks are awesomely efficient; the sheep outnumber the people; the cricketers are unbelievably tedious. New Zealand wines, however, hold some surprises. In fact, the wines of this remote archipelago have made a remarkable impact in a very short space of time. Imports into the UK (much the biggest export market) have grown at a rate which has surprised even the New Zealanders. When the New Zealand Wine Guild was launched in London it declared a five-year target of 600,000 cases by 1995. Despite severe recession, this target was reached two years early in 1993. Growth slowed dramatically in 1994, mainly because the short 1992 and 1993 vintages meant there was not enough wine to go around. Quality was not ideal either in these two vintages, with a number of rather unripe Sauvignons in particular from 1993. Nineteen ninety-four was much better in quality, and yields were improved in Gisborne and Hawkes Bay, though still very low in Marlborough.

How has all this been achieved? New Zealand has followed the well-worn New World route of varietal labelling, but its real trump card has been its Sauvignon Blanc. New Zealand's intensely aromatic, gooseberry and tropical fruit-style of Sauvignon Blanc was just the ticket for a wine world, in the mid-1980s, beginning to look beyond Chardonnay. David Hohnen and Kevin Judd's fastidiously crafted and superbly presented Cloudy Bay was the perfect Rolls-Royce motor for the new style. Montana's reliable and affordable version has been the Model T for the masses. New Zealand soon proved that it had more to offer. The best Chardonnays, unctuously rich or lean and lemony, challenge the finest from Australia and California. Sparkling wine has shown itself to be another strong suit, with Deutz Marlborough Cuvée, Daniel Le Brun and Cloudy Bay's Pelorus impressively refined at the top end, and Lindauer popular in the middle market. Red wine has yet to reach the same heights, apart from the isolated fine Cabernet from Te Mata or Pinot from Martinborough.

White wines – Sauvignon, Chardonnay, Riesling and the rest

New Zealand is overwhelmingly a white wine-producing country, and one imagines that will remain the case for the foreseeable future. The climate belies latitudes which in European terms would range from warm to torrid, and generally justifies its 'cool' tag – though certain North Island Chardonnays taste exotically tropical.

Sauvignon Blanc

From Sauvignon Blanc come wines in New Zealand's most distinctive style. In French terms the wines are closest to Sancerre, but with a touch – often no more than a touch – of tropical fruit, and in the best cases a deft influence of oak. There exists a more obviously oaked style known as Fumé Blanc, but this does not appear to be on the increase. It is the grassy aromatic style which has stormed the market. Undoubtedly distinctive, the sheer undiluted intensity of this style can tire with repetition. The many followers of Cloudy Bay would do well to aspire to that wine's subtlety, in the combination of ripeness and intensity, and in the use of oak.

Chardonnay

Chardonnay may, in the long run, reach greater heights than Sauvignon. The grape itself is richer in possibilities, as even the makers of Cloudy Bay believe. The Cloudy Bay version is predictably among New Zealand's finest, but here the competition is very hot.

Riesling

This noble grape is, as everywhere, underrated in New Zealand. Its potential is very exciting indeed – perhaps greater than in any other New World region. The dry style is fresher and more aromatic than in Australia – not far from Germany's Rheinpfalz. Botrytised wines can be great.

The rest – Chenin Blanc, Müller-Thurgau

New Zealand's wine industry, as it grew in the 1960s, was based on Müller-Thurgau, planted on the advice of German viticulturalists. This was unfortunate, though New Zealand's Müller-Thurgau has the dubious honour of being among the world's best. Chenin Blanc is another unfashionable variety which performs well, but should probably be replaced by Sauvignon and Chardonnay.

Red wines – Pinot Noir, Cabernet Sauvignon, Merlot, Pinotage

New Zealand's red wines still lag far behind her whites. For once the enthusiasm of British wine writers, comparing New Zealand Cabernets to the finest from Bordeaux, California and Australia, has been misplaced. Most New Zealand Cabernet, in the editor's experience, is still far too herbaceous to be recommendable. There are exceptions, however, such as the superb Te Mata reds and good examples from Cloudy Bay, Ngatarawa, Dashwood and Vavasour. Promise is there and the wines are improving. However, the temperamental Pinot Noir may prove more excitingly suited to New Zealand's coolish, well-watered climate. Neudorf, Martinborough, Vavasour and Ata Rangi are leading the field.

The regions

New Zealand's total area under vine is less than half that of a single French region such as Alsace, yet her vineyards stretch over a wider spread of latitudes than all the vineyards of France. At the moment, there is no appellation control and cross-regional blends are common, but the specific strengths of particular regions are increasingly being recognised.

The North Island

Despite its rather damp and, in places, sub-tropical climate, the North Island remains the centre of the New Zealand wine industry. The most exciting quality area is Hawkes Bay, especially for Chardonnay and Cabernet. Gisborne is bulk-producing white wine country. The steamy area around Auckland has three or four fine producers, and Martinborough in the extreme south shows exciting potential for Pinot Noir.

The South Island

This dramatically beautiful, glacier-strewn island was shunned by wine-growers until around 1973. However, the sunny Marlborough region in the north-east has proved to be *the* place for Sauvignon Blanc, source of the grapes for both Cloudy Bay and Montana. Cabernet can also be good when not too grassy.

Pick of the New Zealand producers
Babich Good, rich Irongate Chardonnay from Hawkes Bay.

Le Brun, Daniel Expatriate Champenois producing rich, almost Bollinger-esque *méthode traditionelle* from Pinot and Chardonnay.

Cloudy Bay Seminal winery producing classic Sauvignon Blanc from Marlborough and increasingly fine Chardonnay, Cabernet and sparkling Pelorus.

Collards Auckland-based producer of rich Chardonnay, copybook Sauvignon and excellent Chenin Blanc.

Cooks/Corbans/Stoneleigh New Zealand's second-largest company, with reliable whites under Cooks label, fine Stoneleigh Sauvignon and Cabernet. Only disappointing in the cheaper reds.

Dashwood Second label of Vavasour (q.v.) producing exciting Marlborough Sauvignon, Chardonnay and remarkably good Cabernet.

Delegats North Island producer of good Chardonnay and Sauvignon.

Hunters One of the finest small producers in New Zealand, with hauntingly pure Sauvignon and complex Chardonnay.

Jackson Estate Exciting Marlborough estate producing austere Riesling, intense Sauvignon and complex Chardonnay.

Kumeu River Auckland-based winery specialising in complex, French-influenced styles of Chardonnay and Cabernet/Merlot.

Martinborough One of New Zealand's best Pinot Noirs, from the southern tip of North Island, and underrated Riesling.

Matua Valley Sauvignon good, if not outstanding; decent reds.

Millton Vineyard Fine organic wines, especially Chardonnay and Riesling, made by James Millton at Gisborne.

Montana The colossus of New Zealand wine, accounting for half the country's output. Remarkable quality and value for money, especially Marlborough Sauvignon, sparkling Lindauer and excellent Deutz Marlborough Cuvée. Reds still on the grassy side.

Neudorf Very good, hand-crafted wines, Sauvignon and Pinot Noir, especially, from Nelson in South Island.

Ngatarawa Some of New Zealand's best Cabernets from individualist winery in Hawke's Bay; outstanding botrytised Riesling.

Nobilo Large producer of reasonably priced wines; whites much better than reds.

Selaks Subtle Sauvignon with a touch of residual sugar is best bet from this Auckland-based winery.

Te Mata Outstanding Coleraine Cabernet/Merlot from Hawkes Bay is consistently New Zealand's best red.

Vavasour A red star in the ascendant; some of New Zealand's best Cabernet blends.

Villa Maria Very good, unusually rich Sauvignon and good Cabernet from New Zealand's third-largest producer.

Vintage guide

The great majority of New Zealand wines are made to be drunk in the vibrant intensity of their youth. Sauvignons tend to lose their freshness rather quickly, and two years should be regarded as an upper age limit. Some Chardonnays can age longer, while the best Cabernets and Rieslings will improve over five years and more.

1995 Early reports are optimistic about quantity after favourable summer weather. This could be the largest vintage since 1990.

1994 Very good quality grapes after some cool early summer weather, but quantity again well below average in many areas.

1993 This was the most difficult vintage ever experienced in New Zealand. Uneven flowering and rain disrupted fruit setting, and quantity was 40 per cent less than usual. Quality is variable, some wine showing unripeness and dilution.

1992 A late harvest and some rather austere, underripe wines, though the best Sauvignons and Chardonnays are excellent.

1991 Generally excellent, problem-free vintage.

NORTH AMERICA

CALIFORNIA

This time it was Japan which suffered a major earthquake. But next time, next year, next decade? The threat of truly devastating destruction, last seen in 1906 when the flames of burning San Francisco could be seen from the Mayacamas mountains above the Napa Valley, surely still hangs over the inhabitants of California's coastal strip. This threat colours the nature of the life that is led there, giving it both its remarkable enthusiasm and intensity and its curious sense of unreality.

Where else would you get a perfectly serious winery called Frog's Leap, with the branch of a madrone oak sticking through the upper storey of the winery house ('when there's a wind, we get surf in the bath')? Where else would you find a character like the surreal Randall Grahm, sticking brilliant wines into outrageously jokey bottles? This is the benign side of Californian wackiness. There is a much less benign side, where a lack of forethought and an excess of egos per hectare are prevalent. This lack of forethought led to the use of the only partially phylloxera-resistant rootstock, AxR 1, against the advice of French viticulturalists. The current phylloxera B epidemic means that as many as 40 per cent of California's vines will have to be replanted by the year 2000 – a hugely costly disaster.

The excess of egos is in some ways an even bigger problem. The Californian wine industry has for years suffered from a debilitating hollowness – the giant Gallo winery with its mass-marketed brands at one end, a rabbit-like proliferation of boutique wineries all seeking premium prices at the other. One or two valiantly moderate producers, Fetzer, Benziger of Glen Ellen, Kendall-Jackson, Jason Korman's California Direct initiative, have attempted to bridge the gap, which as far as the export markets are concerned, is absolutely crucial. California, of course, is not terribly interested in exports, but 1993 and 1994 saw the first signs of a concerted effort to target the £5–8 section, where California surely has its best chance.

Not everyone, it must be said, agrees with that assessment. Simon Farr, the thoughtful buying director of Bibendum, feels that 'California cannot compete with Australia in the lower-middle market and ought to go for out-and-out quality and eccentricity'. He has a point. The most exciting tables at the 1994 and 1995 Wine Institute of California tasting were undoubtedly the one where Randall Grahm (in 1994) and the other Rhône Rangers held court. Here were truly original wines, made from varieties such as Grenache, Syrah, Mourvèdre, Barbera – fun yet seriously good. Zinfandel, California's great 'native' variety, also has loads of untapped potential.

In fact, the strange conclusion one reaches is that for all its obsession with marketing, California is doing a pretty lousy job marketing its wines. The wines are far better than the image. Take Pinot Noir. California's best wine-making brains have long been at work on the world's most tantalising variety. The results get better every year, and if this writer was looking for a good-value Pinot Noir, California, not Burgundy, is the first place he would look. But California Pinot Noir is hardly a household name.

What about Cabernet Sauvignon, better known and more closely associated with the Golden State? California makes many marvellous Cabernets, few of them cheap, but the best undoubtedly on a par with Bordeaux's finest. One has to conclude that wines such as Ridge Monte Bello, Mondavi Reserve, Newton, Clos du Val and others are seriously under-rated. And then Chardonnay, the most fashionable of grapes; surely California has made its mark with that? Only up to a point. Australia has run away with the Chardonnay stakes, though very few Australian Chardonnays match the best of California's for refinement. At the 1995 California tasting Acacia's unoaked Caviste Chardonnay took the breath away with its freshness and purity.

California needs to pay serious attention to the lopsided structure of its wine industry. There are signs of this happening. At long last the big contract growers and makers in the San Joaquin Valley are beginning to show interest in tailoring varietals for the UK own-brand market. The industry needs a proper base and a proper middle, as well as a galaxy of stars.

California wine – the basic styles

White wines
Chardonnay California spotted the potential of Chardonnay long before Australia, and now has over 50,000 acres of the grape, more even than France. The styles have shifted enormously over 20 years, from lusciously rich and heavily oaked to the opposite extreme of leanness, before striking an increasingly good balance between the two. The arrogant pride of the winemaker has also

yielded considerably to the recognition of the value of *terroir* – especially the cool microclimates of areas such as Carneros and the valleys of San Luis Obispo and Santa Barbara.

Sauvignon Blanc This grape's current fashionability means that Californian versions abound. Mondavi started the fashion for the oaked style called Fumé Blanc. Nowadays, most aim for a fresher, grassier style with little or no oak. Frog's Leap and Matanzas Creek are among the leaders.

The rest Another of California's unsung glories is botrytised Riesling, especially from Phelps and Chateau St-Jean. At the cheaper end of the market, Chenin Blanc and Colombard abound as quaffers.

Red wines
Cabernet Sauvignon It was the Cabernet Sauvignons from the Napa Valley which first established California as a potentially great wine producer. The best Napa, Sonoma and Santa Cruz Cabernets continue to offer the only serious, concerted challenge to the complexity and longevity of Bordeaux. Some California Cabernets have also changed in style, going from massively powerful and tannic to sometimes undernourished 'elegance', before landing up at a mid-point. A few of the finest, such as Ridge and Clos du Val, however, have never wavered from an ideal of civilised complexity. Bordeaux-style blends, including Merlot, Cabernet Franc and even Petit Verdot, as well as single-varietal Merlot, and possibly even more interesting, single-varietal Cabernet Franc, are on the increase.

Pinot Noir Pinot Noir's increasing success in California remains something of an untold story. The best, seductively fruity, wines come from Carneros, where Saintsbury and Acacia lead the field, the Monterey side-mountains (Calera, Chalone) and the valleys of San Luis Obispo and Santa Barbara (Au Bon Climat).

Zinfandel Wine lovers from outside California cannot understand why Californians underplay their most distinctive variety. In the right, serious hands (Ridge), Zinfandel can offer fascinating layers of thick, sweet, brambly fruit. Most, unfortunately, is vinified hastily either as blush or styleless light red.

Rhône Rangers Randall Grahm of Bonny Doon believes passionately that most of California is better suited to southern European varieties such as Grenache, Syrah and Mourvèdre than to Cabernet Sauvignon and Chardonnay. His brilliant, but inconsistent, wines prove his point, and others have come aboard the Rhône boat, especially Qupé, Phelps (a pioneer), Ojai, Jade Mountain. Others are experimenting with Italian varieties, such as Sangiovese, Barbera and Nebbiolo.

Sparkling wines
California has become a major player in the high- quality *méthode traditionelle* stakes, and if the champagne houses of Reims and Epernay are feeling the heat, they themselves are largely responsible. Several of the champagne houses, such as Moët, Bollinger, Roederer, Mumm and Piper-Heidsieck, have established Californian offshoots. These are challenged by the best indigenous contenders such as Schramsberg, Iron Horse and Jordan.

The regions
California has been developing a very loose appellation system of AVAs or approved viticultural areas. These, however, are merely geographical designations and do not stipulate approved varieties, yields or wine-making procedures in the French fashion.

Napa Valley
California's most famous region has been subdivided into a bewildering number of different AVAs. Napa continues to be the showplace of California wine and sometimes the tour-guides and PR people seem to outnumber the winemakers. However, a large number of California's greatest Cabernets and Chardonnays (increasingly sourced from Carneros, an area split between Napa and Sonoma) still come from Napa.

Sonoma County
A large, straggling region split into a number of AVAs. Sonoma is Robert Louis Stevenson country and preserves, in parts, a charming rural feel. There is less hype and PR, and a more relaxed and down-to-earth approach. Some wines are more relaxed too, though there are wide differences between the warm Alexander Valley and the cool Russian River.

Mendocino and Lake Counties
The two northernmost California wine counties. Good-value wines.

Central Coast

A largely meaningless cover-all AVA including a number of districts stretching most of the way from San Francisco to Los Angeles and incorporating the following:

Santa Cruz Mountain district south of San Francisco with some star wineries, such as Ridge and Bonny Doon.

Monterey The dusty valley around Salinas does not look like high-quality wine country, but cool winds temper the climate. The mountains on either side house some first-rate wineries, especially for Pinot Noir.

Edna Valley Cool valley AVA in San Luis Obispo, producing high-quality Chardonnay and Pinot Noir.

Santa Maria and Santa Ynez Valleys Cool valley AVAs in Santa Barbara county making some of California's best Chardonnay and Pinot Noir.

San Joaquin Valley Best-known part of the hot Central Valley, home of jug wines.

Pick of the wineries

Acacia Excellent Carneros producer of Chardonnay, including new unoaked Caviste, and Pinot Noir.

Au Bon Climat Santa Barbara winery specialising in burgundian Pinot Noir.

Beaulieu One of Napa's most famous names, especially for supple yet long-lived BV Georges de Latour Cabernet Sauvignon. Beautour Cabernet reasonably priced, Rutherford can be good. Possibly living on reputation.

Benziger of Glen Ellen Increasingly good estate Cabernet from producer of extremely successful low-priced Glen Ellen Chardonnay, with residual sugar.

Beringer Very large Napa producer owned by Nestlé, but still managing to achieve top quality, especially with Reserve Cabernet. Also Knights Valley range from Sonoma.

Bonny Doon The Santa Cruz hide-out of chief Rhône Ranger Randall Grahm. Do not let jokey labels distract attention from splendid wines based on southern French and Italian varieties.

Calera One of California's most serious Pinot Noir producers, with single-vineyard bottlings, based in Gavilan mountains, Monterey.

Carmenet Some of California's most Bordeaux-like reds, including remarkable Cabernet Franc.

Chalone Extraordinary vineyard and winery in hot, dry Pinnacles National Monument, Monterey, producing very complex, long-lived Chardonnay, Pinot Noir and Pinot Blanc.

Chandon, Domaine Moët offshoot in Napa, with excellent restaurant and improving sparklers.

Chateau St-Jean Suntory-owned Sonoma winery specialising in wonderful botrytised Riesling and complex Chardonnay.

Clos du Bois Consistently excellent Sonoma winery, equally good at Cabernet and Merlot blends (Briarwood, Marlstone) and Chardonnay.

Clos du Val Pioneering winery in Stag's Leap district of Napa, run with Gallic finesse by Bernard Portet. Superbly sensuous, fine-tuned Cabernet.

Cuvaison Napa winery noted for sophisticated Cabernet and Carneros Chardonnay made by questing winemaker John Thacher.

Duckhorn Napa winery with one of best California Merlots.

Fetzer Successful, large Mendocino winery pioneering in the field of organic viticulture. Good Barrel Select Cabernet and Chardonnay. Second label, Bel Arbors.

Foppiano Sonoma winery with good-value varietals, also under Riverside Farms label.

Frog's Leap Stylish Chardonnay, Cabernet and refreshing Sauvignon from this jokily named Napa Valley winery.

Heitz Classic Napa individualist producing (on best form) great long-lived Cabernet (Napa Valley, Bella Oaks and Martha's Vineyard).

Iron Horse First-class Sonoma producer of ultra-sophisticated sparkling and good still wines.

Jordan Gatsby-esque Sonoma winery of petroleum geologist Tom Jordan, producing velvety, supple Alexander Valley Cabernet, less convincing Chardonnay and very good sparkling wine called J.

Kendall-Jackson Specialist large-scale producer of barrel-fermented Chardonnay based in Lake and Mendocino Counties, though much fruit comes from Santa Maria Valley, Santa Barbara.

Kistler High-class Chardonnay specialist in Sonoma, with many different single-vineyard bottlings.

Mayacamas Obstinately old-fashioned producer in Mayacamas mountains west of Napa Valley, specialising in Cabernet which requires a decade or more to reach maturity.

Mondavi The greatest name in California wine. Remarkable company almost unique in combining top quality and large quantity. Sophisticated Cabernet Sauvignon Reserve, oaky Chardonnay Reserve, recently startlingly improved Pinot Noir, seminal Fumé Blanc.

Monterey Vineyards Seagram-owned producer of good-value Chardonnay.

Newton Leading proponent of mountain vineyards, making excellent, concentrated Cabernet from Spring Mountain, on west side of Napa Valley. Unusual in planting Petit Verdot. Chardonnay also fine.

Phelps Highly versatile Napa winery, adding Rhône Rangers (one of first California Syrahs, in fact) to well-established tannic Cabernet and top-quality botrytised Riesling.

Qupé The best Syrah (as opposed to Petite Sirah) producer in California.

Ridge Philosopher-winemaker Paul Draper, based high in Santa Cruz mountains, serenely goes his own way, making perhaps California's most complex, beautifully textured Cabernets (Santa Cruz Mountains, York Creek – Napa Valley, and Monte Bello from winery vineyard) and Zinfandel.

Roederer Quartet, made from 70 per cent Chardonnay, 30 per cent Pinot Noir grown in Anderson Valley, Mendocino, matches the best *méthode traditionelle* sparklers for finesse.

Saintsbury Dick Ward and David Graves specialise in Pinot Noir (early-maturing Garnet, medium-bodied Carneros and deeper Reserve), perhaps California's most seductive, and satisfying barrel-fermented Chardonnay, both from Carneros fruit.

Sanford Santa Barbara-based specialist in early-maturing Pinot Noir and powerful Chardonnay.

Schramsberg Glamorous but also serious Napa producer of rich, complex sparkling wines.

Shafer Under-rated producer of gloriously supple Cabernet from Stag's Leap in Napa.

Simi Excellent Sonoma producer of Chardonnay; Cabernet recently much improved.

Sonoma-Cutrer The ultimate Chardonnay specialist, with single-vineyard Les Pierres perhaps California's most complex, minerally.

Stag's Leap Wine Cellars Cabernet specialist; Napa Valley, one of best in class; Stag's Leap Vineyard, supple, polished; Cask 23, remarkably rich, lush-textured. Good Petite Sirah.

Trefethen Reliable producer of rich Chardonnay and sometimes rather leafy Cabernet from own vineyards in south of Napa Valley.

Vintage guide

Most California wines are drunk young, but the best Cabernets, from producers such as Ridge, Mayacamas, Newton, require several years – as much as a decade in some cases – to reach optimal maturity. Chardonnays can also improve with up to five years' bottle age.

1994 A long cool end to the growing season, in the top-quality areas of Napa, Sonoma and Central Coast, leading to promising quality, especially for Pinot Noir. Quantities in general up to 20 per cent down on previous year.

1993 A late, difficult harvest with reduced quantities in many areas, but some excellent Chardonnay.

1992 After several years of drought, 1992 saw copious winter rain. A hot summer followed and the harvest was gathered in excellent conditions.
1991 A very late vintage saved by a long Indian summer in September and October. Generally excellent quality.
1990 Very fine year producing extremely rich Chardonnay.
1989 The so-called 'harvest from hell', with conditions more reminiscent of northern Europe than California: a cool, wet growing season followed by torrential rain in September, causing widespread botrytis. Some decent wines, not for long keeping.

Earlier fine Cabernet vintages: 1986, 1985, 1984.

OREGON

Heavily hyped in the mid-1980s as the New World's most promising source of Pinot Noir, Oregon's small-scale wine industry has failed to develop as fast as some starry-eyed critics predicted. Lack of consistency, caused partly by the uncertain climate of the Willamette Valley, but more fundamentally by lack of professionalism in the winery, is a bugbear. The splendidly sophisticated, but overpriced, Pinot Noir made by Robert Drouhin, together with star newcomers such as Cristom and Benton Lane, shows the quality that can be achieved. The challenge of making such quality commercially viable remains to be met. Other good producers: Argyle (traditional method sparklers, Riesling), Elk Cove, Eyrie, Knudsen-Erath, Oak Knoll (fine Chardonnay).

WASHINGTON STATE

The irrigated vineyards of Washington State are situated well inland, to the east of the Cascade Mountains, in zones officially described as semi-arid. The climate is quite different from either California's or the Willamette Valley's, with long hot summer days and very cool nights. This gives fruit of very clear definition and balance; Washington has specialised in white varieties such as Riesling, but the Bordeaux grapes Cabernet Sauvignon and Merlot show exciting promise. So far, the wine industry, hampered by lack of investment, has been slow to translate this promise into really top-class results, though the large Chateau Ste-Michelle winery, together with its second label Columbia Crest, delivers very acceptable quality. Other good producers: Columbia Winery (very fine Otis Vineyard Cabernet), Hedges Cellars (fine Red Mountain Reserve Cabernet/Merlot), Hogue Cellars (good Merlot) and Salishan.

THE REST OF THE USA AND CANADA

Wine is produced commercially in a number of other states, from Idaho in the north-west to Texas in the extreme south. The most important source of quality wine, apart from those discussed above, is undoubtedly New York State. Vineyards tempered by the Finger Lakes in upstate New York can produce sensationally rich Chardonnay (look out for Wagner Vineyards). Long Island, near New York, is proving a highly promising source of both Chardonnay and Cabernet. North of the border, the Okanagan Valley inland from Vancouver has hit the headlines with the award-winning Mission Hill Chardonnay, and a small region of Ontario near Niagara Falls is showing promise with both Chardonnay (look out for Inniskillin) and delicate dry Riesling.

MEXICO

Mexican wine may seem an unlikely concept, but the northern part of the Baja California peninsula, just south of San Diego, is showing itself capable of matching or surpassing the quality of 'upper' California's Central Valley. Indeed, the lush, ripe Petite Sirah and Cabernet from L.A. Cetto put most of Gallo's offerings to shame.

SOUTH AMERICA

CHILE

There is a received story about Chilean wine which runs as follows. Until the late 1980s Chilean wine was hopelessly old-fashioned and out of touch with the international market. Suddenly, around 1990 (coinciding, not fortuitously, with the return to *soi-disant* democracy), the picture changed. Massive investment came from outside, especially from the USA and France. Out went the ancient vats made of Chilean wood (rauli), in came stainless steel. Chilean wine was transformed, became modern, sleek, international. Pats on the back all round.

This story is what many Chilean wine producers would like us to believe, but it is only partially true. Here is another version. Chile had a proud tradition, dating back to the mid-nineteenth century, of making the best wines in South America. Chilean Cabernet Sauvignon won international medals, even in Paris. Because of economic difficulties, Chilean companies were slow to invest in the kind of high-tech equipment necessary for making modern white wine, though they continued to produce excellent reds. Pinochet's dictatorship was replaced by a strange kind of democracy (with Pinochet still in place as head of the armed forces and no reprisals taken against those responsible for state-sponsored massacres and torture). Suddenly it was acceptable for foreign firms to invest. Several did so, including Napa's Franciscan Winery and French names as prestigious as Rothschild of Lafite and Prats of Cos d'Estournel. New equipment was used to make largely characterless modern-style white wines which were enthusiastically promoted by American-trained marketing executives. Unfortunately, few steps were taken to control yields, and, because some wines tasted so thin, they were illegally corrected with sorbitol.

In some ways, the Chilean wine saga is a cautionary tale, the moral being that high-tech wine-making equipment and marketing techniques are not enough to create a successful wine-exporting industry. Fortunately, the best Chilean wine producers either always knew this or have taken the lesson on board. In the past year or so Chile seems to have taken a decisive step forward. Some truly exciting Chilean white wines have appeared, sourced from the Casablanca Valley between Santiago and Valparaiso. Chile could still do with more homegrown winemakers of international calibre, as opposed to visiting flying winemakers, but Alvaro Espinosa Durán of Carmen is a new name to conjure with, as well as the ubiquitous and probably overstrained Ignacio Recabarren. The quality of the reds, apart from one or two exceptional Cabernets, such as the Lafite-inspired Los Vascos, the sophisticated Don Melchor from Concha y Toro, Montes Alpha from Aurelio Montes and the powerful Errázuriz Don Maximiliano, appears rather static, and, in some cases, worse than that.

It always seemed a gross exaggeration to call Chile the Australia of the 1990s: Chile has some way to go to reach that sort of maturity, as both a democracy and a wine producer (maybe there is some connection between the two). Perhaps Chile would do best to concentrate on being Chile and making distinctively Chilean wines.

Red wine – styles and grape varieties

Red wines have always been Chile's main strength.

Cabernet Sauvignon

The great Bordeaux grape has flourished for more than a century in the irrigated vineyards of central Chile. Chilean Cabernet, at its best, strikes a satisfying balance between New World exuberance and Old World restraint. The wines smell of tobacco as well as blackcurrants, though the vegetal tone can easily shade into unripeness when yields are stretched. The influx of French winemakers, and French oak, has led to some extremely Bordeaux-like Cabernets, especially Los Vascos – excellent wines but not terribly Chilean?

Merlot and Pinot Noir

One or two single-varietal Merlots and Pinots Noirs – especially Cono Sur – have appeared and show great promise.

White wines – styles and grape varieties

For a long time, the quality of Chile's whites lagged far behind that of the reds. Temperature-controlled fermentation improved matters, but real varietal character proved elusive, until the discovery of the cool Casablanca Valley as an exciting source of whites in the early 1990s.

Chardonnay
Chile has, inevitably, joined the international consensus in planting
this variety, but it has yet to establish a clear-cut style or styles.
Several examples are competent, and the Casablanca versions,
intensely lemony, look exciting.

Sauvignon
One of the biggest problems with Chilean Sauvignon is that much
of it is not Sauvignon at all, but the greatly inferior Sauvignonasse.
Even true Sauvignon has seldom shone with intense varietal
characteristics (Torres in Curicó has been quite successful), until the
arrival of the New Zealand-influenced Casablanca versions.

The rest
Fair-quality Riesling is produced by Torres, among others.
Recabarren makes aromatic Casablanca Gewurztraminer.

The regions

The 1995 vintage is the first to showcase Chile's new system of
appellations. This divides the long, narrow country into five
viticultural regions, with sub-regions and zones within those.
Under the regulations, a wine labelled with any of the recognised
viticultural areas must have a minimum of 75 per cent of its grapes
sourced from that region. The figure for the proportion of stated
grape varieties in varietal wines is also 75 per cent, but those
imported into the EU must contain 85 per cent of the stated variety.

The two most important regions for quality wines are the small
Aconcagua Region, with its sub-regions of Aconcagua Valley and
Casablanca Valley, source of so many of Chile's most original new
whites, and Central Region, which covers the sub-regions of Maipo
Valley (source of many fine Cabernets), Rapel Valley, Curicó Valley
and Maule Valley.

Pick of the producers

Caliterra Originally a partnership between Errázuriz of Chile and
Franciscan Vineyards of Napa. Now wholly Errázuriz-owned and
producing acceptable, but not outstanding, modern-style wines.

Carmen Although under the same ownership as Santa Rita, Carmen
Vineyards is run quite separately and both white and red wines
benefit from the viticultural and oenological expertise of Alvara
Espinosa Durán. Whites express fresh fruit, reds are fine and
elegant.

Casablanca Confusingly, both a label and an area. Casablanca Santa Isabel Estate whites from Recabarren are outstanding, but plain Casablanca label wines do not necessarily come from Casablanca Valley.

Concha y Toro The largest Chilean producer of always reliable, and sometimes excellent, wines (especially Don Melchor Cabernet).

Cousiño Macul Chile's most traditional producer, with an historic estate just outside Santiago. Antiguas Reservas Cabernet can be magnificent, though erratic.

Errázuriz Unpronounceable winery based in Aconcagua Valley. Good Cabernet, Merlot, Chardonnay and Sauvignon.

Los Vascos Colchagua estate 50 per cent owned by Rothschilds of Lafite. Gilbert Rokvam of Lafite makes Chile's most Bordeaux-like Cabernet.

Montes Dynamic Curicó winery run by Aurelio Montes. Has brought in Hugh Ryman to make international-style Sauvignon. Montes Alpha Cabernet rich and oaky.

San Pedro Large Lontüé firm, now under Spanish control and employing flying winemaker Jacques Lurton as consultant.

Santa Carolina Santiago producer now employing Ignacio Recabarren as chief winemaker. Much-improved whites.

Santa Rita Very well-equipped modern producer with improved whites, including some from Casablanca Valley, and largely disappointing reds.

Torres Well-established Lontüé offshoot of the enterprising Catalan firm. Sauvignon Blanc used to be Chile's best by far (Bellaterra is oak-aged version), now has competition. Reds in elegant style, including experimental Pinot Noir.

Undurraga Renovated family operation near Santiago, making good modern-style whites and reds.

ARGENTINA

Argentina is one of the world's largest wine producers, but exports to the UK, never massive, were badly affected by the war over the islands which the British call the Falklands and the Argentinians refer to as las Malvinas. The Falklands factor is now no longer a factor, at least as far as major chains and supermarkets are concerned, and some very good Argentinian reds – especially the elegant Cabernets from Trapiche and old-fashioned ones from Weinert, and improving whites, especially Catena, are now quite widely distributed. One black grape which performs better in the dry vineyards of Argentina's Mendoza province than almost anywhere else is Malbec. The aromatic white Torrontés is certainly of interest, but has so far failed to capture the imagination of British drinkers. Argentina's wine industry has been opening up to the outside world in the past few years, with input from international winemakers such as Peter Bright and Jacques Lurton, and much can be expected (and we hope much beyond Cabernet and Chardonnay) in the next decade.

THE REST OF SOUTH AMERICA

Wine is produced in other South American countries, especially Brazil, Uruguay and Peru, but very little is seen in the UK, apart from bottles of the surprisingly good Cabernet from Viña Tacama in Peru and leathery Uruguayan Tannat.

SOUTH AFRICA

South African wine-growers can breathe again. After his momentous electoral victory of April 1994 State President Nelson Mandela has given his seal of approval to the wine industry, which some had seen as a possible target of the new ANC government. This comes as a relief for many people in the UK also. Imports of South African wine into the UK have been growing at a remarkable rate over the last three years, and at a time of shortfall from other producers such as Australia, South Africa's role as a provider of, in particular, fresh, fruity whites is increasingly important. The clean, fresh, inexpensive whites made from Chenin and Colombard are excellent value for money, but the Chardonnays are potential world-beaters. Reds have been slower to hit their stride in pace with the international competition, especially since many traditional Cape Cabernets taste dry, dusty and austere, but Merlot shows seductive, juicy promise and Pinotage offers a uniquely South African flavour.

South Africa has had a long way to go to catch up with, say, Australia, mainly because of the isolation caused by years of sanctions, but also because of the doggedly bureaucratic nature of the wine industry. Shortage of good, virus-free vine material has been one of South Africa's main handicaps. Recently, there have been significant steps towards deregulation, with the abolition both of the quota system, which banned wine production in many excellent locations, and of the minimum wine price for exports, which made it difficult for exporters to compete at the low-priced end of the market. South African wine is now at the beginning of an exciting phase of expansion and search for quality, comparable to that of the Australian wine industry in the 1970s and 1980s.

Wine of origin system

South Africa's wine of origin system (WO) specifies origin, variety and vintage but does not control other factors such as yield. Chaptalisation (see glossary) is prohibited, but acid adjustment, as used in Australia, is permitted. A new, less obtrusive wine of origin seal is being introduced to replace the old 'bus ticket' seal.

Varieties and styles

White wines
South Africa is a white-wine country. White grapes account for nearly 85 per cent of all plantings. By far the largest share of this 85 per cent is still taken by Chenin Blanc, often called Steen, which produces pleasantly fruity, dry, off-dry and luscious sweet wines in the Cape. Colombard, taking up some 10 per cent of South African vineyards, can give very attractive, freshly scented wines. Sauvignon covers some 4 per cent of the vineyard area, but South African Sauvignon often seems to lack distinctive varietal character. Chardonnay is the rising star, capable of superb quality and a style interestingly poised between New and Old Worlds. Plantings are increasing rapidly and currently stand at 2.9 per cent of vineyard area.

Red wines
South African red wines do not, on the whole, burst with primary fruit flavours as dramatically as those from Australia and California. Cabernet Sauvignon, in particular, is often unappealingly lean and sinewy, needing up to a decade to reach mellow maturity. For South Africans, these characteristics may be signs of aristocratic restraint, but the outside world remains to be convinced. South Africa's most distinctive red wine grape is Pinotage, a cross between Cinsault and Pinot Noir. Pinotage wines often have a strong tone of nail varnish-remover, and sometimes also a banana-tinged sweetness. However, from an estate like Kanonkop, Pinotage can be wonderfully chocolatey. So far, South Africa has come up with one world-class Pinot Noir, that of Hamilton-Russell. Merlot is a grape which seems to thrive in South Africa, producing delicious, soft juicy reds. Shiraz is also delivering some exciting, spicy, minty wines.

Sparkling wines
South Africa is showing increasing promise as a producer of mid-priced sparkling wines made from Pinot Noir and Chardonnay, though top quality will be obtained only from cool-vineyard fruit.

The regions

Nearly all South African wine is produced within a fairly confined area of the south-western Cape. The original cradle of Cape wine is Constantia, just outside Cape Town and very near the ocean. The two biggest centres of the wine industry are Paarl, headquarters of the KWV, a predominantly red wine area, and Stellenbosch, perhaps the Cape's premier wine-producing district. Warmer inland districts include Olifants River, Worcester and Robertson, a source of excellent Chardonnay. Perhaps the most exciting vineyard developments are taking place in districts with cooler climates, especially Elgin and Walker Bay in the Overberg district.

Pick of the producers

Backsberg Some of South Africa's most agreeable reds, including seductively scented, forward Merlot from this reliable estate.

Bergkelder A uniquely South African mixture of *négociant*, co-operative and estate-owner. Vinifies the wines of many estates, including Meerlust, as well as producing *négociant* wines under such labels as Stellenryck Collection and Fleur du Cap.

Boschendal Large Paarl estate has won awards for its Le Grand Pavillon sparkling Blanc de Blancs.

Buitenverwachting German-owned Constantia estate particularly noted for Chardonnay and Sauvignon Blanc. Also organic wines.

Ellis, Neil Particularly good whites from this recently established winery which works with bought-in grapes.

Fairview Excellent Paarl estate run by Charles Back. Wines consistently excite, with brilliant, New World-style fruit. Very good Charles Gerard Reserve white, an oaked blend of Sauvignon and Semillon, and red blend of Cabernet Franc and Merlot.

Hamilton-Russell Pioneering producer of best South African Pinot Noir and admirable Chardonnay from cool vineyards near Hermanus.

Kanonkop Superb red wines, especially Pinotage, from this Stellenbosch producer.

Klein Constantia A new star in the Cape firmament. Magnificent rich Chardonnay and intense, minty Cabernet, as well as sweet Vin de Constance, from dried Muscat, made by talented winemaker Ross Gower.

KWV The great umbrella organisation of South African wine is undergoing major change. It seems likely that its two roles – as brand-owner and legislator-cum-regulator – may be separated. The export brands are losing ground rapidly but still offer reasonable quality.

Mulderbosch Probably South Africa's best Sauvignon, excellent in both intense, crisp unoaked and rich Graves-like Fumé styles.

Pongracz Excellent traditional method sparkler, two-thirds Pinot Noir, one-third Chardonnay, produced by the Bergkelder.

Rust en Vrede Stellenbosch estate owned by former Springbok rugby player Jannie Engelbrecht and specialising in reds – some of South Africa's best.

Stellenbosch Farmers Winery One of the world's largest wineries, responsible for a wide range of products, including the admirable Zonnebloem range.

Vriesenhof Excellent Stellenbosch estate run by former Springbok rugby player Jan Boland Coetzee. Remarkably understated Chardonnay.

De Wet (De Wetshof), Danie Reliable producer of often quite delicate and judiciously oaked Chardonnay, from Robertson vineyards.

ELSEWHERE IN THE WORLD

NORTH AFRICA

Algeria, Tunisia and Morocco are former French colonies which were once significant wine producers. Now they are independent Islamic states, and wine production is tolerated (barely, one feels in some cases) rather than actively developed. Some decent Algerian reds, especially Coteaux de Mascara, and sturdy Moroccan reds, such as Tarik and Sidi Brahim, occasionally make their way over to the UK and can be good value.

ASIA – INDIA, CHINA, JAPAN

India's one wine of international note is the traditional-method sparkler Omar Kyahham. Developed with assistance from the champagne house Piper-Heidsieck, using Ugni Blanc and Chardonnay grapes grown at a height of 700 metres in the Sahyadri mountains, not far from Bombay, Omar Khayyam is surprisingly good. Still wines are promised from the same source.

China obviously has potential as a wine-producer, given the right market conditions. At the moment, a very fair, buttery, oaky Chardonnay is produced at the Huadong winery with Australian assistance.

Japan's problem as a wine producer is not the market but the scarcity of land suitable for vineyards. The only home-grown Japanese wines we have encountered have been appalling, but experimental efforts from Suntory will surely be a great improvement, given the company's commitment to quality-wine production in France and Germany.

Part III

Where to buy wine

SYMBOLS

☞ Denotes generally low prices and/or a large range of modestly priced wines.

☞ A merchant given this symbol offers exceptionally good service. We rely on readers' reports in allocating service symbols; this means that there may be merchants offering first-class service who appear here with no symbol because such distinction has gone unreported. Readers, please report!

☞ A merchant awarded this symbol makes a special effort to train staff to a high standard in wine knowledge, so advice from behind the counter should be particularly reliable. Other merchants without this symbol may also offer good advice – please report.

☞ Indicates high-quality wines across the range.

☞ This award is given for a wide range of wines from around the world.

Best buys

These are the Editor's choice of four out of a group of wines selected by the merchant in question as being distinguished in terms of value for money, or offering very fine quality regardless of price. In most instances, two wines at under £5 and two at over £5 have been selected. A very few merchants were unwilling to nominate any wines as their best buys and so the recommendations here may be restricted.

William Addison (Newport)

The Warehouse, Village Farm, Lilleshall,   *Tel* (01952) 670200
Newport, Shropshire TF10 9HB   *Fax* (01952) 677309

Open Mon–Fri 8–5, Sat 9–1 **Closed** Sun, public holidays **Cards** Access, Visa;
personal and business accounts **Discount** Negotiable **Delivery** Free within 40-mile
radius (min. 1 case); mail-order available **Glass hire** Not available **Tasting and talks**
Promotional tastings and individual organised tastings **Cellarage** £3 per case per year

'With the improvement in quality of the lower-priced wines,' says
John Horton, 'customers are limiting their purchases to the under-
£10 bracket.' The Addison range does stray above that figure from
time to time, particularly in the impressive set of clarets, which has
four vintages each of Châteaux Gruaud-Larose, Palmer and
d'Angludet, and in the burgundies from Louis Latour, Harmand-
Geoffroy and Jacques Prieur. However, Duboeuf beaujolais, Louis
Sipp Alsace and good ranges of Rhônes and country wines stick
mostly to under a tenner.

The German wines are from Louis Guntrum and Deinhard, the
Spanish from Bodegas Fariña, CVNE and Faustino Martínez while
Bodenham and Halfpenny Green provide English wines. Best of
the New World range are the Beringer Californians, Mouton
Excelsior South Africans, Penfolds Aussies and the New Zealanders
from Matua Valley and Jackson Estate.

Best buys

Syrah, Vin de Pays des Côtes de Thongue 1993, Domaine
Montmarin, £
Chardonnay 1994, Vin de Pays d'Oc, Domaine de Luc, £
Pommard 1er Cru Les Fremières 1992, Domaine Coste Caumartin,
££
Champagne Laurent Desmazières Cuvée Tradition, ££

Addison-Bagot Vintners

13 London Road, Alderley Edge, Cheshire   *Tel* (01625) 582354
SK9 7JT   *Fax* (01625) 586404

Open Mon–Fri 8.30–7, Sat 10–7 **Closed** Sun and public holidays **Cards** Access,
Delta, Switch, Visa; personal and business accounts **Discount** 5% retail; wholesale by
negotiation **Delivery** Within a 25-mile radius (min. order 1 case); mail-order available
Glass hire Free with order **Tasting and talks** Annual tasting; tutored and group
tastings by arrangement **Cellarage** Not available

John Richard Addison-Bagot's first year at the helm of the former
Eaton Elliot has been nothing if not eventful. The effect of a triple
whammy (increased duty rates, uncertainty over currency levels

and price increases from producers) has meant that prices have been forced up in certain areas, but the range available has expanded and is more interesting than ever.

You'll find Alsace wines from the Beblenheim co-operative and Schlumberger, a range of Louis Latour burgundies and some good Loire Sauvignon from Vacheron and Bailly. Most interesting perhaps are the regional whites from Château Theulet in Bergerac and Domaine Cauhapé in Jurançon. There's a small German set from Dr Loosen, Spanish wines from Ochoa and CVNE and an English pair from Kit Lindlar. The Italian list is very impressive, and, while we'd pick on the Tuscans from Castello di Volpaia and Franca Spinola, and Aldo Conterno's Barolos, anything in the range should give pleasure.

The Americas range is slightly dull, but that from South Africa is better, with wines coming from Thelema, Meerlust and Uitkyk. Antipodean interest appears in the shape of Shaw & Smith, Montara and Cape Mentelle from Australia, and Ngatarawa, Neudorf and Coopers Creek from New Zealand.

Best buys

1994 Drostdy Hof Sauvignon Blanc, £
Côtes de Malepère 1992, Château Malvies, £
Sancerre 1993, Domaine Vacheron, ££
Vouvray Demi-Sec 1993, Château Moncontour, ££

Adnams Wine Merchants

The Crown, High Street, Southwold, Suffolk	*Tel* (01502) 727220
IP18 6DP	*Fax* (01502) 727223
The Cellar and Kitchen Store	
Victoria Street, Southwold, Suffolk IP18 6JW	*Tel* (01502) 727220
The Grapevine	
109 Unthank Road, Norwich, Norfolk NR2 2PE	*Tel* (01603) 613998
Adnams Wine Shop	
Pinkneys Lane, Southwold, Suffolk IP18 6EW	*Tel* (01502) 722138

Open (The Crown – mail-order only) Mon–Fri 9–5, Sat 9–12; opening times vary for other outlets **Closed** Sun, public holidays **Cards** Access, Switch, Visa; business accounts **Discount** 5% on 6+ cases **Delivery** Free 2+ cases, £5 for single case orders; mail-order available **Glass hire** Free with order to local customers **Tasting and talks** 4 main events per year, plus others on request; numerous smaller events in Southwold and around the country **Cellarage** £6 per case per year

---

This is perhaps the most difficult entry in the *Guide* to write, since perusing Adnams' wine selection promotes salivation on a grand scale. It's not that Adnams is in a different league (East Anglian competitor Lay & Wheeler provides just as tasty a range), but it plies its trade with elan, with a zeal sadly lacking in today's wine world of price points and 'me-too' varietals. At the time of writing, all the Adnams arrows are pointing towards the spectacular love-it-or-hate-it Recioto Spumante from Bertani, but in another month they will probably point somewhere else. Gigolo-style, they swing mainly to wherever there is good wine to be had, and Adnams customers need to concentrate hard to follow the action.

Besides the frothy Recioto, enthusiasts for Italian viniculture will find plenty of wines from Tuscany and Piemonte, but just as many from the Veneto, including some brilliant stuff from Quintarelli. A reasonable Spanish set has been enlivened by the arrival of the great-value Baso reds from Rioja and Navarra. The Portuguese range has also had new life breathed into it; how many other companies could even contemplate offering a mixed case of 12 different wines from the country? Some of the best and best-known producers are represented in the German list, but you'll also find less famous, though still excellent, Riesling from Josef Leitz. Willi Opitz provides nectar from Austria.

Clarets are competent rather than brilliant, but the Burgundian selection betrays a passion; Rousseau and Domaine Leflaive head the reds and whites, but you'll also find much else besides. The Alsace wines of Deiss, Hugel and Schoffit are all brilliant, as are the Loires from Huet, Domaine des Aubuisières and Vacheron. Rhône-lovers will not be disappointed by the range of great reds and whites from Chapoutier, Château de Beaucastel, Chave and others, and more great southern flavours appear in the pleasing selection of regional wines. Those who enjoy great champagne should not miss the wines of Billiot and Billecart-Salmon, and might also care to try alternative sparklers, such as the Jansz and the Clover Hill from Tasmania and the Californian Schramsberg.

At a time when certain merchants are veering away from New World wines, the Adnams range has grown stronger, particularly its Australian section. We'd go for the wines from Cullens, Mountadam, Jasper Hill and Montara. Interesting New Zealand items include Forrest Riesling, Neudorf Semillon, Martinborough Vineyard's Pinot and Ngatawara Cabernet/Merlot, while the wines of Shafer, Bonny Doon and Saintsbury will please lovers of Californian wine.

Visitors to the Norwich shop and the Cellar and Kitchen Store in Southwold will always find plenty of bottles to sample, but larger tastings are held twice a year in Norwich and London. However, many Adnams customers get no nearer to the shops than the appealing mailshots that land on the mat at roughly two-month intervals. Those who deal with the company only intermittently may not have noticed that the phone numbers have changed recently (the information super-highway has now arrived in Southwold). Even so, Loftus, Marshall, Chase et al. remain on a different planet from much of the rest of the wine world.

Best buys

1994 Baso, Navarra Garnacho, Vinos de la Granja, £
Jean des Vignes vin de table, dry white, £
Semillon/Sauvignon Reserve 1992, Cullen, Western Australia, ££
Vouvray Sec 'Cuvée Victor' 1992, Domaine des Aubuisières, ££

Amey's Wines

83 Melford Road, Sudbury, Suffolk CO10 6JT   *Tel* (01787) 377144

Open Tues–Sat 10–7 **Closed** Mon, Sun, public holidays **Cards** Access, Delta, Visa
Discount 5% on 1 mixed case **Delivery** Free within 20-mile radius (orders over £50)
Glass hire Free with suitable order **Tasting and talks** Regular in-store tastings
Saturdays, occasional tutored tastings **Cellarage** Not available

The number of people mentioning cross-Channel purchases at Peter Amey's store is increasing, but we'd still prefer to fill our cellar at this Sudbury merchant. Value is very much the watchword, but the overall quality level is commendably high (or highly commendable). Sparkling wine fans can enjoy champagnes from Moët and Chartogne-Taillet, cava from Torre del Gall or a long list of Australian fizz, including Seppelt's Sparkling Shiraz. Overall the Australian range is very impressive, and features wines from Mount Langi Ghiran, Mitchelton, Mountadam and Montara. Top of the New Zealand selection are the wines of Te Mata and Martinborough Vineyards, and other New World highlights are mature wines from Newton in California and the Thelema South Africans.

Turning to France, Alsace wines come from Leon Beyer and the Turckheim co-op while the best of the burgundies are the reds from Vallet Frères and Michel Juillot and the Chablis from Domaine de l'Eglantière. A short set of Rhônes includes Châteauneuf from Font de Michelle and Alain Paret's sturdy St Joseph, and tasty regional wines come from Chemins des Bassac and Château Grand Moulin. Ch. Haut Marbuzet '89 tops a sensible claret range. The Riojas from La Rioja Alta, the Ribera del Duero from Paga de Carraovejas and the J. M. da Fonseca Portuguese reds stand out in the Iberian range. Dr Loosen provides tasty German wines, and similarly good Italian bottles come from Giuseppe Mascarello, Felsina Berardenga and La Parrina.

Look out for more newsletters in the coming months. The number of tastings is also set to increase. All are welcome at these – even those who buy wine across the Channel.

Best buys

1994 Villard Casablanca Sauvignon Blanc, £
1993 David Wynn Dry White, £
Côte Rôtie 1990, Guigal, ££
Mercurey Blanc 1992, Domaine du Meix-Foulot, ££

Les Amis du Vin

(mail-order only)
430 High Road, London NW10 2HA

Tel 0181-451 0981
Fax 0181-459 4473

Open Mon–Fri 9.15–5.15 **Closed** Sat, Sun, public holidays **Cards** All accepted;
business accounts **Discount** 5% on 1 case **Delivery** Free in parts of London (1 case
or more); free on UK mainland (3+ cases); charges vary for smaller orders; mail order
available **Glass hire** Free with order **Tasting and talks** 4 or 5 tastings in London
each year **Cellarage** Not available

See 'The Winery'

John Armit Wines

5 Royalty Studios, 105 Lancaster Road,
London W11 1QF

Tel 0171-727 6846
Fax 0171-727 7133

Case sales only **Open** Mon–Fri 9–6 **Closed** Sat, Sun, public holidays **Cards**
Access, Visa; personal and business accounts **Delivery** UK delivery service; 1 or 2
cases £10, 3+ cases free **Glass hire** Not available **Tasting and talks** One large
tasting a year, plus tastings upon request for clients **Cellarage** £6 per case per year

The range of wines assembled by John Armit, former managing
director of Corney & Barrow, bears more than a passing
resemblance to that of his former company. There's plenty of
Bordeaux, much of it from the Moueix properties, and there's
plenty from Burgundy, and not an awful lot else besides. There
similarities end, however. Mr Armit and his cohorts have more
style, more panache, and, if dynamic is hardly the word for the
chaps at Helmet Row, it is quite appropriate here. When Robert
Parker, the famous American wine writer, was over last March, it
was Armit who hosted a lunch and a dinner in his honour.

The burgundy selection is impressive. Joining the two Leflaive
firms in providing whites are such producers as Guy Roulot,
Ramonet and Lamy-Pillot. Reds come from Ponsot, Ghislaine
Barthod, Simon Bize and Domaine de l'Arlot. Other French wines
of note are René Berrod's beaujolais, Sancerre from Paul Millérioux,
André Kientzler's Alsace and regional wines from Aimé Guibert
and Domaines Virginie.

From the rest of Europe, you'll find the superstar Ribera del Duero wines from Pesquera (but only from good vintages) and the Terrebianca Tuscans. A small but fascinating New World selection includes Coldstream Hills and Delatite from Australia, Californian wines from Groth, Ravenswood and Hess, and some great South African whites from Mulderbosch. And don't miss the chance to compare two very different styles of top Argentinian winemaking, represented by the wines of Weinert and Luigi Bosca.

The company is obviously doing something right. Sales were up 50% last year and a new computer system has just been installed to help speed up business. Bin-end sales bring some of the more stratospheric prices to nearer manageable levels, but there's always much of interest available, especially around the £10 mark.

Best buys

House white, Jacques Lurton Cuvée, £
Cuvée des Fleurs 1993, Vin de Pays d'Oc, £
Puligny-Montrachet 1993, Domaine Leflaive, ££
Bourgogne Rouge 1990, Mont Avril, Goubard, ££

ASDA

Head office
ASDA House, Southbank, Great Wilson Street,   *Tel* 0113-243 5435
Leeds, West Yorkshire LS11 5AD   *Fax* 0113-241 8666
(Over 200 stores throughout the UK)

Open (Leeds) Mon–Sat 9–8, Sun 10–4; Hours vary from store to store   **Closed** Easter Sunday, Christmas Day   **Cards** Access, Switch, Visa; personal accounts   **Discount** £2 off any case consisting of 12 bottles, £4 off any case over £48   **Delivery** Not available **Glass hire** Available to customers spending over £20, £10 refundable deposit required **Tasting and talks** Held in stores during hours of trading; outside by prior arrangement   **Cellarage** Not available

---

With the jovial Nick Dymoke-Marr now in charge, aided by Alistair Morrell (late of E H Booth) and Illy Jaffar, ASDA's wine department is currently in as good shape as that of any supermarket. The shelves are now laid out by style, with red wines classified by fullness and whites by sweetness, and bins and barrels containing wines of special interest (Colli di Catone Frascati on our last visit) have added an extra dimension. The rack of 'Wines for Special Occasions' attempts to attract those customers who cross to the other side of the aisle when such words as 'fine' and 'vintage' appear. Such marketing schemes would be of little use if there were nothing to back them up, but the ASDA range deserves credit for its compactness, for the attractive labelling and for many of the wines in the bottles.

From Bordeaux, the Château le Désert Sauvignon and Haut Saric Bordeaux red are reasonable; red burgundy is thin on the ground, but whites are more prolific, with Guy Mothe's Chablis and the St Véran from Domaine des Deux Roches of particular note. The rustic reds of the Rhône and southern France are generally good, while the pick of the regional whites are the Côtes de Gascogne and the Montagne Noire Chardonnay.

German wines include the obligatory Liebfraumilch, Piesporter, Niersteiner and Bernkasteler, plus much more serious fare from van Volxem, von Kesselstatt and Aschrott'sche Erben. The Coltiva wines are reasonable Italian cheapies, but the Castelcerino Recioto di Soave, the Rozzano red from Villa Pigna and the Chianti Colli Senesi from Salvanza are a good deal better for not very much more money. The Spanish selection is generally less inspired, although the Terra Alta Cabernet/Garnacha is good. Eastern Europe is better, and the own-label Hungarian Muscat is delicious.

The Arius wines are the pick of an otherwise lack-lustre Californian range, while Rowan Brook and Cono Sur supply some tasty Chilean fare. The Fairview Shiraz from South Africa is wonderful, while the Woodlands Pinot Noir is actually a more expensive wine in disguise. Undeterred when the supplier of the own-label Chardonnay told them that they could have no wine from the 1995 vintage, the buyers have assembled a decent set of Australian wines: Victoria Park is a great fizz, and the wines of Penfolds, Hardy's and Goundrey will not disappoint.

Discounts are available for case purchases, and glasses are now available for hire when over £20 is spent. The £1.99 wonders that the company is committed to stocking may not please the purists, but they're usually at least clean and well made, and without them many customers would bypass the wine department entirely. ASDA cannot be faulted for trying to make wine-buying more accessible to customers; it's easy to say that the cheaper wines should have more character, but if they did they wouldn't be cheaper.

Best buys

1994 Muscate Sec, Alasia, £
1994 Kasbah Shiraz/Malbec/Mourvèdre, £
1994 Shaw & Smith Chardonnay, ££
1992 Chianti Classico, Isole e Olena, ££

Stéphane Auriol Wines

High Street, Hartley Wintney, Hampshire *Tel* (01252) 843190
RG27 8NY *Fax* (01252) 844373

Open Mon–Sat 9–9; Sun and public holidays 12-2 **Closed** Chr Day **Cards** Access,
Amex, Delta, Switch, Visa; personal and business accounts **Discount** Negotiable
Delivery Free within 10-km radius on any order; free elsewhere with min. £150 order,
otherwise charged at cost; mail-order available **Glass hire** Free with order **Tasting
and talks** Regular monthly tastings, organised tastings available **Cellarage** Not
available

'I have always wanted to farm,' says John Carlisle, MD of Stéphane
Auriol. Anyone interested in grazing in his shop will find much to
ruminate over. Champagne comes from Herbert Beaufort and
Bollinger, with alternative sparklers in the form of Omar Khayyam
from India and Lindauer from New Zealand. The Caves de Hoen
provide Alsace wines, Loires are from Domaine du Rochoy, and
wines from La Chablisienne, Naigeon-Chauveau and Domaine des
Varoilles appear amongst the burgundies. There are three vintages
of Ch. Batailley in a range of clarets that caters for most pockets.
From Spain you'll find Navarra wines from Monte Ory and Rioja
from Faustino Martínez. We'd like to tell you who makes the
German and Italian wines, but the list doesn't say. No such
problem in Australia, with wines coming from Mitchelton, Wirra
Wirra and Plantagenet. The rest of the New World range is not as
healthy, although the Sumac Ridge Canadians, the Simonsig South
Africans and the Grove Mill New Zealanders will not disappoint.
There are also ports, sherries, Madeiras and whiskies aplenty, so
we'd recommend you to visit the quaintly named town of Hartley
Wintney, especially on the first Saturday of each month when there
is a range of wines for tasting.

Best buys

1993 Stéphane Auriol House White, Bordeaux Sauvignon, £
1987 Navarra Crianza, Monte Ory, £
Gewürztraminer 1993, Sumac Ridge, ££
Chatsfield Cabernet Franc 1994, Mount Barker, ££

For merchants who sell a minimum of twelve bottles, we say 'Case
sales only' in the details at the head of an entry.

The Australian Wine Club

Orders
Freepost WC5500, Slough, SL3 9BH   *Tel* 0800-716 893

Case sales only   Open Mon–Fri 9–6; Sat 10–4   **Closed** Sun, public holidays   **Cards**
Access, Amex, Delta, Visa;   **Discount** 10% discount on all purchases for members of
the Four Seasons Wine Plan   **Glass hire** Not available   **Tasting and talks** Annual
tasting in May   **Cellarage** Not available

The AWC's (forced) move in 1994 from retail premises in The
Strand in Central London to become an exclusively mail-order
operation based in Datchet has been a great success. So much so
that the main moan from Messrs Smith and Reedman is that
customers are drinking too much. Stocks are falling rapidly in the
aftermath of their annual Great Australian wine-tasting, in which
1,600 people 'went berserk ordering wine', and anxious eyes are
looking seaward for the arrival of more wine.

The range is certainly not the largest Aussie selection around,
and if you're looking for wines under £5, there are few available.
Similarly, if you're after such familiar names as Penfolds,
Rosemount and Brown Brothers, look elsewhere. Where the AWC
comes into its own is in the number of smaller and less familiar
wineries it lists. St Hallett, Henschke, Coldstream Hills and Penley
Estate are now famous, but keep an eye out for Chapel Hill,
Heritage, RBJ and Primo Estate from South Australia, for David
Traeger, Delatite and the drastically improved Water Wheel from
Victoria, for Allandale from the Hunter Valley and for Wignalls
over in the south-west corner of Western Australia. Perhaps the
best-value wines are those under the own-label Buckley's and
Laraghy's brands.

Another success has been the Four Seasons wine plan, under
which £25 per month automatically brings you four cases of wine a
year, each with a minimum value of £82.50. Demand was such that
supplies of certain wines for the spring 1995 case ran out, and
substitutes had to be found. Customers wanting to make up their
own minds can follow the action via the regular newsletter-cum-
list, the only criticisms of which are an over-reliance on exclamation
marks and the word 'stunning'. It gives greater prominence to the
wines that Australia does best, Rhône-style reds, Riesling and
Semillon, than to Cabernet and Chardonnay, but there are few
wines in its pages that we would not happily drink.

Best buys

St Hallett Poachers Blend 1994, £
Laraghy's Bin 599 Red 1994, £
Tim Adams 'The Fergus' 1994, ££
Primo 'Joseph' Cabernet Merlot Moda Amarone 1992, ££

Averys of Bristol

Head office
Orchard House, Southfield Road, Nailsea,   *Tel* (01275) 811100
Avon, BS19 1JD   *Fax* (01275) 811101
Shop
11 Park Street, Bristol, Avon BS1 5NG   *Tel* 0117-921 4145
Cellars
9 Culver Street, Bristol, Avon BS1 5JE   *Tel* 0117-921 4146

Open (Shop) Mon–Sat 10–6; (Cellars) Mon–Sat 9–7 **Closed** Sun, public holidays
Cards Access, Visa; business accounts **Discount** Available to Averys Bin Club
members **Delivery** Free within 5-mile radius of Bristol; 24+ bottles free, surcharge of
£5.50 under 24 bottles in mainland UK **Glass hire** Free, breakages charged for
Tasting and talks Available at Culver Street Cellars **Cellarage** Available depending
on quantity

Although Averys opened a new shop in 1995, 'new' is hardly the
word for the premises. Part of a labyrinth of cellars dating back to
the seventeenth century, they were the main Averys offices and
warehouse until April. With the amount of containerised traffic
increasing, it was decided to relocate the main storage facilities to
nearby Nailsea and open the old premises as Averys Wine Cellars.
The Park Street shop is still very much in business, but the new
Cellars offer parking outside, daily tastings and more besides. Sales
are by the case (rather than by the bottle as in Park Street), but
making up a dozen from the over 1,000 wines on show shouldn't
pose much of a problem.

The Averys assortment majors on the traditional wine areas of
the world, but still contains much of interest from the less-well-
established areas. John Avery was a pioneer of New World wines,
and in an interesting range, you'll find offerings from Tyrrells,
Mitchell and Coldstream Hills in Australia, C. J. Pask and Nobilo in
New Zealand and Hamilton-Russell, Klein Constantia and
Rustenberg from South Africa, while America is represented from
end to end by Swanson and Far Niente (California), Inniskillin
(Canada), Undurraga (Chile) and Norton (Argentina).

Spanish highlights are the Enate Somontano wines and Rioja
from La Rioja Alta, while reliable Italian fare is provided by
Antinori, Rocca della Macie and Araldica. Serious German wines
come from Drs Loosen and Thanisch, while the wines of Three

Choirs are the pick of the English range. The Yarden range from Israel is also surprisingly good, especially the sweet Muscat.

The wines of Remoissenet and Lupé-Cholet will please lovers of traditional burgundies, and numerous clarets are also available; do ask about the small stocks of older wines (available in quantities too limited to appear on the list or in the shops, but occasionally appearing in mixed cases in the January sales). Duboeuf provides beaujolais, and Rhône wines include several from Jaboulet Aîné and Mark Ryckwaert's great-value Côtes-du-Rhône. Among the Loires, Alphonse Mellot's Sancerre and Huet's Vouvray are most pleasing, and the Alsace wines of Hugel and Kuentz-Bas are also good. The best of the French country wines are those from Domaine de l'Orangerie and Domaines Virginie. Those looking for good-value champagne need look no further than the company's own-label wine.

The informative newsletters and special offers mean that it's worth being on the mailing list, and those wishing to spread the cost of wine-buying over a long period of time can join Averys' Bin Club.

Best buys

Vin de Pays des Côtes de Gascogne 1993/94, Domaine de Rieux, £
Vin de Pays de la Cité de Carcassone 1994, Domaine de L'Orangerie, £
Brauneberger Juffer Riesling Kabinett, 1993 Max Ferd. Richter, ££
Founders Reserve Pinot Noir 1991/92, Willamette Valley Vineyards, ££

Bacchus of Olney

2 Dartmouth Road, Olney, Buckinghamshire MK46 4BH   *Tel* (01234) 711140
Fax (01234) 711140

Open Mon–Fri 11–7, Sat and public holidays 9.30–7 **Closed** Sun, Mon 11–1 **Cards** Access, Delta, Switch, Visa; personal and business accounts **Discount** Negotiable **Delivery** Free Bucks, Northants, Beds and London (min. 2 cases) **Glass hire** Available, £1 per glass if broken **Tasting and talks** Private, corporate, on- and off-site **Cellarage** Not available

---

A welcome newcomer to the Guide, Russell Heap's shop has only existed since the late summer of 1994, but already promises much. You'll find Alsace wines from Pierre Sparr, a range of clarets that includes four vintages of Ch. Gruaud Larose, and burgundies from Bruno Clair, Jean Grivot and Vincent Girardin. Alain Paret and Domaine Durieu provide Rhônes, while tasty country wines come from Château Flaugergues and Domaine de la Fadèze. There's a small but decent Spanish set and a larger Italian set featuring Pinot

Bianco from La Prendina, Tuscan reds from Banfi and Barolo from Giordano. Quality German wines come from Gunderloch, Josef Leitz and Dr Loosen, and there's also a short set from Austria.

Henschke and Penley Estate provide the best of a good Australian selection, and the New Zealand section includes great stuff from Allan Scott and Martinborough Vineyards. Californian bottles are few at present, although you will find the Roederer Quartet sparkler; South Africans are thicker on the ground, with wines coming from de Wetshof, Uitkyk, Kanonkop, Landskroon and many others.

There is a Sampling Club, very much along the lines of that run by Wines of Interest (q.v.). For a fee of £10 per year, members can buy the two recommended wines of the month at half-price and, if they like them, buy further quantities at a reduced rate.

Best buys

Syrah 1994, Collin & Bourisset, £
Chenin Blanc 1992, Vredendal, £
1989 Kanonkop Cabernet Sauvignon, ££
Meursault Les Tillets 1992, Olivier Leflaive, ££

Ballantynes of Cowbridge

3 Westgate, Cowbridge, South Glamorgan CF71 7AQ   *Tel* (01446) 774840
Fax (01446) 775253

Open Mon–Sat 9–5.30 **Closed** Sun, public holidays **Cards** Access, Delta, Switch, Visa; personal and business accounts **Discount** 8% case discount on collections and local deliveries **Delivery** Free in Cardiff, Vale of Glamorgan, Cumbridge and Bridgend (min 1 case); nationwide (min £250 = 5% discount); mail-order available **Glass hire** Free with order **Tasting and talks** 3 times per year **Cellarage** £4.50 per case per year

---

'We do not believe in flying winemakers,' says Peter Ballantyne. Sorry Mr B., they do exist, but for character and style we'd plump for the producers on your list almost every time. The Ballantynes shop is now two years old, although the mail-order business has existed since 1978. The range continues to expand, and, while wines from Burgundy and Italy could be said to be specialities, quality abounds throughout.

New to the admirable Tuscan range is the wonderful Brunello (and Rosso) di Montalcino of Ciacci Piccolomini. The rest of Italy provides satisfaction by way of Valentini's Montepulciano d'Abruzzo and Luigi Ferrando's Carema. The German section of the list concentrates on the top estates of the Rhine and Mosel, and the Spanish section include Rioja from López de Heredia and Ribera del Duero from Félix Callejo. A move away from Australian wine has been noted over the last year, although a range which includes Wirra Wirra, Geoff Weaver's Stafford Ridge and Cullens still deserves attention, as do the wines from Bodegas Weinert in Argentina and Fairview Estate in South Africa.

France remains the most important country in the list, with burgundy a particular passion. Less familiar but good producers, such as J. J. Confuron and Coste-Caumartin, sit very happily alongside the more familiar Domaine Leflaive, Etienne Sauzet and Henri Jayer; regular offers augment the already impressive selection. Marcel Deiss and Domaine Schlumberger provide Alsace wines, Rhônes include several Châteauneufs from top producers, while Loires come from Gitton and Huet. Christian Senez provides a large range of champagne and a very decent group of clarets covers most price ranges and maturities. Highlights of an ever-expanding range of French regional wines are the Madiran from Domaine des Bories and the excellent-value wines of Domaine la Rosière.

With a range such as this the thrice yearly customer tastings should be worth frequenting. Those not close to Cowbridge might care to make use of the free delivery on orders over £120 – equivalent to roughly one glass of that double magnum of 1976 Château Pétrus that no one has yet snapped up.

Best buys

Syrah 1993, Domaine Mas Montel, £
Sauvignon blanc 1994, Château Saint-Flerin, £
Bourgogne Passetoutgrain 1992, Henri Jayer, ££
Pouilly-Fuissé 1992, Vieux Murs, ££

Balls Brothers

313 Cambridge Heath Road, London E2 9LQ
Tel 0171-739 6466
Fax 0171-729 0258

(14 wine bars in London)

Open Mon–Sat 10–6 **Closed** Sun, public holidays **Cards** All accepted; personal and business accounts **Discount** 5% on 1 case; mail order 2.5% on 5 cases, 5% on 11 cases **Delivery** Mail-order available, free delivery for 1+ case in Central London **Glass hire** Free with order, £10 deposit required **Tasting and talks** Tutored and social tastings in our bar/restaurants or customer premises **Cellarage** 5p+VAT per case per week ie; £2.60+VAT per year

---

Many of Richard Balls' customers are traditional City types with fairly traditional tastes who frequent the various Balls Brothers wine bars and restaurants in and around EC2. Richard aims to cater for such tastes, but also introduce customers to more exotic fare. So you will find quality clarets from Tour de Mons, La Lagune and

Ducru-Beaucaillou, burgundies from Michel Lafarge, Chavy and Jean-Marc Brocard and of course plenty of port and champagne. But you'll also find New World stars such as the Mitchell and Peter Lehmann from Australia, C J Pask from New Zealand and South Africans from Klein Constantia and Paradyskloof.

Other French wines of note are the Alsace wines from Paul Blanck, Châteauneuf from Château Mont Redon and Domaine du Vieux Télégraphe and an interesting set from southern France. Germans are rather lacklustre, but the Spaniards from Ochoa and La Rioja Alta, and the Italians from La Parrina and Castello di Volpaia are much better.

Best buys

Château Pech-Celeyran 1993, La Clape, £
1994 Fairview Chenin/Sauvignon Blanc, £
1993 Mitchell Peppertree Shiraz, ££
Pouilly Blanc Fumé 1992, Château de Tracy, ££

Adam Bancroft Associates

57 South Lambeth Road, London SW8 1RJ

Tel 0171-793 1902
Fax 0171-793 1897

Case sales only   Open Mon–Fri 8–6   **Closed** Sat, Sun, public holidays   **Cards** None accepted   **Discount** Available   **Delivery** Free in London elsewhere 1 case £6.50, 2 cases £8.50, 3+ cases free   **Glass hire** Available   **Tasting and talks** Available **Cellarage** Not available

---

So much for the upturn in the economy; the report from Adam Bancroft is that customers are tending to buy cheaper wines. Not that anything on his list is extraordinarily expensive. True, none of the Western Australian wines of Madfish Bay, Devil's Lair and Howard Park is under a fiver, but all offer character and subtlety. They are also the only non-French wines. From Bordeaux, 'a region which I've always regarded as both daunting and inherently less exciting to buy in', famous names are thin on the ground, but Ch. Belregard-Figeac will please claret-lovers everywhere. From the Loire, where there are almost as many red wines as white, Alain Marcadet, Masson-Blondelet and Pierre Girault are the names to look out for. Among the several tasty wines from the Rhône, Cornas from Colombo and red and white Châteauneuf from Domaine de la Janasse stand out; Colombo is also responsible for a Côtes du Roussillon in the regional French range, where it joins Ardèche wines from Domaine des Terriers.

The firm's real area of expertise, though, is Burgundy. From Billaud-Simon's Chablis in the north to François Calot's Morgon in

245

the south the region is covered with a disregard for big names but an eye for quality. Alain Guyard's Marsannay is great affordable white burgundy, the Mâconnais wines of Michel Forest are slightly pricier but still good value, and even Paul Pillot's range from Chassagne never reaches extortionate prices. From the range of reds, try the Côte de Nuits wines from Chopin-Groffier and Frédéric Esmonin, and from the Côte de Beaune, don't miss Bernard Glantenay's Volnay.

Here's a company which is quietly getting on with finding good, unknown wines, which it then offers at good prices with the minimum of fuss.

Best buys

Chardonnay 1994, Domeque, £
Syrah Rose 1994, Domaine de Ferrier, £
Côtes du Roussillon 1993, Jean-Luc Colombo, ££
Madfish Bay Unwooded Chardonnay 1994, ££

Barnes Wine Shop

51 Barnes High Street, London SW13 9LN

Tel 0181-878 8643
Fax 0181-878 6522

Open Mon–Sat 9.30–8.30, Sun 12–2 **Closed** Public holidays **Cards** Access, Amex, Switch, Visa; business accounts **Discount** 5% off mixed cases or full cases if payment made by credit card; 7% payment by cash/cheque **Delivery** Free in central London area; charges for further away; mail-order available **Glass hire** Free with order **Tasting and talks** Regular Saturday tastings; Summer and Winter regular tastings; Private tastings held in customer houses or companies by arrangement **Cellarage** £7.05 per case per year

---

As the *Guide* went to press this establishment was taken over by Lea and Sandeman (q.v.).

We have tried to make *The Which? Wine Guide* as complete as possible, but we would be pleased to hear from you about any other wine merchants you feel deserve an entry, or your comments on existing entries. You can now reach us on e-mail at: *guidereports@which.co.uk*

Barwells of Cambridge

70 Trumpington Street, Cambridge,   *Tel* (01223) 354431
Cambridgeshire CB2 1RJ   *Fax* (01223) 369818

Open Mon–Sat 10–10, Sun 12–3, 7–9 **Closed** New Year's Day, Chr and Boxing Days
Cards Access, Delta, Switch, Visa; personal and business accounts **Discount** 5–10%
on case **Delivery** Cambridge and environs (min. 1 case) **Glass hire** Free with order
Tasting and talks For local societies and colleges **Cellarage** £3.50 per case per year

The past year has seen this Cambridge company become
independent from Barwell and Jones, and so far the future looks
promising. You'll find plenty of claret, with magnums of 1978
Château Latour for those who can afford them, and Châteaux
Plince, Picque-Caillou and Malescasse for the less well-heeled.
Burgundies are mainly from Labouré-Roi, Rhônes include Côte
Rôtie from Burgaud, and there are several good-value country
wines. Grimaldi provides Italian reds from Piemonte, while Veneto
wines are from Guerrieri-Rizzardi. Spanish wines include Rioja
from Marqués de Cáceres and Montecillo, Austrian wines are from
Johann Topf, and Chilford Hundred gives an English interest to the
list. The Australian wines from Virgin Hills, Sandalford and
Woodstock are good, as are the South Africans from Meerlust, La
Motte and Drostdy Hof. America offers Wente Californian wines
and Columbia from Washington State amongst others, and from
further south come the Caliterra Chileans.

Prices were current in summer 1995 to the best of our knowledge but can
only be a rough indication of prices throughout 1996.

This is a young company that is still finding its feet, but we look forward to watching Barwells develop over the next twelve months.

Best buys

Drostdy Hof Steen, £
1989 Flonheimer Adelberg Auslese, Peter Mertes£
Fleur du Clinet 1989, Pomerol, ££
Vosne-Romanée 1985, Marcilly, ££

Benedict's

28 Holyrood Street, Newport, Isle of Wight PO30 5AU	*Tel* (01983) 529596 *Fax* (01983) 826868

Open Mon–Sat 9–5.30 **Closed** Sun, Chr Day and Boxing Day **Cards** Access, Amex, Visa; personal and business accounts **Discount** 5% on full cases (may be mixed); larger orders by negotiation **Delivery** Free delivery in the Isle of Wight; nationwide subject to carriage and packing at cost **Glass hire** Charges £1 per dozen **Tasting and talks** Regular blind tastings Sept–Apr; commissioned tastings as requested **Cellarage** £3 per case per year

Malcolm Rouse may be alone among wine-merchants in having the Wine and Spirit Education Trust diploma and an MBE. From his fortress on the Isle of Wight this retired naval officer has weathered the effects on his wine/delicatessen business of recession ('What recession?' J. Major, Westminster), cross-Channel shopping and (this is the Isle of Wight, remember) smuggling and has emerged bloodied but apparently unbowed.

We say 'apparently' because there are many wines in the range which probably have been in stock for a few years. Where red wines are concerned, this is frequently no bad thing. That 1986 Bulgarian Special Reserve Stambolovo Merlot will still be excellent, as will the Brown Brothers Shiraz of the same year from Australia, and much of the Italian and Spanish ranges will not have suffered from the passage of time; whether the same can be said for the 1986 Coopers Creek Cabernet/Merlot from New Zealand and the 1989 Loron Beaujolais is another matter. Where whites are concerned, though, the situation is different. Bulgarian Chardonnay from 1987, a 1990 Vinho Verde and much of the Spanish range should have been pensioned off many years ago.

Benedict's still deserves attention nonetheless, particularly for the ranges of claret and South African wines. The former boasts an excellent selection from the extra-ripe 1989 vintage, the pick of which are Ch. Nenin, Ch. Pavie and Ch. Branaire-Ducru. From the latter, reds from Meerlust and La Motte and whites from

Boschendal and Neetlingshof are merely the peak of a good solid selection. England, too, stands out, with the local wines of Adgestone, Barton Manor and Rosemary.

We wish Mr Rouse well over the coming year, but we would advise him perhaps to have a bin-end sale of some of his more mature wines and replace them with something fresher.

Best buys

Rosemary Vineyard Bacchus Dry White 1993, £
Neethlingshof Gewurztraminer 1994, £
'Le Ragose' Recioto della Valpolicella Amarone 1985, ££
Chambolle-Musigny Amoureuses 1990, Joseph Drouhin, ££

Bennetts Wines and Spirits

High Street, Chipping Campden,   *Tel* (01386) 840392
Gloucestershire GL55 6AG   *Fax* (01386) 840392

Open Mon–Fri 9–1, 2–5.30, Sat 9–5.30 **Closed** Sun, public holidays and Chr period
Cards Access, Visa; business accounts **Discount** 5% cash/cheque, 2.5% credit cards
on 1–5 cases; 7.5% cash/cheque, 5% credit cards on 5–9 cases; 10% cash/cheques, 7.5%
credit cards on 10+ cases **Delivery** Free nationwide (min 3 cases; (1 case £9, 2 cases
£8); free locally (10-mile radius, min. 1 case) **Glass hire** Free with order or £1 per
dozen **Tasting and talks** 2 main tastings per year, £5 refundable against purchase;
occasional wine dinners with hotels and restaurants **Cellarage** Not available

As Charles and Vicky Bennett concentrate more and more on the upper end of the wine market, business continues to increase at their Chipping Campden establishment. 'It is possible to make a business work while pursuing a policy of only selling the very best,' says Charles. 'We are sometimes accused of being élitist, but you don't go into a Rolls-Royce showroom looking for a Skoda.'

Nonetheless, there is still much for the less well-heeled to find on the shelves. The Cuvée du Cépage range of French country wines is very good value, and Mas de Daumas Gassac red and white are available for deeper pockets. Multiple vintages of Ch. Pétrus and the first growths will make you drool, but the numerous *cru bourgeois* clarets will please your bank manager. Burgundy-lovers will warm to whites from Olivier Merlin, Louis Carillon and Domaine des Comtes Lafon and reds from Daniel Rion, Vallet Frères and Bruno Clair. The Rhône and Alsace sections may be smaller, but wines from Chapoutier in the former and Schlumberger in the latter are certainly pleasing; champagnes include the familiar (Krug, Roederer) and the less familiar but good-value (Georges Goulet and Billion).

The German, Spanish and Portuguese ranges are similarly small, although all three are of high quality; Don Zoilo sherries and ports from Taylors and Ramos-Pinto set the standard. Lovers of Italian wine are better served: reds include Allegrini's Valpolicella, Mascarello's Barolo and Chianti from Isole e Olena and Fontodi, while the white includes Puiatti, Teruzzi e Puthod and Pieropan.

Devotees of the New World are also in for a treat. Californian wines include Calera Pinot Noir, a range of Ridge reds and the eccentric wines of the even more eccentric Randall Grahm of Bonny Doon. Australia yields Bannockburn, Shaw & Smith, Cape Mentelle and Yarra Yering, and fine New Zealand wines come from Kumeu River, Wairau River and Hunters. The Thelema wines from South Africa are also outstanding.

It's encouraging to see businesses such as the Bennetts' thriving by being good at being good. The inhabitants of Chipping Campden are indeed fortunate to have such an excellent wine-merchant on their doorstep.

Best buys

Les Terrassus du Guilmon Rouge 1993, £
Quinta de la Rosa 1992, £
Bannockburn Pinot Noir 1991, ££
François Billion 'Le Mesnil', ££

Bentalls of Kingston

Wood Street, Kingston-upon-Thames,	*Tel* 0181-546 1001
Surrey KT1 1TX	*Fax* 0181-549 6163

Open Mon–Fri 9–6 (Thurs till 9); Sat 8.30–6; Sun and public holidays 11–5 **Closed** Chr Day and Boxing Day **Cards** Access, Amex, Delta, Switch, Visa; personal and business accounts **Discount** 5% on 1 case **Delivery** Free in Kingston, Putney, Wimbledon, Richmond, Esher (minimum £10 order) **Glass hire** Free with order **Tasting and talks** In-store tastings on Sats and tutored cheese and wine tastings every 2 months on Thurs eves **Cellarage** Free for wines bought from Bentalls

---

The wine section of the Bentalls store in the heart of Kingston-upon-Thames is something of a haven of quiet compared with the bustle of the surrounding departments. Wine-lovers can browse at leisure through the selection of wines assembled by Andrew Willy, wine and food buyer for the shop. His range majors on interesting wines mainly from Old World countries but with a fair smattering from newer regions. For example, you'll find South Africans from Meerlust and l'Ormarins, Californians from Grgich Hills and Sonoma Cutrer and Aussies from Capel Vale and Brokenwood. Cousiño Macul provide Chileans, while New Zealanders are from Grove Mill and Esk Valley.

However, the European choice is much wider. Fans of Portuguese wines will find several interesting and serious reds,

João Pires Moscatel de Setubal and a wonderful selection of all styles of ports from Taylor, Niepoort and several other houses. Italian wines are strong too, with a combination of the familiar – Avignonesi, Isole e Olena, Voerzio – with the less well known – Querciabella and Argiolas. Spanish wines include Rioja from CVNE and Marqués de Murrieta, Ribera del Duero from Vega Sicilia and Valduero. German wines are sparse, although names such as Robert Weil and Lingenfelder are reassuring to see.

In France, Alsace comes from Schlumberger, Loires include Joguet Chinon and André Dézat Sancerre while good regional wines include Mas de Daumas Gassac and the Coteaux du Languedoc from Château de Montperzat. The Rhônes from de Barjac and Domaine de la Janasse are good, while claret lovers will find a constantly changing selection which is strong on wines around the £10 mark but which also has loftier fare for those who can afford it – 1966 Lafite and 1961 Léoville las Cases on our last visit. Burgundies too are ever-changing, with producers such as Billaud Simon in Chablis, Louis Carillon in Puligny and Domaine Bertagna in Nuits-St-Georges showing the calibre of the wines available. You'll find champagne from big names, but we'd steer you towards those from growers such as Ilostomme and Jacques Selosse.

Good advice and enthusiasm are very evident from the staff, who are always willing to give suggestions for food and wine partnerships. There are usually wines to taste each Saturday, and occasional promotions give customers the chance to sample food and wine from various regions around the world.

Best buys

1993 Bodegas Valduero Blanco, £
1993 Moldovan Cabernet Sauvignon Blanc, £
1989 Mouchão, Alentejo, ££
1993 Ruché di Castagnole Monferrato, ££

Berry Bros & Rudd

3 St James's Street, London SW1A 1EG

Tel 0171-396 9600
Orders 0171-396 9669
Fax 0171-396 9611

Berry's Wine Warehouse
Houndmills, Basingstoke, Hampshire RG21 2YB   *Tel* (01256) 23566
Berry's Duty-Free Shop
Terminal 3, Heathrow Airport   *Tel* 0181-564 8361

Open (London) Mon–Fri 9–5.30, (Heathrow) Mon–Sun 6–10, (Basingstoke) Tue, Wed
10–5, Thur, Fri 10–8, Sat 10–4 **Closed** public holidays **Cards** All accepted; personal
and business accounts **Discount** 3% on 3+ cases, 5% on 5+ cases, 7.5% on 10+ cases
Delivery Free delivery in mainland UK (min. 1 case); mail-order available **Glass hire**
£3.30 per 30 glasses (inc cleaning) **Tasting and talks** Tastings throughout year; daily
at Heathrow shop **Cellarage** £4.80 per case per year

The 'old dog/new tricks' line seems to have been forgotten by this
venerable merchant from St James's. After last year's expansion
into Heathrow Terminal 3, this year '300 years of wine experience
and expertise come to Basingstoke's first Wine Warehouse.' At the
new premises, close to their old wine shop in Basingstoke, the
company now offers everything from the famous Good Ordinary
Claret to stuff that is extremely good and far from ordinary.
Majestic need not feel threatened yet, but lovers of fine wine who
find themselves whistling up or down the M3 would be well
advised to pop in.

The company is, and always has been, a good place for the
classics, particularly claret, burgundy and German wines.
However, although the 'traditional' wines with which the company
has often been associated (Doudet-Naudin burgundy being the
most obvious) are still listed, the results of more adventurous wine-
buying now grace the range as well. The Rhônes include several
wines from Chapoutier and Château de Beaucastel, Loires include
Vacheron Sancerre and reds from Joguet and Couly-Dutheil, while
Trimbach, Dopff au Moulin and Kuentz-Bas provide the Alsace. A
small set of Italians includes Mascarello's Dolcetto and Fontodi's
Chianti, while the Spanish range includes CVNE Riojas and Chivite
Navarra. Of the nine English wines on offer we recommend those
from Staple St James and Bruisyard St Peter.

The wines of Shafer, Au Bon Climat and Qupé stand out in the
Californian range, and South American representation includes
Chilean wines from Carmen and Argentinian wines from Trapiche.
Of the greatly expanded South African range, try the reds of
Thelema, Kanonkop and Fairview and the whites from Louisvale
and Danie de Wet. From Australia come Wirra Wirra, Wignalls and
Hollick, and from New Zealand Hunters, Martinborough
Vineyards and Forrest Estate.

You'll also find plenty of champagne, sherry, port and Madeira, as well as the company's own bottlings of single malts and other impressive spirits. Wines are now always available for tasting in Basingstoke, and there are large customer tastings six times a year. If you can't visit any of the shops, you can keep in touch with the company via the entertaining newsletters. Those unable to make up their minds which wines to buy might care to take advantage of the 'Like Clockwork' scheme, under which £25 per month ensures the delivery of a mixed case of wines four times a year.

Best buys

Good Ordinary Claret, £
Berrys' French Country White, £
Brauneberger Juffer Riesling Spätlese 1990, Max Ferd. Richter, ££
1990 Fixin, Fougeray de Beauclair, ££

B H Wines

| Boustead Hill House, Boustead Hill, | *Tel* (01228) 576711 |
| Burgh-by-Sands, Carlisle, Cumbria CA5 6AA | *Fax* (01228) 576711 |

Case sales only **Open** Mon–Sat 9–6; other times by arrangement **Closed** Thurs except by appointment **Cards** None accepted; personal and business accounts **Discount** By arrangement **Delivery** Free in Carlisle area and North Lakes (min. 1 case); nationwide mail-order available (3+ cases free, 1/2 cases £10) **Glass hire** Free with order **Tasting and talks** One in-store Chr tasting, regular wine club meetings, talks and tastings to societies by request, wines often open for customers to taste **Cellarage** Not available

---

'We plan to remain a centre of excellence in the North of England for wines of character, quality and value.' Linda Neville's plan for the year is an admirable one; it would be hard for the business that she and husband Richard have built up since 1984 to become much better. They organise Wine and Spirit Education Trust courses in Carlisle, have their own wine-tasting society and dispense invaluable advice to local restaurateurs on how to organise their wine-lists.

They also have a great range of wines. Of particular note are the several mature New World wines at prices that make you check whether VAT is included. Rouge Homme 1985 Cabernet, Evans & Tate 1984 Shiraz, Fetzer 1985 Barrel Select Cabernet, Hamilton Russell 1990 Pinot Noir, Martinborough 1989 Chardonnay, Renaissance 1983 Late Harvest Riesling and a clutch of others from the '80s are all under a tenner. If we've beaten you to Boustead Hill House to mop up such bargains, a quick look at the dozens of younger wines available should ease the pain.

By comparison with the New World representation the French list is sparse, although ferreting about the Burgundy and Bordeaux ranges will unearth a set of wines from Domaine Moillard and clarets from Ch. Léoville-Barton and Ch. Vieux-Château-Certan. The selection from southern France has Mas de Daumas Gassac, Château Simone in Palette and Domaine de Trévallon, while the Rhônes include four vintages of Bernard Burgaud's Côte Rôtie.

The Spanish list is good, but the Italian one is better, with a range of *vini da tavola* from around the country including I Sodi di San Niccolò, Aldo Conterno's Il Favot and Umani Ronchi's Cumaro. The best items in the German selection, from Robert Weil and Mönchhof, are to be found in the sweet wine section – a B H speciality that also includes Austrian wines from Willi Opitz and the luscious Vin de Constance from South Africa. Denbies provide several English wines made from grapes, while Rock's offer a range made from other fruit, including a gooseberry sparkler. How this last stands up against the champagnes of Pol Roger and others is not for us to say; perhaps you should propose a comparative tasting to the B H Wine Society.

Best buys

Côtes de Duras Sauvignon Blanc 1994, £
Montepulciano d'Abruzzo, Umani Ronchi 1992, £
Coteaux de Tricastin 1990, Domaine le Vieux Micocoulier, ££
Côtes de Castillon 1990, Château Puycarpin, ££
Château Theulet Cuvée Prestige 1990, Monbazillac, ££

Bibendum

113 Regent's Park Road, London NW1 8UR

Tel 0171-722 5577
Fax 0171-722 7354

Case sales only **Open** Mon–Thur 10–6.30, Fri 10–8, Sat 9.30–5 **Closed** Sun, public holidays **Cards** Access, Amex, Delta, Switch, Visa; personal and business accounts **Discount** None offered **Delivery** Free mainland England, London and South-East (min. 1 case), elsewhere £10 per delivery **Glass hire** £1 per tray of 24 **Tasting and talks** Monthly tastings **Cellarage** 50p per case per month

The past year has seen the launch of an exciting new list that genuinely achieves its aim of making wine more interesting and accessible. There are profiles of all the producers, and also useful boxes of the 'If you've enjoyed Wine X, why not try Wine Y?' variety. Nor is the list a triumph of repackaging over lack of content. A large number of the wines on offer have a letter 'N' in a star next to the listing, denoting new items.

Joining a good set of regional wines are the Roussillon reds and whites of Gérard Gauby and serious Faugères from Gilbert Alquier. The Vacqueyras of Château des Tours joins some serious Rhône wines. Additions to the Loire range include Nicolas Joly's Coulée de Serrant, although the Rolly Gassmann Alsace wines have not been supplemented. Burgundies are a real Bibendum speciality, and there's plenty of activity early each Spring with a major *en primeur* offer. Don't miss the wines of Ghislaine Barthod, Michel Lafarge and Jean-Marc Boillot.

There are small but tasty German and Spanish selections, but the Italian range is of greater interest. Saffirio's Barolo, Talenti's Brunello, Vallarom Chardonnay and the characterful wines of Cascina Castle't are our favourites. Good-value Australian wines from Basedows join more expensive but very serious bottles from Yeringberg. There are good New Zealand reds and whites, and a totally new South African range from Wildekrans, Bouchard Finlayson and Grangehurst. The Californian list is a mix of excellence and eclecticism; great Pinot and Chardonnay come from Morgan, Acacia and Chalone, while for spicier reds, check out Duxoup Wine Works' Charbono and the Zinfandels from Topolos and Elyse. New from further south are the Caliterra wines from Chile and the tasty Catena range from Argentina.

Best buys

Sauvignon Blanc 1993, Mount Konocti, £
Red Cliffs Colombard 1994, Victoria, £
Catena Cabernet Sauvignon 1993, Agrelo Vineyard, ££
Edna Valley Chardonnay 1993, ££

The Bin Club (Howells of Bristol)

| The Old Brewery, Station Road, Wickwar, | *Tel* (01454) 294085 |
| Gloucestershire GL12 8NB | *Fax* (01454) 294090 |

Open Mon–Fri 9–5.30 **Closed** Sat, Sun, public holidays **Cards** Not accepted; personal and business accounts **Discount** Not available **Delivery** Bristol and Gloucester; nationwide mail-order service (min. 3 cases) **Glass hire** Not available **Tasting and talks** Not available **Cellarage** 28p + VAT per case per month

Much of the business undertaken by this mail-order merchant is with British expatriates who wish to lay down fine wine until their return to the UK. Members (life membership is £25) sign up for a monthly subscription (recommended £40) and build up credit that can then be spent on Bin Club wines. There is no core list as such. Instead, members receive around six offers per year, each of which features a small number of wines: perhaps ten champagnes, or fifteen wines for laying down. The wines in these offers are very good, and the demand from customers is, if anything, for wines of even higher calibre. Those in search of even better wines can sign up for the Bin Club 100. A subscription of £100 or more per month gives a lucky few first bite at the handful of cases of rare wines that occasionally become available, such as Cloudy Bay Sauvignon, Sassicaia, Grange Hermitage and others.

Of course, you don't have to live overseas to buy wine from the Bin Club, but purchasers based in the UK might care to check prices against those of other merchants. However, we are sure that no merchant serves the expatriate community so well. The directors regularly travel and meet members throughout the world, and, from the sound of it, a good time is had by all.

Booths

Head office
4, 5 & 6 Fishergate, Preston, Lancashire PR1 3LJ
Tel (01772) 251701
Fax (01772) 204316

Open Every day, varies from store to store **Closed** Some public holidays **Cards** Access, Switch, Visa; **Discount** 10% on mixed case of 12 **Delivery** Not available **Glass hire** Free with orders over £25 **Tasting and talks** Occasional **Cellarage** Not available

Booths is surely unique in the UK wine trade in being able to set up horizontal tastings of both 1.5 litre bottles of own-label Liebfraumilch, Bereich Nierstein, Hock and Piesporter Michelsberg and of 1988 Châteaux Trotanoy, Gruaud-Larose, Latour à Pomerol and Beychevelle. One might suspect that wines such as these were there only for show, with one case of each spread thinly between the 24 stores, but this is simply not so. Sales of bottles over £8 continue to increase, especially for reds, and, although the full range only appears in the top stores (Knutsford, Windermere and Millbrook Way), you'll find some very decent bottles in every outlet.

Wines from the Buxy co-op figure among the white burgundies, but you'll also find Puligny from Domaine Leflaive and even La Tâche. Grippat's Hermitage Blanc appears among the Rhônes, while Schlumberger provides excellent Alsace wines, and alongside those basic, less appealing German wines there are more impressive offerings at all sweetness levels. Sassicaia tops the list of Italian notabilities, which also includes Conterno e Fantino's delicious Mon Pra. Spanish offerings come from Ochoa, CVNE and Vega Sicilia.

A strong Australian set includes Cape Mentelle Zinfandel, Yarra Yering Pinot and Willespie Semillon, while Cloudy Bay Chardonnay and Wairau River Sauvignon are the pick of the New Zealand range. The Californian list is not as impressive, but Cuvaison Merlot and Opus One appear amid a sea of Gallo.

There are of course plenty of 'normal' supermarket wines, and here Booths is on a par with the competition. However, the Booths range goes on to soar (very successfully) into the realms of fine wine, and it is for these flights of fancy that the stores deserve your custom.

Best buys

Peter Lehmann 1993 Semillon, £
Pauillac 1990, Château Batailley, £
Fetzer Cabernet Sauvignon 1987, ££
Booths Brut Champagne, ££

Booths of Stockport

62 Heaton Moor Road, Heaton Moor, Stockport, Cheshire SK4 4NZ	*Tel* 0161-432 3309 *Fax* 0161-432 3309

Open Mon–Fri 9–7, Sat 8.30–5.30 **Closed** Sun, public holidays **Cards** All accepted **Discount** 5% on mixed case; 8% on unsplit case **Delivery** Free in Stockport area (min. 1 case); nationwide mail-order at cost **Glass hire** Free with order **Tasting and talks** Every Saturday; theme or topic once a month **Cellarage** Not available

Roles are firmly defined in the delicatessen run by the Booth brothers. 'Graham buys the food, leaving John to enjoy talking about, tasting and selling the wines to his heart's content.' This John is quite good at, although those looking for the traditional classics of the wine world might care to look elsewhere. Not that the clarets and burgundies are poor, there just aren't very many of them; the wines of Vallet Frères and Ch. Ramage-la-Batisse stand out. Other French wines worth trying are Henry Pellé's Ménétou-Salon, the Rhônes from Alain Paret and Château Fortia and the Corbières of Château de Lastours. And don't miss the characterful champagne from Jacques Selosse.

Good Italian wines abound, with much of interest under £10. The J. M. da Fonseca Portuguese range, too, is good, and you'll also find some mature Moldovan wines dating back to 1975. Californian offerings from Newton and Frog's Leap, the Chilean and Mexican wines from Viña Porta and L. A. Cetto, and the Jackson Estate New Zealanders are all tasty, but the best range is the Australian. Whether you're after the lofty Yarra Yering, Penfolds Grange Hermitage and Mountadam Chardonnay, or the good-value wines of David Wynn, Salisbury Estate and Peter Lehmann, there's something here for you.

The tasting programme aims to educate as well as entertain and, with prices usually well under £10 per session, is good value. John is just recovering from the ignominy of the Booth's side's defeat in a blind-tasting competition against the nearby Sandiway Wine Company; it was the Beenleigh Manor Cabernet/Merlot that was the team's downfall. Nonetheless, a good time was had by all, even if the losers did have to stand everyone a meal at a Manchester Chinese restaurant.

Best buys

Quinta de la Rosa, Douro, Portugal, £
Mas de la Garrigue, Côtes du Roussillon, £
1992 Mas de Daumas Gassac Rouge, ££
1992 Mountadam Chardonnay, ££

Bordeaux Direct

New Aquitaine House, Paddock Road, Caversham, Reading, Berkshire RG4 5JY	*Tel* (01734) 481711 *Fax* (01734) 461953
Parent company – Direct Wines (Windsor) Ltd as above	
2 Dorna House, Guildford Road, West End, Woking, Surrey GU24 9PW	*Tel* (01276) 856133
3 Holtspur Parade, Beaconsfield, Bucks HP9 1DA	*Tel* (01494) 677564
144 High Street, Bushey, Herts WD2 3DH	*Tel* 0181-950 0747
121 Arthur Road, Windsor, Berks SL4 1RU	*Tel* (01753) 866192

Open (Retail Sat 9–6) (Mail-order Mon–Fri 9–7, Sat 10–5, Sun 10–4) **Closed** Chr Day and Easter Monday **Cards** All accepted; business accounts **Delivery** Free nationally for orders over £50; mail-order available **Glass hire** Free **Tasting and talks** In store tastings by arrangement; annual Vintage Festival in London with producers present; occasional tastings at venues around the country **Cellarage** Not available

---

Although the name may be unfamiliar, Direct Wines (Windsor) is one of Britain's biggest wine-retailers. It is the company behind both Bordeaux Direct and the Sunday Times Wine Club, which between them have a very large section of the mail-order market. There's practically no difference between the companies in terms of the wines they sell; the July 1995 lists from both were identical, barring two wines and a few very minor cosmetic differences. Those lists are well-produced affairs, full of tasting notes and mainly based around mixed-case offers. The wines are generally good, and getting better, with southern France remaining a particular area of strength. The quality of the mailings is as high as those of any company, and the large number of customers has given rise to enthusiastic social activities, topped by the annual Vintage Festival in London at which 4,000+ people have a chance to taste through the range and meet many of the producers.

We had thought that the Vintage Festival was only for the STWC members, but the Bordeaux Direct entry form also claimed it as part of its make-up. If so, this makes it somewhat unnecessary to pay £10 per year (or £35 for life) to join the STWC. However, our main criticism is that the prices remain far too high. Appellation for appellation, the wines are very good, but pound for pound, we would spend our beans elsewhere. Still, the level of service is hard to fault, and the multitude of customers shows that the company must be doing something right.

Best buys

Bianco Vergine Val di Chiana 1994, Renzo Masi (white), £
Farnese Montepulciano d'Abruzzo 1994 (red), £
Le XV du Président 1994, Côtes du Roussillon (red), ££
Château La Clarière Laithwaite 1993, Côtes de Castillon (red), ££

The Bottleneck

7&9 Charlotte Street, Broadstairs, Kent CT10 1LR   *Tel* (01843) 861095
                                                        Fax (01843) 604004

Open Mon–Sat 9–9, Sun, Good Fri and public holidays 12–2, 7–9 **Closed** Chr and Boxing Days **Cards** All accepted; business accounts **Discount** 5% on cases (wine/beer), 7.5% case discount, monthly special offer wines **Delivery** Free in the Thanet local area (min. £20 purchase), rest of East Kent free (min. 1 case) **Glass hire** Free with order to fill glasses three times **Tasting and talks** Every Sat morning - new products **Cellarage** Not available

There are plenty of bottles worth necking at Chris & Lin Beckett's Broadstairs establishment, and we would not doubt their claim to have the best range of wines in Thanet. Cross-Channel shopping remains a threat, but sales are increasing. The New World remains popular, and new arrivals are the South African wines from Hamilton Russell and Weltevrede, the Villard Chilean range and the Flichman Sangiovese/Cabernet from Argentina. Californians are rather ordinary, although William Wheeler's Quintet is especially good. New Zealand offerings come from Ngatarawa, Palliser and Vavasour, while a long list from Australia features wines from Pipers Brook, Wolf Blass and Rockford.

The French range is not as good. Only the clarets have any degree of authority about them, and there are several tasty wines on the sensible side of £15. Spain produces sherries from González Byass and the Enate wines from the Somontano region; Dr Loosen appears in the German range, while Italian bottles include Chianti Classico from Antinori and Pellegrino's scrumptious Moscato.

Best buys

Villard Sauvignon Blanc 1994, Aconcagua, Chile, £
Sutter Home Zinfandel 1992, California, £
Rockford Dry Country Grenache 1993, Australia, ££
Châteauneuf du Pape 1990, Domaine Font de Michelle, ££

Bute Wines

Mount Stuart, Rothesay, Isle of Bute	*Tel* (01700) 502730
Strathclyde PA20 9LR	*Fax* (01700) 505313
2 Cottesmore Gardens, London W8 5PR	*Tel* 0171-937 1629

Case sales only Open Mon–Fri 9–5 **Closed** Sat, Sun, public holidays **Cards** None accepted **Discount** 12+ cases **Delivery** Mail-order available **Glass hire** Not available **Tasting and talks** Various tastings throughout the year **Cellarage** £5 per case per year (or part year)

In 1995 the house and gardens of Mount Stuart, family seat of the Stuarts of Bute, were opened to the public. With this came the winding down of the Isle of Bute office of Bute Wines, and the transfer of all business to the London address. However, Jennifer, Marchioness of Bute, remains at the helm to steer a course over the seas of the fine-wine world. That course is somewhat steadier than it was a few years ago, when she overzealously bought rather a lot of 1989 claret *en primeur*, which still graces the list. The purse-strings have been kept under slightly better control since then, but this is still one of the best ranges of Bordeaux around, with Pomerol in particular in plentiful supply. There's an impressive array of burgundies as well, with a good range of 1986 whites and of reds from 1988-90. Alsace wines comes from Zind-Humbrecht and Théo Faller, fine Vouvray from Domaine de la Saboterie while the wines of Guigal, Chave and Jacques Reynaud stand out from the Rhône list. From outside France, there's a handful of reasonable Australian wines, some excellent Californians, five vintages of Sassicaia and a range from the Massandra collection dating back to 1929.

The Bute office may have closed, but occasional wine weekends are still held at Mount Stuart, usually with a visiting winemaker from properties such as Domaine de l'Arlot or Domaine de Chevalier. In an ideal world Lady Bute would have been allowed to keep buying at the exhilarating rate she once did, but we appreciate that it was probably 'a good thing' for business to exercise slightly more restraint. These days, if you want to benefit from her wine-spotting talent, you'll have to keep in touch with the regular offers of burgundy and bordeaux. The wines are still great, and there are usually several to choose from, but the number of cases of each is slightly more limited than in days gone by.

Best buys

Pomerol 1989, Château Lagrange, ££
Chablis 1990, Tribut, ££

The Butlers Wine Cellar

247 Queen's Park Road, Brighton, East Sussex   *Tel* (01273) 698724
BN2 2XJ   *Fax* (01273) 622761

Open Tue, Wed 10–6, Thur, Fri 10–7, Sat 9–7   **Closed** Mon, Sun, public holidays and Chr   **Cards** Access, Amex, Delta, Switch, Visa;   **Discount** None offered   **Delivery** Within 10-mile radius; nationwide mail-order available (3+ cases free)   **Glass hire** Free with order (min 6 bottles)   **Tasting and talks** Approximately fortnightly **Cellarage** Not available

Hard-nosed commerciality takes something of a back seat to out-and-out enthusiasm at Geoffrey and Henry Butler's Brighton shop. Many merchants sell odd bottles of this and that, but the Butler selection is one of the oddest. Where else can you find 1962 Romanian Pinot Gris, 1953 Liebfraumilch, 1949 Bourgogne Rouge or 1939 Priorato Rancio?

More cautious wine-drinkers will also find much of interest, particularly among the clarets, where a broad range stretches back to 1928 Ch. Cantenac Brown. Lovers of white burgundy will find several mature treats, including a range of Meursaults dating back to 1961. Highlights of the French regional selection are the Sauvignon from Chapelle de Cray and the Viognier from Chais Cuxac.

As well as that venerable Liebfraumilch, the German range contains a 1962 Piesporter plus a large set of fine wines from Deinhard. The Italian wines also look good, whether you go for the heady heights of Sassicaia or the more affordable range from the south of the country. The compact Spanish selection includes the good-value wines of Monte Ory in Navarra, and value is also the watchword for the Moldovan and Romanian ranges. Tatachilla Hill and d'Arenberg form the backbone of the Australian collection, but wines from the United States are thin on the ground. Of greater note are those from South Africa, particularly the mature Zonnebloem reds and the Nederburg sweeties.

The new wine club – subscription £10 per annum, refundable against purchases – gives members discounts, newsletters and first pick at new wines. Membership is essential for those interested in attending the fortnightly tastings: among the most stimulating in the country. The current calendar includes Ch. Haut-Brion v. Ch. La Mission-Haut-Brion and the fascinating prospect of 1992 Domaine de la Romanée-Conti burgundies in a head-to-head with Doudet-Naudin wines from the '50s and '60s.

Best buys

Andes Peaks Chardonnay (Chile), £
Cinco Viñas, Vino de Mesa £
Romanian Pinot Gris 1962, ££
Château La Croix Du Pez (St Estèphe) 1989, ££

Anthony Byrne Fine Wines

Ramsey Business Park, Stocking Fen Road, Ramsey,	*Tel* (01487) 814555
Cambridgeshire PE17 1UR	*Fax* (01487) 710831

Open Mon–Fri 8.30–6, Warehouse 5–10 **Closed** Sat, Sun, public holidays **Cards** Access, Visa; business accounts **Discount** On full case purchases **Delivery** Free for min. 5 cases of £250, below £6 per drop **Glass hire** Not available **Tasting and talks** By invitation only **Cellarage** Not available

Anthony Byrne does the bulk of its business with hotels and restaurants throughout the country, and only 5% is with the general public. However, it's 5% of an awfully big pie. Other companies may be more geared up to deal with private customers, but it's doubtful whether many can compete with Anthony Byrne's range of over 2,000 wines. Burgundy-lovers, in particular, will find much to delight them. Chablis is from Château de Maligny, while other whites are from Gagnard-Delagrange, Domaine Leflaive, Lamy-Pillot and Pierre Morey. For red burgundy, the wines from Domaine de l'Arlot, Rossignol-Trapet and Georges Clerget will not fail to satisfy. The champagnes from Drappier and Henriot may not be the best-known but they are excellent. Clarets cover all the major appellations with thoroughness, with wines up to first-growth level as well as such affordable châteaux as Ch. Lyonnat in Fronsac and Ch. des Annereaux in Lalande de Pomerol. The Alsace range from Zind-Humbrecht is hard to beat, and the Loire range, with wines from Lucian Crochet, Pierre-Jacques Druet and Didier Dagueneau, isn't far behind. Rhône stars include Alain Graillot, Tardy & Ange and Château de Beaucastel.

Noteworthy German wines come from Wegeler-Deinhard and von Kesselstatt, while the Italians from Isole e Olena, Allegrini and Giacomo Ascheri will not disappoint. You'll find a large Penfolds range in the Australian list, plus other wines from Delatite, Pipers Brook and Petaluma. From New Zealand look out for Palliser, Babich and Vavasour; other New World highlights are Merryvale wines from California, Neetlingshof from South Africa and Santa Carolina from Chile.

Those who seek the traditional personal service of an olde worlde wine-merchant will probably not enjoy the Byrne experience. However, the no-frills service does mean that prices are kept down, and the quality and depth of the range is very hard to argue with.

Best buys

Côtes du Lubéron 1993, Château Val Joanis Rouge, £
1994 Neetlingshof Gewürztraminer, £
Tokay Vieilles Vignes 1992, Zind-Humbrecht, ££
Nuits-St-Georges 1er cru Les Forêts 1989, Domaine de l'Arlot, ££

D Byrne & Co

12 King Street, Clitheroe, Lancashire
BB7 2EP

Tel (01200) 23152

Open Mon–Sat 8.30–6 (Thur and Fri till 8) **Closed** Sun, Chr, Boxing and New Year's Days, Easter **Cards** None accepted; personal and business accounts **Discount** £1.50 on 1 mixed case; 5% on orders over £250 **Delivery** Free within Clitheroe (min. 1 case) **Glass hire** Free with order **Tasting and talks** Annual customer tasting Sep to Oct; in-store tastings most Saturdays **Cellarage** £1 per year

It's something of a disappointment to enter the Clitheroe premises of Andrew and Philip Byrne for the first time. Yes, there are some beautiful old shelves above and to the side of the counter; yes, there are wine racks full of bottles; and, yes, there is an exotic whiff in the air, a mixture of coffee and fresh tobacco. But where's all this fine wine that everyone goes on about?

Pass through a narrow opening into the adjoining room and you'll find out. A sea of wooden boxes full of top clarets spreads out before you, and the racks on the walls are stuffed with top French and German wines. Press on, and you'll find a room full of Italian and Australian bottles interspersed with a few bits and pieces from other countries, and then, finally, the New Zealand, Spanish and South African wines.

It's hard to guess how many different wines are in stock, and we wonder if even Philip or Andrew know precisely. Rest assured though, that if you are after a particular wine style, they will have at least one top-class example available. Nor can it be said (as we have heard some competitors say) that they merely buy what others have already recommended. Yes, they keep in touch with the trends, but they also set them, and nothing ends up in the shop unless they enjoy it themselves.

The brothers describe themselves as 'polite, hard-working and happy,' and the customers who regularly travel hundreds of miles to visit the shop obviously approve of the service and the wines. You'll find a constantly evolving and expanding range that already threatens to burst out of every nook and cranny in the shop. The Byrnes are always prepared to advise on any wines in the shop, but

263

you'll bring a special smile to their faces if you enquire about the Alsace wines.

A lack of pretence, the lack of a bank loan and some canny buying, particularly where the clarets are concerned, mean that prices are extremely reasonable. All the same, don't expect to leave the shop without having spent, either physically or just mentally, an alarming amount of money.

Best buys

1992 Trapiche Pinot Noir, Argentina, £
1993 Villard Sauvignon, Chile, £
St-Julien 1988, Château Talbot, ££
1994 St-Véran Terre Noir, Domaine des Deux Roches, ££

Cairns & Hickey

854–856 Leeds Road, Bramhope, Leeds,   *Tel* (0113) 2673746
West Yorkshire LS16 9ED   *Fax* (0113) 2613826

Open Mon–Fri 9–9, Sat 10–9, Sun 12–2, 7–9 **Closed** Chr Day **Cards** Access, Delta, Switch, Visa; personal and business accounts **Discount** 5% discount on cases (can be mixed) **Delivery** Free approx. 30-mile radius; nationwide mail-order **Glass hire** Free with order **Tasting and talks** Regular in-house tastings, normally Sats **Cellarage** Available £3 per year

The ending of the lease has forced Peter Cairns to close his Blenheim Terrace shop, but it's very much business as usual in Bramhope. You'll find a range of claret that sticks mainly to the lesser classed growths, but does include Ch. Margaux and Ch. Mouton-Rothschild. Chablis come from Gérard Tremblay and there are other burgundies from Louis Latour, Drouhin and a clutch of growers. Dopff & Irion provides most of the Alsace wines, Chapoutier does the same for the Rhône, and Loire wines come from Domaine Baumard, Ackerman-Laurence and Paul Millerioux. Canard-Duchêne features among a range of familiar champagnes. The German wines may be good, but the list neglects to say who made them; the Italians are slightly uninspiring, but the Spanish bottles from Marqués de Murrieta and Senorío de Los Llanos are better.

The pick of the Australian list are the wines from Grant Burge, Cape Mentelle and Mountadam; New Zealand offerings include wines from Oyster Bay, Nobilo and Jackson Estate. Beringer Vineyards stands out in the Californian section, and other Americans of interest are the Domaine Drouhin's Oregon Pinot, the Inniskillin Canadian wines and the Chileans from Santa Carolina. We'd pass over the KWV South Africans in favour of the wines from Klein Constantia and Backsberg. Gonzalez Byass sherries, a range of vintage ports and several whiskies are also available, but if we had some spare space in the shopping bag, we'd fill it with a pint bottle of Tim Taylor's Landlord.

Best buys

Côtes de Gascogne Blanc, 1994, Lou Magret, £
1994 Sauvignon Blanc Alondra Chile, Santa Emiliana, £
1994 Nobilo Sauvignon Blanc, Marlborough, ££
Listrac 1990, Château Fourcas Hosten, ££

Cape Province Wines

77 Laleham Road, Staines, Middlesex	*Tel* (01784) 451860
TW18 2EA	*Fax* (01784) 469267

Open Mon–Sat 9–5.30 **Closed** Sun, public holidays **Cards** Access, Switch, Visa **Discount** Available **Delivery** Free delivery within 5-mile radius (min. 1 case); below 1 case orders £6.50 **Glass hire** Free with local order (min. 3 cases) **Tasting and talks** At weekends **Cellarage** Not available

Peter Loose has over 20 years' experience of importing South African wine, so it comes as little surprise that his range from the Cape is one of the best around. Where he scores over many people who have jumped on the South African bandwagon more recently is in his stocks of more mature wines from the 1970s and 1980s. So if you want to see how Zonnebloem's 1979 Pinotage, Meerlust's 1980 Rubicon or Rustenberg's 1978 Cabernet are ageing, or if you'd like to compare them with the current vintages, this is the place to come. Of the younger wines, our favourites are the reds from Hamilton Russell, Simonsig and Delheim, and the whites from Klein Constantia, Dieu Donné and Neetlingshof. If you're a Cape wine fan (or eager to be converted) you're almost certain to find something to your liking here.

Best buys

1991 Nederburg Baronne, £
1994 Neetlingshof Gewürztraminer, £
1991 Backsberg Klein Babylonstoren, ££
1989 Nederburg Weisser Riesling Late Harvest, ££

A Case of Wine ('Pigs 'n' Piglets')

Harford, Pumpsaint, Llanwrda, Dyfed	*Tel* (01558) 650671
SA19 8DT	*Fax* (01558) 650671
A Case of Wine Deli	
Bridge Street, Lampeter, Dyfed	*Tel* (01570) 423771

Open Mon–Sat 9–11, Sun 9–6 (shop Mon–Sat 10–5.30 excluding Wed) **Closed** Public
holidays (shop closed Wed, Sun and public holidays) **Cards** None accepted
Discount 10% discount on £100 order for unmixed wines or 5% discount on any
unmixed case including free delivery **Delivery** Free in most counties in Wales (min. 1
case); mail-order service available in Wales only **Glass hire** Free; breakages charged
for **Tasting and talks** Monthly wine and food events held at restaurant; private
wine-tastings organised to customer requirements, free tuition included **Cellarage**
Not available

From his new deli in Lampeter Aldo Steccanella can now sell wine
by the bottle, along with fresh pasta, cheeses, meats and salamis.
Not that putting together a case was ever a problem, particularly
for fans of Italian wine. However, the expansion of the other
sections of his list now makes this one of Wales's best wine-
merchants. In the French range you'll find underpriced Rhône
wines from Roger Sabon and Domaine de la Soumade, Alsace from
Louis Gisselbrecht, burgundies from Vincent Girardin and Durup,
good affordable clarets and some tasty regional wines. From Spain
come the Navarra wines of Chivite and the Rioja of Marqués de
Cáceres, and there are also Hungarians bottles from Tibor G'al,
winemaker at Tenuta dell'Ornellaia. G'al's Tuscan wines feature in
a strong Italian range, which also includes wines from C. S. Santadi
in Sardinia, Ascheri and Giuseppe Mascarello in Piemonte,
Allegrini and Pieropan in the Veneto and Puiatti in Friuli.
Australian wines come from Shaw & Smith and Mount Langi
Ghiran, New Zealanders from Millton Vineyard and South Africans
from Thelema and Cape Soleil. From the States come the Newton
Californians and the Oregon wines of Willamette Valley Vineyards.

Regular dinners and tastings are held at the restaurant, which is
the main premises, and there are plans to start a series of wine-
appreciation courses at the University of Wales, Lampeter.

Best buys

1994 La Serre Sauvignon Blanc, Vin de Pays d'Oc, £
Araldica Moscato d'Asti, £
1990 Cappello di Prete, Rosso del Salento, Candido, ££
Cabernet Sauvignon Vin de Pays de la Principauté d'Orange 1992,
Domaine de la Soumade, ££

The Celtic Vintner

The Wine Showroom

Star Trading Estate, Ponthir Road, Caerleon	*Tel* (01633) 430371
Gwent NP6 1PQ	*Fax* (01633) 430154
73 Derwen Fawr Road, Sketty,	*Tel* (01792) 206661
Swansea, West Glamorgan SA2 8DR	

Open (Head office; Mon–Fri 8.30–4.30, Sat 8.30–12) (Swansea Mon–Fri 8.30–6, Sat by appointment) **Closed** Sun, public holidays and Bank holidays **Cards** Visa; personal and business accounts **Discount** Negotiable based upon quantity of order **Delivery** Free locally (South Wales, Hereford, Avon) (min. 1 case); rest of UK at cost **Glass hire** Free in multiples of 48 goblets and 24 champagne flutes **Tasting and talks** Available **Cellarage** Not available

The Celtic Vintner business is still very much in a state of flux. The past year has seen the merging of the business with the wine wholesaling side of owners Stedmans. The Celtic Vintner name remains, but although former owner Brian Johnson still has a hand in the wine-buying, his involvement is slowly reducing. Still the range is a good one. You'll find champagne from Joseph Perrier and other major houses. In Bordeaux, the clarets stick mostly to under a tenner but there's also a smattering of classed growths as well, while whites include dry wines from Château Bauduc and stickier fare from Châteaux de Berbec and de Malle. Pierre Sparr provides Alsace wines, Chanson and Parent burgundies while Loires come from Henry Pellé and Jean-Paul Balland. Amid the Rhônes are wines from Vieux Télégraphe, Delas and Chante Cigale, while regional interest appears in the shape of ranges from Philippe de Baudin and Caroline de Beaulieu.

Italians are patchy, but the Germans from van Volxem and von Kesselstatt are better. Spaniards too are worth a look, with a large range of CVNE Riojas and other wines from Torres and Ochoa. The South Africans from Fairview, Allesverloren and Montestell are good, as are the Australians from Alkoomi, Yalumba and Chateau Reynella. Other New World highlights include the Hunters New Zealanders, Weinert Argentinians, Caliterra Chileans and the Palmer wines from Long Island.

Best buys

Côtes de Bordeaux 1993, Domaine du Seuil Premières, £
1994/5 Nederburg Chardonnay, £
1993 St Severin Blauer Zweigelt Kabinett, ££
1990/1 Chateau Reynella Shiraz, McLaren Vale, ££

Châteaux Wines

(Not a shop)

Paddock House, Upper Tockington Road	*Tel* (01454) 613959
Tockington, Bristol, Avon BS12 4LQ	*Fax* (01454) 613959

Case sales only **Open** Mon–Fri 9–5.30; Sat 9–12.30 (most Sats) **Closed** Sun, public holidays **Cards** Access, Delta, Switch, Visa; personal and business accounts **Discount** By negotiation **Delivery** Free on UK mainland (min. 2 case or £100) all orders pay consignment charge of £7.05 per order; mail-order available **Glass hire** Not available **Tasting and talks** Annual tasting and lunch in London (Nov) by invitation **Cellarage** £4.89 per case per year

The Rosemount wines are no more, so Château Musar is the sole non-Frenchman in the Châteaux Wines album. The Miller family's list barely stretches to 100 wines, but there's much of interest. Ch. La Lagune is the most expensive of a sensible range of clarets, which also features wines from Châteaux Potensac, d'Issan and Chasse-Spleen. André Pelletier supplies very quaffable cru Beaujolais, Chablis comes from Simonnet-Febvre, and other burgundies come from Ampeau and Delaunay. The Orschwiller co-op provides Alsace wines, and you'll also find Domaine de l'Aigle's lovely Chardonnay and a fine Coteaux du Tricastin from Domaine le Vieux Micocoulier. Add Laurent-Perrier champagne and that's pretty much it. If you want to check out the range, there is an annual tasting each November, or you could don a cap, grab a satchel and try and sneak into one of the talks that Mr Miller does for schools and colleges.

Best buys

Domaine des Garrigues Lirac Assemat 1993/4, £
Tricastin 1989, Domaine le Vieux Micocoulier, £
Sancerre Blanc 1993, Domaine Reverdy, ££
Morey-St-Denis 1992, Delaunay, ££

Chippendale Fine Wines

15 Manor Square, Otley, West Yorkshire	*Tel* (01943) 850633
LS21 3AP	*Fax* (01943) 850633

Open Mon–Fri (not Wed) 10–5.45, Sat 9.30–5 **Closed** Wed, Sun, public holidays **Cards** Access, Visa; business accounts **Discount** 5% cases (3% off all purchases, 6% off cases for Discount Club members) **Delivery** Free for 6+ bottles within 15-mile radius; nationwide mail-order service at cost **Glass hire** Free glass loan with wine order **Tasting and talks** 2 main tastings per year Feb, Oct **Cellarage** Not available

Our current favourite tasting note comes courtesy of Mike Pollard, proprietor, manager, tea boy, delivery man, etc. of Chippendale Fine Wines. His description of most Pinotage wines as 'a bit like stewed strawberry jam with a small trowel of freshly dug soil added' is as inspired as it is accurate. Mr P.'s prose remains as entertaining as ever, and his selection of wines is nearly as compelling.

Despite the reservations about Pinotage, South African wines, notably those from Fredericksburg and Wildekrans, have made a tentative appearance on his shelves, where they join a large band of Antipodean offerings: those from Martinborough, Neudorf, Cullens, Yarra Yering and Tim Adams are the pick of an interesting range. The Californian selection remains small, although the wines of Newton Vineyards and Saintsbury will not disappoint.

Deinhard provides the German wines, the Spanish selection features the Riojas of Remélluri and Martínez Bujanda, and the Portuguese list includes the toothsome Cartuxa red and ports from Cálem and Niepoort. The expanded Italian selection includes Soave from Anselmi and Pieropan, Allegrini's Amarone and Rocca della Macie's Sergioveto.

No French region is covered in any great depth, but there are many interesting wines. Rhône fans may compare the Condrieu of Pierre Dumazet with the Vin de Pays Viognier he also produces – at half the price. Other *vins de pays* worth sampling are from Mas de Daumas Gassac and La Serre, and Daniel Domergue's Minervois is excellent stuff. Devaux champagne, burgundies from Faiveley and Thévenet, Alsace from Kuentz-Bas and claret from Ch. Belgrave also look good.

We'll leave the last word to Mike: 'I hope I can be included in the sadly dwindling band of enthusiasts who offer good wine at good prices and also friendliness, a little humour and a sense of enjoyment. These last three aspects are a bit nebulous but just as important as discounts, free delivery, etc., in the horrible Brave New World of "clone store" retailing.'

Best buys

La Serre Sauvignon Blanc Vin de Pays d'Oc 1994, £
Candidato, Tinto Plata, £
Cullen Estate Reserve Semillon Sauvignon Blanc, Australia 1992, ££
Mâcon-Clessé 1992, Domaine de la Bon Gran, Jean Thévenet, ££

Classic Wines & Spirits

Vintners House, Deeside Industrial Park   *Tel* (01244) 288444
Deeside, nr Chester, Clwyd CH5 6LE   *Fax* (01244) 280008

Open Mon–Fri 7.30–6, Sat 9–5 **Closed** Sun, public holidays **Cards** Access, Amex, Diners, Visa; personal and business accounts **Discount** By negotiation **Delivery** Free within North-West area (min. 12 bottles); free nationwide mail-order (min. 12 bottles) **Glass hire** Not available **Tasting and talks** Occasional in-house **Cellarage** Not available

The bulk of business undertaken by James Dean (no, not that one), John Lennon (you're kidding!), Paul Newman (honestly?) and the rest of the folk at this Chester wine-merchant is wholesale, but the recent move to larger premises has given them more space to devote to their retail sales.

If you're after something French, you'll find clarets from Barton & Guestier as well as from several *crus classés*, burgundy from Bouchard Père & Fils and Drouhin and plenty of great Alsace wines from Schlumberger and Dopff au Moulin. The Denbies English wines and CVNE Riojas are worth trying, as are the excellent-value Le Veritiere Italians.

A large range of Rothbury wines, plus others from Pipers Brook, Wolf Blass and Baileys, will please fans of Australian wine, while those who favour South African will head for the wines of Meerlust and Allesverloren. Also available are Matua Valley and Montana wines from New Zealand, Santa Rita from Chile, and Californian bottles from Vichon and Mondavi.

The best range of all, however, is from Champagne. Were price no object, we'd guzzle the mature wines from Krug, Lanson and Taittinger, but our bank balance tends to push us towards the still very delicious wines from Charles Heidsieck and Massé. Cheers!

Best buys

Gamay du Haut Poitou 1993, £
Vin de Pays de Gascogne 1993, Domaine de la Hitaire, £
Côtes du Castillon 1989, Château Jouanin, ££
Massé 'Baron Edward', NV, Reims, ££

Brian Coad Fine Wines

66 Cole Lane, Stowford Park, Ivybridge,	*Tel* (01752) 896545
Devon PL21 0PN	*Fax* (01752) 691160

Case sales only **Open** Mon–Fri 8–8; Sat 8–4 **Closed** Sun, public holidays **Cards** None accepted; personal and business accounts **Discount** Available on 10+ cases **Delivery** Free delivery on 1+ case within 40-mile radius **Glass hire** Free **Tasting and talks** Not available **Cellarage** Not available

If Brian Coad doesn't feature on the list of wine-merchants that Bordeaux and burgundy fans regularly deal with, it can only be because they haven't heard of him. There are multiple vintages of clarets from nearly all the first growths and most of the 'super-seconds', as well as more affordable wines from Châteaux de Marbuzet, Tayac and Cissac. Ch. d'Yquem and Ch. Rieussec will satisfy Sauternes fans. Red burgundies come from Armand Rousseau, Méo-Camuzet, Michel Voarick and Remoriquet, whites from Louis Carillon, Bernard Millot and Domaine des Deux Roches. The Rhône section isn't bad either, with the excellent-value Coteaux du Tricastin from Domaine des Grangeneuve and Albert Dervieux's wonderful Côte Rôtie. Three vintages of Mas de Daumas Gassac and tasty Loire wines from Domaine de Terrebrune are also available. There are sketchy ranges from outside France, but that from Australia is full of interest – we'd head for the Coonawarra wines from Rymill, Braidon and Hollick.

Best buys

1993 Talimba Grove Shiraz/Cabernet Sauvignon, £
Merlot 1992, Viña Undurraga, £
Pauillac 1990, Château Batailley, ££
St Véran Vieilles Vignes 1992, Domaine des Deux Roches, ££

Connolly's

Arch 13, 220 Livery Street, Birmingham,	*Tel* 0121-236 9269/3837
West Midlands B3 1EU	*Fax* 0121-233 2339

Open Mon–Fri 9–6, Sat 9–2 **Closed** Sun, public holidays **Cards** Access, Amex, Switch, Visa; personal and business accounts **Discount** 10% on 1 case (un)mixed 'cash & carry' **Delivery** Free within Birmingham and surrounding areas (1+ cases) **Glass hire** Free with order, charge for breakages **Tasting and talks** Tastings held at local restaurants; tutored tastings for customers (in-house or their premises); **Cellarage** Not available

Much has been made in past editions of the *Guide* of the quality of Chris Connolly's poetry. One of his odes about Captain Scarlet and the Mysterons was so dire that we were tempted to omit him from this year's Guide, and a more recent one in which the Famous Five apprehended a band of bootleggers nearly clinched it. However, a glance through his range of wines convinced us that the librettist of Livery Street merited inclusion with honours.

Connolly's customers have been known recently for their penchant for New World wines, but the past year has seen some much more traditional wines offered. An offer of 1993 red burgundy included wines from Réné Engel, Robert Arnoux and Domaine de la Pousse d'Or. 'New' to the claret range, via a 'silly offer', are 1982 Ch. Lynch-Bages, 1983 Ch. Latour and 1986 Ch. Ducru-Beaucaillou. These join a solid French range based around Hugel Alsace, Loires from Henri Bourgeois and Domaine la Saboterie, Rhônes from Jaboulet Aîné and the excellent Chais Cuxac *vins de pays*.

There aren't many German wines, although Deinhard and Dr Loosen are reassuring names to find, as are Torres and Marqués de Murrieta in the Spanish list and Araldica, Allegrini and Capezzana in the Italian section (do try the more exotic Dorigati Trentino wines). Ports come from Warre, Cálem and Martinez Gassiot.

Not much is new in the Californian range, but the Fairview South Africans have been joined by wines from Meerlust and Kanonkop. New Zealand bottles come from de Redcliffe and Grove Mill, while Australian interest is provided by Grant Burge, Parker Estate and Cape Mentelle.

An active tasting programme includes monthly tutored events and various food and wine evenings at local restaurants. As we go to press lucky customers are enjoying Japanese cuisine and fine wines from around the world at the Shogun Teppan-yaki Restaurant. Will Mr C. have composed a haiku for the occasion?

Best buys

Artadi Tinto Rioja Alavesa, 1994, £
Chardonnay Chais Cuxac, Vin de Pays d'Oc, £
Côtes de Castillon 1990, Château de Belcier, ££
Old Vine Shiraz 'The Black Monster' 1992, Grant Burge, ££

If your favourite wine-merchant is not in this section, write and tell us why you think we should include it.

Co-op Wholesale Society

Head Office
New Century House, PO Box 53, Manchester, M60 4ES *Tel* 0161-834 1212
Fax 0161-827 5514

2,500 subsidiary outlets

Open Normal shop trading hours **Cards** Most major credit cards **Discount** None
offered **Delivery** Not available **Glass hire** Not available **Tasting and talks**
Regularly offered in store **Cellarage** Not available

If all its stores were big enough to stock the full Co-operative
Wholesale Society (CWS) wine range, the Co-op would be
mentioned in the same breath as the other major supermarket
chains. But they are not; they vary in size from airport hangar to
hole in the wall, and, unsurprisingly, the bigger the store the
greater the choice of wines. Another complication is that some Co-
operative societies are compelled to take wines from the CWS list,
while others can buy from whom they please.

Generalisation in such a situation is difficult but not impossible.
As with any supermarket chain, the main task for the wine-buyers,
Dr Arabella Woodrow MW and Paul Bastard, is to service the sub-
£4 end of the market, especially the own-label range. This they do
with competence, particularly where France and Eastern Europe
are concerned, but don't look for fireworks. At prices above £4
things get much more interesting. Those willing to fork out the
£10+ for E & E Black Pepper Shiraz, burgundies from Domaine
Rion and 1983 Ch. Cissac will not be disappointed, but there's
plenty of quality to be had for considerably less. Among the most
exciting items are Baileys Liqueur Muscat, Fetzer Valley Oaks
Cabernet, Philippe de Baudin Vin de Pays d'Oc Chardonnay,
Thelema Chardonnay and Viñas de Vero Pinot Noir.

We wouldn't really recommend you to go miles out of your way
to buy wine at the Co-op. All the same, if you use the store only for
grocery shopping, take a look next time at a wine range that is
much more than just a bread-and-butter one.

Best buys

Le Trulle Chardonnay Del Salento, £
Long Slim Red Chilean (Cabernet-Merlot), £
Bernkasteler Badstube Riesling 1993, Kabinett von Kesselstatt, ££
Penfolds Coonawarra Cabernet 1991, ££

Corkscrew Wines

Arch 5, Viaduct Estate, Carlisle, Cumbria CA2 5BN   *Tel* (01228) 43033
                                                     Fax (01228) 43033

Open Mon–Sat 10–6, Sun 12–3 **Closed** Public holidays **Cards** Access, Amex, Delta, Switch, Visa; business accounts **Discount** 5% on mixed cases, negotiable for larger orders **Delivery** Cumbria, N. Yorks, N. Lancs, S. Scotland (min. 2 cases); mail-order available **Glass hire** Free **Tasting and talks** Six annually **Cellarage** Not available

Laurie Scott 'gave up making money to become a wine-merchant'. We'd encourage you to put a little more cash in his pocket by visiting his Carlisle railway arch. You'll find very decent champagne from Drappier and Bollinger, plus alternative sparklers from Pongracz in South Africa, Jordan in California, and Seppelt and Grant Burge in Australia. Further Australian wines come from Mitchelton, Brown Brothers and Bailey's, New Zealanders from Nobilo, Collards and Montana, and South African bottles are provided by Neil Ellis, Meerlust and Fairview. From the Americas come the Andes Peak Chileans, the Inniskillin Canadians and Californians from Morgan, Sutter Home and Mondavi.

The clarets include good-value wines from Châteaux Ramage-la-Batisse and Tour Haut-Caussan. Vallet Frères and Olivier Leflaive represent the top of the red and white burgundy sections. There are Alsace wines from the Turckheim co-op and Loires from Marc Brédif and Jean-Claude Dagueneau. The regional wines from Domaine le Vieux Micocoulier and Domaine de la Soumade are excellent, but the Rhônes from Alain Paret and Domaine du Pégau Feraud are even better. From Spain, you'll find Fariña's Gran Colegiata and Rioja from Vallemayor, while from over the border in Portugal come the characterful wines of J. M. da Fonseca. The German list is patchy, but the Italians from Allegrini, Bartolomeo di Breganze and La Parrina are much better. If fortified wine is your thing, sherry from Barbadillo, ports from Quinta do Vesuvio, Dow and Fonseca, and Madeira from Cossart Gordon should give satisfaction.

Best buys

1994 La Chapelle de Cray Sauvignon de Touraine, £
1990 Stellenvale Cabernet/Shiraz, £
Côtes de Castillon 1990, Château Puycarpin, ££
Châteauneuf de Pape 1990, Domaine du Pégau Feraud, ££

Corney & Barrow

12 Helmet Row, London EC1V 3QJ	*Tel* 0171-251 4051
	Fax 0171-608 1373
194 Kensington Park Road, London W11 2ES	*Tel* 0171-221 5122
Corney & Barrow East Anglia	*Fax* 0171-221 9371
Belvoir House, High Street, Newmarket, Suffolk CB8 8DH	*Tel* (01638) 662068
Corney & Barrow with Whighams of Ayr	
8 Academy Street, Ayr, Strathclyde KA7 1HT	*Tel* (01292) 267000

Open (Kensington) Mon–Sat 10.30–8; (Newmarket) Mon–Sat 9–6; (Ayr) Mon–Sat 9.30–5.30 **Cards** Access, Amex, Visa; personal and business accounts **Discount** Negotiable **Delivery** Free local delivery; Free delivery within M25 (min. 2 cases); Deliveries of 3+ cases in UK £8+VAT **Glass hire** Free **Tasting and talks** 3 major London and City tastings each year, plus regional tastings; bottles open regularly for tasting **Cellarage** £5–20+VAT per case per year

The slip of paper dropping out of the front of the new, ring-bound, jazzy-covered C&B list warns customers that, due to currency fluctuations, prices in the list are increased by 20p per bottle. It is doubtful whether such an increase will have any effect on the customers who buy the wines of Domaine de la Romanée-Conti, Domaine Leflaive and Châteaux Pétrus and Trotanoy from the company. This is a place to come for some of the classics of the wine world, and, although the Kensington Park Road shop does have good stocks of wines from outside France, not many of them are featured in that smart list.

Those that are, with the possible exception of the cheaper Australian wines (and Rudolf Muller's Liebfraumilch, Piesporter Michelsberg and Niersteiner Gutes Domtal) are certainly of interest. No one could complain about the CVNE Riojas, and Dr Thanisch Moselles, or the Castello di Rampolla Italian, Parker Estate Australian and Palliser New Zealand wines, nor about the sherries from Lustau or the vintage ports.

In the French list Cattin's Alsace wines, Jaboulet Aîné Rhônes and some tasty Loire Sauvignons are worth trying, as are the champagnes of Salon, Roederer and Delamotte. A small set of regional wines includes a great white Bergerac, La Combe de Grinou, and the impressive Bordeaux-style Château de Biran from Pécharmant. However, with those exceptions, it's Bordeaux and Burgundy all the way. Clarets major on the wines from the J-P Moueix stable, with Châteaux Pétrus and Trotanoy at the top and some rather more affordable *petits châteaux*. Also worthy of note are the wines from Châteaux de Lamarque and le Tertre-Rôteboeuf. White wines are thin on the ground. However, the same could not be said for the burgundies. The wines of Domaine Leflaive are obviously the big attraction, but less exalted fare is available from

Olivier Leflaive and others. Besides the Domaine de la Romanée-Conti reds, you'll also find wines from Armand Rousseau, Joseph Roty and Rossignol-Trapet, as well as a range of beaujolais from Marc Dudet.

If you can't find your favourite domaine or château in stock, or should you wish to relieve yourself of a few of those cases of Mouton 1982 which are clogging up the back porch, the company's rapidly expanding broking division is on hand to scour the fine wine world for buyers and sellers on your behalf.

Best buys

Vin de Pays des Côtes Catalanes, Chardonnay 1993, Mistral Wines, £
Castillo de Expeleta Crianza 1990 (Rioja), £
Parker Estate Terra Rossa, 1st Growth, 1991, ££
Château la Clotte 1982, Grand Cru Classé, St Emilion, ££

CPA's

44 Queens Road, Mumbles, Swansea, West Glamorgan SA3 4AN	*Tel* (01792) 360707 *Fax* (01792) 362103

Open Tue–Fri 2–6.30, Sat 11–6 **Closed** Mon, Sun, public holidays **Cards** Access, Amex, Visa; personal and business accounts **Discount** 5% on 1+ cases (cash or cheque terms only) **Delivery** Free within 10-mile radius (min. 1 case); mail-order available **Glass hire** Free with order **Tasting and talks** Tutored tastings and wine dinners on request **Cellarage** Not available

P and A (Paul and Andrew) now concentrate on their country-house hotel, leaving C (Caroline Rees) to run the wine side. For a business that is only four years old, CPA seems remarkably mature. The range may not be the largest around, but it's full of fine wines from all over the world, and business is 'on the up, with people willing to try different wines and experiment with different styles'. The French range covers all the major areas well, with the highlights being the regional wines from Domaines Virginie and Domaine la Fadèze, Sancerre from Bailly-Reverdy and the Rhônes from Domaine du Vieux Télégraphe and Château du Grand Moulas.

The Italian wines from Le Ragose and Rocca delle Macie are good, as are the Spanish ones from Campo Viejo and the Welsh wines form Cariad. Australian stars are the Henschke and Penley Estate wines, while the Californians from Frog's Leap and Peter Michael are also impressive. Chileans are from Montes, South Africans from Hamilton Russell and Rust en Vrede, and New Zealanders from Allan Scott and Lincoln Vineyard.

Best buys

Faugères 1993, Château de Laurens, £
Bianco di Custoza 1994, Teresa Rizzi, £
1992 Allan Scott Chardonnay, ££
Pol Roger Demi-Sec, ££

Craven's Wine Merchants

15 Craven Road, London W2 3BP

Tel 0171-723 0252
Fax 0171-262 5823

Open Mon–Fri 11–9.30, Sat 10–9.30, Sun 12–2, 7–9, public holidays 11–9.30 **Closed** Good Friday, Chr and Boxing Days, New Year **Cards** Access, Delta, Switch, Visa; personal and business accounts **Discount** 5%–7.5% for mixed case of 12 or more **Delivery** Free within Paddington area (min. £50 purchase value); nationwide mail-order available **Glass hire** Free with orders over £50 **Tasting and talks** Every third Sat of month **Cellarage** Not available

Craven's is an enthusiastic young company that deserves attention for the effort it has devoted to sourcing its own wines, rather than sticking to the ranges offered by the major wholesalers. Not that there are no familiar wines in stock: witness the Mondavi Californians, Montana New Zealanders and Torres Chileans. However, the best wines are those you may not even have heard of. Henri Germain champagne is very good, particularly the Cuvée President; the Blanquette de Limoux from Domaine Collin is a very acceptable alternative. Tasty regional fare includes Saint Chinian from Caves de Roquebrun, Cahors from Château de Haute-Serre and Côtes de la Malepère from Château de Routier. Grand Listrac and Ch. Dalem provide great-value drinking for those who can't stretch to the first-growth clarets.

From outside France, we'd pick out the Piemonte wines from Baracco de Baracho and the Australians from Mount Bold, Greenock Creek and Peter Rumball. Since much of the range may be unfamiliar to you, we'd urge you to visit Craven's for the tastings that take place on the third Saturday of each month.

Best buys

Vin de Pays de l'Aude, 1992 Domaine Collin Chardonnay, £
Côtes de Malepère, 1993 Château de Routier Rosé, £
Blanquette de Limoux Cuvée Prestige 1992, Domaine Collin, ££
Cahors 1990, Château de Haute-Serre, ££

Croque-en-Bouche

221 Wells Road, Malvern Wells, Hereford & Worcester WR14 4HF

Tel (01684) 565612

Case sales only **Open** At any time by arrangement **Cards** Access, Delta, Visa **Discount** 4% on 48+ bottles, cash and collect **Delivery** Free for 2+ cases within 10-mile radius; mail-order available **Glass hire** Not available **Tasting and talks** Available only for wine-tasting groups **Cellarage** Free for short-term cellarage

With the increased pressures on wine-merchants to generate cash flow and reduce the number of items in stock, it is often difficult to find mature wines in any great depth. But then the Croque-en-Bouche is not your ordinary wine-merchants. It's a restaurant with quite simply one of the best wine-lists in the country; and proprietor Robin Jones is very willing for you to visit and fill yourself a case of goodies from his cellar.

This is not a range put together by a label-watcher, although you will find many famous names in the cellar. There are several delights from younger vintages, but, as we said, the real excitement is to be found in the more mature wines. Californian items include 1984 Ridge Petite Sirah, 1983 Mondavi Reserve Pinot and 1983 Clos du Val Chardonnay, and mature Australians include 1986 Lake's Folly Chardonnay, 1984 Leeuwin Cabernet and wines from Lindemans stretching back to the 1960s. There are some strapping young Super-Tuscans, but you'll also find much more venerable fare from throughout Italy. Amongst the Spanish wines you'll find Marqués de Murrieta Riojas dating back to 1960.

Turning to France, it's difficult to find fault with a Rhône range which offers around 80 Côte Rôties and almost as many Hermitages and Châteauneufs. The Alsace and Loire selections are also breathtaking, with numerous vintages of both Clos Ste Hune and Moulin Touchais available. The lover of mature claret will find much to savour, including some surprisingly affordable wines from the great 1961 vintage. Robert Ampeau's eclectic wines appear with other burgundies from Daniel Rion, Louis Michel and Domaine Leflaive. Domaine de Trévallon and Mas de Daumas Gassac, plus champagne from Billiot and Billecart-Salmon complete an astonishing selection.

The only possible complaint is that there are simply too many good wines available. Restraint must be exercised, unless you are prepared to part with more cash than your bank manager would appreciate. Even so, prices for the mature wines are particularly fair, so it is worth treating yourself a little. And, if you do visit, it would be churlish not to stop for lunch or dinner – after all it will probably take you two hours to wade through the entertaining list!

Best buys

Coddington Vineyard Bacchus 1990, £
Errazuriz Sauvignon blanc 1994, Chile, £
Château Caronne Ste. Gemme 1982, ££
Pinot Noir 1992, Laroche, ££

Davisons Wine Merchants

Head office
7 Aberdeen Road, Croydon, Surrey CR0 1EQ   *Tel* 0181-681 3222
(77 branches in London and the Home Counties)

Open Mon–Sat 10–2, 5–10, some Sats 10–10, Sun 12–2, 7–9; public holidays **Cards**
Access, Delta, Switch, Visa; personal and business accounts **Discount** 8.5% off
(un)mixed cases of wine **Delivery** Free locally; elsewhere by arrangement; mail-order
available **Glass hire** Free **Tasting and talks** Regular store tastings **Cellarage** Not
available

Lovers of fine wines know that there's more than first meets the
eye in their local Davisons. That rack next to the counter, which the
manager keeps a watchful eye on, contains a range of mature
wines (claret and port in particular) that few other companies
selling by the bottle can match. Those ports include the '63, '70 and
'77 vintages of Croft, Graham, Taylor and Warre, and much more
besides. While first-growth clarets, particularly Ch. Mouton-
Rothschild, are available in great depth, affordable Bordeaux is
very much present. In particular, wines from the 1986 vintage such
as Châteaux La Lagune, Batailley and Les Ormes-de-Pez are all on
the friendly side of £20. 'Even wine-buyers from other companies
use us for mature wines for their own table!', says Michael Davies.
Perhaps you'd better nip down there before stocks disappear.

Burgundies never quite reach such heights, although the whites
from Domaine Morey and Jean Germain, and the reds from Jean
Grivot and Machard du Gramont are certainly well above the
mundane. Elsewhere in France, Duboeuf provides beaujolais,
Sancerre comes from Jean-Max Roger, and Alsace wines are
produced by Hugel and Zind-Humbrecht. The Châteauneuf from
Font de Michelle tops the Rhône range, while country wines of
interest include reds from Domaine de Limbardie and James
Herrick Chardonnay from Vin de Pays d'Oc.

The ranges from Italy, Spain, Germany and Eastern Europe are
competent rather than exciting. The Australian wines are better,
and we'd go for the E & E Black Pepper Shiraz, the Ironstone wines
from Western Australia and the Green Point sparkler. Bottles from
California and South Africa are less convincing, but the Chilean
wines from Caliterra and the New Zealanders from Morton Estate
are good.

Service is usually excellent. Most Davisons branches are run by husband-and-wife teams who live above the stores, and so feel more like proprietors than mere shop-workers. Indeed, one manager described it as running 'a family business within a family business'. The takeover of Mayor Sworder (q.v.) should have little effect on the appearance of the shops, although we wouldn't be surprised if the quality of the wines were to rise even higher.

Best buys

Nuragus di Cagliari Dolia, 1994, Sardinia, £
Don Gulias Tinto (Spain), £
Château la Lagune 1982, ££
Château Rieussec 1983, ££

Rodney Densem Wines

Office

4 Pillory Street, Nantwich
Cheshire CW5 7JW

Tel (01270) 623665
Fax (01270) 624062

Open Mon–Fri 9–6; Sat 9–5.30 **Closed** Sun and public holidays **Cards** Access, Switch, Visa; personal and business accounts **Discount** 5% on mixed cases; special rates on 5+ cases **Delivery** Within a 50-mile radius (min. 1 case), nationally £8 per case; mail-order available **Glass hire** Free for standard range, duluxe crystal £4 per box of 24 **Tasting and talks** Every weekend in store, approx. 4 evening sessions per year and 3–4 annual tutored gourmet events **Cellarage** Not available

---

Awards for the Best-dressed window continue to be heaped on Rodney Densem's Pillory Street premises. Beauty is more than skin-deep, too, as the wines inside are also of very good quality. Although customers' interest in the Antipodean wines is reported to be warming, you'll still find much of interest. Australian wines include ranges from Hardy's, Brown Brothers and Yaldara, while New Zealanders come from de Redcliffe and Ponders Estate. Californian bottles come from Mondavi and Sterling Vineyards, South Africans from Boschendal and Fairview, and there's also a small set of Chilean wines.

Among the champagnes Gosset stands out from more famous *grandes marques*. Burgundies come from Domaine Laroche, Charles Gruber and Louis Latour, while clarets include Château Lamothe-de-Haux, a wine with ideas above its premier Côtes de Bordeaux status. There are reasonable Loire and Rhône selections and an Alsace range from Loberger. Riojas from Conde de Valdemar and Faustino Martínez feature in the Spanish list, while Italian wines include Masi Soave, Prunotto Barolo and the Regaleali Sicilians. More wines will appear in the German range when more customers demand them. The own-label sherries from Lustau join others from Don Zoilo and Sandeman, and there are also ports from several famous names.

Besides weekly store tastings, separate dinners and tutored tastings are held regularly throughout the year. Mr Densem also doubles as a clairvoyant; one page of his recent list proclaimed '1995 is the year of white Bordeaux' – we wait with anticipation to see if his prediction will come true.

Best buys

Castillo de Montblanc, Conca Barbera Spain, £
Klippenkop Cinsault/Shiraz, South Africa, £
Sauvignon 1994, Ponders Estate, New Zealand, ££
1990 Château Lamothe 1er Cuvée, Côtes de Bordeaux, ££

Direct Wine Shipments

5/7 Corporation Square, Belfast, Co Antrim	*Tel* (01232) 243906/23870
BT1 3AJ	*Fax* (01232) 240202
Duncairn Wines	*Tel* (01232) 370694
555 Antrim Road, Belfast BT15 3BU	

Open Mon–Fri 9–6.30 (Thur 9–8), Sat 9.30–5 **Closed** Sun **Cards** Access, Delta, Switch, Visa; personal and business accounts **Discount** With orders over 12 bottles, cash discount of 10-12% given in free wine **Delivery** Free in Northern Ireland (min. 1 case); mail-order available, delivery is £10 per case **Glass hire** Available **Tasting and talks** £5 per person for tasting of 6 wines; optional buffet supper (approx. £10) **Cellarage** Free with order

---

Belfast wine-drinkers continue to be among the best-educated in the UK, thanks to the twice-yearly wine courses run by Kevin McAlindon *et al.* in their recently revamped dockside premises. A programme of six lectures is followed by a challenging multiple-choice exam, but DWS can certainly provide several wines with which to celebrate afterwards.

Champagne would be the obvious choice, and we'd choose those from Vilmart and Drappier in preference to the several *grandes marques*. Alternatives include a cava from Segura Viudas and Seppelt's Salinger. If you're after claret, it's here in depth, whether you fancy 1945 Ch. Margaux or more affordable fare such as Ch. Lanessan, five vintages of which are available. Sauternes fans will take comfort from nearly as many vintages of Ch. Coutet. The burgundy range majors on reds from Faiveley and whites from Olivier Leflaive, but in between are good growers such as Simon Bize, Jean Gros and Domaine Leflaive. Domaine Laroche provides Chablis, while beaujolais comes from Jacky Janodet and Pierre Ferraud. Hugel dominates the Alsace range, and the Rhône selection is big on Chapoutier wines, though wines from Château

Rayas, Chave and Clape also feature. From the Loire, Foreau and Joly provide excellent Chenin Blanc, while Charles Joguet's Chinon is similarly tasty. Don't miss the characterful southern reds from Domaines de Trévallon and Tempier.

German wines include Bürklin-Wolf and Verwaltung der Staatsweingüter in Eltville, while Portuguese wines come from Caves Aliança. Italians include the heady heights of Solaia and Gaja's Barbaresco, Mastroberardino's Taurasi and the Sicilian wines of Regaleali. Spain is well covered, whether you're after such familiar names as Torres, Julán Chivite, Vega Sicilia or Marqués de Cáceres, or the less well known Augustus or Peñalba López. Lustau sherry, Cossart & Gordon Madeira and Warre port will please lovers of fortified wine.

The name of Torres appears again in the South and North American ranges. Other United States producers to look out for are Ridge, Sanford and Newton. South African wines listed include whites from Boschendal and Klein Constantia and reds from Hamilton Russell and Rustenburg. Delegats and Hunter's represent New Zealand interest, while in the rapidly expanding Australian range Stoniers Merricks from the Mornington Peninsula, Henschke from the Eden Valley and St Huberts from the Yarra join the reliable Brown Brothers wines.

In fact the whole range has expanded and continues to expand, both in quantity and in quality. That DWS recently introduced a fine wine brokerage service shows that its sights are set firmly on the upper end of the market, and an active programme of tastings and dinners keeps customers happy. If the comprehensive and informative list may not always please sticklers for grammatical perfection, wine lovers everywhere will find it a source of many vinous treasures.

Best buys

Rosso Conero, Monte Schiavo 1989, £
Emilio Lustau Manzanilla, £
Vega Sicilia Valbuena, Ribera del Duero 1988, ££
Rothbury Estate Sauvignon Blanc, New Zealand 1984, ££

Domaine Direct

29 Wilmington Square, London WC1X 0EG

Tel 0171-837 1142
Fax 0171-837 8605

Case sales only **Open** Mon–Fri 8.30–5.30 **Closed** Sat, Sun, public holidays **Cards** Access, Delta, Visa; business accounts **Discount** Not available **Delivery** Free in London (min. 1 mixed case); Home Counties 1 case £9, 2 cases £11, 3+ cases free; mail-order available **Glass hire** Not available **Tasting and talks** Two or three customer tastings a year in London; smaller events by arrangement **Cellarage** £7 per case per year inc. insurance

Domaine Direct's *raison d'être* remains the wines of Burgundy, and lovers of good Chardonnay and Pinot Noir will probably be on the company's mailing list already. The much-heralded 1992 whites and 1990 reds are fast disappearing from the range, but, since burgundy has fared better than much of France in more recent vintages, there are still many fine wines available at (relatively) sensible prices.

The weather may have been reasonable, but it is the quality of the producers which makes the Domaine Direct range worthwhile. Michel Juillot's wines from Mercurey, Roumier's from Morey-Saint-Denis and Jean-Marc Pavelot's from Savigny will please Pinot fans, while names such as Guy Roulot, Blain-Gagnard, Jean Durup and Etienne Sauzet will be familiar to devotees of Chardonnay.

The range from outside Burgundy is in danger of running into three figures. The rest of France in less than 50 wines is impossible, but look out for gems such as the Domaine de la Janasse Châteauneuf. The pick of the Australian wines are Leeuwin Estate, Ashbrook and Heritage; the New Zealand range includes Redwood Valley and Vidal; and Spottswoode and Nalle represent California.

Best buys

Leeuwin Estate Art Series Chardonnay 1990, ££
Mercurey Rouge 1992, Michel Juillot, ££

The Dorking Wine Cellar

Glebelands, Vincent Lane, Dorking, Surrey
RH4 3YZ

Tel (01306) 885711
Fax (01306) 743936

Case sales only **Open** Mon–Sat 9–6, Sun in Dec and public holidays 10–3 **Closed** Sun except in Dec **Cards** Access, Amex, Delta, Switch, Visa; personal and business accounts **Discount** 5% for £100 spent; 10% for £500 spent **Delivery** Free within 25 mile-radius of Dorking (min. 1 case); mail-order available **Glass hire** Free with order **Tasting and talks** Monthly tutored tastings and weekly (mainly Sat) at least 4 wines **Cellarage** Not available

The Dorking Wine Cellar's address will be familiar to people who used to buy wine from wholesalers Whiclar & Gordon. Indeed, the influence of that company is still very much in evidence in the list: the southern French wines from Philippe de Baudin, the Caliterra Chileans and the Australian wines from the BRL Hardy group (Reynella, Hardy's, Moondah Brook and Parrot's Hill). However, the new incumbents have added many wines to the range. Additional regional French delights come from Mas Segala and Château le Raz, and there are some serious clarets from the 1982 vintage and a range of burgundies from Louis Jadot and Domaine Marchand. Franz Reh provides most of the German list, while CVNE features prominently in the Spanish section. Italian wines are good rather than great, although those of Tedeschi and Masi are excellent. Joining those BRL Hardy bottles are Australian wines from Petaluma and Pipers Brook; Nobilo and Ngatarawa provide the New Zealanders, while South Africa is represented by Klein Constantia, Zonnebloem and Rustenberg.

Best buys

Vin de Pays d'Oc 1994, Chais Cuxac Viognier, £
1994 Caliterra Sauvignon Blanc, £
Pomerol 1990, Château Grange Neuve, ££
Cornas 'Chante Perdis' 1990, Delas, ££

Eckington Wines

2 Ravencar Road, Eckington, Sheffield,
South Yorkshire S31 9GJ

Tel (01246) 433213
Fax (01246) 433213

Open Mon-Fri 9–9, Sat 9–8, public holidays open by arrangement **Closed** Sun **Cards** personal and business accounts **Delivery** 10-mile radius (min. 3 cases) £4.75 per case for 1-2 cases; mail-order service available **Glass hire** Free **Tasting and talks** Monthly tasting group **Cellarage** Not available

Even as far north as Sheffield, the effects of cross-Channel sorties have bitten into the wine trade. We doubt whether people buying in France will have access to as good a range as that offered by

Andrew and Cherry Loughran, particularly if they are after New World wines. The Loughrans offer New Zealand wines from Vidal and Goldwater Estate, Argentinians from Norton and Chileans from Caliterra, Santa Carolina and Undurraga. North Americans of note come from Gundlach-Bundschu, Saintsbury and Staton Hills, while Groot Constantia and Neil Ellis provide South Africans. A long list of Australian wines features the wares of Bannockburn, St Hallett and Rockford.

German wines are notably absent, but you'll find Spanish ones from Marqués de Murrieta and Pesquera, and Italians from Isole e Olena and Sassicaia. In the French selection, the wine that the Loughrans are proudest of is Didier Cornillon's Clairette de Die. You'll also find wines from all the major regions, with the best ranges being the clarets and the regional wines. The former includes top classed growths as well as more affordable fare, such as Ch. Pitray and Clos du Marquis. Southern highlights are the wines from Domaines de l'Hortus, de Terrebrune and La Combe Blanche.

There's a tasting group that meets once a month for theme events, and a quarterly wine scheme offers mixed cases of new releases and old favourites at discount prices. Even without such reductions, the Eckington prices are decidedly friendly (particularly for the more expensive wines).

Best buys

1993 Le Champassias, Chatillon en Diois, £
Barbeito Crown Malmsey, £
1982 Norton Estate Malbec, ££
1994 Wairau River Sauvignon Blanc, ££

Edencroft Fine Wines

8-10 Hospital Street, Nantwich, Cheshire CW5 5RJ   *Tel* (01270) 625302
                                                          Fax (01270) 625302

Open Mon–Fri 9–5.30, Sat 8–5.30 **Closed** Wed pm, Sun and public holidays **Cards** Access, Amex, Delta, Switch, Visa; personal and business accounts **Discount** Negotiable **Delivery** Delivery within 15-mile radius £3.50 per case; mail-order available **Glass hire** Not available **Tasting and talks** Twice a year **Cellarage** Not available

The strange genesis of this wine-merchant deserves to be reported. Brookshaw's delicatessen in Nantwich had been in business for several years with little or no thought of selling wine. One Christmas, not too long ago, a local wine establishment approached Mark Brookshaw to tell him that the fruits in alcohol he was selling contravened the licensing laws; unless he withdrew them from sale, said merchant would report him to the appropriate authority. The legal fees necessary to obtain a licence would have taken around ten years to recoup just by selling the preserved fruit so Mark decided to branch out and sell wines as well.

Considering that Mark began from a standing start only three years ago his range of wines is heartening. At present a large proportion of the stock comes from wholesalers Haughton Agencies, who have a Nantwich office, but the range is evolving into something very interesting. Australian wines of note come from Mountadam, Montara Estate and Cullens, New Zealanders from Forrest Estate and Martinborough Vineyards and Californians from Newton and Saintsbury. Aimé Guibert, under different guises, provides several of the regional French wines, with others coming from Daniel Domergue in Minervois. Champagne is from Veuve Clicquot and Canard-Duchêne, Bordeaux from the various Baron Philippe de Rothschild châteaux; Trimbach provides Alsace, while Loire wines are from Marc Brédif and de Ladoucette. Add Rioja from Remélluri and that's almost it. The fruits in brandy are still available, of course, but now there's even more reason to visit this appealing establishment.

Best buys

Merlot 1992, Domaine des Pailhes, £
Terroirs d'Estagnol 1993, Moulin de Gassac, £
1992 Yarra Yering Shiraz No. 2, ££
1992 Cullen's Reserve Semillon/Sauvignon, ££

Eldridge Pope

Head office
Weymouth Avenue, Dorchester, Dorset   *Tel* (01305) 251251
DT1 1QT   *Fax* (01305) 258155
12 branches in Dorchester, Shaftesbury, Sherborne,
Wareham, Westbourne, Weymouth, Wincanton, Winchester,
including 4 Reynier Wine Libraries

Open Mon–Sat 9–5.30 (some local variation) **Closed** Sun, public holidays **Cards** Access, Amex, Switch, Visa; personal and business accounts **Discount** 5% on 1 case **Delivery** Free within 20-mile radius of branch on orders of £30+; mail-order available **Glass hire** Free with order (min 1 case) **Tasting and talks** At all branches; nearly always at weekends **Cellarage** £3 per case per year

---

Joe Naughalty MW, the man responsible for the Eldridge Pope wine range for the past dozen years, is set to retire as this *Guide* hits the streets. His description of himself as 'a traditionalist with a modern outlook' sheds some light on the company's range. Yes, you will find New World wines in the range, but its main thrust is towards the classic areas. This year is the first for several years in which The Chairman's Claret has come not from Ch. Cissac but from the Beaumont. Ch. Cissac fans can still drown their sorrows with vintages dating back to 1961, while most of the other clarets stick to the sensible side of £15. Those who can't afford Sauternes will find alternative sweet Bordeaux from the appellations of Cérons, Ste-Croix-du-Mont and Loupiac. Red burgundies veer towards the Côte de Beaune, with several wines from Domaine Prieur Brunet; the Côte de Nuits wines are provided by Domaine de la Romanée-Conti and Armand Rousseau. Highlights among the whites are the wines from Sauzet, Michel Colin and Jean Durup. Rhônes include Châteauneuf from Domaine de Montpertuis, while tasty Chenin Blanc from Jean Baumard, in a variety of sweetnesses, appears in the Loire range. Alsace is from Dopff & Irion, while regional wines are provided by Abbaye de Valmagne in the Coteaux du Languedoc and Jean-Claude Fontan in Gascony.

German wines are from von Kesselstatt and Schloss Vollrads, Italian from Ascheri and Umani Ronchi, and Spanish from Fariña, Gran Caus and Muga. Bernard Massard's Luxembourg wines and the Hungarians from Château Megyer are also worth trying. Best of those New World interlopers are the Californian wines from Grgich Hills and Gundlach-Bundschu, the Dalwhinnie and Mountadam Australians and the South Africans from Backsberg and Dieu Donné. The Chairman's New Zealand Sauvignon Blanc is one of a set of tasty wines from Redwood Valley. Hidalgo provides the Heirloom sherries, while Madeira fans can find mature wines dating back to the turn of the century.

Best buys

Vin de Pays d'Oc Blanc de Blancs sur Lie 1994, Louis Chatel, £
Coteaux du Languedoc 1992, Abbaye de Valmagne, £
Savennières Clos du Papillon 1992, Baumard, ££
Châteauneuf du Pape Cuvée Classique 1992, Domaine de Montpertuis, ££

Ben Ellis & Associates

Brockham Wine Cellars, Wheelers Lane,
Brockham, Surrey RH3 3HJ

Tel (01737) 842160/844866
Fax (01737) 843210

Open Mon–Fri 9–6, Sat 9.30–1 **Closed** Sun, public holidays **Cards** Access, Visa; personal and business accounts **Discount** None offered **Delivery** Free in Surrey, bordering counties and London (min. 1 case); nationwide 1–4 cases £10, 5+ cases free; mail-order available **Glass hire** Free with order **Tasting and talks** 2 series of tastings per year May/June and Nov/Dec **Cellarage** £4 (exc VAT) per case per year

Ben Ellis & Associates continues to be one of the quiet achievers of the British wine trade. News about the company travels by word of mouth, and the service is of such quality that the number of happy customers continues to increase. Good wines backed by good advice and service, plus an active tasting programme is the winning formula.

Fans of the classics will find a sensible range of clarets around the £10-20 range, with several wines above and below that bracket. White burgundy comes from Carillon, Jadot, Domaine des Comtes Lafon and Domaine de l'Eglantière, red from Daniel Rion and Comte Armand. In the Rhône section look for the wines of Domaine de la Soumade and Bernard Faurie. The Alsace wines come from Albert Mann, while from the Loire, André Dézat provides good Sancerre and Bourgeuil. Billecart-Salmon champagne is wonderful stuff, and the regional wines from Domaine de Regusse, Daniel Domergue and Château Routas aren't bad either.

Compact Italian, German and Spanish ranges focus on such quality producers as Lingenfelder and Dr Loosen, Aldo Conterno and Badia a Coltibuono and Remélluri and La Rioja Alta. The Newton and Bonny Doon items from California are also pleasing, as are those from Warwick, Dieu Donné and Jordan in South Africa. Gramp, Reynolds and Amberley may be unfamiliar Australian names but do try their wines; the same goes for Ngatawara from New Zealand.

The firm's tasting calendar caters for several levels of interest and experience, with recent events ranging from basic wine appreciation classes to a tutored tasting of Taylor and Fonseca ports. This, plus regular *en primeur* offers (such as 1993 burgundy and 1994 claret), serve as icing on an already very appealing cake.

Best buys

Pinot Noir 1994, Domaine de Regusse, £
Agramont Viura/Chardonnay 1994, £
St Hallett Old Block Shiraz 1992, ££
Chablis 1er Cru Montmains Vieilles Vignes 1993, Denis Race, ££

English Wine Centre

Alfriston Roundabout, East Sussex BN26 5QS

Tel (01323) 870164
Fax (01323) 870005

Open Mon–Sat 10–5; Sun 12–3; public holidays 10–5 **Closed** 24 Dec–2 Jan **Cards**
Access, Amex, Switch, Visa; personal and business accounts **Discount** 5% off cases
Delivery Free within 20-mile radius (min 1 case); nationwide at cost; mail-order
available **Glass hire** Free with order **Tasting and talks** Invitation tastings
throughout year **Cellarage** Not available

To commemorate VE Day, the English Wine Centre recommended
customers to try Elderberry Wine from the Lurgashall winery,
which was what many people drank to celebrate the formal end of
the war in Europe. For those who prefer English wine of a grapier
origin, Christopher Ann has one of the best ranges around and has
had since the English Wine Centre was founded in 1967.

The 'retired-major' phase of English wine-making has now,
thankfully passed. Those who run vineyards today are
professionals rather than hobbyists, and as a result the range of
wines available at the English Wine Centre has never been better.
The wines of the Harvest Group (q.v.) can be found here, but look
out also for wines from Breaky Bottom, Chapel Down, Three
Choirs, Berwick Glebe and Staple St James.

The thrice-yearly list gives much less than half the picture,
though. It is far better to visit the Centre and look round the
museum – particularly during the weekend in September when the
English Wine and Regional Food Festival is held (grape-treading
competitions, live jazz, plus a chance to meet the winemakers and
taste their wares).

Best buys

Gildridge white 1992, £
Staple St. James, Müller-Thurgau dry white, £
Seyval Blanc 1992, Breaky Bottom, ££
Vintage Brut Hidden Spring sparkling 1990, ££

Enotria Winecellars

153–155 Wandsworth High Street, London
SW18 4JB

Tel 0181-871 2668
Fax 0181-874 8380

Open Mon–Sat 10–7 **Closed** Sun, public holidays **Cards** Access, Switch, Visa;
personal accounts **Discount** Collection discount on orders over 1 case collected from
Winecellars shop **Delivery** Free nationwide (min 2 cases); min. 1 case within London;
mail-order available **Glass hire** Free with order (min 1 case); deposit required
Tasting and talks Tutored tastings; 2 major annual events; dinners

Despite earlier protestations to the contrary from several of those
concerned, it wasn't too much of a surprise when importers Enotria
finally engulfed Winecellars early in 1995. The bulk of the
Winecellars business had always been wholesale, and although
both companies were Italian specialists, it was surprising how little
the two ranges overlapped. The old Winecellars offices upstairs at
the Wandsworth shop may now be empty, but retail customers will
not have noticed much change, apart from a new name on the
shop and an adjustment in opening hours.

Those Italian wines are still the main reason to visit the shop.
Topping the Piemonte range are Barolos from Roberto Voerzio,
Giuseppe Mascarello and Aldo Conterno, while excellent-value
wines appear under the Araldica and Alasia labels. From the
Veneto, we'd recommend the wines of Allegrini, Pieropan,
Bartolomeo di Breganze and Anselmi. The Alto Adige wines from
Lageder and Franz Haas, and the Friuli whites from Jermann and
Puiatti are also excellent. Tuscans are similarly impressive, and,
although our favourites are the reds from Isole e Olena, Fontodi,
Argiano and Felsina Berardenga, all of the range is good. Heading
south, Umani Ronchi's Rosso Conero and Paradiso's Barbarossa
show the quality available from central Italy, while in the south
itself, C. S. Santadi and Candido produce very characterful stuff.
Those with a sweet tooth might care to try the Sicilian stickies from
de Bartoli and Cantine Florio, the Recioto di Soave from Anselmi
and Pieropan or the range of Vin Santo. (If this range of Italian
wines bears some resemblance to that in your local wine-merchant,
it's because the company is UK agent for all of them and distributes
them very efficiently.)

There are many decent wines from other places as well.
Australians come from Shaw & Smith, Tim Adams and Mount
Langi Ghiran, South Africans from Thelema, and an eclectic bunch
of Californian wines is listed. The Hungarians from Tibor G'al and
Château Megyer are good, and the German items from
Lingenfelder, Bert Simon and Max Ferd. Richter aren't bad either.
France is also covered with admirable thoroughness, and quality is
very much to the fore. Moreover, because most people associate the

company with Italian wines, the shop sometimes has difficulty disposing of end-of-line stock from other regions, so bargains are often available.

Wandsworth may not be the easiest place to get to, but we'd recommend a visit to stock up on wine, olive oil, flour and more besides. You might even care to attend one of the tutored tastings that take place above the shop regularly; they are some of London's most interesting and informative.

Best buys

1994 Muscate Sec, Alasia, £
1994 Kasbah Shiraz/Malbec/Mourvèdre, £
Chardonnay 1994, Shaw & Smith, ££
Chianti Classico 1992, Isole e Olena, ££

Evington's

---

120 Evington Road, Leicester, Leicestershire   *Tel* 0116-254 2702
LE2 1HH

Open Mon–Sat 9.30–6, Suns in Dec   **Closed** Bank hols, Suns   **Cards** Access, Amex, Delta, Switch, Visa; personal and business accounts   **Discount** 5% on 1–3 cases, 7.5% on 4–9 cases, 10% on 10+ cases   **Delivery** Free within Leicestershire   **Glass hire** Free   **Tasting and talks** On and off premises   **Cellarage** Available

---

Simon March's customers keep coming back for the 'friendly unsnobbish advice and brilliant fast service,' and are demanding more and more red wine. Evington's has a pretty good selection of all hues. Alsace is from Schlumberger and Trimbach, Loires from Paul Buisse and Baumard, while the best of the burgundies are the Chablis from Domaine des Malandes and the Parent Pommards. Five different producers provide Châteauneuf, while clarets come from Châteaux la Serre, la Tour de By and Palmer. Champagne is from Devaux and Joseph Perrier, with alternative sparklers including Omar Khayyam, Martini Asti and the Deutz New Zealander.

Still New Zealand wines are courtesy of Grove Mill and Babich, the Australian selection includes familiar fare from Penfolds and Brown Brothers, while similarly well-known Californians are from Mondavi, Quady and Fetzer. Other New World wines to look out for are the South African Dieu Donné Chardonnay and L. A. Cetto's Mexican Nebbiolo. The J. M. da Fonseca Portuguese reds are good value, the Spanish set is fair, while the Italians from Ascheri, Tedeschi and le Casalte are certainly worth trying.

Best buys

Penfolds Rawson's Retreat Cabernet/Ruby/Shiraz, 1993, £
Vaspaiolo Superiore 1993, Bartolomeo di Breganze, £
Fairview Estate Shiraz/Merlot, 1991, ££
Chablis 1er Cru Montmains 1991, Domaine des Malandes, ££

Philip Eyres Wine Merchant

The Cellars, Coleshill, Amersham,	*Tel* (01494) 433823
Buckinghamshire HP7 0LS	*Fax* (01494) 431349
Associated company	*Tel* (01295) 251179
S H Jones & Co, 27 High Street, Banbury	*Fax* (01295) 272352
Oxfordshire OX16 8EW	

Case sales only   Open Mon–Fri 8–10, Sat and Sun 9–10   **Closed** Public holidays and
(partially) during annual holiday   **Cards** Access, Visa; personal and business accounts
Discount 10p per bottle on unmixed cases   **Delivery** Free within surrounding area;
central London, 1 case £6.50, 2+ cases free; rest of UK mainland 1–3 cases £6.50, 4+
cases free; mail-order available   **Glass hire** Free with 1-case order   **Tasting and talks**
Several tastings a year in Coleshill; occasional tastings in London   **Cellarage** Not
available

If a good range of wines backed up by high standards of personal
service is your idea of the ideal wine-merchant, then you could do
far worse than deal with Philip Eyres and his colleagues. Mr Eyres
was one of the founding forces behind the idea of *en primeur*
campaigns in the 1960s through his company Henry Townsend. He
has been trading under his own name for six years now, the last
two in collaboration with Banbury merchant S. H. Jones (*q.v.*). The
Eyres list is now by and large a personal choice from the Jones
selection, with good representation of all wine regions from
throughout that range, but with a particularly strong set of
Germans, notably from the Nahe State Wine Domain. Customers
also receive regular offers, some of them *en primeur*, some focussing
on particular regions – 'Treasures of the New World', for example.

Best buys

Vin de Pays des Côtes de Gascogne 1994, Domaine de Rieux, £
Coteaux du Lyonnais 1993, Cuvée Sélectionée Pierre-Gabriel
Saligny, £
Maximin Grünhäuser Herrenberg Riesling Auslese, von Schubert,
1988, ££
St Georges St Emilion 1990, Château Macquin St Georges, ££

Farr Vintners

Mainly mail-order
19 Sussex Street, Pimlico, London SW1V 4RR

Tel 0171-828 1960
Fax 0171-828 3500

Case sales only **Open** Mon–Fri 10–6 **Closed** Sat, Sun, public holidays **Cards** Access, Delta, Switch, Visa; personal and business accounts **Discount** On orders over £2,000 **Delivery** London, £8.50 per consignment; elsewhere at cost; mail-order available **Glass hire** Not available **Tasting and talks** Frequent dinners and tastings for regular customers **Cellarage** £5 per case per year

Among all the awards Farr Vintners have gained over the few years they have been in business, the Queen's Award for Export takes some beating. In the fine wine market Farr remains the place to look first and the firm that others seek to emulate. The minimum order of £500 may deter some, but wine-lovers the world over are familiar with this dynamic company.

Bordeaux is covered with thoroughness, and multiple vintages from virtually every well-known château are always available. The burgundy list concentrates on such producers as Domaine Leroy, André Ramonet and de Vogüé, and, although the prices of several wines are above cloud level, basic Bourgogne Blanc or Rouge from those same producers is available. Château de Beaucastel and Guigal wines feature prominently among the Rhônes, as does Dom Perignon among the champagnes.

Outside France, the only permanent fixtures in the range are the New Zealand wines from the Kumeu River. Fine offerings from other parts of the wine world come and go with great regularity, however, so it's worth contacting Farr if there's something special you're after.

Best buys

Château de Beaucastel, ££
Pauillac, Château Pichon Longueville Lalande, ££

Fernlea Vintners

7 Fernlea Road, Balham, London SW12 7RT

Tel 0181-673 0053
Fax 0181-673 3559

Open Mon–Sat 10.30–7 **Closed** Sun, public holidays **Cards** Access, Visa; personal and business accounts **Discount** Not available **Delivery** Available by arrangement; mail-order available **Glass hire** Available **Tasting and talks** Individual tastings carried out **Cellarage** Free for 1 year with purchase

Peter Godden reports that trends in Balham indicate '... a reversion back to French wines instead of "Always Australia" – people are still experimenting, which is great.' Those large bottles of Moët are still around for those who can lift them, together with other champagnes from other famous names as well as the less well known but still excellent de Castellane. Chapoutier supplies Rhônes, Sancerre is from Jean Max Roger, while burgundies are supplied by Rossignol Trapet, Drouhin and William Fèvre. Clarets range from humble petit château level up to l'Evangile, Lafite and Gruaud Larose. Among the Germans, there's not much between Piesporter level and more impressive stickies from 1976. The Italian set is fair, the Spanish bottles from Chivite, CVNE and Valformosa are slightly better.

Yarra Yering Cabernet and Mountadam Chardonnay top a neat Australian range, New Zealanders are by way of Mills Reef, Matua Valley and Goldwater, while Domaine Drouhin Oregon Pinot and the L. A. Cetto Mexicans are the highlights of the American selection.

Best buys

Sauvignon Blanc Carta Vieja, 1994, £
Vin de Pays du Gard, Mas Roubaud Rouge/Blanc, £
Brouilly 1992, Domaine Tuilleries, ££
Ruländer Trockenbeerenauslese 1981, Holler, ££

Findlater Mackie Todd

Deer Park Road, Merton Abbey, London	*Tel* 0181-543 7528
SW19 3TU	*Fax* 0181-543 2415
(mail order only)	

Open Customer information line Mon–Fri 9–5.30; 24hr answer machine **Closed** Sat, Sun, public holidays **Cards** Access, Amex, Visa; John Lewis accounts; personal and business accounts **Discount** Not available **Delivery** London, £3.95 single case, free delivery for 2 cases or over £100; mail order available **Glass hire** Free **Tasting and talks** Approximately 6 times a year around the country, often in John Lewis Partnership venues **Cellarage** £5.65 per year

---

The marriage of this long-established mail-order merchant with the John Lewis group (and hence the Waitrose chain) seems to have given an old dog a new lease of life. The FMT selection remains strong in the classics, although the 'Inner Cellar' section of the list has now become part of the main range. Rest assured that you can still find some very classy clarets, going back to the 1970 Ch. La Mission-Haut-Brion, and four vintages of Ch. Laville-Haut-Brion, plus Louis Latour's Corton-Charlemagne and, of course, the famous Dry Fly sherry. Small parcels of other fine wines also appear from time to time for interested customers. The injection of Waitrose's wine-buying talent (five Masters of Wine at the last count) has added many interesting new items, however. Some will be familiar to shoppers at Waitrose, but FMT gives the buyers an additional outlet for special wines, or for those that are available in quantities too small to put on the Waitrose shelves.

South African wines come from Villiera and Thelema, Argentinian from Trapiche and Chilean from Valdivieso and Concha y Toro. Fans of Australian wine might care to try the Simon Whitlam Chardonnay, Chateau Reynella's Basket Press Shiraz and the Green Point sparkler, while New Zealand enthusiasts will relish the wines from Montana's top estates, plus others from Goldwater Estate and Hunter's. Wines from California are few, although those from Dry Creek Vineyards are very good.

Mönchhof is the pick of the seemingly reduced German range, while the wines of Cosme Palacio and Callejo stand out in the short Spanish set. A slightly larger Italian selection offers Santadi's big, juicy Carignano del Sulcis from Sardinia and the Riva wines from Emilia Romagna. If English reds have never impressed you, Chapel Down's Epoch 1 might be the wine to convert you.

The Duc de Marre champagne is great value, as is the slightly cheaper Domaine de l'Aigle brut from Limoux. Other wines of note from regional France are the vins de pays from Grassa, Domaine St-Hilaire and Domaine de St-Louis. The Rhône, Loire and Alsace ranges are small, but the Châteauneuf from Comte de Lauze is textbook stuff. Back in Burgundy, the Chorey-lès-Beaune from Maillard and Nuits-St-Georges from the Caves des Hautes-Côtes are both good affordable Pinot for those who can't stretch to the *grand cru* wines on offer. Similarly for whites, the St-Véran from the Caves des Grands Crus is for the less well-off, while Coche-Bizouard's Meursault is for the well-heeled. Of the less familiar clarets, our favourites are the trio from the 1990 vintage from Châteaux du Piras, Patache d'Aux and Vieux Robin.

Although the company is mail-order only, it's not necessary to buy by the case. However, with a range of wines such as this it would be churlish to order just by the single bottle.

Best buys

Findlater's Club Claret, Bordeaux AC, Peter Sichel, £
Touraine Sauvignon AC, Domaine Gibault 1993, £
Duc de Marre, Special Cuvée Brut Champagne, ££
Urziger Würzgarten Riesling Kabinett 1986, Mönchhof, Robert Eymael, ££

Le Fleming Wines

9 Longcroft Avenue, Harpenden,   *Tel* (01582) 760125
Hertfordshire AL5 2RB

Case sales only **Open** 24-hour answerphone, delivery during normal working hours
Cards All accepted; personal and business accounts **Discount** 5% on large orders
Delivery Free locally (min. 1 case); otherwise negotiable **Glass hire** Free (breakages
charged for) **Tasting and talks** 4 times a year and on request **Cellarage** Not
available

In the face of the onslaught from cross-Channel trade, Cherry
Jenkins, along with many small merchants in the south of England,
has battened down her Harpenden hatches and is doing her best to
weather the storm until some benevolent government sees fit to
change the duty rates. Her shift towards more on-trade business
has not affected the quality of the range, nor her desire to sell more
wine to the general public. Australia remains a strong favourite,
although a recent trip to California has meant that the range from
there has increased. From the former come the wines of Cullens,
Mount Langi Ghiran and Rockford, while from the latter, Newton,
Frog's Leap and Foppiano are available. There are also small
Chilean, New Zealand and South African ranges.

In France, all the major areas are covered well, particularly
southern France. Wines that stand out include Bernard Baudry's
Chinon, the Gigondas from Domaine les Pallières, the burgundies
from Daniel Rion and Olivier Merlin, and the Alsace from Zind-
Humbrecht. The Spanish and German ranges are reasonable, rather
than exciting; Italian bottles of note are the Ca dei Frati Lugana, the
Ascheri Barolo and Selvapiana's Chianti Rufina. Tastings are held
four times a year, and we'd encourage Harpendenizens to drop in.

Best buys

Côtes du Duras Sauvignon Blanc 1993, £
Klippenkop Cinsault/Shiraz 1993, £
Rockford Dry Country Grenache 1993, ££
Frog's Leap Zinfandel 1991, ££

Forth Wines

Crawford Place, Milnathort, Kinross-shire
KY13 7XF

Tel (01577) 863668
Fax (01577) 864810

Case sales only Open Mon–Fri 9–5, public holidays **Closed** Sat, Sun, 25 Dec, 1 and
2 Jan **Cards** Access, Visa; personal and business accounts **Discount** Not available
Delivery Local delivery (min. 3 cases); mail-order available **Glass hire** Not available
Tasting and talks 2 times a year **Cellarage** Not available

Forth is a company which conducts an alarming amount of
wholesale business and relatively little with the general public.
However, the invitation is always there to put together a mixed
case from the 900 or so wines in stock, and it's an invitation that
should be taken up with gusto. Pride of place throughout is
naturally given to producers for which Forth are agents, but the
quality is high enough that this does not usually pose much of a
problem. In the French section, Alsace wines are all from Gustave
Lorentz, Delas dominates the Rhônes, and Louis Latour and
Moreau provide most of the Burgundies. The Bordeaux selection is
more varied, with multiple vintages of Châteaux Grand-Puy-
Ducasse, Calon-Ségur and Latour and some excellent whites from
André Lurton. Vallformosa, Chivite and Marqués de Cáceres are
very much in evidence in the Spanish list, as are Ruffino and Lenz
Moser in the Italian and Austrian selections.

North American wines come from three more agencies,
Mondavi, Sutter Home and Columbia. Torreon de Paredes
provides the Chilean wine, South Africans are from Overgaauw,
Vriesenhof and Neil Ellis, and New Zealanders are produced by
Mills Reef. Rosemount features heavily in an Australian range that
also includes wines from Cape Mentelle and Orlando.

Anyone having difficulty deciding on a dozen might care to buy
one of the mixed cases featured in the Quaffers Club newsletters.

Best buys

Merlot 1990, Torreon de Paredes, Chile, £
1993/4 Pinot Blanc, Gustave Lorentz, £
1991 Elspeth Chardonnay, Mills Reef, ££
1991/3 Lirac, Les Queyrades, Mejan, ££

Fortnum & Mason

181 Piccadilly, London W1A 1ER

Tel 0171-734 8040
Fax 0171-437 3278

Open Mon–Sat 9.30–6 **Closed** Sun, public holidays **Cards** All accepted; personal and business accounts **Discount** 11 bottles for the cost of 12 **Delivery** Free within M25 area, (min. order of £40); £4 for goods under £40; 24-hour mail-order service available **Glass hire** Not available **Tasting and talks** Regular tastings in store 11.30–3 **Cellarage** Not available

Young, educated staff, regular in-store tastings, some of the world's most interesting wines ... Fortnum & Mason? Well, yes. Under the guidance of the unassuming Annette Duce, Fortnum's is now one of the best places to buy wine in central London. The high quality and standards of service that customers have come to expect over the last three centuries remain, but the prices are coming more in line with those of other wine merchants.

The store has always provided the classics, and traditionalists will not be disappointed. There's something for all port drinkers, whether for laying down or for drinking now (how about Cockburn 1935?). Champagne comes from several well-known houses, but you'll also find wines from the less widely-known Gosset, Ruinart and Billecart-Salmon. A broad range of claret from 1990 Ch. Les Charmes-Godard to 1945 Ch. Haut-Brion should cover all tastes and pockets. White Bordeaux lovers will spot dry wines from Châteaux Sénéjac, La Tour-Martillac and Haut-Brion and sweeter fare from Les Justices, Suduiraut, and d'Yquem (ten vintages on our last visit). Burgundy, too, is well covered. Chablis comes from William Fèvre and Louis Michel while the Domaines Leflaive, Comtes Lafon and Louis Carillon provide whites from the Côte d'Or. If red Burgundy is your thing, and you can't afford the wines of de Vogüé and Domaine de la Romanée-Conti, try instead Bruno Clair's Marsannay or Michel Juillot's Mercurey.

From the Loire venerable Bonnezeaux, Sancerre from Jean-Max Roger and Vacheron, and the extraordinary Coulée de Serrant are available. Alsace wines come from Trimbach, Faller and Josmeyer, Rhônes from Château de Beaucastel, Jean-Luc Colombo and Jaboulet Aîné. Among the regional wines are Domaine de Trévallon, vin jaune from Château d'Arlay and mature Corbières from Domaine du Trillol.

German wines are treated seriously. The own-label Mosel Riesling comes from Max Ferd. Richter, the hock from Heyl zu Herrnsheim, while other wines in varying degrees of sweetness come from the likes of Lingenfelder, Robert Weil and Schloss Saarstein; notable, too, are the Austrian sweet wines of Willi Opitz. From Spain, try the Rioja from Bodegas La Rioja Alta and CVNE, the good-value Ochoa wines from Navarra and the Juvé y Camps cava. Italian bottles of note are the Piemonte wines of Bava and Ceretto, the Tuscan wines from Isole e Olena and Selvapiana and the whites from Jermann in the north-east.

If the Fortnum & Mason range pleases the traditionalists, it also caters remarkably well for New World fans. Among the Californian wines Chardonnays from Newton Vineyards, Au Bon Climat and Acacia are excellent, as are the Ridge Cabernet and the Pinot from Saintsbury as well as the Oregon Pinot of Domaine Drouhin. South African reds come from Neil Ellis, Beyerskloof and Kanonkop, while whites include Chardonnays from Danie de Wet and Hamilton Russell, as well as the nectar known as Vin de Constance. None of the New Zealand wines will fail to please, but we particularly like the wines of Te Mata, Daniel le Brun and Jackson Estate. Familiar Australian names appear, but we'd urge you to try the less famous wines of Pierro, Mitchell, David Traeger and Water Wheel.

If you're not sure what to try from this impressive selection, start with one of the own-label wines, which come from top producers around the world.

Best buys

House Vin du Patron Red and White, £
Fortnum & Mason Red Burgundy (Domaine Faiveley's Red Mercurey), ££
Fortnum & Mason Sancerre (Domaine Vacheron), ££

The Four Walls Wine Company

High Street, Chilgrove, nr Chichester,   *Tel* (01243) 535219
West Sussex PO18 9HX   *Fax* (01243) 535301

Open Tue–Sat 9–3, 6–11, Sun and public holidays 9–3 **Closed** Mon and Feb **Cards** Access, Delta, Diners, Switch, Visa; personal and business accounts **Discount** By negotiation **Delivery** Nationwide via Parcelforce or Target at cost; mail-order available **Glass hire** Free **Tasting and talks** Oct and Mar **Cellarage** Free with order

The restraint that Barry Phillips showed when asked to recommend wines over £5 was admirable. It would have been tempting to pick the 1983 Le Montrachet from Ramonet or the 1975 Ch. Pétrus, but he plumped for much humbler fare from his grand list, as shown below. There can be few other wine-merchants with a similar breadth of fine wines available by the single bottle. This pleasing state of affairs occurs because Four Walls is the retail arm of the White Horse Inn, which over the past 26 years has gained much acclaim for its wines.

As befits a restaurant with such a name, the list includes Ch. Cheval Blanc from eight vintages, and the 1972 at £30 is surely worth a punt. Other first growths are also available in depth, but there are also hundreds of less pricey wines: 1982 Ch. Gazin sounds cheap at £17.50. White Bordeaux fans will enjoy Haut-Brion Blanc and Pavillon Blanc du Château Margaux, again both from several vintages, while those with a sweeter tooth will be attracted to Sauternes from Ch. Rieussec, Ch. d'Yquem and many others. Further sweet (and dry) delights are found in the Loire and Alsace ranges, with a broad range from Zind-Humbrecht standing out in the latter. However, the best range of French whites is from Burgundy. From Bourgogne Blanc to *grand cru* level, enticing wines from top producers – Domaine Leflaive, Sauzet, Jean-Noël Gagnard, Louis Carillon – abound, and again, although some prices run well into three figures, there's much of interest under £20.

Red burgundy fans will drool at a similarly comprehensive set of wines. From the Côte de Beaune come offerings from Comte Armand, Chandon de Briailles and Domaine de la Pousse d'Or, while the Côte de Nuits selection contains wines from Joseph Roty, Domaine Mongeard-Mugneret, Chopin-Groffier and many others. The choice of reds from the rest of France looks sparse in comparison, but Domaine de Trévallon, Château de Beaucastel and Hermitage La Chapelle will not disappoint.

The Italian selection does not cover the cheaper wines, concentrating instead on Gaja's Barbaresco, Aldo Conterno's Barolo, Tignanello and Sassicaia. It's the same with Germany. Don't come here for Liebfraumilch; what you will find instead is a broad range of some of the world's greatest Rieslings – among them Rheingaus from Schloss Rheinhartshausen and Wegeler-Deinhard and Mosels from von Schubert – at all sweetness levels. The small Spanish selection includes four vintages of Torres Black Label.

New World wines are of the classier variety. South Africa provides Thelema, Nederburg and Warwick, New Zealand offers Cloudy Bay and Kumeu River, while Australian wines come from Petaluma, Henschke and Yarra Yering. In the Californian range are Peter Michael's excellent Chardonnay and Cabernet, several vintages of Hanzell Pinot Noir, as well as big names such as Cask 23, Opus One and Heitz Martha's Vineyard.

Best buys

Touraine Sauvignon 1993, L'Oisly et Thésée, £
Van Loveren Blanc de Noir, South Africa, £
Pauillac, Château Batailley 1978, ££
Vouvray Moelleux, 1990, Didier Campelou, ££

John Frazier

Warehouse

Stirling Road, Cranmore Industrial Estate,   *Tel* 0121-704 3415
Shirley, Solihull, West Midlands B90 4NE   *Fax* 0121-711 2710
Branches in Billesley, Bromsgrove, Henley in Arden,
Lapworth, Shirley, Solihull, Streetly and Tanworth in Arden

Open Mon–Sat 10–10, Sun and public holidays 12–2, 7–10   **Cards** All accepted;
personal and business accounts   **Discount** Available   **Delivery** Available within a 50-mile radius, min 4 cases; mail-order available   **Glass hire** Available at 45p per dozen
Tasting and talks Contact stores for details   **Cellarage** Free with order

There are eight shops now in the Frazier empire, but the firm continues to be everything a good family wine-merchant should be. For innovation and excitement, you may want to look elsewhere, but for solid wines at fair prices, Frazier's cannot be faulted.

New World wines continue to gain in popularity according to the company. From Australia, they offer customers the familiar Penfolds, Brown Brothers and Wolf Blass wines as well as bottles from the less widely seen Mitchell's and Knight's Granite Hills.

Alongside the KWV South African wines are Hamilton Russell Pinot Noir and Meerlust Rubicon, and from New Zealand Montana is joined by C. J. Pask and Palliser Estate. Sutter Home, Gallo and Mondavi constitute most of a slightly dreary Californian range, while Concha y Toro represents Chile. Spanish highlights are Riojas from CVNE and Contino, and Navarra from Ochoa; stars from Italy are hard to find, though. Deinhard provides most of the German wines.

The claret is of the good, solid type: Châteaux Cissac, Meyney, d'Angludet and Palmer. Burgundies are mainly from Chanson and Louis Latour, although Jean Grivot's Vosne-Romanée, Defaix's Chablis and Lafarge's Meursault make appearances. In the Rhône section Jaboulet, Chapoutier and Domaine du Vieux Télégraphe are reassuring, as are the many grande marque champagnes; we'd go for the Joseph Perrier. Schlumberger's Alsace, de Ladoucette's Pouilly Fumé and vins de pays from Domaine Virginie also look good.

Best buys

1991 Concha y Toro Cabernet Sauvignon Merlot (Chile), £
Vin de Pays d'Oc Marsanne 1993, Domaine Virginie, £
Vosne-Romanée 1989, Domaine Jean Grivot, ££
Sauvignon Blanc 1992, Palliser Estate, ££

Fuller, Smith & Turner

Head office
The Griffin Brewery, Chiswick Lane South, *Tel* 0181-996 2000
London W4 2QB *Fax* 0181-995 0230
chain of 65 shops

Open Mon–Sat 10-10; Sun 12–3, 7–10; public holidays **Closed** Chr Day **Cards**
Access, Switch, Visa; personal and business accounts **Discount** Varies depending on
on-going promotions; 1 bottle free per case, 10% discount on 5+ cases **Delivery** Free
within 10-mile radius of any store (more for large orders) **Glass hire** Free **Tasting
and talks** Tastings every Sat 2–5 **Cellarage** Not available

Wine bargain of the moment (and it will still be around when the
Guide comes out) is the range of 1985 and 1989 German Kabinetts
from Dr Thanisch that Fuller's has on offer for under a fiver. 'They
just weren't selling,' wine-buyer Roger Higgs told us. Other things
are selling, however, and the Fuller's chain looks more attractive by
the minute. The 65 stores no longer look as embarrassed as they
once did, the knowledge of the people behind the counter seems to
be improving, and the wines are very appealing.

We're not sure how the classy clarets sell in the shops, but the
selection features 1988 wines from Châteaux Mouton-Rothschild,
Gruaud-Larose and Palmer as well as several more affordable
wines. Burgundies include whites from Domaine des Deux Roches
and reds from Philippe Naddef; Jean-Luc Colombo provides three
wines in the Rhône section, and other French highlights are the
good range of vins de pays, the pick being Domaine
Roquenegade's Cabernet Sauvignon.

The Augustus wines from Penedés are rather better than the
Torres range, and wines to note from Italy include Casal di Serra
Verdicchio and some reasonably priced Tuscan vini da tavola. Ports
come from Taylor, Graham, Dow and Fonseca. Bypass the KWV
South Africans and head for the wines of Saxenberg and Dieu
Donné. From the Americas, the Thornhill range shows that
California can produce good cheap wine, the Cono Sur Chileans
are very good, and the Catena Argentinians are a revelation. Look
out for New Zealand bottles from Blackbirch, Kumeu River and
Waimarama, and for Australians from Devil's Lair, Rockford,
Leasingham and Wirra Wirra.

Not all the stores are obliged to stock the full range, but if we've
mentioned anything that isn't in your local branch, the manager
will be able to obtain some for you. Given sufficient notice, the
manager should also be able to locate something suitable for
celebrating an anniversary; most vintages of the past fifty years are
represented in Fuller's stock. And if you need that bottle of Taylor's

1945 chilled (remember, the customer is always right!) the Chilla machines in the larger stores will do it in around four minutes.

Best buys

Côtes du Rhône 1994, Domaine Vieux Manoir de Maranson, £
1994 Rioja Basa Garnacha, Viña Artadi, £
1993 Catena Agrelo Vineyard Chardonnay, ££
1992 Rockford Basket Pressed Shiraz, ££

Elizabeth Gabay and Partners

| 20 Grange Road, Highgate, London N6 4AP | *Tel* 0181-342 9247 |
| | *Fax* 0181-347 6322 |

Case sales only   Open No fixed hours **Cards** None accepted **Discount** Not available **Delivery** £3.50 London postal codes (min. 1 case) **Glass hire** Not available **Tasting and talks** 2–3 times a year **Cellarage** Not available

As well as being a member of the tasting panel that selects wines for Wine Finds (q.v.), Elizabeth Gabay is a very handy wine-merchant in her own right. We're not sure who the partners are, but the chances are that if you contact the company you'll speak to Elizabeth herself. There is no core list as such, but the monthly newsletters keep customers in touch with an ever-changing range of wines, with food suggestions to accompany each one. By the time this *Guide* appears, the range may be totally different from the current one (Spring 1995), so anything we mention here serves only to show the type of wines on offer. France and Italy make up the main weight of the range, although New World bottles, such as the Australian Skillogalee Riesling, Flynn Vineyards Pinot Noir from Oregon and the Thelema South Africans do make an appearance. From France, there are Alsace wines from Albert Seltz, decent clarets (such as 1990 Ch. Belgrave and Ch. Lascombes) and good regional fare, for example the Pic St Loup wines from Domaine de l'Hortus. Italians include Villa Vetrice's Vin Santo, Allegrini Amarone Classico della Valpolicella and Carmignano from Capezzana. Tastings of the range take place two or three times a year, and, although the wines on show may change, the quality remains very high.

Best buys

Not really appropriate given the nature of the list

Gauntley's of Nottingham

4 High Street, Exchange Arcade,   *Tel* (0115) 9417973
Nottingham, Nottinghamshire NG1 2ET   *Fax* (0115) 9509519

Open Mon–Sat 9–5.30, Sun in Dec **Closed** Sun, public holidays **Cards** Access,
Delta, Switch, Visa; personal and business accounts **Discount** 5% on 1 case **Delivery**
Nottingham, Derby, Newark (min. 1 case); £6.50 if outside area; mail-order available
Glass hire Free with order **Tasting and talks** Tastings conducted by growers and
shop; private tastings on request **Cellarage** Not available

A friend of the *Guide* who probably spends more per year on wine
than our entire editorial budget cites Gauntley's as one of the few
companies in the country in which he has absolute confidence.
We're sure that there are many other customers who would say the
same about this Nottingham wine (and cigar) merchant,
particularly if they are fans of the Rhône and Provence.

The nature of John Gauntley's business is such that the wine list
often tells less than half the story. Customers are kept in touch with
the real action by regular newsletters that feature small parcels of
rare and unusual wines, and anyone who is slow in responding to
such offers often misses out. Even so, the core wines of the range
are still extremely attractive. The Rhône is covered with passion,
and the ranges of wines from Cornas and St Joseph show that there
is much more to the Syrah grape than Hermitage and Côte Rôtie;
we'd choose wines from Noël Verset and Emile Florentin, but
might find a space in our cellar for a bottle or two of Hermitage
from Florent Viale. As an alternative to a Châteauneuf from
Château de Beaucastel or Clos des Papes, try one from Domaine
Pegau, Mallière or St Benoît. The basic Côtes du Rhône from
Domaines Remejeanne and Gramenon are anything but basic.
Provence brings fine wines from Domaines Rabiaga and Tempier,
and customers should keep an eye out for some new wines from
Mas Bruguière in the Languedoc; French country wines include
characterful stuff from Domaine Peyre Rose and Domaine de
l'Hortus.

The Loire range concentrates on Chenin Blanc, with Vouvray
from Huet, Foreau and Fouquet, and Quarts de Chaume from
Baumard, but expansion is planned for the very near future.
Vilmart champagne is excellent, as are the Alsace wines of Ostertag,
Zind-Humbrecht and Trimbach. Clarets are thin on the ground, but
Burgundy is much better represented. John has just begun to
import André Brunet's Meursault, but whether, like the wines of
Comtes Lafon and Jobard, they will ever make it on to the list
before customers snap them up is debatable. Reds come from
Patrice Rion, René Engel and Michel Lafarge, although again, you'll
have to be quick if you want to buy some.

After such delights in France, the ranges from the rest of the world are something of a bonus. German wines come from Theo Haart and Bassermann Jordan, and Italian from Pieropan (Soave) and Fugazza (Oltrepò Pavese). New from Australia are wines from Cullens in Western Australia and Dalwhinnie in Victoria, and the Californian selection now includes Joseph Swan's characterful wines. South African offerings from Thelema, Warwick and Hamilton Russell complete a fine range.

Best buys

1992 Coteaux de Murviel, Domaine de Limbardie, £
1992 Côtes de Thongue, Domaine de Montmarin, £
1989 Muscat Moenchreben, Domaine Rolly Gassmann, ££
1993 Côtes du Rhône Les Genèvrieres Remi Klein, ££

General Wine Company

25 Station Road, Liphook, Hampshire
GU30 7DW

Tel (01428) 722201
Fax (01428) 724037

Open Mon–Sat 9–9, Sun and public holidays 12–2, 7–9 **Closed** Chr Day **Cards** Access, Amex, Delta, Switch, Visa; personal and business accounts **Discount** 5% on mixed case purchase; other discounts up to 15% **Delivery** Free within 30-mile radius, nationwide delivery £2.50 per case; mail-order available **Glass hire** Free with order **Tasting and talks** Every Sat **Cellarage** Not available

Alan Snudden may be a failed accountant, but he's a proficient wine-merchant. He describes his company as 'a small but aggressive independent shipper'. We might be tempted to add the word 'quality-minded' as well. Anyone who is keen on South African wine will find much of interest from producers such as Backsberg, Neetlingshof, Glen Carlou and Saxenberg. The Australian range is impressive, too, with Coldstream Hills, Tisdall and Hollick providing just a selection from the many wines on show. The New Zealanders from Palliser Estate are good, as are the L. A. Cetto Mexican wines and the Chileans from Undurraga and Caliterra.

From Spain, we'd recommend the Somontano wines from Viñas del Vero, and the Riojas from Marqués de Cáceres and Campo Viejo, while from Italy, we'd choose the Masi Valpolicella and Soave and Villa Lanata's Langhe Chardonnay. Peter Mertes and Schmitt provide Germans. France is not covered in great depth, but good wines abound. Alsace comes from Trimbach and the Turckheim co-op, and the Corbières from Château Grand Moulin is very tasty, as are the Loire wines from Crochet and La Chapelle de Cray. Not all the claret is as pricy as the 1959 Ch. Latour, and there's much of interest at around a tenner. The burgundy and Rhône ranges feature many good producers, and the champagnes from Chartogne-Taillet and Canard-Duchêne are as satisfying as many of their more expensive competitors.

Customers now have the opportunity of buying ex-cellars, by adding their orders (minimum two unmixed cases) to what the company is already shipping, and obtaining attractive savings.

Best buys

Corbières 1991, Château Grand Moulin, £
Cheverney 1993 'Le Portail', £
Domaine des Berthiers 1993 Pouilly Fumé, ££
Lirac 1991, Les Queyrades, ££

Matthew Gloag & Son

Bordeaux House, 33 Kinnoull Street, Perth,   *Tel* (01738) 621101
Perthshire PH1 5EU   *Fax* (01738) 628167

Open Mon–Sat 9–5 **Closed** Sun, public holidays **Cards** Access, Visa; personal and business accounts **Discount** 5% on 1 case if collected **Delivery** Scotland, 1+ case free; England and Wales, 2+ cases free, otherwise £3.95 per consignment; mail-order available **Glass hire** Free **Tasting and talks** Occasional tastings in shop; regular tutored tasting evenings; large summer and Chr tastings **Cellarage** Not available

---

The opening of the Kinnoull St shop on Saturday has given the inhabitants of Perth more of a chance to sample the compact Matthew Gloag wine range. The list is compact too, and now starts with Australians. Quite reasonable ones they are too, the pick being the wines from Woodstock, Capel Vale and Katnook. The Selaks wines join a new Zealand range that also includes wines from Redwood Valley. South African representation is provided by Drostdy Hof, Meerlust and Uitkyk, Californian bottles come from Wente Brothers, and Viña Porta provide those from Chile. The Domaine de Montmarin wines from the Côtes de Thongue are the best of a short regional French range. Other French wines of note are the Domaine Servin Chablis, Clos de Nouys Vouvray, red burgundies from Machard du Gramont and Bachelet and the Rhônes from Château de Beaucastel. Clarets are good too, with several affordable wines from good recent vintages. The German selection stems from Deinhard, the Spanish from Guelbenzu and Navajas, and the Italian section has a clutch of good value wines. You'll also find Taylor's ports and sherries from Barbadillo. The bimonthly newsletters are not the most lavishly produced, but the wines featured are always good value.

Best buys

Marqués de Aragòn 1994 Calatayud, £
Domaine de Montmarin Sauvignon 1994, £

Shiraz Capel Vale 1991, Western Australia, ££
Selaks Sauvignon Blanc 1994, Marlborough, New Zealand, ££

Goedhuis & Co

6 Rudolf Place, Miles Street, London SW8 1RP   *Tel* 0171-793 7900
                                                     Fax 0171-793 7170

Case sales only   Open Mon–Fri 9–5.30 **Closed** Sat, Sun, public holidays **Cards**
Access, Visa; personal and business accounts **Discount** Subject to size of order
Delivery Free within M25 area (min 3 cases), elsewhere £10; mail-order available
Glass hire Not available **Tasting and talks** Available **Cellarage** £5.95 per case per
year

At first glance, the latest Goedhuis fine wine list is crammed with
Bordeaux, Burgundy and ... that's about it. Not that the company
fails to offer wines from other parts of the world; there are good
Rhônes from Beaucastel and Chapoutier, champagne, port and
Tokay, even some Cloudy Bay and Tignanello on the list.
Recipients of the regular mailings will know that the company is
UK agent for the Bernardus winery in California's Carmel valley,
and the wines from there are good value (when we asked
Goedhuis for wines costing under £5, we were surprised at the
choice available).

All the same, the main emphasis of the business is on the fine
wines of Bordeaux and Burgundy. Such wines don't come cheap,
but not all command the £2,000+ per case of 1982 Ch. Mouton-
Rothschild. Relatively affordable burgundy from growers such as
Mongeard-Mugneret, Ponsot, Serafin and Méo-Camuzet is
available, although you'll also find their more expensive bottles
should you wish. In the claret list there's plenty of wine left from
the good vintages of the late 1980s, including most of the first
growths, but you'll also find such affordable châteaux as
Beaumont, Lalande-Borie, Sociando-Mallet and Potensac on offer.

Those interested in easing the purchase of wine can take
advantage of the Bottle Bank scheme, which spreads the cost of
wine-buying over 12 months. Bargain-hunters might prefer to wait
for the bin-end offers which bring some of those high prices down
to slightly more manageable levels.

Best buys

Domaine Perriere, Les Amandiers 1992, £
Côtes de Thongue Chardonnay 1993, Domaine Boyer, £
Châteauneuf de Pape 1990, Château de Beaucastel, ££
Pauillac, Château Duhart Milon Rothschild 1985, ££

Gordon & MacPhail

58-60 South Street, Elgin, Moray IV30 1JY

Tel (01343) 545110
Fax (01343) 540155

Open Mon–Fri 9–5.15, Sat 9–5 **Closed** Sun, public holidays **Cards** Access, Switch, Visa; personal and business accounts **Discount** 10% on 12 bottles **Delivery** Free within 30-mile radius; mail-order available **Glass hire** Free with order, min 1 case **Tasting and talks** Not offered **Cellarage** Not available

First of all, Happy 100th Birthday to the company which James Gordon and John Alexander MacPhail established on 24 May 1895. John Urquart joined the company that year and his descendants now run the Elgin shop from the same premises. The range of malt whiskies is quite simply the largest and best in the world, whether your taste is for 1936 Mortlach or something more recent.

Wines take something of a back seat in such company, but the range is still a good one. It errs on the traditional side, so you'll find good, solid claret from Châteaux Cissac, Feytit-Clinet and d'Angludet, burgundy from Chanson and ports from Croft, Graham and Taylor dating back almost as far as the whiskies. There are also Rhônes from Chapoutier and Roger Combe, some serious Germans, Italians from Frescobaldi and Antinori, and Iberians from J. M. da Fonseca and Torres. Highlights in the New World are Chateau Tahbilk and Mitchell from Australia, C. J. Pask and Delegats from New Zealand, Santa Carolina from Chile and from South Africa Neetlingshof and Backsberg.

Best buys

Buda Bridge Chardonnay, 1993, £
Peter Lehmann Vine Vale Riesling, 1994, £
Haut-Médoc 1987, Château Caronne-Ste Gemme, ££
Gewürztraminer Hornstein 1992, Cave Vinicole de Pfaffenheim, ££

Grape Ideas

3/5 Hythe Bridge Street, Oxford,   *Tel* (01865) 722137
Oxfordshire OX1 2EW   *Fax* (01865) 791594

Open Mon–Fri 10–7; Sat 10–6 **Closed** Sun, public holidays **Cards** Access, Delta,
Switch, Visa; personal and business accounts **Discount** 5% off all unmixed cases,
2.5% off mixed cases **Delivery** Free locally (min. 1 case); mail-order available **Glass
hire** Free with order **Tasting and talks** One major tasting each year **Cellarage** Not
available

What else would you expect of an Oxford wine merchant than staff
who are 'educated, polite, numerate and knowledgeable'? Well
how about some classic claret, Burgundy and port? Grape Ideas can
certainly supply those, as a look in the Fine Vintage Wines annexe
will show. However, given the impoverishment of students (and
dons) this wine warehouse list is geared mainly towards more
affordable fare.

The French country wines are certainly good value, and we'd go
for the Côtes de Duras from Berticot and Philippe de Baudin's Vin
de Pays d'Oc. The prices of the cru bourgeois and petit château
clarets are distinctly grant- (and loan-) friendly, as are those of the
Loire wines from Guy Saget. Among the Noémie Vernaux
burgundies are more interesting wines from Domaine des Deux
Roches and Faiveley. Schlumberger provides Alsace wines, while
among the champagnes (Taittinger and Roederer) the House
champagne from Garnier offers good value.

The Rioja from Campillo and the Marqués de Monistrol Penedés
wines are worth a try, and the Sogrape range from Portugal is well
represented. The Italian range seem to have contracted slightly,
although the Vino Nobile de Montepulciano from le Casalte and
the Isole e Olena Chianti Classico are very good; a short set of
Germans appears to be reasonably serious, but the list omits the
names of most producers.

From the New World, mature Californian Cabernets from
Kenwood, Pine Ridge and Z-D are still available, while the South
American list includes Carmen from Chile and Trapiche and
Weinert from Argentina. The Zonnebloem South African wines
deserve more attention than the rather dreary KWV range, and the
reliable Cooks New Zealand selection is joined by more inspiring
fare from Redwood Valley. The wines of Plantagenet in Western
Australia are certainly decent, especially the Muscat and the Shiraz.

Best buys

Domaine de Fontjun St Chinian AC, £
Duras, Bertiot Sauvignon, £

1994 Cairanne, Domaine de la Presidente, Max Aubert, ££
1994 Plantagenet Omrah Vineyard Chardonnay (Western
Australia), ££

The Grape Shop

135 Northcote Road, London SW11 6PX

Tel 0171-924 3638
Fax 0171-924 3670

Open Mon 10–2, 5–9.30, Tue–Sat 10–9.30, Sun & public holidays 12–3, 7–9 **Closed**
Chr and Boxing Days **Cards** Access, Amex, Delta, Switch, Visa; business accounts
Discount Negotiable **Delivery** Free in London (min. 1 case) **Glass hire** Free with
order **Tasting and talks** Tastings held on Saturdays **Cellarage** Not available

The success of The Grape Shop's French outlets combined with
rather stagnant trade in SW11 have made Martin Brown put his
Northcote Road shop up for sale. There has been little interest from
prospective buyers, and Martin expects to be around well into 1996.
It will be a shame when the shop eventually does go, as this has
been one of south London's best independent wine-merchants.
The shop resembles a chaotic Oddbins more than anything, with
too many wines crammed into too small a space. The wines are
good, mind you, and, like Oddbins, are heavy on the Australian
wines. You'll find wines from Hollick, Henschke, Rymill, Grant
Burge and many others, with plenty of older vintages available.
The rest of the New World range is poor by comparison, although
the L. A. Cetto Mexicans and the South African wines from Klein
Constantia and Rustenberg will not disappoint.

Claret fans will find a good selection ranging from mature first
growths to some decent *cru bourgeois* and second wines.
Burgundies come from a healthy mixture of merchants and
growers, with a 1971 Doudet-Naudin Corton-Charlemagne there to
tempt the brave. You'll also find wonderful champagne from
Vilmart, Henri Bourgeois Sancerre and Alsace wines from Scherer,
and on our last visit, a few cases of Guigal's single vineyard Côtes
Rôties were being delivered.

There are very few German wines on offer but the Spanish
selection is healthier, with wines from Vega Sicilia, Marqués de
Monistrol and Chivite. Italian wines are even better, whether your
budget restricts you to the Via Nova wines and Santadi's
Carignano or whether you care to try the heady heights of
Sassicaia, Solaia or Argiano's Brunello.

Club members (£10 per annum) receive regular discounts, plus
occasional 20% off at weekends. Everyone can take advantage of the
seafood stall which appears outside the shop at the weekend and
offers bargain crustaceans to those who get there early. The range
available through the French shops is a somewhat slimmed down

version of the full range, with fewer interesting wines. However, it's still one of the best merchants on the French side of the Channel.

Best buys

Petite Sirah 1992, L. A. Cetto, £
Cosme Palacio y Hermanos Rioja Blanco, 1992, £
Basedows Shiraz, 1989, ££
Champagne Vilmart Grand Réserve NV, ££

Great Northern Wine Company

Granary Wharf, Leeds Canal Basin, Leeds,	*Tel* (0113) 2461200
West Yorkshire LS1 4BR	*Fax* (0113) 2461209
The Warehouse, Blossomgate, Ripon, North Yorkshire	
HG4 2AJ	

Open Mon–Fri 9–6, Sat 9.30–5, Sun 10.30–4 **Closed** public holidays, Chr and Boxing Days **Cards** Access, Amex, Delta, Switch, Visa; personal and business accounts **Discount** 8% on 1 case (un)mixed **Delivery** Free within 30-mile radius (min. 1 case); mail-order service available **Glass hire** Free with order **Tasting and talks** Monthly tutored tastings and large annual tasting **Cellarage** Not available

Still living up to its name, the Great Northern Wine Company remains the best place for the inhabitants of Leeds and Ripon to find a range of top bottles from around the globe. Current trends among Yorkshire wine-drinkers show a move away from New World wines towards more traditional styles. Undeterred, the company has expanded its already decent Australian range (Grant Burge, Brown Brothers, Cape Mentelle) with wines from Henschke and Chateau Xanadu. The New Zealand list includes Kumeu River, Hunters and de Redcliffe wines, while Fairview and Rustenberg provide South African interest. A marginally less interesting Californian range nonetheless includes Ridge Vineyards' Mataro and Foppiano's Petite Sirah, while from the other side of the States come wines from Palmer. Mexican and Chilean wines come from L. A. Cetto and Undurraga respectively.

The German and Portuguese ranges are slightly half-hearted, although the Calem ports are good. Italy is slightly better with Chianti from Vicchiomaggio and Barolo from Giordano. Lovers of Spanish wine will take pleasure in the wares of CVNE, La Rioja Alta, Torres, Ochoa and COVISA in Somontano. Do try the Moldovan reds and Hungarian whites.

Turning to France, champagne from Joseph Perrier always goes down well, and Alsace comes from Louis Gisselbrecht. The Loire and Rhône ranges never get fully into their stride, but the range of country wines, including Châteaux de Lastours and Tours des Gendres, is more interesting. Pick of the burgundies are Chablis from Domaine des Malandes and Vosne-Romanée from Réné Engel, while the *cru bourgeois* claret range includes Ch. Ramage-la-Batisse, Ch. MacCarthy and Ch. Beaumont.

There is also a range of fine and rare wines but you'll have to visit the dark arches of the Leeds shop to look at those (a small range of interesting whiskies might act as an incentive). There are gaps in the GNWC range, but the enthusiastic staff will always do their best to plug them with a suitable alternative. Customers unable to visit either shop should look out for the monthly tutored tastings in and around Leeds.

Best buys

Artadi Tinto, Rioja DO, Cosecheros Alaveses 1994, £
Faugères 1992, Château de Laurens, £
Hunter's Sauvignon Blanc 1994, New Zealand, ££
Coteaux du Tricastin 1990, Domaine les Vieux Micocoulier, ££

Great Western Wine Company

The Wine Warehouse, Wells Road,	*Tel* (01225) 448428
Bath, Avon BA2 3AP	*Fax* (01225) 442139

Case sales only **Open** Mon–Sat 10–7 **Closed** Sun, public holidays **Cards** Access, Switch, Visa; personal and business accounts **Discount** Approximately 5% on 3+ cases **Delivery** Free within 20-miles radius (min. 1 case); nationwide mail-order service available **Glass hire** Free **Tasting and talks** Some wines always open to taste, regular tutored tasting **Cellarage** £5 per year

We're sure it's not just the move to more spacious premises that has led to Philip Addis *et al.* increasing their sales over the past year; the quality of their wines must have something to do with it. You'll find a good range of claret that majors on good but not overpriced wines, such as Châteaux Citran and Beychevelle, but is augmented from time to time by offers of finer and rarer fare (Ch. Pavie 1961 anybody?). Domaine des Malandes provides Chablis, while other burgundies come from such top growers as Méo-Camuzet, Carillon and Guy Prieur. Turckheim co-op Alsace, Georges Gardet champagnes, a good regional French selection and Rhônes from Delas are also worth plundering. The Spanish range includes Riojas from CVNE, the Viñas del Vero Somontano wines and the excellent Ribera del Duero from Pago de Carraovejas. Italian wines of interest come from Teruzzi e Puthod, Allegrini and le Casalte, while the German ones are mostly from Gustave Adolf Schmitt. Bath's own Mumfords Vineyard provides five wines.

From Australia the Goundrey wines from Mount Barker and those of Pipers Brook in Tasmania are notable; New Zealand offers Matua Valley, while Fairview and Boschendal represent South

Africa. From the Americas come the Norton wines from Argentina, L. A. Cetto's from Mexico and Californian bottles from Beringer and Marimar Torres. Blandy Madeiras, Dow ports and Barbadillo sherries complete the range.

Of the many dinners, tastings and other events that take place, our favourite is 'An evening of Questionable Taste', at which participants play boules, drink wine, eat canapés and have the chance to fail utterly to answer such questions as, 'what was the wine you've just drunk?'

Best buys

Coteaux du Languedoc 1993, Château Coujan, £
Vin de Pays d'Oc Chardonnay/Sauvignon, 1994, Domaine St Hilaire, £
Champagne Jean Moutardier Carte Noir Brut, ££
Côte Rôtie Brune et Blonde 1991, Chapoutier, ££

Peter Green

37a/b Warrender Park Road, Edinburgh	*Tel* 0131-229 5925
EH9 2PG	*Fax* 0131-229 5925

Open Mon–Fri 9.30–6.30, Sat 9.30–7 **Closed** Sun, public holidays **Cards** Switch, Delta; personal and business accounts **Discount** 5% on 1 case **Delivery** Free delivery in Edinburgh; mail-order available **Glass hire** Free **Tasting and talks** Monthly tastings; also, tastings to groups on request **Cellarage** Not available

---

If customers at this excellent Edinburgh merchant notice Michael Romer appearing more bleary-eyed than usual, it's not the result of over-enthusiastic late-night tasting sessions, but the effects of stuffing his new computer with information. As his is a particularly vibrant and extensive range of wines it must have taken a long time to feed into his system. The set of over 30 Alsace wines features bottles from Schlumberger, Hugel and Trimbach and there are clarets to suit all pockets.

Burgundies are mainly from merchants such as Bouchard Père et Fils and Faiveley, with Duboeuf providing beaujolais, but there are also wines from growers such as Daniel Rion and Tollot-Beaut. Whether Loire fans enjoy Chenin or Sauvignon Blanc, there is something here for them. Paul Jaboulet and Chapoutier provide Rhônes, while regional interest is provided by four vintages of Mas de Daumas Gassac red and the range of Philippe de Baudin Vin de Pays d'Oc.

Niersteiner Gutes Domtal is there for those who must have it, but there's also proper Niersteiner from Senfter as well as several other excellent estate-bottled German wines. A similarly impressive set of Italian offerings include proper Soave from Pieropan and Anselmi, Brunello from Colombini and a range of Super-Tuscans. The range from Spain is also superb. There are several Riojas as well as more unusual offerings such as the Somontano wines of Enate, the Señorio de Sarria Navarrans and the Torremilanos range from Ribera del Duero. The Portuguese reds from J. M. da Fonseca are also worth trying, as are seven vintages of Château Musar.

New Zealanders of note include reds from Lincoln Vineyards and whites from Hunters and Jackson Estate. Top Australian producers such as Yarra Yering, Tim Adams and Bannockburn are very much the order of the day. There's a vast amount from Chile, both red and white, as well as Trapiche from Argentina. North American highlights are Firesteed Pinot Noir from Oregon and the Californian wines from Crichton Hall and Carneros Creek. The Meerlust, Thelema and Hamilton-Russell from South Africa are also excellent.

Add champagnes, ports, sherries and around 100 malt whiskies and you have a merchant well worth doing business with. The monthly tastings at The Queen's Hall must be particularly worthwhile events to attend.

Best buys

Best's Colombard, 1993, £
Vin de Pays d'Oc 1993, Philippe de Baudin, £
Campofiorin, Masi, 1990, ££
Los Carneros Pinot Noir, Carneros Creek, 1991, ££

Alexander Hadleigh Wines

The Old School House, 216 Barnes Lane,   *Tel* (01489) 885959
Sarisbury Green, Southampton, Hampshire SO31 7BG   *Fax* (01489) 885960

Case sales only Open Mon–Fri 8.30–5.30 **Closed** Sat, Sun, public holidays **Cards** Access, Visa; business accounts **Discount** 5% on unmixed cases **Delivery** Free within 50-mile radius (min. 1 case) **Glass hire** Available **Tasting and talks** Private tastings for groups **Cellarage** Not available

It's mainly trade sales at Delwyn Lea Taylor's School House, but there's plenty for members of the general public to stay behind for after lessons, provided they are willing to buy by the case. You'll find Alsace wines from Muré and Hugel, Duboeuf beaujolais, and clarets dating back to 1895 Ch. Calon-Ségur and featuring several vintages of Ch. Batailley. The burgundy range is impressive, with several top producers on show, and the Rhônes from Jaboulet Aîné, Chapoutier and Château de Beaucastel will not disappoint either. Loires are reasonable, and there are plenty of good-value regional offerings.

Serious German wines come from Balthasar Ress and von Kesselstatt, and similarly impressive Italian wines include Fattoria San Leonino's Chianti Classico and the Brunello from Val di Suga. From Spain come CVNE and Principe de Viana, and you'll also find John Charnley's excellent Wickham English wines.

The New World range is very comprehensive. St Helena and Longridge appear alongside more familiar New Zealand wines from Morton Estate and Hunters. From South Africa come Boschendal, Buitenverwachting and Simonsig, while Craigmoor, Tarrawarra and Henschke form just part of a large Australian set. North American offerings include Canadian wines from Mission Hill, Gray Monk and others, and Californians from Beringer, Pedroncelli and Clos du Val. Norton in Argentina, and Montes and Concha y Toro in Chile represent South America. Ports date back to 1847, but there are also plenty of wines from more recent vintages.

Best buys

1994 Drostdy Hof Chenin Blanc, £
Moorook NV, Kingston Estate, Australia, £
1992 McGuigan Brothers Black Shiraz, ££
1992 Gigondas, Domaine les Safres, ££

Hall Batson & Co

168 Wroxham Road, Sprowston,	*Tel* (01603) 415115
Norwich, Norfolk NR7 8DE	*Fax* (01603) 484096

Case sales only   Open Mon–Fri 8.30–6, Sat 9.30–12.30   **Closed** Sun, public holidays   **Cards** Access, Visa; personal and business accounts   **Discount** By negotiation   **Delivery** Free in Norfolk, Suffolk, Cambridge and Essex (min. 1 case); mail-order available   **Glass hire** Free with order   **Tasting and talks** Groups by appointment; telephone first   **Cellarage** Not available

The prize for the smallest bottles of wine we have met goes to this energetic East Anglian company, whose latest list features four wines that are each available in a 3.75-cl size. Those looking for something slightly more substantial will find plenty of appetising full-size bottles (and magnums) available. Regional French stars include Domaine de Montluc's Côtes de Gascogne and Louis Latour's Ardèche wines. Louis Latour also contributes wines to a burgundy range that features such growers as Simon Bize, Michel Bouzereau and Robert Ampeau. For those with large wallets, 1970 Ch. Pétrus is available, but wines such as 1988 Ch. Liversan and 1989 Ch. La Tour-de-Mons are rather more affordable. The Châteauneuf from Château la Nerthe stands out in the Rhône selection, Guy Saget provides several Loire wines, and those from

Alsace are supplied by François Runner. Champagnes include large ranges from Joseph Perrier and Charles de Cazanove.

Notable items come from von Kesselstatt and Romerhof in Germany, CVNE and Bodegas Berberana in Spain, and Masi and Antinori in Italy. The Fairview South African, Dry Creek Californian and Concha y Toro Chilean wines are good, but the best New World bottles are the Antipodeans. Hunters, Te Mata and Coopers Creek provide those from New Zealand, while Australian wines come from Hay Shed Hill in Margaret River, Rockford, Petaluma and many other top wineries.

The staff are 'young and enthusiastic, with a passion for wine and life'. They also have a good range of wines to back them up, which makes it a pleasure rather than a chore to put together the minimum purchase of a dozen.

Best buys

Côtes de Duras, Sauvignon Blanc 1994 Cave Berticot, £
Vin de Pays de l'Hérault, 1993 Domaine de Seriège Rouge, £
Châteauneuf du Pape 1990/1, Château la Nerthe, ££
1994 Hay Shed Hill Pitchfork Pink, Australia, ££

Halves

Wood Yard, Off Corve Street, Ludlow, Shropshire   *Tel* (01584) 877866
SY8 2PX   *Fax* (01584) 877677
(Head office and mail-order – see also The Wine Treasury)

Case sales only **Open** Mon–Fri 9–6, occasional Sat 9–5 **Closed** Sun, public holidays
Cards Access, Amex, Delta, Switch, Visa; business accounts **Discount** 5% on
unmixed cases; £4.80 per case on 2+ cases **Delivery** To UK mainland (prices include
delivery) (min. order 1 mixed-case) **Glass hire** Not available **Tasting and talks**
Tasting dinners arranged at restaurants throughout the year **Cellarage** £4.99 per case
per year

Tim Jackson's link up with the Wine Treasury (q.v.) proved to be something of a marriage of inconvenience, so his less-than-pint-sized company is now back to dealing by mail-order only from the Ludlow office. You'll still find champagnes from Bruno Paillard and Boucheron, plus sherry from Hidalgo, including what Tim terms 'cooking sherry' wines, which are remnants from earlier shipments and have lost the freshness of current releases. Ports are in good supply, whether you're after something for current drinking or to lay down. There are Loire reds from Couly-Dutheil and whites from Château de Tracy and Fabien Colin. Alongside the Rieflé Alsace range are other wines from Paul Blanck and Kuentz-Bas. Louis Michel provides a range of Chablis, while other burgundies come from René Monnier and Alain Burguet. Clarets form the largest section of the range, with Vieux Château Certan at the pricy end and Châteaux de Pitray and de France at more affordable levels. There are also several Sauternes and Barsacs. Southern France is a bit sparsely represented at present, but Tim is on the lookout for wines to join the Cahors from Château de Gaudou. Rhônes are more abundant, with the wares of Jaboulet Aîné, Graillot and André Perret available.

New Zealand wines come from Redwood Valley, Chileans from Santa Rita (while stocks last) and Australians from Taltarni, Pipers Brook and Best's. The half-litre Vin de Constance from South Africa is a welcome intruder. Californians of note include Shafer Merlot, Matanzas Creek Chardonnay and Joseph Phelps' stunning Late Harvest Riesling. There are a few (sweeter) German wines, and Spain is represented by Torres and La Rioja Alta. A good set of Italian wines features Pieropan Soave, Chianti Classico from Isole e Olena and Barbaresco from Brigaldara. Truffles, oils, dried mushrooms and sun-dried tomatoes are also available.

Just as this *Guide* appears, the company will be celebrating its fifth birthday. If you are unable to grab a last-minute place for the various dinners and events being held around the country, there will be a special anniversary list to enjoy.

Best buys

Manzanilla la Gitana, Hidalgo, £
Muscat 1991, Paul Blanck, £
Condrieu 1993, Vernay, ££
Savigny les Vergelesses 1992, Simon Bize, ££

H & H Wines

29 Roman Way Industrial Park, Godmanchester,   *Tel* (01480) 411599
Cambridgeshire PE18 8LN   *Fax* (01480) 411833

Case sales only   **Open** Mon–Fri 9–5.30   **Closed** Sat, Sun, public holidays, between Chr and New Year   **Cards** Amex; personal and business accounts   **Discount** Not available   **Delivery** Free in Cambs, Beds and Northants (min. 1 case); elsewhere in UK at cost; mail-order available   **Glass hire** Not available   **Tasting and talks** Organised tutored tastings   **Cellarage** Not Available

The past year has seen Messrs Scicluna and Honorez move to new premises, but their company still shows the same attention to quality that has made them one of Britain's most interesting small merchants.

Bordeaux is not the firm's forte, but the claret range does contain many wines at the sensible end of the price range. Burgundy is much more noteworthy. From the Côte d'Or, Louis Carillon, Guy Roulot and Jean Philippe Fichet supply the white wines, de Montille, Joseph Roty and Mongeard-Mugneret the reds. Elsewhere in Burgundy, Réné Berrod Beaujolais, Maconnais wines from Jean-Jacques Vincent, Michel Juillot's from the Côte Chalonnaise and Chablis from Durup, R & V Dauvissat and Vocoret are all of top quality. Among the Rhône wines are Côte Rôtie from Réné Rostaing, Châteauneuf from Bosquet des Papes and Hermitage from Pierre Gaillard.

As well as reds and whites from Alain Brumont, the impressive regional French range also includes Cahors from Triguedina, Jurançon from Charles Hours and Chardonnay from Domaine de l'Aigle. Fans of red Loires will head for the wines of Marionnet, Joguet and Druet, while devotees of Sauvignon Blanc will not be disappointed by Didier Dagueneau's Pouilly Fumé, Vatan's Sancerre or Pellé's Menetou-Salon. Marc Kreydenweiss Alsace and champagne from Veuve Clicquot and Pierre Moncuit complete a classy French selection.

Class, too, is the word for the wines of Alois Kracher from Austria and Dr Loosen from Germany, and for the Italian offerings of Isole e Olena and Giuseppe Mascarello. Quality is very much to the fore in the New World section. California provides Ridge, Calera, Newton and Cuvaison, while New Zealand brings Martinborough Vineyards, Wairau River and Forrest Estate; the pick of the Australian section are Brokenwood, Hickinbotham and Mountadam.

A small set of ports, Armagnac from Léon Lafitte and the olive products of Mas de la Dame in Provence conclude a fascinating and reasonably priced range.

Best buys

Côtes de Gascogne, Blanc de Brumont 1993, £
Château Viranel, St Chinian 1993, £
Marsannay en Ouzelois, Vieilles Vignes 1993, Joseph Roty, ££
Pacherenc du Vic-Bilh, Château Montus 1992, Alain Brumont, ££

Roger Harris Wines

Loke Farm, Weston Longville, Norfolk NR9 5LG   *Tel* (01603) 880171
                                                   Fax (01603) 880291

Case sales only **Open** Mon–Fri 9–5 **Closed** Sat, Sun, public holidays **Cards** All accepted; personal and business accounts **Discount** Negotiable **Delivery** Local delivery service; mail-order available **Glass hire** Not available **Tasting and talks** Available on request **Cellarage** Not available

---

'Claret is your wife, Burgundy your mistress, but Beaujolais is the young girl with whom you flirt.' Yes, it was a Frenchman who said it, but no, we won't say who. Roger Harris's flirtation has been going on for 20 years and shows no sign of abating. Indeed, 'I have such an enduring love of beaujolais that I would from preference drink nothing else.' Not that the purity of Gamay is the only thing to appear on the list. You'll find some Mâconnais Chardonnays, some Aligoté-based wines from the Coteaux du Lyonnais, an occasional good-value *vin de pays* and even champagnes (from Ruelle-Pertois). However, with those exceptions, it's beaujolais and its ten *crus*, in a selection assembled with love. Rather than list particular producers, we would recommend that you put yourself on the mailing list and buy one of the mixed cases which feature in the six-weekly newsletters. We would also ask you to take note of Mr Harris's plea: 'Don't jump into your cars and head for Calais – we might not be here when you return!'

Best buys

Moulin-à-Vent 1993, Château du Moulin-à-Vent, ££
Brouilly 1994, Château Thivin, ££

Harrods

Knightsbridge, London SW1X 7XL

Tel 0171-730 1234
Fax 0171-584 8235

Open Mon, Tue, Sat 10–6; Wed–Fri 10–7; some public holidays **Closed** Sun and some public holidays **Cards** All accepted; personal and business accounts **Discount** 1 free bottle per case exc. classed-growth clarets, vintage ports and prestige champagnes **Delivery** Free within the M25 (min order £50); £5 charge for orders under £50; mail-order available **Glass hire** Not available **Tasting and talks** Full programme of diverse tastings run by Harrods Gourmet Club **Cellarage** Not available

---

Another year on and there are new faces in Harrods wine department. Alastair Llewellyn-Smith has been lured away to Roberson and in his place are Andrew Montague, formerly of the Californian Wine Institute, and Nick Mason, ex-Bibendum. The department looks better and better on each visit, with a constant stream of new and exciting wines to augment the classics, which are still there in depth. Prices, while certainly not falling, seem to be more in line with what you would expect to pay in an independent merchant. The own-label range is good, but the treasures lie beyond.

You'd expect champagne to be here in quantity, but you might not expect it from a grower such as Henri Billiot. Clarets range back to 1961, but there's plenty from 1989 and 1990 for those who prefer younger wines. Amid the *grand cru* burgundies are tasty Mâconnais wines from Guffens-Heynen and Olivier Merlin. The Vouvrays from Gaston Huet are the highlights of the Loire range, while Trimbach, Schlumberger and Hugel appear in the Alsace range.

Dervieux-Thaize Côte Rôtie and the Ardèche wines of Domaine des Terriers are also worth trying.

Valpolicella from Le Ragose, Aldo Conterno's Barolo and Tuscans from Lodovico Antinori and Isole e Olena stand out in the Italians, CVNE and La Rioja Alta provide Spanish interest, while German fans will find a large range from Dr Loosen, Max Ferd. Richter and Lingenfelder. And don't miss the Austrian wines from Stiegelmar and Willi Opitz. The New World range continues to improve, and there are good selections from all the major countries. Rare wines worth looking out for are the Chardonnays from Kistler in California and Wignalls in Western Australia, Fleur du Cap's Special Late Harvest from South Africa and Ata Rangi's New Zealand Pinot Noir.

Ports and sherries are in plentiful supply, and there's also a decent range of malts. There are plans for a major refit for the department in the very near future, which among other things will ensure that the majority of bottles can be stored on their sides.

Best buys

Vin de Pays de Maures 1993, Domaine des Astros Rosé, £
San Crispino Sangiovese, 1992, £
Harrods Chablis 1993, William Fèvre, 1993, ££
Wairau River Sauvignon Blanc, 1994, Marlborough, ££

Harvest Wine Group

Clocktower Mews, Stanlake Park, Twyford, Reading, Berkshire RG10 0BN	*Tel* (01734) 344290 *Fax* (01734) 320914

Open Mon–Fri 9–5, Sat 10–5, Sun 12–3, public holidays 10–5   **Closed** Chr and New Year   **Cards** Access, Delta, Switch, Visa; business accounts   **Discount** 5–10% dependent on order   **Delivery** Reading postcodes RG1–RG12, 1–11 cases £7.50–15, 11+ cases free; nationwide mail-order service   **Glass hire** Not available   **Tasting and talks** Group talks given on and off site   **Cellarage** Not available

---

When not making wine in Brazil, Czechoslovakia, South Africa or other parts of the globe, 'Wandering' John Worontschak is to be found in various places around the south of England overseeing production of England's best wine. That's not just John talking (although he's almost as good at that as he is at wine-making): England's top wine trophy, the Gore Brown, has been awarded to a Worontschak wine for the past three years.

The thirteen English vineyards in which he is involved band together under the Harvest umbrella for marketing purposes, and all produce wines that are eminently drinkable. Ten of these have cellar-door outlets where they sell their own wine and that of other Harvest wineries. Our pick would be the wines of Thames Valley

Vineyards, Sharpham, Wickham and Pilton Manor (especially the Westholme sweetie), but all can be recommended. The special release Clocktower wines from Thames Valley show the potential of Chardonnay and Pinot Noir for table wines in England, and a recent bottle of the 1989 Pinot Noir was remarkably tasty. Look out for the unique Gamay: white and sparkling!

Best buys

Pilton Manor Westholme 1991, £
Thames Valley Medium Dry, £
Northbrook Springs Dessert 1994, ££
Sharpham Barrel Fermented 1993/4, ££

John Harvey & Sons

Order office and shop
12 Denmark Street, Bristol, Avon   *Tel* (0117) 9275010
BS1 5DQ   *Fax* (0117) 9275001

Open Mon–Fri 9.30–6, Sat 10–1 **Closed** Sun, public holidays **Cards** Access, Delta, Switch, Visa; personal and business accounts **Discount** £1 per case (10+ cases) **Delivery** Free within Bristol and Environs (min. 4 cases; 3 or less £10 per delivery); nationwide mail-order service **Glass hire** Loan small quantities, arrange hire where necessary **Tasting and talks** Two public tastings per year, private tastings by arrangement **Cellarage** Can be arranged

---

Ask someone to pick a list of traditional wine merchants, and the chances are that before very long, they'll come up with this venerable Bristol firm, now in its 200th year. Yes, of course you'll find plentiful supplies of Bristol Cream in the Denmark Street shop, but there are other things besides. There are some good 1990 clarets around, whether you're after a *petit château* wine or Ch. Lynch-Bages, and the range is enhanced by *en primeur* offers in suitable vintages. Chablis is from Moreau, with other burgundies mostly from Louis Latour and Louis Jadot. Gabriel Meffre dominates the Rhônes. The Australian selection from Wynns, Rymill and Willespie is worth trying, as are the Jordans wines from South Africa and Kendall Jackson's from California. Everything Chilean comes from Errazuriz, and all the New Zealander wines from Villa Maria. Perhaps the most interesting wines in the range are the Austrians from Freie Weingärtner Wachau.

Innovation is noticeably absent from much of this range, though. The practice of sticking with just one producer in many regions may have been acceptable in the past, but at a time when so much good wine is available, it smacks of complacency. John Harvey tells us, '1996 will be our bicentenary year and we will be celebrating suitably with a special prestige price list.' Such a document is all very well, but, unless the wines in that list give it a rapid dose of rejuvenation, the phrase 'mutton dressed as lamb' could spring to mind all too readily.

Best buys

Muscadet de Sèvre et Maine sur Lie 1993, Domaine La Haute Carizière, £
Côtes du Rhône, Syrah Ma Garrigue 1994, Gabriel Meffre, £
St Emilion Grand Cru, Château Lassègue 1990, ££
Chablis 1er Cru Vaillons Vieilles Vignes 1993, Cuvée Prestige, Guy Moreau, ££

Harvey Nichols

109–125 Knightsbridge, London SW1X 7RJ	*Tel* 0171-235 5000
	Fax 0171-235 5020

Open Mon–Fri 10–8; Sat 10–6; Sun 12–2, public holidays 10–6   **Closed** Chr and Boxing Days   **Cards** All accepted   **Discount** 5% on mixed cases; 10% box cigars, 12 bottles for the price of 11 on unsplit cases   **Delivery** Local delivery service available; nationwide mail-order available at £7.50 for a case of wine and £8 for a case of champagne   **Glass hire** Not available   **Tasting and talks** Every Sat   **Cellarage** Not available

---

Clued-up diners in London look forward to Monday nights, when all the wines in Harvey Nichols' 5th floor restaurant are on sale at shop prices. Buyer Alexander Ignatieff is responsible for both restaurant and shop wines, and in the short space of time since the wine department opened in November 1993, he has put together an interesting range of wines from throughout the world. The house champagne is from Deutz, and there are several other top champagnes. The rest of the French range, too, concentrates on quality rather than price, and you'll find plenty of *cru classé* clarets, Burgundy domaines such as Ramonet, Armand Rousseau and Carillon and top Loire Chenin from Coulée de Serrant among others. The range from the rest of Europe is a case of quality rather than quantity, but the New World wines are more prolific. Californians of note come from Qupé, Au Bon Climat and Bonny Doon, while Australian offerings are provided by Madfish Bay, Cape Mentelle and Pipers Brook. Te Mata and Jackson Estate New Zealanders, and Chileans from Santa Rita are also available. Prices are on the high side, but it's almost worth paying that little bit extra to get a glimpse of someone famous.

Best buys

Harvey Nichols Bordeaux Sauvignon Blanc, £
Le Veritière Chardonnay, 1994, £
Harvey Nichols Champagne, ££
Harvey Nichols Bourgogne Rouge, ££

Richard Harvey Wines

Not a shop

Bucknowle House, Bucknowle, Wareham,	*Tel* (01929) 480352
Dorset BH20 5PQ	*Fax* (01929) 481275

La Maison du Vin

71 Avenue Carnot, 50100 Cherbourg, France	*Tel* (010 33) 33 43 39 79

Mainly telephone and mail order
12 Rue Gardens, Clemenceau, 35400 St Malo

Case sales only **Open** Mon–Sat 10–7, Sun 10–1 **Closed** Chr **Cards** Access, Visa;
personal and business accounts **Discount** 2.5% on 1 unsplit case; 5% on 5+ cases
Delivery Within 30-mile radius (min. 3 cases); min. 7 cases for delivery elsewhere;
mail-order available **Glass hire** Free with order **Tasting and talks** 1 annual tasting;
others by request **Cellarage** £4 per case per year + insurance

'Please supply a brief biography of yourself,' we asked politely.
'Sex, wine and rock'n'roll,' replied Richard Harvey. Not quite what
we had in mind, but then this Master of Wine is hardly your typical
wine merchant. The illogicalities of British duty law have prompted
him to open a second outlet in France, this time in St-Malo. You can
still buy wine from his Wareham office, but only by the case; the
French outlets sell by the bottle as well, and Mr Harvey also
delights in offering advice not just on the wines but also on 'where
to eat and go to the beach'.

There are several wines in his range which we'd happily sup *au
bord de la mer*, especially the Alexandre Bonnet champagnes. Of the
burgundies, Chablis comes from Droin, and Guy Roulot's
Bourgogne Blanc and Rouge are anything but basic. Regional
French wines come from Domaines de Ribonnet and de l'Aigle,
while Ch. Sociando-Mallet and Ch. Haut-Bailly stand out amid the
clarets. Henri Marionnet's Loire wines and Alsace from Zusslin are
good, as are Rhônes from Noël Verset and Clos des Papes. New
World interest is catered for with Wakefield and Goundrey wines
from Australia and the New Zealand wines of Wairau River.
Offerings from Riccardo Falchini in Italy, Amezola de la Mora in
Rioja and Mönchhof in Germany complete the range.

Best buys

Merlot 1993, Domaine de Ferrandieres, Vin de Pay d'Oc, £
Muscadet de Sevre et Maine, Domaine du Vieux Chai 1993, £

Château Rolier 1990, Côte de Francs, ££
Vin de Pays de la Haute Vallée de l'Aude 1993, Chardonnay
Domaine de' L'Aigle, ££

Haslemere Cellar

Rear of 2 Lower Street, Haslemere, Surrey   *Tel* (01428) 645081
GU27 2NX   *Fax* (01428) 645081

Open Tues–Fri 9.30–6.30 (closed Wed afternoons), Sat 9–5 **Closed** Sun, public
holidays **Cards** Access, Amex, Delta, Switch, Visa; business accounts **Discount** 5%
on 1+ case (may be mixed) **Delivery** Free along the A3 and within Central London
(min. order £35); nationwide mail-order available **Glass hire** Free with order
Tasting and talks Regular tutored tastings in-store (usually twice a week) **Cellarage**
£4 per case per year + insurance

Still small but perfectly formed, Richard Royds' shop remains a
stimulating place to buy wine. The clarets are worth a look,
covering all prices and maturities with efficiency; Ch. La Tour de
Mons 1971 is surely worth a punt at £13.50. Burgundies are
appealing too, with wines from Comtes Lafon and Jean-Philippe
Fichet for the flush, Emile Juillot and René Perraton for the less
well-off. The Loire whites concentrate mostly on Chenin Blanc,
with Vouvray from Boutet-Saulnier and Coteaux du Layon from
Domaine de la Roche Moreau; don't miss the clutch of Loire reds
either. Catin and Mittnacht-Klack provide the Alsace wines, René
Balthazar's Cornas and Alain Graillot's Crozes both represent top-
notch Syrah from the Rhône. The selection of Banyuls and the
Provence wines from Château Routas also deserve attention.

German wines are taken seriously, with Fritz Haag
demonstrating very ably what Piesporter should be like. The
Spanish and Italian ranges are smaller, but tasty wines abound.
Stanton & Killeen and Merricks Estate stand for Australia, and
Wairau River for New Zealand. Port-drinkers might care to try one
of the range of '63s, although lovers of fortified wine who have a
sense of adventure and plenty of cash might prefer to splash out on
a madeira, or try the 1900 Moscatel from João Pereira d'Oliveira.

The Haslemere Cellar is expanding slowly but sensibly, and
promises much for the future.

Best buys

1993 Côtes du Roussillon Villages, Cuvée des Celliers, £
1987 Castillo de Almansa Reserva, Almansa (Spain), £
1991 Gewurztraminer Grand Cru Rosacker, Domaine Mittnacht-
Klack, ££
Collioure 1990, Domaine de Baillaury, ££

Haynes Hanson & Clark

Head office and wholesale warehouse
Sheep Street, Stow-on-the-Wold, Gloucestershire   *Tel* (01451) 870808
Gl54 1AA   *Fax* (01451) 870508
Retail outlet
25 Eccleston Street, London SW1W 1AA   *Tel* 0171-259 0102
          Fax 0171-259 0103

Open Mon–Fri 9–7, Sat 9.30–6 **Closed** Sun, public holidays **Cards** Access, Switch, Visa; personal and business accounts **Discount** 10% on unmixed cases **Delivery** Free to Central London and Gloucestershire; UK mainland mail-order available **Glass hire** Loan with wine purchase **Tasting and talks** By invitation held Central London, The City, Gloucestershire, Cheshire and Derbyshire **Cellarage** Not available

Last year the HHC head office moved from London to Gloucestershire; this year, the London shop in Kensington Church Street closed and a larger one in Belgravia opened. The company duly celebrated the second move with a tasting in conjunction with the Society of Garden Designers during the Chelsea Flower Show. Who said wine merchants had no sense of occasion?

Apparently customers have become bored with the heavier wines, so much of the New World range is of the subtle variety: Cape Mentelle and Plantagenet from Australia, Louisvale and Hamilton Russell from South Africa, Saintsbury from California and C J Pask from New Zealand. Marqués de Murrieta and Marqués de Cáceres cater for Rioja fans, while Pieropan, Castello di Volpaia and Isole e Olena do the same for Italophiles. Lovers of German wines had better look elsewhere.

Champagnes include many major grandes marques, but prudent party-givers might care to opt instead for the well-aged Pierre Vaudon. The Rhône selection is small, but everything from the Château du Grand Moulas Côtes du Rhône up to Bernard Faurie's impressive Hermitage is worth trying. Loire whites are good, and don't miss Charles Joguet's great Chinon reds. A solid claret range, still with plenty of wines from the excellent '89 and '90 vintages, is augmented by regular offers of small parcels of mature wines as well as en primeur campaigns. Pick of the regional selection are the wines from Domaine du Limbardie and Domaines Virginie.

The most important part of the list, however, is the Burgundy range. Raveneau Chablis, Volnay from Michel Lafarge and Hubert de Montille, Savigny and Corton from Chandon de Briailles, Vosne-Romanée from Jean Grivot . . . the list of top producers goes on and on. In between Michel Large's Bourgogne Rouge at under a tenner and Gagnard-Delagrange Montrachet at over £100, there is something for Burgundy-lovers everywhere.

Best buys

Domaine de L'Ameilland 1994 Rouge, £
Rowlands Brook Semillon/Chardonnay 1994, £
Viognier Domaine de Rogusse 1994, ££
Savigny lès Beaune ler cru Les Lavières 1988, Chandon de Briailles,
££

Hedley Wright

Unit 11 The Twyford Centre, London Road,	*Tel* (01279) 506512
Bishop's Stortford, Hertfordshire CM23 3YT	*Fax* (01279) 657462

Case sales only Open Mon–Wed 9–6, Thur–Fri 9–7, Sat 10–6, Sun (Dec only) 10–2
Closed Sun, public holidays **Cards** Access, Delta, Switch, Visa; personal and business
accounts **Discount** 5% discount for Bonus Club members **Delivery** Within 20-mile
radius; mail-order available **Glass hire** Free with order **Tasting and talks** Tastings
every Sat, numerous offers throughout the year; phone to be added to mailing list
Cellarage £4.50 per case per year

Apologies for exaggerating the problems that Hedley Wright face
in selling wine in Bishop's Stortford; the competition comes from
only five supermarkets, not the six we reported last year. In the
face of such competition, the company has wisely chosen to
concentrate on the quality end of the market, and, although the
bulk of the business is wholesale trade, the number of cases sold to
the general public, plus the growing customer base, shows that it
must be doing something right.

The backbone of the list is the group of producers for which
Hedley Wright is agent: these include Daniel le Brun and Jackson
Estate from New Zealand, Montes in Chile, and Churchill port.
However, the range is fleshed out with quality wines from around
the world. Pedroncelli, William Wheeler and Monteviña represent
California, and the Australian list includes Shiraz from Taltarni and
Henschke, plus Chardonnay from Moss Wood. The company is
looking for replacements for the Montestell South African wines
(winemaker Julius Laszlo has retired to fish at his beach house), but
you'll still find some of these excellent bottles in the list.

Alsace wines come from the co-op at Kientzheim-Kayersberg,
while the Couillaud brothers provide Muscadet and Chardonnay
from the Loire. Gérard Brisson's Morgon reminds not a few people
of red burgundy. For the real thing though, Fougeray de Beauclair
and Vincent Girardin are the producers to look for; white
burgundy is mainly from Louis Latour and Olivier Leflaive. Stocks
of claret change constantly, but affordable fare such as Ch. Andron-
Blanquet 1985 is very much the order of the day. Other French
wines to look for are the reds and whites of Mas de Daumas Gassac
and the Rhônes from Domaine de Cabasse.

Joining the Riojas of Bodegas Monteleiva in the Spanish range are the good-value Valdepeñas wines of Bodegas Los Llanos. An expanded Italian set ranges from the Cepparello and Ornellaia Super-Tuscans to such southern Italian delights as Candido's Salice Salentino. German wines are mainly the rather dull Peter Mertes range, so why not liven your palate with the distinctly un-Germanic English duo from Warden Abbott and Old Luxters.

En primeur campaigns, regular newsletters and 'a commitment to serve our customers in the knowledge that if we don't succeed, neither will our business' all make Hedley Wright very capable of surviving among the supermarket giants.

Best buys

Montes Merlot Cabernet 1992, £
Chardonnay 1993 Domaine de la Croix, £
'Quintet' 1990 William Wheeler, ££
Churchills Traditional LBV 1988, ££

Charles Hennings (Vintners)

London House, Lower Street, Pulborough,	*Tel* (01798) 872485
West Sussex RH20 2BW	*Fax* (01798) 873163
Golden Square, Petworth, West Sussex GU28 0AP	*Tel* (01798) 343021
10 Jengers Mead, Billingshurst, West Sussex RH14 9PB	*Tel* (01403) 783187

Open (Pulborough) Mon–Sat 8.30–6 (closes at 7 on Fri), (Petworth) Mon–Sat 9–1, 2–6 (closes at 7 on Fri), (Billingshurst) Mon–Sat 9–1, 2–9 **Closed** Sun and public holidays (except Billinghurst 12–2, 7–9) **Cards** Access, Delta, Switch, Visa **Discount** Wine – 5% off 6 bottles, spirits – 3% off 12 bottles **Delivery** Free in Sussex (min. 1 case); mail-order available **Glass hire** deposit required **Tasting and talks** Every weekend in all shops, two large tastings twice a year, separate venue **Cellarage** Not available

'Our customers are always ready to try something new!' Ted Hennings continues to offer his customers in Pulborough, Billingshurst and Petworth much to keep them interested, as well as plenty of old favourites. Clarets range from the good-value Ch. Lamothe-de-Haux up to Ch. Haut Brion; Rhônes include Pascal's fine Côtes-du-Rhône, and Louis Latour and Charles Vienot provide several burgundies. CVNE Riojas and Ochoa Navarras are the highlights from Spain, while Dr Loosen provides the best of the German range. In the South African section of the list we'd head for the wines from Kanonkop, Neil Ellis and Danie de Wet, while Sonoma-Cutrer's Chardonnay stands out in an otherwise ordinary Californian selection. The New Zealand wines – Jackson Estate, Te Mata, Montana's top estates – are much better, and the Australians from Mitchelton, Morris and Penfolds will certainly not disappoint.

Best buys

Bergerac Blanc Sec 1994 Château Boudigand, £
1994 Neetlingshof Gewürztraminer, £
1990 Mick Morris Cabernet Sauvignon, ££
Sauternes, 1988 Château Lafaurie Peyraguey, ££

Hicks & Don   ❀ 🌐 🤝

Order office
Blandford St Mary, Dorset DT11 9LS   *Tel* (01258) 456040
    Fax (01258) 450147

The Old Bakehouse
Alfred Street, Westbury, Wiltshire BA13 3DY   *Tel* (01373) 864723
    Fax (01373) 858250

Park House, North Elmham, Dereham, Norfolk   *Tel* (01362) 668571
NR20 5JY   *Fax* (01362) 668573

Open Mon–Fri 8.30–5 **Closed** Sat, Sun, public holidays **Cards** Access, Visa; personal and business accounts **Discount** By negotation **Delivery** Free in local area for 3+ cases, 1–2 cases £3 per case; mail-order available **Glass hire** Free **Tasting and talks** Normally late Autumn in London, Oxford, Cambridge, Norfolk, Wiltshire and Dorset **Cellarage** £4.92+VAT per case per year

The Hicks & Don main list is a personal selection by Masters of Wine Robin Don and Ronnie Hicks from the Woodhouse Wines (q.v.) range. These include Alsace from Schlumberger and Louis Gisselbrecht, a set of decent clarets, and burgundies that come from Drouhin, Jean-Marc Brocard and Jean Gros. 'Wines from minor districts' include Côtes de Gascogne from Domaine de Rieux and Domaines Virginie, while Loire Sauvignon is provided by Henri Bourgeois. In the Rhône range, the stars are the Font de Michelle Châteauneuf and the great-value red and white Côtes-du-Rhônes from Château St Estève d'Uchaux.

The English wines from Elmham Park (made by Robin Don) are worth trying, as are the German from von Schubert, Max Ferd. Richter and Langewerth von Simmern. A short Italian selection features Felsina Berardenga's excellent Chardonnay, Masi Valpolicella and Chianti Rufina from Villa di Vetrice. The Spanish range includes wines from Torres and Raimat and sherries from Barbadillo. Ports are from many major houses.

The Californian wines from Mondavi, Sutter Home and Glen Ellen are not the most exciting around, but Australian representation is better, with Mountadam, Goundrey and David Wynn. Chilean wines come from Cousiño Macul and Concha y Toro, New Zealanders from Matua Valley and South Africans from Thelema and Villiera.

Hicks & Don also specialise in selling wine ex-cellars. Customers benefit by being able to pay for wines in two instalments (the first for the cost of the wine in the country of origin, the second for shipping charges, duty and VAT) and by avoiding the storage charges a merchant would incur by having the wine in his cellar. Wines on offer range from classed-growth claret and Sauternes to East European bottles and beaujolais.

Best buys

Hicks & Don Claret, £
1993 Norfolk Oyster, £
1990 Goundrey Windy Hill Cabernet Sauvignon, ££
Champagne, Joseph Perrier Cuvée Josephine 1985, ££

High Breck Vintners

Bentworth House, Bentworth,	*Tel* (01420) 562218
Nr Alton, Hampshire GU34 5RB	*Fax* (01420) 563827

Open Mon–Fri 9.30–5, Sun by appointment only   **Closed** Sat, public holidays   **Cards** None accepted   **Discount** Not available   **Delivery** Local delivery; nationwide mail-order service available   **Glass hire** Available   **Tasting and talks** 3–4 times annually **Cellarage** £5 per case per annum

---

The French exchange rate at the time of writing was a distinctly wine-merchant-unfriendly 7.60 francs per pound, so Howard Baveystock's response when asked to recommend wines below £5 was 'Forget it!' However, those willing to spend more will find some memorable wines in his selection, which (with the notable exceptions of sherries from Garvey and Lustau, Rioja from Berberana and ports from Quinta de la Rosa) are nearly all French. House specials include Bentworth House plonk, but we'd nudge you in the direction of the wines from south and south-west France, such as the Bergerac and Saussignac from Château Richard and Domaine des Chaberts' Coteaux Varois red and rosé. From the Rhône comes the Gigondas of Domaine des Tourelles, Gitton provides wonderful Sancerre and Pouilly Fumé, and the Alsace is from Daniel Wiederhirn. As well as a fine selection of beaujolais from the Eventail organisation, other burgundies include Hervé Olivier's Santenay and Alain Pautré's Chablis. Among the clarets you may still find some top wines from the '88/'89/'90 vintages; if not, you may want to console yourself with a glass of champagne from either Bauget-Jouette or Lamiable Frères.

Best buys

Chablis 1993, Alain Pautré, ££
Graves 1989/90, Domaine la Grave, ££

George Hill of Loughborough

59 Wards End, Loughborough,	*Tel* (01509) 212717
Leicestershire LE11 3HB	*Fax* (01509) 236963

Open Mon–Sat 9–5.30 **Closed** Sun and public holidays **Cards** Access, Delta, Switch, Visa; personal and business accounts **Discount** 5% on 6 bottles, approx. 10% on case **Delivery** Local delivery service available **Glass hire** Free with order **Tasting and talks** Sometimes in store; evening groups by request **Cellarage** Available

Andrew Hill ('single, fun-loving, 48 going on 28') admits to making mistakes and being complacent about certain areas in his wine-buying in the past. We don't notice too many such howlers in this range. It is not as exciting as some, but good solid wines appear throughout.

Perhaps the New World representation needs a slight revamp. The Fairview South African wines are more interesting than the KWV range; Nobilo Vintners provides most of the New Zealand list; and the Sutter Home and Mondavi-Woodbridge wines from California are not the most exciting. Australia fares better, with wines from Pipers Brook, Simon Hackett and Baileys. The Latin American wines of L. A. Cetto from Mexico and Echeverría and Concha y Toro from Chile are also worth trying.

The Spanish list includes Navarra wines from Ochoa, Ribera del Duero from Callejo and CVNE Riojas, while Italian interest is provided by Argiano (Brunello di Montalcino), Colli di Catone (Frascati) and the good-value Araldica wines from Piemonte. German wines come from Louis Guntrum and Schloss Vollrads. Alphonse Mellot's Loires, Michel Mourier's Rhônes and Alsace from Kuehn are all reasonable. Better are the burgundies, especially the Domaine des Malandes Chablis and the Parent reds. The clarets include first-growth wines, but the accent is mostly on affordable cru bourgeois and Right Bank wines. Improvements are under way in the regional French range, so watch this space. Mr Hill knows as well as anybody where he needs to improve his range and he is doing so with the minimum of fuss.

Best buys

Barbera d'Asti, Araldica, 1991, £
Pinot Gris, Fairview Estate, South Africa, £
Conde de la Salceda Rioja Gran Riserva, ££
Chablis ler Cru, Côte de Lechet 1992, Domaine de Malandes, ££

J E Hogg

61 Cumberland Street, Edinburgh, Lothian EH3 6RA   *Tel* 0131-556 4025
Fax 0131-556 4025

Open Mon–Fri (exc. Wed) 9–1, 2.30–6; Sat and Wed 9–1 **Closed** Sun and public
holidays **Cards** Switch **Discount** On some orders **Delivery** Free to Edinburgh and
East Lothian (min. 1 case) **Glass hire** Free; breakages and washing at cost **Tasting
and talks** On request for customers **Cellarage** Not available

'Continued downward lurching of the pound' prevented Jim Hogg
publishing his new wine list in time for our perusal, but the reports
we hear of his Edinburgh shop continue to be very favourable. Mr
H. is something of a traditionalist at heart, but his shelves have
space for any wines which appeal to him. So you'll find a large set
of Penfolds reds, together with Tyrrells and Wolf Blass,
representing Australia, the excellent Meerlust and Klein Constantia
from South Africa and classy Californian fare from Swanson,
Cuvaison and Dry Creek. Babich, Hunters and Mills Reef fly the
New Zealand flag. Italian wines of interest include Marco Felluga's
Collio whites, Chianti from Ruffino and Fontanafredda Barolo,
while similarly tasty offerings from Spain include Rioja from
Martínez Bujanda and La Rioja Alta. Mr Hogg obviously enjoys his
German wines and we'd recommend you to plunder his range for
the many tasty Rieslings on offer.

More good Riesling can be found in an Alsace range that
includes wines from Schlumberger, Dopff & Irion and Hugel.
Jaboulet Aîné provides much of the Rhône range, while prominent
among the burgundies are the wines of Champy, described by
Anthony Hanson as 'frank and open-faced, their characters varied
and interesting'. The sweet Loire wines of Jean Baumard and
Foreau are tasty, as are Sauvignons from de Ladoucette and
Alphonse Mellot. Clarets are in great supply, and lovers of
Sauternes should be able to find something of interest, whatever
their financial means. There's also plenty of champagne, port and
large ranges of sherry and malt whisky. Like the wines, the prices
demanded are distinctly on the friendly side, so if you find yourself
with a few pounds left in the kitty, why not stock up on Brodie's
teas, coffees and hand-made chocolates?

Best buys

Deidesheimer 'Heritage Selection Deinhard', £
Nederburg 'Edelrood', £
Vosne Romanee 1990, Bouchard Père et Fils, ££
Swanson Estate Chardonnay, 1991/2, ££

331

Holland Park Wine Company

12 Portland Road, London W11 4LA

Tel 0171-221 9614
Fax 0171-221 9613

Open Mon–Fri 10–8.30, Sat 9–8.30 **Closed** Sun and public holidays **Cards** Access, Amex, Delta, Switch, Visa; personal and business accounts **Discount** 5% on 1 case, 10% on 6 cases **Delivery** Free in Central London (min. 1 case); free nationwide mail-order (min. £120 otherwise +£7.50) **Glass hire** Free with order **Tasting and talks** Shop and tutored tastings **Cellarage** £4.50+VAT per case per year

How long does one remain a bright young wine merchant? Master of Wine James Handford's company has now been in existence for over six years, but he and his business show few signs of middle-age spread. This is a good, economical range of wines with something to suit all tastes and pockets. The Bordeaux range includes affordable petits châteaux as well as 1989 Ch. Pichon-Baron and 1986 Ch. Rieussec. Burgundies include several growers' wines in a Louis Latour selection, while Alsace wines come from Trimbach and Willm. The Domaine de Terriers country wines and Alain Marcadet's Loire reds and whites are good value. Our favourite among the champagnes is the wine from Gosset.

Items of note from Italy include Vino Nobile di Montepulciano from Tenuta Trerose, Prunotto Barbera and several offerings from Antinori, while interesting Spanish wines come from Nikeas, Ochoa and Marqués de Murrieta. Sherries come from Lustau, and there are ports from Taylor, Fonseca and others. Top of the Australian list are Moss Wood Chardonnay and Rockford Shiraz, but there's much else besides; the Hunters wines from New Zealand and those of Simi from California are also good.

A separate fine-wine list is updated monthly, occasionally accompanied by offers such as en primeur claret on a rather generous '12-for-the-price-of-10' scheme. For those interested in learning more about wine, James runs a series of classes once a year over five evenings. Other tutored tastings are held roughly once a month, often with a visiting winemaker in attendance. These are usually free, but do ring to check that there is space first.

Best buys

Chardonnay 1994, Domaine du Fraisse, £
Riparosso, Montepulciano d'Abruzzo 1992, £
Saint Aubin 1993, Domaine Gérard Thomas, ££
Rioja Crianza 1990, Bodegas Zugober, ££

House of Townend

Head office
Red Duster House, 101 York Street, Hull, *Tel* (01482) 326891
North Humberside HU2 0QX *Fax* (01482) 587042
(15 branches in Yorkshire)

Open Mon–Sat 10–10; Sun 12–2, 7–10 **Closed** Chr Day **Cards** Access, Switch, Visa; personal and business accounts **Discount** 5% off mixed case **Delivery** Available within 70-mile radius of Hull (min. 1 case); free nationwide mail-order service for orders over £75 (+£6 if under £75) **Glass hire** Free with order **Tasting and talks** Tastings most weekends in retail outlets; private tastings on request; Monthly Wine Club meetings **Cellarage** £2.70+VAT per case per yearly +insurance

The fourth generation of the Townend family is now in charge at this Hull-based merchant, which remains as reliably solid as ever. However, we do notice undercurrents of something rather more up-tempo, rather like a merchant banker wearing flowery boxer shorts beneath his pin-striped suit. You'll still find plenty of wine from the traditional areas, with the Bordeaux range in particular being good. Someone is going out of his (or her) way to include new producers and growers in the burgundy range, and this should be applauded. Rhône fans will enjoy the wines of Chapoutier, Vieux Télégraphe and many others, although the Loire and Alsace ranges are rather limited at present.

Italian and Spanish wines are reasonable, but those from Germany are better and include mature Schloss Vollrads wines, plus younger fare from Rudolf Müller. The Henschke reds and whites are the highlights from Australia, Mondavi and Sutter Home provide the bulk of the Californian list, and C J Pask does the same for New Zealand. A broader South African selection comes from Hamilton-Russell, Klein Constantia and Boschendal.

Although much of the company's current expansion is geared towards the wholesale side of the business, private customers are not neglected. A programme of tastings includes informal events in the shops plus more structured events once a month. For £5 per year you can become a member of the House of Townend Wine Club and receive discounts, newsletters and other goodies.

Best buys

Dolcetto Del Piemonte 1993, Castello Del Poggio, £
Sunnycliff Colombard Chardonnay 1993, £
Bourgogne Chardonnay 1993, Domaine Michelot, ££
Shiraz 'Mount Edelstone' 1991, Henschke, ££

Irvine Robertson

10-11 North Leith Sands, Edinburgh	*Tel* 0131-553 3521
EH6 4ER	*Fax* 0131-553 5465

Case sales only **Open** Mon–Fri 9–5.30, public holidays, Sat by appointment **Closed** Sun, New Year's Eve **Cards** None accepted; business and personal accounts **Discount** 5–10 cases 40p per case, 11–20 cases 50p per case, 21–50 cases 60p per case **Delivery** Free for 3+ cases, 1–2 £6.50 per case + VAT; mail-order available **Glass hire** Free with order **Tasting and talks** In customers' place of business, private houses, wine clubs **Cellarage** Not available

An increasing amount of Sandy Irvine Robertson's business is based around the producers that his company represents in Scotland. These include Guigal in the Rhone, Taittinger, Billecart-Salmon in Champagne, Jaffelin in Burgundy, Muga in Rioja, Esk Valley in New Zealand, Nederburg in South Africa and the port houses of Warre and Churchill Graham. However, you will find plenty of wine from other producers, and, although the bulk of the trade is with hotels and restaurants, private customers willing to assemble a dozen bottles are most welcome. There are sensible clarets from Ch. de Sours and Ch. de Pez, burgundies from Fichet and Daniel Rion, Alsace from Heim, and Loire wines from Henri Bourgeois and Pierre & Yves Soulez. The German wines are reasonable, while those of Jermann and Umani Ronchi stand out among the Italians. Fans of South African wine can find bottles from Louisvale, Klein Constantia and Hamilton Russell, while the Australian high notes come from Penfolds and Carlyle Estate. Chilean wines are provided by Echeverria, Californians by Stag's Leap Wine Cellars and New Zealanders by Esk Valley.

Best buys

Rocheburg Cabernet Sauvignon 1992, £
Mauvezin d'Armagnac 1994, Domaine de l'Esperance, £
St-Julien 1991, La Réserve de Léoville-Barton, ££
1994 Carlyle Estate Marsanne Semillon, ££

Michael Jobling Wines

Suite 2, Baltic Chambers, 3-7 Broad Chare,	*Tel* 0191-261 5298
Newcastle upon Tyne, Tyne and Wear NE1 3BQ	*Fax* 0191-261 4543

Case sales only Open Mon–Fri 9–5.30; Sat by appointment **Closed** Sun, public holidays **Cards** Access, Visa; business accounts **Discount** 5% on 4 cases; 4+ cases by negotiation **Delivery** Free within 25-mile radius of Newcastle (min. 1 case); mail order available **Glass hire** Free with order **Tasting and talks** 2 major tastings per year; smaller groups by appointment **Cellarage** Not available

Every time we look at Michael Jobling's range of wines, it seems to have expanded. It's still not the largest around, but it's stuffed full of interesting wines from around the world. Pol Roger and Billecart-Salmon champagne kick off the list, there's Alsace from Schlumberger and Théo Faller, plus small sets of claret, Rhônes, Loires and regional wines. The burgundies include wines from Sauzet, Michel Niellon and Tollot-Beauts. The few German bottles are on the serious side, as are the Italians from Allegrini and Tenuta dell'Ornellaia and the Riojas from Remélluri and La Rioja Alta. New World appeal is provided by Hunter's from New Zealand and Shaw & Smith and Pipers Brook from Australia, and American wines are from Los Vascos, Stag's Leap Wine Cellars and Château Ste Michelle. Special dinners are held at Newcastle's Michelin-starred restaurant, 21 Queen Street, often with visiting winemakers.

Best buys

Maccabeo 1992, Château Pech-Celeyran, £
1993 Les Terrasses de Guilhem, Les Vignerons de Villeveyrac, £
Pinot Réserve 1991, Théo Faller, ££
1994 Hunter's Sauvignon Blanc, ££

S H Jones

Shop

27 High Street, Banbury, Oxfordshire OX16 8EW	*Tel* (01295) 251179
	Fax (01295) 272352

S H Jones and Company

9 Market Place, Bicester, Oxfordshire OX6 7AA	*Tel* (01869) 322448

Open Mon–Fri 8.30–6; Sat 9–6 **Closed** Sun, public holidays **Cards** Access, Switch, Visa; personal and business accounts **Discount** Available **Delivery** Within 40-mile radius; mail-order available **Glass hire** Free with order **Tasting and talks** 2 programmes of tastings per year spring/autumn £5 per head refunded against orders **Cellarage** Available

First Banbury, then Bicester, next ... the world? The people at S. H. Jones are on the lookout for additional retail premises in Oxfordshire, so business must be booming. It's not hard to see why.

They have a wonderful range of wines at very reasonable prices, and we have had good reports about the service the company offers, both in the shops and through the associated company Philip Eyres (q.v.).

As befits a traditional family merchant of long (150 years') standing, French wines occupy a major amount of the shelf space. There are still stocks of impressive clarets from good vintages, as well as numerous mature Sauternes including several vintages of Ch. Rieussec. The burgundy-lover too will not be disappointed by some tasty reds and some even better whites. The regional French range is good, too, particularly the reds. Among the many Rhônes, Marc Ryckwaert's Château de Grand Moulas is great value, while the Vieux Télégraphe, Châteauneuf and Chave's Hermitage are simply great wines, both reds and whites. More great wines come from Huet in Vouvray, Schlumberger in Alsace and Henri Billiot in Champagne.

Germany, too, receives thorough coverage, with wines from von Schubert, the Friedrich-Wilhelm-Gymnasium and the Nahe Staatliche Weinbaudomänen available. Decent Italian wines include Pieropan Soave, Vino Nobile from Le Casalte and a set from Prunotto in Piemonte. The Spanish list is reasonable rather than outstanding. From Australia, we'd choose the wines of Mitchells, Cape Mentelle and Rothbury Estate, while from New Zealand (if the Cloudy Bay had run out) we'd settle for the wares of Jackson Estate and Palliser Estate. In the American range, Mondavi Californians are joined by Domaine Drouhin Pinot from Oregon, Etchart and Weinert from Argentina and Undurraga and Los Vascos from Chile. While the luscious Vin de Constance is our favourite from South Africa, we don't object to drier whites from Klein Constantia, nor to reds from Fairview and Hamilton Russell.

Hidalgo and Lustau provide sherries, and there's plenty of port available from good recent vintages. Rather older bottles appear in the shape of the Pereira d'Oliveira madeiras that date back to 1907. Besides all these delightful wines, and some equally outstanding whiskies, the programme of tastings offers remarkable value. Prices seldom rise above the £5 mark, and the charge is redeemable against orders over £50.

Best buys

1993 Syrah la Condamine l'Evèque, £
1994 West Peak Sauvignon Blanc, £
Mâcon Chardonnay 1993, Talmard, ££
Carignano del Sulcis 'Riserva' Rocca Rubia, 1990, ££

Justerini & Brooks

61 St James's Street, London	*Tel* 0171-493 8721
SW1A 1LZ	*Fax* 0171-499 4653
45 George Street, Edinburgh, EH2 2HT	*Tel* 0131-226 4202
	Fax 0131-225 2351

Open Mon–Fri 9–5.30 **Closed** Sat, Sun and public holidays **Cards** All accepted; personal and business accounts **Discount** £1 per case on 2-4 cases; £2 per case on 5-7 cases; £3 per case on 8+ cases **Delivery** Available in mainland UK and N. Ireland, 1-23 bottles £9, 24+ bottles free; mail-order available **Glass hire** Free **Tasting and talks** Specialist tastings involving growers and interested customers **Cellarage** £6.50 per case per year

There's no secret about what makes Justerini & Brooks consistently one of England's (the world's?) very best wine-merchants. The backing of the giant Grand Metropolitan group is undoubtably very important, and the 240-year heritage is also significant. However, they would count for little unless backed up by efficient service, excellent advice and a truly great selection of wines.

While the list focuses on the classics, interesting wines appear throughout the range. Those from South Africa include Chardonnays from Dieu Donné and Thelema, the tasty wines of Fairview and Neetlingshof's unctuous Late Harvest Riesling. Joining the California range from Husch and Saintsbury are the Sonoma wines of Chalk Hill, and Charles Cimicky (great Shiraz) and Neil Paulett join other Australian wines from Scotchman's Hill and Cape Mentelle. Ata Rangi Pinot, Palliser Chardonnay and Dry River Sauvignon stand out in the New Zealand section.

The Spanish representation ranges from the Don John cheapie via Pesquera to Vega Sicilia and venerable vintages of Castillo Ygay. There's not too much for fans of Portuguese table wine, although the range of ports and Madeiras more than compensates. Lovers of Italian wine will notice Aldo Conterno's great Barolo as well as the Super-Tuscans from the successful '88 and '90 vintages, and enthusiasts for Germany are in for even more of a treat; if such names as Egon Müller, von Schubert, Dr Thanisch, Schloss Schönborn, Bürklin-Wolf and Fritz Haag excite you, this is the place to visit.

There can be little to say against a Bordeaux list which lets you arrange a horizontal tasting of 1928 Châteaux Pétrus, Ausone, Lafite, Cheval Blanc and Latour - and a vertical of Ch. d'Yquem back to 1921. Nor will those looking for more recent vintages be disappointed, since the firm has large stocks from the good years of the 1980s. Should you still not find what you're after, the recently established broking department is at your disposal. Rhônes are similarly serious; a winter offer from the region featured Côte Rôtie from Clusel-Roch and Bernard Burgaud, Hermitage from Bernard

337

Faurie and Chapoutier and Châteauneuf from Font de Michelle and Vieux Télégraphe.

The Burgundy list reads like a roll call of the good and the great, and those who haven't stocked up on their '92 whites and '90 reds will still find much available. For (relative) affordability, we'd go for Albert Grivault's Meursault and Jean-Noël Gagnard's Chassagne-Montrachet from the whites, and have reds from Bruno Clair and Ghislaine Barthod. From the Loire, look for the Joguet and Druet reds, Lucian Crochet's Sancerre and Huet's Vouvray, and try the Alsace wines of Domaine Weinbach and Hugel. Good value describes the French country wines and the House champagne from Sarcey, but those who fancy trying the 1947 Krug will have to dig somewhat deeper.

In sum, a first-rate wine-merchant. Indeed, the only thing one can possibly grumble at is the miserly discount system; buyers of over 8 cases of those first-growth clarets, *grand cru* Burgundies and impressive Rhônes can knock 25p off the price of each bottle. The regular offers of Burgundy and Rhône are often backed up with tastings of many of the wines, so it's worth ringing up for details of these. The Selected Cellar Plan scheme is available for those wishing to build up their wine stocks, whether for now or for the future. For an introduction to the J&B range and to their excellent service, why not put together a mixed case of 24 half-bottles from the hundreds on offer?

Best buys

Vin de Pays de Vaucluse, Domaine du Vieux Chêne, £
House claret, £
Nuits-St-Georges, Les Cailles, Chevillon 1992, ££
Mâcon Uchizy, Domaine Talmard 1992, ££

King & Barnes

Vintners Fine Wine Merchants
16 Bishopric, Horsham, West Sussex RH12 1QP

Tel (01403) 270870
Fax (01403) 270570

Open Mon–Sat 9–5.30 **Closed** Sun, public holidays **Cards** Access, Delta, Switch, Visa **Discount** 5% on 1+ case **Delivery** Free in Horsham area (min. 2 case) **Glass hire** Free with order **Tasting and talks** Regular store tastings on most Sats, occasional organised tastings for invitees **Cellarage** Not available

Gareth Jones, manager of the recently refurbished King & Barnes shop in Horsham, reports that customers are becoming more discerning and are prepared to fork out extra pennies for a bottle of wine. The shop has plenty to satisfy their thirsts. Fetzer wines from California, Hamilton-Russell from South Africa and Montes from

Chile will do for starters. Of the many Australian listings, we'd recommend the wines from St Hallett, Piper's Brook and Wirra Wirra. The CVNE Riojas are good, as are the wines from Dr Loosen in Germany and Sogrape in Portugal. The Italian list remains patchy. Also, while we usually disapprove of things labelled as British wines, we find those on offer quite acceptable, since they are the Broadland Wineries range of fruit wines.

In the French range are some good burgundies, including very affordable Chablis from Guy Mothe and first-class Brouilly from Château des Tours. You'll have no trouble finding something to your liking among the clarets, and André Dézat's Loire wines will not disappoint. The range from the rest of France is not as strong, although good wines do appear. And if one night you don't feel like a bottle of wine, the shop now sells beer from the King & Barnes Horsham Brewery (proper stuff, not that widget muck) straight from the barrel.

Best buys

1993 Klippenkop Cinsault/Shiraz, £
1993/4 Torres Viña Esmerelda, Penedés, £
Graves 1989, Château Cabannieux, ££
1992 St Hallett Old Block Shiraz, ££

Kwik Save

Head office

Warren Drive, Prestatyn, Clwyd LL19 7HU	*Tel* (01745) 882826
Approx. 950 branches in England and Wales	*Fax* (01745) 882880

Open Mon–Sat 9–5 (Thur–Fri open til 8), Sun 12–3 (some stores only) **Cards** Delta, Switch **Discount** Not available **Delivery** Not available **Glass hire** Not available **Tasting and talks** Very selective **Cellarage** Not available

The no-frills Kwik Save chain may not be the first place you would think of to buy wine, but for good value, it is hard to beat. The brief for consultant Angela Muir MW is to find wines that will sell at under £3. This she does with considerable success, and comparisons with wines from other supermarkets in the same price range are very favourable.

What Angela calls the 'housekeeping wines' (Muscadet, claret, hock, Soave, etc.) are OK, but the best wines are the less familiar ones. All wines have point-of-sale tasting notes, should you need guidance. Our favourites in the sub-£3 range are Kym Milne's Atesino Chardonnay and Puglian Red, White Pacific from Chile, Pedro Rovira Garnacha/Cabernet and Don Fadrique Cencibel from Spain, Alta Mesa from Portugal, and from Eastern Europe the

Hungarian Pinot Gris and Macedonian Merlot. Over £3, the Barefoot Californian wines are reasonable, while from the south of France, the Domaine Fontenille Marsanne, Domaine St Martin Pinot Noir and Fortant de France Grenache are all tasty. Fizz lovers will find the Louis Raymond champagne and the Cadenza Asti very palatable.

Poor wines are very little in evidence throughout. Yes, there's still buckets of British Wine, Liebfraumilch and Lambrusco, but hard-up wine-drinkers looking for character will find more bang for their buck here than in most places.

Best buys

White Pacific Chilean Sauvignon, £
Skylark Hill Very Special Red, £

Lay & Wheeler

Head office and wine shop

The Wine Market, Gosbecks Road, Colchester,   *Tel* (01206) 764446
Essex CO2 9JT   *Fax* (01206) 560002
Culver Street Wine Shop, 6 Culver Street West,   *Tel* (01206) 764446
Colchester, Essex CO1 1JA

Open Mon–Sat 9–7 **Closed** Sun, public holidays **Cards** Access, Amex, Delta, Switch, Visa; personal and business accounts **Discount** 5% on 120+ bottles **Delivery** Essex and South Suffolk delivery service (min. 1 case mixed wine); free nationwide mail-order service for two cases or £150 **Glass hire** Free with order **Tasting and talks** Tutored tastings and wine workshops twice a week **Cellarage** £5.64 per case; 5+ cases £5.22

For flamboyance and eclecticism in the choice of wine you might want to look elsewhere, but for the complete package that is a wine-merchant there are few companies in the same league as Lay & Wheeler. This is the sort of wine-merchant your mother wouldn't mind you marrying; one who, though well able to surprise and delight, can always be relied on.

The 15% discount available on full-case purchases of a range of champagnes is not heralded with a plethora of capital letters and exclamation marks, even though it is better value than the familiar 'seven-for-the-price-of-6' offers. The large range of country wines is admirable, as are the Rhônes, where you'll find Châteauneufs from Vieux Télégraphe and Clos des Papes and plenty of characterful northern Syrah. The Alsace from Schlumberger, Hugel et al. will give immense pleasure, as will the Couly-Dutheil Chinon and the numerous Sancerres. There's plenty of claret, whether you're after affordable fare such as Ch. Tour du Pas St Georges or the several vintages from the rather loftier Ch. Pichon-Lalande. Burgundies are, if anything, better. New to the list are wines from Domaine

Leroy, Comtes Lafon, Mugneret-Gibourg and Hubert Lignier. We particularly like the Boisson-Vadot Meursaults.

The South African range is worth investigating; you may find several good wines from unfamiliar producers – the Claridge wines in particular are excellent. Our favourites among the many Australian items are the rich reds from Rolf Binder, Stephen Henschke and Penley Estate. The New Zealand stars are Allan Scott, Martinborough Vineyards and Redwood Valley, while the Californian wines from Duckhorn, Peter Michael and Jordan can also be recommended.

The Spanish list is good rather than great, but a German range with wines from von Schubert, Fritz Haag and Selbach-Oster is hard to beat. There are plenty of great Italian bottles ranging from the level of Super-Tuscans and Aldo Conterno's Barolo to the characterful Salice Salentino from Candido. The Austrian range is certainly worth investigating, especially for the wines of Heinrich and Kracher.

If you need a hand to guide you through the world of wine, the Wine Discovery programme may just be the thing. For around £35 per month, the company will send you six cases of wines per year, together with detailed tasting notes and information on the producers. Those with a bit more confidence might care to buy the sample cases offered in the regular newsletters. Tastings and workshops take place frequently, and there are also several formal winemaker dinners each year; a recent one involved Mme de Lencquesaing from Ch. Pichon-Lalande. Lay & Wheeler is simply very hard to fault.

Best buys

Sauvignon Blanc 1994, West Peak, South Africa, £
Vin de Pays de l'Herault, Terret Blanc 1993/4, Domaine la Fadéze, £
1987 Schramsberg, Blanc de Noirs, ££
Eden Valley Riesling 1993, Henschke, ££

Laymont & Shaw

The Old Chapel, Millpool, Truro,	*Tel* (01872) 70545
Cornwall TR1 1EX	*Fax* (01872) 223005

Case sales only Open Mon–Fri 9–5 **Closed** Sat, Sun, public holidays **Cards** None accepted; personal accounts **Discount** Available on 2+ cases **Delivery** Available locally (min. 1 case); mail-order available **Glass hire** Free with order **Tasting and talks** Available **Cellarage** Available

---

From the old Methodist chapel that is home to Laymont & Shaw, John Hawes, his wife and daughter continue to stick to what they do best: peddling wine from Spain and nothing else (except brandy from Spain, oil from Spain and vinegar from Spain). His customers are on 'a ceaseless search for value for money', but, rather than offer them the bland £2.49 reds and whites that have dragged the standards of Spanish wine into new levels of mediocrity, Mr H. has much better fare on offer.

There are several wines under £5 available, notably the Don John red and white which the company 'invented'. However, not very much more money will get you some far better stuff. Martínez Bujanda provides good modern Rioja, while more traditional fare comes from La Rioja Alta. The Ribera del Duero wines from Valduero stand up very well in comparison. From Valdepeñas come the affordable Los Llanos wines, while Navarra produces similarly good value in the shape of the Príncipe de Viana Agramont wines, as well as the innovative reds and whites from Castillo de Monjardín: great Chardonnay. The Torres Penedés range will be familiar to most, but we find the Jean León wines much more appealing. Masia Barril Priorato, the varietal range from Viñas del Vero in Somontano and the Albariño from Lagar de Cervera are also good. Juvé y Camps and Codorníu provide cava, while the sherries from González Byass and Barbadillo are joined by the own-label wines from Hidalgo and Lustau. The Scholtz Hermanos Malagas also appear on the list, perhaps for the last time, since a large part of this producer's business has closed down.

The thrice-yearly Iberian Independent newsletter contains details of special parcels of rare wines, offers on mixed cases, crosswords, strong opinions and more. Should you need further advice, the helpful Hawes clan will be more than willing to give it, either in English or in Spanish.

Best buys

'Don John' Tinto Red, £
Castillo de Monjardín Tinto Joven 1994, £
Viña Ardanza Rioja Reserva 1986/87, ££
Viña Valduero Ribera del Duero Crianza 1989, ££

Layts

20 Midland Road, London NW1 2AD	*Tel* 0171-388 4567
	Fax 0171-383 7419
50–52 Elizabeth Street, London SW1W 9PB	*Tel* 0171-730 8108
	Fax 0171-730 9284
14 Davies Street, London W1Y 1LJ	*Tel* 0171-499 9144
	Fax 0171-495 2002
21 Motcomb Street, London SW1X 8LB	*Tel* 0171-235 3723
	Fax 0171-235 2062

Open Mon–Fri 9–6, Sat 10–4 **Closed** Sun, public holidays, Chr, Easter **Cards** All accepted; personal and business accounts **Discount** Rarely **Delivery** UK mainland (£10 delivery charge for orders less than £150); mail-order available **Tasting and talks** By arrangement; one public tasting yearly **Cellarage** £6+VAT per case

'Time to fill the cellar again,' trumpeted the four horses on the front of a recent Laytons newsletter. The shops may be rather reserved and the main list itself relatively sparse, but these regular missives, with a refreshing combination of tasty new wines and plenty of adjectives, give you the best overall view of this wine merchant. On his regular trips to France's major wine areas, buyer Graham Chidgey uncovers some really fine wines, which most of the time live up to the purple prose.

That's not to say that those seeking wines from other parts of the world should ignore Laytons. The Italian selection from Fenocchio and La Spinosa in Piemonte and the South African and Australian wines from Fleur du Cap, and Taltarni respectively are certainly tasty; it's just that the French selection forms the lion's share of the range.

The Laytons champagne has been excellent for the past few years, putting many a *grande marque* to shame. The regional wines from Domaine Piccinini and Domaine de Bellevue are worth trying, as are the Alsace wines of Paul Blanck. The Sancerre from the Cotat brothers is even better, but do give it plenty of time in your cellar before drinking. Amid the Rhônes from Delas Frères are Châteauneufs from Vieux Télégraphe and Domaine de la Janasse. Burgundy-lovers will appreciate the selection from Guffens Heynen/Verget, Chartron et Trébuchet and many others, while fans of Bordeaux will warm to an ever-changing selection of young and mature wines.

The offers are often accompanied by invitations to taste the new arrivals at the Midland Road premises. Do take them up; you'll find some rather unfashionable, but fantastic wines.

Best buys

Vin de Pays d'Oc Merlot 1993, Domaine Piccinini, £
Château de la Pelissiere, Vieilles Vignes 1994, £
Châteauneuf du Pape, Domaine de la Janasse, Christophe Sabon 1989, ££
Chassagne-Montrachet Blanc, Verget 1993, ££

Lea & Sandeman   ❀ ☞ ◉

301 Fulham Road, London SW10 9QH	*Tel* 0171-376 4767
	Fax 0171-351 0275
211 Kensington Church Street, London W8 7LX	*Tel* 0171-221 1982
	Fax 0171-221 1985

Open Mon–Fri 9–8.30; Sat 10–8.30 **Closed** Sun and public holidays, Easter and Chr
Cards Access, Amex, Switch, Visa; personal and business accounts **Discount** 5–15%
on mixed-case sales **Delivery** Free London (min. 1 case), free nationwide delivery on
orders over £150 **Glass hire** Free with order **Tasting and talks** 4 main tastings per
year **Cellarage** Not available

'We were thrilled to bits to be awarded "Independent of the Year" last year,' says Charles Lea. If he and Patrick Sandeman carry on as they are doing, more awards can surely not be far behind. It has been a busy year for the pair, culminating in the takeover of the Barnes Wine Shop in July. There have been special offers on a range of Viognier, 1990 Super-Tuscans (now mostly all gone, although grab the Camartina from Querciabella while you can), some excellent winter warmers in the shape of southern French reds and, last but not least, lever-action Screwpull corkscrews (buy two for only £60 each!).

Those southern French reds give a good introduction to the L&S philosophy. None is really cheap, but all are stuffed with character and will appeal to those who love wine rather than famous names. The Coteaux du Languedoc from Château Lascaux and Domaine de la Coste, and the wines of Domaine de la Croix Belle are excellent. More guts and spicy fruit appear in the Rhône range, with Châteauneuf from Domaine de la Mordorée, Côte Rôtie from Clusel-Roch and exemplary Côtes-du-Rhône-Villages from Domaine Ste Anne.

Burgundies are also commendable, although stocks of the best wines flit in and out of the shop rather speedily. Names such as R & V Dauvissat, Jobard, Comte Armand and Ponsot show the calibre of what is on offer. Clarets, too, form an ever-changing range. You'll always find something, whether you want wine to drink now or to lay down. From Alsace Marcel Deiss provides the goods (the very, very goods), and among the many champagnes, you'll probably find your favourite *grande marque* (we like the Gosset wines).

In the Italian section look for the Oberto Barolo and the Querciabella Tuscans; in the Spanish section the CVNE Riojas will not fail to please. The wines from Niebaum-Coppola in California, Bannockburn in Australia, de Leuwen Jagt in South Africa and Wairau River in New Zealand are also very tasty.

Those seeking famous names may find themselves disappointed in Lea & Sandeman. However, we'd advise attending one of the four-yearly tastings in order to find a new set of producers to add to your 'must-buy' list.

Best buys

Bergerac Blanc Sec, Château Tour des Gendres 1994, Luc De Conti, £
Vin de Pays d'Oc Merlot 1993, Domaine de Terre Mégère, £
Coteaux du Languedoc 1993, Château de Lascaux, ££
Mâcon Vire 1991, Domaine Emilion Gillet, Jean Thévenet, ££

O W Loeb

not a shop
64 Southwark Bridge Road, London SE1 0AS

Tel 0171-928 7750
Fax 0171-928 1855

Open Mon–Fri 9–5.30 for telephone enquiries only   **Closed** Sat, Sun, public holidays
Cards None accepted; personal and business accounts   **Discount** Not available
Delivery Free in Central London for deliveries of 1+ cases; nationwide mail-order service free for 6+ cases (1–2 £10+VAT, 3–5 £3+VAT per case)   **Glass hire** Not available   **Tasting and talks** Not available   **Cellarage** £5+VAT per case per year

---

Dominus anyone? Perhaps the Australian Tolleys? Loeb's have these New World wines, but we feel that their presence is rather token. We'd give our business to the company for their fabulous ranges from the Rhône, Alsace, Burgundy and Germany.

True, there is a reasonable set of clarets, and we'd consider stocking up with those '88s, '89s and '90s before the prices rise higher. But for real passion we'd head for the burgundies first. Reds come from Tollot-Beaut, Armand Rousseau, Domaine Dujac, de Montille and others, while the whites are produced by Sauzet, Ramonet, Gagnard Delagrange and Louis Michel. The company is agent for the Paul Jaboulet wines from the Rhône, but we are just as keen to drink the wines of Château Rayas. In the Loire range, Joguet provides great Chinon, while equally good Vouvray comes from Foreau. Alsace wines from Hugel and Madame Faller's Domaine Weinbach complete the French range.

The introduction to the Mosel-Saar-Ruwer section of the list says it all: 'a virtual roll-call of the great growers in the three river valleys.' Robert Eymael, von Hövel, Egon Müller, J. J. Prüm, von

Schubert, and many more top producers are represented. Aschrott'sche Erben from the Rheingau, Bürklin-Wolf and von Buhl from the Rheinpfalz and the Staatliche Weinbaudomäne from the Nahe complete a fabulous German range.

Many of the most interesting wines never appear on the main wine list because customers have been so quick to buy from the regular offers. We'd suggest you put yourself on this company's mailing list – especially for the remnant sales, which are full of genuine bargains for those who get there early.

Best buys

1990 Seigneurie de Peyrat rouge, Vin de Pays de l'Hérault, £
1993 Drovers Dry White, Tolley, £
1992 Auxey Duresses, J. Pascal, ££
1990 Tokay Jubilee, Hugel, ££

London Wine Emporium

86 Goding Street, Vauxhall Cross,   *Tel* 0171-587 1302
London SE11 5AW   *Fax* 0171-587 0982

Case sales only   **Open** Mon–Fri 10–7, Sat 10–5, Sun before Chr 10–4, Good Fri 10–5 **Closed** Sun, public holidays   **Cards** Access, Amex, Delta, Diners, Switch, Visa; business accounts   **Discount** 5% on 1+ cases   **Delivery** Free 1+ cases within the M25 area; Free 3+ cases outside M25 area (1–2 cases £5 per case); Nationwide mail-order available   **Glass hire** Free with order   **Tasting and talks** Tutored tastings given on a regular basis   **Cellarage** Not available

Since the London Wine Emporium was granted a retail licence last autumn, it's no longer case sales only at Colin Barnes's Vauxhall railway arch. Not that putting a case together here would be a problem; it's just that being one arch away from a branch of Majestic, you need all the help you can get.

The company no longer shares the premises with Alex Findlater, but both firms share a love of things Australian. A fine range features Brokenwood, Grant Burge, Hollick, Mount Mary, Clyde Park and Seville Estate, plus over a dozen different liqueur Muscats. New Zealand is similarly well represented, with whites, reds and sparkling wines; you'll be familiar with many of the names, but do look out for the less-well-known wines from Ata Rangi, St Nesbit, Ngatawara and Rippon. South Africa is another speciality, with over 70 wines on offer; producers such as Delheim, Warwick, Thelema, Neil Ellis, Hamilton-Russell, Neetlingshof, Villiera and Boschendal will be familiar to Cape-wine lovers everywhere, but there's much more besides.

France looks rather skimpy by comparison, but Alain Paret's Côtes-du-Rhône, Olivier Merlin's Mâcon and the clutch of affordable clarets are all good. An expanding range of country wines includes the wonderful wines of Château des Estanilles. A range from Moldova, Greek wine from Boutari and Mexican from L. A. Cetto share the shelves with the excellent Valpolicellas of Le Ragose and Portuguese bottles from J. P. Vinhos. The Spanish selection includes Felix Callejo's Ribera del Duero and several Riojas, while highlights from the United States are the Willamette Valley Vineyards reds and whites.

Colin Barnes is the driving force behind 'Women in Wine', a scheme aimed at highlighting the efforts of female winemakers. Around two dozen estates from around the world are featured, although no one has yet satisfactorily explained why so many of the women involved come from New Zealand.

Best buys

Vin de Pays de Vaucluse NV, £
Paul Thomas, Columbia Valley White 1993, £
Ployez-Jacquemart NV Champagne, ££
Warwick Farm 1991 Trilogy, ££

Luvians Bottle Shop

Faval (Cupar) Ltd, 93 Bonnygate, Cupar,	*Tel* (01334) 654820
Fife KY15 4LG	*Fax* (01334) 654820

Open Mon–Sat 9–7, Sun 12–5.30, public holidays **Closed** Chr and Boxing Days, 1 and 2 Jan **Cards** Access, Delta, Switch, Visa; personal and business accounts **Discount** By negotiation **Delivery** Free within 15-mile radius (min. 1 case in town, 2 cases out of town) nationwide mail-order available **Glass hire** Free with order **Tasting and talks** Malt, whisky, cognac, sherry etc. on a day-to-day basis, port and wine 3–4 times a year **Cellarage** Free for regulars

Fancy seeing how those 1971s are developing? Vincent Fusaro can help you out. He can offer a horizontal tasting of Millburn, Glenlossie, Dailuaine, Balmenach, Macallan, Speyburn and Craigellachie. Whisky, not wine. The range of malts here is truly stunning, although the wines aren't bad either.

Dow, Fonseca and Taylor ports are here in depth, as are sherries from González Byass. Clarets range from 1982 Ch. Lynch Bages to several *cru bourgeois* wines from the late 1980s; burgundies are from Moreau and Faiveley, while Guigal provides Rhônes. Alsace fans will warm to wines from Trimbach and Hugel, while lovers of the Loire can enjoy Marc Brédif's Vouvray and Pouilly Fumé from de Ladoucette. For those who can't stretch to the numerous *prestige cuvées* in the champagne range, Canard-Duchêne will amply suffice.

There are several Riojas to tempt the palate, but the Italian wines deserve attention. Borgogno's Barolo, Mastroberardino's Taurasi, Chianti from Selvapiana and Pagliarese plus the Cepparello and I Sodi Super-Tuscans stand out among the reds, while the whites from Tiefenbrunner, Jermann and Umani Ronchi are very good too.

Amid the many Australian wines listed you'll find Cape Mentelle's awesome Zinfandel, Plantagenet's classy Shiraz and great Semillon from Tim Adams. Oyster Bay from New Zealand, Montes from Chile and South African wines from Neil Ellis and Zonnebloem stand out from the rest of the New World range.

From a standing start 11 years ago, when the core business was entirely ice-cream, the Luvians drinks range has blossomed. In some places, it needs pruning, in others, controlled doses of fertiliser would pay dividends. However, enthusiasm seems to be in plentiful supply in what, according to Mr Fusaro, is 'probably Scotland's largest selection of fine drink under one roof'.

Best buys

Salice Salentino, Cosimo Taurino, £
Tiefenbrunner Pinot Grigio, £
Château Haut Marbuzet 1988, ££
Gewurztraminer 1991, Trimbach, ££

Majestic Wine Warehouses

Head office
Odhams Trading Estate, St Albans Road,   *Tel* (01923) 816999
Watford, Hertfordshire, WD2 5RE   *Fax* (01923) 819105
44 branches

Case sales only   Open Mon–Sat and public holidays 10–8, Sun 10–6   **Closed** Chr and Boxing Days and New Year's Eve and Day   **Cards** All accepted; business accounts **Discount** Available   **Delivery** Free within 5-mile radius (min 1 case); nationwide mail-order service available   **Glass hire** £9 per dozen   **Tasting and talks** Themed tasting weekends, tasting counter available at all times; private tastings for groups **Cellarage** Not available

As we go to press, celebrations are being planned for the opening of the 50th Majestic store. The inhabitants of Southampton will now have a chance to experience the company that has done more than any other for the concept of the wine warehouse. The rocky patch of the late 1980s and early 1990s is now long past, and the stores have regained the vitality which made them such refreshing places to buy wine in the early eighties.

The core range of wines is very reasonable, but to get the most out of Majestic, you have to visit the place regularly. We'd recommend clubbing together with friends for monthly trips, otherwise you'll miss out on the special parcels which Tony 'Del-Boy' Mason has unearthed.

Even if you miss these, you'll always find champagne at very keen prices, whether the inexpensive de Telmont and Oeil de Perdrix or such *prestige cuvées* as Veuve Clicquot's La Grande Dame. The Californian Roederer Quartet, Cloudy Bay's Pelorus and Pongracz from South Africa lead the challenge to Champagne. The clarets on display are reasonable, although it's worth getting to know your local manager, as there are often some cases of finer wines somewhere in the Majestic system (if the staff haven't bought them first). Faiveley and Louis Latour provide burgundy, Rhônes come from Vidal Fleury. More flair is to be found in the regional French section. Our favourites are the rich, spicy Château Flaugergues, the Galet vineyards Viognier and the varietals under the Les Jumelles label.

The Italian wines are just as interesting and good-value, particularly at the cheaper end of the range. Spanish representation is reasonable, while the star of the Portuguese wines is the characterful Serradayres red. Grans-Fassian and von Kesselstatt provide the most inspiring German bottles.

We'd avoid the cheaper end of the Californian range and head for the impressive Pinots, Zinfandels, Chardonnays and Cabernets, plus the spicy reds from Jade Mountain and Joseph Phelps. Along with the numerous Penfolds offerings are Australian wines from Chateau Tahbilk, Cape Mentelle and Vasse Felix. The Coopers Creek and Oyster Bay from New Zealand are good, but the South African range has yet to find its feet.

Case sales only is still the order of the day, but putting together a dozen bottles is seldom a problem, particularly when eight bottles of certain big-name champagnes are offered for the price of six. There's usually a £1.99 wonder around if you're desperate to fill those final spaces, and, if wine hasn't taken up all the space in your car, the deals on beer and mineral water are difficult to ignore.

There are hits and misses in the wine range, and we'd like to see the innovation in the Italian and French regional wine ranges creep into a few other areas, particularly at the cheaper end. However, even if you don't share the manager's taste in music, Majestic is once more a very enjoyable place to buy wine.

Best buys

Château la Perrière 1993, Bordeaux, £
Marsanne, Chateau Tahbilk 1992, £
Coteaux du Languedoc, Château Flaugergues 1994, ££
Beringer Chardonnay 1992, Napa Valley, ££

Marks & Spencer

458 Oxford Street, London W1N 0AP

Tel 0171-935 7954
Fax 0171-486 5379

Over 283 branches

Open Varies from store to store, Sun 10–4 or 11–5; some stores open public holidays
Closed Easter Sunday, Chr and Boxing Days **Cards** Delta, Switch; M&S Chargecard
Discount Available to M&S Chargecard owners **Delivery** Mail order available
Glass hire Not available **Tasting and talks** In store **Cellarage** Not available

A comparison of Waitrose and Marks & Spencer is interesting. Both stand somewhat apart from other supermarkets, attracting (or perhaps being perceived as attracting) a higher class of customer. Neither feels the need to indulge in petty pricing wars, and both are known for the high quality of their food selection. However, Waitrose has now won our supermarket wine-merchant award for three years running, but M&S hasn't even made the shortlists.

All the same, the wines on offer are improving. There are still a number of 'misses' – wines that are not bad, just actively mediocre. The same can be said of any supermarket, but perhaps the 'misses' stand out more in the M&S range, since it is smaller than those of, say, Sainsbury's and Tesco. The M&S wine departments still seem rather sterile, but the stuff on the shelves is increasingly worth putting your fingerprints on. The burgundy section (with Chablis from La Chablisienne, Montagny from the Buxy co-op and some good reds from Jadot) is, wine-for-wine, as good as any of the competition. The champagnes from Union Champagne are reliably good, as are the own-label clarets from the J-P Moueix range. The selection of southern French whites is patchy, but that of the the reds is generally better, and the Côtes du Roussillon in litre bottles is excellent value. Giordano's Il Caberno is the star of a decent range of Italian reds, Gran Calesa is a fine Spanish red, and the Australian bottles from Peter Lehmann, Coldstream Hills and Rosemount are delicious. Trapiche's Medalla Tinto from Argentina, which appeared early in 1995, was a winner, and the Kaituna Hills New Zealand wines are also impressive.

It's still hard to get very excited about the range, but the number of good wines at around the £5 mark does seem to be increasing. We would be surprised if M&S ever gained the reputation for its wines that it enjoys for its clothes and food, but at least the company seems to be trying a lot harder than in the past. Wines can also be delivered to your home (£3.99 per delivery) through the Marks & Spencer Wine Cellar scheme, for which a list (issued every three months) features some wines that are available in store together with some Cellar exclusives.

Best buys

1994 Giordano Chardonnay del Piemonte, £
Vin de Pays de l'Hérault 1993, Domaine St Pierre, Domaines
Virginie, £
1993 Rosemount Orange Vineyards Chardonnay, ££
1990 Gran Calesa, Costers del Segre, ££

Martinez Fine Wines

36 The Grove, Ilkley, West Yorkshire LS23 9EE	*Tel* (01943) 603241
Martinez Fine Wine and Food	*Fax* (01943) 603241
The Ginnel, Harrogate, North Yorkshire HG1 2RB	*Tel* (01423) 501783
Martinez Fine Wine	
22 Union Street, Halifax, West Yorkshire HX1 1PR	*Tel* (01422) 320022

Open Mon–Sat 10–6, public holidays 10–6 **Closed** Sun **Cards** Access, Delta, Switch, Visa; personal and business accounts **Discount** 5% on mixed cases; 10% on unmixed cases **Delivery** Free North and West Yorkshire (min. 1 case), UK mainland £6 per case; mail-order available **Glass hire** Free **Tasting and talks** Regular tutored and non-tutored tastings and gourmet dinners **Cellarage** £2.50+VAT per case per year

With the opening of the Halifax shop in October 1994, Martinez Fine Wines now mount a three-pronged attack on the Yorkshire fine-wine market. It's a very efficient assault, too. Even without the Mad March Sale, offering 15% discounts on all cash or cheque purchases of six bottles or more, Danny Cameron and his companions have much to attract you.

Don't expect a big range from the traditional classics, though. Wines earn their place here by quality not by reputation. Still, there's a decent array of claret, and burgundy-lovers will enjoy the reds from Vallet Frères. The Rhônes and Loires are decent, and the Schlumberger Alsace won't disappoint, but the best range from France covers the many regional wines, particularly the Domaine Jougla St Chinian and Daniel Domergue's Minervois. German listings include Georg Breuer's concentrated Rieslings, and Mouchão from the Alentejo in Portugal is an astonishing wine. There are plenty of good Spanish reds, plus an unpronounceable white called Txomn Etzanoz from the Basque country. The Italian list is not quite as profuse but still includes plenty of interesting wines.

There's much to commend in the South African range, with Thelema and Klein Constantia being the pick of around a dozen wineries on show. California is less in evidence, although the wines of Newton and Saintsbury will not disappoint. Interesting Australian offerings include Stafford Ridge Chardonnay, Hickinbotham Pinot Noir and Long Gully Cabernet Sauvignon,

351

while the New Zealand wines of Neudorf and Martinborough Vineyards are also good.

The chatty Noble Rot newsletter keeps customers in touch with new wines, tastings, dinners and other events. In surveying the ranges of many merchants we come across several identikit wine lists that result from buying almost entirely from the same half-dozen specialists; the folks at Martinez deal with those same companies too, but they list many more interesting and rare wines besides – which makes this one of Britain's more stimulating places to buy wine.

Best buys

1990, Chiltern Valley Dry, England, £
1993, Chianti Classico Geografico, £
Bordeaux Supérieur 1990, Château Beaufresque, ££
Allesverloren Shiraz 1989, ££

F & E May

27 Brownlow Mews, Bloomsbury, London WC1N 2LA   *Tel* 0171-405 6249
                                                  Fax 0171-404 4472

Case sales only **Open** Mon–Fri 9–5.30 **Closed** Sat, Sun, public holidays **Cards** Switch; personal and business accounts **Discount** Various **Delivery** Free within London (min. 1 case) **Glass hire** Not available **Tasting and talks** By request **Cellarage** Available

---

F & E May is very much a traditional company, and, with the exception of the Redwood Valley New Zealanders and the Nottage Hill Australians, its list concentrates on French and German wines. The Châteauneuf from Domaine de Nalys and a range from Leon Revol feature in the Rhônes, Alsace wines are from Klipfel, and Sancerre of various hues comes from Paul Millérioux. Louis Tête provides beaujolais, and other burgundies include Chablis from Lamblin and a large selection from Domaine Prieur. Clarets are available in depth, dating back to the 1979 vintage, while the white Bordeaux range includes Pavillon Blanc du Château Margaux, a set of classed-growth Sauternes and the somewhat cheaper Cadillac of Ch. Fayau. In the German selection, you'll find Mosel wines from von Schubert, Friedrich-Wilhelm-Gymnasium and Bischöfliches Priesterseminar and hock from Bürklin-Wolf and the State domaines of Nahe and Eltville.

Best buys

1989 Maximin Grünhauser Riesling Auslese, von Schubert, ££
1990 Erbacher Marcobrunner Riesling Spätlese, Staatsweingüter Eltville, ££

Mayor Sworder & Co

7 Aberdeen Road, Croydon, Surrey CR0 1EQ   *Tel* 0181-681 3222

Open Mon–Fri 9–5 **Closed** Sat, Sun, public holidays **Cards** None accepted;
personal and business accounts **Discount** By negotiation on bulk orders **Delivery**
Free within M25 (min. 1 case) elsewhere £6.50+VAT per order; mail-order available
Glass hire Free with order **Tasting and talks** One tasting annually for account
holders; small, informal tastings occasionally **Cellarage** £5.20+VAT per case per year

The quiet, unassuming Mayor Sworder is now owned by J. T.
Davies, parent company of Davison's (q.v.), but apart from a move
of offices from Kennington to Croydon, customers will notice little
difference. This has never been the flashiest of companies, and the
range has erred on the small side, but when it comes to the quality
of the wines, the company can stand with the best of them. The
selection befits a wine-merchant which has been in business for
over 90 years, concentrating on the classic regions, but sticking
fairly firmly to the more sensibly prices wines. The available New
World wines are jolly good particularly the Australians from
Château Xanadu, Hillstowe and Idyll and the Fetzer Californians.
Italians are sparse, and Spaniards even more so, although the Rioja
Alavesa from Valserrano is good. Germans too run to little more
than a dozen wines, with the pick being the Vereinigte Hospitien
Mosel Rieslings.

France is where most of the action is. The Richemont sparklers
are excellent alternatives to the various grande marque
champagnes. Country wines of interest include the St Chinian from
Prieuré Donnadieu and Domaine la Serre's Merlot. The
Monbazillac from Château la Borderie would put many a Sauternes
to shame, while Fournier's Loire Sauvignon makes a good cheap
substitute for those who cannot afford the Millet-Roger Sancerre.
Robert Michel's Cornas and André Perret's Condrieu top a Rhône
range that also features Château La Nerthe's Châteauneuf and the
stylish Vacqueyras from Château des Roques. The Bordeaux range
features several good wines under a tenner as well as loftier classed
growths. Burgundies stick mostly to the sensible side of £20, and
we'd pick out Gérard Martin's St Amour and St Véran in particular.

Best buys

Chardonnay 1994, Père Ventura (Spain), £
Vin de Pays des Côtes de Thongue 1993, Domaine de la Serre
Merlot, £
St-Véran 1992, Domaine l'Ermite de St-Véran, ££
Moulin-à-Vent 1993, Domaine Amédée Dégrange, ££

Michael Menzel

297–9 Ecclesall Road, Sheffield,   *Tel* (0114) 2683557
South Yorkshire, S11 8NX   *Fax* (0114) 2671267

Open Mon–Sat 10–7 **Closed** Sun, Chr, Boxing and Easter Days **Cards** All accepted
Discount Available **Delivery** Local delivery free for 3+ cases, free outside local area
for 5+ cases **Glass hire** Free with order **Tasting and talks** Available **Cellarage** Not
available

Michael Menzel's wine bar and restaurant finally emerged from a
very long pupation and opened its doors in April 1995. If just a few
of the wines available at the shop appear on the restaurant list,
then diners are in for a treat.

This is a place to come for good, solid, traditional wines, with
sprinklings of more modern fare just to add spice. Deinhard
provides the German range, the Australian comes from Brown
Brothers, and Mondavi wines make up most of the Californian list:
more esoteric New Zealand bottles come from Rongopai and de
Redcliffe. Rioja fans will not be disappointed by wines from the
Marqués de Murrieta, Faustino Martínez and La Rioja Alta, while
Masi Valpolicella, Jermann whites and Tignanello will please Italian
enthusiasts (you'll also find Bertani's astonishing sparkling
Recioto).

Fans of more classical fizz will appreciate the champagne from
several famous *grandes marques*, although we'd also recommend the
Philipponnat wines. Elsewhere in France, Hugel's Alsace, Provence
wines of Domaine Ott and Chapoutier Rhônes are all good solid
fare. In the Loire range, De Ladoucette provides Pouilly Fumé, and
Vouvray comes from Marc Brédif. Clarets are admirable, with
wines up to first-growth level and several affordable classed
growths from the classic 1985 vintage. Burgundies are provided by
Drouhin, Louis Latour, Bouchard Père et Fils and Faiveley, a
reliable quartet of merchants if ever there was one. But that's only
what you'd expect from Mr Menzel.

Best buys

Mercurey 1989, Domaine de la Croix Jacquelet, Faiveley, ££
Pauillac, Château Batailley 1985/88, ££

Milton Sandford Wines

Head office
The Old Chalk Mine, Warren Row Road, Knowl Hill, Reading, Berkshire RG10 8QS

Tel (01628) 829449
Fax (01628) 829424

Case sales only **Open** Office open Mon–Fri 9–6; it is requested that visitors arrange appointment in advance **Cards** None accepted; personal and business accounts **Discount** Only to the trade **Delivery** Free Central London, M4 and M3 corridors, M40 and A40 up to Stratford (min. 3 cases; £5 for orders under 3 cases); nationwide mail-order available **Glass hire** Not available **Tasting and talks** By appointment only **Cellarage** Not available

When customers describe this company as 'the pits', they are not disparaging the wine range; Milton Sandford is based in an old chalkpit in the heart of Berkshire. This provides conditions that are remarkably good for storing wine, but it seems to affect the prices as well. Even if they do exclude VAT (the bulk of business is wholesale) we're sure they're a bit on the low side. Not that we're complaining!

Nor are we carping about the range on offer. It's a compact selection of interesting wines that focuses on lesser known names from Australia but manages to come up with the goods from several other regions. Among those Australian wines are Shottesbrooke and Jeffrey Grosset from South Australia, and Fermoy Estate, Hay Shed Hill and Ashbrook from Margaret River. All err on the subtle side, although you will find St Hallett Old Block Shiraz if you want more of a mouthful of muscle. Stag's Leap Wine Cellars lend interest to the Californian list, and there's a clutch of wines from other New World countries.

The Nahe wines of Paul Anheuser are good, as are the Los Llanos Valdepeñas and Hidalgo sherries. In the French section the many affordable clarets are joined by a smaller range of burgundies from some excellent producers. Beaucastel Rhônes, Pouilly Fumé from Jean-Claude Chatelain and champagne from Bruno Paillard may give you further incentive to contact this company and go mining for wine.

Best buys

Stewart Point Shiraz Cabernet 1993, S.E. Australia, £
Cape Charlotte 1994 Dry Muscat à Petits Grains, S.E. Australia, £
Bruno Paillard Cuvée Première NV, ££
Les Tourelles de Longueville 1989, (second wine) Pichon-Longueville-Baron, ££

Mitchell & Son

21 Kildare Street, Dublin 2
Tel (01) 6760766
Fax (01) 6611509

Open Mon–Wed, Fri 10.30–5.30, Thurs 10.30–8; Sat 10.30–1 **Closed** Sun, public
holidays **Cards** All accepted; personal and business accounts **Discount** 5% on 1–2
cases, 7% on 3–5 cases, 10% on 6+ cases **Delivery** Free within Dublin county (min. 3
cases); mail-order available **Glass hire** 11p per glass **Tasting and talks** Tastings
every Thur evening in shop. Also organised tastings in cellars for groups/wine clubs
Cellarage Not available

If the UK wine trade complains about the activities of the
Chancellor, pity the poor wine-merchants of Ireland, who have to
suffer a duty rate of £1.65 per bottle, plus VAT at 21%. No £1.99
wine in Dublin. What you will find, though, is Mitchells, a
traditional wine-merchant with a heritage dating back through six
generations of Mitchells and nearly 200 years.

Venerable the firm may be, but it is far from stagnant. The past
year has seen the introduction of Mitchells white burgundy and
claret, the first of what is hoped to be many own-label wines. And a
new club has been launched, Mitchells Wine Guild, which offers
members regular tastings, discounts, exclusive offers and the
chance to visit European wine-growing regions.

The range of wines remains very good. Fonseca ports, Lustau
sherries and Pommery champagne form the bulk of their respective
ranges. Clarets from Ch. de Sours up to several vintages of
Châteaux Rausan Ségla, de Lamarque and Lynch-Bages are
available, as is a large set of Mommessin burgundies. Mommessin
are also responsible for several of the Rhône wines, although do try
the Domaine Brusset Gigondas. Dopff au Moulin Alsace, Domaine
Ott Provence and top notch *vin de pays* from Mas de Daumas
Gassac complete the French wines.

Deinhard provides the German range, and the Spanish list
includes wines from Marqués de Riscal and Vega Sicilia. The J. M.
da Fonseca Portuguese range is full of character, and the same can
be said for the Atesino Italian wines. Highlights from the New
World are Sequoia Grove from California, Babich from New
Zealand and the wines of Esslemont Estate in Australia's Hunter
Valley.

Director Peter Dunne says the company is kept on its toes by
rivals, but 'we feel our staff are the best you can find.' If you're
interested in experiencing the Mitchell touch, tastings are held
every Thursday in the shop. We can think of many worse ways to
spend an evening.

Best buys

Mitchell's White Burgundy 1993, Mommessin, ££
Mitchell's Claret 1990, Chateau bottled, ££

Mitchells Wine Merchants

Head office and main outlet
354 Meadowhead, Sheffield, South Yorkshire   *Tel* 0114-274 5587/0311
S8 7UI   *Fax* 0114-274 8481
Branches
148 Derbyshire Lane, Sheffield, South Yorkshire   *Tel* 0114-258 3989
S8 8SE
25 Townhead Road, Dore, Sheffield, South Yorkshire   *Tel* 0114-236 6131
S17 3GD

Open Mon–Thur 9.30–10, Fri–Sat 9.30–10.30, Sun and public holidays 12–2, 7–10
Closed Chr Day and New Year's Day   **Cards** Access, Switch, Visa; personal and
business accounts   **Discount** 5% on mixed cases, 7.5% on full cases   **Delivery** Free for
local deliveries within 30-mile radius; mail-order available   **Glass hire** Free with wine
purchase   **Tasting and talks** Every Fri and Sat in store; group tastings by request
Cellarage 5p per case per week; initial £1 per case charge

'I've been in the trade 28 years and I'm still only 42,' says genial
John Mitchell. His Sheffield shop may have nothing of the rarefied
atmosphere of St James's, but an enthusiastic welcome is
guaranteed to all. You'll find some great wines on his shelves as
well (and beers, and malt whiskies).

The ranges from Spain and Australia remain excellent. Besides
wines from Vallformosa in Penedés and Ochoa in Navarra, there
are several Riojas to whet the appetite. From Australia, try the
wares of Andrew Garrett, Hardy's and Cape Mentelle. The
Americas range includes wines from Echeverria in Chile, L. A.
Cetto in Mexico and Hogue Cellars in Washington State, while
from New Zealand come Mills Reef and Vidal. The pick of the
South African wines are those from Neil Ellis.

Italian wines come from Cesari and Villadoria, and the German
range includes wines from Deinhard. In the French section claret
fans will be able to line up a vertical tasting of Ch. Lascombes; red
burgundy comes from Pierre André, Chablis from Moreau, and
Georges Duboeuf provides a good range of beaujolais. Montaudon
champagne offers good value in a range from many of the major
houses. De Ladoucette Loire, Trimbach Alsace and Delas Rhônes
are also listed.

Wines are available for tasting each weekend, and there are also
regular 'Call My Bluff' evenings in which a panel describes a wine
(tasted blind) and the audience has to guess which of them is
telling the truth. A bistro has opened up this year next door to the

Meadowhead shop. If the food is as good and as honest and John and his wines, it should be a great success.

Best buys

Echeverria 1994 unwooded Chardonnay, Chile, £
Vin de Pays d'Oc 1992 Cabernet Sauvignon, Philippe de Baudin, £
Conde de Valdemar Reserva Rioja 1990, ££
Châteauneuf du Pape, Delas Frères 1990, Les Calcerniers, ££

Moreno Wine Importers

2 Norfolk Place, London W2 1QN

Tel 0171-706 3055
Fax 0171-724 3813

11 Marylands Road, London W9 2DU

Tel 0171-286 0678
Fax 0171-286 0513

Open (Norfolk Place) Mon–Sat 10-7 (Marylands Road) Mon–Fri 4–10, Sat 10–10, Sun 12-3 **Closed** Public holidays and Norfolk Place closed Sun **Cards** Delta, Switch, Visa; personal and business accounts **Discount** 5% on 1 case; 5% off any sale to Wine Club Members **Delivery** West and North London (min. 1 case); free mail-order service Central London, £9 outside of London **Glass hire** Free with order (£1 refundable deposit per glass) **Tasting and talks** Moreno's Wine Club on the last Friday on every month; contact Juanito on 0171-286 0678 **Cellarage** Not available

Last year we were promised some wines from outside Spain – from such outlandish places as South Africa, Australia and New Zealand. On our last visit, these had not materialised, and the only non-Spanish wines worth investigating were the Chileans from Viña Porta and Viña Casablanca, and the healthy Portuguese range. To be honest, though, even if such foreigners did appear, we don't think it would do much to change our mind about Moreno. This is the place for lovers of Spanish wine to come and drool. Where the company scores in particular is in having mature wines, such as 1964 Protos Gran Reserva from Ribera del Duero, 1962 Castillo Ygay Rioja Blanco and even Federico Paternina's Rioja Gran Reserva from 1928. However, there's also plenty of younger fare. Riojas come from 18 bodegas, with especially good ranges from Marques de Murrieta and La Rioja Alta, but those keen to find out what else Spain has to offer will have their eyes well and truly opened. Good dry whites come from Marqués de Alella (particularly the two Chardonnays) and Santiago Ruiz in Rias Baixas. The Mari Dulcis Moscatel from Bodegas Bordejé in Campo de Borja is a luscious dessert wine and of course there are sherries from de Soto and Valdespino. Reds of character are provided by Guelbenzu (Navarra), Pago de Carraovejas (Ribera del Duero) and Cellers de Scala Dei (Priorato). You'll also find the familiar Torres wines, with nine vintages of Black Label/Mas la Plana on offer.

Conde de Caralt and Parxet are just two of the bodegas providing cava.

If you wish to improve your acquaintance with Spanish wine, we'd suggest either buying one of the mixed cases on offer, or else attending one of the monthly tastings that the Moreno Wine Club holds at the Spanish Chamber of Commerce in the West End.

Best buys

1994 Navajas Rioja Blanco Sin Crianza, £
Cristalino Brut Cava, £
1994 Ochoa Vino de Moscatel à Petits Grains, ££
1989 Guelbenzu Evo Tinto Navarra Gran Reserva, ££

Morris & Verdin

10 The Leathermarket, Weston Street	*Tel* 0171-357 8866
London SE1 3ER	*Fax* 0171-357 8877

Case sales only   Open Mon–Fri 9–6   **Closed** Sat, Sun, public holidays   **Cards** None accepted; personal and business accounts   **Discount** Negotiable   **Delivery** Free within Central London (for 6+ cases); £7.05 up to 5 cases; mail-order available   **Glass hire** Not available   **Tasting and talks** Approximately 7 annual tastings (charged)   **Cellarage** £6 + VAT per case per year

The over-educated oenophiles at Morris & Verdin (their description, not ours) have moved from the cramped Churton Street premises, site of many an office cricket match, to something rather more spacious near London Bridge. The company will be well known to lovers of burgundy, and the range continues to be one of the most satisfying around, offering wines of individuality and character, not all at rich man's prices. You'll find Bourgogne Rouge from Michel Esmonin and Patrick Rion, and Bourgogne Blanc from Jean-Philippe Fichet and Gérard Chavy for under a tenner. The Grand Burgundy Offer that appears each January is certainly worth investigating.

However, Morris & Verdin is increasingly worth turning to for the wines of other regions. There's always a reasonable set of clarets, ranging from Ch. Sénéjac up to first-growth levels, and this is boosted by occasional *en primeur* campaigns. Other French highlights are the Alsace wines from Domaine Ostertag, regional fare from Château Routas, Châteauneuf from Beaucastel and the Vouvray of Bourillon Dorléans. The company has just become agent for Vega Sicilia, and you'll also find a range of Tokaji from Bodegas Oremus which Vega Sicilia set up in 1993. Quinta de la Rosa provide port and red wine. There are small ranges from the southern hemisphere, but the best New World selection comes from California. Au Bon Climat, Dominus and Bonny Doon are the stars, but Jade Mountain, Qupé and Frog's Leap aren't far behind.

Best buys

Domaines Virginie Marsanne 1994, Vin de Pays d'Oc, £
Vin de Pays des Coteaux de Murviel, Domaine de Limbardie 1993, £
1993 Gevrey Chambertin Clos St Jacques, Esmonin, ££
1994 Gewürztraminer d'Epfig, Domaine Ostertag, ££

Morrisons

Head office

Hilmore House, Thornton Road, Bradford,	*Tel* (01274) 494166
West Yorkshire BD8 9AX	*Fax* (01274) 494831

Approximately 70 branches, north of England and Midlands

Open Mon–Sat 8–6, Sun 10–4 **Closed** Chr and Boxing Days, Easter Sunday **Cards** Access, Switch, Visa **Discount** None offered **Delivery** Not available **Glass hire** Free with order (deposit required) **Tasting and talks** To selected groups normally in store in evening **Cellarage** Not available

With the number of its stores now pushing 80, Morrisons is pressing even more good-value wines into trolleys in the Midlands and North of England. This is not the place to come to stock a cellar with great wines, but, as buyer Stuart Purdie knows, that's not what his customers want.

You will find Ch. Caronne-Ste-Gemme and Michel Lynch in the claret section, and the Tremblay Chablis and Marqués de Murrieta Rioja don't come cheap either, but the best sets of wines are from Eastern Europe and southern France. In the former the Romanian reds are very impressive at the price, while the latter offers Big Frank's Red, Château de Lastours, Laperouse White and the tasty wines from Chais Cuxac. Australian offerings include reds from Wolf Blass and Jamiesons Run, whites from Goundrey and Brown Brothers. Chilean wines are from Santa Carolina and Cousiño Macul, but the rest of the New World range is less inspiring, with KWV from South Africa, Gallo from California and Cooks from New Zealand.

Being a medium-sized chain means that Morrisons has access to parcels of wines that larger supermarkets are unable to take. Keep an eye on the shelves, because these will be in and out of the shop before you can say 'More reasons to shop at Morrisons.'

Best buys

Solana Cencibel Tinto, £

Romanian Classic Pinot Noir, £
Barolo 1990, Feyles, ££
Paul Herard Brut, NV, ££

The Newbridge Wine Centre

287 Tettenhall Road, Newbridge, Wolverhampton,   *Tel* (01902) 751022
West Midlands WV6 0LE   *Fax* (01902) 752212

Open Mon–Fri 9–6.30, Sat 10–6   **Closed** Sun and public holidays   **Cards** Access, Amex, Delta, Switch, Visa; business accounts   **Discount** 5% on mixed case; 7% on unmixed case   **Delivery** 5 mile radius of shop and West Midlands (free over £100)   **Glass hire** Free with order   **Tasting and talks** Monthly in shop plus organised outside events   **Cellarage** Not available

The name outside the shop has changed, and the interior has been refurbished, but Pierre Henck is still as firmly at the helm as he has been since the shop opened in 1974. Australian wines continue to be popular with his customers, and, although there may be larger ranges elsewhere, Craigmoor Chardonnay, E & E Black Pepper Shiraz and Cape Mentelle Cabernet/Merlot will provide great satisfaction. Other New World notabilities are the Babich and Hunter's New Zealand wines, the Echeverria wines from Chile, and the Columbia Crest Merlot from Washington State. French bottles to look out for are the Chablis from Droin, burgundies from Bouchard Père et Fils, Alsace from Schlumberger and Bordeaux from Châteaux la Tour de By, Nenin and Suduiraut. CVNE Rioja, German wines from Dr Dahlem and Italian wines from Allegrini and Ascheri are also worth keeping an eye cocked for, while from closer to home come the white wines from Halfpenny Green in Staffordshire.

Best buys

Vin de Pays des Côtes de Gascogne 1993, Lasserre du Haut, £
Coteaux du Languedoc, Château Delranc 1993, £
Morey St Denis 1er Cru La Forge 1987, Société d'Exploitation du Clos de Tart, ££
1993 Hunters Oak-Aged Sauvignon Blanc, ££

Le Nez Rouge

12 Brewery Road, London N7 9NH   *Tel* 0171-609 4711
                                                  Fax 0171-607 0018

Pagendam Pratt & Partners
Thorpe Arch Trading Estate, Wetherby,   *Tel* (01937) 844711
West Yorkshire L23 7BJ   *Fax* (01937) 541058

Open Mon–Fri 9–5.30 **Closed** Sat, Sun, public holidays, Chr and Easter **Cards**
Access, Delta, Switch, Visa; personal and business accounts **Discount** Available
Delivery Free within the M25 area (min 1 case); nationwide mail-order service
available **Glass hire** Not available **Tasting and talks** In conjunction with 6-weekly
offers, plus Spring/Summer and Winter/Autumn tastings **Cellarage** £3 per year, first
year free

After a few years of existing only in name under the umbrella of
parent company Berkmann Wine Cellars, the red nose has finally
re-emerged with Andrew Bewes at the helm as Club Secretary.
Many areas of the selection still have fully to find their feet, notably
the German, Italian and Spanish ranges, and much of the New
World range is confined to the wineries for which Berkmann is
agent: Santa Monica in Chile, Morton Estate in New Zealand,
Norton in Argentina and Beringer in California. The delicious
Coldstream Hills Australian wines are joined by a set from
Rosemount and a lone 1986 Hunter Valley Semillon from Petersons
which is great value at £5.50.

The French list is more diverse, although again the agencies
dominate in certain areas, notably the Muré Alsace but especially
the Duboeuf beaujolais. Lucian Crochet provides tasty Sancerre,
and there are plenty of interesting regional wines. Clarets are good,
but the best range is the burgundies, particularly the whites. The
champagnes from Bruno Paillard and Pommery are also rather
fine.

At present, Le Nez Rouge is little more than Berkmann Wine
Cellars with a retail hat on. Not that the range on offer lacks its
appeal, but it will be interesting to see whether the company
establishes a truly separate identity from Big Brother. In the
meantime, for a taste of Le Nez Rouge, why not try one of the
suggested sample cases, and perhaps add some of the wares of The
Cheese Cellar Co. to your order.

Best buys

Torrontes 1994, Bodega Norton, Argentina, £
1994, Lievland Sauvignon Blanc, South Africa, £
Morgon Jean Descombes 1994, Georges Duboeuf, ££
Black Label Chardonnay 1993, Morton Estate, New Zealand, ££

James Nicholson Wine Merchant

27a Killyleagh Street, Crossgar, Co Down
BT30 9DQ

Tel (01396) 830091
Fax (01396) 830028

Open Mon–Sat 10–7 **Closed** Public holidays, Sun, Chr and Boxing Day, Easter Mon, 12 July **Cards** Access, Visa; business accounts **Discount** By negotiation **Delivery** Free in Northern Ireland (min. 1 case); mail-order available **Glass hire** Free with order **Tasting and talks** Regular in-store tastings and organised events **Cellarage** Free first year, then £3 per case per year

A new format for James Nicholson's list this year, but the same attention to detail and quality which has made his company into one of the best wine-merchants not only in Northern Ireland but in the whole UK. The lack of dead weight is probably the most impressive thing. Other companies may have larger ranges, but, wine-for-wine, the range available in Crossgar is hard to beat.

From Burgundy you'll find not only a large set from Drouhin but also wines from growers such as Vincent Girardin, Claude Maréchal, Michel Forest and Jean-Marc Boillot. Clarets are good, dating back to 1966 Ch. Léoville-Las Cases, and (although a gremlin attacked that page of the new list) we know that there's usually a decent selection of Sauternes available. There are several wines from Colombo, Beaucastel and Jaboulet Aîné among the Rhônes, and the Schlumberger Alsace and the Loire wines of Huet and André Dézat can also be recommended. However, our favourites from France appear in the regional red section: Château Grand Moulin Corbières, Coteaux du Languedoc from Château de Lascaux and the *vins de pays* from Chemins de Bassac.

Serious German Riesling from J. J. Prüm, Gunderloch and Joseph Leitz can be found here, as can top-notch Rioja from Marqués de Murrieta, Remélluri and Martínez Bujanda. The Italian wines from Aldo Conterno, Umani Ronchi and Candido, and all (both) wines in the Portuguese range are good. Ports come from Graham, and Hidalgo provides sherries.

The Meerlust and Drostdy Hof wines from South Africa, Casablanca's from Chile and Norton's from Argentina should all be tried. The pick of the Australian bunch are Garry Farr's Bannockburn wines, Hollick from Coonawarra and Holm Oak from Tasmania. If you miss out on the Cloudy Bay New Zealanders, the Neudorf wines are excellent. Our favourites from California are the wines of Ridge, Saintsbury, Bonny Doon and, for those with plenty of money, the Kistler Chardonnays.

The regular newsletters usually have a regional theme – Bordeaux, Burgundy, southern France, Italy – as well as a featured grape variety, and customer tastings and some delicious-sounding (and -tasting) mixed cases are offered to back these up. Recent attractions at the winemaker dinners held at top local restaurants have included Jean-Marc Boillot, James Halliday and Gérard Jaboulet.

Best buys

Telmo Rodriguez Garnacha (Navarra), £
Mount Auriol Sauvignon Blanc, Vin de Pays, £
Patrick Campbell's Laurel Glen Terra Rosa 1992, ££
Margaux 1990, Château Pontet Chappaz, ££

Nickolls & Perks

37 High Street, Stourbridge, West Midlands DY8 1TA	*Tel* (01384) 394518 *Fax* (01384) 440786

Open Mon–Fri 9–7, Sat 9–6 **Closed** Sun, public holidays **Cards** All accepted; personal and business accounts **Discount** Available **Delivery** Free delivery in West Midlands (min. 6+ cases); nationwide mail-order available **Glass hire** 10p per item plus deposit **Tasting and talks** Monthly talks **Cellarage** Charges vary

The MD of Nickolls & Perks tells us that his company opened in June 1970, although the logo says 'Established 1797'. We forgive this discrepancy, because this is one of the country's best traditional independent wine-merchants. You will find a clutch of wines from 'newer' regions, and a particularly good set of Riojas, but the main reasons for dealing with the company are its exceptional Bordeaux range and selections of champagne, burgundy and port that are almost as good. The range of claret is vast, whether you're looking for such affordable fare as Châteaux Liversan, Larose-Trintaudon or Sociando-Mallet or the classiest of the classed growths. Much of it is available by the bottle rather than by the case – yes, you can visit the seventeenth- century cellars in Stourbridge and actually touch these bottles! One of the best things about it is that it belongs to the company. Those whose fingers were burned by various merchants going belly-up will find the company as reliable as any for *en primeur* purchases.

The Pierre Ponnelle burgundies from the late 1940s, will have their fans, but those whose palates crave something fresher may care to wet them with the reds from Rossignol-Trapet, Domaine Moillard and Lucien Boillot. Kopke Colheita ports date back to 1937, vintage ports to Cockburn 1904, with a good selection from recent vintages. The thrust of Nickolls & Perks may not be to everyone's liking, but lovers of traditional fine wines will find excitement hard to repress.

Best buys

1993 Orvieto Classico Amabile, Bigi, £
Corbières 1993, Château de Bellevue, £
St Emilion Grand Cru 1989, Château Rolland-Maillet, ££
1993 Cloudy Bay Chardonnay, ££

Nicolas UK Ltd

6 Fulham Road, London SW3 6HG   *Tel* 0171-584 1450
(8 stores in London and the South-East, 300 in France)   *Fax* 0171-589 1807

Open Mon–Sat 10–10, Sun 12–2, 7–9   **Closed** Public holidays, Chr Day, Good Fri
Cards All accepted; personal and business accounts   **Discount** Negotiable   **Delivery**
Within London area   **Glass hire** Not available   **Tasting and talks** Available
Cellarage Not available

The eight Nicolas shops in and around London give Brits a chance to try what the French really do adore. You will find some 'foreign' wines (as one shop manager put it) on the shelves, and these are generally good, but going to these shops for anything other than French wine is rather like eating fish and chips in a Chinese restaurant.

Bordeaux reds and (sweet) whites are theoretically available in quantity and date back to the last century, but if you do want some of those more special wines, there is a chance that they may have to be ordered for you. Burgundies are slightly less good, and tend to concentrate on wines from Bouchard Père et Fils and other merchants, rather than from growers. Rhône offerings include Lirac from Domaine de la Mordorée and various wines from Delas and Jaboulet Aîné, while Loires come from Domaine de Chatenoy and Domaine des Roches Neuves. Schlumberger provides Alsace, while Provence wines come from Domaine Ott. Other regional wines of note include Château Simone Palette, Bandol from Domaine de Terrebrune and Château Peyros Madiran. There's also an eye-catching range of own-label *vins de pays* from Languedoc-Roussillon. Famous-name champagnes complete the range.

Prices can be on the high side, but special offers over the past year have lived up to their name (three bottles for the price of two on a range of *cru bourgeois* clarets; 20% off all champagnes for a limited period, regardless of quantity). We're pretty sure that the eight English shops would not survive without the 300 on the opposite side of the Channel, but we'd still recommend you to take a look around and experience some genuinely polite and efficient service – and free gift-wrapping.

Best buys

Nicolas Vin de Pays des Côtes de Gascogne blanc 1993, £
Vin de Pays d'Oc 1994, Domaine les Tuilleries d'Affiac, £
Cahors 1992, Clos de la Coutale, ££
Saint Véran les Ombrelles, 1994, ££

Noble Rot Wine Warehouses

18 Market Street, Bromsgrove, Hereford and Worcester B61 8DA	*Tel* (01527) 575606 *Fax* (01527) 574091

Open Mon–Fri 10–7; Sat 9.30–6.30 **Closed** Sun (exc late Nov and Dec), public holidays **Cards** Access, Delta, Switch, Visa; business accounts **Discount** By negotiation **Delivery** Free within 20-mile radius (min. 1 case), otherwise at cost **Glass hire** Free, breakages charged for **Tasting and talks** Major tastings in May and Nov; occasional tutored tastings **Cellarage** Not available

Why the plural in the company name we don't know. We do know that Julie Wyres' and Peter Weston's approach to the wine business is an admirable one. Pretence is refreshingly absent, and the pair continue to find new avenues to explore. Moreover, they're prepared to listen to what customers have to suggest; hence the recent decision to move to sales by the bottle, rather than just in dozens.

Not that finding twelve good bottles on the shelves is a problem, nor will they cost an arm and a leg, since prices seldom stray over £10. French country wines from Domaine de Maubet and Château de Grézan in Faugères are good value, as is the Turckheim Alsace range. Chablis from Simonnet-Febvre and Bernard Legland are the best of the smallish burgundy selection, while the Loire wines of Chapelle de Cray and Henry Pellé are also tasty. Good value from Spain appears in the shape of the Navarra Las Campañas wines and the Solana Valdepeñas, and the Portuguese Aliança range is similarly affordable. Italian highlights are the Alasia whites, especially the Muscat, and the reds from Santadi and La Parrina. And do try the Hungarians from Château Megyer.

The New World range is solid rather than exciting, but we'd point out the Riddoch Australians, Lincoln New Zealanders and Bon Courage South Africans. Barbadillo sherry and ports from Ferreira and Dow are also available.

A monthly newsletter keeps customers in touch with special offers and events, including the two major tastings each year, in May and November. However, bottles are always available for tasting in the shop, so why not pop down? It's next to Wilson's Pet Centre (the hair of the dog takes on a new meaning!).

Best buys

Minervois 1991, Domaine des Combelles, £
Château Boulay 1994, Montlouis, £
Brouilly 1993, Benoît Trichard, ££
Bon Courage Noble Late Harvest 1994, ££

The Nobody Inn

Doddiscombsleigh, nr Exeter, Devon EX6 7PS

Tel (01647) 252394
Fax (01647) 252978

Open Mon–Sat and public holidays 11–11, Sun 12–10.30 (phone for appointment between 3–6) **Closed** Chr Day **Cards** Access, Amex, Delta, Switch, Visa; personal and business accounts **Discount** 5% on 1 case **Delivery** Free within 15-mile radius, elsewhere approx. £4.90 per case; nationwide mail-order available **Glass hire** Free with order (min. 1 case) **Tasting and talks** Monthly tutored tastings; daily blind wine-tasting competition **Cellarage** Not available

Even without the wines, the Nobody Inn is a jolly decent pub. The food is good (particularly the Devon cheeses), the dozens of whiskies are very impressive, and the beer isn't half bad either. But the most important reason for visiting is to see the eccentric and enthusiastic collection of wines. This is a range put together by a wine-lover, not a marketing man. That wine-lover is Nick Borst-Smith, who for 25 years has been piling up wines in every nook and cranny in the pub – to the point where precise stock levels of certain wines are difficult to determine. You'll find classics ancient and modern here, and at all price levels: Hugel and Trimbach Alsace, burgundy from Jean Thévenet, Domaine des Deux Roches and Domaine de la Romanée-Conti ('barbecue wine for the lottery winner'), several clarets at different stages of maturity and Rhône wines from Alain Graillot, Guigal and Guy de Barjac. The Loire is something of a speciality, with the accent firmly on Chenin rather than Sauvignon Blanc. Lovers of sweet wine in particular will appreciate a range going back to a 1935 Bonnezeaux and including several wines from the fabulous '89 and '90 vintages. The regional French range is set to expand, but for now the wines of Mas de Daumas Gassac, Domaine Cauhapé and Alain Brumont will do very nicely, thank you.

Austrian wines come from Willi Opitz, English from Boze Down and Pilton Manor, and from Germany, in which Nick discerns a 'rekindling of interest', Schloss Johannisberg and Dr Loosen provide the goods. The Italian selection is on the pricey side, but all are worth trying, especially the range of 1985 Super-Tuscans. The range from Spain is generally less interesting, although Remélluri Rioja and four vintages of Torres Milmanda Chardonnay are available. And if your experience of Greek wine has hitherto been one of anguish, try the Hatzimichalis Merlot.

From New Zealand the Wairau River and Martinborough Vineyards offerings are good; the best from Chile come from Viña Casablanca, and Argentinian wines come from Weinert, Norton and Navarro Correas. The South African range, consisting of Boschendal, Warwick, Allesverloren and others, should be expanding shortly. Those in search of cheapies in the Californian list will be disappointed, but those looking for great wine will find plenty of it from Mayacamas, Kistler, Ridge, Dunn, Duckhorn and Silver Oak. The Australian section is similarly impressive: five vintages of Grange, the rare and classy wines of Giaconda, plus other delights from Cassegrain, Rockford and Dalwhinnie.

Since sweet wines are one of Nobody Inn's fortes you'll also find numerous liqueur Muscats, as well as Sauternes from Ch. d'Yquem and Ch. Rieussec, Joseph Phelps Late Harvest Riesling, all those Loires and a string of the sweeter German wines. Not much imagination is needed to put together a rather high-class wine and cheese evening.

Best buys

Mavrodaphne of Patras, Tsantalis, £
1994 Moscato D'Asti, Araldica Vini Piemontesi, £
1992 Cape Mentelle Shiraz, Margaret River, Australia, ££
1990 Ridge Chardonnay, Santa Cruz Mountains, ££

Oddbins

Head Office
31-33 Weir Road, London SW19 8UG

Tel 0181-944 4400
Fax 0181-944 4411

201 branches

Open Mon–Sat 10–9; Sun 12–3, 7–9 **Closed** Chr, Boxing and New Year's Days
Cards Access, Amex, Visa; business accounts **Discount** 5% on mixed case; 10% on mixed case from Sat tastings; 7 for 6 on sparkling wines and champagne **Delivery** Free in local area (min. 1 case or £50) **Glass hire** Free, returnable deposit required
Tasting and talks Every Sat in-store; tutored tastings given periodically **Cellarage** Not available

The Victoria Wine Cellars wine fair at a smart London hotel? The Majestic wine tour of Australia? Tutored customer tastings by famous winemakers in a branch of Wine Rack? It just doesn't ring true, does it? It does with Oddbins. Great wines and staff who not only are interested in wine but, despite working more hours than a junior doctor for rather less money, also want to sell it to you – these have kept Oddbins ahead of any serious competition.

The range from Australia is still one of the best around, if not the best. The Chilean range is also hard to beat, but then Oddbins did latch on to the newer, more innovative styles of winemaking quite a long time before anyone else. A much smaller selection from New Zealand nonetheless offers impressive fare from Waipara Springs, Martinborough Vineyards and Dashwood. The South African wines listed are increasing in number, with the Stellenzicht 'Block Series' offering particularly good value. The Californian range has the very affordable Ravenscourt wines as well as headier fare from Ridge, Bonny Doon and Franciscan.

There's plenty of good Spanish wine to be had, particularly from Navarra, and Müller-Catoir is still the highlight of a little-changed German range. The Italian list remains uncharacteristically ordinary, though only by comparison with the standards of Oddbins' offerings from other parts of the world. Still, the Gaetane Carron wines are good at the cheaper end of the range, and the Lamaione Merlot should cost twice as much as it does.

France is much better represented. Among the Loire wines, Gitton provides characterful Sancerre, while the Vouvray from Bernard Fouquet's Domaine des Aubuisières is hard to beat. Alsace wines (Ralph Steadman's latest subject in the chatty list) come from Hugel, Schoffit and Théo Faller, while the wines of Réméjeanne and Richaud's Cairanne are far from basic Côtes-du-Rhône. You'll find more good value in the regional range, and our favourites are the wines from Châteaux de Lascaux, Villerambert-Julien and Paul Blanc. The expansion of the claret range in the wake of the 1989 and 1990 vintages has slowed somewhat (due to lack of good wines), but the progress in the burgundy list continues. There are still some of the fabulous 1992 whites around, plus some good 1993s.

Those in search of finer wines used to be forced to look elsewhere. No longer. There are now six branches of Oddbins Fine Wine, packed to the gills with brilliant wines. Nor does the list confine itself to big names; label-watchers will not be disappointed by the many clarets and burgundies, but some of the stars of the past year are virtually unknown on these shores: Rocca Albino Barbaresco, La Jota Cabernet Sauvignon, Green & Red Zinfandel, Rutz Pinot Noir. Add to all this great beers, great whiskies, tastings every Saturday and some of the best offers available on champagne . . . it's no wonder that Oddbins is still the most exciting place to buy wine in the country.

Best buys

Costières de Nîmes 1993, Paul Blanc, £
Palacio de la Vega Cabernet 1993, Tempranillo, £
1993 Rheboskloof Chardonnay, ££
Château de Lascaux 1993, Les Noble Pierres, ££

Parfrements

68 Cecily Road, Cheylesmore, Coventry,	*Tel* (01203) 503646
West Midlands CV3 5LA	*Fax* (01203) 506028

Open 24 hours a day, every day, all year **Cards** personal and business accounts
Discount Available **Delivery** within 15-mile radius; mail-order available **Glass hire**
Free with order **Tasting and talks** On request, groups only **Cellarage** Not available

Quite how much licence there is in Gerald Gregory's offer of 'the opportunity to taste any wine up to £16 per bottle before purchase' is not clear. Suffice it to say that after one sip of many of the wines in his range it would be hard not to want to try some more at home. This is a compact selection, which shows a discerning palate. New World wines run to less than twenty, but include Gundlach-Bundschu's Zinfandel, Dalwhinnie Shiraz and a New Zealand pair from Jackson Estate. We're not sure who makes three of the Italian quartet, but we do know and like the Riojas from La Rioja Alta and the German wines from Graf Matuschka- Greiffenklau. From France, there's Alsace from Dopff & Irion, Marcel Juge's Cornas, Ménétou-Salon from Henry Pellé and a decent range of regional wines. Clarets are mainly good *cru bourgeois* wines and include five vintages of Ch. Cissac. The largest section in the range is the burgundies. Whites include Chassagne-Montrachet from Michel Colin and Chablis from Durup, while reds come from Georges Roumier and Prieur-Brunet, with André Pelletier's Juliénas also available. Add ports from Churchill Graham and sherries from Manuel de Argueso and that's about it. It may be a small selection but we'd very happily drink anything listed – even without trying it first.

Best buys

1993 Kenyon Ruby Cabernet, £
1991 L.A. Cetto Petite Sirah, £
1987 Viña Ardanza Rioja Reserva, La Rioja Alta, ££
1988 Churchills Traditional LBV Port, ££

Pavilion Wine Co

Finsbury Circus Gardens, London EC2M 7AB

Tel 0171-628 8224
Fax 0171-628 6205

Case sales only **Open** Mon–Fri 8.30–8.30 **Closed** Sat, Sun, public holidays **Cards** Access, Amex, Delta, Switch, Visa; personal and business accounts **Discount** 2% on 6–11 cases; 2.75% on 12–25 cases **Delivery** Nationwide 1 case £8; 2 cases £6; 3 cases £3; mail-order available **Glass hire** Not available **Tasting and talks** Annual tasting for all customers **Cellarage** £7.50 +VAT per case per year inc. insurance

No, Pink Floyd fans, it's not *that* David Gilmour. We're not sure whether this one plays the guitar but he has learned a thing or two in his thirty years in the wine trade. This is the classic 'small but perfectly formed' range; the number of wines listed barely stretches to a hundred, but quality is very much to the fore. You have to buy by the case, although there's the chance to buy just a bottle of any of the range if you consume it in the wine bar (same address as the office – there's no shop). There are only around ten New World wines, but they come from the likes of Bonny Doon, Au Bon Climat, Cloudy Bay and Cullens. Rioja is from Martínez Bujanda, Soave from Pieropan, sherry from Hidalgo. Languedoc wines of note come from Mas de Daumas Gassac and Domaine Teisserenc, while Rhône reds and whites are from Domaine du Vieux Télégraphe and Jean-Yves Liotaud. Loires to watch out for come from the Soulez brothers and Lucien Thomas, while Bernard Staehlé provides Alsace wines. Among the burgundies (the largest range) are Vincent Girardin's Maranges, Jayer-Gilles' Nuits-St-Georges and Manciat-Poncet's Pouilly-Fuissé.

Best buys

Corbières 1992, Domaine Baillat, £
Côte Roannaise 1993, Domaine Picatier, £
Bourgogne Blanc 1993, Domaine Darnat, ££
Vin de Pays des Coteaux des Baronnies 1993, Domaine du Rieu Frais, Viognier, ££

Thos Peatling

Head office
Westgate House, Bury St Edmunds, Suffolk IP33 1QS   *Tel* (01284) 755948
(27 branches throughout East Anglia, including   *Fax* (01284) 705795
Peatlings Wine Centre in London)

Open Varies from store to store **Cards** Access, Amex, Visa; personal and business
accounts **Discount** 5% on mixed case **Delivery** Free in East Anglia and London;
nationwide mail-order service available **Glass hire** Free with order **Tasting and
talks** Weekly at most shops; evening tastings by invitation; tutored tastings
Cellarage Free

There seems to be more to this East Anglian chain every time we
take a look. The smart new catalogue still contains plenty of claret,
with the first growths on display next to several lesser wines that
have been bottled in the company's own cellars. The producers in
Burgundy who are willing to send barrels for bottling in Bury St
Edmunds are of a higher calibre: Etienne Sauzet, Lucien Boillot,
Jean-Paul Droin and others. Rhônes are good, and include great
Côtes-du-Rhône from Domaine Gramenon, while the regional
selection features a real star in the shape of Domaine Maby's
Coteaux de Cèze red. Alsace is from the Caves de Benniwihr,
Vacheron Sancerre appears in the Loire range, and characterful
champagne is provided by Brusson.

German wines include Egon Müller's Scharzhofberg from the
Saar and several other wines we'd tell you more about if the list
mentioned who'd made them. The Italian list is very sound, with
Soave from Pieropan, Valpolicella from Allegrini and the Ser
Gioveto Super-Tuscan. New in the Spanish range are some fine
Riojas from Viña Valoria, while Quinta da Foz de Arouce from
Beiras heads an impressive set of Portuguese reds.

We commented in last year's *Guide* that the New World range
lacked excitement. The arrival of new ranges from two Australian
producers may not warrant major fanfares, but the wines of Peter
Dennis in McLaren Vale and the Hanging Rock winery in Macedon
are exceptionally good. The Californians from Bouchaine, QC Fly
and Pine Ridge are also worth trying, as are Paul Thomas's
Washington State wines. The Chilean bottles are decent, and the
South Africans from Fairview and Thelema are even better.

The description of a day's activities at the Peatling's Wine
Festival, which takes place one weekend each September, reads
like a leaf out of a modern-day Pepys's diary. Rest assured that,
though it is possible, it is not obligatory to attend two tutored
tastings, eat a huge meal and order several cases of wine, with
pauses only for beer and champagne.

Best buys

Chardonnay 1993, Vin de Pays d'Oc (UK-bottled), £
Vin de Pays des Coteaux de Cèze 1991, Domaine Maby Rouge, £
1994 Jim Jim Sauvignon Blanc, Hanging Rock Winery, ££
Pessac-Léognan 1990, Château Lafargue, ££

Penistone Court Wine Cellars

The Railway Station, Penistone,	*Tel* (01226) 766037
Sheffield, South Yorkshire S30 6HG	*Fax* (01226) 767310

Case sales only **Open** Mon–Fri 10-6; Sat 10–3 **Closed** Sun and public holidays
Cards Personal and business accounts **Discount** Negotiable on large orders
Delivery Free to Yorkshire, Lancashire, Derbyshire (min. 1 case), other areas charged
at courier cost; nationwide mail-order service available **Glass hire** Free with order
Tasting and talks Regular testings **Cellarage** Not available

The bulk of Chris Ward's business may be wholesale, but private
customers visiting his premises are made most welcome. You'll find
a large range of champagnes from famous names, as well as
competition in the form of Austrian wines from Schlumberger.

Burgundies are predominantly from merchants such as Louis
Latour, Bichot, Moillard and Bouchard Père et Fils, while most of
the Rhônes come from Delas. Of the Loires, we'd jump at the
Joseph Mellot Sancerre, and take a gamble on the mature Muscadet
from Château de Chasseloir. Claret stocks turn over with some
rapidity, but there should be something good to suit all palates. As
well as those Schlumberger sparklers, you'll find still Austrian
wines from Lenz Moser and Anton Wöber; Bert Simon and
Deinhard lend German interest. From Italy look out for Banfi's
Tuscan wines and the eminently quaffable Cavalchina range from
the Veneto. A strong Spanish set comes from Martínez Bujanda,
CVNE, Vega Sicilia, Ochoa and Viñas del Vero.

The Australian list is reasonable – Brown Bros, Cape Mentelle,
Tyrrell's, Piper's Brook – but do try the lesser-known South African
wines from Rozendal, Eikendal, Taillefert and others. Babich and
Grove Mill provide New Zealand wines, while the Californian
range has mature wines from Sonoma-Cutrer, Swanson,
Renaissance and Franciscan, which have probably been on the
shelves rather longer than Chris would like. Why not pay a visit
and relieve him of some of them?

Best buys

Côtes du Ventoux 'Escarlate' Delas 1993, £
Barbera del Piemonte, Giordano 1993, £
Anton Wöber Riesling, 1993, ££
Mounier Bleue, Austria, ££

Philglass & Swiggot

21 Northcote Road, Battersea, London
SW11 1NG

Tel 0171-924 4494

Open Mon–Sat 11–9, Sun 12–3, 7–9 **Closed** Public holidays, Mon 11–5 **Cards** All accepted; business accounts **Discount** 5% on mixed cases, 7% sparkling wines, 15% unmixed champagne **Delivery** Free London SW postcodes and West End (min. 1 case); mail-order available **Glass hire** Free with order (min. 2 case) **Tasting and talks** Regular in-store tastings and annual summer tasting – tutored tastings for wine clubs regularly undertaken **Cellarage** Not available

Time was when this friendly Battersea merchant was the place to come for a great set of Australian wines but not much else. Antipodeans are still very much the speciality, but they are now outnumbered by wines from other parts of the world, and Karen Rogers has shown that she can spot good'uns regardless of their origin. From the Americas, you'll find wines from Alamos Ridge in Argentina and Villard in Chile, and Californians from Acacia and Duxoup. Hamilton Russell and Meerlust appear in the South African range. Those as yet unconvinced by Austrian wines should try the selection from Freie Weingärtner Wachau, particularly the Riesling, and further good Riesling appears in the shape of the Dr Loosen's German offerings. The Italian range includes bottles from Franz Haas and La Parrina, while the Enate wines from Somontano top the Spanish range. The French selection is small but carefully chosen. It includes burgundies from Armand Rousseau and Louis Carillon, Bordeaux from Châteaux Pitray and Rahoul, Alain Paret's Rhônes and great *vin de pays* from Les Chemins de Bassac and Château de Jau.

However, the Antipodean range puts all others to shame. Notable New Zealand wines come from Rothbury, Palliser, Giesen and The Brothers. The Australian offerings range from the good-value David Wynn wines, through Montara and Mitchelton, up to Henschke, Mountadam and Cape Mentelle, with great fizz coming from Peter Rumball and Green Point. The mail-order operation is just getting off the ground, and those keen to be first in the queue for the few cases of Grange Hermitage and Hill of Grace that occasionally appear should get themselves on the mailing list pronto.

Best buys

1994 Drostdy Hof Chenin Blanc, £
Vin de Pays d'Oc Merlot 1994, Bellefontaine, £
1993 Riesling, Freie Weingärtner Wachau, ££
1993 Mitchelton III Grenache/Mourvèdre/Syrah, ££

Christopher Piper Wines

1 Silver Street, Ottery St Mary, Devon   *Tel* (01404) 814139
EX11 1DB   *Fax* (01404) 812100

Open Mon–Fri 9–1, 2–5.30; Sat 9–1, 2.30–4.30   **Closed** Sun, public holidays   **Cards**
Access, Visa; personal and business accounts   **Discount** 5% on 12 mixed bottles, 10%
on 36+   **Delivery** South-West 1–3 cases £6+VAT, 4+ cases free; UK 1–5 cases
£6+VAT, 6+ cases free   **Glass hire** Free   **Tasting and talks** Every Saturday in store
plus 5–6pm every day; 4 main tastings per year plus 2 wine weekends   **Cellarage**
£4.20+VAT per case per year

If you mistrust scrawny wine-merchants who look as if they only drink the stuff they sell once a week (and then only one glassful with a dry crust), then Christopher Piper is your type of man. Not that he's portly. He's ... well, jolly. He looks as if he enjoys being a wine-merchant (and a winemaker, at Château des Tours in Brouilly) very much. He's also very good at both.

Château des Tours takes pride of place in a decent range of beaujolais, but better still is the range from further north in Burgundy. Côte de Beaune whites come from Paul Garaudet and Gérard Chavy, Chablis from Pinson, while reds are from Rossignol-Trapet, Tollot-Beaut and Comte Armand. Clarets include decent *cru bourgeois* wines plus a manageable set of classed growths. Excellent-value wines from Domaines Virginie, St Hilaire and de l'Aigle can be found among the regional French wines. Rhônes come from Domaine des Entrefaux and Bernard Faurie, while Loire wines include Serge Laporte's Sancerre, Masson Blondelet Pouilly Fumé and the heady sweet Coteaux du Layon of Domaine des Maurières. Louis Gisselbrecht provides Alsace wines, while champagne comes from Gremillet and several of the major houses.

Ottery St Mary is experiencing an upturn in demand for German wines, and Mr P. obliges with excellent Riesling from Louis Guntrum, von Kesselstatt and Josef Leitz (try a comparison with the Austrian Riesling from Malat-Brundlmayer). Masi Valpolicella and Ceretto Barolo form just a small part of the interesting Italian range; the Spanish selection consists mostly of CVNE Riojas, and J. M. da Fonseca wines dominate the Portuguese.

Among the Californian items are Joe Phelps's delicious Viognier and Syrah, as well as Pinot Noir from Calera and a full range from Beringer. From further south come the Monte Chilean and Norton Argentinian wines. You'll also find a very worthwhile set from Australia, with Cullens, Henschke and Coldstream Hills standing out in particular, as well as New Zealand wines from Highfield Estate and Hunters. From South Africa the wines of Neetlingshof, Danie de Wet and Kanonkop are also good.

The bimonthly *Noble Rot* newsletter gives details of special offers, tastings plus potted views of what is happening in the wine world. Entertaining, forthright and full of good wine (a bit like Mr Piper himself).

Best buys

Vin de Pays de L'Hérault, Domaine Guillaume Delcoeur, £
Namaqua Colombard 1995, Vredendal, £
Bourgogne Blanc Chardonnay 1993, Domaine Gérard Chavy, ££
Juliénas 1994, Château de la Bottiére, ££

Terry Platt Wine Merchant

Head Office
Ferndale Road, Llandudno Junction, Gwynedd   *Tel* (01492) 592971
LL31 9NT   *Fax* (01492) 592196
World of Wine
29 Mostyn Avenue, Craig Y Don, Llandudno,   *Tel* (01492) 872997
Gwynedd LL30 1DQ

Open (Terry Platt) Mon–Fri 8–5.30; (World of Wine) Mon–Sat 10–8, Sun 12–2, Pub hols 10–8 **Closed** (Terry Platt) pub hols **Cards** Access, Switch, Visa; personal and business accounts **Discount** By negotiation **Delivery** Free within local area (min. 1 case); out of area at cost **Glass hire** Free with order, otherwise 25p per dozen **Tasting and talks** Held at World of Wine **Cellarage** Not available

After last year's whopping 110% increase in New World sales, Jeremy 'I live for food and wine' Platt has noticed slight resistance to the wines of New Zealand and Australia. However, this hasn't prevented wines from Hunters and Vavasour being added to the range from the former, nor Rockford and Craigmoor joining the Pipers Brook and Cape Mentelle wines in the latter. South Africa is booming, and customers will find Blue Rock and Mouton-Excelsior wines on offer. Californians come from Au Bon Climat, Bonny Doon and El Camino Real, while a large set from Canada includes the wares of Mission Hill, Henry of Pelham and Stonechurch Vineyards. South America offers the Montes wines from Chile, Castel Pujol from Uruguay and Trapiche from Argentina.

More traditional fare appears in the French selection, which is solid rather than exciting, although the Alsace wines (Schlumberger, Trimbach, Dopff au Moulin) and the regional selection, particularly the Tissot duo from Arbois, are worth a look. You'll find several drinkable clarets, not many of which cost above £20, a good range of beaujolais from the Eventail de Vignerons Producteurs, burgundies from Louis Latour, Antonin Rodet and Machard de Gramont, and Bruno Paillard champagne.

Spain offers plenty of Riojas to choose from, plus the good-value Viñas del Vero Somontano wines. The three Portuguese wines are all good, and the Monnow Valley Welsh wines are stocked for more than just patriotic reasons. Von Kesselstatt provides the pick of the German selection, and from Italy the Pighin wines from Friuli-Venezia Giulia stand out.

Visitors to Llandudno are assured of a warm welcome by Jeremy and his staff – 'after all, they pay the bills!'

Best buys

L. A. Cetto Petite Syrah 1991, £
1993 Viñas del Vero Chenin Blanc, £
Champagne Bruno Paillard Première Cuveé, NV, ££
1992 Le Sophiste, Bonny Doon, ££

Playford Ros

| Middle Park House, Sowerby, Thirsk, | *Tel* (01845) 526777 |
| North Yorkshire YO7 3AH | *Fax* (01845) 526888 |

Case sales only   Open Mon–Sat 8–7   **Closed** Sun, public holidays, Chr, Boxing and New Year's Days   **Cards** Access, Visa; personal and business accounts   **Discount** 5% for early settlement (within one week of delivery), 2.5% for orders of 6+ mixed cases   **Delivery** Free within Yorkshire, Derbyshire, Durham boundaries (min. 1 case); mail-order service available   **Glass hire** Free, refundable deposit required   **Tasting and talks** Restaurant customers, one large annual tasting, 7–8 themed tastings throughout the year   **Cellarage** Free

---

The latest Playford Ros list has a decidedly juvenile air about it. A young man of no more than eight months old graces the cover, while the first spread is devoted to pictures of members of staff at tender ages. Those seeking wines that will age as gracefully as the staff will find much to choose from, as well as several bottles for more immediate consumption. There's Chablis from Daniel Dampt, plus other burgundies from Domaine Leflaive, Louis Latour and a clutch of top growers. Rhône wines include Châteauneuf from Domaine Grand Tinel and a range from Chapoutier, while Alsace is provided by Hubert Krick. There's also a good set of Loire wines and *vins de pays* from Hugh Ryman and others. In the Bordeaux section Ch. de Sours provides excellent-value red, white and rosé, and other wines range from some tasty *cru bourgeois* châteaux right up to Ch. Pétrus.

The Spanish, German and Italian representation is much sparser, although good wines abound. South Africans of note come from Dieu Donné, Hamilton Russell and Klein Constantia, Chileans from Montes and Argentinians from Weinert. In the North American range, Domaine Drouhin's Pinot, Cline Cellars Zinfandel and the Renaissance wines are all very good. A fine set of Australian bottles includes Yarra Yering, Mountadam and Grant Burge, while similarly impressive New Zealand fare comes from St Nesbit, Cloudy Bay and Redwood Valley.

This is an impressive range that wine-lovers from North Yorkshire and further afield should consider carefully. The bulk of the Playford Ros business is wholesale, but there is always one of those youngsters on hand to help assemble your mixed case.

Best buys

Castillo di Montblanc Blanco 1994, Conca del Barbera, £
1994 Stoney Vale Cabernet/Shiraz, £
1989 Diezmo Rioja Crianza, ££
Tokay Pinot Gris Herrenweg 1993, Hubert Krick, ££

Le Pont de la Tour

36d Shad Thames, Butler's Wharf, London   *Tel* 0171-403 3403
SE1 2YE   *Fax* 0171-403 0267

Open Mon–Sat 12–8.30, Sun 12–3, public holidays 12–8.30 **Closed** Chr, Boxing, Easter and New Year's Days **Cards** All accepted **Discount** 5% on mixed case **Delivery** Free within M25 **Glass hire** Hired by dozens, £1 per glass **Tasting and talks** Themed tastings alternate months **Cellarage** Not available

---

The Le Pont de la Tour shop is actually the cellar of the eponymous restaurant. For those interested in comparing prices, the 1993 Ch. Haut Rian Bordeaux Blanc is £4.95 in the shop and £13.95 in the restaurant, and the 1989 Bannockburn Shiraz £12.50 in the shop and £27.50 in the restaurant.

We would gladly buy our wine at the shop though. It has a broad range that concentrates mainly on France but also takes in great wines from other parts of the world. Good Australian bottles come from Mad Fish Bay and Balgownie, California is represented by Shafer, Matanzas Creek and Kistler, and Louisvale and Simonsig provide South Africans. Among a good set of Italian wines are the delicious Vigneto Rancia from Felsina Berardenga and the Trentino wines of Alois Lageder. Top Spanish reds come from La Rioja Alta and Vega Sicilia, while similarly serious German fare is provided by Max Ferd. Richter and J. J. Prüm. Willi Opitz's amazing sweet Austrian whites are also available, plus Château Musar from 1967.

Champagne-lovers will find plenty of mature wines dating back to the early 1960s, as well as fresher fizz from Billecart-Salmon and Louis Roederer. Top names provide the wines from Alsace, the Rhône and the Loire. The same can be said of the burgundy range, with producers such as Robert Ampeau, Bruno Clair, Sauzet and

Dujac all contributing wines. The Bordeaux range is brilliant, whether you're a lottery winner or just want a decent bottle to go with the steak-and-kidney pudding (1990 Château des Annereaux would be perfect).

Best buys

House Red, Domaines Virginie 1993, £
Château Haut Rian Bordeaux Blanc 1993, £
Santenay 'Clos de la Confrèrie' 1992, Girardin, ££
Balgownie Estate Cabernet Sauvignon, ££

Portland Wine Company

16 North Parade, Sale, Greater Manchester M33 3JS	*Tel* 0161-962 8752
	Fax 0161-905 1291
152a Ashley Road, Hale, Greater Manchester WA15 9SA	*Tel* 0161-928 0357
82 Chester Road, Macclesfield, Cheshire SK11 8DL	*Tel* (01625) 616147

Open Mon–Sat 10–10, Sun 12–3, 7–9.30, public holidays **Cards** Access, Switch, Visa; personal and business accounts **Discount** 10% on mixed cases, mixed case of 6 wines 5%, beers 5% **Delivery** Open to negotiation or normal postal rates; small scale mail-order service **Glass hire** Free with order **Tasting and talks** Regular evening tutored tastings; 3 large events a year **Cellarage** Not available

---

The paucity of good wine-merchants in Manchester city centre is more than compensated for by the presence of Geoff Dickinson's mini-chain on the southern outskirts of the city. The Nelson shop has been closed ('too far away and too many shopping centres'), but the other three shops are doing very well, thank you.

It's not difficult to see why. Whether you're after the oldest from the Old World or the newest of the New, you'll find it here. Last year's Bordeaux offer featured 1953 Ch. d'Yquem and 1964 Ch. Latour as well as many more affordable wines from the vintages of the late 1980s. Burgundy fans will find the good, old-fashioned wines of Vallet Frères, Olivier Merlin's great Mâcon and (if you time it right) brilliant Meursault from Comtes Lafon. The Rhône, Loire and Alsace ranges are small but full of interesting stuff, while from other parts of France, you'll find Domaine de Maubet Côtes de Gascogne and Mas de Daumas Gassac from the Hérault.

Italian highlights are Altesino's Brunello, Foradori's Teroldego and Pieropan's Soave, while the Quinta de la Rosa and Cartuxa reds are good in the Portuguese range. From Spain come three vintages of Jean León Cabernet, the ubiquitous Torres wines and several Campo Viejo Riojas. Fans of the more exotic might care to try instead the mature Moldovan reds or the eight vintages of Château Musar from the Lebanon.

In the New World range, you'll find excellent New Zealand wines from Vavasour, Goldwater and Martinborough Vineyards and South Africans from Meerlust, Rustenberg and Hamilton Russell. The Echeverria and Villard Chilean wines are highly acceptable, as are the rather more expensive Californians from Au Bon Climat, Newton and Bonny Doon. The love affair with Australia continues, and the selection features some of the country's best and most characterful producers. We'd choose the wines from Henschke, Grant Burge, Penley Estate, Yarra Yering and Cape Mentelle.

Tutored tastings are held frequently, and the £5–10 charged for these is very reasonable. Those who miss the major tastings two or three times a year at the nearby Bowdon Hotel will always find wines available for tasting on Saturdays at the Hale shop. If you need more information about any wine, genial Geoff and his crew are on hand to assist, or you can tap into the VinDATA database and cellar-management system for a computerised guide to the world of wine.

Best buys

Sauvignon Blanc 1994, Villard, £
1993 David Wynn Shiraz, £
St Véran Les Terres Noires 1994, Domaine des Deux Roches, ££
1992 Martinborough Vineyards, Pinot Noir, ££

Quellyn Roberts

15 Watergate Street, Chester, Cheshire CH1 2LB	*Tel* (01244) 310455
	Fax (01244) 346704

Open Mon–Sat 8.45–5.45 **Closed** Sun, public holidays **Cards** Access, Amex, Switch, Visa; business and personal accounts **Discount** 5% off mixed cases **Delivery** Free within 25-mile radius of Chester (min. 1 cases); nationwide mail-order available **Glass hire** Free **Tasting and talks** Saturday tastings; tutored tastings organised **Cellarage** Available to customers only; £4 + VAT per case per year

Ships from Oporto and Bordeaux no longer sail up the River Dee to Chester, as they did when Paul Quellyn Roberts' great-grandfather established his wine-merchant's business in 1863. The closure of Watergate Street to traffic has meant that wines are now stored in a new warehouse, but the shop remains in the 12th-century cellars that have been the company's home for over 130 years. There's plenty of Bordeaux from good recent vintages. Chablis is provided by Alain Geoffroy, beaujolais by Duboeuf, and there are other burgundies from Louis Latour and Robert Arnoux. Alsace comes from the Turckheim co-op, Loire wines from de Ladoucette and Marc Brédif.

The Italian, Spanish and German ranges are unimpressive, and Portuguese table wines are totally absent, although there is some compensation in the form of some good vintage and tawny ports. The New World selection is much better. You'll find Australians from Yalumba, Wolf Blass and Peter Lehmann and New Zealanders from Oyster Bay and Hunter's. South African wines are provided by Meerlust, Backsberg and Boschendal, while South America yields the Weinert Argentinians and Montes Chileans, among others.

Best buys

Bordeaux Supérieur 1992, Château La Dominante, £
Chardonnay 1994, Sable View, £
1994 Sauvignon, Marlborough, Jane Hunter, ££
1988 Rubicon, Meerlust, ££

Raeburn Fine Wines

21-23 Comely Bank Road, Edinburgh EH4 1DS

Tel 0131-332 5166
Fax 0131-332 5166

Open for tastings but not to the public
The Vaults, 4 Giles Street, Leith, Edinburgh
EH6 6DJ

Tel 0131-554 2652
Fax 0131-554 2652

Open Mon–Sat 9–6; Sun 9.30–5 (12.30–5 for alcoholic drinks) **Closed** Public holidays **Cards** Access, Delta, Switch, Visa; business accounts **Discount** 5% on unsplit cases, 2.5% on mixed cases **Delivery** Free in Edinburgh (min. 1 case) otherwise at cost; mail-order available **Glass hire** Free with order **Tasting and talks** Offered throughout he year **Cellarage** Not available

Every time we glance through Zubair Mohamed's range of wines, we find it hard not to gulp in astonishment. There are no token vines, no names for names' sake. What there is is a superb array of great wines from around the world, the vast majority of which have been imported by the company.

Much effort has gone into the range of regional French wines, and we'd particularly point you towards the Roussillon wines of Domaine Gauby and Gilbert Alquier's Faugères. For champagne, Henri Billiot is hard to beat, and the Alsace wines of Rolly Gassmann will find many fans. Burgundies are quite simply brilliant: Coche-Dury, Domaine Leflaive, Méo-Camuzet, Michel Lafarge, Ghislaine Barthod, Jobard, and several more. Amid an ever-changing array of Bordeaux wines, certain properties are followed regularly, including Châteaux des Trois Chardons, Canon, Léoville-Poyferré and Rabaud-Promis and Domaine de Chevalier (red and white). Tasty Rhônes include Noël Verset's Cornas and Gentaz-Dervieux's Côte Rôtie, while similarly exciting fare from the

Loire include the Cotat brothers' Sancerre and a range of Huet Vouvray dating back to 1947.

A serious approach is also applied to non-French wine. Germany provides Schloss Schönborn and Mönchhof, and Spain brings Amezola and Marqués de Murrieta. The Italian list is even better; try the Chiantis from Riccardo Falchini, Monte Bernardi and Monsanto. Serious Australian wines include Geoff Weaver's Stafford Ridge and the Seville Estate Yarra Valley wines, while equally intense Californian items include Mount Eden, Rochioli and Joseph Swan's wonderful Zinfandels. The wines from Warwick Estate in South Africa and from Cloudy Bay and Selaks in New Zealand are also very fine.

If you still need convincing about the Raeburn range, ports from Niepoort and Quinta de la Rosa, and a range of own-label whisky ('The Bottlers') might help sway you. There's also a programme of tastings and offers throughout the year, details of which appear in the regular newsletters. As we finish writing this *Guide* lucky Raeburn customers are sitting down at Martin's restaurant in Edinburgh for a dinner hosted by Noël Pinguet, winemaker at Huet in Vouvray, just one of a selection of similar events featuring top (and we mean top) names from the world of wine.

Best buys

1992 Domaine de Paguy Blanc, £
Vin de Pays Rouge 1990, Domaine de Callory, £
1990 Seville Estate Cabernet Sauvignon, Yarra Valley, Australia, ££
Meursault 1989, François Jobard, ££

Reid Wines (1992)

The Mill, Marsh Lane, Hallatrow,	*Tel* (01761) 452645
Nr Bristol, Avon BS18 5EB	*Fax* (01761) 453642

Open Mon–Fri 10.30–6 (other times by appointment) **Cards** Access, Visa; personal and business accounts; 3% premium charged on credit card transactions **Discount** Not available **Delivery** Within 25-mile radius; mail-order available **Glass hire** Free with order if returned clean **Tasting and talks** Available **Cellarage** £5+VAT per case per year

If a wall collapsed while you were cleaning your basement, and you suddenly found you had discovered the remains of Uncle Mort's wine cellar, we know a man (or men) in Hallatrow who would be very interested to talk to you. Buying parcels of old and rare wine is a Reid Wines speciality, but if you have something for sale, be prepared for a brutally frank appraisal. Of 1975 clarets, for example: 'It is fashionable to denigrate the '75s as tannic and fruitless. This is not strictly true, but if you want a tannic and fruitless wine, try the Montrose or the Rausan-Ségla.'

The Reid claret list runs to several pages, and many items are available only in tiny quantities; two bottles here, five bottles there. It's the same for Sauternes, with several vintages of Ch. d'Yquem and Ch. Rieussec available. Among the red burgundies lurk some good wines from the wonderful '88/'89/'90 trio, as well as several more venerable bottles going back to 1923 La Tâche. Whites include some delicious '92s from Jadot as well as 1944 Chassagne-Montrachet, Bordeaux-bottled for the 11th Hussars ('certainly one of the stupidest bottles to be offered in this list'). Mature Hermitage and some great Côtes-du-Rhône feature in the Rhône section, while the Alsace list offers much of interest from Schlumberger, Hugel and Trimbach. As well as Reid Wines Blanc de Blancs champagne, you can content yourself with the wines of Roederer, Pol Roger and Ruinart. From the regional wines, try the very affordable varietals from Domaines Virginie and Alain Brûmont's delicious Madiran and Pacherenc du Vic Bilh.

German and Spanish representation are good, although quantities again are small. The Italian section is more numerous and we'd point you towards Jermann's whites, a steady range of Tuscan reds, Gaja's Barbaresco and Aldo Conterno's majestic Barolo. The concession to Eastern Europe appears in the shape of Tokay from the Royal Tokay Wine Company. Lustau provides sherries, ports date back to early this century, and madeiras stretch back well into the last.

The Californian range majors on the sturdy wines of Clos du Val and Niebaum Coppola, while among some mature Australian bottles are younger wines from St Hallett, Taltarni and Cape Mentelle. Wairau River from New Zealand and Thelema and Warwick from South Africa are also to be found.

A perusal of the Reid list never fails to please. You'll find wit, wisdom and wine in plentiful supply. Bottles appear and disappear with regularity, but, even if they've run out of your first-choice wine, the second-choice will still be pretty good.

Best buys

Minervois 1992, Château de Gourgazaud, £
Vin de Pays d'Oc 1994, Domaines Virginie, £
Médoc 1990 Château La Tour St Bonnet, ££
Brunello di Montalcino Pieve San Restituta 1990, Gaja, ££

La Réserve

Mark Reynier Fine Wines Ltd
56 Walton Street, London SW3 1RB

Tel 0171-589 2020
Fax 0171-581 0250

The Heath Street Wine Co
29 Heath Street, Hampstead NW3 6TR

Tel 0171-435 6845
Fax 0171-431 9301

Le Picoleur
47 Kendal Street, London W2 2BU

Tel 0171-402 6920
Fax 0171-402 5066

Le Sac A Vin
203 Munster Road, Fulham, London SW6

Tel 0171-381 6930
Fax 0171-385 5513

Clapham Cellars (Wholesale/by the case only)
7 Grant Road, London SW11 2NU

Tel 0171-978 5601
Fax 0171-978 4934

Open Mon–Fri 9.30–9, Sat 9.30–7, The Cellar 12–10.30 **Closed** Sun, public holidays
Cards Access, Amex, Switch, Visa; personal and business accounts **Discount** 5% on 1
case **Delivery** Free Central London, nationwide free for orders over £200; nationwide
mail-order service available **Glass hire** Free with order **Tasting and talks** Regular
in-store tastings **Cellarage** £5 per case per year

Although this tome is intended as a guide to wine, we feel obliged
to draw your attention to the whisky offers that Mark Reynier has
put together. For an investment of around £1,000 you can become
the proud owner of a hogshead of one-year-old Springbank
(occasionally Longrow or Glenfarclas), which will sit maturing in
Scotland until you choose to have it bottled. After fifteen years
you'll find yourself with around 25 cases of some extremely
pleasant whisky, and, although a dram or two may be needed
when you face the hefty bill for duty (currently £75 per case) you'll
have a bargain.

Back to wine. Of the five shops in Mark Reynier's empire, La
Réserve is the flagship (flagshop?), but you'll find some very
pleasant stuff in all the other stores. Burgundy is a real area of
passion, and a dizzy array of wines from fine growers includes
Puligny from Etienne Sauzet, Chablis from Jean Collet, Meursault
from Michelot-Buisson, Vosne-Romanée from Méo-Camuzet and
Gevrey-Chambertin from Armand Rousseau. Bordeaux-lovers are
less well served (though the comparison is only relative), but there
are several wines of classed-growth level in the range. The Loire
wines of Domaine Baumard and Lucien Thomas's Sancerre deserve
attention, as do Marcel Deiss's Alsace offerings. The Côtes du
Ventoux from Domaine des Anges stands up very well against
more famous names from the Rhône. The best of the regional
wines are the set from Domaines de Triennes, while the Charles

Leprince champagne is a respectable alternative to the many *grandes marques*.

The Spanish selection is fair, but the Italian range is spectacularly good – particularly in Piemonte, where you'll find wines from Bruno Giacosa, Ceretto, Gaja, Vietti and many others. California fans will appreciate the wines of Calera, Grgich Hills and Ridge, while lovers of Australian wine should not miss the wares of Mount Bold, Brokenwood and Greenock Hills. Dieu Donné from South Africa and New Zealand wines from Hunter's, Vavasour and Palliser Estate are also available.

Regular offers, a lively tasting programme and dinners enhance the customer's life. In 'The Cellar' below the La Réserve shop, you have a chance to drink wines at shelf prices, and sample pâtés, cheeses, terrines, salads, fruit and cover all for £10. We say 'bargain'!

Best buys

Côtes du Duras Sauvignon 1993, Les Peyrières, £
Montepulciano d'Abruzzo 1993, Ronchi, £
Bourgogne Blanc 1992, Domaine Etienne Sauzet, ££
Calera Reed Mount Harlan Pinot Noir 1992, ££

Howard Ripley

35 Eversley Crescent, London N21 1EL

Tel 0181-360 8904
Fax 0181-360 8904

Case sales only **Open** Mon–Fri 9–10, Sat 9–1, Sun 9–12 **Closed** Public holidays **Cards** None accepted; business accounts **Discount** None offered **Delivery** Free in North London (min. 5 cases), otherwise £8.50 per case; mail-order available **Glass hire** Free **Tasting and talks** To groups on request **Cellarage** For short periods only

With a growing list of Burgundy's best producers, dentist/wine-merchant Howard Ripley is certainly not looking down in the mouth. Economics takes something of a backseat to out-and-out enthusiasm in a range which covers Burgundy with a thoroughness that few can match. You won't find much Chablis, there's hardly anything from the Mâconnais and the Ch. Chalonnaise never gets a look in. If you want wines from the Côte d'Or, though, you will not be disappointed. Big names are here, but only those making good wine, and you'll also find up-and-coming producers who are keen to be listed in Howard's range. Prices are seldom staggering, and although you won't find much under a tenner, there's plenty on offer under £15 (exc VAT). For an introduction to great burgundy, might we suggest that you club together with some friends and sample wines from twelve different producers. Our mixed case would include whites from Gérard Thomas, Gérard Chavy, Jean-Marc Boillot, Henri Germain, Ramonet and Pierre Morey, plus reds from Comte Armand, Rousseau, Leroy, Hudelot-Nöellat, Michel Lafarge and Roumier.

Best buys

Chassagne-Montrachet 1er cru Morgeots 1992, Domaine Ramonet, ££

Volnay 1er cru 1991, Domaine Michel Lafarge, ££

Roberson

348 Kensington High Street, London W14 8NS

Tel 0171-371 2121
Fax 0171-371 4010

Open Mon–Sat 10–8, Sun and public holidays 12–3 **Closed** Chr, Boxing and New Year's Days **Cards** Access, Amex, Delta, Switch, Visa; personal and business accounts **Discount** 10% on mixed case of wine, no discount on spirits **Delivery** Free in the London area, at cost outside London; mail-order available **Glass hire** Free with wine purchase (refundable deposit required) **Tasting and talks** Informal tastings on Saturdays; monthly tutored tastings **Cellarage** No

Customers must be getting better at dodging traffic wardens at the Olympia end of Kensington High Street, for Roberson's sales have increased markedly over the past year. Since its inception this has always been one of London's most stylish wine-merchants, but the shop somehow seems a more relaxed place to buy wine than it has been in the past. The staff are young and keen (but not aggressively so), and you won't feel intimidated as you wander round the spacious premises. All the bottles are stored lying down, even in the (locked) dark cases which house the more expensive stuff.

These venerable bottles include classed-growth reds and sweet whites stretching back to the 1920s, but more affordable fare appears in the shape of Châteaux de Rayne-Vigneau, Potensac and Patache d'Aux. Amid pricey burgundies from Domaine Leflaive and Domaine de la Romanée-Conti more reasonably priced wines from Bruno Clair and Louis Carillon are interspersed. The Rhônes include red and white Châteauneuf from Vieux Télégraphe and Robert Michel's Cornas, while among the Loires you'll find Vacheron Sancerre and Pouilly Fumé from de Ladoucette. A small Alsace range contains much of interest, and regional French highlights include Château-Chalon from Henri Maire and Monbazillac from Château Theulet.

Serious German wines come from Dr Loosen and Robert Weil, and Iberia provides the CVNE Riojas, Torres wines and a clutch of tasty Portuguese reds for enthusiasts to enjoy. Fans of Italian wine are well served by Allegrini Valpolicella, Prunotto Barbaresco and d'Angelo's Aglianico del Vulture, and you'll also find several vintages of Château Musar. Ports and sherries are available in depth, although sales of the Croft and Taylor 1927s could probably be speedier.

North American highlights are Au Bon Climat Pinot and Chardonnay, Hess Cabernet and Hogue Cellars Merlot, and the Australian list is just as interesting, with the wines of Bannockburn, Hugo and Petaluma the pick of the bunch. A New Zealand range with Matua Valley, Martinborough Vineyards and Hunter's looks good, but the firm reports that many customers are moving away from Antipodean wines in favour of their expanding ranges from Chile and South Africa.

Quality has it price, and this is not always the cheapest place to buy wine. However, we'd encourage you to visit the shop, perhaps for the informal tastings each Saturday or for one of the monthly tutored events.

Best buys

Chardonnay de l'Aude 1994, Vin de Pays de la Haute Vallée de l'Aude, £
Montepulciano d'Abruzzo 1993, Citra, £
Pinot Bianco 1992, Jermann, ££
Château Rausan-Ségla 1986, ££

The Rose Tree Wine Co

15 Suffolk Parade, Cheltenham, Gloucestershire   *Tel* (01242) 583732
GL50 2AE   *Fax* (01242) 222159

Open Mon–Fri 9–7; Sat 9–6 **Closed** Sun, public holidays **Cards** Access, Delta, Switch, Visa; personal and business accounts **Discount** 5% on mixed cases **Delivery** Free in Gloucestershire, Avon, Central London, South Devon (min. 1 case), outside areas £5 + VAT per case; mail-order available **Glass hire** Free **Tasting and talks** Trade, private and tutored talks; main yearly tasting in November **Cellarage** £2.60 per case per year

---

It is now nearly nine years since Rose Tree was established, and the business has expanded steadily, evolving into the sort of sensible wine-merchant of which any town would be proud. Lovers of Spanish wine are the best served by the range on offer. You'll find the Viñas del Vero wines from Somontano, Chivite Navarra wines, cava from Juvé y Camps, Riojas from CVNE and Viña Salceda, and sherries from Lustau and Don Zoilo. Good-value Italian wines include the Canaletto Veneto whites, while rather more money will buy you reds from Santadi, Isole e Olena and Argiano. The Tokays of Château Megyer, both dry and sweet, are very pleasant. French highlights include burgundies from Fichet and Yvon Clerget,

Vouvray from Christian Chaussard, some impressive yet affordable clarets and the excellent Côtes du Lubéron from Château la Verrerie. Georges Gardet champagne deserves as much attention as the wines of grander houses.

New World enthusiasts are catered for by wines from Salisbury Estate and Mount Langi Ghiran from Australia and enjoyable New Zealand Sauvignons from Te Mata, Jackson Estate and Nobilo. The Californian range is not the most exciting around, although the Mondavi Napa wines should not disappoint; Chilean wines come from Undurraga, and Weinert provides great Argentinian Cabernet.

Plans are in hand to extend the burgundy and Rhône ranges over the next year, so we wait with keen interest to see what Messrs Brown and Maynard will uncover.

Best buys

1987 Castillo de Almansa Reserva, £
Vin de Pays l'Aude 1992, Domaine Perrière, £
Viñas del Vero (Somontano) 1990, Merlot/Cabernet Sauvignon Reserva, ££
Côtes du Luberon 1992, Bastide la Verrerie, ££

R S Wines

32 Vicarage Road, Southville, Bristol,	*Tel* (0117) 963 1780
Avon BS3 1PD	*Fax* (0117) 953 3797

Case sales only   Open Mon–Fri 9–6   **Closed** Sundays, Public holidays   **Cards** Not accepted; personal and business accounts   **Discount** Sometimes   **Delivery** Free locally; nationwide mail-order service available   **Glass hire** Available   **Tasting and talks** Available   **Cellarage** Approximately £2 per case per year

---

Raj Soni's first entry in the *Guide* coincides with his company's tenth anniversary. Not that he's only now achieved the required quality standard, just that we're sometimes a bit slow on the uptake. Much of the R S business is wholesale, but interested members of the public are very welcome to put together a dozen wines from the many on offer.

Says Raj, 'I taste everything listed regularly.' We'd be very happy to join him in such a monitoring session, particularly if he included the burgundies from Pierre Bourée, Maroslavac Leger and Simon Bize. The clarets aren't bad either, and a separate fine-wine supplement contains more impressive stuff. An expanding set from the Languedoc includes the smashing reds and whites from the Roquebrun cooperative, while the Alsace wines of Albert Mann,

Rhônes from Alain Paret and Vouvray from Bourillon d'Orléans are also good. The Vilmart champagne is exceptional.

Among the many Australians listed, you'll find Hunter wines from Reynolds Yarraman, Coonawarra wines from Hollick and Western Australians from Chatsfield and Cape Mentelle. American input comes from Saintsbury and Niebaum Coppola in California, L. A. Cetto in Mexico, Weinert in Argentina and Caliterra from Chile. The Wairau River and Cloudy Bay New Zealanders and Thelema South Africans are also excellent. German wines are few, but Dr Loosen's wines will not disappoint, and neither will those from Isole e Olena and Araldica in Italy. There are several Riojas in the Spanish selection, but we'd highlight the Navarra wines from Senorío de Sarria and Chivite.

Were other, more venerable merchants in Bristol to take a leaf from the R S book, perhaps we would recommend them as strongly as we do this company.

Best buys

Côtes du Rhône 1993, Union des Vignerons de Tavel, £
Vin de Pays d'Oc, Chardonnay 1993, Philippe de Baudin £
Vilmart Grand Cellier Champagne NV Brut, ££
Reynolds Hunter Yarraman Valley Cabernet Sauvignon 1992, ££

Safeway

Head Office

Safeway House, 6 Millington Road, Hayes,	*Tel* 0181-848 8744
Middlesex UB3 4AY	*Fax* 0181-573 1865
367 branches	

Open Mon–Fri varies from store to store, Sat 8.30–8 (most stores), Sun 10–4 **Closed** Public holidays **Cards** Access, Delta, Switch, Visa; business accounts **Discount** Available **Delivery** Not available **Glass hire** Not available **Tasting and talks** Occasionally in some stores **Cellarage** Not available

---

There are some things which Safeway gets very right. Anyone who thinks of the various Bulgarian reds as just the same wine repackaged in several different ways should try the single-vineyard wines that the company offers. The prices are seldom much more than is asked for other Bulgarians, but the wines are a lot more appealing, and even more serious. Of the other Eastern Europeans, the reds are much better than the rather ordinary whites, and the Kirkwood Moldovan Cabernet/Merlot is a delicious young wine. In the New World list it is worth trying the Chilean and Australian ranges, although the Stony Brook wines from California, which come from Fetzer, are very good.

Southern France offers much of interest, but the quality is somewhat more erratic; where flying winemakers have been involved in the blends, quality is often remarkably ordinary. Our favourites are the Château Montner Roussillon, Laperouse white, La Cuvée Mythique and the Galet Syrah. In a batch of clarets that appeared just before last Christmas, much was made of some big-name 1992 wines (Ch. Léoville-Barton, Ch. de Fieuzal and others), but the best wines in the range were the less-known Ch. Andron-Blanquet and Ch. Peymartin. Burgundies were until recently rather disappointing, but an influx of new wines, mainly from Luc Javelot/Labouré Roi but from some growers as well, has breathed new life into the range. Of the champagnes, the Albert Etienne wines have shown reliability over the past few years, and the Chartogne Taillet brut is also fine stuff.

You'll find reasonable Italian and Spanish ranges (including the Viña Albali Cabernet in the latter), and the Lustau sherries will not fail to please. The Portuguese wines are very good, from the exotically perfumed own-label Bairrada to the supple, oaky Vinha do Monte. English wines are refreshingly in evidence, although what your local store sells may very well depend on which is your nearest vineyard.

Organic wines are more prominent than in other supermarkets, although whether the public are as interested in this as they once were is debatable. Unsurprisingly, the best organic wines on offer are the Penfolds red and white. You'll also find wines labelled Vegetarian White (Côtes de Gascogne) and Red (Bordeaux), both perfectly decent – but doesn't this imply that the other wines in the range are not vegetarian?

The twice-yearly Wine Fairs take place for four weeks in May and November and have proved extremely successful. Parcels of wine too small for the normal range appear on the shelves, and then disappear with a speed that pleases the company. As with the main range, there are misses, but there are usually a good many more hits. Safeway seems prepared to take risks with its wine-buying in a way that other supermarkets don't, and this is particularly refreshing.

Best buys

Vin de Pays d'Oc Syrah 1994, Galet Vineyards, £
Chardonnay del Salento 1993/4, 'Le Trulle', £
Albert Etienne Brut, ££
Gevrey-Chambertin premier cru 1990, Domaine Rossignol-Trapet, ££

J Sainsbury

Stamford House, Stamford Street, London SE1 9LL *Tel* 0171-921 6000
360 branches *Fax* 0171-921 7610

Open Regular late night opening **Cards** Access, Amex, Switch, Visa **Discount** Not offered **Delivery** Wine Direct mail-order service **Glass hire** Not available **Tasting and talks** Tastings on an ad-hoc basis **Cellarage** Not available

Lousy exchange rates combined with a succession of poor vintages in Europe have made the supermarket wine-buyer's task a difficult one in recent months. It is to this climate that Allan Cheesman returns after a few years' sabbatical in fruit and veg. It was Cheesman who in the 1980s made Sainsbury's the supermarket to beat, and his return has prompted much speculation. Certainly, since his move Sainsbury's has not been the force it was under his regime, although much of that is due to the improvement in the competition rather than to any drop in standards at Stamford House.

It's still too early to say what effect his return has had on the wine department, but already we have heard inspiring noises along the lines of 'we have tended to concentrate too much on price points rather than quality'. He arrives to find one of the healthiest of the supermarket ranges, although that's not saying much at the moment. What is good to see is the increase in the number of top-quality wines and the decision to feature these on the dusty rack which used to sit between the red and the white wines. (From our own observations of this section, it was where the men browsed while the women picked something cheaper off the main shelves.)

Fortunately, the main shelves contain much of interest. The Bordeaux range is as good as any at the cheaper end, with Château Carsin providing good reds and whites. At a higher level, the company has chosen the wines of lesser châteaux from good vintages, rather than big names from the dreadful years, a policy we approve of. The Languedoc-Roussillon wines from James Herrick and Chais Baumière are also good, and, although Geoff Merrill's Italian wines are not the stunners that Sainsbury's would have us believe, they are quite good. Peter Bright's Portuguese range is better, and the Do Campo Tinto is a bargain. The Australian range seems to have settled down to more manageable proportions, and includes some rather ordinary wines under the Tarrawingee label plus tastier stuff from Yarra Ridge, now at a more sensible price than when first introduced. The Washington State wines under the Washington Hills label are the best of a poor North American range, but the South Americans are generally better. South African wines of interest come from Fairview and Kanonkop, while Oyster Bay Chardonnay heads the New Zealand range.

Those who don't care to pick their way between those large stock trolleys that always seem to be double-parked in the wine aisle might care to take advantage of the Wine Direct mail-order service. This is now also accessible via the Internet, and those wishing to pay a virtual visit can find the Sainsbury Homepage at *http://www.j-sainsbury.co.uk/*. A further development this year has been the expansion of Sainsbury's French operation. The decision to open in the Mammouth centre in Calais has proved successful, and the number of wines, beers and spirits stocked now tops 300.

Best buys

1993 Barrique-aged Cabernet Sauvignon Atesino, Geoff Merrill, £
1994 Chais Baumière Sauvignon Blanc, Vin de Pays d'Oc, £
Sainsbury's Blanc de Noirs Champagne, ££
Fronsac 1990, Château La Vieille Curé, ££

Sandiway Wine Company

Chester Road, Sandiway, nr Northwich, Cheshire CW8 2NH	*Tel* (01606) 882101 *Fax* (01606) 888407

Open Mon–Fri 9–1, 2–10 (Wed 9–1, 5.30–10); Sat 9am–10pm; Sun 12–2, 7–10, public holidays usually Sunday hours **Closed** Wed 1–5.30, Chr, Boxing, New Year's Days **Cards** Access, Amex, Delta, Switch, Visa; personal and business accounts **Discount** 5% on 1 case **Delivery** Free within 10-mile radius (min. 1 case) **Glass hire** Free with order **Tasting and talks** Monthly informal tastings; also tutored events **Cellarage** Not available

---

Graham Wharmby might like to give the impression that chaos rules in his establishment, but it is a chaos that results from offering some of the best wines available in Britain in the least po-faced way imaginable. You won't find anything resembling a wine list, so a visit to this wine-shop-cum-post-office-cum-general-store is essential. Australian sales continue to increase, and customers will find a broad range from the likes of Grant Burge, Cassegrain, Reynolds and many others. Queue now for the tiny allocation from Cloudy Bay, or alternatively try one of the many other New Zealand offerings. Californian wines come from Bonny Doon, Jade Mountain and Qupé, South Africans from Thelema. The Spanish list includes the excellent-value Solana red and white, while Quinta de la Rosa from Portugal is lovely wine. Italy is another area of enthusiasm, and has benefited from the arrival at Sandiway of Philip Beavan, formerly with Eaton Elliot. Aldo Conterno's Barolo and the Chianti from Felsina Berardenga head a fine range.

From France, you'll find Alsace from Trimbach and Château d'Orschwihr, Rhônes from Alain Paret and impressive burgundy from Patrice Rion, Olivier Merlin and Denis Bachelet. Clarets include good, sensibly priced wines such as Châteaux Sénéjac, and Tour du Pas St-Georges, while regional wines of interest come from Mas de la Dame and Château Theulet. The champagne from Jacques Selosse has considerable character, but you'll find more familiar fare from Pol Roger and Veuve Clicquot. A close link with Reid Wines (q.v.) means that there's always something old and interesting in store (and we don't just mean Graham!). There's also The Sticky Patch, with a variety of sweet wines from throughout the world of wine.

The shop also contains a variety of locally-produced foods, including Montgomery Moore chocolates (when the shop isn't too warm), Wendy Brandon's pickles and jams. Customers have a chance to taste a selection of these and of the wines every weekend, and there's a more formal programme of wine-tastings, which in the past has attracted winemakers of the calibre of Jean Trimbach, François Billecart and Randall Grahm. There's a regular newsletter that gives details of tastings, special parcels of wine and offers, and the company also holds one of the best January sales around. If you buy one bottle, you get 1% discount, 2 bottles, 2%, etc. right up to 20 bottles, 20% off virtually every wine in the shop. No doubt about it, the tongue may be firmly in the cheek, but this is a seriously good wine-merchant.

Best buys

Domaine de Limbardie 1993, Henri Boukandoura, £
Côtes de Gascogne 1994, Domaine de Rey, £
Jade Mountain les Jumeaux 1993, Douglas Daniellak, ££
Felsina Berardenga Chianti Classico Vigneto Rancia 1990, ££

Santat Wines

| Cavendish House, Sydenham Road, Guildford, | *Tel* (01483) 450494 |
| Surrey GU1 3RX | *Fax* (01483) 455068 |

Case sales only Open Mon-Sat 9-7 **Closed** Sun, public holidays **Cards** Access, Amex, Visa; business accounts **Discount** Negotiable **Delivery** Free local delivery; mail-order available **Glass hire** Free with order **Tasting and talks** Free to customers on mailing list and tasting always available on premises **Cellarage** Not available

'Famous for rich gastronomy, love of song and rugby-playing.' The description could be applied either to Gascony or to one of its sons, Eric Narioo, director and wine-buyer for this enthusiastic Guildford company. It's no surprise to find a good range of wines from the south-west corner of France, with the highlights being the Jurançon of Clos Lapeyre and the Madiran from Domaine Berthoumieu. From further east come excellent Languedoc wines courtesy of Les Chemins de Bassac and Domaines Virginie and the Provence wines of Château Simone in Palette and Domaine le Galantin in Bandol. Rhônes of note include Lirac from Domaine de la Mordorée and Domaine Mathieu's Châteauneuf. Alsace is from Scherer, Vouvray from Champalou and there's also a small range of decent clarets. Gérard Tremblay supplies Chablis, while other burgundies are provided by Joseph Belland and Emile Juillot. And, if you've never tasted the wines of Savoie, try the pair from Domaine la Gentilhommière.

There is vinous life here outside France, with small but good ranges from Italy, Spain and Germany, and a New World selection featuring the Goundrey Australians, Ata Rangi Pinot from New Zealand and the Gundlach-Bundschu Californians.

Director Liz Reid tells us that Santat is run 'by a youthful team of enthusiasts for whom enjoyment of wine always goes hand in hand with the love of food.' Those attending the regular evening tastings (which are free) will find not only wines to sample but also 'elaborate and visually stunning food'. Bon appetit!

Best buys

Côtes de Duras Blanc 1993/4, Domaine des Arnauds, £
Gamay, Vin de Pays du Jardin de la France, Domaine les Hautes Noelles, £
Madiran Cuvée Charles de Baatz 1990, Domaine Berthoumieu, ££
Abymes 1992/3, Domaine la Gentilhommière, Savoie, ££

Scatchard

4 Temple Court, Liverpool, Merseyside L2 6PY   *Tel* 0151-236 6468
                                                      Fax 0151-236 7003

Open Mon–Fri 9.30–6, Sat 10–2 **Closed** Sun, Public holidays **Cards** Access, Amex, Delta, Switch, Visa; personal and business accounts **Discount** 5% case discount for wines and beers; greater discounts on larger orders **Delivery** Free locally (min. 3 cases) **Glass hire** Free with order **Tasting and talks** With guest speakers once a month; weekly informal tastings in shop **Cellarage** Only for existing customers

City-centre Liverpool's only independent wine-merchant has a name as a Spanish specialist, but offers much more besides. You'll find decent champagnes from Gosset and Louis Roederer, Alsace from the Turckheim co-op, Guy Saget Loires and some respectable regional fare such as Mas de la Garrigue Côtes du Roussillon. Clarets come and go, but there's usually something reasonable and affordable around, such as Châteaux Fourcas-Hosten and Kirwan.

Burgundies (and the Germans and Italians) are adequate rather than great. Best of the New World wines are Orlando's St Hilary Chardonnay and St Hugo Cabernet from Australia, Carmen from Chile, Grove Mill from New Zealand and Paul Thomas's Washington State wines. That Spanish list includes a range from Torres, plus additional Penedés wines from Marqués de Monistrol, Rioja from CVNE, La Rioja Alta and Campillo, Ribera del Duero from Valduero and sherry from José de Soto.

We should like to recommend Scatchard's with more enthusiasm than we do. We have had good reports of the standards of service offered, but, rather like Willoughby's in Manchester, we would prefer to see a little more adventurousness shown in the selection on the shelves.

Best buys

Favor 1991 Brut Reserve Cava, £
Penedés Chardonnay 1994, Marqués de Monistrol, £
Pomerol, Château Sainte Marie 1990, ££
De Soto Don José 'Anada 1830', Oloroso, ££

Sebastopol Wines

Sebastopol Barn, London Road, Blewbury,   *Tel* (01235) 850471
Oxfordshire OX11 9HB   *Fax* (01235) 850776

Case sales only   Open Tues–Sat 10.30–5.30   **Closed** Mon, Sun, public holidays (exc. Good Friday)   **Cards** Access, Visa; business accounts   **Discount** 5% on 6 bottles of wine; 5% on specific cases; £1 collection discount per case; otherwise by negotiation **Delivery** Free within 10-mile radius (min. 1 case); mail-order available   **Glass hire** Free with order (min. 1 case wine)   **Tasting and talks** Monthly theme tastings (Sat) **Cellarage** Not available

---

Barbara & Caroline Affleck's range is as admirably efficient as ever, covering most of the wine world with style and good taste, and with nothing included just for the sake of it. So there are no German wines, no Eastern Europeans and (with the exception of Cossart Gordon madeiras and a handful of good ports) no Portuguese wines. There are Spanish wines (and good ones too), including mature Jean León Cabernet, Alejandro Fernández's Tinto Pesquera and Rioja from Marqués de Murrieta. Italians too are excellent, with the pick being the wines of Allegrini, Aldo Conterno and Fontodi. Shaw & Smith, Henschke and Dalwhinnie provide great Australian contributions, New Zealanders come from Palliser Estate and Grove Mill, and the short South African list features wines from Thelema. From California, you'll find Chardonnay from Calera, Zinfandel from Ridge and Cabernet Sauvignon from

Carmenet, while from further south in Chile, there are Cabernets from Los Vascos and Montes.

Alsace fans will enjoy the wines from Marcel Deiss and Albert Boxler, while Loire enthusiasts will spot the Pouilly Fumé from Jean-Claude Chatelain and sweeter wines from Jean Baumard. In the Rhône selection, there are several vintages of Beaucastel available, together with Crozes-Hermitage from Alain Graillot and Côte Rôtie from Bernard Burgaud. Sauternes of note come from Châteaux Rieussec and Guiraud, while the range of red Bordeaux features several good to very good wines from the 1985 vintage onwards. The white burgundy selection, including wines from Domaine Leflaive, Marc Colin and Michel Barat's Chablis, is impressive, but the reds from Domaines Leroy, Dujac, de Vogüé and Fernand Lecheneaut are even better.

Tastings are held each Saturday, to which customers receive advance invitations together with a list of the eight to ten wines that will be on offer. There are worse things to do in Oxfordshire on a Saturday.

Best buys

Riesling 1993, Wynns Coonawarra Estate, Australia, £
Côtes du Ventoux la Vieille Ferme 1991, Jean-Pierre Perrin, £
Sauvignon Blanc 1994, Palliser Estate, New Zealand, ££
Chardonnay 1994, Thelema Mountain, South Africa, ££

Seckford Wines

2 Betts Avenue, Martlesham Heath, Ipswich,	*Tel* (01473) 626681
Suffolk IP5 7RH	*Fax* (01473) 626004

Case sales only Open Tue–Sat 10–6 **Closed** Sun, Mon and usually bank holiday before weekend **Cards** Access, Switch, Visa; personal and business accounts **Discount** 5% off 6 cases **Delivery** Free within 25-mile radius (min. 1 case); national mail-order service available **Glass hire** Free except for breakages **Tasting and talks** Tutored tastings by arrangement, min. 15 people; twice yearly tastings in warehouse of new arrivals **Cellarage** Not available

Wine-drinkers who have plenty of money will know Seckford for their broking activities, through which the likes of Domaine de la Romanée-Conti, Guigal's single-vineyard Côte Rôtie, all the first-growth clarets and multiple vintages of Dom Perignon are usually available. However, there's also plenty on the retail side for people who think £100 is a lot to spend on a case of wine. Heading the French country range are wines from Domaine de l'Hortus and Domaine Peyre Rose. Affordable clarets come from Châteaux Puygueraud and Malescasse, while similar value can be found in the burgundy section with the Marsannay from Fougeray de

Beauclair and Henri Jayer's Passetoutgrains. Château de Beaucastel appears prominently in the Rhônes, and Alsace comes from Rolly-Gassmann, while Gaston Huet's Vouvray features among the Loire wines. Christian Senez champagne will suit those with more sense than money.

Spanish bottles are thin on the ground; a slightly larger set from Germany features Dr Loosen wines, and a broader range from Italy includes Barolo from Ascheri, Vajra and Elio Altare. New World interest appears in the shape of Delheim South Africans, Rochioli Californians and New Zealanders from Wairau River and Dashwood. Australian offerings are in plentiful supply, with the best wines coming from Moss Wood, Seville Estate and Hollick.

Visitors to Martlesham Heath will always find around a dozen wines available for tasting, kept fresh by the Verre du Vin system – although we doubt whether these will include Sassicaia, Ch. d'Yquem, Fonseca '63, etc.

Best buys

Minervois, Château de Cordes 1993, £
Chardonnay de la Portallière 1993, £
Côtes de Francs 1989, Château Puygueraud, ££
Champagne Christian Senez NV Brut, ££

Selfridges

400 Oxford Street, London W1A 1AB	*Tel* **0171-629 1234**
	Fax **0171-491 1880**
Wine Dept Direct Line	*Tel* **0171-318 3730**

Open Mon–Sat 9.30–7 (Thurs to 8), 5 Sundays before Chr and Good Fri 12–3, public holidays as usual **Closed** Sun, Chr and Boxing Days **Cards** All accepted; personal and business accounts **Discount** 12 bottles for the price of 11 **Delivery** Free within M25 on orders over £100, otherwise £6.95 outside London and £3.95 inside London **Glass hire** Free with order, breakages charged for **Tasting and talks** Call for details **Cellarage** Not available

---

'We see ourselves as a wine-merchant within a department store,' says William Longstaff, wine-buyer for Selfridges. Certainly any merchant would be proud to have such an extensive range of wines (1,200 and still growing) and also such a high average spend per bottle (£8 and, again, still rising). Those wines are good and interesting as well, whatever your budget. Champagnes include multiple vintages of Krug and Dom Pérignon, but also much more affordable fare, such as the non-vintage wines from Charbaut and Georges Goulet. Clarets include three 1945 first growths as well as cru bourgeois wines from Châteaux de Pez, Greysac and Chasse-Spleen. Moderately priced white Bordeaux come from Châteaux Haut-Rian and Loupiac-Gaudiet, but there's Ch. d'Yquem for those with a few more pennies. Red burgundies come from Domaine Moillard, Faiveley and Domaine de la Romanée-Conti, whites from Sauzet, Daniel Defaix and Louis Latour. Alsace from Schlumberger and Trimbach will not disappoint, and neither will the Loire wines from Lamé-Delille and Henry Pellé. Chapoutier and Vieux Télégraphe supply Rhônes, and decent regional wines come from Chais Cuxac and Daniel Domergue.

Italian wine is the company's fastest-growing area, and the range is impressive. There are the I Sodi di San Niccolò and Querciagrande Super-Tuscans, mature Borgogno Barolo dating back to 1952, good Valpolicella from Tedeschi and Masi and a range of whites from Jermann. The German list is less profuse but still excellent. Spanish wines include Cabernet Sauvignon from Marqués de Griñón and Torres, Rioja from Contino and Montecillo and Navarra wines from Ochoa. Top of an interesting Portuguese range is the super Quinta de Foz de Arouce, while Denbies' Noble Harvest is the best of the short English selection. There are several wines from Eastern Europe, including Tokay Eszencia from 1957, plus the Israeli wines from Yarden.

Grange tops an Australian range that also features great wines from Devil's Lair, Howard Park and Tim Adams. New Zealanders include reds from Goldwater and Martinborough Vineyards, and whites from Te Mata and Neudorf. Wines from the States include Paul Thomas's Washington wines, great Merlot from Crichton Hall and Newton, fine Viognier from Joseph Phelps and brilliant Chardonnay from Au Bon Climat and Matanzas Creek. South Africans are also available in depth, and the whites from Neil Ellis and Dieu Donné, and reds from La Motte and Hamilton Russell, should bring satisfaction.

Madeiras date back to 1952, ports to 1945 and you'll also find plenty of delicious sherries. Add to this numerous whiskies, liqueurs and beers coming from over 30 countries, and you have an extraordinarily good wine-merchant. There are bottles available for tasting in store most days from 1pm to 6pm. In addition, a programme of tutored tastings with visiting winemakers is planned for this autumn, but these will be just for Selfridges Gold Account customers. Those not able to visit the store for fear of traffic wardens might care to take advantage of the free delivery service for orders over £100.

Best buys

1993 Sorbiano Montescudaio DOC Tuscany, £
Sauvignon Vin de Pays d'Oc, Domaine de Subremont, £
Chablis 1er Cru Côte de Lechet 1990, Defaix, ££
Newton Merlot 1989, Napa Valley, ££

Edward Sheldon

New Street, Shipston-on-Stour, Warwickshire *Tel* (01608) 661409
CV36 4EN *Fax* (01608) 663166

Open Mon 9–5.30, Tue–Fri 9–7, Sat 9–5 **Closed** Sun, public holidays **Cards** Access,
Delta, Switch, Visa; personal and business accounts **Discount** Volume based
Delivery Warwickshire, Gloucestershire, Oxfordshire, Beds, Herts, London,
Northants, Berkshire, Bucks (min. 1 case); mail-order available as The Coaster Club
Glass hire Free with order **Tasting and talks** Available **Cellarage** Not available

Over the past year a few more New World wines have crept into
the Edward Sheldon list, but the range still remains one geared to
serve 'a conservative area where trends are slow to come through.'
That's not to say that there's nothing of interest here.
Traditionalists may prefer to stick to the Hunting Port and House
Claret, but we would urge you to experiment. Familiar New World
wines come from Montana, Mondavi, Cousiño Macul and KWV,
but we'd point you towards the Goundrey and Hardy's Australian
wines, Te Mata New Zealanders, Caliterra Chileans and Fairview
South Africans. German wines of note come from Dr Loosen and
Bert Simon, Spaniards from Ochoa, Torres and CVNE. The Italian
selection is rather jaded, but J. M. da Fonseca provides good
Portuguese reds.

French country wines are 'a most interesting and rewarding
section of our list', although you will find much larger ranges
elsewhere. Champagnes come mostly from the major houses, such
as Joseph Perrier and Taittinger, while Trimbach and Kuentz-Bas
provide Alsace. There are reasonable Loire and Rhône selections,
with Châteaux de Tracy and de Beaucastel in evidence. Clarets
include an extensive range from the excellent 1989 vintage as well
as older wines dating back to the early 1960s. As well as burgundies
from merchants such as Louis Latour and Chanson, growers on
show include Jayer-Gilles, Ponsot, Henri Clerc and Sauzet.

Best buys

Sauvignon Blanc Caliterra 1994, £
Corbières 1993, Château Combe Loubière, £
Hautes Côtes de Nuits 1989, Domaine Gros, ££
E&E Black Pepper Shiraz 1992, ££

Sherston Wine Company (St Albans)

97 Victoria Street, St Albans,
Hertfordshire AL1 3TJ

Tel (01727) 858841

Open Tue–Fri 12–7, Sat 9.30–6 **Closed** Sun, public holidays and Mon **Cards** Access, Delta, Diners, Visa; personal and business accounts **Discount** 5% on cases **Delivery** Hertfordshire, Bedfordshire, Buckinghamshire, Cambridgeshire and London; St Albans free for orders over £20 **Glass hire** Free with order **Tasting and talks** Every 8-10 weeks. Tastings are tutored and a fee is charged depending on the wines tasted **Cellarage** Not available

May we first of all congratulate Ernest Jacoby on the recent arrival of grandson Jack. Then we must applaud him on a range of wines that is a model for small wine-merchants everywhere. From France, it offers Alsace from Schlumberger, good Rhônes from Domaine Ste Anne, André Dézat's Sancerre and champagne from Hostomme. Michel Lafarge's Volnay and Chablis from Alain Gautheron feature among the burgundies, while clarets range from 1982 Cos d'Estournel to the delicious Lalande de Pomerol from Ch. des Annereaux. Regional French highlights are the Côtes de Gascogne from Domaine des Maubet and Domaine Berthoumieu's Madiran.

The pleasing Italian range covers the country thoroughly, with a clutch of mature Piemonte wines and the Trentino wines of de Tarczal standing out. Spain too is well represented by a range that extends from the good-value Callejo wines of Ribera del Duero right up to Castillo Ygay Rioja from 1952 at £99 a bottle. There are also some chunky Portuguese reds from Quinta da Cismeira. Californian wines are noticeably absent, but you will find South Africans from Hamilton Russell and Zandvliet, Australians from Cape Mentelle and Plantagenet, and New Zealanders from Esk Valley and (if you're lucky) Cloudy Bay.

A subscription of £5 buys annual membership of the Sherston Wine Club, which entitles you to discounts, special tastings and dinners and a periodic newsletter. In addition, visitors to the shop on Fridays and Saturdays will always find wines available for tasting.

Best buys

Sauvignon de Touraine 1993, La Chapelle de Cray, £
Minervois 1991, Domaine Des Combelles, £
Cabernet Franc 1991, de Tarczal, ££
Pinot Gris Grand Cru Kitterle 1985, Schlumberger, ££

Smedley Vintners

Rectory Cottage, Lilley, Luton, Bedfordshire
LU2 8LU

Tel (01462) 768214
Fax (01462) 768332

Case sales only **Open** Mon–Fri 9–6, Sat 9–5, Sun and public holidays 10–1 **Cards** None accepted; personal and business accounts **Discount** £1.20 per unmixed case, other discounts negotiable **Delivery** Free within 50-mile radius (min. 1 case); nationwide at cost; mail-order available **Glass hire** Free with order **Tasting and talks** 2 main tastings per year; smaller tutored tastings **Cellarage** £4 per case per year + insurance

Derek Smedley's range of wines is as compact, pleasant and efficient as the man himself. Sales are by the case, but there's plenty of good wine at sensible prices to make putting a mixed dozen together a pleasure rather than a chore. You'll find Laurent Perrier champagnes, and a great alternative in the shape of Daniel le Brun's excellent New Zealand fizz. Up-market Côtes-du-Rhône comes from Domaine de Cabasse, while good country wines include Château Quattre Cahors and Berticot Sauvignon from the Côtes de Duras. A small Bordeaux range concentrates on *petits châteaux* wines under £10, while burgundies are mostly from the Antonin Rodet stable. Guy Saget's Loires, and Alsace from the Kientzheim-Kayersberg co-op complete the French range.

The German range lacks conviction; Portuguese presence is provided by Churchill ports and Cossart Gordon madeira, and Spanish representation is limited to little more than the wines of Marqués de Riscal and sherries from Manuel de Argueso. The Italian wines from Prunotto, Antinori and Bartolomeo de Breganze are much better. The Bataapati Hungarians have disappeared from the list, but in their place have come a couple of Tokays from the Royal Tokaji Wine Company. Mr Smedley will be more than willing to give you details of the English wines from Warden Abbot; he is the winemaker. The search is currently on to find South African replacements for the wines from Montestell and Dieu Donné. Californians come from William Wheeler, Chileans from Montes and Argentinians from Weinert. Antipodean bottles include wines from Jackson Estate in New Zealand and Rosemount, Mitchelton and Goundrey in Australia.

There are several tastings, events and dinners throughout the year, often in aid of local charities. Mr Smedley provides what he describes as, 'a classic wine-merchant service, personal and friendly.' A growing number of customers obviously agree with him.

Best buys

Cabernet Franc 1994, Domaine d'Il Saint Pierre, £
Rueda 1994, Marqués de Riscal, £
Graves 1990/92, Château de Landiras Blanc, ££
Montes Alpha Cabernet Sauvignon 1990, ££

Gateway/Somerfield

Somerfield House, Hawkfield Business Park,	*Tel* (01179) 359359
Whitchurch Lane, Bristol, Avon BS14 0TJ	*Fax* (01179) 780629
650 branches	

Open Mon–Sat 8.30–6, Sun 10–4, public holidays **Closed** Chr, New Year's Day, Easter Sunday **Cards** Access, Amex, Delta, Diners, Switch, Visa **Discount** None offered **Delivery** Not available **Glass hire** Not available **Tasting and talks** Tastings of 6 wines once a month in the top 100 stores **Cellarage** Not available

The process of converting all the Gateway stores to Somerfield continues, and should be completed within two years. It shouldn't make too much difference to the wine department. For much of the past year the majority of the wine trade has been focusing on Somerfield's heavy discounting policy, which has often meant that wines that were on sale at, say, £3.79 would be available at £2.29 for a fortnight before reverting to their normal price. Wine Buying Controller Angela Mount admits that the company is losing money on wines at the reduced rates, but says that after such promotions sales are typically up by 30% on what they were before. Such a policy may get up some people's noses, but it's hard to fault in marketing terms, and it does get people buying wine who perhaps would not have done so.

The range is one that can compete very adequately with those of other supermarkets on the standard products (Frascati, Liebfraumilch, Bordeaux Rouge, etc.) that make up the bulk of supermarket wine sales. However, for the wine-lover in search of that little bit more, excitement is rather hard to find. Highlights from France are the Chablis from La Chablisienne, 1988 Ch. Haut-Marbuzet, country wines from Hugh Ryman and Château de Caraguilhes, and the Prince William range of champagne. Italian wines of interest include Rocca delle Macie's Riserva di Fizzano and Taurino's Salice Salentino. Wines from Penfolds, Lindemans and Chateau Reynella top the Australian range, and New Zealanders include wines from Stoneleigh and Coopers Creek; Beringer Cabernet seems slightly out of place in an otherwise ordinary set of Californians.

Best buys

Berberana Tempranillo, Rioja 1992, £
1994 Somerfield Australian Chardonnay, Penfolds, £
St Joseph 1990, Cave de St Désirat, ££
Chablis 1er Cru Grand Cuvée 1990, La Chablisienne, ££

Sommelier Wine Company

The Grapevine, 23 St George's Esplanade,   *Tel* (01481) 721677
St Peter Port, Guernsey GYI 2BG   *Fax* (01481) 716818

Open Mon–Fri 10–5.30, Sat 9.30–5.30 **Closed** Sun, public holidays **Cards** Access,
Delta, Switch, Visa; personal and business accounts **Discount** 5% on 1+ cases
Delivery Free in Guernsey (min. 1 case) **Glass hire** Free **Tasting and talks** Monthly
dinners and tastings twice a year **Cellarage** Not available

'We hope you have as much enjoyment drinking the wines as we
did finding them,' says Richard Allisette to his customers. He's
certainly put together a very satisfactory range, and if it does reflect
some of his preference for Italian wines and his customers'
penchant for things Australian, so what? There's much else besides
to satisfy all palates. You'll find champagnes from Gardet and Pol
Roger, vin de pays from Domaine Virginie, Saint Chinian from
Domaine des Jougla and some good Loire whites from Henri
Bourgeois. White burgundies come from Drouhin and Jobard, reds
from Daniel Rion and Bachelet. Domaine Ostertag provides Alsace,
while Rhônes include reds and whites from Château St Estève,
Domaine du Vieux Télégraphe and Guigal. The range of clarets
sticks to sensibly-priced wines, such as Châteaux Sénéjac and de
Sours.

The best in the Spanish section are the Chardonnay from
Castillo de Monjardin and the Riojas from La Rioja Alta. Those
Italian wines that Richard is so keen on include Vernaccia from
Teruzzi e Puthod, Vin Santo and Chianti Classico from Isole e
Olena, Argiano's Brunello and the characterful Duca d'Aragona
from Puglia. You'll also find the Chateau Megyer Tokay, both dry
and sweet.

The Australian range is impressive, and we'd recommend Pipers
Brook, Montara Estate and Shaw & Smith for whites, Charlie
Melton, Wirra Wirra and St Hallett for reds. New Zealand wines
include great Sauvignon from Forrest Estate and Wairau River, and
Semillon and Pinot Noir from Neudorf. Interesting Californians
come from Qupé, Bonny Doon, Newton, Calera and Ridge, and
you'll also find the excellent Thelema South Africans.

Best buys

St Hallett Poachers Blend 1994, £
Salice Salentino, Candido 1990, £
Vouvray, Champalou Petillant NV, ££
Châteauneuf du Pape Red, Domaine Mathieu, 1990, ££

Spar

32-40 Headstone Drive, Harrow, Middlesex HA3 5QT   *Tel* 0181-863 5511
                                                            Fax 0181-863 0603

1,831 licensed branches

Open All year 8am–11pm (some 24 hours)   **Closed** Chr Day   **Cards** At individual stores' discretion   **Discount** Only on promotion   **Delivery** Not available   **Glass hire** Not available   **Tasting and talks** During wine festivals   **Cellarage** Not available

It's difficult to be specific about the Spar range, because the 1,831 licensed stores are all, in effect, independent shops that buy whatever they choose from the company's range through the head office. Also, there is nothing to stop each retailer buying wines from other sources (not cross-Channel bootleggers, of course). However, even if your local manager sticks to the core selection, there will still be some decent stuff available.

The highlights from France are the Chais Cuxac vins de pays, Chablis from La Chablisienne and the Baron Villeneuve-de-Cantemerle claret. Iberians of note include the Ribera del Duero from Senorío de Nava and the Dão from Duque de Viso, while the Riesling from Grans Fassian will probably prove more satisfying than the various sized bottles of Liebfraumilch. The Nottage Hill and Moondah Brook Australians are the best of the New World selection.

Rather like Kwik Save, this is not an obvious first choice as a place to buy quality wine, but there's plenty of value available on the shelves (and for 24 hours a day in some shops).

Best buys

St Chinian, Château Prieure des Mourgues, £
Spar Viognier Cuxac, £
Nottage Hill Chardonnay, £
Senorío de Nava, Ribero del Duero, ££

Frank E Stainton

3 Berry's Yard, Finkle Street, Kendal, Cumbria   *Tel* (01539) 731886
LA9 4AB   *Fax* (01539) 730396

Open Mon–Sat 9–5.30   **Closed** Sun, public holidays   **Cards** Access, Delta, Switch, Visa; personal and business accounts   **Discount** 5% on 1 case   **Delivery** Free within a 45-mile radius of Kendal (min. 1 case); mail-order available   **Glass hire** Not available **Tasting and talks** On request in own tasting room for min. 20 people @ £10 per head **Cellarage** Available

Whether the E stands for excellence or not, this Lake District merchant is certainly a source of wonderful wines from across the world. Clarets offer everything from petit château to first-growth level, and, while Bordeaux whites are not as plentiful, you'll find good stuff from Châteaux Couhins-Lurton and Rieussec. In Burgundy, Chablis comes from William Fèvre, while most of the Côte d'Or wines are from merchants such as Louis Latour and Joseph Drouhin. Duboeuf provides beaujolais, Alsace comes from Schlumberger and Hugel, and Chapoutier and Paul Jaboulet supply Rhône wines. Pricey Provence from Domaine Ott, classy Muscadet from Chéreau-Carré and champagnes from Devaux and Ruinart are also available.

Sparkling wines from elsewhere include Cloudy Bay's Pelorus and the Taltarni Australians from Tasmania and central Victoria; Other Antipodean offerings of note come from Pipers Brook, Cape Mentelle, Grant Burge and Redwood Valley. There are also Chilean wines from Cousiño Macul and Concha y Toro, South Africans from Glen Carlou and Allesverloren, and Californians from Mondavi and Clos du Val.

In the Spanish section, don't miss the sherries from Lustau and Burdon, the CVNE Riojas or the many vintages of Torres Mas la Plana. The Italian wines are impressive, with the affordable offerings from Araldica joining more expensive bottles, such as Allegrini Recioto and Barolo from Ascheri. Whenever interest in German wines rekindles, there's plenty here to whet the appetite, including several wines from Bürklin-Wolf, Louis Guntrum and S A Prüm.

Expect good advice on the range since 'all wines stocked have been tasted by all members of staff at some point.' Not a bad job to have since these include Ch. d'Yquem, La Tâche, Ch. Latour, Sassicaia, Opus One and Grange.

Best buys

Vin de Pays d'Oc Cabernet Sauvignon 1994, Chantefleur, £
Entre Deux Mers 1994, Château la Freynelle, £

Stonyridge Vineyard 1991 Cabernet, Waiheke Island, New Zealand, ££

Deidesheimer-Hohenmorgen Riesling Kabinett, Dr Bürklin-Wolf, 1988, ££

John Stephenson & Sons (Nelson) Ltd

254 Manchester Road, Nelson, Lancashire BB9 7DE   *Tel* (01282) 698827
Fax (01282) 601161

Open Mon–Thur 10.30–10, Fri–Sat 10-10   **Closed** Closed, some public holidays
Cards Access, Amex, Delta, Switch, Visa; personal and business accounts   **Discount**
5% on full and mixed cases   **Delivery** 20-mile radius (min. 1 case); mail-order service
available   **Glass hire** Free   **Tasting and talks** Weekly   **Cellarage** Not available

John Stephenson & Sons was established in 1914 as a grocery business and, following a spell in the Spar organisation, moved solely into the wine and spirit business in 1976. A large amount of business is cash-and-carry with local hotels and restaurants, but the general public is very welcome, and sales are not restricted to case purchases. Recent expansion and refurbishment has meant that producing a wine-list for customers is on a back burner at present, but manageress Jeni Cockett sent us a 55-page computer-generated list of what's currently available.

Clarets include first-growth wines as well as sensibly priced wines from Châteaux Anthonic and Beaumont. Burgundies come from Vallet Frères, Château de Meursault and Jadot, while other French wines of note are Corbières from Château de Lastours, Henry Pellé Sancerre and Domaine de Nalys Châteauneuf. The German wines appear to be serious, although the computer hasn't told us who made them. The Spanish selection includes Rioja from Contino and Faustino Martínez and the good-value Solana red and white. Accompanying a range of Penfolds Australians are other wines from Hickinbotham, Carlyle Estate and Peter Lehmann. Chilean wines are provided by Errazuriz Panquehue and Santa Rita, New Zealanders by Babich, Jackson Estate and Villa Maria. We're not sure how fresh the 1988 Buitenverwachting Sauvignon will be, so we'd steer fans of South African wine towards the 1993 Dieu Donné Chardonnay and the Allesverloren Shiraz.

Best buys

Côtes du Rhône 1994, Le Mistral, £
Pinot Blanc 1992, Cave Vinicole de Turckheim, £
1994 Coopers Creek Marlborough Sauvignon Blanc, ££
Château Musar 1988, ££

Stones of Belgravia

6 Pont Street, London SW1X 9EL

Tel 0171-235 1612
Fax 0171-235 7246

Open Mon–Fri 10–8, Sat 10–7 **Closed** Sun, Chr day, Good Fri, Boxing Day, Easter Mon and all bank hols **Cards** Access, Amex, Delta, Switch, Visa; personal and business accounts **Discount** 5% for a case **Delivery** Free within London (min. £50 order) **Glass hire** Free with order **Tasting and talks** In-store promotions **Cellarage** Not available

'In Belgravia,' says Stones' buyer and director Mike Hall, 'they still want plenty of claret, burgundy and champagne.' His shop offers all three in style. Grande marque champagnes are available in some depth, although those who try the Georges Vesselle wines instead will find a treat. The clarets range from Stones Claret (courtesy of Calvet) at under a fiver to Châteaux Pétrus, Lafite and Latour at considerably more, while burgundies are mostly from Louis Latour and Pierre André. Other French wines worth trying are the Champet Côte Rôtie, the Hugel Alsace and the Sancerre from Henri Bourgeois. From elsewhere in Europe, CVNE Riojas are the Spanish highlights, and Prunotto provides Barolo. Stones are now agents for Moss Wood in Margaret River, and their wines join other Australians from Mount Bold and Wolf Blass. Chileans are provided by Echeverria, Californians by Durney and Mondavi, and New Zealanders by Palliser and Dashwood. Residents of Belgravia are also probably partial to a drop of port or whisky; the Stones' range will cater for their needs very adequately.

Best buys

Mâcon-Villages 1993, Fromont-Moindrot, £
Stones Claret, Patrice Calvet, £
Champagne 1988, Georges Vesselle Grand Cru, ££
1993 Moss Wood Cabernet Sauvignon, Margaret River, ££

Stratfords Wine Shippers

The Old Butcher's Wine Cellar
High Street, Cookham, Berkshire
SL6 9SQ

Tel (01628) 810606
Fax (01628) 810605

Open Mon–Fri 9–5.30, Sat 10–5.30 **Closed** Sun, public holidays **Cards** All accepted; personal and business accounts **Discount** 5% on 1 case **Delivery** Free within 30-mile radius; nationwide £9 per case; gift service and mail-order available **Glass hire** Free with order **Tasting and talks** Available in-store 4 times a year **Cellarage** Not available

Paul Stratford now has another Australian string to his bow: Best's winery in Great Western, Victoria, source of delicious Colombard and one of Australia's best Shirazes. Best's joins a portfolio that also includes Yaldara in the Barossa and Goundrey in Western Australia – all wineries that produce good-value wines with some top-end stunners. Whether three wineries makes a company an Australian specialist is debatable; however, visitors to The Old Butcher's Cellar will find much else besides. New Zealand wines come from Nobilo and Lincoln, South Africans from Klein Constantia, while Californians include rather dull fare from Christian Brothers plus more interesting bottles from Sonoma-Cutrer and Swanson. Among the Spanish wines are Torres and Campo Viejo, the Germans include a pair from Schloss Johannisberg, and the most interesting of the Italian bottles are the Barone Ricasoli Tuscans. French highlights are the Charbaut champagnes, Turckheim Alsace, burgundies from Rossignol-Trapet and Gérard Thomas, and a good range of clarets dating back to 1975 Ch. Latour.

Best buys

1992 Yaldara Reserve Shiraz, £
Sauvignon de Touraine 1993, Domaine de Cray, £
Champagne Charbaut Sélection Brut, ££
1990 Goundrey Windy Hill Cabernet Sauvignon Reserve, ££

Summerlee Wines

Summerlee Road, Finedon, Northampton,	*Tel* (01933) 682221
Northamptonshire NN9 5LL	*Fax* (01933) 682221
London Office (telephone enquiries)	
Freddy Price, 48 Castlebar Road, London W5 2DD	*Tel* 0181-997 7889
	Fax 0181-991 5178

Open Mon–Fri 9.15–12.30 **Closed** Sat, Sun, public holidays **Cards** None accepted; personal and business accounts **Discount** 5% for 5 mixed cases **Delivery** Free in London, Oxford, Cambridge and Northamptonshire (min. 2 cases, less than 2 cases £6.50+VAT); nationwide mail-order available **Glass hire** Free **Tasting and talks** 3 tastings per year in Oxford, Cambridge and London; occasional in-house **Cellarage** £4 per case per year

The Earls Barton off-licence has closed, but Freddy Price is still very firmly in business in both Northampton and London. Case sales only is the rule, but assembling a dozen bottles should be no problem, especially if you love fine German wines. Few can match this German range. The Mosel-Saar-Ruwer region is very ably covered by wines from Max Ferd. Richter, Schloss Saarstein and Karthäuserhof; Balthasar Ress represents the Rheingau, Paul Anheuser the Nahe, and Weingut Pfeffingen the Rheinpfalz. If the thought of these great wines gets your juices flowing, Summerlee will definitely be a port of call.

The Bordeaux range is fairly compact, but is augmented by occasional *en primeur* offers. David Thomas's reds and whites from Château Bauduc are excellent value. Burgundies come from Georges Clerget, Domaine Auffray and Patrick Javillier, while Rhônes are from Guigal and Domaine des Entrefaux. If you're an Alsace enthusiast, all the wines of Domaine Bott-Geyl, from the far-from-basic Pinot Blanc up to *grand cru* level, are stunning. There are small Loire and regional French ranges, plus several Jura wines from Château d'Arlay. Bodegas Bilbainas provide classic Rioja, sherries come from Barbadillo, and the small New World range includes wines from Stafford Ridge, St Hallett in Australia and Groot Constantia in South Africa.

Best buys

1993 Château Bauduc Blanc Sec Bordeaux, £
1991 Bernkasteler Kurfurstlay Riesling Qba Max Ferd. Richter, £
Château Quinault 1990 Grand Cru, St Emilion, ££
Tokay-Pinot Gris Réserve 1992, Domaine Bott-Geyl, ££

Sunday Times Wine Club

New Aquitaine House, Paddock Road, Caversham,   *Tel* (01734) 481711
nr Reading, Berkshire RG4 7UB   *Fax* (01734) 471928
Holding company – Direct Wines (Windsor) Ltd
New Aquitaine House, Paddock Road, Reading   *Tel* (01734) 481711
Berkshire RG4 5JY   *Fax* (01734) 471928

Open Mon–Fri 9–7; Sat 10–5, Sun, public holidays 10–4   **Closed** Chr Day and Easter
Monday   **Cards** All accepted   **Discount** Not available   **Delivery** Free nationwide on
orders over £50; mail-order available   **Glass hire** Not available   **Tasting and talks**
Annual Vintage Festival in London with producers present; programme of tastings at
venues around the country   **Cellarage** Not available

See Bordeaux Direct

T & W Wines

51 King Street, Thetford, Norfolk IP24 2AU   *Tel* (01842) 765646
    Fax (01842) 766407

Open Mon–Fri 9.30–5.30; Sat 9.30–1   **Closed** Sun, public holidays   **Cards** Access,
Amex, Diners, Visa; personal and business accounts   **Discount** None offered
Delivery Free within 15-mile radius (min 1 case); nationwide (min 4 cases); mail-order
available   **Glass hire** Free with order   **Tasting and talks** Yes   **Cellarage** £4.75 per
case

'We have very few wines costing less than £5,' said Trevor Hughes
when we asked him for some low-cost recommendations; he did,
however, propose a magnum of 1961 Krug at £323.13 a bottle.
Those in search of cheap and cheerful wines should look
elsewhere, but enthusiasts for fine wine will find much to attract
them. As well as that Krug, other champagnes come from Michel
Arnould and André Clouet. There are long lists of Alsace wines
from Trimbach and Hugel, while the Rhône range features wines
from Jean-Luc Colombo, Bernard Gripa in St Joseph and Jean-
Michel Gerin in Côte Rôtie. Clarets are available in depth from all
the good vintages of the '70s and '80s, but if you're quick you may
catch that last bottle of 1921 Ch. Gruaud-Larose. Sauternes fans can
try multiple vintage of Ch. les Justices and the extraordinary Ch.
Gilette. Burgundy-lovers are treated to good ranges from Jean
Thévenet, Olivier Leflaive, Faiveley and Domaine de la Romanée-
Conti, as well as a host of wines from other top producers. From
outside France, you'll find the bizarrely delicious Austrian wines of
Willi Opitz, wonderful Piemonte wines from Bava and Gaja and
characterful Rioja from Cosme Palacio. New World wines to look
out for include classic Californians from Silver Oak, Duckhorn and
Flora Springs, New Zealanders from Jackson Estate and Australians

from Hollick and Taltarni. The 600 or so wines on display in the well-appointed Thetford shop represent only around one-third of what is available, so don't be afraid to ask if you can't find precisely what you're looking for.

Best buys

1990 Volnay-Santenots, Domaine Pierre Matrot, ££
1987 Flora Springs Cabernet Sauvignon, Napa Valley, ££

Tanners Wines

26 Wyle Cop, Shrewsbury, Shropshire SY1 1XD	*Tel* (01743) 232400
	Fax (01743) 344401
4 St Peter's Square, Hereford,	*Tel* (01432) 272044
Hereford & Worcester HR1 2PG	*Fax* (01432) 263316
36 High Street, Bridgnorth, Shropshire WV6 4DB	*Tel* (01746) 763148
The Old Brewery, Brook Street, Welshpool, Powys	*Tel* (01938) 552542
SY21 7LF	*Fax* (01938) 556565

Open (Shrewsbury) Mon–Sat 9–6, (Hereford, Welshpool and Bridgnorth Mon–Sat 9–5.30, Welshpool Sat 9–12), all open Sun in December   **Closed** Sun, public holidays **Cards** Access, Amex, Visa; personal and business accounts   **Discount** On delivered orders (2.5% on 3 cases, 5% on 5 cases, 7.5% on 10 cases); larger discounts on cash and collection of orders   **Delivery** Free for local deliveries (min. 1 case); nationwide free on orders of £75+, £6 on orders under £75; mail-order available   **Glass hire** Available **Tasting and talks** One annual event; tutored and group tastings available   **Cellarage** £4.11 per case per year

Richard Tanner sent a list of all the promotional activities undertaken by his company during 1994. Those who think of Tanners as a rather good but fairly sedate outfit stand to have the latter notion rapidly dispelled by a round of dinners, tastings and other events. These vary from large trade fairs to tastings for 20 parishioners of the Pipe-cum-Lyde church. By being seen to be part of the local community, and by serving that community well, Tanners continues to thrive.

The quality of the wines probably has something to do with it as well. As befits such a good, solid company, there's plenty of good, solid wine available. A large claret range is supplemented by *en primeur* campaigns, and fans of white bordeaux will also find much of interest. Lofty burgundies come from the Domaine Leflaive and Armand Rousseau, although Vincent Girardin's Santenay and Dauvissat-Camus Chablis may prove more to your pocket's liking. Standing out in good ranges from the Loire and the Rhône are Didier Dagueneau's Pouilly Fumé and Châteauneuf from Beaucastel and Vieux Télégraphe. The Schlumberger Alsace will not disappoint, and neither will the regional wines from Domaine de l'Arjolle and Château Villerambert Julien.

411

The German range is good, particularly the unusual Schales wines; the Spanish and Italian ranges, too, are hard to fault. Those looking for something from closer to home will find English wines from Three Choirs and Wroxeter Roman Vineyard and Welsh wine from Monnow Valley. There's also a strong set of New World wines, many of which will be familiar, but with some surprises. These include Gauchos Lurton from Argentina, Vriesenhof from South Africa and Jim Barry's excellent Australian wines (don't miss the spectacular Armagh Shiraz). The range of ports should cover all needs, while those in search of sherry can do much worse than try the own-label wines from Hidalgo. Indeed, the whole range of own-label wines is very reliable, and the champagne (from Duval Leroy) is excellent.

We have heard no complaints from customers who deal with the company only by mail-order. The regular offers and Talking Tanners newsletters are conservatively laid out but contain many delicious and tempting wines. Expect good service and advice in the four shops as well. A recent memo to all sales staff read, 'It is Tanners' policy that all recruits and promoted staff are sales persons by nature and that all actually in sales should acquire product knowledge as quickly as possible, both parts of the Diploma being the minimum goal.' Why not go in and ask one of them how to spell Len de l'Elh?

Best buys

Tanners Chardonnay, Vin de Pays d'Oc, £
Tanners Claret, £
Vin de Pays des Côtes de Gascogne, Domaine de Rieux, £
Mâcon-Clessé Quintaine Guillemont-Michel 1993, ££
Chateau du Grand Moulas Villages 1994, ££

Charles Taylor Wines

Cornwall Road, Waterloo, London SE1 8TW   *Tel* 0171-928 8151
                                                  Fax 0171-928 3415

Case sales only Open Mon–Fri 8–6 **Closed** Sat, Sun, public holidays **Cards** None accepted; personal and business accounts **Discount** Not available **Delivery** Free delivery for 4+ cases, otherwise £8 per delivery in London, £12 England and Wales, Scotland at cost **Glass hire** Available **Tasting and talks** Regular tastings every 2–3 months **Cellarage** Not available

---

As we go to press, builders are just finishing Charles Taylor's new office in London. But the move from Epsom won't affect the range he has: decent wines, offered in a frill-free manner to keep prices low – so, unmixed cases please.

Burgundies form the core of the list. Of the whites, Chablis comes from Domaine des Malandes and Ancien Domaine Auffray, Puligny-Montrachet from Carillon and Gérard Chavy, Meursault from Philippe Bouzereau and Boyer-Martenot and St Aubin from Gérard Thomas. Reds include Gevrey-Chambertin from Lucien Boillot and Rossignol-Trapet, Nuits-St-Georges from Bertrand Ambroise and Savigny-lès-Beaune from Girard Vollot. There's still plenty of wine from the 'famous' vintages – ('92 for whites, '90 for reds) but recent tastings of this range have shown that who makes the wine is usually more important than the year. So don't ignore the many brilliant 1993 wines, reds and whites.

From Bordeaux, there's usually some oddments of classed-growth claret and Sauternes, but the dry whites of Château Thieuley and Vieux Château Gaubert, and the reds from Châteaux Fourcas-Dupré and La Tour du Haut Moulin should always be available. Loire wines come from Fournier, Jean-Claude Chatelain and Domaine de la Motte, Rhônes include Marc Sorrel's excellent Hermitage, while Jean-Luc Mader provides tasty Alsace wines. The Australian wines of Evans & Tate provide a single non-French range, but a very palatable one.

Best buys

Mâcon-Prissé Les Clochettes 1993, Cave de Prissé, £
Côtes du Rhône 1993, Vieux Manoir de Frigoulas, £
Puligny-Montrachet 1992, Domaine Louis Carillon, ££
Haut Médoc, Château Tour du Haut Moulin 1989, ££

Tesco Stores Ltd

Head Office

Tesco House, Delamare Road,   Tel (01992) 632222
Cheshunt, Hertfordshire EN8 9SL   Fax (01992) 644235

Tesco Plc
420 branches throughout England, Scotland
and Wales; one in Coquelles, Calais

Open Mon–Thur 9–8, Fri 9–9, Sat 8–8, Sun 10–4; public holidays as advertised **Cards** Access, Switch, Visa **Discount** Available in some stores **Delivery** Not available; Tesco Wine Select (mail-order) freephone; 0800 403403 **Glass hire** Available in larger stores **Tasting and talks** Regularly in larger stores **Cellarage** Not available

Congratulations to Tesco for being the first supermarket to introduce a pair of own-label Canadian wines (made by an Australian resident in England). They're not going to set the world on fire (although the red is very pleasant) but that's not really the point in the supermarket wine game. Any gimmick that attracts attention to your wine range rather than someone else's is worth it.

The Tesco range is the largest among the major multiples, and has a correspondingly high number of misses. The main criticism at a recent tasting was not of faulty wines but of boring ones, and the southern French whites, in particular, were curiously dissatisfying. On the bright side, though, there are several stars.

Australia is currently an area of real strength. How many bottles of Penfolds Bin 707 and Rosemount Balmoral Syrah are sold is not really the point. However, the own-label wines are excellent, especially the Botrytis Semillon, and we applaud the decision to charge that little bit extra rather than skimp on quality to get something on the shelf at a price. A little more money will get you super Shiraz from Maglieri and Kingston Estate and Mick Morris's blockbuster Durif. South African wines are almost as good, and improving by the minute. Fans of Italian wine are well served, with the highlights of the range being Kym Milne's Puglians, Villa Pigna from the Marches and a surprisingly healthy range of own-label Chianti. The champagnes from Forget-Brimont and Herbert Beaufort remain impressive, although the Tesco 1982 Vintage Champagne can be somewhat variable in quality. The range of estate-bottled Germans is not as wide as it once was, but it's hard to blame the company for that when even specialist merchants have difficulty selling such wines. The Tesco Rioja Reserva and the Viña Mayor red from the Ribera del Duero are good solid wines, but the real bargains from Spain are to be found in one of the best ranges of own-label sherry around.

Don't expect every store to have all the wines, particularly items such as 1985 Les Forts de Latour at £25.99 and 1989 Grange Hermitage at £44.99. The company grades its stores into ten categories, according to the space available for drinks in each, and only twenty carry the full range. (These top-notch stores also have in-store wine advisers whose job it is to help customers choose wine and to offer tastings, party planning and other services more often associated with a 'real wine-merchant'.) Whatever the standard of your local Tesco, though, there will be plenty of drinkable wines on those shelves. If there are no shops near you, Tesco Wine Select will deliver a range to your door, some of which are exclusive to the mail-order operation. Cross-Channel shoppers can now shop on familiar territory in the Coquelles branch close to Calais, where the range is one of the best around.

Best buys

Tesco Canadian Red, £
Tesco Superior Palo Cortado Sherry, £
1986 Villa Cerro Amarone, ££
Tesco Barossa Valley Merlot, ££

Thresher Wine Shops/ Wine Rack/Bottoms Up

Head Office
Sefton House, 42 Church Road, Welwyn Garden City   *Tel* (01707) 328244
Hertfordshire AL8 6PJ   *Fax* (01707) 371398
Whitbread Plc, split by 5 main branches = 1,604

Open Mon–Sat 9–10.30, Sun 12–3, 7–10.30, public holidays **Closed** Chr Day and
Easter Sun **Cards** Access, Amex, Delta, Switch, Visa; personal and business accounts
Discount Available **Delivery** Free locally around branches nationally; nationwide
mail-order available **Glass hire** Free **Tasting and talks** By brand **Cellarage** Not
available

The multifarious Thresher group is Britain's largest wine retailer,
with over 1,600 outlets. Lumping them all together under one
heading is something the company objects to, since it would have
us believe it is impossible for anyone not to know the difference
between the various incarnations. Sorry chaps, you're wrong! The
presenter of Channel 4's *Pot Night* in Spring 1995 said of cannabis-
buying, 'for many people, it doesn't seem any more unusual than
going into Threshers and buying a can of Special Brew.' We doubt
if anyone jumped up and asked, 'does he mean Food & Drinks
Stores from Thresher, Drinks Stores from Thresher, or Thresher
Wine Shops?'

In wine terms, the main interest is to be found in Bottoms Up,
Wine Rack and Thresher Wine Shops. An increasingly confident-
looking Bottoms Up sits at the top of the tree and offers the largest
range of wines in surroundings that are spacious but just cluttered
enough. The atmosphere, the wines on the shelves and the usually
keen and bright staff combine to make the stores more appealing
than competitors Wine Cellar and Victoria Wine Cellars. The Wine
Rack stores offer a slightly smaller range, although it's difficult to
tell the difference between many of the smaller ones and the
supposedly inferior Wine Shops, and the staff do not seem as
enthusiastic as those in Bottoms Up. Some people scan the window
displays of the Thresher Wine Shops and wonder whether they
should not be called Beer Shops, but there's still a very respectable
range of wines inside.

The wine-buying continues to improve, and is now more
focused than in the past (although there are still ten New Zealand
Sauvignons). Recent promotions have featured some very
impressive wines. The southern French range contains gems at all
levels, including a delicious Malvoisie from the Côtes Catalanes
and further lovely wines from Mas Faussie and Domaine Gauby.
Tasty South Africans include the good-value Winelands range and
loftier stuff from Villiera and Warwick. Chile is the current

favourite, with the Las Colinas range and the Lontue wines from Valdivieso deserving particular mention.

In all other areas, the company offers at least competence, and often much more. The range of *petits châteaux* clarets introduced last year is good, not great, and those in search of exciting Bordeaux might care to look elsewhere. The burgundy selection, too, is solid rather than stunning, with the whites being more rewarding than the reds. Champagnes are very decent, with good but lesser-known names including Hamm and Drappier; we like the idea of the six J. L. Malard wines from different villages in the region, but we wonder whether customers will find it a bit too much to assimilate. The Alsace selection has been very strong of late and, although it has shrunk slightly, still offers some great whites from Zind-Humbrecht, Rolly-Gassmann and Hugel. The English range is also not as large as it has been, but, with most of the wines made by John Worontschak of the Harvest Wine Group (q.v.), the quality is excellent. The German selection has been improved by the arrival of some fine wines from Castel Vollmer and the Ruppertsberger co-op. Iberian wines of note include Rioja from Martínez Bujanda and Luis Pato's Portuguese wines. As well as more familiar fare from Rosemount and Penfolds, the Australians include a range of fine wines, under the Samuel's Bay label, that has been developed by Thresher in conjunction with Adam Wynn of Mountadam. Californians worth trying come from Voss, Duxoup and Firestone, and you'll also find the good-value King's Canyon range, made by Hugh Ryman in conjunction with the Arciero winery.

We should also mention the 'no-quibble guarantee' recently launched by the Wine Shops. Return any product you are dissatisfied with, and the staff will refund your money, no questions asked, even if the bottle is empty. Although the company is making rather a song and dance about it (there are several other merchants who will do exactly the same) the campaign has produced one of our favourite stories of the year. An old lady didn't enjoy the 3-litre cask of South African Chenin Blanc she had bought, but it was too heavy to take back to the shop on the bus. So she brought back a medical sample bottle filled with a small amount of the stuff (or at least no one doubted her word that it was wine). She was chauffeured home by the manager of the store bearing something different – and not in a sample bottle.

Best buys

Vin de Pays des Coteaux de Peyriac Blanc 1994, Mas Faussie, £
Quinta de Lamelas Red 1993, Douro, £
Samuel's Bay Eden Valley Riesling 1994, ££
Newtonian Cabernets 1991, Napa Valley, ££

Trout Wines

Nether Wallop, Stockbridge, Hampshire	*Tel* (01264) 781472
SO20 8EW	*Fax* (01264) 781472

Open Mon–Fri 9.30–1, 5–8 (early closing Mon), Sat 9.30–8 **Closed** Sun, public holidays, Monday from 1 **Cards** None accepted; personal and business accounts **Discount** 5–10% on mixed cases **Delivery** Free within 30-mile radius and in London **Glass hire** Free with order **Tasting and talks** Regular free tastings on Saturdays **Cellarage** Not available

Now into his third year as a wine-merchant in Nether Wallop, Anthony Whitaker is noticing a gradual increase in sales at the 'idyllic thatched cottage' that is his premises. Customers are becoming increasingly adventurous, and the range of wines is expanding, but the bottom line is 'I can only sell it if I like it'. It's still not a massive selection, and the last list we saw contained some wines which perhaps should have been pensioned off by now. However, you'll find a good set of regional French wines, decent oddments of claret and burgundy, and lovely champagne from Le Brun de Neuville and Ruinart. Several Sicilians from Pellegrino appear among the Italian bottles, Spanish offerings include good-value Navarra from Las Campañas, and you'll also find Riesling Forellenwein from Germany (Forellenwein translates as 'Trout wine'). Australian interest is provided by Mitchelton, Rothbury and Echo Point; Bonny Doon, Sequoia Grove and Oak Knoll top the range from the US, while the Warwick reds from Stellenbosch are the stars of the South African range.

Further incentives for a visit include Weston's cider, some tasty local beers, a range of Spanish nibbles from Borges and locally grown asparagus, when in season. Anthony's motto isn't exactly 'we never close', but if you should find yourself in Nether Wallop outside his opening hours and gasping for a glass of the strawberry-flavoured vermouth known as Chamberyzette (it could happen), he is more than willing to open his door to you if just ring the bell.

Best buys

Auxerrois, Danebury Vineyards 1992, £
1993 Finca Flichman Sangiovese/Cabernet, £
Rosso Bonera 1990, Settesoli, ££
St Emilion Grand Cru 1990, Clos des Menuts, ££

Turville Valley Wines

The Firs, Potter Row, Great Missenden,
Buckinghamshire HP16 9LT

Tel (01494) 868818
Fax (01494) 868832

Case sales only **Open** Mon–Fri 9–5.30 **Closed** Sat, Sun, public holidays, Xmas and Easter **Cards** Not available; business accounts **Discount** Not available **Delivery** Within 10-mile radius, £8 for first case, £3 for further cases (min. 1 case) **Glass hire** Not available **Tasting and talks** Not available **Cellarage** £5 per case per annum

The introduction of a minimum order price of £250 (before VAT) will probably have very little effect on most of this Buckinghamshire fine-wine merchant's customers. This is the place to come for fine and rare wine, particularly from Bordeaux and Burgundy, and overseas customers anxious for such goodies outnumber the Brits. The range is not as extensive as that of Farr Vintners, but one advantage is that the company is more willing to sell mixed cases. The commodity nature of the business means that wines listed one day could well have been sold to a Japanese customer the next; however, if they don't have your favourite claret available, they probably know a man who has. The range of producers in the burgundy selection is impressive, with broad ranges from Domaine de la Romanée-Conti, Leroy, Domaine Leflaive and Ramonet, plus good selections from other top growers. There are heavy-duty Rhônes from Jaboulet Aîné and Guigal and good stocks of ports ranging back to 1963, as well as various oddments such as Grange Hermitage, Sassicaia and Vega Sicilia. The range of madeiras must be the best around, with a choice from their birth year for 1995's centenarians, and even something for those celebrating their bicentenary.

Best buys

Côtes du Rhône 1991, Guigal, £
Haut-Médoc, Château Caronne Ste Gemme 1986, ££
Hermitage La Chapelle 1967, Jaboulet, ££

Ubiquitous Chip Wine Shop

8 Ashton Lane, Hillhead, Glasgow G12 9SJ

Tel 0141-334 7109
Fax 0141-337 1302

Open Mon–Fri 12–10; Sat 11–10 **Closed** Sun, Chr and New Year's Days **Cards** All accepted **Discount** 5% on 1 case (cash) **Delivery** Available within 10-mile radius of Glasgow (min. 3 cases) **Glass hire** Free with order **Tasting and talks** Tastings held in the restuarant **Cellarage** Not available

It would have been easy for Cliff Scott to develop an air of complacency in the absence of serious competition from other wine-merchants in Glasgow. However, we're pleased to say that his range shows no sign of slipping in quality, and if anything is growing stronger. Other merchants may cover certain regions in more depth, but, with the notable exception of German wines, the range here provides a good example of virtually every style of wine one could desire.

Customer demand is for wines from the southern hemisphere. Cliff offers a good range, including several impressive Australians. New Zealanders from Esk Valley, Redwood Valley and Martinborough, and South Africans from Neil Ellis, Warwick and Klein Constantia. From South America, you'll find Concha y Toro Chileans and Norton Argentinians. Edging north of the Equator, there are L. A. Cetto's Mexican Petite Syrah and some great Californian wines: Joseph Swan Zinfandel, Sonoma Cutrer Chardonnay and Le Cigare Volant, to name but three.

Riojas from Montecillo and La Rioja Alta stand out in a good Spanish range, and the robust Portuguese reds provide further Iberian interest. Notable Italian wines are the Duca Enrico from Sicily, the Jermann whites from Friuli and Cascina Castle's astonishing Passum from Piemonte. France is covered with an admirable thoroughness. There's plenty of claret, young and old, cheap and not so cheap. Burgundies include whites from Domaine Leflaive and Vocoret, and reds from Tollot-Beaut and Leroy. The Rhônes are good, as are the Alsace wines from Rolly-Gassmann and Dopff & Irion. In the Loire range there's a 1928 Anjou moelleux, plus less ancient wines from Joguet, Domaine des Baumard and Henry Natter. French country wines feature the reds from Domaine de Trévallon and Mas de Daumas Gassac and much more besides.

If you need yet further temptation, over 100 malt whiskies are available, and there are occasional dinners and tastings in the adjoining restaurant. Indeed, the wine shop grew out of the restaurant, and as a consequence is able to offer stocks of wines maturer than might be available in some other places.

Best buys

Cent'are Rosso, Duca di Castlemonte 1992, £
Aligoté, Châtillon-en-Diois 1993, Domaine de la Gouyarde, £
Barolo Riserva 1985, Franco-Fiorana, ££
Sauvignon Blanc 1994, Mulderbosch, ££

Unwins

Head Office

Birchwood House, Victoria Road, Dartford,   *Tel* (01322) 272711
Kent DA1 5AJ   *Fax* (01322) 294469
Approximately 300 branches in South-East England

Open Mon–Fri 9–10, Sat 9–10.30, Sun and public holidays 12–3, 7–10 **Cards** All
accepted; personal and business accounts **Discount** 5% on case of 6; 10% on 1 case
(table and sparkling wine and own-label champagne); 12.5% on case of 12 champagne;
12.5% on all orders over £200 **Delivery** Within South-East England; mail-order
available **Glass hire** Free **Tasting and talks** Most Saturdays in selected branches
Cellarage Not available

Rather a strange company, Unwins. No other high-street chain can
compete with their range of classed-growth claret (six vintages of
Ch. Latour, five of Ch. Haut-Brion and much more besides at prices
that only those who managed to lay down *en primeur* stocks can
match). The recently introduced Portuguese range, including the
splendid Quinta da Foz de Arouce, is again difficult to beat. And
the Australian wines from Penfolds and Rosemount, if rather
familiar, are reliably good. But similar depth and quality from other
regions is lacking. There are several outcrops of quality, such as the
Loires from Vacheron and Couly-Dutheil, Châteauneuf from
Château des Fines Roches, Opus One from California and Grove
Mill Chardonnay from New Zealand, but the rest of the landscape
is still somewhat drab.

Unwins really should look closely at the areas that its high-street
competitors are focussing on, and seek to bolster the ranges from
South Africa, Chile and the south of France; a little more shopping
around in the Rhône and Burgundy would also not go amiss.
Claret at £75 a bottle and a pair of (rather good) Canadian wines
are all very well, but they do seem to be the icing on a rather
ordinary cake.

Best buys

Fitou 1991, Les Producteurs du Mont Tauch, £
Vin de Pays d'Oc, Domaine Collin Rosier Chardonnay, £
Pauillac 1989, Château Haut-Batailley, ££
Rougeon 1988, Calona Vineyards, British Columbia, ££

Valvona & Crolla

19 Elm Row, Edinburgh, Lothian EH7 4AA
Tel 0131-556 6066
Fax 0131-556 1668

Open Mon–Sat 8.30–6 (Thur and Fri till 7.30); most public holidays **Closed** Sun,
Xmas, Boxing Day until 2 Jan **Cards** Access, Amex, Switch, Visa; business accounts
Discount 5% on 12 bottles **Delivery** Free within Edinburgh (min. order £30);
nationwide at cost; mail-order available **Glass hire** Free with order **Tasting and
talks** Tutored and informal tastings given periodically **Cellarage** Not available

'I started at the bottom rung of the family wine and deli ladder,'
says Philip Contini. 'I am now at about rung number four, with 50
to go!' Judging by Valvona & Crolla's already extremely impressive
standards, the quality that will have been achieved when he finally
reaches the top will be staggering. The shop's latest award is that of
Britain's Best Specialist Food Shop: if you ever need to do a tasting
of Italian olive oil, this is the place to visit. For Italian wines as well,
the shop is extremely hard to beat. Prizes for Italian wine-merchant
of the year usually alternate between this company and Enotria
Winecellars in Wandsworth.

Non-Italian wines are limited to port and champagne, but
complaints about such vinous bigotry are rapidly defused by the
many fabulous bottles available. While Tuscany, Piemonte and
Veneto offer the healthiest selections, only Valle d'Aosta, Liguria
and Molise of Italy's 20 wine regions are unrepresented. Deep
pockets will find two dozen wines from Gaja, thirteen vintages of
Sassicaia and Maurizio Zanella's Ca' del Bosco wines, but anyone
with upwards of £4 to spend on a bottle will find a fabulous choice.
Those with a sweet tooth will find plenty to attack the fillings,
including first-rate Vin Santo from Avignonesi and Selvapiana.
We'll let Philip have the last word: 'Italian wine is a difficult subject
to understand and requires time and dedication. Our only and best
solution to assist the customer is to allow them to taste, taste and
taste again, and it seems to work.'

Best buys

Pinot Bianco La Vis 1994, Trentino, £
Barbera d'Asti 'Ceppi Storici' 1992, Araldica, £
Lugana 'I Frati' 1994, Dal Cero, ££
Valpolicella Classico Superiore La Grola 1991, Allegrini, ££

Helen Verdcourt Wines

Spring Cottage, Kimbers Lane, Maidenhead,   *Tel* (01628) 25577
Berkshire SL6 2QP

Case sales only **Open** All hours (24 hour answerphone) **Cards** None accepted;
personal and business accounts **Discount** 5% on 12+ case order **Delivery** Free
locally and in West and Central London (min. 1 case); nationwide at cost; mail-order
available £5 per case **Glass hire** Free **Tasting and talks** Regular tastings **Cellarage**
Not available

Come on all you Maidenheadians! When there is a wine-merchant
of the calibre of Helen Verdcourt on your doorstep, only a fool
would choose to cross the Channel to buy wine in Calais. Hers is a
range that changes according to where good wine is available, and
she says at the start of her most recent list that she is not importing
most of her usual French stars, due to a run of poor vintages. What
she is left with is still pretty impressive. There's a range of reds and
whites from Château de Beaucastel, plus other Rhône wines from
Guigal, Jaboulet Aîné and Jamet. Vincent Girardin provides great
affordable burgundy, while the Alsace wines from the Turckheim
co-op are similarly friendly to pocket and palate. The claret section
sticks mostly to *crus bourgeois*, with a clutch of wines from the
excellent 1990 vintage. Henry Pellé's Menetou-Salon, the Philippe
de Baudin Vins de Pays d'Oc and Granier champagne are also
tasty.

In the wake of those poor French vintages the Italian range has
been bolstered, and you'll find many tasty wines, particularly the
Piemonte wines from Vietti. Spanish wines, too, are good, and
include Martínez Bujanda Riojas, Augustus Cabernet Sauvignon
and the stunning Clos Mogador from the Priorato region. Ridge
and Newton head the Californian list, Oyster Bay and Palliser
Estate provide great New Zealanders, and South African wines
come from Saxenberg and Jordan. A long Australian list features
wines from Rockford, Hollick Cape Mentelle and St Hallett.

Such a range would be hard to match on either side of the
Channel, and the prices asked are distinctly on the reasonable side.
Even if you don't buy wine from Helen, you might want to join
one of the three wine clubs she runs in and around Maidenhead.

Best buys

Vin de Pays d'Oc Merlot 1992, Philippe de Baudin, £
Sauvignon de Touraine 1993/94, La Chapelle de Cray, £
Coudoulet de Beaucastel 1992, ££
Barbera d'Alba, Vigna Vecchia Scarrone 1993, Vietta, ££

Victoria Wine Company

Head Office
Dukes Court, Duke Street, Woking, Surrey
GU21 5XL
1,531 branches

Tel (01483) 715066
Fax (01483) 755234

Open Varies from shop to shop generally Mon–Sat 10–10 **Closed** Chr Day **Cards** Access, Delta, Switch, Visa; business accounts **Discount** 5% on 1 case; 7 for 6 on champagne, sparkling wine (over £5.99) (Victoria Wine Cellars only) **Delivery** Varies by shop **Glass hire** Free with larger order **Tasting and talks** Occasionally in selected shops **Cellarage** Not available

With the launch of the Gare du Vin and South of the Bordeaux shops in the late 1980s, Victoria Wine anticipated 1990s fashions for wine retailing. The idea was a sound one, but the execution (a triumph of style over content) was far from perfect; the shops soon closed. Since then, the company has spent time shoring up the defences, acquiring Augustus Barnett and becoming the second-largest retail chain in the country. The upmarket Victoria Wine Cellars shops were launched in 1994 from much stronger foundations, and the company now looks the healthiest it has done for several years.

As yet there are only 31 Victoria Wine Cellars shops, but there are plans for up to 150 in the next two to three years, several of which will be on former Augustus Barnett sites. Raising the expectations of customers in these areas overnight does have its problems, but it is a slightly easier task than the one that Wine Cellar (q.v.) faces in converting Cellar Five shoppers. First indications are that wine sales are exceeding expectations, and are typically up 25% year on year. The rest of the VW empire consists of 822 'Destination' Wine Shops and 504 Neighbourhood Drinks Stores (sounds remarkably similar to the Thresher set-up). The Drinks Stores are just basic off-licences, although the wines on the shelves continue to improve, while Wine Shops offer a much larger range: 75–90% of the Victoria Wine Cellars range, depending on the store, and wines not in stock can be ordered by the single bottle. There are also 179 Haddows stores in Scotland, plus a brand-new shop with 450 wines in the Cité Europe complex adjacent to the entrance to the Channel Tunnel in Calais (early reports of it are favourable).

The classier clarets, like many of the more interesting (and expensive) wines, are Victoria Wine Cellars exclusives. If a famous name is more important to you than something that tastes pleasant, you can find Léoville-Las-Cases 1992. We'd spend our £25 on a bottle each of Châteaux La Tour-Carnet and Teyssier from the infinitely more joyous 1990 vintage. However, wines from

Châteaux Laclaverie and le Meynieu are in wider distribution and are certainly worth trying. Southern French highlights are the Galet range and Big Frank's Red and White. The Jadot burgundies are usually good, although some of the older parcels can be variable in quality. There are several German wines at bargain prices which will be drinking well now, although they'll probably still be on the shop shelves for some time to come. The Italian section is not brilliant, but the Spanish is better and includes Contino Rioja and the Chivite Navarra wines. There's an impressive range of ports dating back to the 1960s and a recently introduced set of sherries in half-bottles. There is also what has been for several years one of the best own-label vintage champagnes in existence.

Turning to the New World, the Stratford Californians are the best of a rather pedestrian range, but the Chileans from la Fortuna, Canepa, Caliterra and Co are much better value. The pick of an excellent Australian range are the wines of Green Point, Katnook and Basedow. Notable South Africans come from Fairview and Graham Beck, while the excellent Shingle Peak wines, exclusive to the company, form part of a good New Zealand range.

Counter staff undergo a rigorous instruction programme before they're let loose on the public; even so, the standard of the shop staff, even in the Victoria Wine Cellars, still needs to rise to reach the Bottoms Up and Oddbins level. However, the company continues to improve, and, although the motto 'Connoisseurs Who Make Sense' is rather high falutin, it is increasingly appropriate.

Best buys

El Liso Barrel-aged Tempranillo, La Mancha, £
Vin de Pays d'Oc Chardonnay 1994, Galet Vineyards, £
1992 Katnook Botrytised Chardonnay, ££
1992 Fairview Estate Shiraz/Merlot, ££

La Vigneronne

105 Old Brompton Road, London SW7 3LE	*Tel* 0171-589 6113
	Fax 0171-581 2983

Open Mon–Fri 10–9, Sat 10–7 **Closed** Sun, public holidays **Cards** All accepted **Discount** 5% on 12 bottles; special discount to subscribers paying £10 per annum **Delivery** Nationwide up to £100 order, £10 delivery, £100-£200 is £5 delivery, £200+ free delivery, Scotland and Northern Ireland at cost; mail order available **Glass hire** Not available **Tasting and talks** Twice weekly tutored tastings **Cellarage** For existing customers only

---

If you don't see Liz and Mike Berry much in the La Vigneronne shop now, it is because they have moved to Provence, leaving day-to-day running of the shop in the very capable hands of Dion

Gunson. They aim to set up a business selling New World wines to French winemakers. Talk about coals to Newcastle!

Both of them return to these shores frequently, and the Berry touch is still very evident in the list; no one can beat the company for the regional French wines. As well as the familiar Mas de Daumas Gassac (although who else has so many vintages?) you'll find guts and passion throughout the range. Our favourites are the Vaquer whites, the good-value Terre Mégère wines and anything from Mas Jullien; and, if you want to see who is threatening to take the Hérault crown from Aimé Guibert, try the stunning Domaine de la Grange des Pères. Those bored with port but seeking something along the same lines might care to try the range of Banyuls, Maury and Rivesaltes.

If you're after wines from the Rhône or Alsace, you won't be disappointed. Chapoutier, Château Rayas and Jaboulet Aîné from the former, Marc Kreydenweiss, Léon Beyer and Trimbach from the latter are just some of the excellent producers whose wares are on show. Claret- and burgundy-lovers, too, will find much to savour, whether from recent vintages or one of the much more venerable offerings. From the Loire too, there's great wine available, notably the Lamé-Delille reds and Nicolas Joly whites.

If France receives the bulk of the attention, other countries are not neglected. Few merchants have a more eclectic and focused New World range (don't ask for Gallo wines here, unless you're after the expensive stuff from Sonoma). The shop also has plenty of German, Spanish and Italian wines to grab your attention. However, many of the more interesting wines only appear on the enticing newsletters. There's usually a theme behind each month's missive, but there should be something to take your fancy whatever your taste. Don't miss the bin-end sales either, when the sometimes quite high prices are slashed dramatically.

The La Vigneronne programme of tastings has to be one of the most invigorating. The past year's subjects have included Australian Semillon, Ch. d'Angludet, Savennières, Jermann, a decade of Domaine de Trévallon and the wines of Gaja, tutored by Angelo Gaja himself.

Best buys

Merlot d'Oc 1993, Domaine Terre Mégère, £
1994 Viognier d'Oc, Domaine Terre Mégère, £
Château Simone Palette 1992, ££
Mas Jullien Languedoc 'Cailloutis' 1992, ££

Villeneuve Wines

37 Eastgate, Peebles, Borders EH45 8AE

Tel (01721) 722500
Fax (01721) 729922

Open Mon–Thur 9–8, Fri–Sat 9–9, Sun 12.30–5.30, public holidays **Closed** 25 and 26 Dec, 1 and 2 Jan **Cards** Access, Delta, Switch, Visa; personal and business accounts **Discount** 5% off cases **Delivery** Free delivery within 50-mile radius (min. 1 case); nationwide mail-order available **Glass hire** Free **Tasting and talks** By invitation to regular customers **Cellarage** 5p per case per week

The disturbingly vivid horse on the cover of the Villeneuve wine-list sports something between a grin and a grimace. Perhaps it has just tasted its way through the company's commendable range of wines and is bracing itself to start on the 150 or so malt whiskies. Those wines include a Loire range from Langlois-Chateau and Alsace from Trimbach and the Ribeauvillé Co-op. There are Rhônes from Jaboulet Aîné and Chapoutier, burgundies from La Chablisienne and Faiveley and a range of Pierre Ferraud beaujolais. Amid several first-growth clarets are less pricy wines from Châteaux Cissac and de Sours. Most impressive of the regional French wines are the Domaine de Trévallon reds. Champagne come from Jean Lefebvre, and the company rates it as being at least as good as many of the grandes marques.

The Italian list is profuse and includes the Canaletto wines from Veneto, the Jermann whites from Friuli and Chianti Rufina from Villa de Vetrice. Iberian interest is provided by the Spanish wines of Jean León, Enate and La Rioja Alta and a range of tasty Portuguese reds. Best amid a large Eastern European selection are the Bataapati Hungarian wines. Fetzer supplies good-value Californians, with pricier fare coming from Sonoma Cutrer and Saintsbury. Chilean wines are impressive, and there is a huge range from the Antipodes. South Africa is nearly as well represented, with wines from Thelema, Klein Constantia and de Wetshof.

After last year's expansion of the retail premises there has been a corresponding expansion in sales. With a range such as this, it's not hard to see why.

Best buys

Rothbury Trident 1992, £
Beyerskloof Pinotage, NV, £
Grand Cru St Emilion 1990, Château Pasquette, ££
Hautes Côtes de Nuits Blanc 1993, Dufouleur, ££

Vinceremos Wines

(Mail-order only)   *Tel* (0113) 257 7545
261 Upper Town Street, Bramley, Leeds,   *Fax* (0113) 257 6903
West Yorkshire LS13 3JT

Case sales only   **Open** Mon–Fri 9–5.30; Sat (by arrangement)   **Closed** Sun, public holidays   **Cards** Access, Visa   **Discount** 5% on 5+ cases; 10% on 10+ cases   **Delivery** Free locally (min. 1 case), nationally 1–4 cases £5.95, 5+ cases free; nationwide mail-order service   **Glass hire** Free locally only   **Tasting and talks** Bi-annual tasting in Leeds   **Cellarage** 5p per week per case

The idea behind organic winemaking is a good one. The absence of added chemicals from both vineyard and the winery means that what ends up in your glass is a much more natural and healthy drink. Not many years ago the standards of organic winemaking left much to be desired. Reducing the use of sulphur dioxide, the winemaker's disinfectant, was philosophically sound, but in practice wines oxidised all too frequently. The number of such wines is now far less than it was; producers have learned to keep their juice clean, and wines calling themselves organic have never been better.

Vinceremos does have wines that are not organic, notably the range of vegetarian Vins de Pays de l'Aude from Domaine Saint Michel and the Moroccans from Sincomar. However, most of the wines do belong to one or other of the range of organic organisations around the world. The stars of the French range are the Vacqueyras from Domaine le Clos de Caveau, Pierre André's Châteauneuf, the Provence wines from Domaine du Jas d'Esclans and Domaine Richeaume, and Jacques Frelin's southern offerings. There are a few clarets, but burgundies (red and white) are noticeably absent. Fizz on offer includes champagne from José Ardinat and Clairette de Die from Achard Vincent. Highlights from the rest of the list are James Millton's New Zealand whites and the selection of organic beers and ciders.

Best buys

Rabbi Jacob, Sincomar, £
Vin de Pays de l'Hérault 1993, Domaine de Savignac, £
Millton Vineyard Barrel-Fermented Chenin Blanc 1994, ££
Muscadet de Sèvre et Maine Sur Lie 1994, Guy Bossard, ££

Vin du Van Wine Merchants

Colthups, The Street, Appledore, Kent TN26 2BX

Tel (01233) 758727
Fax (01233) 758727

Open Mail-order only; Mon–Sun and public holidays 9–6 **Closed** Xmas and Boxing Days **Cards** Cash or cheques only **Discount** Not available **Delivery** Free delivery within 30-mile radius (min. 4 bottles); nationwide mail-order service **Glass hire** Not available **Tasting and talks** Occasional tutored tastings **Cellarage** Not available

Mr Bonkers of Appledore, aka Ian Brown, continues to cock a snook at wine snobs everywhere, sometimes accompanying it with a mean 12-bar blues on his Strat. 'It's strange but spookily true that those who hanker in mode nostalgic for the good old days when wine was wine and Lafite was a tenner a Nebuchadnezzar are, of course, talking complete, utter and total cobblers.' The style will grate with many, but a growing band of customers finds it a welcome breath of fresh air in an often stuffy wine world. Over half of them are doctors and surgeons who respond to his offers in General Practitioner (we always did worry about the medical sense of humour!). The business is all mail-order, so don't turn up on his doorstep unless you want Stanley the Cat MW (Moggy of Wine?) to set his claws into you.

The Chilean and Spanish wines that Ian used to stock are no more, since customers were ignoring them with vigour. However, his Australian range continues to expand and must be one of the biggest around. Indeed, with the exception of Château Musar, Californians from Beringer and Noceto, L. A. Cetto's Mexican wines and some great New Zealanders from Seifried and Jackson, there's nothing else on offer. The big names are all there, but lesser-known wineries such as Glenara, Coriole, Chatsfield and Reynolds Yarraman are also worth exploring. Unusually for a mail-order merchant, it's not necessary to buy by the case, and indeed, case purchases attract no discount. However, with prices that are some of the keenest around, it would be very easy to put together a rather large order.

Best buys

Houghton HWB 1994, £
Penfolds Bin 2 Shiraz/Mourvèdre 1992, £
Charlie Melton Sparkling Shiraz 1991/2, ££
Chambers Rutherglen Liqueur Muscat, ££

The Vine Trail

5 Surrey Road, Bishopston, Bristol,   *Tel* (0117) 9423946
Avon BS7 9DJ   *Fax* (0117) 9423946

Case sales only   **Open** Can be contacted from 8–11pm, 7 days a week   **Cards** None accepted; personal and business accounts   **Discount** 2% on 5+ cases; 3% on 10+ cases; 5% on 25+ cases; trade discounts negotiable   **Delivery** Free in Bristol; mail-order available   **Glass hire** Free with 3+case order   **Tasting and talks** Tutored and informal tastings held regularly in Bristol; annual tasting in London and Cheshire **Cellarage** £4+VAT per case per year

Stretching (just) to 80 wines, Nick Brookes' range is certainly not the largest around. With none of the wines coming from outside France, it is also not the most comprehensive. However, for the efficiency with which it covers France's major areas, and for the number of good but unfamiliar winemakers represented, it is something of a gem.

There's a small range of champagne plus 'the world's best sparkling white' Vincent Raimbault's Vouvray brut. M. Raimbault also knows how to make decent still Vouvray (dry and semi-dry), and his wines sit in the Loire range alongside a more familiar Pouilly Fumé from Jean-Claude Chatelain. André Thomas may not be the most familiar of names in Alsace, but his wines are excellent, particularly the Riesling. Stars in the Rhône section include Pierre Gonon's white St Joseph and the reds from Domaine Brusset, while perhaps the best of some very quaffable beaujolais is the Côte de Brouilly from Château Thivin. Burgundy fans will enjoy Jean Collotte's red and white Marsannay and the full, nutty Pouilly-Fuissé from Jacques Saumaize. There's a set of decent clarets but little white Bordeaux, apart from the Ch. de Rolland Barsac, but the dry Montravel from Domaine de Perreau is wonderfully clean and fresh. Of the three Jurançon wines on offer, the best is the sweet, full and fleshy Clos Thou, while of the wine from the Languedoc, the wines of Terre Mégère stand out.

Those not living in the south-west need not miss out on this range, because, besides two major Bristol tastings, there are annual events in Cheshire and London.

Best buys

Montravel Sec 1994, Domaine Perreau, £
Côtes du Ventoux 1993, Domaine Peysson, £
Chénas 1993, Bernard Broyer, ££
Canon Fronsac 1989, Château Cassagne Haut Canon, ££

El Vino

47 Fleet Street, London EC4Y 1BJ	*Tel* 0171-353 5384
	Fax 0171-936 2367

Open Mon–Fri 11–8, Sats before Chr **Closed** Sun, public holidays, most Sats **Cards** Access, Amex, Visa; personal and business accounts **Discount** Negotiable for large orders **Delivery** Within City and West End; mail-order available **Glass hire** Free **Tasting and talks** 12 per year, plus tutored (with speaker) tastings on demand **Cellarage** £4.50 per case per annum

El Vino has been serving the City with wine for well over 100 years, so it comes as no surprise to hear Graham Mitchell (fourth generation of Mitchells in the family business) say, 'whilst there has been a significant increase in the purchase of New World wines, traditional claret and burgundy remain our specialities.' Many of the burgundies are El Vino's own selection (either that or they have missed the producer's name off the wine list), and the quality of those we've tried has been good, with a 1992 Petit Chablis from Durup, in particular, being excellent. There are clarets ranging from Communard Bordeaux Rouge to Ch. Latour and Ch. Lafite. There are small Spanish and Italian ranges and a slightly larger (producerless) set of Germans. Those encroaching New World bottles include Australian wines from Basedows, New Zealanders from Redwood Valley, and the Beyerskloof Pinotage from South Africa. Ports are from several of the major houses, or you could settle for a bottle of Magnificent Old Tawny. The three wine bars in the City will soon be joined by a fourth on London Wall.

Best buys

El Vino Choisi de Boyier French white table wine, £
1991 El Vino Rioja Crianza, £
1993 El Vino Pinot Blanc d'Alsace, ££
Bordeaux 1985, Château Brun-Labrie, ££

Vintage Roots

Sheeplands Farm, Wargrave Road, Wargrave,	*Tel* (01734) 401222
Berkshire RG10 8DT	*Fax* (01734) 404814

Case sales only **Open** Mon–Fri 9–6 **Closed** Sat, Sun, public holidays **Cards** Access, Visa; business accounts **Discount** 5% on 5+ cases; £1.50 per case collection discount **Delivery** Available within a 30-mile radius of Reading (min. 1 case); 1 case £3.95, 2 cases £5, 6+ cases £6; mail-order service available **Glass hire** Free with order **Tasting and talks** 1–2 per year, or by arrangement to groups **Cellarage** Not available

Unlike Vinceremos, the only other serious organic wine specialist, Neil Palmer and Lance Pigott's company offers only organic wines. There is some overlap between the two companies' lists, but this range does seem fuller. Domaine St Apollinaire provides toothsome Côtes-du-Rhône, while the star of the Loire range is Huet's Vouvray. White burgundies come from Jean Javillier and Guyot, and reds are provided by Jean-Claude Rateau. Penedés wines come from Albet i Noya, Sedlescombe English wines are available, and Australian bottles include the Botobolar Mudgee range and the company's own Robinvale red and white. There's even a 1985 Californian Cabernet Sauvignon from Frey Vineyards. The list gives details of which wines are vegetarian, which are vegan, and which are made using biodynamic farming methods.

A final word (which could also have appeared with the Vinceremos entry). The trophy winner in the 1994 Organic Wine Challenge was Penfolds' first organic white. The winner the following year was its first organic red. It's not surprising that such a vast organisation should produce good organic wine. All the same, the ease with which the company won these awards first time out would seem to indicate that wine-making standards in other parts of the organic world still have some catching up to do. Perhaps the good reports of biodynamic methods emanating from several producers around the world deserve even more widespread attention. (Those interested in finding out more about biodynamic methods can obtain a leaflet from Vintage Roots, written by St-Emilion producer Guy Meslin of Ch. Laroze, outlining the main principles.)

Best buys

Soave Superiore 1994, Gino Fasoli, £
1994 Albet y Noya Tempranillo, Penedés, £
Meursault 1992, Jean Javillier, ££
Côtes de Bourg 1990, Château Falfas 'Le Chevalier', ££

The Vintry

Park Farm, Milland, Liphook, Hampshire GU30 7JT	*Tel* (01428) 741389
	Fax (01428) 741368
Plastow Farm, Plastow Green, Newbury, Berkshire RG19 8LP	*Tel* (01635) 268230
	Fax (01635) 269276
Manor Farm, Nyland, nr Gillingham, Dorset SP8 5SG	*Tel* (01963) 370848
	Fax (01963) 370253

Case sales only **Open** Never closes **Cards** None accepted; cheques only **Discount** By negotiation **Delivery** Not available **Glass hire** Free **Tasting and talks** Held twice a year at each of the three outlets **Cellarage** Available by arrangement

---

Alan Johnson-Hill makes decent claret at Château Méaume. Nigel Johnson-Hill works as a stockbroker in London but finds time to sell his brother's wine, as well as other French wines with a British connection. These include Ch. de Seuil Graves from Bob & Sue Watts and David Thomas's Ch. Bauduc. There are always some classy clarets available (Ch. le Bon-Pasteur and Ch. d'Angludet on the last list) and a range of burgundy from Louis Latour. Regional wines include Chais Cuxac Chardonnay and Corbières from Domaine du Révérend. Sparklers include wonderful champagne from Charbaut, and one non-French wine in the shape of Roederer Quartet from California. The list is one of the smallest around, but customers obviously appreciate the very personal touch brought to the wine business by the Johnson-Hills and the two other couples they work with.

Best buys

Bordeaux Rosé 1994, Château Méaume, £
Chais Cuxac Chardonnay NV, £
Margaux Réserve 1993, Peter Sichel, ££
Vin de Pays d'Oc 1993, Muscat à Petits Grains, Hugh Ryman, ££

Waitrose

Head Office
Southern Industrial Area, Bracknell,   *Tel* (01344) 424680
Berkshire RG12 8YA   *Fax* (01344) 305662
111 subsidiary outlets; John Lewis Partnership

Open Mon–Sat 8.30–6, Sun 10–4 (some stores open on a Sun) **Closed** most public holidays **Cards** Access, Delta, Switch, Visa **Discount** 5% on unsplit case, promotion wines 12 for 11 **Delivery** mail-order available **Glass hire** Free **Tasting and talks** Available at some branches **Cellarage** Not available

---

Despite the vast improvement in supermarkets over the past ten years, there are still small, grotty branches of virtually all the chains somewhere in the country. We can't recall visiting or hearing of a grotty branch of Waitrose though; perhaps they don't exist. Customers prepared to pay that bit more (and not just for wine) will, not surprisingly, find higher quality, both on the shelves and in the character of the stores themselves.

This is particularly true where wine is concerned. The aim is that customers should feel they are in a distinct part of the shop, and not just another aisle full of barcodes (this is evidenced by the separate tills for wine purchases in many branches). The only wines you'll find at £1.99 are half-bottles and the obligatory Lambrusco, although wine-for-wine, the prices are not much different from those in other supermarkets.

The main activity at the moment is in the ranges from South Africa, Chile and the South of France. From South Africa the Delheim Cabernet and the Chardonnays from Avontuur and Klein

Constantia are excellent, as are the Valdivieso Chilean wines. The recent batch of new wines from southern France is slightly hit-and-miss, although don't miss the Chais Cuxac Viognier and the Laperouse white. Eastern Europe and Australia continue to be popular, but the most impressive range is the clarets. The stars are the 1990 Biston-Brillette and La Roseraie de Gruaud Larose, a surprisingly good 1992, but several other good wines (notably from 1990) are available. The own-label champagne is also special, and anyone after great but unfashionable wine should check out the mature German Rieslings.

Having no less than five Masters of Wine in the buying department is an asset of which any company would be proud, but the fact that they also have a very reasonable commercial sense is, if anything, more important. If for any reason the wine range does not reach the heights a customer would like, there is always the Waitrose Direct mail-order service offered by Findlater Mackie & Todd.

Best buys

Tokay Pinot Gris d'Alsace 1993, Cave de Beblenheim, ££
Costières de Nîmes 1993, Château de Nages, £
Leasingham Shiraz 1992, Clare Valley, South Australia, ££
Wairau River Sauvignon Blanc 1994, Marlborough, ££

Waterloo Wine Company

59–61 Lant Street, Borough, London SE1 1QL

Tel 0171-403 7967
Fax 0171-357 6976

Open Mon–Fri 10–6.30, Sat 10–5 **Closed** Sun and public holidays **Cards** Access, Delta, Switch, Visa; business accounts **Discount** None offered **Delivery** Central London, other areas by arrangement; mail-order service available **Glass hire** Returnable deposit required **Tasting and talks** Monthly **Cellarage** Not available

By the time this edition of the Guide appears, the sense of expectation will be rising at the Waterloo Wine Company. Proprietor Paul Tutton has a vineyard in Waipara, New Zealand that has been producing excellent wine for some time, but this year will see the arrival of the first wines that Paul himself has made. Whether it will be known, as in the case of a certain Ottery-St-Mary-based wine-maker/merchant, as Chairman's Plonk remains to be seen.

There are other New Zealand wines available, including Redwood Valley Chardonnay and the St Nesbit Cabernet/Merlot blend. The Stoniers Merricks wines from Australia show the great potential of the Mornington Peninsula, while the Caliterra Chileans improve with every vintage. The Italian list concentrates on Piemonte, with Barolo from Aurelio Settimo and Barbaresco from Punset, and there are decent German wines from the Staatsweingüter Eltville, plus a set from CVNE in Spain.

Best among the burgundies are the Perrot-Minot reds and Roger Belland's whites. The bordeaux and Rhône ranges are good rather than great, but the Loire selection is very impressive, and anyone who favours Sauvignon Blanc, Cabernet Franc or Chenin Blanc (of whatever age or sweetness) will find something tasty here. In particular, those who have never seen the point of Loire reds should try the wines from Couly-Dutheil, Lamé-Delille and Mabileau. Seltz provides Alsace wines, and good regional wines include Domaine la Tour Boisée Minervois and Corbières from Château Hélène. We would recommend you to eschew the champagnes from more famous names and try those under the Le Brun de Neuville label, which are extraordinarily good.

Best buys

Minervois 1991, Domaine la Tour Boisée Rouge, £
1993/4 Azay-le-Rideau Rosé, Pibaleau, £
Pinot Noir 1993, Mark Rattray Vineyard, Waipara, New Zealand, ££
Barolo Vignette Roche 1988, Aurelio Settimo, ££

Waters of Coventry

Collins Road, Heathcote, Warwick,	*Tel* (01926) 888889
Warwickshire CV34 6TF	*Fax* (01926) 887416

Case sales only **Open** Mon–Fri 9–5 **Closed** Sat, Sun, public holidays **Cards** Access, Visa; personal and business accounts **Delivery** Within 40-mile radius Warwick (min. 2 cases); nationwide mail-order £6+VAT on 1 case, 5+ free **Glass hire** Not available **Tasting and talks** Not available **Cellarage** Not available

Robert Caldicott acknowledges that his modern warehouse premises are not the ideal place for presenting wines to the general public, rather than to the hotel and restaurant trade that forms the bulk of his sales. 'However,' he adds, 'we do have quite a keen following.' Looking at the wines he stocks, it's not hard to see why.

Devaux provides the keenly priced Paul de Richebourg champagne as well as wines under its own label. Ch. Palmer heads a claret range that also contains such affordable wines as Ch. La Tour St-Bonnet and Ch. d'Angludet. Burgundy comes from Rodet, Jacques Prieur and Louis Latour, with the range augmented by Daniel Dampt's Chablis and Duboeuf beaujolais. Highlights from the rest of France are the Couly-Dutheuil Chinon, Louis Sipp's Alsace and lovely Chenin Blanc from Domaine des Sablonettes. The

German selection lacks conviction, but the Italian wines from Antinori and the Spanish from CVNE and Senorío de Sarria are much better.

The South African range features wines from Boschendal and Zonnebloem, while those of Jackson Estate stand out in a short New Zealand selection. Montes, Concha y Toro and Cousiño Macul represent Chile, Australian bottles come from Taltarni, Rothbury and Brown Brothers, and Mondavi, Clos du Bois and Ridge provide Californian interest.

There's also a large range of malt whiskies, ports from most of the major houses and sherry from González Byass. If such things interest you, why not join Mr Caldicott's 'keen following'?

Best buys

Côtes du Roussillon 1992, Domaine Força Réal, £
Villa Rosa Sauvignon, Chile, £
Graves Blanc 1990, Château Montalivet, ££
Chablis ler cru Côte de Lechet 1992, Domaine Daniel Dampt, ££

Weavers of Nottingham

Vintner House, 1 Castle Gate, Nottingham,	*Tel* (0115) 9580922
Nottinghamshire NG1 7AQ	*Fax* (0115) 9508076

Open Mon–Sat 9–5.45 **Closed** Sun, public holidays **Cards** All accepted; personal and business accounts **Discount** By negotiation **Delivery** Free within 50-mile radius (min. 6 bottles) **Glass hire** 10p per dozen if delivered and collected **Tasting and talks** Available **Cellarage** Not available

Weavers has been selling wine in the heart of Nottingham for over 150 years, with the Trease family at the head of the company since 1887. The range assembled by Alan Trease and fellow-director Keith Whitehead is a solid one. Champagne comes from Joseph Perrier, beaujolais from Duboeuf and Chablis from William Fèvre, with other burgundies from Louis Latour. Clarets are commendable, as are the Alsace wines from Schlumberger and the Rhônes from Domaine du Vieux Télégraphe. Spanish highlights are CVNE Riojas and the Somontano wines from Viñas del Vero, while Italians of note include Poggio Antico's Brunello and a selection from Antinori.

The West Peak whites are good cheap South African bottles, although the Boschendal wines are better. Other New World wines of note are Concha y Toro's from Chile, Jackson Estate's, from New Zealand and the Australians from Goundrey, Mitchell and Cape Mentelle. There are several sherries to tickle your fancy, with the best being the Lustau almacenista range. There are also ports dating back to 1970 Graham and a large range of malt whiskies. Chances to further your acquaintance with the range include in-store tastings and more formal events at No. 17 Castle Gate, the Georgian town house that is home to the company's growing agency division.

Best buys

Buda Bridge Hungarian Chardonnay, £
1991 Orla Dorada Crianza, £
Graves 1986, Château Smith-Haut-Lafitte, ££
Sauvignon Blanc 1994, C. J. Pask Hawkes Bay, ££

Whitesides Wine Merchants

Shawbridge Street, Clitheroe, Lancashire
BB7 1NA

Tel (01200) 22281
Fax (01200) 27129

Open Mon–Sat 9–5.30 **Closed** Sun, public holidays **Cards** Access, Delta, Switch, Visa; personal and business accounts **Discount** 5% on cases **Delivery** Free within Lancashire, Cumbria and North Yorkshire (min. 1 case); mail-order service £6 per case **Glass hire** Free with order **Tasting and talks** On site to groups, charged at cost **Cellarage** Not available

While not stocking anywhere near the same number of wines as their Clitheroe colleagues D Byrne & Co, Whitesides nonetheless have a very reasonable set of wines. Retail and admin. manager Sue Lewtas, who also writes a fortnightly wine column for the local paper, tells us that customers are drinking less wine but of better quality. There's plenty of interest in French regional wines, and Whitesides satisfies this demand with some fine wines from the Coteaux du Languedoc. You'll also find Muscadet from Chéreau-Carré, Alsace wines from Louis Sipp and Rhônes from Max Aubert and Jaboulet Aîné. Highlights among the burgundies are Laroche Chablis, Pommard from Comte Armand and Jacques Prieur's Meursault. A smaller bordeaux range concentrates on the sub-£10 level, and champagnes come from Bruno Paillard and several of the larger houses.

The Friedrich-Wilhelm-Gymnasium Rieslings stand out in the German section of the list, and the Spanish selection includes Riojas from Marqués de Cáceres and Faustino Martínez. Italians of interest come from Tiefenbrunner, Frescobaldi and Taurino. The Californian range is slightly lacklustre, but the Washington State wines of Paul Thomas and the Oregon pair from the Willamette Valley are more interesting. Mount Hurtle, Willespie and Penfolds provide the best of the Australians, while the New Zealand wines from Coopers Creek, Grove Mill and Delegats are also good. In the

South African section we'd steer you past the KWV wines to those from Blue Rock and Mouton Excelsior.

This is a range which hits more than it misses, but we'd like to see a little more adventurousness shown in choosing some of the wines.

Best buys

Coteaux du Languedoc 1993, Château de Granoupiac Blanc, £
St Chinian 1993, Château Guiraud Rouge, £
Oregon Pinot Gris 1992, Willamette Valley, ££
Monthélie 1992, Domaine du Château de Puligny-Montrachet, ££

Whittalls Wines

Darlaston Road, Walsall,   *Tel* (01922) 36161
West Midlands WS2 9SQ   *Fax* (01922) 36167

Case sales only   **Open** Mon–Fri 9–5.30   **Closed** Sat, Sun, public holidays   **Cards** None accepted; personal and business accounts   **Discount** By negotiation on 5+ cases   **Delivery** Free within 10-mile radius, nationwide £8+VAT per consignment (5+ cases free); mail-order available   **Glass hire** Free with order   **Tasting and talks** Tastings either by shop or foreign winemakers   **Cellarage** £1.75 per case per year

---

Whittalls Fine Wine Manager Richard Vodden reports that the effect of cross-Channel shopping is felt even as far north as Walsall, particularly on sales of cheaper wines. However, he counters such assaults with 'a fast, efficient service offering traditional and modern wines backed with sound advice.' The traditional type includes clarets up to first-growth level, but with much of interest around the £10 mark, and an array of Sauternes from the good vintages of the 1980s. White burgundies come from Domaine Laroche, Henri Clerc and Jean Germain, reds from Coste-Caumartin, Domaine des Varoilles and Antonin Rodet. From among more familiar Rhônes, try the Gigondas from Domaine les Goubert and Marcel Juge's Cornas. Other French wines to look out for are Schlumberger Alsace, Domaine Daulny's Sancerre and champagnes from de Venoge.

Michel Schneider provides much of the German range, while Spanish wines come from Marqués de Cáceres and Faustino Martínez. Best of the Italians are the Piemonte wines from Ascheri. New World interest is provided by Peter Lehmann and Yaldara from Australia, Babich and Dashwood from New Zealand, South Africans from Blue Rock and Paul Thomas's Washington State wines.

If you attend one of the regular tutored tastings, you may find a visiting winemaker or Richard himself speaking. Whittalls runs a programme of special offers and occasional *en primeur* campaigns.

If you buy wines from the company but don't feel like having them delivered just yet, the cellarage charge of £1.75 per case per year is one of the lowest around.

Best buys

Bordeaux Supérieur 1990, Château Saint Marten Baracan, £
Côtes du Rhone 1988, Domaine Brune, £
Sancerre 1992, Domaine Daulny, ££
Gevrey-Chambertin premier cru 1985, Clos Des Varoilles, ££

Wickham & Co

New Road, Bideford, Devon EX39 2AQ
Tel (01237) 473292
Fax (01237) 472471

Open Mon–Fri 9–5, Sat 9–1 **Closed** Sun and public holidays **Cards** Access, Switch, Visa; personal and business accounts **Discount** 5% on 1+ case; larger orders by negotiation **Delivery** Free in Devon (min. 1 case); mail-order available **Glass hire** Free with order **Tasting and talks** Occasional tutored tastings, other tastings throughout the year **Cellarage** Not available

This Bideford merchant is owned by London-based Balls Brothers (q.v.) but operates independently. Membership of the Merchant Vintners buying consortium means that many of the wines (for example the Rowlands Brook Australians, Marc Ryckwaert's Côtes-du-Rhône and the C. J. Pask New Zealanders) will be familiar to customers of such companies as House of Townend, Adnams, Lay & Wheeler and Tanners. Clarets are impressive, with plenty of sensibly priced wines such as Châteaux Montalivet (Graves), de Pez (St-Estèphe) and Moulin-à-Vent (Moulis). Burgundies are mainly from merchants, although wine-buyer Ron Harris is particularly proud to have found the wines of Domaine Dupont-Fahn. The Alsace, Loire and Rhône ranges contain plenty of interesting wines; champagne is from Joseph Perrier and other more famous *grandes marques*. The regional fare from Domaine de l'Arjolle and Château Fonscolombe are certainly worth trying.

The Italian range is rather dull, but the Spanish selection from Ochoa and CVNE is better and the German wines from Friedrich-Wilhelm-Gymnasium and Bischofliches Priesterseminar better still. Apart from the ubiquitous Penfolds, Australian wines of note come from Mitchell and Wolf Blass. Californians are poor, but the New Zealanders from Goldwater Estate and Hunter's are excellent. The Chilean bottles are from Concha y Toro and the South Africans from Boschendal, Fairview and Klein Constantia. Local colour appears in the shape of Mark Sharman's Sharpham wines from near Totnes.

Best buys

Bordeaux Rouge 1993, Château la Combe des Dames, £
Rowlands Brook Shiraz, South Australia, £
Champagne Joseph Perrier Cuvée Josephine 1985, ££
1989 Don Melchior Cabernet Sauvignon, Concha y Toro, ££

Windrush Wines

The Ox House, Market Place, Northleach,	*Tel* (01451) 860680
Cheltenham, Gloucestershire GL54 3EG	*Fax* (01451) 861166
142 Old Brompton Road, London SW7 4NR	*Tel* 0171-244 8118
	Fax 0171-244 6014
The Knightsbridge Pantry, 12 William Street,	*Tel* 0171-235 0460
London SW1 9HL	*Fax* 0171-235 0783
85 High Street, Oxford, Oxfordshire OX1 4BG	*Tel* (01865) 798085
	Fax (01865) 798893
25 High Street, Hungerford, Berkshire RG17 0NF	*Tel* (01488) 686850
	Fax (01488) 686850

Open Mon–Sat 8–10, Sun 8–5, public holidays **Closed** Chr Day, Boxing Day, Easter Sun **Cards** All accepted; personal and business accounts **Delivery** Free within 6-mile radius (over 5 cases); 1–2 cases £6, 3 cases £8, 4 cases £10; nationwide mail-order service available **Glass hire** Free **Tasting and talks** Weekly in shops or by request **Cellarage** Not available

With five shops now in the chain (and plans for possibly seven more by the end of 1996), Windrush Wines is threatening to swamp the south of England with its wares. The food is of a very high calibre (dry goods from Fauchon, Innes breads and much more besides), and the wines are also excellent. This has always been a place to find wines from America's Pacific north-west, and the current selection does not let you down, featuring Eyrie, Ponzi and Adelsheim from Oregon, plus Salishan from Washington. In addition, you'll find some super Californian bottles, particularly the Storybook Mountain Zinfandels. Australian wines of note come from Chateau Xanadu, Leconfield and Goundrey, New Zealanders from Neudorf and Jackson Estate, and South Africans from Warwick and Wellington. The Italian and Spanish ranges are small but carefully chosen.

From France, there's a small Bordeaux range and a larger set from Burgundy that includes beaujolais from Trénel and Thévenet's impeccable Mâcon. From the Loire comes Château Gaudrelle's succulent Vouvray, while the Rhônes feature Domaine Maby's rich, perfumed wine from the Coteaux de Cèze and Châteauneuf from Domaine de Nalys. The Jurançon from Clos Lapeyre and Domaine Tempier Bandol form just part of a

fascinating set of regional wines, and the champagnes from
Billecart-Salmon and Bollinger will not fail to please.

Even without the food, this eclectic range would merit attention.
With it, it looks even better. And if the wines ever start to lose their
appeal, you can always try the exquisitely named beers from the
Bavarian Scherdel brewery: Weissbier Hell and Doppelbock
Dunkel.

Best buys

Bergerac Sec 1991, Château Richard, £
Dão Tinto Quinta Do Serrado, 1991, £
Collioure Cuvée Les Piloums 1987, Domaine Du Mas Blanc, ££
Pinot Gris 1993, Adelsheim Vineyards, ££

The Wine and Beer Company

Marco's Wines and Spirits

13 Ferrier Street, London SW18 1SN	*Tel* 0181-875 1900
	Fax 0181-875 9797
Rue de Judeé, Zone Marcel Doret, 62100, Calais	*Tel* 00 33 21 97 63 00
567 King's Road, London SW6 2EB	*Tel* 0171-731 0773
Centre Commerciale Continent, Quai de L'Entrepôt 50100 Cherbourg	*Tel* 00 33 33 22 23 22
Quai Frissard, Bassin Vantan, 76600 Le Havre	*Tel* 00 33 35 26 38 10

Open Mon–Fri 11–10, Sat 10–10, Sun 12–3 **Closed** Public holidays **Cards** Access,
Delta, Switch, Visa **Discount** 17.5% on champagne, 15% wine, 20% discount Fri and
Sat **Delivery** Within M25 (£50 min. order) **Glass hire** Free, breakages charged for
Tasting and talks Daily **Cellarage** Not available

With the sale of a number of London shops and the opening of
further ones in Le Havre and Cherbourg, Marco Attard's French
outlets now outnumber the English ones by three to two. Who can
blame him? The selection has never been marked by major
innovation but has tended to concentrate on familiar names at
razor-sharp prices, with *grande marque* champagnes in particular
available at hefty discounts for large purchases. Bordeaux is one of
the few areas where an attempt has been made to stock something
more unusual, with parcels of such interesting wines as 1982 Ch.
d'Issan, 1976 Ch. Lagrange (St-Julien) and 1979 Ch. Potensac in
stock at the time of writing. The Australian list is as healthy as ever,
with the best wines coming from Heggies, Penfolds and Rothbury.
The South African selection from Allesverloren, Meerlust and
l'Ormarins also looks good, while other highlights are the Novarro
Correas Argentinian wines and Californians from Foppiano and
Fetzer. Beer buyers will also find a visit is well worth it, not for the
depth of the range but (again) for the ultra-keen prices. The no-

frills service may not appeal to all, but the value for money is difficult to argue with, especially on the other side of the Channel.

Best buys

Vega Rioja 1989, Crianza, £
Chardonnay, NV Sable View, £
Médoc 1990, Les Brulières de Beychevelle, ££
Yalumba Rutherglen Show Reserve Muscat, ££

The Wine Bureau

5 Raglan Street, Harrogate, North Yorkshire HG1 1LE	*Tel* (01423) 527772 *Fax* (01423) 563077

Open Mon–Fri 9–11, Sat 10–11 **Closed** Sun and public/bank holidays **Cards** Access, Delta, Visa; personal and business accounts **Discount** 5% for 1+ case **Delivery** Free within 50-mile radius (min. 1 case); mail-order available **Glass hire** Not available **Tasting and talks** 2–3 per annum; specialist tutored and advanced blind tastings **Cellarage** Free

We consider ourselves privileged to have copy number four of draft two of the first-ever list from this Harrogate merchant. The list has been produced partly as a result of increased interest from customers for bottles to take home from The Tannin Level wine-bar, but also with a view to providing much more of the services one would expect from a wine-merchant. The range on offer is but a small selection from the 400 or so items available in the wine-bar, but the quality throughout is very good. Champagne is from George Goulet and Jacquesson, beaujolais from the Eventail organisation, good-value clarets include Ch. Beaumont and Amiral de Beychevelle while tasty Menetou-Salon is provided by Domaine de Chatenoy. Kuentz-Bas Alsace and the *appellation-contrôlée*-flouting Rebelle are certainly very good. Noteworthy Spanish bottles come from Marqués de Griñon and Somontano, while the Italian whites from Jermann are among the country's best. In the New World range, you'll find Hamilton Russell from South Africa, Echeverria from Chile, Grant Burge from Australia and Babich from New Zealand.

Best buys

Echeverria Sauvignon Blanc 1994, £
Vin de Pays d'Oc, Vigneaux Merlot, £
Grant Burge Old Vine Shiraz 'The Black Monster' 1992/3, ££
Chassagne-Montrachet 1992, Michel Niellon, ££

Wine Cellar

Head Office
PO Box 476, Loushers Lane, Warrington *Tel* (01925) 444555
Cheshire WA4 6RR *Fax* (01925) 404040
11 branches North East/North West/Midlands,
Central England, Epsom and Chiswick

Open Varies from store to store **Cards** Access, Amex, Switch, Visa; personal and business accounts **Discount** 10% on case purchases **Delivery** Free within 20-mile radius **Glass hire** Free with order (72 hours' notice required) **Tasting and talks** Sat tastings and talks for local groups **Cellarage** Not available

'What are your areas of speciality?' asked the questionnaire (not for this *Guide*); 'crisps and snack food,' came the reply from Cellar Five. That was five years ago. Now, Greenalls Cellars is one of the most-talked about wine companies in the country, and, with nearly 500 shops (mostly in the North of England), is the third-largest chain after Thresher and Victoria Wine. The top level in the chain is Wine Cellar, of which there are expected to be around 20 shops by the end of 1995, with southern branches in Chiswick, Epsom and Banstead. Then come the 40+ Berkeley Wines shops, which stock around 450 of the 600 or so wines that Wine Cellar carries. The rest of the stores are Cellar Five, basic off-licences but still with some interesting wines on the shelves.

The man largely responsible for blasting the company from almost nowhere to such a position is Nader Haghighi, ex-Thresher marketing supremo who arrived in the middle of 1994 and turned the place upside down. Almost from a standing start, the wine range has become one of real excitement, and the arrival of former William Low buyer Kevin Wilson early in 1995 should ensure continuing interest and quality.

Since the company is in effect so young, it's difficult to say which are its speciality regions. Australian and Chilean wines are in plentiful supply, and there are some good South Africans, from estates such as Kanonkop and Backsberg, and some top Californians from Ridge and Shafer. There are some impressive wines in the burgundy and Bordeaux ranges too, particularly the Matrot Meursault and the 1990 Ch. Haut-Marbuzet. Alain Paret's Rhônes are excellent, as are Henry Pellé's Loire Sauvignons. There are competent ranges from the rest of Europe as well, with unusual highlights being the Austrian Siegendorf Rot and Quinta da Foz de Arouce from Portugal. Whiskies, ports and sherries are in good supply, and there are also champagnes from several *grandes marques* and a grower called Ariston.

All is not absolutely rosy, though. The company is learning that customers used to shopping in the old-style Cellar Five do not change their wine-buying habits and move upmarket overnight. The staff at head office may be bright, but those in the shops still have a long way to go to catch up with their counterparts at Oddbins, Wine Rack and Bottoms Up. The Thornton's chocolate cabinets that Haghighi considered getting rid of remain in the stores, largely because of the amount of money they generate. And the busy wine list has been criticised for looking too much like an Oddbins list (though some would take that as a compliment). However, the transformation achieved in such a short space of time is remarkable. Haghighi wants Wine Cellar to win awards. It hasn't so far, but it will very soon.

Best buys

Peter Lehmann Grenache 1994, £
Vin de Pays d'Oc Sauvignon Blanc 1994, Jacques Lurton, £
Hedges Red Mountain Reserve 1991, Washington State, ££
Bourgogne Aligoté 1993, Domaine Pillot, ££

Wine Finds

| The Bath Brewery, Toll Bridge Road, Bath | *Tel* (01225) 852711 |
| Avon BA1 7DE | *Fax* (01255) 858632 |

Case sales only **Open** Mail-order only; (Sales office) Mon–Fri 9–6, Sat 10–1 **Closed** Sun, public holidays **Cards** Access, Amex, Delta, Switch, Visa; personal and business accounts **Discount** None available **Delivery** Free UK mainland (min. £90) **Glass hire** Not available **Tasting and talks** Quarterly tastings **Cellarage** Not available

---

Wine Finds is a mail-order company that aims to provide the next step up the ladder for those who have begun to demand more than their local supermarket can offer. Every two months, customers are offered a range of around 100 wines selected through a process of blind tasting by a panel consisting mainly of Masters of Wine. For something to be listed, it must be not only good, but good value as well, and everything receives ratings for quality and value for money. Says Simon Thompson, 'We are saddened that the results of our evaluation indicate, time and time again, that so much wine sold at higher prices, and with a supposedly better pedigree, is in fact little better – and often worse – than the cheap and reliable commodity wines sold by the major retailers.'

A region-by-region summary is given, but wines in the main body of the list are grouped together by style rather than country (Fruity & Aromatic Whites, Bordeaux-inspired Reds, and so on), which leads to an interesting mix of wines in each section. A recent list of Softer, Riper Whites included two wines from Alsace, a Mâcon, a Vouvray, a Châteauneuf and an Australian

Sauvignon/Semillon. Typically 30% of the wines in each list are new to the range, so if you have enjoyed a wine and wish to reorder, it's best to do so as soon as possible. The vast majority of wines on offer are under £10, and prices are made more attractive by the Rebate Scheme. Following an initial purchase, customers are entitled to a discount of 20% of the value of that order on subsequent orders. It's a very refreshing way of buying wine that we hope (and expect) will do very well over the next few years.

Best buys

Impossible, given the nature of the business

The Wine House

| 10 Stafford Road, Wallington, Surrey SM6 9AD | *Tel* 0181-669 6661 |
| | *Fax* 0181-401 0039 |

Open Mon–Sat 10–6, Sun 12–2 **Closed** Chr and Boxing Days, some public holidays **Cards** Access, Amex, Delta, Visa; business accounts **Discount** 10% on 1 case (cash/cheque/Delta); 7% on 1 case (credit cards/Amex) **Delivery** Free local delivery over £50, other deliveries at cost; mail-order service available **Glass hire** Free with order **Tasting and talks** Two major tastings per year, smaller events throughout year; groups by arrangement **Cellarage** Not available

An experimental layout this year for Morvin Rodker's list. It's split into three sections according to price – since that is how most of his customers (and indeed the vast majority of wine-drinkers) buy their wine. List A (100 Wines for Everyday Use) features wines between £3 and £5. The most interesting of the bottles falling into this category are the Serradayres Portuguese red, the Enate Spaniards from Somontano, the several *vins de pays* and a handful of rather underpriced estate- bottled German wines. Middle-range wines on List B fall into the £5–10 bracket, and sparkling wines appear for the first time: those from Freixenet and Seppelt. Iberian wines include Luis Pato's wonderful Bairrada and Riojas from Remélluri and Muga, and the Italians from Maculan and Masi look good too. French reds are all lumped together here, and include a fine set of mature clarets and several sturdy southern wines. Red burgundies are not very much in evidence, although you will find St Véran from Domaine des Deux Roches and Bernard Legland's Chablis. The New World gets fully into its stride here, and alongside a fine Australian range there are Californians from Villa Mount Eden and New Zealanders from Te Mata and Seifried Estate.

Above £10 (Classic and Prestige Wines) champagnes from Pol Roger and F. Bonnet make an appearance, clarets become very serious and there are some great burgundies from Joseph Roty,

Domaine Vocoret and Jean-Marc Bouley. Other highlights are René Rostaing's Côte Rôtie, several Rioja *gran reservas* and several delicious German wines, with still some from the '75 and '76 vintages. The three lists aim to whet the appetite and are by no means a comprehensive inventory of what's in stock. Why not pay a visit and see what else is available?

Best buys

Vin de Pays d'Oc 1994, Syrah Pin d'Alep, £
Palacio de Bornos 1993, Rueda, £
Haut-Médoc 1989, Château Lamothe-Cissac, ££
Chateau St Jean La Petite Etoile Fumé Blanc 1991, Russian River, ££

Wine Raks (Scotland) Ltd

21 Springfield Road, Aberdeen,	*Tel* (01224) 311460
Grampian AB1 7RJ	*Fax* (01224) 312186
1 Urquhart Road, Aberdeen, Grampian AB2 1LU	*Tel* (01224) 641189

Open Mon–Sat 10–10; Sun 12.30–6 **Closed** Chr, Boxing and New Year's Days **Cards** Access, Delta, Switch, Visa; personal and business accounts **Discount** 5% on cases **Delivery** Local delivery (min. 1 case); mail-order available **Glass hire** Free with order **Tasting and talks** Bi-annually at Aberdeen Art Gallery and upon request **Cellarage** £5.99 per case per year

'In continual pursuit of excellence' is Tariq Mahmood's motto. His range is full of interesting wines, some familiar, some less so. There are several country wines, including Corbières from Château de Lastours and Bergerac from Château le Raz. Cattier provides champagne, while Alsace comes from the Turckheim co-op. In the Loire range, Gitton's Sancerre stands out, while much of the burgundy range comes from Vallet Frères. There's plenty of claret for all tastes and pockets, and the Rhônes from Cave de Tain l'Hermitage are also available.

Of the New World wines, the most interesting are the New Zealanders from Ata Rangi and the Fairview South Africans. Italian offerings include Piemonte wines from Burlotto and Tuscans from Dei and San Giusto. Bodegas Murua provide Rioja, while Senorío de Sarria in Navarra supply good-value alternatives. The ports include a range of own-label *colheita* wines dating back to 1941.

The matching of food and wine is something that Mr Mahmood takes seriously, and the centre pages of his list give his recommendations on what to serve with dishes as varied as smoked eel, wild duck and haggis. There's also a separate fine-wine list, which, when we last saw it, contained a large range of clarets, 1961 Huet Vouvray and Barolos dating back to the 1950s.

Best buys

Senorío de Sarria Reserva 1985, Navarra Tinto, £
Chianti Putto 1992/93, Poggio Capponi, £
Cornas 1989/90, Cave de Tain, ££
Barolo Neirane 1988, Burlotto, ££

The Wine Schoppen

3 Oak Street, Heeley, Sheffield,	*Tel* (0114) 2553301
South Yorkshire S8 9UB	*Fax* (0114) 2551010
Barrels & Bottles Ltd	
1 Walker Street, Wicker, Sheffield, South Yorkshire	*Tel* (0114) 2769666
S3 8GZ	*Fax* (0114) 2799182

Open Mon–Fri 9.30–6; Sat 9.30–5 **Closed** Sun, public holidays **Cards** Access,
Switch, Visa; personal and business accounts **Discount** 11.5% off full case **Delivery**
Free within 15-mile radius (min. 1 case); nationwide any quantity at cost; mail-order
available **Glass hire** Free with order **Tasting and talks** Offered periodically
Cellarage £2.60 per case per year

A move to new, purpose-built premises has enabled Anne Coghlan
to increase her range. Pride of place goes to a German range that
features Nahe from Wilhelm Schweinhardt, Franken from Ernst
Gebhardt and Kuehling-Gillot's Rheinhessen wines. Few wine-
merchants can offer a range that covers so many of the German
provinces, and we would urge you to forget your prejudices and
try some of these wines.

Turning to the French section of the list, Ogier provides Rhônes,
Chablis comes from Domaine Bersan, and the champagne is
produced by Gremillet and Pol Roger. Spanish wines include Viña
Salceda Rioja, while best of the Italians are the Villa di Vetrice
Chianti and Teruzzi e Puthod's Vernaccia. New in from Australia
are the excellent Bethany wines. These join a slightly lacklustre
New World range, although the L. A. Cetto Mexican wines and
Swanson Californians are good. A range of Churchill's port is also
available.

There are separate newsletters for the main outlet and for
Barrels & Bottles. These still seem to be in the teething stages, and
we trust that future editions will include the names of the
producers of all of the wines, VAT-inclusive prices and fewer
spelling mistakes. Both shops run very active tasting programmes,
and there are even plans for a weekend trip to Champagne.

Best buys

Corbières 1993, Seigneur de Vairan, £
Chardonnay 1993, Les Plantanes de Marquise, £

Grenache 1994, Bethany Vineyard, ££
Langenlonsheimer Scheurebe Auslese 1989, Nahe, W.
Schweinhardt, ££

The Wine Society

Gunnels Wood Road, Stevenage,
Hertfordshire SG1 2BG

Tel (01438) 741177
Fax (01438) 741392

Open Mon–Fri 9–5 (Order Office); Mon–Fri 9–5.30, Sat 9–4 (Showroom) **Closed** Sun,
public holidays **Cards** Access, Visa **Discount** Available **Delivery** Nationwide
delivery; mail-order service available **Glass hire** Free **Tasting and talks** Available
throughout the year **Cellarage** £4.44 per case per year

Of all the fees demanded for membership of mail-order wine clubs,
the £20 asked by the Wine Society must surely be one of the best-
value. If you are scared that your application for membership will
be refused, don't worry; even if you don't know anyone who is
already a member, a proposer can easily be found.

Having become a member, what is on offer? Quite simply one of
the best ranges of wines in the country, particularly for the
traditional wine drinker, but increasingly also for anyone who
loves good wines wherever they come from. We reported last year
that those interested in New Zealand wine were not well catered
for. New for 1995 are wines from Neudorf, Kumeu River, Hunter's
and Te Mata; not bad for beginners. The Chilean range has also
increased, and there's no shortage of stylish Australian wines. Only
enthusiasts for South Africa and California could claim to be
neglected; even here, though, those wines that are available
(Warwick and Shafer in particular) are very good.

People who enjoy Portuguese reds will find much to savour,
and *aficionados* of Spanish wine will not be disappointed by Rioja
from CVNE, Marqués de Murrieta and La Rioja Alta. The Italian
and German ranges both contain some splendidly characterful
stuff, whether you are looking for something to drink now or in
ten, even twenty, years' time.

The same can be said of the range of clarets and burgundies. If
you can't stretch to the vast amounts demanded for some of the
wines, you will still find great pleasure available for under £10,
notably from Michel Lafarge's Bourgogne Rouge and Château
Méaume. You'll find several wines for laying down among the
Rhônes, although the 1964 Jaboulet Aîné Cornas is probably ready
to drink. There is an ample choice for fans whether they favour
Sauvignon Blanc, Chenin Blanc or Cabernet Franc, while Alsace
wines include a strong set from Hugel and Trimbach. There's also a
plentiful array of regional wines ranging from good cheap quaffers
to more serious fare: Domaine Cauhapé Jurançon *moelleux*,

Domaine Tempier Bandol and Domaine Gauby Côtes du Roussillon.

Although the value offered by the Wine Society is good, particularly where the own-label wines are concerned, cross-Channel travellers in search of further bargains might care to visit the Hesdin showroom, where an abbreviated range of the Society's wines is available. Customers tied to the UK will not be disappointed by the service they receive, though. The regular newsletters keep them in touch with the Society in between the thrice-yearly lists, and there will probably be a lively group of members not very far from you that meets regularly for dinners, tastings and other vinous events.

Best buys

Montado, Alentejo, 1991, £
Duca di Castelmont, Alcamo, 1994, £
Maximin Grünhaus Abtsberg Riesling Spätlese, 1992, ££
Grosset Gaia, 1992, Clare Valley, ££

The Wine Treasury

143 Ebury Street, London SW1W 9QN
Tel 0171-730 6774
Fax 0171-823 6402

Open Mail-order only; Mon–Fri 8.30–10 **Closed** Sat, Sun, public holidays **Cards** Access, Visa; business accounts **Discount** 10% on 1–9 unmixed cases (min. order £200) 15% on 10+ cases; mixed case prices (24 bottles) 12–24 bottles surcharge 40p a bottle **Delivery** Free mainland England and Wales; Scotland 70p a case (min. charge £7 per delivery); mail-order available **Glass hire** Not available **Tasting and talks** Throughout year, please enquire **Cellarage** Not available

---

The closure of the Wine Treasury's retail shop in Fulham Road in early summer came as little surprise to observers of the wine trade. Passing trade just did not exist at that end of Fulham Road, as the shop's previous tenants, The Fulham Road Wine Centre, found out. However, the Wine Treasury range is one of the more interesting around and we would encourage you to contact the company and put together a mixed case, maybe even two.

You'll find some great Californian bottles, including wines from Shafer, Kistler and Cline Cellars, similarly impressive Australian ones from Penley Estate and Dalwhinnie, and some of South Africa's top reds from Warwick Farm and Rust en Vrede. Expensive Spanish offerings come from Vega Sicilia, with better value appearing in the shape of Jean León's Penedés wines and Riojas from La Rioja Alta. The Italian wines may not be the most familiar around, but we'd suggest you try those from Vigneto della Terre

Rosse, La Prendina and de Tarczal. Germany is little in evidence, but Walter Skoff and Alfred Fischer provide Austrian wines of note.

Regional French highlights include excellent Vin de Pays d'Oc from Les Chemins de Bassac and Coteaux des Baronnies from Jean-Yves Liotaud. Joseph Rieflé provides Alsace wines and there are some decent Loires from Fabien Colin and Château de Chenonceaux. Amid the Rhône wines, try the great Côtes-du-Rhône from Jean-Michel Gerin and Domaine Richaud, the Gigondas from Domaine Montvac and André Perret's Condrieu. The Bordeaux selection is fair, but the burgundies are excellent, particularly when the company sees fit to offer 20% off anything in the range. In particular, look out for Etienne Boileau's Chablis, Côte de Nuits reds from Perrot-Minot and Chevillon, Côte de Beaune whites from Domaine Leflaive and Pierre Boillot and a large range of Champy wines from throughout the region.

The marriage with Halves (q.v.) was not a great success, but there are still plenty of wines in half-bottle sizes. Plentiful supplies of interesting spirits, dried mushrooms, truffles and oils are also available. The Treasury Wine Club is still alive and kicking, membership of which entitles you to a package of tastings, dinners, discounts, newsletters (the *Bacchus Bugle*) and more besides.

Best buys

Vin de Table Blanc 1993, Domaine Léon Barral, £
Touraine Sauvignon 1993/94, Caves des Vignerons des Coteaux Romanais, £
Médoc 1991, Château Rollan de By, ££
Cotes d'Oakley 1993, Cline Cellars, ££

Wine World

Owlet, Templepan Lane, Chandlers Cross,	*Tel* (01923) 264718
Rickmansworth, Hertfordshire WD3 4NH	*Fax* (01923) 264718

Open Mon–Sun and public holidays 8–11 **Cards** None accepted **Discount** Not available **Delivery** Free within Hertfordshire, Bucks, Beds, Middlesex and London (min. 3 cases) elsewhere £3 per case **Glass hire** Free with order **Tasting and talks** Regular tutored tastings for workshops and gourmet evenings **Cellarage** Free for limited period

It wasn't really necessary for Lilyane Weston to enclose a CV with her form for entry in the *Guide*. However, we are pleased to inform you that she is one of the few wine-merchants to hold a private pilot's licence. Fittingly, her range is full of high-fliers, most of them, French, like Lilyane. The Alsace range comes from the Turckheim co-op, while Loires include Henry Pellé's Menetou-

Salon and the great-value Chapelle de Cray Touraine Sauvignon. Interesting regional items include Corbières from Château de Lastours and Domaine de Maubet's Côtes de Gascogne. Ch. Haut-Marbuzet tops a small range of clarets, burgundies come from Jaffelin, and there's an interesting range of *cru beaujolais*. Most of the Rhône wines are from the reliable Cave de Tain l'Hermitage, while the champagne is Perrier Jouet's. From outside France, you'll find Campo Viejo Riojas, Brown Brothers Australians, Villard Chileans and Don Zoilo sherries. If you're interested not only in drinking the wines but in hearing about them as well, Lilyane lectures regularly, though the problem may be to find a space in her diary.

Best buys

Gaillac Rouge 1990/92, Château Clement-Termes, £
Pinot Blanc d'Alsace 1993/4, CVT, £
Chianti Classico Riserva DOCG 1988, Brolio Estate, ££
Champagne Marniquet Brut, ££

The Winery

Subsidiary of Les Amis du Vin
4 Clifton Road, Maida Vale, London W9 1SS   *Tel* 0171-286 6475

Open Mon–Fri 10.30–8, Sat 10–6.30 **Closed** Sun, public holidays **Cards** All accepted; business accounts; Forte gold card **Discount** 5% on (un)mixed cases; negotiable for bulk orders **Delivery** Free (min. 3 cases); see Les Amis du Vin **Glass hire** Free with order **Tasting and talks** 4/5 throughout year **Cellarage** Not available

Sorry, The Winery's Summer Champagne Festival will be ending just before the *Guide* hits the streets. Major-name fizzes were available at prices which even Odd.... (You Know Who) couldn't match. Don't be too dispirited, though; the normal charges for Ayala, Ruinart, Gosset, Charles Heidsieck and several other *grandes marques* are still very friendly.

The shop (an old chemist's with the original shelving up to the high ceiling, piled with wine) is one of London's most welcoming. The first growths lie protected behind the counter, but there's plenty of more affordable claret as well, such as 1988 Ch. Maucaillou and 1990 de France, both under a tenner. Burgundies are fair rather than very good; Joseph Mellot provides Loire whites and very decent Rhône reds come from Ogier and Château d'Aqueria. Domaine Jux and Trimbach appear in the Alsace range, while the Australian-influenced La Porcii Chardonnay tops the Languedoc-Roussillon range.

Those looking for real Australian wines will find good ranges from Yalumba, Bannockburn, Redbank and Vasse Felix. New Zealand bottles are mainly from Delegats and Oyster Bay, Chileans from Santa Rita, and the South African selection includes offerings from Saxenberg and l'Ormarins. Although the Californian range no longer includes the mature wines it once did, it's still one of the best around: Fetzer, Cuvaison, Ridge, Phelps, Sanford, Calera, Voss, etc. The Cortese Barbarescos, the Tedeschi wines from the Veneto, the Tuscan range from Frescobaldi and the wonderful Puglian reds from Taurino stand out in the Italian list. Monte Vannos Ribera del Duero and the Chivite Navarra wines look good in the Spanish section.

The Les Amis du Vin mail-order operation is undergoing some restructuring, but, although a list hasn't been produced for over two years, it is still very much alive, and any of the wines mentioned above can be delivered to your door. When the Les Amis du Vin restaurants were sold, the logo was sold too, so the next few months could see a change of name.

Best buys

Vin de Pays de l'Aude 1994, Moulin Grandet Rouge, £
Fetzer Vintage White 1993/4, £
Bannockburn Chardonnay 1992, Geelong, ££
Notarpanaro Vino da Tavola 1986, Taurino, ££

Wines of Interest

46 Burlington Road, Ipswich, Suffolk IP1 2HS · *Tel* (01473) 215752
Fax (01473) 280275

Open Mon–Fri 9–6, Sat 9–1 **Closed** Sun, public holidays **Cards** None accepted; business and personal accounts **Discount** 5% on unmixed cases **Delivery** Free to Ipswich, Norwich and City of London; free elsewhere for 6+ cases, otherwise at cost **Glass hire** Free with order **Tasting and talks** Regular tutored tastings in London, Norwich and Clacton **Cellarage** Approx £3 per case per year

---

It may be first-division football for Ipswich this season, but much of the range put together by Tim Voelcker and Jonathan Williamson is firmly in the Premier League. This is not a large range, but you should easily be able to find something to your liking somewhere in the selection. The Bordeaux range is dotted about with classed-growth wines as well as mature *petits châteaux* wines from good vintages, and among the burgundies the Chablis from Domaine des Malandes stands out. There is also a separate fine-wine list containing details of wines available in quantities too small to appear in the main range. The Pascal Côtes-du-Rhône Cuvée Personelle is obviously a favourite of the company (they organised a vertical tasting of it in spring 1995), and Jaboulet Aîné and Domaine de la Mordorée provide other Rhône wines. Other French wines that deserve mention are the Rolly Gassmann Alsace and the Château de Lascaux *vin de pays*.

The German range contains some mature bottles from Mönchhof, while fans of Italian wines will enjoy Santadi's Carignano del Sulcis and Mascarello's Nebbiolo delle Langhe. There's plenty of good value from Spain and Eastern Europe, although we reserve judgment on the sweet Hungarian Cabernet Sauvignon. Both American continents are lumped together on the list. We'd go for the Ridge Geyserville from California and the Echeverria Chilean wines. Fairview and Thelema from South Africa are good, but the best of the New World wines are the Australians from Wirra Wirra, Yaldara and Wakefield. Hidalgo sherries, Cossart Gordon madeira, and some decent ports and malt whiskies are also available.

Inhabitants of Norwich, Clacton and London are treated to a programme of tutored tastings with events usually at least once a month. They look very appealing. Our favourite ploy from Wines of Interest, though, is the Sampling Club. Members (£1.20 a month) are sent details of two wines per month; they then have the opportunity to buy their first bottle of these at half the list price, and subsequent bottles at the sealed-case rate, regardless of the quantity. Full marks for initiative! Now, do they have any tips for the football team?

Best buys

Vin de Pays d'Oc 1993 Sauvignon, Domaine de la Done, £
Manzanilla 'La Gitana' Hidalgo, halves, £
Cabernet Sauvignon 1992, 'The Angelus' McLaren Vale, Wirra Wirra South Australia, ££
Viña Amezola 1990, Rioja Crianza, ££

Wines of Westhorpe

Marchington, Staffordshire	*Tel* (01283) 820285
ST14 8NX	*Fax* (01283) 820631

Case sales only   **Open** Mon–Fri 8.30–6, Sat 8.30–12 **Closed** Sun, public holidays, Chr week **Cards** Access, Delta, Switch, Visa; business accounts **Discount** 6–15 cases £2.60, 16–25 £3.60, 26–35 £4.60, 36–45 £5.10, 46–55 £5.30 **Delivery** Not available; mail-order available **Glass hire** Not available **Tasting and talks** Occasionally on request **Cellarage** Not available

Much of Alan Ponting's business is with the trade (we don't know how many *Guide* readers will take the discount of £5.60 per case offered to those buying by the pallet). There are Chilean wines from Peteroa and Australians from Tatachilla Hill (soon to be called Karanga) and the increasingly impressive d'Arenberg. However, with those exceptions, the range concentrates entirely on Eastern Europe, and particularly on Hungary and Bulgaria. The Bulgarians especially will be familiar to anyone who has spent much time in wine-shops over the past few years. However, if you find yourselves drinking such wines in reasonable quantity, the no-frills service offered by Wines of Westhorpe means that you'll probably find them cheaper here than anywhere else.

Best buys

Ialoveni Cabernet Sauvignon 1988, Moldova, £
Bulgarian Special Reserve Mavrud 1989, £
D'Arenberg Ironstone Pressings 1991/2, ££
Tokaji Aszú 1986/8, ££

Woodhouse Wines

The Brewery, Blandford St Mary   *Tel* (01258) 452141
Dorset DT11 9LS   *Fax* (01258) 450147
9 branches in Southern England

Open Mon–Sat 10–10, Sun 12–3, 7–10, public holidays open subject to licensing requirements **Closed** Chr Day **Cards** Access, Visa; business accounts **Discount** Negotiable **Delivery** Local delivery service available; nationwide mail-order available **Glass hire** Available **Tasting and talks** Available **Cellarage** Not available

---

Philip Clive is still settling into his Dorset surroundings after moving south from his position as head of ASDA's wine department. Ten off-licences is a slightly different proposition from the hurly-burly of a major supermarket chain, but he is looking forward to the change of scene. The Woodhouse range errs towards traditional tastes, with several *petits châteaux* clarets as well as a wide choice of sherries and ports. However, Australia is also strongly represented, and Philip plans to maintain that strength and bolster the ranges from South Africa and Eastern Europe. For a flavour of the wines available, see the entry for Hicks & Don, a company that, like Woodhouse Wines, is owned by the Hall & Woodhouse Brewery.

Best buys

Solana Torrontes & Treixadura 1994, £
Lindemans Cawarra Colombard/Chardonnay 1994, £
Cahors 1991, Domaine Eugenie, ££
Barolo 1989, Arione, ££

Wrightson & Co

Manfield Grange, Manfield, Nr Darlington,	*Tel* (01325) 374134
North Yorkshire DL2 2RE	*Fax* (01325) 374135

Case sales only Open Mon–Fri 9–6 **Closed** weekends and public holidays **Cards** Access, Visa; personal and business accounts **Discount** Not available **Delivery** Free within 40-mile radius; mail-order available **Glass hire** Free with order **Tasting and talks** Tastings for companies and wine clubs **Cellarage** £5.88 per case per annum +VAT

Simon Wrightson (formerly with Justerini & Brooks, Corney & Barrow and John Armit) is now sole proprietor of this North Yorkshire business (which used to be Pease & Wrightson). Our past criticisms about list quality have been firmly put to flight by a smart new document that gives detailed descriptions of all the wines available. This is a compact range, with quality to the fore, majoring on France but with smatterings from elsewhere. The best of these are the Jackson Estate Chardonnay from New Zealand and the Oak Knoll Pinot from Oregon. Clarets range from Ch. Méaume right up to Ch. Pétrus; there are also several tasty wines from the Languedoc, as well as small but worthwhile sets from Alsace and the Loire. Guigal provides Rhônes; red burgundies are from the splendid Pierre Bourrée, and whites from Olivier Leflaive. Expect the ranges from Italy and Spain to expand over the next year.

Best buys

Caves de Berticot Sauvignon 1994, £
Vin de Pays des Coteaux de Bessilles 1993, Domaine St Martin La Garrigue, £
Vin de Pays d'Oc 1994, Château de Gourgazaud Viognier, ££
Canon-Fronsac 1991, Château Pichelèbre, ££

Wright Wine Company

The Old Smithy, Raikes Road, Skipton, North Yorkshire	*Tel* (01756) 700886
BD23 1NP	*Fax* (01756) 798580

Open Mon–Sat 9–6; public holidays 11–4 **Closed** Sun **Cards** None accepted; business and personal accounts **Discount** 5% on mixed cases **Delivery** Free within 30-mile radius **Glass hire** Free with order **Tasting and talks** Sometimes **Cellarage** Negotiable

Bob Wright's new list came out with a warning to customers: 'Ignore the prices in this list!' He is not the only wine-merchant to feel the effect of unfriendly exchange rates, but he keeps his enthusiasm and maintains a fine selection. Stocks of the old South African wines that used to grace the range have now gone, but you'll find younger wines from Warwick and Delheim, together with some excellent sweeties from Nederburg. North American bottles include four Canadians, Chateau Saint Michelle Washington State Cabernet and Californians from Sonoma-Cutrer, William Wheeler and Inglenook. Chilean, New Zealand and Australian wines are also in plentiful supply. The Italian selection is fair, the Portuguese range comes mainly from the reliable J. M. da Fonseca, and the German list offers much for those wishing to rise above Liebfraumilch level. From Spain, you'll find Rioja from Martínez Bujanda and Marqués de Murrieta, and a range from Torres.

There's plenty for the claret-lover, particularly in the £10–15 bracket. Burgundy fans are treated to reds from Emile Juillot, Domaine Moillard and Faiveley, and whites from Maroslavac-Léger and Domaine Servin in Chablis. Chapoutier and Desmeure provide Rhônes, Alsace is produced by Schlumberger and Albert Mann, while Jean-Claude Dagueneau and de Ladoucette furnish Loire wines. Topping the regional French range are five vintages of Mas de Daumas Gassac, and those wishing to celebrate can try champagnes from Hostomme and Pol Roger, the latter in several sizes up to a Nebuchadnezzar.

Best buys

Syrah Coteaux du Languedoc 1992, Domaine Les Embals, £
Aramon 1994, Terrasses de Landoc, Création de Gassac, £
Muscadet de Sèvre et Maine Sur Lie 1990, Vieilles Vignes,
Comte Leloup de Chasseloir, ££
Châteauneuf du Pape 1985, Père Caboche, J. P. Boisson, ££

Peter Wylie Fine Wines

Plymtree Manor, Plymtree, Cullompton, Devon	*Tel* (01884) 277555
EX15 2LE	*Fax* (01884) 277557

Open Mon–Fri 9–6, Sat 9.30–1 **Closed** Sun, public holidays **Cards** Not accepted; personal and business accounts **Discount** Available **Delivery** 15-mile radius (min. order 1 unit); mail-order service available **Glass hire** Not available **Tasting and talks** By invitation only **Cellarage** £7+VAT per case per year

---

'1905 Cos d'Estournel ... unhealthy colour, like most 90-year olds!' Not the oldest wine on the Peter Wylie list, this, and at £35 a bottle by no means the most expensive (the 1865 Yquem at £1,865 fits both descriptions). Those interested in finding out what mature Bordeaux, of whatever hue, tastes like will find Mr Wylie's range excellent, and those after younger bottles will not be disappointed either. Ports and champagnes of considerable venerability are also in evidence. The burgundies do not date back as far, but again there are several wines from good recent years, mainly from Louis Latour and Drouhin, but also from growers such as Rossignol-Trapet and de Vogüé. There are oddments from the Rhône, the Loire and California, but not much else. 'I am quite content to look after the one-off and the modest-value customer,' says Mr Wylie. Those in search of a wine for an anniversary year will probably find something already in stock, and those in search of large-format bottles – double magnums, jeroboams and imperials – will also find a large selection. But it's the old wines that are the most appealing, and we would encourage enthusiasts everywhere to club together with friends to buy a mixed case of these senior citizens.

Best buys

Margaux, Château Palmer 1983, ££
Barsac, Château Climens 1983, ££

Yapp Brothers

| The Old Brewery, Water Street, Mere, Wiltshire | *Tel* (01747) 860423 |
| BA12 6DY | *Fax* (01747) 860929 |

Open Mon–Fri 9–5; Sat 9–1 **Closed** Sun, public holidays **Cards** Access, Diners, Visa; personal and business accounts **Discount** 6–10 cases £1 per case, 11–20 cases £2, 21+ £2.50; collection discount £3 per case **Delivery** Free Dorset, Wiltshire and Avon (2+ cases); £4 charge for smaller quantities; mail-order available **Glass hire** Free with order **Tasting and talks** Annually at dinners and restaurants, Summer and Chr sale with 30+ wines on tasting, constant shop tastings **Cellarage** £4 per case per year

Robin Yapp's two mistresses, the Loire and Rhône valleys, continue to intrigue him, and we are fortunate that he chooses to share their pleasures with us. Those who would share his passion should make sure they have a copy of his simply laid out and beautifully illustrated wine list. The wistful Yapp prose (Yapping?) details how his growers continue to live sheltered lives, undisturbed by the hurly-burly of the late twentieth century, persevering in the face of adversity while crafting wines which are a true expression of their origins.

Regardless of whether the prose style appeals to you, or occasionally reminds you of Peter Mayle, the wines in the list are the real items of interest. A range of excellent Sauvignons includes Gérard Cordier's Reuilly, Sancerre from André Vatan and Pouilly Fumé from Jean-Claude Guyot, who also provides a wine made from Chasselas. Good, dry Chenin Blanc is provided by Daniel Jarry in Vouvray, Yves and Pierre Soulet in Savennières and the Château at Azay-le-Rideau. Sweeter nectars come from Jarry again, Vincent Lecointre in the Coteaux du Layon and Jean & Michel

Berger in Montlouis. For reds, Druet's Bourgeuil is the most serious and long-lived, but do try Paul Filliatreau's Saumur Champigny.

It's difficult to put a foot wrong in choosing from the Rhône selection, with the possible exception of the somewhat erratic and expensive Château Grillet. Our favourite white from the range is Chave's Hermitage, although Vernay's Condrieu runs it a close second. For Syrah fans, Chave's red Hermitage is magnificent, and the Clape Cornas and the Côte Rôties from Jasmin, Champet and Burgaud are also splendid. From the southern Rhône, Lucien Michel provides spicy ripe Châteauneuf, and the Meffre Gigondas is lovely. Those in search of good value could do far worse than try Château Valcombe's Côtes du Ventoux and the Domaine de Grangeneuve Tricastin.

Provence is not strictly the Rhône in wine-world terms, but we can only thank Robin for straying a little from his chosen patch. The reds from Domaine de Trévallon, Château Simone and Mas de la Rouvière are the pick, but you'll also find the whites from Château de la Canorgue in the Luberon and François Sack in Cassis quite delicious.

The Yapp list also includes a spot of Alsace from Charles Schleret, some very decent champagne from Bruno Paillard and Jacquesson, and an occasional item from the Jasper Hill Vineyard in Australia. Anyone interested in seeing these or the Rhône and Loire wines in a more appropriate setting should find out about the tasting dinners and luncheons held around the country.

Best buys

Gamay de l'Ardèche 1994, £
Saumur Blanc 1994, Saint Cyr en Bourg, £
Gigondas 1990, Domaine Saint Gayan, Meffre, ££
Hermitage Blanc 1992, Chave, ££

Noel Young Wines

56 High Street, Trumpington, Cambridgeshire
CB2 2LS

Tel (01223) 844744
Fax (01223) 844736

Open Mon–Sat 10–9, Sun and public holidays 12–2 **Closed** Chr, Boxing and New Year's Days **Cards** Access, Delta, Diners, Switch, Visa; personal and business accounts **Discount** 10% on 1 case, 7% if paid by credit card **Delivery** Free within a 25-mile radius (min. 1 case), nationally £5 case charge; mail-order available **Glass hire** Free **Tasting and talks** Every weekend; tutored tastings available **Cellarage** Not available

Or Noel Very Young as perhaps he should be known. Although only 26, he has built up business over the past four years to a stage where he is one of Britain's best small wine-merchants. Gaps in the range are being plugged continually with new and interesting stuff. The man even blends his own Australian wines under the Magpie Estate label – and very good they are too, particularly the reds. They join a large range which concentrates on smaller wineries such as Lake's Folly, Veritas and Hollick. A similar approach to New Zealand means that wines from Te Mata, Allan Scott and Ngatarawa are available. South Africans of note come from Weltevrede, Boschendal and Thelema, while South American offerings include wines from Viña Montes and Viña Port in Chile, and from Navarro Correas and Luigi Boscain in Argentina. From North America, you'll find ranges from Au Bon Climat and Bonny Doon, together with the former's Oregon Pinot Noir (called La Cagoule, under the Ici/La Bas label), plus the Rief Estate Canadians.

There's much of interest in the regional French selection, and the Rhônes from Bosquet des Papes and Domaine Durieu are also good. Top of the Loire range are Didier Dagueneau's Pouilly Fumé and the sweet Vouvray from Bourillon D'Orléans. Alsace comes from Marc Kreydenweiss, clarets from some of the less expensive crus classés and crus bourgeois. Burgundies are impressive, with whites from Jobard, Thévenet and Vocoret, and reds from Comte Armand, Joseph Roty and Robert Chevillon.

The Italian contingent rarely strays much above £10, but there's plenty of tasty stuff on offer. Most interesting of the Spaniards are the Penedés wines of Albet y Noya and the range from the Priorato region. In the German selection, pass over the Liebfraumilch and head for the wines of Dr Loosen, Paul Basten and Paul Anheuser. The Austrians are all worth trying, particularly Aloïs Kracher's impeccable sweet wines.

If some of the wines are unfamiliar, you'll get a chance to taste from the range each weekend, with more formal events, often tutored by such visiting winemakers as Ernst Loosen and Robert O'Callaghan (of Rockford in the Barossa), roughly once a month. The launch of a nationwide mail-order service in the very near future will serve to bring the wares of this promising young merchant to a wider public.

Best buys

Gilberts Peak 1994, Colombard Sauvignon, Australia, £
Corbières, Château Bellevue 1993, £
Nebbiolo Delle Langhe 1991, Mascarello, ££
Alois Kracher 1992, Chardonnay Eiswein, ££

WHO'S WHERE

This is a gazetteer of individual wine stockists listed in the *Guide*. See also the directory of chains and supermarkets that follows.

London

E2
Balls Brothers 244

EC1
Corney & Barrow 275

EC2
Pavilion Wine Co 371

EC4
El Vino 430

N6
Elizabeth Gabay and Partners 303

N7
Le Nez Rouge 362

N21
Howard Ripley 385

NW1
Bibendum 254
Laytons 343

NW3
La Réserve 384

NW10
Les Amis du Vin 236

SE1
Charles Taylor Wines 412
Morris & Verdin 359
Le Pont de la Tour 378
O W Loeb 345
Waterloo Wine Company 433

SE11
London Wine Emporium 346

SW1
Berry Bros & Rudd 252
Farr Vintners 293
Harrods 319
Harvey Nichols 322

Haynes Hanson & Clark 325
Justerini & Brooks 337
Laytons 343
Stones of Belgravia 407
Windrush Wines 439
The Wine Treasury 448

SW3
La Réserve 384
Nicolas UK Ltd 365

SW6
Marco's Wines and Spirits 440
La Réserve 384

SW7
La Vigneronne 424
Windrush Wines 439

SW8
Adam Bancroft Associates 245
Goedhuis & Co 307

SW10
Lea & Sandeman 344

SW11
Philglass & Swiggot 374
The Grape Shop 310
La Réserve 384

SW12
Fernlea Vintners 293

SW13
Barnes Wine Shop 246

SW18
Enotria Winecellars 290
The Wine and Beer Company 440

SW19
Findlater Mackie Todd 294

W1
Fortnum & Mason 298

Laytons 343
Selfridges 397

W2
Craven's Wine Merchants 277
Moreno Wines 358
La Réserve 384

W8
Bute Wines 260
Lea and Sandeman 344

W9
Moreno Wine Importers 358
The Winery 450

W11
Corney & Barrow 275
Holland Park Wine Company 332
John Armit Wines 236

W14
Roberson 386

WC1
Domaine Direct 283
F&E May 352

England

Avon

Bath
Great Western Wine Company 312
Wine Finds 443

Bristol
Averys of Bristol 241
Châteaux Wines 268
John Harvey & Sons 321
RS Wines 388
The Vine Trail 429

Hallatrow
Reid Wines (1992) 382

Bedfordshire

Luton
Smedley Vintners 401

Berkshire

Cookham
Stratfords Wine
  Shippers 408

Hungerford
Windrush Wines 439

Maidenhead
Helen Verdcourt Wines
  422

Newbury
The Vintry 431

Reading
Bordeaux Direct 258
Harvest Wine Group 320
Milton Sandford Wines
  355
Sunday Times Wine
  Club 410

Wargrave
Vintage Roots 430

Windsor
Bordeaux Direct 258

Buckinghamshire

Amersham
Philip Eyres Wine
  Merchant 292

Beaconsfield
Bordeaux Direct 258

Great Missenden
Turville Valley Wines
  418

Olney
Bacchus of Olney 242

Cambridgeshire

Cambridge
Barwells of Cambridge
  247

Godmanchester
H&H Wines 317
Ramsey
Anthony Byrne Fine
  Wines 262

Trumpington
Noel Young Wines 457

Cheshire

Alderley Edge
Addison-Bagot Vintners
  232

Chester
Quellyn Roberts 380

Hale (near Altrincham)
Portland Wine
  Company 379

Macclesfield
Portland Wine
  Company 379

Nantwich
Rodney Densem Wines
  280
Edencroft Fine Wines
  285

Sandiway
Sandiway Wine
  Company 392

Warrington
Wine Cellar 442

Cornwall

Truro
Laymont & Shaw 341

Cumbria

Carlisle
BH Wines 253
Corkscrew Wines 274

Kendal
Frank E Stainton 405

Devon

Bideford
Wickham & Co 438

Cullompton
Peter Wylie Fine Wines
  455

Doddiscombsleigh
The Nobody Inn 367

Ivybridge
Brian Coad Fine Wines
  271

Ottery St Mary
Christopher Piper
  Wines 375

Dorset

Blandford St Mary
Hicks & Don 328
Woodhouse Wines 453

Gillingham
The Vintry 431

Wareham
Richard Harvey Wines
  323

Essex

Colchester
Lay & Wheeler 340

Gloucestershire

Cheltenham
The Rose Tree Wine Co
  387

Chipping Campden
Bennetts Wines and
  Spirits 249

Northleach
Windrush Wines 439

Stow-on-the-Wold
Haynes Hanson &
  Clark 325

Wickwar
The Bin Club 255

Greater Manchester

Sale
Portland Wine
  Company 379

Stockport
Booths of Stockport 257

Hampshire

Basingstoke
Berry Bros & Rudd 252

Bentworth
High Breck Vintners 329

Hartley Wintney
Stéphane Auriol Wines 239

Liphook
General Wine Company 305
The Vintry 431

Southampton
Alexander Hadleigh Wines 314

Stockbridge
Trout Wines 417

Hereford & Worcester

Bromsgrove
Noble Rot Wine Warehouses 366

Hereford
Tanners Wines 411

Malvern Wells
Croque-en-Bouche 278

Hertfordshire

Bishop's Stortford
Hedley Wright 326

Bushey
Bordeaux Direct 258

Harpenden
Le Fleming Wines 296

Rickmansworth
Wine World 449

St Albans
Sherston Wine Company 400

Stevenage
The Wine Society 477

Isle of Wight

Newport
Benedict's 248

Kent

Appledore
Vin du Van Wine Merchants 428

Broadstairs
The Bottleneck 259

Lancashire

Clitheroe
D Byrne & Co 263
Whitesides Wine Merchants 436

Nelson
John Stephenson & Sons 406

Leicestershire

Leicester
Evington's 291

Loughborough
George Hill of Loughborough 330

Merseyside

Liverpool
Scatchard 394

Middlesex

Staines
Cape Province Wines 265

Norfolk

Dereham
Hicks & Don 328

Norwich
Adnams Wine Merchants 233
Hall Batson & Co 315

Thetford
T & W Wines 410

Longville
Roger Harris Wines 318

Northamptonshire

Finedon
Summerlee Wines 409

Nottinghamshire

Nottingham
Gauntleys of Nottingham 304
Weavers of Nottingham 435

Oxfordshire

Banbury
S H Jones 335

Bicester
S H Jones 335

Blewbury
Sebastopol Wines 395

Oxford
Grape Ideas 309
Windrush Wines 439

Shropshire

Bridgnorth
Tanners Wines 411

Ludlow
Halves 316

Newport
William Addison 232

Shrewsbury
Tanners Wines 411

Staffordshire

Marchington
Wines of Westhorpe 452

Suffolk

Ipswich
Seckford Wines 396
Wines of Interest 451

Newmarket
Corney & Barrow 275

Southwold
Adnams Wine
    Merchants 233

Sudbury
Amey's Wines 235

Surrey

Brockham
Ben Ellis and Associates
    288

Croydon
Mayor & Sworder 353

Dorking
The Dorking Wine
    Cellar 284

Guildford
Santat Wines 393

Haslemere
Haslemere Cellar 324

Kingston-upon-Thames
Bentalls of Kingston 250

Wallington
The Wine House 444

Woking
Bordeaux Direct 258

Sussex (East)

Alfriston
English Wine Centre 289

Brighton
The Butlers Wine Cellar
    261

Sussex (West)

Billingshurst
Charles Hennings
    (Vintners) 327

Chilgrove
The Four Walls Wine
    Company 299

Horsham
King & Barnes 338

Petworth
Charles Hennings
    (Vintners) 327

Pulborough
Charles Hennings
    (Vintners) 327

Tyne & Wear

Newcastle upon Tyne
Michael Jobling Wines
    335

Warwickshire

Shipston on Stour
Edward Sheldon 399

Warwick
Waters of Coventry 434

West Midlands

Birmingham
Connolly's 271
Parfrements 370

Solihull
John Frazier 301

Stourbridge
Nickolls & Perks 364

Walsall
Whittalls Wines 437

Wolverhampton
The Newbridge Wine
    Centre 361

Wiltshire

Mere
Yapp Brothers 456

Westbury
Hicks & Don 328

Yorkshire (North)

Harrogate
Martinez Fine Wines
    351
The Wine Bureau 441

Manfield
Wrightson & Co 454

Ripon
Great Northern Wine
    Company 311

Skipton
Wright Wine Company
    454

Thirsk
Playford Ros 377

Yorkshire (South)

Sheffield
Eckington Wines 284
Michael Menzel 354
Mitchells Wine
    Merchants 357
Penistone Court Wine
    Cellars 373
The Wine Schoppen
    446

Yorkshire (West)

Halifax
Martinez Fine Wines
    351

Ilkley
Martinez Fine Wines
    351

Leeds
Cairns & Hickey 264
Great Northern Wine
    Company 311
Vinceremos Wines 421

Otley
Chippendale Fine
    Wines 268

Scotland

Borders

Peebles
Villeneuve Wines 426

Fife

Cupar
Luvians Bottle Shop 347

Grampian

Aberdeen
Wine Raks (Scotland)
    Ltd 445

Elgin
Gordon & MacPhail 308

Kinross-shire

Milnathort
Forth Wines 297

Lothian

Edinburgh
J E Hogg 331
Justerini & Brooks 337
Peter Green 313
Raeburn Fine Wines 381
Irvine Robertson 334
Valvona & Crolla 421

Strathclyde

Ayr
Corney & Barrow 275

Glasgow
Ubiquitous Chip Wine
    Shop 418

Rothesay, Isle of Bute
Bute Wines 260

Tayside

Perth
Matthew Gloag & Son
    306

Wales

Clwyd

Deeside
Classic Wines & Spirits
    270

Dyfed

Lampeter
A Case of Wine Deli 266

Llanwrda
A Case of Wine 266

Gwent

Caerleon
The Celtic Vintner 267

Gwynedd

Llandudno Junction
Terry Platt Wine
    Merchant 376

Mid Glamorgan

Powys

Welshpool
Tanners Wines 411

South Glamorgan

Cowbridge
Ballantynes of
    Cowbridge 243

West Glamorgan

Swansea
CPA's 276
The Celtic Vintner 267

Northern Ireland

Co Antrim

Belfast
Direct Wine Shipments
    281

Co Down

Crossgar
James Nicholson Wine
    Merchant 363

Republic of Ireland

Dublin
Mitchell & Son 356

Channel Islands

Guernsey

St Peter Port
Sommelier Wine
    Company 403

CHAINS AND SUPERMARKETS

Part IV

Find out more about wine

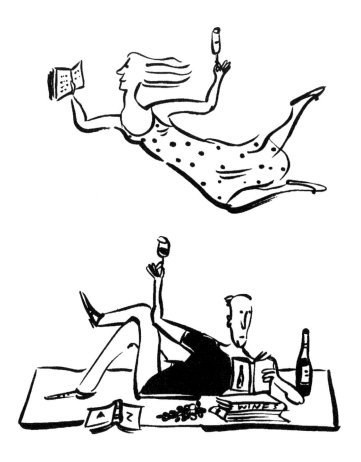

FIND OUT MORE ABOUT WINE

As the popularity of wine grows and it becomes increasingly accessible there are more opportunities to learn about it. Wine clubs operate all around the country, offering tutored tastings, dinners and other events. There are tours to vineyards and wine regions enabling you to sample local cuisine and broaden your knowledge. Some travel companies deal exclusively with wine-related tours and holidays. Wine courses are available for absolute novices and knowledgeable enthusiasts alike; some courses concentrate on grape varieties while others focus on regions.

WINE CLUBS

Association de la Jurade de St-Emilion (Grande Bretagne) Peter Shamash, 7 Tower Court, Overstone Park, Northants NN6 0AS TEL (01604) 642379 A regular series of gastronomic dinners, lunches and visits to St-Emilion, intended to increase knowledge and appreciation of the wines of this region.

Bramhope Wine Appreciation Group Kelvyn Chapman, 20 Ayresome Avenue, Leeds, W Yorks LS8 1BE TEL (0113) 2666322 Tutored tastings are held twice a month with the cost of wines shared (usually £3–£5 per session for six wines). Activities include visits from guest speakers, occasional visits to merchants, dinners and tours of wine-making regions abroad. Annual subscription £18. A smaller group also meets every Monday at the Garforth School Evening Centre during term-time.

Civil Service Wine Society Stan Baker, 131 Gordon Road, Chatham, Kent ME4 5LX TEL (01634) 848345 Fortnightly tastings on Wednesday evenings at the Civil Service Club, Great Scotland Yard, Whitehall, London between March and December. Founded in 1975 the Society welcomes non-Civil Servants – there is no membership charge, payment is made for each tasting attended. All members are invited to verbally assess product quality.

Cornwall Wine Tasting Group Peter Portwood, 3 Belmont Villas, Truro, Cornwall TR1 1HS TEL (01872) 73856 Although the group is affiliated to the Wine Society, membership is open. There is a one-off joining fee of £10, but a supplement is charged for each tasting attended. Meetings are held monthly with the exception of August and December when the tasting is substituted by a dinner.

Harrogate Medical Wine Society 86 Station Parade, Harrogate, N Yorks HG1 1HH TEL (01423) 503129 FAX (01423) 561820 Open to members of the medical and related professions. Tutored tastings are held monthly and social functions, visits to wine shows and other societies are also organised. Membership is £5 a year with a charge for each tasting.

The International Wine & Food Society 9 Fitzmaurice Place, Berkeley Square, London W1X 6JD TEL 0171-495 4191 FAX 0171-495 4172 Membership terms on application; special rates for members under 25. The International Secretariat in London has a library and club and residential facilities. Nearly 200 regional branches organise dinners, tastings, lectures and visits. The annual *Food and Wine*, regular newsletters and an annual *Vintage Guide* to wine-buying are free to members.

Lay & Wheeler, Hugo Rose MW, 6 Culver Street West, Colchester, Essex CO1 1JA TEL (01206) 764446 FAX (01206) 560002 Full details of Lay & Wheeler's services, including 128-page illustrated wine list, wine workshops, tutored tastings, the Wine Discovery Programme, monthly newsletters and the Cellar Plan are available on request. Tastings, some of which are blind, cover a variety of themes. (See also the Where to buy section.)

The Lincoln Wine Society Norman Tate, 8 Green Lane, North Hykeham, Lincoln, Lincs LN6 8NL TEL (01522) 680388 Meetings are held once a month and activities include guest experts and wine-merchants, fine wine and food evenings, trips to merchants and wine areas, and a grand annual function. Membership is £7 annually (£12 joint). (See also Lincoln Wine Course.)

Northern Wine Appreciation Group DM Hunter, 21 Dartmouth Avenue, Almondbury, Huddersfield, W Yorks HD5 8UR TEL (01484) 531228 Meetings weekly from September to June. Graded tutored tastings and special events are held for new members. Activities include visits to merchants for tastings and dinners.

Ordre Mondial des Gourmets Dégustateurs Martin Mistlin, 41 Kingsend, Ruislip, Middx HA4 7DD This is a French wine guild with a British chapter (the headquarters are in Paris). Various tastings and dinners are held regularly with access to meetings abroad. Initial subscription is £75 for professionals, then £24 annually, and £50 for amateurs, then £24 annually. Martin Mistlin also runs the Fine Wine Dining Club (annual subscription £5), which has six events or more per quarter, meeting in central London hotels and Pinner, Middlesex. This subscription includes the Cofradia Riojana, Lega del Chianti and the Alsace Club of Great Britain.

The Petersham Wine Society John Trigwell, Tanglewood House, Mayfield Avenue, New Haw, Addlestone, Surrey KT15 3AG TEL (01932) 348720 FAX (01932) 350861 Regular tastings in cellars of The Petersham Hotel, Richmond, Surrey with wines of fine quality providing special tasting opportunities, followed by small finger-buffet, in the form of a regional speciality, also bread and cheeses. Annual membership £7.50 (£12 joint). Tastings £17.50/£30 per head.

Tanglewood Wine Society Tanglewood House, Mayfield Avenue, New Haw, Addlestone, Surrey KT15 3AG TEL (01932) 348720 FAX (01932) 350861 The Society has branches in Cobham and Reigate holding regular monthly tastings and social events. Annual membership costs £7.50 (£12 joint at the same address). A charge is made at each tasting: average £9 a head. (See also Tanglewood Wine Tours.)

The Wine & Dine Society 96 Ramsden Road, London SW12 8QZ TEL 0181-673 4439 Weekly tastings (many with guest speakers) and theme dinners are held at various locations in London. Workshops are also held regularly. Tasting evenings start at £10.

The Wine Schoppen Wine Tasting Circle Mrs Anne Coghlan, 3 Oak Street, Heeley, Sheffield S8 9UB TEL (0114) 2553301 FAX (0114) 2551010 A wide range of tutored tastings are hosted by guest speakers. 'Open days' are held on the first Saturday of each month, tasting one special or rare wine; cheese and wine tastings and dinners are also organised. A wine tour abroad and a weekend away are arranged every year. Annual fee is £6 (£11 joint).

The Winetasters PN Beardwood (Secretary), 44 Claremont Road, London W13 0DG TEL 0181-997 1252 This is a non-profit-making club with academic connections which organises tastings, seminars, dinners and tours. Annual subscription £10 (£3 if you live more than 50 miles from London).

Wine World Lilyane Weston, 'Owlet', Templepan Lane, Chandlers Cross, Rickmansworth, Herts WD3 4NH TEL/FAX (01923) 264718 A selection of courses and fine wine tastings, 10–12 wines tasted on average, cost £15–£18 per session. Gourmet Evenings matching at least 6 wines with a 3-course meal, cost £25. Training offered to restaurant staff.

Available to lecture to business and social clubs, consumer groups, colleges and universities, wine trade events of any size, daytime or evening throughout the UK. Extensive library of slides, videos, maps and literature. Member of Circle of Wine Writers.

TRAVEL AND TOURS

ACT (Accompanied Cape Tours and A la Carte Tours) Virginia Carlton, Hill House, Much Marcle, Ledbury, Hereford & Worcester HR8 2NX TEL/FAX (01531) 660210 Runs personalised tours to Natal and the Western Cape of South Africa, visiting wine estates, historical houses and private gardens. Fully inclusive holidays £2,178; 10-day self-drive Cape Town and the Winelands £1,098; Wine and Game Safaris and Wine and Train Itineraries a speciality.

Allez France 27 West Street, Storrington, W Sussex RH20 4DZ TEL (01903) 745319/742345 Allez France offers wine holidays for the independent traveller based in hotels chosen for their setting, cuisine, character and comfort, including a 'unique' selection of hotels with their own vineyards. Travel arrangements are flexible and tailor-made wine tours for groups, clubs or associations can be arranged. Also gastronomic breaks and family holidays.

Arblaster & Clarke Wine Club Tours 104 Church Road, Steep, Petersfield, Hants GU32 2DD TEL (01730) 266883 FAX (01730) 268620 A wide selection of wine tours throughout France, Italy, Spain, Portugal, Australia and South Africa is available on a selection of dates throughout the year. Parties are escorted by knowledgeable wine guides – often a wine journalist or Master of Wine and a bilingual tour manager. Champagne weekend tours start from just £199 per person and depart throughout the year. Walking routes, through the Burgundy Grand Cru, the Beaujolais Crus and the Loire, and self-drive tours are available. Private tours are arranged for companies and wine clubs.

Backroads 9 Shaftesbury Street, Fordingbridge, Hants SP6 1JF TEL (01425) 655022 FAX (01425) 655177 Backroads specialises in walking and cycling holidays, some incorporate touring wine regions in America and Europe. Tours include cycling in the Loire, the Galicia and Minho wine regions and walking in the Napa Valley and Chianti regions. Choose from luxury inn-to-inn or camping.

DER Travel Service Ltd 18 Conduit Street, London W1R 9TD TEL 0171-290 1111 FAX 0171-629 7442/7501 As well as Rhine cruises, DER arranges air and rail holidays to Germany and Austria in wine-growing areas and in 1995 offers visits to the wine festivals in Boppard and Koenigswinter. With your own car you can tour the wine-growing areas of the Rhine and Mosel on a 'Wine Regions tour'. An 8-night tour in 1995 costs from £365 to £307 per person depending on the number of passengers in the car.

English Vineyards Association 38 West Park, London SE9 4RH TEL 0181-857 0452 FAX 0181-851 4864 Many English vineyards are open to the public and offer guided tours, tastings and sales. A free leaflet giving details is available from the address above (send an s.a.e.).

Eurocamp Canute Court, Toft Road, Knutsford, Cheshire WA16 0NL TEL (01565) 626262 (Reservations only: 28 Princess Street, Knutsford, Cheshire WA16 6BG) Eurocamp arranges self-drive camping and mobile home holidays at over 270 sites in Europe, many of which are 'among the grapes'. These include Bergerac, Cahors, Bordeaux, the Mosel and Rhineland. 'Eurocamp Independent' TEL (01565) 755399 offers a ferry/pitch reservations 'package' for campers and touring caravan-owners.

Francophiles Discover France 66 Great Brockeridge, Westbury-on-Trym, Bristol BS9 3UA TEL (0117) 9621975 FAX (0117) 9622642 Coach tour company offering superior, expertly-led cultural tours in 'off-the-beaten-track' France.

Friendship Wine Tours Collins Court, High Street, Cranleigh, Surrey GU6 8AS TEL (01483) 273355 FAX (01483) 268621 On offer are 'tailor-made', escorted tours to the 'Fine Wine' regions of Europe and beyond. Areas covered include wine-production in Champagne, Burgundy, Alsace, the Rhône, the Loire, Bordeaux and Languedoc regions of France; Piedmont and Tuscany in Italy; Rioja, Navarra and Galicia in Spain; Costa Verde and Douro in northern Portugal; the Rhine, Mosel and Baden in Germany. A personal service for the Wine Group worldwide.

HGP Wine Tours Melville House, Melville Street, Torquay, Devon TQ2 5SS TEL (01803) 299292 FAX (01803) 292008 These tours are run by Helen Gillespie-Peck, chairman of L'Académie du Vin, Devon.

Destinations include France, Spain, Italy and Portugal. Short breaks and gourmet weekends are also included in the programme. Up-to-date information from 'Talking Pages' South Devon Freephone (0800) 600 900.

KD River Cruises of Europe GA Clubb, River Cruise Agency, 28 South Street, Epsom, Surrey KT18 7PF TEL (01372) 742033 FAX (01372) 724871 In 1995, a week-long 'Floating Wine Seminar' (from £895) visited six famous wine-growing areas in the Mosel, the Rhine, Alsace and Baden, and included lectures, tutored tastings and optional sightseeing tours.

Moswin Tours Moswin House, 21 Church Street, Oadby, Leics LE2 5DB TEL (0116) 2714982 FAX (0116) 2716016 Wine tours to Germany by air or coach. Some are arranged around special events like the Bernkastel Wine Festival or the Moselle Harvest. Tastings and lectures included. The Moselle Harvest tour offers the chance to get involved in the vineyard work. Other areas covered include the Rhine and Ahr Valley, Franconia, Baden, Elbe Wineland and Saale-Unstrut Wineland. Individual itineraries can be arranged.

Page & Moy 136–140 London Road, Leicester, Leics LE2 1EN TEL (0116) 2542000 Page & Moy offers a range of wine, art, history, architecture and music tours in Europe, in particular, Italy, France and Spain, the Baltic States and Israel.

Tanglewood Wine Tours Tanglewood House, Mayfield Avenue, New Haw, Addlestone, Surrey KT15 3AG TEL (01932) 348720 FAX (01932) 350861 This family business specialises in coach tours to the vineyards of France, including Bordeaux, Burgundy, the Rhône Valley and Provence, the Loire Valley, Alsace and Champagne. (See also Tanglewood Wine Society.)

Wessex Continental Travel PO Box 43, Plymouth, Devon PL1 1SY TEL/FAX (01752) 846880 Described as 'holidays with wine', a range of 7- and 8-day coach tours are offered around France. Prices are from £355 to £385, with a maximum of 36 people per tour. For private/corporate groups, independent arrangements can be made to other wine regions of the world. Pick-up points in London, Portsmouth or Dover. Also, wine cruises to Rioja and Navarra in Spain: seven days from £349.

Wine Journeys Alternative Travel Group, 69–71 Banbury Road, Oxford, Oxon OX2 6PE TEL (01865) 310399 Wine Journeys are led by wine experts Rosemary George MW, Clive Coates MW and Remington Norman MW. The focus is on exploring the wine regions, visiting the best estates, tasting wines and matching them with the local cuisine. For active people, walking and cycling tours to some of the main wine regions are also available. In 1995, a five-day tour in Bordeaux cost £845 plus airfare.

Winetrails Greenways, Vann Lake, Ockley, Dorking, Surrey RH5 5NT TEL (01306) 712111 FAX (01306) 713504 Winetrails offers a variety of gentle walking holidays in grape-growing territory around the world. The emphasis is on good food, wine, nature and local culture. 1996 destinations include Provence, Rhône, Burgundy, Bordeaux, Roussillon, Loire Valley, Languedoc, Haute Savoie, Navarra & Rioja, Jerez & Andalucia, Madeira, Bulgaria, the Cape in South Africa, South Australia, Tuscany, Piedmont, Umbria, California, Cyprus, Majorca, UK (walking weekends). Private 'Tailor Made' trips are available on request worldwide.

Wineweekends Jon and Heather Hurley, Upper Orchard, Hoarwithy, Hereford & Worcester HR2 6QR TEL (01432) 840649 The Hurleys have been organising their Wineweekends since 1973 at their seventeenth-century house on the River Wye. There is a Beginner's Weekend (£125), a Fine Wine Weekend (£155) or a 'Classics' Weekend (£225) to choose from. Meals, wine-tasting and accommodation included. They also have 18 different walks from the house, each with a pub halfway.

COURSES

Association of Wine Educators 20 The Square, Earls Barton, Northants NN6 0NA TEL/FAX (01604) 811993 The Association of Wine Educators is an independent organisation, set up in 1993, of tutors qualified in the field of wine education. It sends out information on members, the type of work they do, wine education programmes, tutored tastings and presentations. Contact them to get on the mailing list.

Christie's Wine Course Caron Williamson (Secretary), 63 Old Brompton Road, London SW7 3JS TEL 0171-581 3933 FAX 0171-589 0383 The Introduction to Wine Tasting course runs for five consecutive Tuesday evenings and offers comparative tastings of a full range of French wines. Six courses are held during the academic year and the cost is £160. Christie's also offers Master Classes with fine and rare wine tastings. Cost is £55–65.

Ecole du Vin Château Loudenne 33340 St-Yzans-de-Médoc, France
TEL (00 33) 56 73 17 80 FAX (00 33) 56 09 02 87 Six-day courses are
held at the château for a dozen students five times a year. Aimed at
the public and professionals in the trade, the lectures and tastings
cover all aspects of viticulture and vinification. Price in 1994 was
11,900FF inclusive. A new three-hour introductory course for both
intermediate and advanced levels is held daily from 9.30–12.30.

German Wine Academy German Wine Information Service,
Chelsea Chambers, 262a Fulham Road, London SW10 9EL
TEL 0171-376 3329 FAX 0171-351 7563 A twelfth-century German
monastery is the setting for courses (delivered in English), which
include lectures by wine experts, vineyard visits and tastings. The
7-day course is run in September and October (DM2100 plus
airfare).

Heart of England School of Wine 20 The Square, Earls Barton,
Northants NN6 0NA TEL (01604) 811993 The proprietors of the
school founded the AWE (see Association of Wine Educators) in
1993. Courses are offered for wine enthusiasts and those working
in the wine trade. Seminars range from half-days to residential
weekends and evening courses. The Wine & Spirit Education Trust
Course is also available to Higher Certificate level. Details of
courses in wine appreciation, tutored tastings and themed wine or
wine and food evenings are available on request. A consultancy
service is also offered to the trade.

Huddersfield Technical College School of Catering, New North
Road, Huddersfield, West Yorks HD1 5NN TEL (01484) 536521 FAX
(01484) 511885 Tastings are held every six weeks at the college and
cost around £8.50. The Wine and Spirit Education Trust's Certificate
and Higher Certificate can be taken and short courses can be
arranged to suit requirements.

Leith's School of Food and Wine 21 Alban's Grove, London W8
5BP TEL 0171-229 0177 Two evening courses are available leading to
the award of Leith's Certificate or Leith's Advanced Certificate of
Wine (roughly analogous to the Wine and Spirit Education Trust's
Higher Certificate, without the sessions on licensing and labelling
laws). Priced £215 and £400 respectively. Other courses are also
sometimes available.

The Lincoln Wine Course Norman Tate, 8 Green Lane, North
Hykeham, Lincoln, Lincs LN6 8NL TEL (01522) 680388 A wine
appreciation course is offered at North Hykeham Evening Institute
starting in September each year. This is a two-term course (two

hours a week) with the emphasis on tasting and gaining a good general knowledge of wine. Participants have the opportunity to take the Wine and Spirit Education Trust's Certificate examination. The cost is divided between the course fee (£30) and a weekly supplement to cover the cost of the tastings. (See also Lincoln Wine Society.)

Wink Lorch, Independent Wine Consultant, 15 Pymers Mead, Dulwich, London SE21 8NQ TEL/FAX 0181-670 6885 Wink Lorch offers tutored tastings on all wine subjects. Tailor-made wine evenings, courses and holidays are provided for a wide range of consumers. She organises regular holidays in the French alps which include visits to Savoie vineyards, local Savoie meals, mountain walks and tastings of wines from other regions. She also leads a residential wine weekend at Missenden Abbey. Member of the Association of Wine Educators.

Plumpton College nr Lewes, East Sussex BN7 3AE TEL (01273) 890454 FAX (01273) 890071 Plumpton College offers courses in vine-growing and winemaking for both amateurs and professionals. Other courses include the Sensory Evaluation of Wine and Practical Wine Analysis. Occasional seminars on wine production are also held at the College. Plumpton College has a 1,400-acre estate with its own well-equipped vineyards and winery.

The Scala School of Wine 24 Scala Street, London W1P 1LU TEL/FAX 0171-637 9077 A full programme of courses and tastings on offer, including novice and intermediate courses which last for five weeks, one evening per week. Separate tutored tasting evenings are also held. The 5-week courses cost £115 and £150 respectively. This includes course notes and up to ten wines in each tasting.

Sotheby's Wine Department 34–35 New Bond Street, London W1A 2AA TEL 0171-408 5051 FAX 0171-408 5961 Varietal and Regional Wine Courses alternate and run throughout the year (except during the summer holiday period), on consecutive Wednesday evenings. £160 per course of five sessions. Wine Seminars, Dinners and Tutored Tastings with top wine producers are also held. Sales of Fine & Rare Wines take place monthly in London, five times a year with Sherry-Lehmann Inc in New York and twice a year in Switzerland.

The Wine & Spirit Education Trust, Five Kings House, 1 Queen Street Place, London EC4R 1QS TEL 0171-236 3551 FAX 0171-329 8712 The aim of the Trust is to promote education and training among those working in the wine and allied industries. Courses are also open to the general public. Wine & Spirit Education Trust courses are offered at three levels: Certificate, Higher Certificate and Diploma. Seminars, Masterclass Tastings and Food and Wine Matching Workshops are also available. In addition, the Trust approves external examination centres to conduct WSET examinations.

The Wine Education Service Philip Cooper, 76 St Margaret's Road, London N17 6TY TEL 0181-801 2229 Offers wine courses for the consumer in the London area, plus Oxford and Tunbridge Wells. Courses combine tasting with both structured tuition and informal discussion, plus a presentation of background knowledge on the world's wine regions. The Level 1 Introductory course features 55 wines and runs for one evening per week over 10 weeks. Cost is £135.

Winewise Michael Schuster, 107 Culford Road, London N1 4HL TEL 0171-254 9734 FAX 0171-249 3663. In addition to fine wine tastings of individual estates and vintages, and blind tastings each spring, Winewise runs two regular wine-tasting courses: a Beginners' Course and a Fine Wine Course. The Beginners' Course is £126 (VAT incl) for six evenings; 40 wines are tasted from round the world ranging in price from £3 to £18 retail, the average price being £8 a bottle. The Fine Wine Course costs £186 for six evenings; 56 wines are tasted from the classic French regions ranging in price from £8 to £60 retail, the average price being £20 a bottle.

Wine Club Tours Clarke House, The Green, West Liss, Hants GU33 6PQ TEL (01730) 895353 FAX (01730) 892888 Wine Club Tours offer a series of tours each year.There are also trips to Bordeaux, where a wine school at Château Lascombes is offered, the Champagne Bus, where tasting begins at Calais; and the vineyards of Burgundy and Beaujolais are annual favourites. Spain, Portugal and Italy also feature regularly, and for late 1996–early 1997 a tour to Chile and Argentina is planned. There is also a new tour to South Africa (18–27 February 1996 £1,599). Six-month membership of the Sunday Times Wine Club is offered for non-members wishing to join these tours.

WINE GLOSSARY

abboccato (Italy) medium-dry

abocado (Spain) medium-dry

adega (Portugal) winery

almacenista (Spain) a small-scale sherry stockholder

amabile (Italy) medium or medium-sweet

amarone (Italy) dry passito (*q.v.*) wine from Valpolicella

amontillado (Spain) an aged fino (*q.v.*) sherry on which yeast flor (*q.v.*) has ceased to grow but which is matured further without flor to develop delicate nutty flavours; commercial 'medium amontillados' are not made in this way, but are blended, sweetened sherries

amoroso (Spain) medium-sweet style of sherry

Anbaugebiet (Germany) growing region

appassimento (Italy) drying of grapes to concentrate their sugars

appellation d'origine contrôlée (AOC) (France) the best category of French wine, with regulations defining the precise vineyard area according to soil, grape varieties, yields, alcohol level, and maybe vineyard and cellar practices

Ausbruch (Austria) dessert wine, between Beerenauslese and Trockenbeerenauslese, from nobly rotten grapes

Auslese (Germany) wine from selected ripe grapes, possibly with noble rot (*see* botrytis)

barrique 225-litre barrel, usually of French oak, in which both red and white wines are matured and white wines sometimes fermented. Normally replaced every 2-3 years, as new barriques have more effect on taste

Beerenauslese (Germany) wine from specially selected ripe berries, probably with noble rot

Bereich (Germany) region, larger than Grosslage, smaller than Anbaugebiet (*q.v.*)

blanc de blancs white wine or champagne made from white grapes only

blanc de noirs white wine or champagne made from red grapes vinified without skin contact (the juice of most red grapes is colourless; all the colouring matter is found in the skins)

bodega (Spain) cellar, winery

botrytis cinerea a form of rot that shrivels grapes and concentrates their sugars ('noble rot')

botte/i (Italy) large oak or chestnut barrel/s

brut (Champagne) dry or dryish (up to 15g sugar/litre)

brut (Madeira) smokily sweet madeira

cantina sociale/cantine sociali (Italy) co-operative winery/ies

carbonic maceration fermentation of whole bunches of grapes in vat filled with carbon dioxide to give fruity wines with low tannin

cava (Spain) champagne-method sparkling wines; now a DO in its own right

chaptalisation the addition of sugar to the must to increase the final alcohol content of the wine

classico (Italy) heartland of a DOC zone, producing its best wines, e.g. Soave

clos (Burgundy) vineyard site that was walled in the past, and may still be walled

colheita (Portugal) vintage (table wine); single-vintage tawny (port)

cosecha (Spain) vintage

cream (Spain) sweet sherry

criadera (Spain) literally 'nursery'; signifies a stage in a sherry solera system (*q.v.*)

crianza, sin (Spain) without wood-ageing

crianza, vino de (Spain) basic wood-aged wine, with one year's oak-cask ageing and one year's bottle- or tank-ageing

cru (France) literally 'growth', meaning either a distinguished single property (as in Bordeaux) or a distinguished vineyard area (as in Beaujolais or Burgundy)

cru (Italy) wine from grapes of a single vineyard, usually of high quality. Term is in common use but not officially permitted

cru bourgeois (Bordeaux) 'bourgeois growth', indicating a wine from the bottom tier of the Médoc region's secondary classification system

cru classé (Bordeaux) 'classified growth', indicating a wine from the Médoc's primary classification system, divided into five strata (premiers, deuxièmes, troisièmes, quatrièmes and cinquièmes crus classés); or from the classification systems of the Graves, Sauternes or St-Emilion

cru grand bourgeois (Bordeaux) 'a fine bourgeois growth', indicating a wine from the middle tier of the Médoc's secondary classification system

cru grand bourgeois exceptionnel (Bordeaux) 'exceptionally fine bourgeois growth', indicating a wine from the upper tier of the Médoc's secondary classification system

crusting/crusted (Portugal) a blend of port of different years for short-term cellaring; needs decanting

cuve close a method of making sparkling wines by carrying out the second fermentation inside a sealed tank rather than in bottle. Also known as the 'tank method' and 'Charmat method'

cuvée (France) vat or tank; sometimes means a 'selected' wine, but the term has no legal status on labels

demi-sec (Champagne, Loire) sweet (up to 50g sugar/litre)

Denominación de Origen (DO) (Spain) wines of controlled origin, grape varieties and style

Denominación de Origen Calificada (DOCa) (Spain) as DO, but entails stricter controls including bottling at source; so far, only Rioja has been given a DOCa status

Denominazione di Origine Controllata (DOC) (Italy) wine of controlled origin, grape varieties and style

Denominazione di Origine Controllata e Garantita (DOCG) (Italy) wine from area with stricter controls than DOC

domaine (Burgundy) estate, meaning the totality of vineyard holdings belonging to a grower or *négociant*

dosage (Champagne) the sugar added with wine to champagne after disgorgement, to determine the degree of sweetness of the final blend, from brut, through extra sec, sec, demi-sec to doux. Extra brut has no dosage

doux (Champagne, Loire) sweet to very sweet (over 50g sugar/litre)

Einzellage (Germany) single vineyard site

Eiswein (Germany) wine made from frozen grapes

English table wine (England & Wales) all English wines, including the very best, are, as yet, classed as 'table wine' by the EC. A pilot scheme for quality wine has been introduced, but has yet to make much impact

Erzeugerabfüllung (Germany) estate-bottled (co-operative cellars may also use this term)

extra brut (Champagne) absolutely dry (no added sugar)

extra dry (Champagne) off-dry (12-20g sugar/litre)

fino (Spain) light, dry sherry matured under flor (*q.v.*)

flor (Spain) a layer of yeast growing on sherry in a part-empty butt; gives fino (*q.v.*) its character

frizzante (Italy) lightly sparkling

garrafa (Portugal) bottle

garrafeira (Portugal) better-than-average table wine given longer-than-average ageing; a producer's selection of his best wine; a colheita port given bottle as well as cask age

grand cru (Alsace) classified vineyard site

grand cru (Burgundy) finest category of named vineyard site

grand cru classé (Bordeaux) 'fine classed growth', indicating a wine from the second level of the St-Emilion classification system

grand vin (Bordeaux) 'fine wine': the top wine of a Bordeaux château, blended from selected cuvées only, as opposed to the 'second wine', which is blended from less successful cuvées and perhaps the wine of younger vines, and which is generally sold at a lower price; in other regions the term is used more loosely

gran reserva (Spain) red wine aged for a minimum of two years in oak casks and three in bottle; white (or rosé) wine aged for a minimum of four years, of which six months must be in oak casks

Grosslage (Germany) collective vineyard site

halbtrocken (Germany) semi-dry

Kabinett (Germany) first category of Prädikat wine (*q.v.*), light and delicate in style

Landwein (Germany) country wine

Late-Bottled Vintage (LBV) (Portugal) a medium-quality red port of a single year

late harvest (Australia, New Zealand, North America) sweet wine made from grapes picked in an over-mature or maybe botrytised condition

lieu-dit (Burgundy) named, but unclassified, vineyard site

liquoroso (Italy) wines fortified with grape alcohol

maceration process of leaving grapes to 'stew' on their skins before, during and after fermentation

maduro (Portugal) a term, meaning 'matured', used loosely of any non-verde (*q.v.*) young wine

malmsey (Madeira) the most sweet and raisiny of madeiras

malolactic fermentation a secondary, non-alcoholic 'fermentation' that converts malic acid into lactic acid. The process is accomplished by bacteria rather than yeast

manzanilla (Spain) salty fino from Sanlúcar de Barrameda

manzanilla pasada (Spain) aged manzanilla (*q.v.*)

méthode traditionnelle (France) replaces méthode champenoise in France to describe the champagne method

metodo classico (Italy) champagne-method sparkling wines

método tradicional (Spain) champagne-method sparkling wines

mis en bouteille par (France) bottled by

moelleux (France) medium-sweet to sweet

mousse (France) term used to describe the effervescence in sparkling wine

mousseux (France) sparkling

muffa nobile (Italy) noble rot

naturale (Italy) natural; describes non-sparkling or slightly sparkling Piemontese Moscato wines with lowish alcohol

négociant (France) wholesale merchant and wine trader

noble rot *see* botrytis

non-vintage (nv) a wine or champagne made from a blend of wines of different years

normale (Italy) non-riserva; most commonly mentioned for Chianti

nouveau (particularly Beaujolais) new wine sold from the third Thursday in November after the harvest. Other areas may be earlier

novello (Italy) new wine, for drinking very young, on sale from October or November

Oechsle (Germany) measure of sugar in grape must; determines quality of wine in Germany and Austria; also used in New World

oloroso (Spain) sherry aged oxidatively rather than under flor (*q.v.*)

palo cortado (Spain) light and delicate style of oloroso (*q.v.*)

passerillage (France) the process of leaving grapes to dry and dehydrate on the vine with the eventual aim of producing a dessert wine from them

passito (Italy) dried or semi-dried grapes or wine made from them

perlant (France) with a slight prickle of gas, visible on the side of the glass

pipe (Portugal) a port cask containing between 534 litres (shipping pipe) and 630 litres (lodge pipe)

Port with an Indication of Age (Portugal) true tawny port, in four styles: 10 Years Old, 20 Years Old, 30 Years Old, over 40 Years Old

Prädikat (Germany and Austria) a category of wine with a 'special attribute' based on natural sugar levels in must, such as Kabinett, Spätlese, Auslese, Beerenauslese, Trockenbeerenauslese or Eiswein

predicato (Italy) category of merit used for new-style Tuscan wines

premier cru (Burgundy) second highest category of named vineyard site. If no vineyard name is specified, wine made from a number of different premier cru sites

premier grand cru classé (Bordeaux) 'first fine classed growth', indicating a wine from the top level of the St-Emilion classification system

propriétaire (France) vineyard owner

puttonyos (Hungary) in practical terms, an indication of sweetness of Tokaj Aszú wines (*q.v.*). The more puttonyos specified (3-6), the sweeter will be the Tokaj

Qualitätswein (Germany) quality wine

Qualitätswein bestimmter Anbaugebiet (QbA) (Germany) quality wine from a specific region

Qualitätswein mit Prädikat (QmP) (Germany) quality wine with a 'special attribute' (*see* Prädikat)

quinta (Portugal) farm, estate. In the port context, any style may be branded with a quinta name, but 'Single Quinta' port generally refers to a single-farm port from a lesser year

rainwater (Madeira) a medium-dry madeira based on the Tinta Negra Mole variety

recioto (Italy) sweet passito (*q.v.*) wine from the Veneto

récolte (France) harvest

reserva (Portugal) better-than-average wine; slightly higher (0.5%) in alcohol than legal minimum; at least one year old

reserva (Spain) red wine aged for a minimum of one year in oak casks and two years in bottle; white (or rosé) wine aged for a minimum of six months in oak casks and one and a half years in tank or bottle

reserve (Bulgaria) wine which has spent two years (white) or three years (red) ageing in wood

reserve (Madeira) madeira with a minimum age of five years

réserve (France) 'reserve': this term has no legal status on labels

riserva (Italy) wines aged for longer than normal. If DOC wines are riserva, then a minimum (but variable) ageing period is laid down. Usually the best wines are held back for riserva

sec (Champagne, Loire) medium-dry (17g-35g of sugar per litre of wine); (other wines) dry

secco (Italy) dry

seco (Portugal, Spain) dry

second wine (Bordeaux) *see* grand vin

Sekt (Germany) sparkling wine

sélection de grains nobles (Alsace) wine made from botrytis-affected grapes (*see* botrytis)

semi-seco (Spain) medium dry

sercial (Madeira) the driest madeira, though cheap examples are rarely fully dry

solera (Spain) sherry ageing system which, by fractional blending, produces a consistent and uniform end product

sous-marque (France) a wine sold or labelled under a secondary, possibly fictional, name

Spätlese (Germany) wine from late-picked grapes, possibly with noble rot

special reserve (Madeira) madeira with a minimum age of ten years

spumante (Italy) sparkling

stravecchio (Italy) extra old

sulfites (US) sulphur dioxide, present in all wines (including organic wines), used as a preservative and disinfectant

supérieur (France) higher alcohol content than usual

'sur lie' (Loire) this should refer to a wine (generally Muscadet) bottled directly from its lees, without having been racked or filtered. The term has, though, been used in a lax fashion in recent years; grant it credence only in conjunction with an indication of domaine-bottling, such as 'mis en bouteille au domaine'; may contain some CO_2

superiore (Italy) wine with higher alcohol, and sometimes more age

Super Tuscan (Italy) non-DOC wine of high quality from Tuscany

Süssreserve (Germany) unfermented grape juice which may be added to fully fermented wine to sweeten it; the process is known as 'back-blending'

Tafelwein (Germany) table wine

tank method *see* cuve close

tawny port (Portugal) basic light port. True wood-aged tawny ports are either marketed as colheitas (*q.v.*) or as Ports with an Indication of Age (*q.v.*)

transfer method a method of making sparkling wines in which the second fermentation takes place in bottle, but the sediment produced by this process is eliminated by decanting and filtering under pressure. The wine is then rebottled

trocken (Germany) dry

Trockenbeerenauslese (Germany) very sweet wine from raisined grapes affected by noble rot

varietal a wine based on a single grape variety

vecchio (Italy) old

velho (Portugal) old

vendange tardive (Alsace) 'late harvest', meaning wine made from especially ripe grapes

verde (Portugal) 'green', meaning young

verdelho (Madeira) medium-dry madeira

viejo (muy) (Spain) old (very)

vigna (Italy) vineyard or 'cru' (*q.v.*)

vigneto (Italy) vineyard or 'cru' (*q.v.*)

viña (Spain) vineyard

vin de pays (France) literally translates as country wine, and describes wine that is better than basic vin de table, with some regional characteristics. Usually vins de pays are determined by administrative geography, with more flexible regulations than for appellation contrôlée (*q.v.*)

vin de table (France) the most basic category of French wine, with no precise provenance other than country of origin given on the label

vin gris (France) pale rosé wine

vinifera (North America) a grape variety that is a member of the European *Vitis vinifera* family, as opposed to some of the other vine families (such as the native American *Vitis labrusca* family)

vinificato in bianco (Italy) juice from black grapes fermented without skin contact to make white wine

vino da tavola (VdT) (Italy) table wine: wine that is neither DOCG,

DOC nor fortified nor sparkling nor low in alcohol. Quality may be basic or exceptionally fine

vino de la tierra (Spain) country wine

vino de mesa (Spain) table wine

vin santo (Italy) type of passito (*q.v.*) wine from Trentino, Tuscany and Umbria

vino tipico (Italy) new category for vino da tavola with some regional characteristics

vintage champagne champagne made from a blend of a single year, sold after at least three years' ageing

Vintage Character (Portugal) medium-quality red port. This style may cease to exist in the near future

vintage madeira (Madeira) the finest madeira; declared only after 20 years' maturation

vintage port (Portugal) very fine port, bottled young and requiring long cellaring (8 to 40 years); needs decanting

vitivinicoltura (Italy) the whole process of wine-making, from the vineyard through to the finished wine

VDQS (France) (Vin Délimité de Qualité Supérieure) covers the very much smaller category, below appellation contrôlée (*q.v.*), with very similar regulations

VQPRD (Italy) 'quality wine produced in a specified region'; EU term indicating appellation contrôlée, DOC, DOCG, DO, DOCa and other similarly controlled quality categories

Weinbaudomäne (Germany) wine estate

Weingut (Germany) wine estate

Weinkellerei (Germany) wine cellar

Weissherbst (Germany) rosé

Winzergenossenschaft (Germany) growers' co-operative

INDEX